W9-CCU-909

FINANCIAL ACCOUNTING

An Integrated Approach

SECOND EDITION

MICHAEL GIBBINS, PHD, FCA

Winspear Professor of Professional Accounting
University of Alberta

Nelson Canada

I(T)P An International Thomson Publishing Company

Toronto • Albany • Bonn • Boston • Cincinnati • Detroit • London • Madrid • Melbourne
Mexico City • New York • Pacific Grove • Paris • San Francisco • Singapore • Tokyo • Washington

I(T)P™
International Thomson Publishing
The trademark ITP is used under licence

Published in 1995 by
Nelson Canada,
A Division of Thomson Canada Limited
1120 Birchmount Road, Scarborough, Ontario M1K 5G4

Canadian Cataloguing in Publication Data
Gibbins, Michael, 1942–
Financial Accounting: An Integrated Approach
2nd ed.
Includes bibliographical references and index.
ISBN 0-17-604816-2
1. Accounting 2. Financial statements
I. Title.
HF5635G53 1994 657'.48 C94-932006-4

Acquisitions Editor	Craig Dyer
Production Editor	Tracy Bordian
Senior Developmental Editor	Maryrose O'Neill
Senior Production Coordinator	Sheryl Emery
Art Director	Liz Harasymczuk
Interior Design	Avril Orloff
Cover Design	Avril Orloff
Composition	VISU*TronX*
Input Operators	Elaine Andrews and Michelle Volk

Printed and bound in Canada

1 2 3 4 (BG) 98 97 96 95

To all students of the art of accounting

CONTENTS

CHAPTER 4

The Cash Flow Statement's Analysis of Cash Flow

CHAPTER 5

Financial Reporting, Accounting Principles, and Auditing

CHAPTER 6

Recordkeeping and Control

CHAPTER 7

Revenue and Expense Recognition in Accrual Accounting

CHAPTER 8

Prelude to Financial Accounting Analysis

CHAPTER 9

Analysis: Ratios, Cash Flow, and Change Effects

CHAPTER 10

Accounting Policy Choices: Inventories, Long-Term Assets, Liabilities, and Related Expenses

Appendix 1: Financial Statements for The North West Company, Inc.

Appendix 2: Creating a Computer Spreadsheet to Represent a Company's Accounts

PREFACE

This book presents a balanced and integrated introductory view of financial accounting. Both the use of financial accounting information and the preparation of that information are emphasized, as are both concepts and techniques. The result is that the chapters attend to four components of an integrated understanding of financial accounting: use concepts, preparation concepts, preparation techniques, and use techniques. Understanding is the central objective, but it rests on the foundation provided by these four components.

Financial accounting is presented as a utilitarian discipline, producing accounting information that is to be used, and responding, even if not always perfectly, to the needs of the people who use it and to changes in those needs over the years. This presentation is aimed both at students who want to become managers or other users of accounting information and at students who want to become accountants, because intelligent use and intelligent preparation of financial accounting information require the balanced understanding that is this book's objective.

Financial Accounting provides a strong conceptual foundation and includes insights from accounting and related research. It also grounds the subject in the practicalities that make financial accounting a challenging discipline and accounting an interesting profession. While providing structure to the learning task to help the student gain understanding, it avoids excessive structure that might give the student the impression that financial accounting is more straightforward and less subtle than it is. The student must do the cognitive work of integrating the ideas into a personal understanding, because otherwise the understanding won't last.

The book is structured to foster an integrated understanding. Chapter 1 introduces both financial accounting and the users and preparers of the information. Chapter 2, 3, and 4 introduce the four main financial statements (balance sheet, income statement, retained earnings statement, and cash flow statement), including both extensive discussion of the use and history of development of the statements and examples of their preparation and interrelationships. Chapter 5 pulls several concepts and practical issues together into an examination of the generally accepted accounting principles behind the statements, including brief attention to auditing, ethics, governmental and not-for-profit accounting, and accounting for corporate groups (to enable students to understand published financial statements, which are usually consolidated). Chapters 6 and 7 are preparation oriented, covering the recordkeeping system and accrual accounting concepts and techniques behind the financial statements, including revenue and expense recognition and accounting for income tax. As a reminder that financial statements are not the only purpose of accounting records, Chapter 6 also introduces "internal control." Chapters 8 and 9 swing back toward the use of the financial statements, focusing on the concepts and techniques used in analyzing and interpreting financial statement information, including some content about capital markets, managerial contracts, present value analysis of cash flows, and change effects ("what if") analysis. Chapter 9 contains an analysis of the financial statements of The North West Company, to illustrate the presentation and analysis of financial accounting information. Chapter 10 is the capstone, bringing it all together by reviewing accounting policy choices regarding inventories, depreciation, and other topics, including both the presentation issues and the analysis of the effects of making one choice versus others.

Each chapter begins with an overview and, in addition to the various topics the chapter covers, includes several features to assist students and instructors. After every one or two sections of each chapter, short "How's Your Understanding?" questions are asked, so that students can check some aspects of their understanding of what has just been read. Toward the end of each chapter are sections examining managers' perspectives on the issues, which help place the chapter in the world of the business manager. Also near the end are findings from accounting research to illustrate contributions by that research to understanding financial accounting. Each chapter includes an instalment of the "continuing case," which tells the story of a small company operating at a scale students may be able to identify with. The story develops with the topics covered throughout the book and thus provides a progressive (mostly preparation-oriented) illustration of the ideas. At the end of each chapter is a set of problems for use in homework and class discussions. These problems reinforce the balance of conceptual and practical analysis and so are designed to allow the exploration of interesting issues rather than dictating particular approaches. However, they also provide considerable mechanical practice.

The book ends with several sections designed to help students develop their understanding. There are an extensive glossary of terms and an index, solution outlines for selected homework and discussion questions, and a supplement showing how to create a computer spreadsheet to facilitate analysis of any company's financial statements.

The book's purpose is to help students develop their own understanding of financial accounting, not to deliver "the answer"—financial accounting's answers are many and varied. The homework solutions, for example, reinforce thoughtful analysis, rather than suggesting that only one answer is to be expected. Much of the material in the book has an informal style, directed toward easing the student into the material and generally lightening up what students feel is serious stuff. It is hoped that students and instructors will enjoy themselves, and especially that students will find financial accounting to be a lot more interesting than they might have expected.

An Instructor's Manual has been prepared to assist in course delivery. The manual includes teaching notes, an exam bank, and transparency masters. Solution outlines for unmarked homework and discussion problems are available to instructors in a separate Solutions Manual. Students can purchase the Study Guide (ISBN 0-17-604818-9) to accompany *Financial Accounting: An Integrated Approach, Second Edition*, through their campus bookstore.

ABOUT THE AUTHOR

Michael Gibbins is the Winspear Professor of Professional Accounting in the Faculty of Business, University of Alberta. He was born and raised in British Columbia, where he married, earned a B. Com. from the University of British Columbia and obtained his chartered accountancy designation in the Prince George office of what is now Deloitte & Touche. Wending his way east, he worked for the Canadian Institute of Chartered Accountants in Toronto, getting an MBA from York University and becoming a father along the way. After a trial at teaching as an assistant professor at Queen's University School of Business, he obtained his Ph.D. in accounting and psychology at Cornell University. A return to the west as assistant professor at University of British Columbia preceded his move to Alberta.

The author's research and teaching interests lie in how people make decisions and judgments, and in the way accounting information is used in making important decisions in business and other economic spheres. A particular interest is in the professional judgment of public accountants, managers, and other professionals who cope with the the pressures and risks of modern business life. He has published widely on judgment, accounting, financial disclosure, and educational subjects, is currently editor of the Canadian accounting research journal *Contemporary Accounting Research*, has been on numerous editorial boards of academic journals, and is active in the Canadian Academic Accounting Association, the American Accounting Association, and other professional bodies. He has received a number of education and teaching awards. The honour of becoming a Fellow of both the Alberta and British Columbia Institute of Chartered Accountants was awarded to him in 1988. Balancing his professional and academic interests, the author collects beer bottles, ceramic frogs and other art featuring frogs, and cycles as much as the northern climate of Edmonton permits.

ACKNOWLEDGMENTS

This book began in development work done as a project for the Centre for the Advancement of Professional Accounting Education (now called the Chartered Accountants' Centre), Faculty of Business, University of Alberta. I am grateful for the Centre's assistance.

All material originally published elsewhere is used with permission. Thanks are due to all the people and companies who gave their permission and therefore helped bring the book to life. For the large contribution their materials have made to the book, I particularly thank The North West Company (especially Pat Easton), Barcol Doors (especially Rosalie Laibida), Glenrose Rehabilitation Hospital (especially Louise Weklych), Canadian Broadcasting Corporation, Cara Operations Ltd., Dominion Textile Inc., Intrawest Corporation, Magna International Inc., Microsoft Corporation, Paychex, Inc., Royal Bank of Canada, Telus Corporation, TSC Shannock Corporation, Tyson Foods Inc., Michael McDonald and Bill Scott.

Many people helped along the way, as this book developed over several years. I am grateful to them all, and apologize to those I do not mention specifically. Special thanks are due to the students of Accounting 311 at the University of Alberta for their patience, and especially for all their ideas and criticisms, as the book developed. I am especially indebted to past co-authors of the annual "Accounting 311 Course Package," who helped me work out many of the ideas in the book: Laurie Beattie, Philip Beaulieu, Richard Chandler, Anona Lukawiecki, Christine Newton, and Duncan Sinclair. For other assistance and support, I am grateful to David Annand, Elaine Aultman, Peggy Barr, Andrea Berman, Allison Brooks, Dwayne Budzak, Mike Chiasson, Tad Drinkwater, Joan Finley, Stefan Gibbins, Tanis Gibbins, Mary Hemmingsen, Dave Jobson, Jocelyn Johnston, Henry Kennedy, Janet LeBlanc, Mary Lea McAnally, Sandra Namchuk, Jim Newton, Linda Olsen, Simone Phillips, Remi Racine, Lorraine Sherwood, Ken Sutley, John Waterhouse, and Kathy West. Particularly helpful in preparing the second edition were: Loretta Amerogen, Lane Daley, Wendy Degner, Ross Denham, Don Easton, Karim Jamal, Dave Jobson, Steve Salterio, Tom Scott, and Heather Wier.

I am also grateful to the following people for their suggestions and constructive comments: Robert Anderson (Brock University), H. Donald Brown (Brock University), Ray F. Carroll (Dalhousie University), Maureen Fizzell (Simon Fraser University), Leo Gallant (St. Francis Xavier University), Duncan Green (University of Calgary), Al Hunter (University of Lethbridge), Terry Litovitz (University of Toronto, Scarborough Campus), Don Lockwood (University of British Columbia), Carol McKeen (Queen's University), and Nicola M. Young (St. Mary's University).

The support of Craig Dyer, Peter Jackson, Maryrose O'Neill, Tracy Bordian, and others at Nelson Canada have been great. Francis Winspear has supported me as the Winspear Professor and given much other support to the University of Alberta. He has also been a fine example to me of the combination of conceptual strength and practicality that this book attempts to transmit. Finally, thanks to my parents for the example of care and thoughtfulness they have always set, and to my wife Betty for her support over the years.

Chapter 1 Introduction to Financial Accounting

1.1 Book Overview

Welcome to an exploration of one of business's most important and, to many people, mysterious subjects: **financial accounting**. The goals of this book are to help you:

- Understand this subject well enough to be able to use accounting reports and explain them to others;
- Acquire the basics of how **accounting** works and how to prepare accounting reports.

Meeting these goals will benefit you whether or not you become an accountant. Non-accountants are affected by accounting in many ways, as this book will show. For their part, accountants need to know how and why accounting reports are used, as well as how to prepare them.

Understanding financial accounting involves both concepts about and techniques for the use and the preparation of accounting reports. Putting these together leads to four kinds of related knowledge: use concepts, preparation concepts, use techniques, and preparation techniques. The connections among the four and the understanding that results from bringing them all together are illustrated in Figure 1.1.

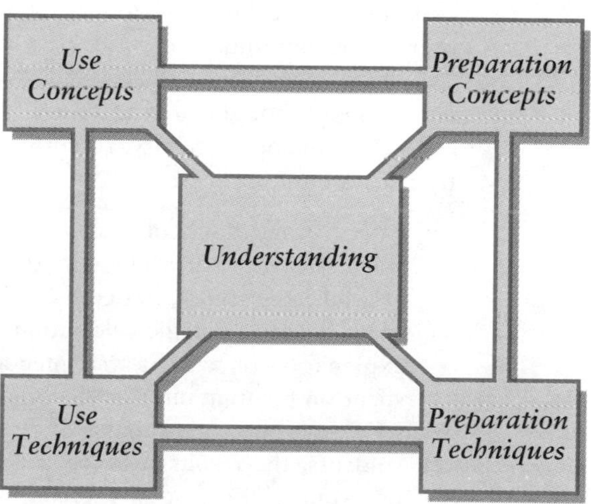

FIGURE 1.1

The first few chapters concentrate on the financial accounting reports, called the **financial statements**, and contain a balanced discussion of the four kinds of knowledge listed above, so that you will begin by seeing the subject from all sides.

(By the way, in addition to an index, this book has a glossary of terms at the back. Any term, such as ***financial statements****, that is printed in bold is included in the glossary. If you are not sure what the term means, look it up right away.)*

After those introductory chapters, emphasis is put on preparation, building up your knowledge of both the technical procedures behind the financial statements and the concepts that bind these procedures together. Then the book swings over to the use of the financial statements in analyzing financial position and performance. The final chapter returns to the balanced mixture, explaining both how accountants come up with some important figures and notes in the financial statements and how to do "what if" analyses to see how the figures would be affected by different events or assumptions.

The going will not all be easy, but if you give it your best effort, you may be surprised at the high level of sophistication you will reach.

1.2 CHAPTER OVERVIEW

This chapter introduces you to the subject of financial accounting and illustrates some useful concepts and techniques. It also suggests a way of thinking about financial accounting that will be important to your career, whether you become an accountant or a user of accounting in business or in other walks of life. Despite what some people think, accounting is not just number-crunching: there is challenge in it, and much of that challenge is in figuring out which numbers to use—deciding what "story" the numbers should tell. Adding and subtracting the numbers is often the easy part. This makes accounting both easier and harder to learn than you might have thought. Don't expect it all to make perfect sense at the beginning; it will take a while to acquire the knowledge that creates an understanding of business and accounting as they really are in our world. This understanding will be based on your knowledge of both concepts and techniques, and of the viewpoints of both accountants and the users of accounting.

"Education," it has been said, "is the process of moving from confident ignorance to thoughtful uncertainty!" A successful business leader, then chancellor of a major university, recently said the following about business education:

> I hope business school students are taught that there are no straightforward answers to anything important. Once, as "Executive in Residence" at a business school, I attended a course. One day, most of the time was spent working out the calculation of a complicated formula with much explanation of what it was intended to prove but almost no time was spent on pointing out that the original inputs to the formula were themselves uncertain and capable of different interpretation. In the eyes of the students, the results took on a certainty that was not justified by the uncertainty of the original premises. I thought it a dangerous concept to be teaching future business people. One thing it took me a long time to learn is that even accounting depends very much upon philosophy and that one must understand where the figures come from before passing judgment on them.[1]

1.3 FINANCIAL ACCOUNTING

Financial accounting measures an enterprise's performance over time and its position (status) at a point in time, and does so in dollars, yen, francs, or whichever currency is relevant to the enterprise. This measurement of **financial performance** and **financial position** is done for all sorts of enterprises: large and small businesses, governments from local to national levels, universities, charities, churches, clubs, international associations, and many others. The financial statements summarize the measurements of financial performance and position in standard ways thought to be useful in evaluating whether the enterprise has done well and is in good shape. These financial statements include **notes to the financial statements**, which contain many words of explanation and interpretation in addition to the numbers. The statements report on the economic and financial side of things and are largely for the use of people outside the enterprise, such as investors, club members, regulatory agencies, and taxation authorities.

As we will see throughout the book, financial performance and position are highly related. Good performance is likely to lead to a healthy financial position: if you make money at your job, you are more likely to have money in the bank. On the other hand, a healthy financial position facilitates performance: if you have money in the bank, that helps you afford the activities that lead to good performance and avoid the risks and worries that come from being broke.

Another branch of accounting, **management accounting**, is oriented toward helping managers and others inside the enterprise. While management accounting is not examined in this book, students interested in how financial accounting measures managerial performance will find frequent references to the relationship of managers with financial accounting.

AN EXAMPLE: GRADES

To outline how financial accounting works, let's use an analogy: the example of students going to university and getting grades for their efforts. The parallel with financial accounting isn't exact, but it will illustrate the main issues.

Students go to university to learn, among other reasons, and they get grades as a measure of their learning. Grades are not a perfect measure of learning, but they are a very important part of the process in modern universities.

- They are used by the students themselves and by others, including parents and university administrators, to assess students' knowledge at various stages and to monitor their performance over time. They are also used by employers to predict future job performance, by scholarship agencies to allocate awards, and so on. Many good and bad things can happen because of a student's grades, even though the student and other people who use grades may feel that they are not necessarily the best reflection of the learning they are supposed to measure.
- Grade reports come out at standard times of the year and in standard formats, and preparing them occupies much of professors' and administrators' time. Great effort goes into minimizing error and fraud. For example, official transcripts are prepared carefully and certified so that

anyone using them can be confident that they have not been tampered with. Cheating and other tampering with the grading system can land a student in very hot water indeed.

- Because of the importance of grades, students may make course and other choices in the expectation that these choices will mean better grades, whether or not they care much about what they are learning. Sometimes the grades, which are only supposed to reflect the learning, seem so important that they drive the system instead!

Here are some parallels between the grade example and financial accounting:

1. The student is in university to learn, but not only for that reason. Similarly, businesses and other organizations are concerned about financial position and financial performance, but not only those. They are, however, the ones financial accounting focuses on.
2. Learning has many dimensions, and course grades represent only some of them. Financial performance and position also have many dimensions. While financial accounting keeps track of several of these dimensions, it does not track all of them. In spite of their imperfections, grades and financial accounting have been with us for a long time and will continue to be important.
3. Individual course grades are measures of performance, and a good cumulative grade point average is an indication that the student's knowledge at that time is good. We also expect students with good grade point averages to do well in subsequent courses. In accounting, good performance also is expected to accumulate to provide a healthy financial position, and a healthy financial position is expected to lead to good subsequent performance. These expectations do not always work out, either for students or enterprises, but we should be able to make some prediction of what is likely to happen in the future, based on what has happened so far.
4. Like grades and grade reports, which summarize the results of many tests, projects, and other activities, financial accounting's reports (financial statements) are summaries of a large number of individual events. In a course, the final exam may matter more than the term paper does in calculating the course grade. In accounting, too, some events may be more important than others in compiling the financial report.
5. Knowing how grade transcripts are used by employers, student loan offices, graduate schools, parents, students, and others helps to understand why they are as they are. Similarly, the use of financial accounting's reports must be understood in order to appreciate the role they play. A company president may be just as anxious about how people will interpret and use an accounting report as is a student about people's reaction to a grade transcript.
6. Grade transcripts are available at the end of each term and summarize the students' performance over specific periods of time such as the school year. Comparisons to performance in other years are made easier by the format of the transcripts. Financial statements also appear at regular intervals (at least once a year and often on a quarterly or even monthly basis) and are prepared using a fairly standard format to increase their useful-

ness as a tool of comparison for different companies or the same company in different years.

7. Much trouble is taken to minimize error and fraud in both grading and the preparation of financial statements. So that people may rely on the statements, auditors verify that they are prepared in a fair manner and in accordance with accepted principles.
8. It is unfortunate, but understandable, that some students choose courses not because they are interesting but because they have heard that a high grade can be obtained. Because financial statements are so important, some managers similarly seem to worry more about "getting the numbers right" than about running the business properly.

1.4 ACCRUAL ACCOUNTING

Financial accounting's task of producing financial statements is a complex one. For even a small business, thousands of events (**transactions**) have to be recorded and their financial effects evaluated. For large corporations like Eaton's, Inco, McDonald's, the Bank of Montreal, and Toyota, or organizations like the University of Alberta, the City of New York, or the Red Cross, the number of transactions runs into the millions or billions. Frequently, when the time comes to prepare the financial statements, transactions have not been completed, are in dispute, or have an otherwise unclear status. Here are examples in which appropriate figures may be difficult to determine:

- The value of Inco's supply of nickel ore depends on the cost of digging it out, smelting and finishing it, and on international nickel prices that can vary significantly from one day to the next.
- The value of the Bank of Montreal's loans to third-world countries (that is, the money actually to be received back from those loans) depends on the health of the borrowing countries' economies, stability in international money transfer arrangements (often disrupted by wars, politics, and natural disasters), and the relative values of various countries' currencies, which, like nickel prices, can change a lot from day to day.
- The value of donations promised to the Red Cross but not yet received depends on how committed donors are to actually producing the cash, which can be affected by unemployment, rising prices for food and other goods the donors need, and other things beyond the Red Cross's control.

To cope with these complexities, financial accounting for most businesses and organizations uses the **accrual accounting** approach. This means that in preparing the financial statements, attempts are made to measure the value of incomplete transactions, to estimate figures when exact amounts are unknown, and generally to make an economically meaningful assessment of awkward problems. For example:

- Someone tries to estimate how much money Inco has spent on nickel ore and whether nickel prices are higher or lower than Inco's cost to produce more nickel, in order to determine whether Inco's supply of nickel is worth what it cost to produce.

- Someone studies the loan repayment record of various countries for the Bank of Montreal and estimates how much money the bank will be able to collect, in order to judge the value of the bank's uncollected loans.
- Someone advises the Red Cross on how much, if any, of the promised donations are likely to be received to help the Red Cross make its spending plans.

Accrual accounting has been developed because financial statements cannot be based just on the routine accounting records of what has happened. Measuring economic performance is more complex than that, and the "truth" can be elusive or depend on one's point of view. Many augmentations (estimates, adjustments, judgments, and verbal explanations) must be made so that the statements will be meaningful. The resulting statements, therefore, depend to a great extent on the quality and fairness of such augmentations.

Financial accounting, because it relies on many judgments, is far more imprecise than most people, even many regular users of financial statements, realize. To help students understand the reality of modern financial accounting, much time must be spent on the real-life imprecisions of preparing and using financial statements. *Accrual accounting is therefore the presumed method in this book*, though there will be some comparisons between it and simpler cash-based accounting.

AN EXAMPLE: GURJIT'S VENTURE

Here is an example of how accrual accounting works. The example is of a small business, one you should be able to imagine easily, but the accounting issues it raises are exactly the same as those faced by big businesses.

Gurjit works in an office during the day, but in the evenings and on weekends she makes silver jewellery in a studio she has set up in her basement. The jewellery is sold in local craft stores, and Gurjit keeps a separate bank account to deposit the cash from her sales and pay the bills for supplies. Accounting is a way of portraying an enterprise; another way, a visual image, may help you. Try to picture her working in her studio, driving around to craft stores to deliver her products and collect cash, and relaxing with her friends when things are going well.

Last year, which was her first year in business, Gurjit received $4,350 in cash from the craft stores for sales of her jewellery and paid $1,670 in cash for silver and for other supplies and expenses. How much money did she make from her business? Well, the simple answer is that she made a **cash income** of $2,680 ($4,350 cash collected minus $1,670 cash paid out). That amount was the increase in her bank account balance during the year.

The notion behind accrual accounting is that maybe the simple answer is too simple, that it really does not properly measure what Gurjit accomplished during the year. Accrual accounting tries to take into account a number of things.

- At the end of the year, Gurjit was still owed $310 for sales by one craft store because the owner had been out when she stopped by. The store paid her a few weeks later, but shouldn't that amount be counted as income for the year the sales were made?
- At the end of the year, Gurjit had supplies and both finished and unfinished jewellery on hand that had cost $280. These were paid for dur-

ing the year, but because they will be used to produce sales in the next year, shouldn't their cost be deducted next year instead?

- At the end of the year, Gurjit had some unpaid bills for business expenses totalling $85. She paid those early in the next year, but aren't they really expenses for the year in which she incurred them, rather than for the year in which she paid them?
- In making the jewellery, she used some equipment she had bought a few years earlier for $1,200. The equipment would be expected to last about ten years; so, shouldn't the wear and tear on it during the year be counted as an expense? It is not easy to figure out how much wear and tear results from a particular period, but say that she feels the year was a normal one of the ten the equipment should last. The cost of the wear and tear, therefore, was about 10% of the original cost of the equipment, or $120. (This $120 figure is what accountants call **amortization.** It can be calculated in several ways, as we will see later on.)

Accounting is continually evolving. An example is in the terms **amortization** and **depreciation.** Both terms apply to the idea of measuring the "consumption" of the economic value of long-term resources such as equipment. Amortization is slowly supplanting depreciation as the more general term for this idea, but you will see both terms (and other terms) used in companies' financial reports and in this book.

Just using these four additional pieces of information, accrual accounting would calculate her business income for the year in the following way, taking into account the various estimates and incomplete transactions described:

Revenue	
($4,350 collected plus $310 still to be received)	$4,660
Expenses	
($1,670 paid minus $280 goods still on hand plus $85 unpaid plus $120 amortization)	1,595
Accrual income based on the information provided	$3,065

You can see that the accrual income is a more complete measure of Gurjit's business performance than is the cash income of $2,680, which is the change in cash balance alone.

But there are some difficulties.

- The accrual income requires extra calculation and so is more complex. This might confuse some people, and it leaves more room for error than the simpler calculation.
- The accrual income doesn't match the change in bank account balance any more, so Gurjit might be less sure of how much she can take out of the bank for her next holiday. The accrual income and cash income can always be reconciled, however. Considerable attention will be given to this in later chapters, but let's do that reconciliation for Gurjit as an example:

Accrual income, as calculated earlier	$3,065
Deduct revenue not yet received in cash	(310)
Deduct cost of goods paid for but unsold, so still on hand	(280)
Add expenses not paid in cash this year ($85 + $120)	205
Cash income, as mentioned earlier	$2,680

- Accrual accounting is a bit of a "slippery slope." Once you start trying to add and subtract things in calculating income, where do you stop? For example, should there be some deduction for the cost of Gurjit's time in making all the jewellery? The preceding calculation seems to imply that her time was free, yet she would probably not agree with that. What about the costs of using the room in her basement for her studio and her car for deliveries? Should some calculation of such costs be made, even though it would be hard to be exact about them? What about income tax? If she has to pay income tax on what she earns from her business, should that tax also be deducted as a business expense? Or is it a personal expense that does not belong in the business's financial statements?

This example is beginning to sound a little complicated! For now, just remember that accrual accounting tries to provide a more thorough measurement of financial performance and other aspects of an enterprise than simple cash-based accounting. In order to do so, it incorporates more complex ideas, as well as estimates and judgments. Much of your task is to understand the complexities, estimates, and judgments so that you will be able to understand the resulting financial statements and what they say about the enterprise.

How's Your Understanding

Here are two questions you should be able to answer, based on what you have just read. If you can't, it would be best to reread the material.

1. Your cousin, a medical student, says, "In our course on how to manage a medical practice, we were told that our financial reports will use accrual accounting. What does that mean?"
2. Fred started his delivery business a year ago. Since then, he has collected $47,000 from his customers and has paid $21,000 in expenses. At the end of his first year, his customers owe him $3,200; he owes his suppliers $1,450; and his truck amortization (depreciation) for the year was $4,600. Using just this information, what is his first year's accrual accounting income? What is his cash income? (You should get $23,150 and $26,000. The two figures reconcile: $23,150 – $3,200 + $1,450 + $4,600 = $26,000.)

1.5 THE PEOPLE INVOLVED IN FINANCIAL ACCOUNTING

There are many actors in the drama that is financial accounting. The main ones are the information **users** (the decision makers), the information **preparers**, who put the information together for the users, and the **auditors**, who assist the users by providing a professional opinion that the information is fair and appropriate. Relationships among these groups are complex, but we can say that in general, users make decisions, preparers facilitate users' decision-making by providing information, and auditors enhance the credibility of the information.

USERS (DECISION MAKERS)

In financial accounting, a user or decision maker is someone who makes decisions on the basis of the financial statements, on his or her own behalf, or on behalf of a company, bank, or other organization. Several users are described below.

Financial accounting is utilitarian: ultimately, the nature and contents of financial statements are functions of the demand for decision information from users. This is not to say that such people are the only ones who matter in the process, nor are they always clear about what information they need or necessarily satisfied with what they get. User demand, however, is the fundamental reason for financial statements, therefore understanding the demand is important.

A user's main demand is for credible **periodic reporting** of an enterprise's financial position and performance.

Credible means that the information in the reports (the financial statements) appears to be sufficiently trustworthy and competently prepared for it to be used to make decisions. There is a **cost–benefit** issue here: huge amounts of money could be spent trying to make the reports absolutely perfect, but since that money would have to come out of the enterprise's funds, spending it would make its performance and position poorer. Users, such as owners and managers, may not want that to happen, so credibility is a relative term, not an absolute one. Accounting information has to be worth its cost.

Periodic means that users can expect reports on some regular basis (for example, yearly or quarterly). The longer the wait, the more solid the information. But waiting for information usually is not desirable: users are willing to accept some imprecision in the information in return for more timely, decision-relevant information. This trade-off is central to accrual accounting because the shorter the period between reports, the fewer the events that will have been completed during the period, hence the more estimates and judgments that will be needed to prepare the reports.

The main groups of users are:

Owners: individual business **owners**, such as proprietors, partners, and other entrepreneurs; individual investors (shareholders) in shares on stock markets who can vote on company affairs; companies that invest in other companies; pension plans and other institutions that invest in companies; people with quasi-ownership interests, such as members of clubs or voters in municipalities; and so on.

Potential owners: people of the same sort as the owners listed above, who do not at present have funds invested in the enterprise, but may be considering making such an investment. Because potential owners often buy shares from present owners, for example, by trading shares on the stock market, rather than investing directly, there is often a significant difference in outlook between present owners, who would like to sell their shares for as much as possible, and potential owners, who would like to pay as little as possible. Saying that accounting responds to demands from users does *not* mean that all the users will have the same demands!

Creditors and potential creditors: suppliers, banks, bond-holders, employees, and others who have lent money to the enterprise, or who are owed funds in return for supplying something of value, or who are considering taking on such a role. Creditors do not have the legal control of the enterprise that owners have, but they often have a large say in enterprise decisions, especially if the enterprise gets into difficulty. In cases of extreme difficulty, creditors may have the right to take over control of the enterprise from the owners. Sometimes the difference between creditors and owners is hard to discern, because it may depend on subtle legalities about who has what rights, and some people may play both roles for a given enterprise; for example, an owner invests money in a business, but in addition may lend the business further money, becoming a creditor as well as an owner.

Managers: those who run the enterprise on behalf of the owners. They have a great interest in the way accounting reports on their activities and results. Often managers' salaries, bonuses, and the likelihood of staying in their jobs are directly affected by the contents of the financial statements. Especially in small businesses, the owner may also be the main manager.

Employees: nonmanagement employees and their unions or other associations. These groups are interested in the enterprise's ability to pay wages, maintain employment levels, and keep such promises as paying pensions.

Taxation authorities, regulators, and other government bodies and agencies: groups that may use the financial statements to calculate taxes payable or to evaluate whether the enterprise is following various rules and agreements.

Financial and market analysts: people who study companies' performance and prepare reports for others by analyzing those companies. Analysts often make recommendations about whether to invest, lend, or do neither.

Competitors: some of the people who get the financial statements may be trying to understand the enterprise's operations for the purpose of making life more difficult for the enterprise. Sometimes managers are reluctant to disclose information to shareholders, for example, because competitors can then also obtain it and act to reduce the enterprise's prospects.

Accounting researchers: people, mostly university professors, but also some based in public accounting firms and other organizations, who study accounting with the objective of understanding it and contributing to its improvement.

Miscellaneous third parties: various other people who may get access to an enterprise's financial statements and use them in various ways. Once statements have been issued, many people may make use of them. Politicians may make judgments about industry efficiency or taxation levels, for example. News reporters may write stories about employment practices. Judges may evaluate the enterprise's ability to pay if it loses a lawsuit.

Think about all these users and decisions! It is a great challenge to develop one set of periodic financial statements for an enterprise so that they can be useful for all. Perhaps you will not be surprised that there is much controversy about whether financial statements do this well, and whether financial accounting methods serve some users or decisions better than others.

PREPARERS (DECISION FACILITATORS)

Three main groups are responsible for the information in the financial statements:

Managers: people responsible for running an enterprise, including issuing accounting and other information, and controlling its financial affairs. The fact that managers are also users, vitally interested in the results, has created a fundamental conflict of interest for them and has led to the development of the auditing function (see below). Managers are often referred to as a group, as management.

Bookkeepers and clerks: under the direction of management, those who do the enterprise's basic recordkeeping, creating the transactional data upon which accrual accounting is built. Many of the bookkeeping and clerical functions are now performed by computers, with all the benefits and frustrations those machines provide.

Accountants: people whose job it is to shape the financial statements by applying the principles of accounting to the enterprise's records, under the direction of management. Many accountants are members of professional societies, such as those of CAs (chartered accountants), CGAs (certified general accountants), CMAs (certified management accountants), and CPAs (certified public accountants). Accountants and their societies also often have auditing experience and interests, and sometimes auditing roles, but the task of preparing the financial statements is quite different in principle from the task of verifying those statements once they are prepared.

AUDITORS (CREDIBILITY ENHANCERS)

Auditors have the job of assisting the users, by verifying that the financial statements have been prepared fairly, competently, and in a manner consistent with accepted principles. The auditing role is a very old one, arising because users demanded some assurance that managers' reports on their performance were not self-serving, biased, or downright untruthful. While auditors may be asked for advice in preparing the statements, especially for small companies, they must avoid responsibility for the statements, because their role is to scrutinize the preparation process. They cannot credibly audit statements they have prepared! (Professional accountants often do prepare financial statements, but in doing so they are not acting as auditors, and they make this clear in covering letters and footnotes attached to the statements.)

The auditor's role falls between those of the preparer and the user, so he or she must be acceptable to both. This usually means the auditor must be *"external"* and *"independent"*—a professional from outside the enterprise, who will collect his or her fee whether the financial results are good or bad, or whether the managers or users are happy or unhappy. The external auditing function is considered so important that the right to perform it is usually restricted to members of recognized professional accountants' societies who have auditing expertise and experience.

External auditors may work alone, but most work in partnership with other auditors in public accounting firms. Some of these firms are very large, having thousands of partners and tens of thousands of employees, and offices in many cities and countries. Public accounting firms offer their clients not only external auditing, but also advice on income tax, accounting, computer systems, and many other financial and business topics. In offering such other advice to enterprises that they also audit, public accountants are not supposed to get so involved that they are in effect auditing their own work, or creating any conflict-of-interest problems. Managing this requires considerable professional skill and attention to ethics and rules of professional conduct.

PEOPLE AND ETHICS

Ethics, mentioned just above, will be raised throughout this book. Ethical issues were involved in the "grades" example in Section 1.3, where cheating and fraud were mentioned. They can arise in just about any area of accounting. Here are some examples:

- An enterprise has been sued by a recently fired employee, who claims that the firing was based on the employee's age and so broke employment laws. The enterprise's president denies any impropriety. The enterprise's chief accountant, who personally feels the former employee's claim is justified, has suggested to the boss that the lawsuit should be mentioned in a note to the financial statements, so that users of the statements will know there is a potential for loss if the former employee wins. The president feels the chief accountant should ignore the lawsuit in preparing the financial statements, to avoid embarrassment and to avoid the appearance of admitting guilt. The president fears that such an apparent admittance could be used against the enterprise in court and so could cause the enterprise to lose the lawsuit. What should the chief accountant do?
- While doing the audit, another enterprise's external auditor learns that the enterprise may have been cheating one of its customers. The customer, who is unaware of this and quite happy with things, is another client of the auditor. The auditor, who is bound by rules of conduct designed to protect the confidentiality of information gained during the audit, knows that saying anything to anyone could result in lawsuits in all directions. Should the auditor just keep quiet about what was found?
- A third enterprise's president is paid a bonus each year, calculated as a percentage of accrual income. The president is considering a proposed change of amortization method that will reduce amortization expense and therefore raise accrual income and increase the president's bonus. So the proposal would put money in the president's pocket. Should the president refuse to implement the accounting change, or request that the bonus calculation ignore the change, or just go ahead and enjoy the higher bonus?

These illustrative problems do not have easy answers, so none are offered here. They are dilemmas for the chief accountant, the auditor, and the president. This book will address ethical issues from time to time and so help you sharpen your ethical sense along with your accounting knowledge, for the two are inseparable.

HOW'S YOUR UNDERSTANDING

Here are two questions you should be able to answer, based on what you have just read:

1. Who is a "user" of financial reports, and why would such a person want them?
2. What is the difference between a "preparer" and an "auditor," and why is the difference important?

1.6 WHY SHOULD A MANAGER CARE ABOUT FINANCIAL ACCOUNTING?

If you plan to be an accountant, the value of studying financial accounting is clear. It may not be so clear, however, if you have other plans, such as a career in management, marketing, finance, engineering, law, human resources, or production. To provide some perspective for those of you not planning an accounting career and to help you understand the managers you will work with if you do become an accountant or auditor, comments will be made frequently about managers and financial accounting. These comments are intended simply to broaden your view of accounting and are not definitive. Give them some thought, and try to relate them to how you see the world.

Let's consider one idea now. As already suggested in the grades example, financial statements are directly relevant to managers because they report on the managers' performances as decision makers, as caretakers of the enterprise, as representatives of the owners, as legal officers of the enterprise, and so on. Only the most numb or cynical manager could fail to be interested in how her or his performance is being measured and in how that performance is analyzed, projected, and otherwise evaluated. Many businesses, professions, government departments, and other organizations base their evaluations of managers, especially senior managers, on the financial results shown in financial statements. Bonuses, promotions, dismissals, transfers, and other rewards and penalties are often directly based on the numbers and commentaries prepared by accountants.

Every manager should have an intimate understanding of how accounting is measuring his or her performance. This will lead to more intelligent decisions, even (or especially) when decision results are uncertain, delayed, or complex. It also leads to more intelligent use of both accounting information and advice from accountants in evaluating one's own performance or that of others. Accounting has its share of jargon, but this will not stop the manager who believes it is important to know what the accountants are doing when they calculate important results or make important projections. Every manager should be able to conduct a "reasonableness check" of the information being provided to her or him and have a comfortable understanding of the accounting implications of what is going on.

1.7 WHAT IS ACCOUNTING RESEARCH?

You might wonder what sort of research is done by accounting professors and other researchers of accounting, auditing, tax, computerized accounting systems, and related fields. Obviously there are no white rats, lab coats, hikes through unexplored terrain, or digging up of ancient pottery shards. What can be researched about accounting?

There is a lot of accounting research going on; there are many accounting research journals, with titles such as *Accounting, Organizations and Society*, *The Accounting Review*, *Contemporary Accounting Research*, *Journal of Accounting and Economics*, and *Journal of Accounting Research*. Here are ten examples of topics accounting researchers around the world are now studying.

1. How do stock and bond markets react to accounting information? Is the reaction more related to accrual income or to cash income?
2. How can bonus plans, budgets, and other accounting-oriented performance rewards and measures be designed to motivate the best management performance?
3. How do auditors, managers, security analysts, and others who use accounting information make their decisions?
4. How does the judgment of professionals, such as accountants and auditors, work and how can such professional judgment be improved?
5. How do owners, managers, creditors, and other parties use accounting information to help manage their business relationships with one another?
6. What historical role has accounting played in the development of our society and our commercial system?
7. How can managers, auditors, accountants, and others involved in accounting be motivated, or assisted, to act ethically in complex, ever-changing circumstances?
8. How can statistics, computer analysis, mathematical modelling, and other aids be used to improve the quality of accounting information or help people to use it better?
9. How do companies decide what financial information to disclose, to whom, and how?
10. How can legal, cultural, and other international differences be taken into account in designing accounting reports for international companies or when comparing companies operating in different countries?

This list could go on for some time! Several of the above examples will be re-encountered as we work through the topics of financial accounting. If you would like to learn more about accounting research, you might try asking an accounting professor what research interests him or her.

1.8 CONTINUING DEMONSTRATION CASE

INSTALMENT

1

Toward the end of each of the chapters in this book is an instalment of the Continuing Demonstration Case. The case describes the founding and initial growth of a wholesale distribution company, Mato Inc., and develops as the chapters' topics develop. Each instalment presents additional data and then shows the results of using that data. The main purpose is to illustrate the technical side of the chapter's topics, so that you can use it to reinforce your learning. Make whatever use of the case is helpful to you, but remember to think about the data provided each time and sketch out what you would do with it *before you look at the suggested results.* If you look at the results before thinking about them, the case will be less helpful to you.

This first instalment provides background information about the two people who run Mato Inc. The founding of the company will be dealt with in Instalment 2.

Data for Instalment 1

"Hi, Tomas, this is Mavis. Just calling to thank you for attending my grandfather's funeral last week. I appreciate the support. Gramps was a great person and always encouraged me to make my mark in the world. Even now he's encouraging me, because in his will he left me some money that he said was to help start my own business. Maybe in a while we could get together and talk about that."

Mavis Janer and Tomas Brot have been friends for several years, ever since their days studying business together at the university. They have often talked about going into business for themselves. Mavis majored in marketing and, since graduation, has worked for a national retailer, moving up the ladder to become a department head in one of the retailer's local stores. While she likes the company and seems to be doing well, she would really prefer to be on her own, making decisions and taking risks. She is full of ideas that cannot be implemented at her level in the retailing company and is afraid that if she stays there too long she will lose her entrepreneurial zeal.

Tomas majored in finance and has worked as a commercial loans officer for a bank since graduating. As he puts it, "After I'd seen a hundred business plans from people wanting to borrow money, I was sure I could put together a better plan for myself, if only I had the opportunity. The local economy hasn't been terribly encouraging, but I have seen lots of good ideas and know there's room for mine to succeed too."

With the catalyst of Mavis's inheritance, and being a careful pair, the two decided to get together and get started on a business plan by writing down (a) the objectives they would have for any business they might operate together, such as to make money, and (b) the risks, constraints, and worries they'd want to avoid or minimize, such as losing their own money. Tomas was more interested in list (b) than Mavis was: he already saw himself playing the role of keeping her entrepreneurial enthusiasm "within bounds," as he called it. Their two lists are given below. *Before looking at them, jot down some of the things you think they might have listed.*

Results for Instalment 1

Below are the lists summarizing what Mavis and Tomas agreed on. The lists will help determine the context within which the accounting for their eventual business will operate and the uses to which the business's financial statements will be put. Financial statements and the accounting system behind them must fit the needs of the company, its owners, its managers, and other interested parties.

a. Objectives

- Be a source of personal pride and satisfaction;
- Be able to continue as an independent business indefinitely;
- Be a business both can contribute to, so both will want to be fully involved;
- Be a challenge to their skills and even be fun to be involved in;
- Provide enough cash income to support both Mavis and Tomas (moderate support now, but greater support in the future, when both expect to have families);
- Grow in value so that it will be a future source of wealth for financing a desired comfortable lifestyle and eventually selling out at retirement;
- Be a useful learning experience that will help them restart their careers if it does not work out.

b. Risks and constraints

- Disagreements or problems that will strain their friendship or make it difficult for them to continue working together in the business;
- Catastrophic financial loss (they don't want to lose what they will invest, but they especially don't want to lose even more than that);
- Environmental degradation related to the business or its products;
- A weak start by being undercapitalized (having too little money invested to give the business a good chance to succeed—a problem Tomas had often seen in his banking work);
- Loss of control because of having to raise significantly more capital than they can find themselves;
- Excessive initial business growth that may be hard to handle;
- Excessive time demands that will damage their family lives and other life quality factors;
- Physically difficult or dangerous products;
- Distant physical locations, which will mean frequent, long commutes;
- Unethical products or services (they did not define what they meant, but thought they would know something was unethical when they saw it).

1.9 HOMEWORK AND DISCUSSION TO DEVELOP UNDERSTANDING

Some homework problems are marked with an asterisk (*). For each of these, there is an informal solution outline at the end of the book. These outlines are intended to facilitate self-study and additional practice: don't look at the solution for any of these without giving the problem a serious try first, because once you have seen the solution it always looks easier than it is. Please note that *a problem can have several solutions*—it is possible for your answer to differ in some details from the solution outline provided and still be a good answer, especially if you have made valid, alternative assumptions or happen to know a lot about the particular situation in the problem.

PROBLEM 1.1* Review of some basic ideas

Answer the following questions:

1. What is the difference between an accountant and an auditor?
2. What is the difference between accrual income and cash income?
3. Are users of financial accounting information all the same in their information needs? Why or why not?

PROBLEM 1.2* Principles of performance evaluation

Suppose you have the job of designing a general system for measuring and evaluating the performance of managers on behalf of an enterprise's owners. List the principles (characteristics) that you think such a system would need in order to be acceptable to both the owners and the managers. Which principles would you expect the owners and managers to agree on fairly easily, and which would you expect to be more controversial?

PROBLEM 1.3* Cash balance and accrual accounting income

Calculate (1) the cash in bank as at the end of 1995 and (2) the 1995 accrual accounting income for Dawn's Diving Trips, according to the following information:

Cash in bank as at the end of 1994	$12,430
Owing from customers as at the end of 1994 (collected in 1995)	1,000
Cash collected from customers during 1995 for 1995 trips	68,990
Owing from customers as at the end of 1995 (collected in 1996)	850
Payable to suppliers as at the end of 1994 (paid in 1995)	1,480
Cash paid to suppliers during 1995 for 1995 expenses	36,910
Payable to suppliers as at the end of 1995 (paid in 1996)	2,650
Amortization on diving equipment during 1995	3,740
Cash used by Dawn for personal purposes during 1995	28,000

PROBLEM 1.4* Bank reconciliation

This problem involves a "bank reconciliation," which was not introduced in the chapter but which you should be able to think through on your own.

Wayne has been facing some cash flow problems, specifically he has been having trouble keeping his bank account straight. He went to the bank to find out his balance and was told that it was $365 as of September 15. As far as he could remember, he had made a deposit of $73 that had not yet been credited by the bank and had written cheques of $145, $37, $86, and $92 that had not yet been deducted from his account by the bank.

At the same time a good, but impatient, friend is demanding repayment of a loan of $70. Does Wayne have enough money in his bank account to repay it?

PROBLEM 1.5 Should management be able to choose accounting methods?

Do you think professors should have the right to use their own judgment in determining course grades, or should those grades be based on objectively set exams administered by someone other than professors? Why? Do you think companies' management should have the right to choose the accounting policies and methods by which their performance is measured? Why? How do these two cases differ, if at all?

PROBLEM 1.6 Resentment of auditor by the person audited

Student radio station CBBS is owned by the student association of the university. The student treasurer of the club that operates the station prepares an annual financial report to the executive committee of the association, and that report is audited. A local accounting firm does the audit for a minimal fee, in order to help the students out. The club treasurer was heard the other day complaining a little about the audit, because having one seemed to imply that the treasurer was not trusted and because the audit fee had to be paid by the club, which was always short of money.

The auditor thus has to deal with some resentment by the treasurer. Make a list of the difficulties the auditor might have because of this resentment, and any other difficulties you think might face such an auditor. (These problems are likely to be encountered by any auditor who is responsible for verifying financial statements prepared by management for use by owners and creditors.)

PROBLEM 1.7 Calculate and reconcile cash and accrual income

Leslie has a part-time business, Quick Crack-Fix, repairing small cracks and stars in car windshields, using a special polymer filler that makes the damage almost invisible and stops cracks from spreading. The repair takes only a few minutes, using equipment and supplies stored in the trunk of Leslie's car. The main customers are used car lots, car rental companies, service stations and insurance companies, but some business is done with individual customers in the driveways of their homes.

For the current year, Leslie's business records showed the following:

Collections from customers	$24,354
Payments to suppliers	5,231
Royalty payments to owner of Crack-Fix trademark	2,435
Money taken out of the business by Leslie	14,000
Depreciation (amortization) on business equipment and car	3,200
Amounts owing by customers at end of previous year	1,320
Amounts owing by customers at end of current year	890
Amounts owing to suppliers at end of previous year	436
Amounts owing to suppliers at end of current year	638
Supplies on hand at the end of previous year	0
Cost of supplies on hand at the end of current year	345

Leslie's business bank account showed a balance of $1,332 at the end of the previous year.

1. Calculate the business's cash income for the current year, explaining whether you have treated the money Leslie took out of the business as a business expense (deducting it in calculating cash income) or a personal withdrawal (not deducting it in calculating cash income).
2. Calculate the bank account balance at the end of the current year, using your answer from part 1.
3. Calculate the business's accrual income for the current year.
4. Reconcile your answers to parts 1 and 3.

PROBLEM 1.8 Calculate accrual income and change in cash

I just don't understand it!" Dwight Benat had received his accountant's calculation of Dwight's business income, showing an accrual income for his first year in business of $45,290. "If I made so much money, why don't I have that much in the bank? My bank account shows only $7,540 on hand!"

Dwight operates Benat Supply, which provides stationery and office supplies to business customers. He has no store, just a small rented warehouse, and only one employee. Here are the data he and his accountant used. Explain clearly to Dwight (1) how the accountant calculated the $45,290 income and (2) why there is only $7,540 on hand.

Collected from customers during the year	$143,710
Still owing from customers at the end of the year (collected next year)	15,220
Paid for products to resell and for other expenses, including wages, during the year	128,670
Owing for products and other expenses at the end of the year (paid next year)	9,040
Cost of unsold products on hand at the end of the year (all sold next year)	26,070
Amortization (depreciation) on equipment during the year	2,000
Personal withdrawals by Dwight during the year	7,500

PROBLEM 1.9 Why is accrual accounting valued?

(Challenging)

An executive of an international economic consulting firm recently said, "I find it interesting that as companies, or even countries, grow in sophistication, they tend to move from simple cash-based financial reports to accrual accounting reports." If this observation is valid, why would you suppose this movement to accrual accounting is happening?

PROBLEM 1.10 Discuss ethical problems

(Challenging)

Discuss the example ethical problems given at the end of Section 1.5. What ethical issues do you see? What do you think the chief accountant, the auditor, and the president should do?

PROBLEM 1.11 Factors in comparing companies' performance

(Challenging)

The president of Gobble Gobble Foods Inc., which makes everything from soup to nuts out of turkey meat, is comparing Gobble Gobble's performance to that of Curdled Products Inc., which does much the same using tofu and other bean curds. The president has the following data for Curdled Products, which she saw in the *Glower and Flail* newspaper yesterday (note that figures inside brackets indicate a loss):

Income for 1989	$1,565,000
Income for 1990	2,432,000
Income for 1991	(985,000)
Income for 1992	123,000
Income for 1993	1,249,000
Income for 1994	2,915,000
Income for first half of 1995	873,000

Without knowing much about accounting except the introductory ideas of this chapter, use your intelligence and experience in comparing things to make a list of the factors you think the president of Gobble Gobble should take into account in comparing her company's performance to that of Curdled.

PROBLEM 1.12 Objectives and risks in investment

(Challenging)

Suppose you had a few thousand dollars on hand and were offered a chance to invest in a small local business. What would be the objectives you would like to see such an investment meet? What risks would you want reassurance about before committing your funds? (You can get some hints about this from the Continuing Case.)

CASE 1A Accrual and cash income in measuring performance

Manitoba Wings is an airline services company with a plant near the Winnipeg Airport and service centres in several provinces. It provides meals, napkins and other food-related items, airplane cleaning, interior maintenance, and several other services to various airlines. The company has been fairly successful, though recessions and deregulation of air services have put significant pressure on its operations. When the company began in the late 1970s, it had a relatively weak financial position (mainly because of borrowing to get set up) and its financial performance, while satisfactory, has not enabled it to reduce its debt load very much. It seems that every time the company gets a little ahead, new equipment must be purchased or new product lines developed, and the company finds itself borrowing again.

A recent year provides a good example. The company's accrual income was $188,000 and its cash income was $241,000. (The difference was due to amortization expense of $96,000 and uncollected revenue being $43,000 higher at the end of the year than at the beginning. In the company's financial statements, the phrase "net income for the year" was used to describe the accrual income and "cash generated by operations" described the cash income.) The president had looked forward to using some of the cash to pay down debts, but late in the year the company had to buy new food handling and wrapping equipment for $206,000 to meet revised standards announced by its airline customers. Therefore, the company ended up only a few thousand dollars ahead in cash, not enough to make much of a dent in its debts.

The president has a regular half-yearly meeting with the company's external auditor to discuss accounting and auditing issues. After the above results were known, the president phoned the auditor and made the following comments: "I thought I'd ask you to think about a few things before our meeting next week. When it comes to our accounting, I think the company has too many masters and too many measures. What I mean is first that too many people are concerned with what our financial statements say. Why can't we just prepare financial statements that meet my needs as president—why do we have to worry about all the other people outside the company? Sometimes I'm not even sure who all those other people are, since you accountants and auditors often just talk about 'users' without being too clear what you mean. Also, I'm confused by the existence of both a 'net income figure' and a 'cash generated by operations' figure in our financial statements. Why can't we just have one or the other to measure our performance?"

The president raised issues that will be addressed frequently as this book develops your understanding. But for now, what would you say to the president?

CASE 1B Who would be interested in a company's financial statements?

The "financial highlights" and "corporate profile" excerpts that follow accompanied the 1993 financial statements of Intrawest Corporation, a Canadian ski resort operator. Based on these excerpts, who do you think would be interested in the financial statements of Intrawest, and why?

Intrawest Corporation
Financial Highlights

For the Years Ended September 30	1993	1992	1991
Operating Results (millions of dollars)			
Revenue			
Real estate	111.8	51.2	42.4
Ski and resort operations	58.6	55.5	34.5
Refinancing and dilution gains	—	15.6	—
	170.4	122.3	76.9
Net Income (loss)	16.9	19.6	(3.2)
Cash Flow			
Real estate	25.0	12.9	6.3
Ski and resort operations	12.7	11.2	9.7
Unallocated corporate expenses	(10.6)	(6.7)	(5.4)
	27.1	17.4	10.6

CORPORATE PROFILE

Intrawest is the leader in mountain resort development in North America, combining expertise in resort real estate development with resort and ski operation management. Intrawest owns and operates Blackcomb, Tremblant and Panorama and in the fall of 1993 entered into a real estate joint venture with Ralston Purina Company to transform the Colorado ski resort of Keystone into a world-class four-season destination resort.

Intrawest's real estate business focuses on residential multi-family developments and niche industrial and commercial markets. Real estate operations are concentrated in British Columbia and the state of Washington. Intrawest is a publicly traded Canadian company with shares listed on the Toronto, Montreal and Vancouver stock exchanges. The majority of Intrawest's shares are held by major Canadian financial institutions. Intrawest's head office is in Vancouver, British Columbia.

REPRODUCED COURTESY OF INTRAWEST CORPORATION, ANNUAL REPORT, SEPTEMBER 30, 1993.

1. Chancellor Sandy A. Mactaggart of the University of Alberta; letter to the author, January 24, 1991. Reprinted by permission.

CHAPTER 2

Financial Position: The Balance Sheet

2.1 Chapter Overview

This chapter introduces financial accounting's oldest and most basic report, the **balance sheet.** This statement is increasingly called the **statement of financial position**, because the longer title describes exactly what the statement does. (This book will use the older, shorter title, which is still more frequently used by companies. As in other areas where accounting is evolving, you should be prepared for variation in terminology.) The balance sheet summarizes, at a particular date, the enterprise's financial position:

- Resources (cash, products on hand, land, buildings, etc.);
- Obligations (loans owing, debts to creditors, etc.); and
- Owners' interests (what's left after subtracting the obligations from the resources).

The balance sheet also turns out to be the accumulation of everything financial accounting has recorded about the enterprise since the day it began. It is, therefore, the anchor to which all the other financial statements are tied.

In this chapter, you will learn:

Use concepts: how the demand for reliable financial information, which has existed for centuries, has shaped financial accounting;

Preparation concepts: how the balance sheet has been designed to respond to the demand for reliable financial information;

Preparation techniques: how to use accounting data to make a balance sheet, focusing on a simple balance sheet for now;

Use techniques: the beginnings of how to use a balance sheet to evaluate the enterprise's financial condition.

2.2 A Brief History of Early Accounting

We begin with a history review, because understanding how we got to where we are helps a lot in understanding why we do the things we do now and how to do them. Financial accounting is an ancient information system indeed, with many of its ideas originating hundreds of years ago.

Like other complex human inventions, financial accounting did not just appear one day fully formed. It has developed over thousands of years and has been thoroughly intertwined with the development of civilization. A science writer, quoting a brewery owner, had this to say on the topic of accounting and beer:

> Whatever the reason, [the early farmers in Mesopotamia] grew grain [and] "if you have grain, you need storehouses; if you have storehouses, you need accountants; if you have accountants, bang — you're on the road to civilization" (or the world's first audit).[1]

Our focus here is on accounting, not on history. Nevertheless, the past has a bearing on accounting in that accounting evolves as business, government, and other institutions in society evolve. As the needs for information change, accounting changes to meet those needs. Accounting's evolution is not always smooth, and not always efficient; at any given time there are aspects of accounting that may not seem to fit current needs well, but over time we can expect that accounting will, as it has in the past, meet those needs if they persist. Two terminological changes happening now, from "balance sheet" to "statement of financial position" (above) and from "depreciation" to "amortization" (Chapter 1) are minor examples of accounting's ongoing evolution.

When commerce consisted mainly of trading among families or tribal units, information demands were not complicated. Money had not been invented, so that even the simple financial reports we saw in Chapter 1 could not have been prepared. People would want to know what they had on hand and would need some sort of documentation to accompany shipments, so that they and their customers would agree on what was being traded. To meet such needs, accounting began as simple list-making. Especially important would be lists of the family or tribe's resources and, later, lists of debts to traders or other families. Later still, as commercial activities became more complex, families began to employ others to run aspects of their businesses and began also to create large business units with several locations. Accounting had to become more complex too, providing records that could be used to monitor the activities of employees and businesses in far-flung locations. People found that they needed to be able to verify what employees and traders said was happening. Because of these needs, the practice of having systematic records that could be audited later was begun.

To help you understand how present-day financial accounting concepts and techniques arose, a brief history, taking us from about 4500 B.C. in Mesopotamia to the early A.D. 1800s in England, follows. Chapter 3 will cover the two succeeding centuries, bringing the history up to the present. Keep in mind that the purpose of the review is to help you understand accounting, not to explain general history!

Because modern accrual accounting, as practised in North America and much of the rest of the world, has its roots in the development of Western civilization, our review of accounting history is oriented to that development. The interesting stories of the development of accounting in other parts of the world, such as China, India, and Africa, are, therefore, not included. The comments below are necessarily brief. If you would like to read further, some reading suggestions on accounting history are provided at the end of the chapter.[2]

MESOPOTAMIA TO ROME: 4500 B.C. TO A.D. 400

For a society to demand accounting it must have active trade and commerce, a basic level of writing, methods of measuring and calculating, and a medium of exchange or currency.[3] The earliest known civilization with an active record-keeping system flourished in Mesopotamia (now Iraq and Syria). Generally, a common language (such as Babylonian) existed for business, and there was also a good system of numbers and currency and of recordkeeping using clay tablets. As far as we know, ordinary merchants and general traders did not keep official records. Officials of the government and religious leaders of the temples decided what records were to be maintained for official purposes, and scribes did the recordkeeping. A scribe apprenticed for many years to master the craft of recording taxes, customs duties, temple offerings, and trade between governments and temples. Records consisted of counts and lists of grain, cattle, and other resources, and of obligations arising from trade. We can still see that today: the balance sheet of any enterprise includes items like unsold products and equipment, and trade obligations such as amounts due from customers and due to suppliers. All of these balance sheet figures are summaries supported by detailed lists.

When a scribe determined that a particular record was complete and correct, the scribe's seal was pressed into a clay tablet to certify that this was so, and the tablet was baked to prevent alteration.[4] The scribe was a forerunner of today's accountants and auditors. (However, today's auditors do not use seals; they instead sign an audit report to indicate that the financial statements are fairly presented.) This scribe-based form of recordkeeping was used for many years, spreading across land and time to Egypt, Greece, and Rome. Media other than clay tablets, such as papyrus, were used as time passed.[5] (Do you suppose people accustomed to clay tablets would have resisted the introduction of papyrus, just as some people accustomed to pencil and paper now

Figure 2.1 *A rare example of an early system of accounting, this marble slab documents the disbursements of the Athenian state, 418 B.C. to 415 B.C.*

Reproduced by courtesy of the Trustees of the British Museum.

resist the introduction of computers for accounting?) Figure 2.1 shows a rare example of an early system of accounting.

Trade and commerce grew over thousands of years, from small, family operations to very large activities involving kings, religious leaders, and various levels of government. For example, as the Greek civilization spread and then the Roman empire grew very large, administrative regions were organized in conquered lands in order to simplify governing them. These regions were managed by local administrators or governors, who generally could neither read nor write. When an accounting of their management was required, an official of the central government would come out and listen to an oral report. This event was, therefore, a "hearing," and the listening official was there to "audit" (from the Latin word for "hear"). Today, the person who comes to inspect and approve the financial statements of an enterprise is called an auditor, though a lot more goes on today than just listening!

THE DARK AGES TO THE RENAISSANCE: A.D. 400 TO A.D. 1500

With the fall of the Roman Empire in about the 5th century A.D., both trade and associated recordkeeping became stagnant in Europe, though activities still continued in Constantinople, the Middle East, India, China, and elsewhere. In Europe, great stimulus to trade began with the period of the Crusades, around the 11th century, when kings and princes could not themselves provide the material to support their retinues of crusaders bound for the Holy Land. This was a prosperous time for the lesser nobles and private merchants, who supplied the crusaders from ports such as Venice. A shift of supply and economic power from governments to the private sector began, and large merchant banks developed, such as that of the Medici in Florence. These banks got heavily involved in the businesses and governments they helped to finance.

Because of all these activities, a more exact system of recordkeeping was developed in order to keep track of materials supplied, cash received and spent, and especially who owed whom how much money.[6] For the traders, merchants, and bankers, the stimulus provided by the Crusades set recordkeeping off in a more organized and systematic direction. The new direction was made possible also by refinements in the use of numbers and arithmetic that had taken place in Arab countries during Europe's Dark Ages. The number system we use in accounting and in our daily lives originated from these refinements.

The exact way that accounting, or more precisely, the recordkeeping basis of accounting we call **bookkeeping**, evolved during this busy time is a subject of debate among accounting historians. A major event, however, was the publication in 1494 of a treatise on "double-entry" bookkeeping by Friar Pacioli of Venice. In the book, he referred to the method as an established procedure that had been in use in the Medici banks of Italy and in other businesses for some time. Pacioli's book was an important contribution to the knowledge of algebra and arithmetic, and of value specifically because of its detailed description and codification of the double-entry system. It was rapidly translated into all the major European languages, and, using these translations, European scholars extended Pacioli's ideas.

DOUBLE-ENTRY BOOKKEEPING

Pacioli's concepts were revolutionary but sound: they form the fundamental basis of modern financial accounting, providing a method of pulling together

FIGURE 2.2 *During the Reformation, European merchants and bankers established companies that were early versions of modern business corporations. One such merchant is the subject of this 1630 engraving by Rembrandt. The merchant's scale and ledger book demonstrate his reliance on organization, documentation, and qualification. Careful attention to these facilitates his control of capital (bags of money or gold) and trade goods (casks and chest).*
REPRODUCED BY PERMISSION OF THE BETTMANN ARCHIVE.

all the lists of resources and obligations in a way that helps to prevent errors. The idea is that each trade or other commercial transaction is recorded (entered) twice, hence **double entry**

- once to recognize the resource involved in the transaction (a); and
- once to recognize the source or effect of that resource change (b).

Instead of the disconnected lists that existed before double-entry bookkeeping was invented, the lists of resources and sources were now connected to each other.

If a dollar amount (or that in any other medium of exchange—pounds, francs, yen, marks, and so on) can be assigned to each transaction, that amount can be used to record both the (a) and (b) sides of each. Then, by adding up all the (a) amounts and all the (b) amounts, the two sides act as a check on each other. If errors are made, they are likely to be found because the two sides will not add up to the same amount. If they do add up, we say they "balance." Hence, the "balance sheet," which shows that the two sides do add up. For reasons that may have been important once but are now lost in the mists of time, the (a) sides are called **debits**, and the (b) sides are called **credits**. (Confusingly, negatives on the (a) side are also called credits, and negatives on the (b) side are also called debits.) Thus the balance sheet looks like this:

Resources	Sources
Positive items (debits)	Positive items (credits)
Negative items (credits)	Negative items (debits)

As you can see, the labels are arbitrary: debits are additions to the left or subtractions to the right, while credits are additions to the right or subtractions to the left.

FIGURE 2.3 *A portion of an antique bookkeeping poster. The linking ribbons in the illustration suggest the relationship between financial accounts and business decisions.*
COURTESY OF URSUS BOOKS AND PRINTS LTD., NEW YORK.

In later chapters, we will see much more about the recordkeeping system Pacioli introduced to the world; it is one of the most far-reaching of human inventions. For now, look at two simple examples of double entry.

1. Purchasing goods for resale:
   a. The resource (**asset**) is an addition to the inventory of unsold products;
   b. The source (a **liability**, because a creditor is the source) is that an obligation is created to pay the supplier, so there is a debt owing to the supplier.

If the goods cost, say, $452, we have

- an addition to the account for the resource represented by the list of inventory of unsold products, a *debit* of $452; *and*
- an addition to the account for the obligation represented by the list of amounts owing to suppliers, a *credit* of $452.

The balance sheet stays in balance due to this *double entry*, because both resources and sources are increased (are "up") by $452:

Resources	Sources
Up (debit) $452	Up (credit) $452

2. Borrowing money from the bank on a long-term loan:

   a. The resource (asset) is an addition to the amount of cash on hand;

   b. The source (a liability again) is that an obligation is created to repay the bank, so there is a debt owing to the bank.

   If the borrowed cash is, say, $1,000, we have

   - an addition to the asset "cash," so total resources go up $1,000; and
   - an addition to the liability "long-term bank loan," so the total sources also go up $1,000.

   Again, the balance sheet stays in balance:

Resources		Sources	
Up (debit)	$1,000	Up (credit)	$1,000
Total debits now	$1,452	Total credits now	$1,452

BRITAIN: FROM 1500 TO THE EARLY 1800S

In the several hundred years since Pacioli's treatise, accounting developed to suit the social and business circumstances of each country. France, for example, had a strong, centralized government and developed a national accounting system written by a central board of administrators. On the other hand, England had less government involvement in commerce and trade and a smaller civil service and relied more heavily on the initiatives of the private sector and the courts.[7] The financial accounting system now used in the United Kingdom, Canada, the United States, and many other countries relies heavily on the precedents set in England during this period. (Financial accounting in continental Europe developed on a somewhat different path. Russia, China, Japan, and many other countries have different financial accounting too.)

Prior to Pacioli, English recordkeeping had much in common with Roman methods used hundreds of years earlier. "Stewards" were employed to manage the properties of the English aristocracy, much as local governors had been in Roman-held areas. In 1300, Oxford University offered an accounting course: Roman recordkeeping for stewards![8] The concept of **stewardship**, of a person managing something on behalf of someone else, is still an important aspect of accounting. It is often said, for example, that an enterprise's financial statements demonstrate the quality of management's stewardship of the enterprise on behalf of its owners.

Until the mid-1600s accounting and recordkeeping (bookkeeping) were largely synonymous. Records were a private matter for the attention of the lord, merchant, or banker. But then a significant development occurred (explored further in Chapter 3): the advent of companies that sold stocks (shares of ownership) to private citizens. These citizens could not all crowd into the company's office to inspect the records, even if they could understand them. This produced a demand for some form of reporting to the shareholders, for financial statements that could be relied on as accurate summaries of the records. There was a demand that the balance sheet be more detailed in its description of the owners' equity and the changes in it than had been necessary before there had been such dispersed ownership. There was even some demand for regulation of such reports: for example, in 1657 Oliver Cromwell, as regent of England, required the East India Company to publish its balance sheet.[9] Accounting was on its way to developing the standards of calculation and **disclosure** that are very important in modern accounting and that distinguish accounting from the underlying recordkeeping. Progress in this direction was not rapid, but it picked up steam with the arrival of the Industrial Revolution.

FIGURE 2.4 *An invaluable accounting tool, the first successful European mechanical calculator was invented by Blaise Pascal in 1642 and soon became an international marvel. Pascal was already known as a scientist and mathematician when he invented the adding machine at the age of 19. Among many other things, Pascal is also known as the inventor of the barometer.*
REPRODUCED BY PERMISSION OF THE BETTMANN ARCHIVE.

However, there were some interesting events in the interval. In 1670, a famous company was formed, namely, The Governor and Company of Adventurers of England Trading into Hudson's Bay. The Hudson's Bay Company, or "the Bay," as it now calls itself in its advertisements, has played a very significant role over the centuries, and is still an important part of Canadian business. Many of the records kept by its far-flung employees still exist and provide detailed pictures of business and society over the years.[10] In 1720, the spectacular collapse of the South Seas Company prompted the first known written audit, conducted in order to determine the assets of the company.[11] The developing Industrial Revolution of the late 1700s and early 1800s helped to fuel the emerging commercial sector of Britain, and accounting practices became an important part of the enterprise. In 1825, the British Parliament eased hundred-year-old prohibitions on trading shares in companies, and the modern era of stock markets and publicly owned companies began in earnest. A few years later, Parliament required annual audits of the balance sheets of such companies.[12] Accounting and auditing continued to develop in response to the changing needs of the society of which they were a part.

From this point on in Britain's commercial development, accounting's emphasis shifted from recordkeeping to the topics of: choice of accounting method, professional ethics, and the various standards and laws governing financial reporting and financial disclosure. We will continue this story in Chapter 3.

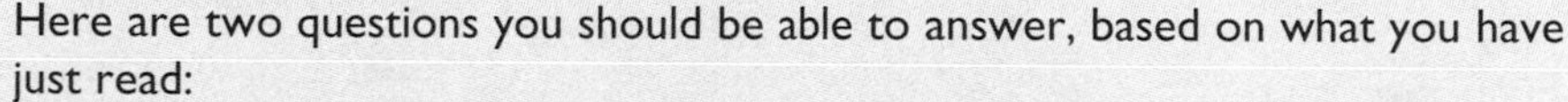

HOW'S YOUR UNDERSTANDING

Here are two questions you should be able to answer, based on what you have just read:

1. Describe a development in business or society that had an impact on the development of financial accounting, or vice versa.
2. Why has financial accounting become more and more sophisticated and comprehensive over the centuries?

2.3 INTRODUCTION TO THE BALANCE SHEET

Corporations, which are legally incorporated **companies** such as Noranda, Bank of Montreal, General Motors, and Nestlé, produce financial statements at least annually. So do many other kinds of organizations, such as the City of Halifax, Foster Parents Plan of Canada, and your university's Student Union. For large corporations, such statements are included in a larger document called an **annual report**. An annual report typically begins with narrative material on the corporation's performance and prospects, before turning to the financial statements, one of which is the balance sheet.

The balance sheet got its name, as we have seen from the comments about double entry, because its two sides (resources and their sources) have the same total, they balance. For example, if you get $100 by borrowing from the bank, your balance sheet would list the $100 as a cash resource (a debit) and $100 as a bank loan (a credit), the source of the money. It lists the set of resources and sources of the enterprise *at a point in time*, thereby describing the enterprise's *financial position* at that point. See Exhibit 2.1 for a simple example (an explanation of the terms used follow the exhibit).

Let's review some features of this balance sheet:

- The title identifies the enterprise (Sound and Light Corporation), the point in time at which it is drawn up (April 30, 1995), and the currency in which amounts are measured (thousands of dollars).
- The balance sheet balances! As of April 30, 1995, total resources of $495 thousand are exactly equalled by the total sources of these resources. It is a summary, so we cannot tell exactly which source produced which resource, for example, the $50 thousand of cash came partly from bank borrowing and partly from other sources, such as past earnings. (More about resources and sources shortly.)
- The positive items on the left-hand side are debits, and those on the right are credits. Because the assets side deducts a $122 thousand credit,

EXHIBIT 2.1

Sound and Light Corporation
Balance Sheet as at April 30, 1995
in Thousands of Dollars

Resources: Debits			**Sources of Resources: Credits**		
Shorter-term assets:			Shorter-term liabilities:		
Cash	$ 50		Owing to the bank	$ 30	
Due from customers	75		Owing to suppliers	73	$103
Unsold products	120	$245	Longer-term liabilities:		
Longer-term assets:			Land mortgage owing		87
Land (cost)	$100		Owners' equity:		
Factory (cost)	272		Share capital issued	$130	
Accum. amort.*	(122)	250	Past income retained	175	305
Total		$495	Total		$495

*Accum. amort. is the total amortization on the factory recorded so far (accumulated). It is bracketed because it is negative (a credit on the debit side), reflecting the factory's economic value estimated to have been consumed to date.

the total debits without that credit are $245 thousand + $100 thousand + $272 thousand = $617 thousand. Adding that credit to those on the right-hand side also gets $617 thousand ($495 thousand + $122 thousand). So, we can also say, for any balanced balance sheet, that debits = credits. The balance sheet may rearrange them or subtract some credits from debits or vice versa (called "netting" the figures), but the underlying equality is always maintained.

Now some terms:

- The resources, which accountants call **assets**, are a mixture of the things that the company needs to do business, for instance, products to sell and a building to operate from, and the things that it has accumulated as a result of doing business, including amounts due from customers for past sales.
  - Assets are usually separated into shorter-term ones (**current assets**) and longer-term ones (**noncurrent assets**). (More about these categories is in Section 2.5.)
- The sources, which accountants call **liabilities** and **owners' equity**, tell us where the resources came from, how they have been financed.
- Liabilities are amounts due (**debts**) to creditors, such as to banks and suppliers, or amounts estimated to be due later, such as future pension payments to retired employees.
  - Like assets, liabilities are usually separated into shorter-term ones (**current liabilities**) and longer-term ones (**noncurrent liabilities**).
- **Equity** is the owners' interest in the enterprise. That interest can come from direct contributions by the owners, or from the accumulation of earnings that the owners choose not to withdraw.
  - Contributions from owners can come in many forms. For a corporation like Sound and Light, the most usual is **share capital:** people give the corporation money in exchange for **shares**, which are portions of

ownership interest. Sound and Light owners (**shareholders**) have contributed $130 thousand to the corporation. For example, some owners probably contributed cash to get Sound and Light started, so they would be one of the sources of the cash asset. More on owners and shares is in Section 2.7. (Many corporations' shares, also called **stocks**, are traded on **stock markets**. In such markets, shares are traded between owners; the corporations issuing the shares got money only when the shares were issued by them to the first owners.)

- Past income retained, usually called **retained earnings**, represents past accrual income not yet given to owners. (The terms **earnings, income,** and **profit** are used pretty much interchangeably, but they all refer to accrual income, as described in Chapter 1.) As we'll see in later chapters, earning income means that there will be more assets (such as cash) and/or fewer liabilities. The owners could have withdrawn cash or other assets from the company, for instance by declaring themselves a **dividend**, but they have chosen instead to leave the assets in the corporation. Thus these assets are resources of the corporation and retained earnings is the source of those resources. The corporation can use these assets to earn more income in the future.

From this simple Sound and Light balance sheet we can answer some questions about the corporation's financial condition:

1. Is the enterprise soundly financed? Sound and Light has financed its $495 thousand in assets by borrowing $103 thousand short-term and $87 thousand long-term, and by getting $130 thousand in contributions from owners and not paying past earnings of $175 thousand out to owners. Its $495 thousand in assets are therefore financed by $190 thousand (38%) from creditors and $305 thousand (62%) from the owners. So, it is not much in debt, proportionately. (What would you think if the creditors were owed $450 thousand and the owners' equity was only $45 thousand? This would be a lot more risky for the creditors.)
2. Can the enterprise pay its bills on time? Sound and Light owes $103 thousand in the short term and has only $50 thousand in cash. Therefore, to pay its bills it will have to collect cash from its customers either by getting them to pay what they already owe or selling them some unsold products for cash. There is likely no problem here: collections and sales, and payments to creditors, are probably going on continuously. The company has $245 thousand of current assets that it should be able to turn into cash to pay the $103 thousand of current liabilities (it is said to have $245 thousand – $103 thousand = $142 thousand in **working capital**). But you can see that if the company had a slow period of sales or collections, it could have difficulty paying its bills. So, we might want to know what times of the year are the company's busy and slow seasons. (What would you think if the company had only $10 thousand in cash and $160 thousand in unsold products? In that case, though its working capital would be the same, it would likely be overstocked and cash short, and might have trouble paying bills.)
3. Should the owners declare themselves a dividend? If so, how large should it be? Legally, the **board of directors** (who manage the company on behalf of the shareholders) might be able to declare a dividend to shareholders of

$175 thousand, the full amount of the retained earnings. But there is not nearly enough cash for that. Those past earnings have been reinvested in unsold products, building, equipment, and so on, and are therefore not sitting around in cash waiting to be paid to owners. This is true of nearly all corporations: they invest past earnings in operating assets and so do not have a lot of cash on hand. Probably a dividend of more than about $25 thousand, only one-seventh of the retained earnings, would cause Sound and Light some cash strain. (What would you think if the corporation had no buildings or equipment but $300 thousand in cash instead? It would appear to be cash rich in that case and should either invest the cash productively or pay a dividend to the owners so they can do what they like with the money.)

So you see that the balance sheet provides interesting information if you know how to read it. Your skill in reading it will grow as you work with it. There are different styles of presentation of the balance sheet; all have the same information, but it is arranged differently. Three common styles are illustrated here, using the Sound and Light figures:

EXHIBIT 2.2

Sound and Light Corporation
Balance Sheet as at April 30, 1995
in Thousands of Dollars

Side-by-side style

Assets		**Liabilities and Equity**		
Current assets	$245	Current liabilities		$103
Noncurrent assets	250	Noncurrent liabilities		87
		Owners' equity:		
		Contributed capital	$130	
		Retained earnings	175	305
TOTAL	$495	TOTAL		$495

Vertical style

Assets		
Current assets		$245
Noncurrent assets		250
TOTAL		$495
Liabilities and Equity		
Current liabilities		$103
Noncurrent liabilities		87
Owners' equity:		
Contributed capital	$130	
Retained earnings	175	305
TOTAL		$495

EXHIBIT 2.2 continued

Working capital style

Net Assets		
Current assets		$245
Less current liabilities		103
Working capital		$142
Noncurrent assets		250
TOTAL		$392
Financing Sources		
Noncurrent liabilities		$ 87
Owners' equity:		
Contributed capital	$130	
Retained earnings	175	305
TOTAL		$392

HOW'S YOUR UNDERSTANDING

Here are two questions you should be able to answer, based on what you have just read.

1. The balance sheet is a summary of certain things at a point in time. What things?
2. Assemble a balance sheet for Northern Inc. from the following information and comment on the company's financial position at that point in time: Share capital, $1,000; Due from customers, $1,100; Owing to suppliers, $2,100; Unsold products, $1,700; Retained earnings, $2,200; Cash, $500; Equipment, $2,000. (You should get current assets $3,300, noncurrent assets $2,000; total assets $5,300; current liabilities $2,100, noncurrent liabilities $0; contributed capital $1,000, retained earnings $2,200; total liabilities and equity $5,300. Liabilities of $2,100 are 40% of total sources, so the company's financing is similar to Sound and Light's. It does not have enough cash to pay all its retained earnings to owners as dividends.)

2.4 MAINTAINING THE BALANCE SHEET EQUATION

Following the double-entry concept, the balance sheet has two parts, and the two parts have the same total. This financial statement, therefore, demonstrates the following equality (the **balance sheet equation**):

Assets = Liabilities + Owners' Equity

As illustrated above, the various items can be arranged in different ways, so that the assets on the left could have some credits (such as accumulated amortization) subtracted from the debits, and the liabilities and equity on the right could have some debits subtracted from the credits (examples later in the book). If you untangle all these format decisions and line up all the debits and all the credits separately, they will be equal, so another way of stating the balance sheet equation is to say that Debits = Credits.

You will recognize, therefore, that the following are all versions of the balance sheet equation:

Assets = Liabilities + Owners' Equity
Assets – Liabilities = Owners' Equity
Assets – Liabilities – Owners' Equity = 0
Debits = Credits

The point of this is to emphasize that the balance sheet will balance, whether all the debits are on one side and all the credits are on the other, or whether the debits and credits are mixed up, some of each on both sides of the balance sheet. This means that the totals of each side of the balance sheet are usually *net* figures. The assets total is the net of all the positive assets minus any negative amounts, and the liabilities and owners' equity total is the net of all the positive liabilities and equity items minus any negative amounts. This method gives accounting great flexibility, because amounts can be moved around on the balance sheet to produce the most useful presentation of the information without disturbing the rule that the balance sheet must balance.

Here is another example. Suppose a company has a bank overdraft of $500, which means that its cash-in-bank asset is negative (the bank has allowed the company to remove $500 more cash from the account than there was in it, in effect lending the company the $500). The company's other assets total $12,400. Its *net* assets are therefore $11,900, and this is also the total of its liabilities and owners' equity. The company can choose one of two ways of presenting this information:

Other assets of $12,400 minus bank overdraft of $500	=	Liabilities and owners' equity of $11,900
	or	
Other assets of $12,400	=	Liabilities and owners' equity of $11,900 plus bank overdraft of $500

For bank overdrafts, it is customary to use the second method, to move the negative bank amount to the other side of the balance sheet. The reason is that even if the company normally has cash in the bank so that the account is normally an asset, it really is a liability at this point because the bank has, in effect, lent the company $500 and will want the money back. Moving items around within the balance sheet (or within other financial statements) is called **reclassification** and is done by accountants whenever it is thought to improve the informativeness of the financial statement. Reclassification may change the totals on both sides of the balance sheet, but it keeps the new totals equal (balanced).

Some negative amounts are left as deductions, not moved to the other side to make them positive, like the overdraft. We have already seen an important credit balance account that is located on the asset side of the balance sheet and treated as a deduction from the rest of the assets: the **accumulated amortization** (or **accumulated depreciation**) figure. It is the amount of all the amortization calculated to date on assets such as buildings and equipment. For accumulated amortization, there are at least three ways of presenting the information, all of which maintain the balance sheet equation. Using the Sound and Light example, the three ways are:

- It could be shown with other credits on the right side of the balance sheet (in former times, it was, and in some countries, still is). In North America, most accountants feel that it is more informative for users to deduct it from the asset figures so that the **net book value** of the assets is shown. The net book value is the assets' original value (cost) minus their accumulated amortization; it tells the user how much of that original value has yet to be amortized.
- It could be separately disclosed as a deduction on the left side of the balance sheet, as it was in the Sound and Light balance sheet at the beginning of Section 2.3. This is very common, but if there are a lot of different kinds of assets and amortization amounts, it can make the balance sheet a little cluttered.
- It could be deducted from the assets' cost and just the net book value could be disclosed on the balance sheet. In the Sound and Light example, the noncurrent assets would be listed in the following sort of way: Noncurrent assets (net) $250. This method, which is becoming quite popular, would be accompanied by a **note** to the financial statements, listing the cost and accumulated amortization amounts separately, and so keeping the balance sheet uncluttered and allowing some additional explanations of the figures if that were thought useful.

This discussion illustrates an important characteristic of the balance sheet equation. It is an invention maintained by the double-entry system and thought to be useful as a conceptual tool for the measurement of financial position. It is an arithmetical result, not some sort of basic truth. As we will see in several examples later on, the bookkeeping task of making sure that the balance sheet is in balance is really just the starting point for the fundamental accounting question of how to measure and describe financial position most appropriately.

HOW'S YOUR UNDERSTANDING

Here are two questions you should be able to answer, based on what you have just read:

1. How can there be debits, and/or credits, on both sides of the balance sheet?
2. Prepare the balance sheet of Mike's Tire Repair (owner, Mike) from the following account balances: Bank overdraft, $250; Due from customers, $640; Inventory of supplies, $210; Equipment cost, $890; Accumulated amortization on equipment, $470; Due to suppliers, $360; Owner's equity, $660. (The first account listed is a credit, the next three are debits, and the last three are credits. You should get net total assets of $1,270 and total liabilities and owner's equity also of $1,270.)

2.5 A CLOSER LOOK AT BALANCE SHEET CONTENT

The balance sheet balances, but what are these assets, liabilities, and owners' equity accounts that so neatly balance with each other? To help you understand, the recent balance sheet of a real company, Paychex, Inc., has been provided in Exhibit 2.3. Paychex, Inc. is an American payroll processing and human resource consulting company, based in Rochester, New York. According to its 1993 annual report, the company has 90 locations, serving 167,000 mostly small business clients across the United States. Among the things you may notice as you review the balance sheet are:

1. It is *comparative*: it contains figures both for the most recent year and for the preceding year to help the users recognize changes. It is standard practice for the more recent figures to be to the left, closer to the words describing those figures.
2. To avoid clutter, the figures are shown in thousands of dollars, not exact amounts to the cent.
3. References are made to various notes. It is not possible to explain every important item on the face of the balance sheet, so extensive explanatory notes are referred to on and appended to most balance sheets. Paychex's notes are not provided here because they raise issues we have not yet covered; just remember to look for notes when you are using balance sheets and other financial statements.
4. The company has many different kinds of asset, liability, and equity accounts. They are not necessarily easy to classify into the categories we saw in the Sound and Light Corporation example. You likely will not understand all the accounts and the way the company has categorized them; that understanding will develop as you work through the book.
5. The balance sheet date is May 31, not December 31. December 31, the end of the calendar year, is the most popular accounting year-end ("fiscal" year-end), but many companies choose other dates.
6. Paychex has two categories of contributed capital: $199 thousand in issued shares and $13,946 thousand in "additional capital." This shows that the company has received more capital from shareholders than the official "par value" of the shares indicates. Such "additional capital" (also called "contributed surplus" by some companies) is rare in Canada because most Canadian companies have "no-par" shares, that is, all capital received is part of the official contributed capital. If Paychex had been a Canadian company, you would have seen only one line for share capital, showing an aggregate amount of $14,145 thousand. This sort of international difference in balance sheets, which may reflect legal or business differences, is common. Usually you can figure out what is causing such differences, but sometimes the reason is obscure.

Some explanation of the detailed content of balance sheets would be helpful now, before some examples of preparing balance sheets are given.

An *asset* is a resource that an individual, an enterprise, or a country owns or controls, and that can provide some benefit now or in the future. Some of Paychex's assets are: cash and near-cash equivalents such as savings certificates, accounts receivable (money due from customers), land, and buildings. All of these assets would appear on the balance sheet of most Canadian enterprises. Most companies also have another asset that Paychex does not seem to have: **inventories** of manufactured or purchased products for future sale or use. (The reason is that Paychex sells services, not products, so it does not have products on hand to sell.)

Exhibit 2.3

PAYCHEX, INC.
BALANCE SHEET

	(in thousands)	May 31 1993	1992
Assets	**Current Assets**		
	Cash and cash equivalents	$ 5,023	$ 5,215
	Investments	33,092	14,810
	Interest receivable	3,293	2,040
	Trade accounts receivable	18,889	17,489
	Prepaid expenses and other current assets	2,612	1,142
	Deferred income taxes	1,316	925
	Total Current Assets	64,225	41,621
	Property and Equipment *(Notes B & E)*		
	Land and improvements	2,663	2,564
	Buildings	21,026	20,729
	Data processing equipment	42,680	38,504
	Furniture, fixtures and equipment	21,442	19,312
	Leasehold improvements	891	846
		88,702	81,955
	Less allowance for depreciation and amortization	46,586	38,080
	Net Property and Equipment	42,116	43,875
	Other Assets	579	746
	Total Assets	$106,920	$86,242
Liabilities and Stockholders' Equity	**Current Liabilities**		
	Trade accounts payable	$ 3,422	$ 3,519
	Accrued compensation and related items	8,581	7,298
	Accrued income taxes	1,011	252
	Other accrued expenses	3,026	1,716
	Deferred revenue	1,399	562
	Current portion of long-term debt *(Note B)*	397	390
	Total Current Liabilities	17,836	13,737
	Other Liabilities		
	Long-term debt *(Note B)*	1,237	1,634
	Unamortized lease incentives *(Note E)*	1,334	1,770
	Deferred income taxes	1,324	1,696
	Total Liabilities	21,731	18,837
	Stockholders' Equity *(Notes C & H)*		
	Common Stock, $.01 par value, authorized 50,000,000 shares: Issued, 19,868,451 in 1993 and 19,765,738 in 1992	199	198
	Additional capital	13,946	11,756
	Retained earnings	71,044	55,451
		85,189	67,405
	Total Liabilities and Stockholders' Equity	$106,920	$86,242

See notes to financial statements. *(Not included)*

REPRODUCED COURTESY OF PAYCHEX INCORPORATED, ANNUAL REPORT, MAY 31, 1993.

Other "assets" of a firm would be happy employees and a safe working environment, yet these do not directly appear on a balance sheet. The reason for the distinction between the assets that accounting recognizes and these other "assets" is that there are objective, standard measures for, and economic control of, the first group but not the second group. An inventory of machine parts is owned by the enterprise and has a dollar cost that can be verified by anyone. A happy employee is, in theory, more productive than an unhappy employee, but it is difficult to measure with any consistency how much more productive a very happy employee is compared with an only mildly happy employee. Moreover, at least in our society, an enterprise does not own its employees! Accounting generally records assets only where there is economic control and where there can be a reasonable level of consistency in measurement techniques and results. This places limits on the scope of the accounting statements.

A *liability* is a presently existing commitment to transfer an individual's, enterprise's, or country's resources to others in the future. Liabilities can be legally owed debts, such as loans from the bank, mortgages, or amounts due to suppliers, but they also can be estimates of future payments based on past agreements, such as those arising from promises of health care or other benefits to employees after they retire, or of warranty repairs for customers when products break down. As examples of the first group, Paychex has "trade accounts payable" due to its suppliers and long-term debt. As examples of the second group, Paychex has "accrued" (current estimated) income taxes and "deferred" (long-term estimated) income taxes.

Following the same rule as for assets, liabilities generally include only obligations with objective, standard measures. If you are in debt to a friend for $10, that would appear on your balance sheet. But, if you are "in debt" to a friend for saving your life, that would not appear on your balance sheet.

A full understanding of what assets and liabilities are and how to measure them will take time and many examples. One thing you may be wondering about is where the figures—the debits and credits—used to measure these things come from. In the history review, it was noted that a precondition for financial accounting as we know it is a medium of exchange. The measuring unit for financial accounting is the currency unit relevant to the enterprise in question. In Canada, the Canadian dollar, not surprisingly, is the usual measuring unit. However, some Canadian companies use other units; for example, Alcan, a large Canadian company active across the country, measures its assets and liabilities in U.S. dollars. Around the world, almost every conceivable monetary unit is used in somebody's accounting, so do not be surprised if you see a balance sheet in pounds, or lira, or rubles, or yen, or whatever.

But, again, where do the dollar figures come from? This turns out to be a very deep and controversial question indeed. Only a superficial answer can be given now, but after a few more chapters, you will have a deeper understanding of it. Accounting is a historical measurement system: it records what *has happened*, not what will happen or would have happened if conditions had been different. Therefore, asset and liability values are derived from the past. Assets are generally valued at *what they cost when they were acquired*, and liabilities are generally valued at *what was promised when the obligation arose*. Assets and liabilities are not valued at the current prices they might fetch if sold or marketed right now. This is something that confuses many users: looking at a balance sheet, a user might think that assets such as land and buildings are shown at what those assets would be worth right now if they were sold. They are instead valued at what they cost when acquired. The differences in these values can be large. For example, a company may have bought land in the downtown area of a city 20 years ago for $50,000. The land may now be worth millions of dollars. But the balance sheet normally will show the land asset at a figure of $50,000, its original cost. This is because the only thing that has happened is that the land was acquired 20 years ago, and the cost incurred then can be verified. Nothing further has happened: the land has not been sold, so its current value is hypothetical and difficult to verify.

The third term in the balance sheet equation is *owners' equity*. It represents the residual ownership interest in the enterprise. This interest has two general forms. First, the owners usually contribute cash or other assets in return for shares or other evidence of ownership. The assets contributed are on the left side of the balance sheet: equity accounts, called share capital or having other names indicating direct contribution by owners, represent the source of such assets. As we saw already, Paychex has $14,145 thousand of contributed capital.

Second, the enterprise usually earns income (also called earnings or profit, as we have seen) and does not return all of the assets representing the accumulation of that income to owners, for instance, in the form of dividends to shareholders. So an enterprise usually has assets produced by the excess of past income accumulated over amounts paid out to the owners. (These assets may include cash, but not necessarily, because accrual income also involves increases in noncash assets such as accounts receivable, and because any cash earned may have been spent to reduce liabilities or acquire other assets.) The equity account called retained earnings represents the source of such income-generated assets. Paychex has $71,044 thousand of retained earnings, more than five times the $14,145 thousand contributed capital.

The details of the owners' equity section of the balance sheet depend on the legal structure of the enterprise and its ownership arrangements. (These will be examined further a little later in this chapter.) Like assets whose sources are liabilities, assets provided by owners are mixed in with the rest: the equity section of the balance sheet represents the owners' *residual* interest because normally, if the enterprise is ended, the liabilities must be paid first and the owners get whatever is left over. You can represent this residual interest by one of the versions of the balance sheet equation given in Section 2.4:

Assets – Liabilities = Owner's Equity
Owners' Equity = Assets – Liabilities

Equity is, therefore, a net figure and is often referred to as the **book value** of the whole enterprise. You will notice that if the assets are less than the liabilities, which would indicate an enterprise with more obligations than resources (not a good position to be in!), the owners' equity will be *negative*. Such a situation is a sign of serious financial problems and is likely to be followed by bankruptcy or other unpleasant results.

Balance sheets are usually designed to separate short-term assets and liabilities from long-term ones.

- Usually, *current* (short-term) assets and liabilities are those that will be converted to cash, paid off, or used up within a year.

- *Noncurrent* (longer-term) assets and liabilities will remain assets and liabilities for at least a year.

The reason for drawing the distinction is to help the reader of the balance sheet judge the short-term financial position (current assets minus current liabilities) of the firm. Paychex has $64,225 thousand of current assets and $17,836 thousand of current liabilities. Its short-term assets, therefore, exceed the short-term debts by $46,389 thousand; they are 360% of the short-term debts. We say that the company's

- **Working capital** (current assets minus current liabilities) is $46,389 thousand;
- **Working capital ratio** or **current ratio** (current assets divided by current liabilities) is 3.60:1.

Low or negative working capital (which is the same thing as a ratio of one or less) is usually an indication of short-run financial difficulties that, if not corrected, can lead to bankruptcy or other serious problems. The interpretation of the working capital ratio depends very much on the nature of the enterprise and its way of doing business: more about interpretation of ratios is given later, especially in Chapter 9. However, you can see that Paychex is in quite a strong position. Not only are current assets more than three times current liabilities, but the company has enough cash and investments alone to pay off the current liabilities twice over.

The balance sheet is a measure of assets, liabilities, and owners' equity at a certain date: it is a snapshot of the organization, listing its stock of resources, obligations, and ownership interest at that date. As in the Paychex example, last year's balance sheet is also usually provided in an annual report to permit a comparison between this year and the previous one. One deficiency with the balance sheet is that it is a static snapshot, not a video: it does not tell us how the organization arrived at the position of having a particular set of assets or liabilities. For that information, we need to look at the other parts of the financial statements, which we will do in later chapters.

2.6 AN ILLUSTRATION OF PREPARING A BALANCE SHEET

For illustrative purposes, we will now construct a balance sheet for John Graham, who decided to set up a business as a downtown courier. Before he could operate his courier service there were a few things he needed: a bicycle, a bike lock, a delivery bag, and a good pair of running shoes. He had $200 in savings, but quickly realized that he would need more funds to purchase all of the required items. John asked his Aunt Elizabeth for a loan of $200 and promised that he would pay her back as soon as he could. She said yes.

John purchased a bike for $500, placing $275 down and promising to pay the rest later. He then bought a bike lock for $15, a pair of shoes for $60, and a delivery bag for $25, paying cash for all these items. He began his business on April 15, 1995, under the name QuickJohn Courier.

From this information we can make the following balance sheet:

EXHIBIT 2.4

QuickJohn Courier
Rough Balance Sheet as at April 15, 1995

Assets		**Liabilities and Owner's Equity**	
Cash (what's left)	$ 25	Loan from Aunt Elizabeth	$200
Bicycle (cost)	500	Amount owing on bicycle	225
Bike lock (cost)	15		
Shoes (cost)	60		
Delivery bag (cost)	25	John's investment	200
Total	$625	Total	$625

Under assets on the balance sheet, we have placed the bicycle (valued at its total purchase price, not at the amount of cash John has paid so far), bike lock, shoes, and delivery bag. These are considered assets because presumably John will be receiving future benefit from these items, in that they will enable him to earn courier revenue. He also has $25 in cash as an asset. He had a total of $400 [$200 (his savings) + $200 (Aunt Elizabeth's loan)], but so far has paid out $375 [$275 (bicycle) + $15 (bike lock) + $60 (shoes) + $25 (delivery bag)].

As to liabilities, John owes his aunt $200 and the bike store $225. These amounts are claims on his resources and are therefore liabilities. He invested $200 of his own savings into his venture: this is the owner's equity portion of the balance sheet. You can see that the $625 on the right-hand side of the balance sheet constitute the total ways in which John raised the funds represented by the assets on the left. The items on the left (cash, bike, and so on) are real: they can be used, spent, or counted. The items on the right account for how those real things arose.

Notice that the right-hand total of the balance sheet, because it contains all of the sources of the assets on the left, is equal to the left-hand total; that is, the resources equal the sources. Both resources and sources are valued at the amounts that arose when the resources were acquired: at the "historical amounts" based on the transactions by which John assembled his small business. This simple balance sheet illustrates the principles upon which all balance sheets are based, regardless of the size of the organization or the amount of money involved.

We cannot classify John's assets and liabilities as current or noncurrent, and so analyze his working capital, without more information. Cash seems to be his only current asset, but, because we do not know when he has to repay Aunt Elizabeth or the money borrowed for the bike, we do not know what his current liabilities are. Determining this is an example of a decision the accountant who prepares the balance sheet has to make, so that the financial statement will be useful to its users.

Rather than leave John's balance sheet in this incomplete state, let's interview him and get some information.

"John, when do you have to repay your Aunt Elizabeth?"
"She never said. But my intention is to pay her back by the end of 1996. I'm sure she would complain if I took longer than that."
"How about the amount you owe on the bicycle: when is that due?"
"The store wants the money right away. I told them I would have to raise the funds by sales in my business, so they said they wanted me to pay just as soon as I could. They made me sign a form saying they could take back the bike and the other stuff if I don't pay."

With this information and some rearranging, we can produce the following balance sheet:

EXHIBIT 2.5

QuickJohn Courier *(Note 1)*
Balance Sheet as at April 15, 1995

Assets		Liabilities and Owner's Equity	
Current assets:		Current liabilities:	
Cash on hand	$ 25	Account payable for equipment *(Note 2)*	$225
Noncurrent assets:		Noncurrent liabilities:	
Equipment, at cost	600	Due to Aunt Elizabeth *(Note 3)*	200
		Owner's equity:	
		John's investment	200
Total	$625	Total	$625

Notes to the Balance Sheet:

1. QuickJohn Courier is an unincorporated business owned by John Graham. It began operating on April 15, 1995.
2. The account payable for equipment is due and is secured by the equipment, which may be seized if the debt is not paid.
3. The amount due to Aunt Elizabeth is expected to be repaid by the end of 1996.

This balance sheet has more information about liabilities and owner's equity than the first version had, but also less detail about the equipment in the assets column. You may or may not like it better. But this version does permit an analysis of John's working capital. He has $25 of current assets and $225 of current liabilities, for a negative working capital of $200 and a working capital ratio of .11 ($25/$225). His business is not in a strong financial position: he is depending on future revenues to bring in the cash needed to pay the bike store. In common, unfortunately, with many new businesses, his courier service is starting out financially weak, and if the future is not as rosy as he hopes, he may be out of business before long.

HOW'S YOUR UNDERSTANDING

Here are two questions you should be able to answer, based on what you have just read:

1. The balance sheet of Paychex, Inc. shows its assets and liabilities. What is an asset and what is a liability in financial accounting?
2. Suppose John Graham came to you wanting you to lend him $300, repayable in two years, to help him pay off the bike store and get his new business on better financial footing. If you did lend the money to him, what would the balance sheet look like after your loan and the payment to the store? (You should get a new cash balance of $100 ($25 + $300 – $225) and a long-term debt of $300 owing to you, instead of the $225 owing to the bike store. This would produce total assets of $700 ($100 current), liabilities of $500 (all non-current), and the same owner's investment of $200. John's business is relatively more in debt, but the short-term position is stronger because no debts have to be paid until next year.)

2.7 HOW DEBITS AND CREDITS MAKE THE ACCOUNTING SYSTEM WORK

This section offers an example of how financial accounting uses debits and credits to record events and, from those records, produce financial statements. The focus will be on the balance sheet for now; in Chapter 3, the example will be extended to cover more financial statements.

We will use a few necessary terms here without much explanation so that the mechanical workings of accounting can be emphasized. You will see more about the terms as later chapters develop your understanding. For now:

- Accounting records certain kinds of events measured in the country's currency (dollars in Canada). We will call those events **transactions**, a word used a few times already.
- Accounting's way of recording transactions is called the **entry**, and, as you saw in Section 2.2, the method follows the double-entry recordkeeping system described by Pacioli 500 years ago. (Entries are summarized in records usually called **journals** and so are also called **journal entries**.)
- The entries are transferred to and summarized in **accounts**, which lie behind all the amounts and descriptions shown on the balance sheet. Each account has a numerical balance that is either a debit or a credit. (All the accounts collected together are usually referred to as a **ledger**.)
- As you know, it is important that all the accounts together produce a balanced balance sheet. Prior to preparing the balance sheet from the accounts, accountants usually make a list of the account balances from the ledger and make sure that the sum of all the debit balances equals the sum of all the credit balances. Because you never know for sure if it will work, this list is called the **trial balance**!

Let's consider an example, CappuMania Inc., a small corporation that operates a coffee bar in the concourse of an office building. At the end of March 1995, the company's balance sheet (Exhibit 2.6) was:

EXHIBIT 2.6

CappuMania Inc.
Balance Sheet as at March 31, 1995

Assets		Liabilities and Shareholders' Equity	
Current assets:		Current liabilities:	
Cash	$ 4,000	Owing to suppliers	$ 1,200
Inventory of unsold food	800	Sales and other taxes owing	600
Inventory of supplies	1,900		$ 1,800
	$ 6,700	Non-current liabilities:	
Noncurrent assets:		Loan to buy equipment	5,000
Equipment cost	$ 9,000		$ 6,800
Accumulated amortization	(1,500)	Shareholders' equity:	
	$ 7,500	Share capital contributed	$ 3,000
		Retained earnings	4,400
			$ 7,400
	$14,200		$14,200

These accounts are assets and so have *debit* balances:

◆ Cash, Inventory of unsold food, Inventory of supplies, and Equipment.

This account is a negative asset and so has a *credit* balance:

◆ Accumulated amortization.

These accounts are liabilities and equities and so have *credit* balances:

◆ Owing to suppliers, Sales and other taxes owing, Loan to buy equipment, Share capital contributed, and Retained earnings.

We already know the accounts are in balance because the balance sheet balances (left side total = right side total). But let's do a trial balance anyway, to demonstrate that the sum of all the debits equals the sum of all the credits (we will drop the $ signs):

Account names	Account balances	
	Debits	Credits
Cash	4,000	
Inventory of unsold food	800	
Inventory of supplies	1,900	
Equipment cost	9,000	
Accumulated amortization		1,500
Owing to suppliers		1,200
Sales and other taxes owing		600
Loan to buy equipment		5,000
Share capital contributed		3,000
Retained earnings		4,400
	15,700	15,700

So it balances! Note that because Accumulated amortization, a credit balance account, is deducted from the Equipment cost on the balance sheet, the sum of the debits is not the same amount as the total of the assets side of the balance sheet, nor is the sum of the credits the same as the total of the liabilities and equity side of the balance sheet. But, as we have seen already, this sort of rearrangement of the *presentation* of accounts in the balance sheet still keeps the accounts in balance even though totals change.

Now let's see how the following four transactions, all happening on April 1, 1995, are recorded using accounting's double-entry method (ignoring the details of the particular computer or manual recordkeeping system):

1. CappuMania pays $500 of its taxes owing.
2. CappuMania buys $450 more supplies, paying $100 cash and owing the rest.
3. A shareholder is given more shares in return for personally paying $1,100 on the equipment loan.
4. CappuMania buys a new coffee urn for $200 cash.

Here are the entries:

	Debit	**Credit**
1. *Resource effect:* Cash is reduced. Cash is a debit, so a negative effect on cash would be a credit (abbreviated CR).		
Source effect: Tax liability is reduced. A liability is a credit, so a negative effect would be a debit (abbreviated DR, for some reason!).		
Entry:		
DR Sales and other taxes owing (liability)	500	
CR Cash (asset)		500
Double-entry method: There is both a DR and a CR and the two are the same. (There is a tradition to list the DR(s) first in an entry, but all that really matters is that for each entry, $DR = $CR.)		
2. *Resource effects:* Inventory is increased $450. It is an asset, so this is a debit. Cash is decreased $100 so this is a credit, as above.		
Source effect: The liability to suppliers is increased $350, so this is a credit.		
Entry:		
DR Inventory of supplies (asset)	450	
CR Cash (asset)		100
CR Owing to suppliers (liability)		350
Double-entry method: There are both DRs and CRs and the sum of the DRs equals the sum of the CRs. (An entry can have any number of DRs and CRs as long as the sums of each are equal.)		
3. *Resource effect:* None.		
Source effects: The equipment loan, a liability, is decreased $1,100, so this is a debit. The share capital, an equity, is increased $1,100, so this is a credit.		

	Debit	Credit
Entry:		
DR Loan to buy equipment (liability)	1,100	
CR Share capital contributed (equity)		1,100

Double-entry method: This transaction affects only the right side of the balance sheet, but the balance sheet stays in balance because one account on the right side goes up and another goes down.

4. *Resource effects:* Equipment, an asset, is increased $200, so this is a debit. Cash is decreased $200, which is a credit as in transactions 1 and 2.

Source effect: None.

Entry:		
DR Equipment cost (asset)	200	
CR Cash (asset)		200

Double-entry method: This transaction also affects only one side of the balance sheet, this time the assets side, but again the balanced entry keeps the balance sheet in balance.

These entries are recorded (**posted**) by adding them to, or subtracting them from, the previous (March 31) balances in the accounts. This is done in Exhibit 2.7, using a computer spreadsheet format (in this case, *Microsoft Excel®*, but the particular spreadsheet does not matter). *Arbitrarily*, the debits are recorded as positive and the credits as negative. This does not mean debits are good and credits are bad!

EXHIBIT 2.7

	A	B	C	D		E		F
1		CappuMania Inc. Example, in Spreadsheet Form						
2								
3			March 31/95					April 1/95
4			Trial balance	Transactions*				Trial balance
5			Debit or credit	Debits		Credits		Debit or credit
6								
7	Cash		4000			(1)	-500	3200
8						(2)	-100	
9						(4)	-200	
10	Inventory of unsold food		800					800
11	Inventory of supplies		1900	(2)	450			2350
12	Equipment cost		9000	(4)	200			9200
13	Accumulated amortization		-1500					-1500
14	Owing to suppliers		-1200			(2)	-350	-1550
15	Sales and other taxes owing		-600	(1)	500			-100
16	Loan to buy equipment		-5000	(3)	1100			-3900
17	Share capital contributed		-3000			(3)	-1100	-4100
18	Retained earnings		-4400					-4400
19								
20		Totals	0		2250		-2250	0

* The numbers in brackets have been added to the spreadsheet printout to refer to the four transactions described in the text.

You can see from the spreadsheet that the March 31 trial balance was in balance because the total of adding all the debits and subtracting all the credits is zero. The transaction entries are in balance because the sum of the debits equals the sum of the credits. The April 1 trial balance is in balance too, just as the March 31 one was. (If you want to review the use of spreadsheets in accounting, please see Appendix 2 "Creating a Computer Spreadsheet to Represent a Company's Accounts.")

It would be unlikely that another balance sheet would be prepared, just one day after the March 31 one, but to complete the example, let's see what the balance sheet, after recording the four transactions, would be (Exhibit 2.8):

EXHIBIT 2.8

CappuMania Inc.
Balance Sheet as at April 1, 1995

Assets		**Liabilities and Shareholders' Equity**	
Current assets:		Current liabilities:	
Cash	$ 3,200	Owing to suppliers	$ 1,550
Inventory of unsold food	800	Sales and other taxes owing	100
Inventory of supplies	2,350		$ 1,650
	$ 6,350	Noncurrent liabilities:	
Noncurrent assets:		Loan to buy equipment	3,900
Equipment cost	$ 9,200		$ 5,550
Accumulated amortization	(1,500)	Shareholders' equity:	
	$ 7,700	Share capital contributed	$ 4,100
		Retained earnings	4,400
			$ 8,500
	$14,050		$14,050

In summary, that is how accounting works.

- First, transactions are recorded in a two-sided (double) entry in a journal.
- Then the journal's entries are recorded (posted) in the accounts.
- Then the ledger of accounts is checked for balancing via a trial balance.
- Then the trial balance is used to prepare the balance sheet.

There are many choices, judgments and details behind this that later chapters will examine (in particular, Chapter 6, Section 6.6), and most accounting systems have their own particular formats for entries and accounts, but now you have the basics.

HOW'S YOUR UNDERSTANDING

Here are two questions you should be able to answer, based on what you have just read:

1. CappuMania's March 31, 1995, balance sheet shows total assets of $14,200. The trial balance of the company's ledger for the same day shows total debits of $15,700. Why are the two totals different?
2. Suppose on April 1, 1995, a fifth transaction had occurred: CappuMania paid $800 on its equipment loan. What would the following revised figures have been on the April 1, 1995, balance sheet: cash, current assets, total assets, total liabilities, total liabilities and shareholders' equity? ($2,400; $5,550; $13,250; $4,750; $13,250)

2.8 BACKGROUND: PROPRIETORSHIPS, PARTNERSHIPS, CORPORATIONS, AND FINANCING

The balance sheet is a summary of much of the organization's financing: it shows what sources of debt and equity were used to produce the list of resources (assets). Just in case you are unfamiliar with the main kinds of business organizations and their financing, this section provides a few explanations. Remember the balance sheet equation:

Assets = Liabilities + Owners' Equity

In this section, we will focus on the right-hand terms, examining how the form of business organization determines the way owners' equity is shown on the balance sheet and outlining how both right-hand terms indicate how the assets are financed. This short introduction will help you deal with the material in this book. While such information is explored more deeply in books or courses on corporate law and finance, many details will also necessarily come up here as we proceed. This book's glossary will also provide help in understanding terminology.

There are many important forms of organization, such as businesses organized as partnerships, corporations or cooperatives, and nonbusiness organizations such as clubs, charities, governments, and political parties. However, they cannot all be described here. Instead, we will focus on the four main kinds of business organization and their main methods of financing.

FOUR KINDS OF BUSINESS ORGANIZATION

We have seen that each balance sheet has an owners' equity section. The Sound and Light Corporation and Paychex, Inc. examples indicated that the equity could be considered to be of two general kinds for a business enterprise:

- *Directly* contributed equity, in which owners have provided money or other assets to the enterprise; and
- *Indirectly* contributed equity (retained earnings), in which owners have allowed income earned by the enterprise to remain there, to help earn more income in the future.

The legal meaning of being an owner depends on what kind of organization exists. The equity section of the balance sheet reflects that legal meaning, so that owners and other users will understand the status of their equity. Four main kinds of business organizations are the **proprietorship**, the **partnership**, the **corporation**, and the **corporate group**.

Proprietorship

A proprietorship, like Gurjit's venture in Section 1.4 and QuickJohn Courier in Section 2.6, is a business owned by one person (the *proprietor*) and does not legally exist separate from the owner. Because the business does not exist as a separate legal entity, it is said to be *unincorporated*. If John, the bicycle courier, just starts up a business one day on his own and without further legal steps, the business is a proprietorship. Legally, such a business is not distinguishable from John's nonbusiness affairs. If he wishes, he can use the business cash to buy groceries, and if he does not pay his business bills, his creditors can claim against any nonbusiness assets he has.

Because a proprietorship has no legal existence, the equity section of the balance sheet does not distinguish between the owner's direct contributions to the business and the indirect contributions by retained earnings. Both kinds of equity are simply lumped together as *owner's capital*. A proprietorship's balance sheet can list whatever assets and liabilities the owner considers relevant to the business (there being no separate legal entity to own any assets or owe any liabilities), and the owner's equity section of the balance sheet just says:

Owner's equity	
Owner's capital	$XXXX

Partnership

A **partnership** is also unincorporated, but it has more than one owner. Again, the owners' personal assets can be claimed by business creditors, so there is the same somewhat arbitrary distinction between business affairs and personal affairs. But the fact that there is more than one owner introduces some formality into the business. For example, there is (or should be) an agreement about how the earnings of the business are to be split among the partners and about how much each partner can withdraw from the business. Because stress can develop in partnerships (as with friendships), provinces, states, and countries have partnership laws that provide some structure if the partners do not do so themselves. A partnership's balance sheet may, like proprietorship's, list whatever assets and liabilities the owners consider relevant to that business. Also, the owners' equity section, like that for a proprietorship, does not distinguish between owners' direct contributions and retained earnings. The only difference is that each owner's total capital is identified on the face of the balance sheet (or, if there are many partners, as in firms of lawyers, accountants, or engineers, in a separate schedule). Therefore, the owners' equity section of the partnership's balance sheet just shows:

Owners' equity	
Partners' capital:	
Partner A	$XXXX
Partner B	XXXX
Partner C	XXXX
Total capital	$XXXX

Corporation

A corporation, like the Sound and Light Corporation and Paychex, Inc., is an incorporated entity that has a legal existence of its own, separate from that of its owners. The corporation continues to exist even if the owners die or quit working, and if the business fails, owners' losses are limited to their equity in the business. Unless they have signed personal guarantees to creditors such as banks, owners will not lose personal assets if the business goes under. A corporation can own property, employ people and otherwise conduct business just as a person can. It can even sue and be sued by its owners. You can usually tell that a business is incorporated because it will have some indication at the end of its name, like "Limited," "Ltd.," "Inc.," or other indications that the incorporating jurisdiction (province, state, or country) will specify.

Corporations can be very complex; just two complexities will be mentioned here.

a. *Forms of Share Capital*

People become owners of a corporation by buying *shares* that give them voting or other powers in it. When a share is first issued by a corporation, the money received for it is put in the corporation's bank account and the source of that asset is called **share capital**, which is an owners' equity item. (If the person who paid the corporation for that share sells it later to someone else, the money for that sale goes to the person who owned the share, not to the corporation. Therefore, the corporation's share capital shows only the amount received by it the first time the share is sold. Most of the millions of share sales and purchases that take place on the world's stock exchanges every day have no effect on corporations' balance sheet accounts for share capital, because they are trades among owners, not issues by the corporations.)

Canadian companies usually have *no-par* shares, which means they can issue their shares for whatever amount seems appropriate. *Par value* shares, rare in Canada but used elsewhere (such as by Paychex, Inc.), have a legal minimum issue price, the par value. Such a minimum share price was used in the past to prevent corporations from abusing present shareholders by selling newly issued shares cheaply, but other protections exist nowadays, so corporations now tend to have no-par shares.

There are several classes of shares, including

- **Common shares** or *ordinary* shares: owners of these vote; they are the corporation's basic (*residual*) owners, the ones who decide who shall be on the board of directors that manages the corporation for the owners and declares dividends to owners;
- **Preferred shares** or otherwise special shares: owners usually do not vote unless there is a problem, but in return they have rights such as receiving a fixed dividend each year or converting their preferred shares to common shares;
- Class A, Class B, and other such categorizations: whether these are more like common shares or preferred shares depends on the specific rights they carry. Many corporations use these vague terms because the complexity of rights often prevents a simple categorization as common or preferred.

The face of the balance sheet or a separate schedule will list all the kinds of shares the corporation is authorized to issue, specify any special rights, and show the amount of share capital obtained on the original issuance of each kind of share. The cash received for such share capital is the property of the corporation: except in specific circumstances, the owners (**shareholders**, or **stockholders** as they are often also called, especially in the United States) have no right to get it back.

b. *Retained Earnings*

Earnings of a corporation belong to the corporation, not to its owners. The shareholders (stockholders) can receive the earnings only if the board of directors declares a dividend. The balance sheet shows the amount of any retained earnings (past earnings minus past dividends) as a separate owners' equity item.

Thus, in addition to its lists of assets and liabilities, a corporation's balance sheet has an owners' equity section showing various legal details to assist present owners and potential future owners:

Shareholders' equity	
Share capital:	
Authorized (narrative describing all the classes of shares authorized)	
Issued capital received:	
Class A shares (for example)	$XXXX
Class B shares (for example)	XXXX
Total issued capital	$XXXX
Retained earnings	XXXX
Total shareholders' equity	$XXXX

Other items than issued capital received and retained earnings may appear in a corporation's owners' equity. Such items reflect legal and accounting complexities that are not important at this point. If you are doing an analysis of the balance sheet, just lumping these with the share capital amount is usually satisfactory.

Corporate Groups

Many companies we are familiar with, such as General Motors, John Labatt, Sears, and Pepsico, are not single corporations but are rather groups of many, often hundreds, of corporations. The balance sheet of such a corporate group attempts to represent what that group looks like as a "consolidated" **economic entity**, even though there is no such entity legally. Doing this requires complex accounting techniques that are mostly beyond the scope of this book. The balance sheet of a corporate group looks a lot like that of a single corporation, with the shareholders' equity section representing the equity of the primary, or *parent*, corporation in the group. In Chapter 5, a brief examination will be made of the assumptions behind financial statements for corporate groups: for now, just remember that such **consolidated** financial statements are aggregations of many legally separate corporations.

EXHIBIT 2.9

Summary of Kinds of Business Organizations

Kind	Legality	Owner(s)	Equity accounts
Proprietorship	Not separate from owner	One proprietor	Capital and retained earnings are combined
Partnership	Partly separate from owners	Several or many partners	Capital and retained earnings are combined, but each partner's total is calculated
Corporation	Separate from owners	Usually several or many shareholders	Legal share capital is disclosed separately from retained earnings
Corporate Group	Consists of legally separate corporations	Usually several or many shareholders	Legal share capital of parent corporation is disclosed separately from retained earnings

BUSINESS FINANCING

The balance sheet's right side lists the sources of the assets listed on its left side. As this book proceeds, many details about both sides of the balance sheet will be explained; for now, here is a list of the main sources:

Current Liabilities (due within a year):

- Loans from banks due on demand or otherwise, at least potentially payable sooner rather than later;
- Financing provided by suppliers and other trade creditors by allowing the enterprise to charge its purchases and pay for them later;
- Wages earned by, but not yet paid to, employees and taxes withheld from them that are to be turned over to the taxation authorities;
- Estimates of amounts owing for things such as power, interest charges, legal costs, and other debts building up, but not yet actually billed to the enterprise;
- Income and other taxes owed by the enterprise;
- Dividends owed by the enterprise (if it is a corporation), declared by the board of directors, but not yet paid to the shareholders;
- Short-term portions of longer-term debts, such as the principal payments due over the next year on long-term mortgages.

Noncurrent Liabilities (debts due more than a year in the future):

- Mortgages, bonded debt (**bonds** are certificates of debt issued by the enterprise that include detailed legal requirements), equipment-purchase agreements, and other debts extending over several years;
- Certain long-term liabilities, such as special loans from owners in addition to their share capital, long-term tax estimates, and estimated liabilities for pensions to be paid to employees when they retire (in excess of money already put aside [funded] for such pensions).

Owners' Equity:

- For a proprietorship: owner's capital (contributed capital and income not withdrawn by owner);
- For a partnership: owners' capital (contributed capital and income not withdrawn by owners);
- For a corporation: share capital received for each kind of share plus retained earnings (plus some other items if legal or accounting complexities require them).

HOW'S YOUR UNDERSTANDING

Here are two questions you should be able to answer, based on what you have just read:

1. The owners of Blotz Consulting Partnership wonder if they should incorporate their business as Blotz Consulting Inc. What difference would this make to the owners' equity section of the business's balance sheet?
2. What are some common examples of current and noncurrent liabilities, and how do the two types differ?

2.9 MANAGERS AND BALANCE SHEETS

Why do managers care about their companies' balance sheets? The basic reason is that many outsiders do, including owners, creditors, tax authorities, and unions. Read any issue of a business newspaper or magazine, and you will see opinions like the following expressed:

> Thinn Inc. has a weak financial structure. Management must solve this problem before risk-shy investors can be expected to take an interest in the company.
>
> Huge Ltd. has large cash reserves, so one can only guess that management is looking to buy another company to add to Huge's consolidated group.
>
> The prices for corporate bonds have responded poorly to recent changes in interest rates because too many corporate balance sheets show too much debt.
>
> In the current turbulent business climate, managers must pay more attention to financing short-term assets with something other than bank borrowing.

The balance sheet reports what the organization's position (assets, liabilities, and owners' equity) is at a point in time (the fiscal year-end or any other date the balance sheet is prepared). It shows the assets (resources) that management has chosen to acquire for the organization, and how management has decided to finance those assets. Therefore, it provides a useful picture of the state of the company and is used by many outsiders to evaluate the quality of management's decisions on obtaining, deploying, and financing assets. For better or worse, it is the summary of all the information recognized by accounting and is, to many people, the basic scorecard of management's stewardship of the company. To emphasize this, in Canada a corporation's balance sheet is usually signed by members of the board of directors, which is the uppermost level of management, responsible to the owners and creditors.

The balance sheet does not directly state how management has performed in using assets to earn income or in controlling cash flows to enable prompt payment of debts. Such information is contained in other financial statements, as will be seen later in this book, but all of it correlates with the basic double-entry information contained in the balance sheet. Good income performance, for example, is reflected by increased assets and owners' equity (retained earnings). The strengths and weaknesses of the balance sheet, which will be explored throughout this book, are therefore fundamentally important to managers, who are responsible for managing companies' assets and liabilities. Managers' own incomes, promotions, careers, pensions, and reputations depend on other people's decisions that, in turn, rest to some extent on balance sheet information.

2.10 ACCOUNTING RESEARCH: ENTITY OR PROPRIETOR APPROACH?

A balance sheet, as we have seen, lists an organization's assets and liabilities and puts a dollar value on each. Double-entry accounting records values for the assets, liabilities, and owners' equity that keep the balance sheet in balance. We have the balance sheet equation, Assets = Liabilities + Owners' Equity, or its equivalent form, Assets – Liabilities = Owners' Equity. Let's think about the second version:

- The equation's left side is the list of resources minus the claims on those resources. We might say that this is a description of the organization, regardless of what its ownership is.
- The equation's right side describes the organization's ownership interests, as were outlined in Section 2.8.

We might ask whether, in the balance sheet and in the double-entry system underlying it, we should give more emphasis to the left side of the equation (the description of the organization) or the right side (the description of the ownership). If there is doubt about how to record something, for example, should we resolve that doubt in favour of the left side of the equation, by making sure that is accurate and letting the right side be a balancing figure, or should we focus on getting the right side correct and force the left side to add up to that predetermined amount?

Here is a simple example. GTX Inc. has one asset (land) and one liability (mortgage on the land). The land cost $1,000 and the mortgage is for $600. So we could focus on the left, report that the assets total $1,000, the liabilities total $600, and therefore the right side owners' equity is whatever is left, $400. But what if the owner of GTX Inc. could sell the company for $700? Shouldn't that be the equity? If it is, then there must be a reason; perhaps that the land is now worth $1,300. So should we list the assets as $1,300, the liabilities as $600, and the owners' equity as $700?

The first approach, focusing on the assets and liabilities and considering the equity to be a residual, is called the *entity* approach. It emphasizes the business as an economic (and legal, if incorporated) entity separate from whoever happens to own it.

The second approach, focusing on the owners' equity, is called the *proprietor* or *proprietorship* approach to accounting. It emphasizes the interests of the owner (or owners, in the case of a partnership or incorporated company) and tries to figure out what the equity is worth to the owner, or, put another way, what the value to the owner is of the assets and liabilities. It looks on the business as just an extension of the owner. A problem here is in figuring out just who the owner is, or who the owners are. Just the voting common shareholders? The holders of nonvoting shares too? What about holders of bonds that can be converted to shares? A simple answer might be to take a strict legal view and consider only those who bear the final legal responsibility for the company, which would probably mean that just the voting shareholders, or the partners, or the sole proprietor would be considered the owner(s).

The proprietor approach views the business through the owner's (or owners') eyes. The business is not separate from the owner(s), and questions of a proper mix of assets or combination of debts and equity are asked from the point of view of the owner(s). The entity approach has a broader orientation, considering the business in its own right and asking what assets and financing are best for that entity.

Accounting research in the 1950s and 1960s considered a number of conceptual approaches to financial statements and tried to establish principles that would permit a choice to be made as to whether the proprietor or entity way of looking at the business should be preferred. (Other conceptual choices were also addressed, but we will consider only this one.) In the 1970s and 1980s, the research began to show that no one conceptual approach to financial statements would satisfy all the criteria that were proposed, nor could any be equally satisfactory to such competing interests as owners, potential owners, creditors, and managers. Accounting, it appears, has to incorporate *both* approaches as much as it can because, on the one hand, organizations such as businesses are separate economic entities that can be transferred among owners at any time, and, on the other hand, every owner is certainly interested in the value of the business to him or her.

Therefore, we find that accounting principles are a mixture of both entity and proprietor concepts and that most people involved in using financial statements are satisfied with the mixture. For example, all assets are valued at what they are worth to the organization, not to the owner (entity approach), but a company's income (profit) is calculated after deducting interest paid to creditors, but before deducting dividends to owners (proprietor approach). When a company is sold to a corporate group, the company's assets and liabilities are revalued to show its overall equity worth according to what the new owners paid for it (proprietor approach), but the assets and liabilities of the other companies in the group are not changed (entity approach).

This book emphasizes that accounting is utilitarian (use-oriented) because it is shaped by people's information needs rather than by theoretical principles. Therefore, the book does not advocate "right" and "wrong" answers. Accounting research has shown (at least so far) that there is no one conceptual principle that can be used to answer important accounting questions. Several apparently reasonable principles, each supported by particular groups of people or replaced by theoretical approaches, give conflicting results when applied to accounting. We are forced to view financial accounting as a complex creature of a complex world, and not as a simple, straightforward crunching of numbers.[13]

2.11 CONTINUING DEMONSTRATION CASE

INSTALMENT 2

Data for Instalment 2

In Instalment 1, Mavis Janer and Tomas Brot were thinking about starting a business together and began working on a business plan, by listing their objectives in having a business and the risks and constraints they were concerned about. If you have forgotten about those, you might look back to the "Results for Instalment 1" in Section 1.8 to see the lists.

After much investigation and debate, Mavis and Tomas came up with a proposal for a business. They had observed a large growth in boutique-style retail stores, usually managed by families, in their region of the country, but felt such stores were not well supported either by supplies of attractive merchandise or marketing ideas. They saw a niche they could fill by setting up a regional wholesale distribution company that would provide the boutique retailers with better access to national and international suppliers of goods, and help in both fitting their product lines to local markets and marketing the products well.

There were other such wholesale distributors in North America, but the local region seemed not well serviced by them, and Mavis and Tomas felt they had some ideas the other distributors had not thought of. The field would be very competitive, but they saw considerable opportunity for growth as baby boomers reached middle age and increased the demand for boutique retailers, and as international trade opened more opportunities for supplying interesting products at attractive prices.

Many things had to be done before the business could start. Here are some of the actions Mavis and Tomas took. First, they decided to incorporate a company, to provide a financing focus and some limited liability for themselves. They decided to call it Mato Inc., after their first names, and because it sounded vaguely exotic and international.

Second, they had to raise initial capital. Tomas felt they needed about $125,000 in share capital and substantial additional bank financing to support the inventory the company would carry. They planned to use modern techniques to minimize inventory levels, but, still, inventory would be a significant asset in the business as they foresaw it. After some analysis and discussion with relatives and friends, they assembled the following capital: Mavis would buy 40% of the issued voting shares with $50,000 cash from her inheritance, and Tomas would buy 24% of the shares. He did not have the $30,000 cash to make the purchase, but would contribute his car to the business, at an agreed value of $10,000, and $20,000 in cash from his savings. Five friends and relatives agreed to contribute $45,000 cash for the remaining 36% of the shares. In addition, Tomas's father agreed to lend the business $15,000. He wanted to be a creditor of the new company; he did not want shares because he was worried about his health and wanted to be able to get the money back if he needed it.

Third, the company needed a management structure. It was decided that the board of directors would consist of Mavis (as chairperson), Tomas, and a representative of the five relatives and friends. Mavis would be president, and Tomas would be vice-president. Basically, Mavis was to look after business development and marketing, and Tomas would see to financing and day-to-day operations.

Fourth, they found a vacant warehouse building that could be rented at an attractive rate and was located both centrally in the region they wanted to serve and reasonably close to their homes. The building would require some renovation to meet their needs, but otherwise they could move right in and get going.

Fifth, Tomas put together a business plan and approached several banks and other financial institutions for support. On the strength of his and Mavis's background and of having their business plan and the above investments already arranged, he was able to secure the support he required: basically, a line of credit (a pre-approved borrowing limit) under which the company would have approved credit of up to $80,000 now, and further credit based on inventories and accounts receivable once operations got underway. Mavis and Tomas had to personally guarantee the line of credit to the company and pledge their shares in the company as collateral on any loan.

On March 1, 1994, the new business was established. On that day:

- The company was officially incorporated, having only one class of no-par shares;
- The company received its first bill (a fee of $1,100 to be paid to the lawyer handling the incorporation);
- The various investors paid their cash;
- A five-year lease was signed for the warehouse space;

- Tomas signed his car over to the company; and
- Mavis left her job to become the new company's only full-time employee at a monthly salary of $2,500.

Tomas would stay in his bank job for a while, and Mavis would spend most of this initial period making contacts with suppliers and retailers, supervising renovations, and doing other tasks necessary to get the business started. They felt it would be better if Tomas kept his paying job at the bank, instead of quitting and increasing the demands on the new company's cash. Until he left his bank job, Tomas would keep track of the time he put in on the company and be paid later at the same rate as Mavis, prorated over 200 hours per month, which was the number of hours per month Mavis expected to put in while getting the business started.

Tomas wanted to have a starting balance sheet for the new company, partly for use in dealing with the bank. So, on the evening of March 1, he and Mavis sat down to prepare it.

Results for Instalment 2

Mavis and Tomas prepared two balance sheets, one with details of everyone's contributions and a second in a more normal format. Exhibit 2.10 shows the first one:

EXHIBIT 2.10

Mato Inc.
Balance Sheet Details as at March 1, 1994

Assets		Sources of Assets	
Cash:		Due to lawyer	$ 1,100
From Mavis	$ 50,000	Investments:	
From Tomas	20,000	Mavis's shares	50,000
From other shareholders	45,000	Tomas's shares	30,000
From Tomas's father	15,000	Other shareholders	45,000
Car	10,000	Tomas's father	15,000
Incorporation costs	1,100		
Total	$141,100		$141,100

The second balance sheet is shown in Exhibit 2.11. In it, they classified the loan from Tomas's father as a current liability because he had said he might want it back any time. The cost to the company of Tomas's car was the agreed value, as discussed above. The incorporation costs were shown as an asset, because Tomas and Mavis felt there was a benefit to the future resulting from the incorporation of the company. However, they were not entirely sure about that, because it was hard to say what the benefit actually was or for how long it would have value.

Exhibit 2.11

Mato Inc.
Formal Balance Sheet as at March 1, 1994

Assets		**Liabilities and Shareholders' Equity**	
Current assets:		Current liabilities:	
Cash	$130,000	Account payable	$ 1,100
Noncurrent assets:		Loan payable	15,000
Automobile (at cost)	10,000	Shareholders' equity:	
Incorporation costs	1,100	Share capital	125,000
Total	$141,100	Total	$141,100

HOMEWORK AND DISCUSSION TO DEVELOP UNDERSTANDING

PROBLEM 2.1* Prepare a simple balance sheet, calculate working capital

Bluebird Bakery, a partnership that rents its bakery premises, had the following account balances at July 31, 1995. Decide if each account is a debit or credit, then prepare a balance sheet for the partnership by placing each account in the appropriate location in the balance sheet. From the balance sheet, calculate the partnership's working capital and working capital ratio.

Bakery equipment cost	$129,153	J. Bird partner's capital	$52,921
Demand loan from bank	14,500	Accumulated amortization	43,996
Supplies inventory cost	13,220	Cash on hand	895
Owing to suppliers	11,240	Owing by customers	3,823
B. Blue partner's capital	27,425	Cash in bank	4,992
Wages owing to employees	2,246	Unsold baked goods cost	245

PROBLEM 2.2* Prepare a balance sheet from simple transactions

South Shore Manufacturing Ltd. had this balance sheet:

South Shore Manufacturing Ltd.
Balance Sheet as at July 31, 1995

Assets		**Liabilities and Owners' Equity**	
Current assets:		Current liabilities:	
Cash	$ 24,388	Bank indebtedness	$ 53,000
Accounts receivable	89,267	Accounts payable	78,442
Inventories, cost	111,436	Taxes payable	12,665
Expenses paid in advance	7,321	Current part of mortgage	18,322
	$232,412		$162,429

continued next page

Assets continued		Liabilities and Owners' Equity continued	
Noncurrent assets:		Noncurrent liabilities:	
Land, cost	$ 78,200	Mortgage, less current	$213,734
Factory, cost	584,211	Pension liability	67,674
	$662,411	Loan from shareholder	100,000
Accum. amortization	(198,368)		$381,408
	$464,043	Shareholders' equity:	
		Share capital issued	$ 55,000
		Retained earnings	97,618
			$152,618
	$696,455		$696,455

On August 1, 1995, South Shore Manufacturing experienced the following transactions:

1. $10,000 of the shareholder's loan was repaid.
2. A customer paid one of the accounts receivable, $11,240.
3. Additional inventory costing $5,320 was purchased on credit.
4. The company issued new shares for $22,000 cash.
5. The proceeds of the share issue were used to reduce the bank loan.
6. More land costing $52,000 was purchased for $12,000 cash plus a new long-term mortgage for the rest.
7. More factory equipment costing $31,900 was purchased on credit, with $13,900 due in six months and the rest due in 24 months.

Prepare a new balance sheet for the company as of August 1, 1995, taking these transactions into account. You can do this directly, by just reasoning out the effect of each transaction on the balance sheet accounts given above, or using a computer spreadsheet, or using a paper worksheet following the format of the spreadsheet illustrated in Section 2.7.

PROBLEM 2.3* Prepare separate and then combined balance sheets for a couple

Janet and Sam, who were engaged to be married, each made lists of their financial resources and the claims on these resources on Friday, June 9, 1995. Here are their lists:

Janet's list:

Cash in chequing account	$ 500
Stereo	2,000
Damage deposit on hall (for wedding)	300

Sam's list:

Cash in chequing account	$1,000
Student loan	2,100
Furniture	500
Prepaid rent on hall (for wedding)	400

1. Prepare a June 9, 1995, balance sheet for Janet using her list.
2. Prepare a June 9, 1995, balance sheet for Sam using his list.
3. On Saturday, June 10, 1995, Janet and Sam were married. Their wedding presents included:

Cash	$2,000
Household gifts	1,500
Parents' payment toward Sam's loan	2,100

The couple paid $1,000 immediately for the band that played at their wedding. There were no damages to the hall during the reception. After the party, they took a honeymoon weekend (lasting until Tuesday evening) and charged all their expenses on Janet's American Express card, which they knew would be due at the end of July 1995. The honeymoon cost $600.

Prepare a balance sheet for the couple as at Wednesday, June 14, 1995. Be sure to include all the financial information given above.

PROBLEM 2.4* Examples of balance sheet categories plus working capital

1. Define each of the following and choose an example of each from the Paychex balance sheet in this chapter (or from the balance sheet of any company familiar or interesting to you).
   a. a current asset;
   b. a noncurrent asset;
   c. a current liability;
   d. a noncurrent liability;
   e. an owners' equity item.
2. Do you think the examples you selected will always be classified in the same way by all enterprises? Why or why not? Give examples if possible.
3. Calculate the company's working capital and working capital ratio for the two years shown in the balance sheet. Has the company's short-term position improved or deteriorated over the two years?

PROBLEM 2.5* Personal balance sheet and debt–equity ratio

1. List your own personal resources and obligations and try to fit them into accounting's standard balance sheet format in which the resources are listed on one side and debts and claims against the resources are listed on the other, keeping in mind that total resources must balance total debts plus residual equity. In doing this, think about: which of your resources and obligations would or would not be reported in the balance sheet; what would likely be disclosed about each; which are short term or long term; and which are easy or difficult to value numerically. (If you have completed a credit application or student loan application, the things you reported there might be a good starting point.)
2. What decision-making information might your list of resources and obligations provide?
3. Calculate your personal **debt–equity ratio** (total liabilities divided by total equity). Are you soundly financed?

PROBLEM 2.6 Purpose and origin of balance sheet

You have been working at a summer job as a clerk in a small store. The new owner of the store comes over to you, waving the balance sheet for the store and saying, "You're studying accounting, I hear. Can you explain to me what my balance sheet is supposed to be telling me and why it is designed to have two sides? Where did such a way of measuring a business come from, anyway?" Give your reply.

PROBLEM 2.7 Historical influences still present in today's balance sheet

It has been asserted that business and accounting have developed along parallel lines as accounting has responded to people's demand for information, and that traces of this development pattern can still be seen in a modern financial report. Take the balance sheet of any modern company (such as the Paychex example in this chapter) and identify *two* items in, or characteristics of, that balance sheet that you think can be traced back to a historical development or demand. Why do you think those items or characteristics are still present at the end of the 20th century?

PROBLEM 2.8 Users and uses of the balance sheet

Consider any company you are familiar with or interested in and make a list of all the people who might be interested in its balance sheet. Make your list using the headings, *Person (decision maker)* and *Use (decision to be made)*.

Try to think about the "use" issue broadly: your list could easily be a long one. You might make it even more broad by including people you think might *like* to use the balance sheet but whose needs are not served by it as you understand it, or who do not have timely access to it.

PROBLEM 2.9 A real company's resources, sources, and debt–equity ratio

Using the Paychex balance sheet, or that of any other company as an example, answer the following questions:

1. What resources does the company have?
2. How are those resources financed?
3. What is the company's relative reliance on debt versus equity financing? Calculate the ratio of total liabilities to total equity (the **debt–equity ratio**) as a measure of this relative reliance. Are there any accounts in the balance sheet's right side that do not seem clearly either debt or equity?

PROBLEM 2.10 Balance sheet information and a nonaccounting career

Write a paragraph in which you identify a nonaccounting career you or someone you know may pursue, and explain the interest in balance sheet information that this career might imply. If you really cannot see any relationship between that career and anything reported in a balance sheet, explain why not.

PROBLEM 2.11 Explain balance sheet ideas to a business executive

You are the executive assistant to Stephane Solden, a particularly hard-driving and successful owner of a chain of restaurants. Not long ago, Solden and you were flying to another city and the in-flight movie was so bad the two of you ended up talking about all sorts of things. One subject was Solden's impatience with accountants and accounting, which, probably because the annual audit of the company's accounts was then taking place, seemed particularly strong. Solden asked you the following questions; what did you say in response?

1. The main thing that sticks in my mind about the balance sheet is that the thing balances! Who cares? Where did that idea come from, anyway, and why should it matter?

2. My auditor keeps wanting to talk to me about what the balance sheet says about the company's finances and how I've managed them. But I always look to the future—why should I care about the balance sheet when it's just a history?
3. Last year, I had a really good idea about the balance sheet. You know, I consider our restaurant managers to be the most important asset the company has. I was going to have the managers added to the balance sheet as assets, so it would show all our assets. But the accountants and auditors didn't seem interested in my idea. Why not?
4. Someone told me once that the balance sheet is a photograph of the business at a particular instant in time, and that you have to be careful because some accountant might have touched up the photo, airbrushed away the warts. What did they mean? Isn't the balance sheet an exact list of all the company's assets and liabilities?

PROBLEM 2.12 Prepare simple balance sheet, notes, what-if analysis

Clambake Kate's Inc. is a maritime eatery specializing in shellfish and soups. The premises are rented and all sales are for cash, so the company has only a few balance sheet accounts. The accounts as at May 31, 1995, are as follows.

Debit balance accounts		**Credit balance accounts**	
Food supplies cost	$ 2,100	Payable to suppliers	$ 5,300
Equipment cost	64,900	Long-term loan	25,000
Other supplies cost	4,500	Wages payable	900
Cash in bank	2,200	Share capital issued	10,000
		Accumulated amortization	27,400
		Retained earnings	5,100
	$73,700		$73,700

1. Prepare a balance sheet for Clambake Kate's Inc. as at May 31, 1995. Include any notes to the balance sheet that you think might be useful.
2. Comment on the company's financial position as shown by your balance sheet.
3. Suppose, when you were reviewing the company's accounts after preparing the balance sheet, you found an error in the records. The company had paid a supplier $2,900, but that payment had inadvertently not been deducted from the company's bank account record nor from its record of accounts payable to suppliers. You decided to record that payment. What changes resulted in the balance sheet you prepared in Part 1 and in your comments in Part 2?

PROBLEM 2.13 Identify debit and credit balances, and prepare a balance sheet

Blue Moon Love Products Ltd. manufactures and sells various aids to middle-aged romantics, including special flower bouquets, French "beer for lovers," seductive apparel, and recipes for aphrodisiac cookies. Here are the company's balance sheet accounts as at June 30, 1995, in alphabetical order.

Blue Moon Love Products Inc.
Balance Sheet Accounts as at June 30, 1995

Account	Amount	Account	Amount
Accumulated amortization	$ 63,700	Owing from customers	$ 6,200
Bank account balance	14,300	Owing to suppliers	21,900
Bank loan	21,200	Retained earnings	47,500
Building	102,100	Share capital issued	25,000
Cash on hand	2,500	Short-term part of mortgage	8,000
Employees' tax not yet remitted	600	Unpaid employee wages	1,800
Fixtures and equipment	37,900	Unsold finished products	29,600
Land	48,000	Unused office supplies	1,400
Long-term part of mortgage owing	71,000	Unused product raw materials	18,700

1. Decide which accounts have debit balances and which have credit balances. According to the company's accounting system, total debits = total credits = $260,700.
2. Based on your answer to #1, prepare the company's June 30, 1995, balance sheet from the above accounts.
3. Comment briefly on the company's financial condition as shown by the balance sheet.

PROBLEM 2.14 Identify items as asset, liability, or owners' equity

State whether or not, and why, each of the following items is likely to be an asset, liability, or owners' equity account (perhaps both an asset and a liability in some cases) of the company indicated:

Company	Item
1. Walt Disney Co.	List of subscribers to *Discover* magazine
2. Canadian Utilities Ltd.	Funds collected from employees, to be repaid to them after retirement as pensions
3. T. Eaton Co. Ltd.	Eaton's satisfied customers
4. Branko Inc.	A lawsuit against the company by a plumber who alleges that Branko failed to pay for work done on the company's premises
5. Canada Safeway Ltd.	Land that Safeway has agreed to sell to a real estate developer once it has been surveyed
6. T. Eaton Co. Ltd.	Eaton's dissatisfied customers
7. Dow-Jones Inc.	The *Wall Street Journal*'s skilled group of editors and reporters
8. Imperial Oil Ltd.	Oil discovered on Imperial's property, but still underground and likely to stay there for many years

9. Edmonton Eskimos Football Club	Players under contract to the team
10. The Brick Warehouse	Deposits received from customers of The Brick for furniture not yet delivered to them
11. Torstar Corp.	Profits earned by the *Toronto Star*, but not yet paid out to the owners as dividends
12. Sears Inc.	A fleet of delivery trucks leased by Sears from several truck-leasing firms
13. Downtown Buick Sales Ltd.	A car Downtown Buick leases to real estate salesperson Don Wharton
14. Redpath Industries Ltd.	Funds owing to Redpath by a customer who recently declared bankruptcy
15. Keg Restaurants Ltd.	The phrase "The Keg" and the round logo, both registered trademarks
16. Triple Five Corporation	The parking lot surrounding Triple Five's West Edmonton Mall
17. Grand Centre Ltd.	A guarantee Grand Centre has made on a bank loan owed by an associated company
18. National Bioengineering Ltd.	A newly developed chemical that shows promise in curing adolescent blemishes once and for all, but that has yet to be approved by the government

PROBLEM 2.15 General versus specific-user balance sheet

(Challenging)

Write a paragraph giving your considered views on the following question: Can a single balance sheet ever satisfy all the users of a company's financial statements, or should there be different balance sheets prepared to meet the differing needs of users?

PROBLEM 2.16 Balance sheets without dollars

(Challenging)

In the high mountains of Whimsia two shepherds, Doug and Bob, sit arguing about their relative positions in life, an argument that has been going on for years. Doug says that he has 400 sheep, while Bob has only 360 sheep; therefore, Doug is much better off. Bob, on the other hand, argues that he has 30 acres of land, while Doug has only 20 acres. But Doug's land was inherited, while Bob traded 35 sheep for 20 acres of land ten years ago and this year gave 40 sheep for 10 acres of land. Bob also makes the observation that, of Doug's sheep, 35 belong to another man and he merely keeps them. Doug counters that he has a large one-room cabin that he built himself and claims to have been offered 3 acres of land for the cabin. Besides these things, he has a plough, which was a gift from a friend and is worth a couple of goats, 2 carts, which were given him in trade for a poor acre of land, and an ox, acquired in return for 5 sheep.

Bob goes on to say that his wife has orders for 5 coats to be made of homespun wool and that she will receive 25 goats for them. His wife has 10 goats already, 3 of which were received in exchange for 1 sheep just last year. She also has an ox for which she traded 3 sheep and a cart, which had cost her 2 sheep. Bob's two-room cabin, though smaller than Doug's, should bring him 2 choice acres of land in a trade. Doug is reminded by Bob that he owes Ted, another shepherd, 3 sheep for bringing him his lunch each day last year.

Who is better off? State any assumptions you make. Try to develop a common numerical representation of the shepherds' situations to support your evaluation.[14]

PROBLEM 2.17 Develop a research idea re: the balance sheet

(Challenging)

Section 2.10 described a question addressed by accounting research: whether the balance sheet should be prepared according to an entity or a proprietor orientation. Go back to the list of possible research questions given in Section 1.7, or think up a question on your own, and apply that to the balance sheet. (For example, item 1 in Section 1.7 might raise this question: How do stock and bond markets react to the information included in the balance sheet?) State what your research question is, explain why it might be worth studying, and suggest how you might study it. Just exercise your curiosity here—think about the balance sheet, and do not try to guess what accounting researchers might actually be doing about the question you come up with.

PROBLEM 2.18 Accountants, ethics, and balance sheets

(Challenging)

As has been indicated several times so far, for example in Section 2.9, managers of businesses and other organizations are very concerned about how the balance sheet reflects their management of the enterprise. This is very natural, and generally appropriate too, because such concern is likely to lead managers to want to do a good job of managing. But it can also lead to a temptation to alter the information in a manager's favour. The possibility of such a temptation is part of the reason auditors are employed to examine financial statements, including the balance sheet. This temptation can also produce ethical problems for professional accountants employed by the enterprise. On the one hand, such an accountant is bound by the ethical rules of the profession to see that proper accounting methods are followed in preparing the company's balance sheet, which would imply that the information should not be altered in management's favour. On the other hand, such an accountant works for senior management and is likely bound by the contract of employment to put the enterprise's interests first. What does such an accountant (for example the chief accountant responsible for preparing the enterprise's financial statements) do if senior management (for example the president) wants to alter the balance sheet to make things look better and makes a good case that such an action will help the enterprise get bank loans and other assistance it needs?

Discuss this situation, from the point of view of both the president and the chief accountant.

PROBLEM 2.19 Prepare a balance sheet from transactions

(Challenging)

Fed up with her dead-end career with a big company, Tanya decided to start her own business, manufacturing and selling fresh pasta and a line of associated sauces, and selling cookware and other equipment to go with the food. It took her several weeks to get set up, before she made a single sale.

Design an approximate balance sheet format for Tanya's new company, PastaPastaPasta Inc., record (using a piece of paper or a computer spreadsheet) the events (transactions) below, which happened in those preparatory weeks, and prepare the company's balance sheet at the end of Tanya's business set-up time.

1. Tanya put personal savings of $45,000 into a new bank account opened in the company's name. She decided that $35,000 of that would go for shares of the company and the rest would be a loan she hoped the company could pay back in a few years.
2. Tanya also provided her large set of recipes and her minivan, to be owned by the new company. She thought the recipes would be worth about $500 and the minivan about $7,500. She was in no hurry to be paid for these items, but thought they should be included in the company's assets.
3. A group of friends and relatives gave her company $25,000 in cash, in return for shares.
4. The company rented space in a small strip mall and paid $2,000 as rent in advance.
5. Another friend, who had no cash but wanted to help, agreed to do some renovations and repainting in the new space, in return for some shares in the company. Tanya and the friend agreed that the work done would have cost $4,500 if she had paid someone else to do it.
6. The company bought a large amount of food processing and storage equipment for $63,250, paying $28,000 in cash and agreeing to pay the rest in five equal annual instalments, beginning in six months.
7. Pasta-making supplies costing $4,720 and cookware for resale costing $3,910 were purchased for $1,000 in cash, with the remainder to be paid in 60 days.
8. The company got a $20,000 line of credit from the bank and actually borrowed $2,500 of that, repayable on demand. Tanya had to sign a personal guarantee for anything borrowed under the line of credit.
9. The company paid a lawyer $1,800 for costs of incorporation.

CASE 2A Interpret a real balance sheet

The 1993 balance sheet (without notes) of TSC Shannock Corporation, a Burnaby, B.C. distributor of pre-recorded video cassettes, audio cassettes, compact discs, laser discs, and similar items, follows. The company's 1993 annual report indicated that there were eight distribution centres across Canada and that aggressive company growth was planned, through acquisitions of other companies, competitive pricing, high product quality, and continued attention to customer satisfaction.

Using the balance sheet, discuss the following questions:

1. Point out some ways in which the company seems to be different from most companies, such as those mentioned in this chapter. What do those differences tell you about how the company operates and how it is financed?
2. What sort of assets probably lie behind the balance sheet figures?
3. What are some things you would like to know about the company, in order to feel comfortable about what the balance sheet tells you and to evaluate the soundness of the company's resources and financing strategy?

TSC SHANNOCK CORPORATION

BALANCE SHEETS

	May 31	
ASSETS	**1993**	**1992**
Current Assets		
Cash	$ 1,600,239	$ 997,723
Accounts receivable	6,007,741	5,722,261
Inventory	4,335,948	3,786,437
Prepaid expenses and deposits	73,422	119,249
	12,017,350	10,625,670
Equipment and leasehold improvements (Note 3)	486,597	514,641
Other assets	275,870	0
	$12,779,817	**$11,140,311**
LIABILITIES AND SHAREHOLDERS' EQUITY		
Current Liabilities		
Accounts payable and accrued liabilities	$ 8,424,243	$ 7,275,305
Income taxes payable	133,803	492,389
	8,558,046	7,767,694
Shareholder's Equity		
Capital stock (Note 4)	3,019,721	2,564,548
Retained earnings	1,202,050	808,069
	4,221,771	3,372,617
Lease commitments (Note 5)		
	$12,779,817	**$11,140,311**

See accompanying Notes To Financial Statements. *(Not included)*

REPRODUCED COURTESY OF TSC SHANNOCK CORPORATION, ANNUAL REPORT, MAY 31, 1993.

CASE 2B Examine the CBC's balance sheet

The Canadian Broadcasting Corporation (CBC) is wholly owned by the Government of Canada (the proprietor of the CBC). About 75% of the CBC's revenue is operating grants from the Government, and most of the rest is advertising revenue. The Government also provides general advances to ensure that the CBC has sufficient working capital to operate properly.

Even though it has only one owner and its balance sheet is prepared as that of a proprietorship, the CBC is a corporation and owns property, signs contracts, and employs people. It also has a number of **capital leases** (primarily to do with its recently completed broadcasting centre in Toronto)—such leases do not give the CBC legal ownership of the property, but they are so close to doing so that they are accounted for as if they were owned property, by debiting noncurrent assets for the economic value of the assets involved and crediting capital lease liability for the future payment obligations.

Below is the CBC's March 31, 1993, comparative balance sheet and Note 8 regarding capital assets. (No other notes are provided because they are rather complex.)

CANADIAN BROADCASTING CORPORATION
SOCIÉTÉ RADIO—CANADA
BALANCE SHEET
As at March 31, 1993

	1993	1992
		(thousands of dollars)
Assets		
Current		
Cash and short-term investments	68,330	40,865
Accounts receivable	86,177	102,145
Programs completed and in process of production	96,626	74,694
Prepaid film and script rights and other expenses	50,042	50,707
	301,175	**268,411**
Investment *(Note 7)*	2,200	—
Capital assets *(Note 8)*	1,266,936	787,892
Deferred charges *(Note 9)*	12,530	16,508
	1,582,841	**1,072,811**
Liabilities		
Current		
Accounts payable and accrued liabilities	166,093	169,559
Accrued vacation pay	61,180	55,999
	227,273	**225,558**
Long-term		
Employee termination benefits	112,121	113,391
Advances from Government of Canada *(Note 10)*	33,000	33,000
Obligations under capital leases *(Note 11)*	436,126	811
	581,247	**147,202**
Proprietor's Equity		
Proprietor's equity account	774,321	700,051
	1,582,841	**1,072,811**

The accompanying notes and schedule A form an integral part of the financial statements. *(Not included)*

8. Capital Assets

	1993			1992
	(thousands of dollars)			
	Cost	Accumulated Amortization	Net Book Value	Net Book Value
Land	36,188	—	36,188	36,155
Bulidings	308,748	149,036	159,712	161,215
Technical equipment	896,178	469,932	426,246	384,954
Furnishings, office equipmnet and computers	64,169	32,174	31,995	21,635
Automotive	18,492	12,660	5,832	5,222
Leasehold improvements	4,780	3,628	1,152	1,822
Peroperty under capital leases	501,617	733	500,884	785
Uncompleted capital projects	104,927	—	104,927	176,104
	1,935,099	**668,163**	**1,266,936**	**787,892**

REPRODUCED COURTESY OF CANADIAN BROADCASTING CORPORATION, FINANCIAL STATEMENTS, MARCH 31, 1993.

Based on this information, and your own knowledge of the CBC and radio and television in general:

1. What does the balance sheet tell you about the way the CBC does its business and how it is financed?
2. How is the CBC's balance sheet similar to or different from the balance sheets of ordinary business corporations?
3. How fully do you think the balance sheet represents the CBC's real value to the country and the risks the CBC faces?

NOTES

1. Judith Stone, "Big Brewhaha of 1800 B.C.," *Discover*, January 1991, p. 14. (The words quoted in the excerpt are those of Fritz Maytag, owner of the Anchor Brewing Company of San Francisco.)
2. Information about the history of accounting and business is published in many places. A variety of professional and academic journals have shown an interest in such material, and there is a journal devoted specifically to it: the *Accounting Historians Journal*. See also the references below.
3. George J. Coustourous, *Accounting in the Golden Age of Greece: A Response to Socioeconomic Changes* (Champaign, Ill.: Center for International Education and Research in Accounting, Univ. of Illinois, 1979).
4. Orville R Keister. "The Mechanics of Mesopotamian Record-Keeping," in *Contemporary Studies in the Evolution of Accounting Thought*, ed. Michael Chatfield (Belmont, Calif.: Dickenson Publishing Company Inc., 1968), 12–20.

5. O. ten Have, *The History of Accounting* (Palo Alto, Calif.: Bay Books, 1976), 27–30.
6. Ibid., 30–46.
7. Ibid., 56–74.
8. Michael Chatfield, "English Medieval Bookkeeping: Exchequer and Manor," in *Contemporary Studies in the Evolution of Accounting Thought*, 36.
9. ten Have, *History*, 67.
10. Peter C. Newman, *Company of Adventurers* (Markham, Ont.: Viking/Penguin Books, 1985), xii.
11. C.J. Hasson, "The South Sea Bubble and M. Shell," in *Contemporary Studies in the Evolution of Accounting Thought*, 86–94.
12. Ross M. Skinner, *Accounting Standards in Evolution* (Toronto: Holt, Rinehart and Winston, 1987), 15–16.
13. For an explanation of the entity and proprietorship concepts, see, for example, the Canadian Institute of Chartered Accountants' research study *Corporate Reporting: Its Future Evolution* (Toronto: CICA, 1980), 15–16. This study considers a large number of other accounting concepts as well. For larger-scale works relevant to the difficulty of fitting any one approach to accounting's various problems, see Skinner, *Accounting Standards in Evolution*, or R.L. Watts and J.L. Zimmerman, *Positive Accounting Theory* (Englewood Cliffs, N.J.: Prentice–Hall, 1986).
14. Adapted from *Accounting Education: Problems and Prospects* (Sarasota, Fla.: American Accounting Association, 1974).

Chapter 3 Financial Performance: The Income Statement

3.1 Chapter Overview

The balance sheet is the fundamental cumulative record of the results of an enterprise's financial activities. Its picture of the enterprise's financial position is not the only story to be told, however. The balance sheet's picture is static: it tells us what the position is. Most managers, owners, and creditors also want to know how well the enterprise is performing and how it got to where it is. Comparing the balance sheets at two different times would show some changes but would not really explain why they happened. To provide that explanation, three additional financial statements have been developed. In this chapter, you will learn about the most important one, the **income statement.** You will also learn about a statement used to connect the income statement to the balance sheet, called the **statement of retained earnings.** In Chapter 4, you will learn about the third one, which focuses on cash inflows and outflows.

In this chapter you will learn:

Use concepts: how increasingly sophisticated managers, owners, governments, and capital markets have produced a demand for information to use in assessing businesses' financial performance over time;

Preparation concepts: how the concept of accrual income, which was introduced in Chapter 1, and the income statement that describes the enterprise's income performance over a period have been designed to respond to the demand for performance information;

Preparation techniques: how to use accounting data to make an income statement and to connect it to the balance sheet through the statement of retained earnings, focusing on simple versions of the statements for now (including the first income statement for continuing case Mato Inc.);

Use techniques: introductory ideas about how to interpret the income statement and statement of retained earnings.

In this chapter, we will focus on business enterprises, because governments and other nonbusiness organizations, such as charities and churches, do not have income statements or retained earnings. Their objectives and operations are different, as will be described briefly in Chapter 5.

3.2 FINANCIAL ACCOUNTING'S MORE RECENT HISTORY

In Chapter 2, we saw how the development of commercial activity and the demand for information contributed to the development of double-entry accounting and the balance sheet. We left that review of history at the early 1800s. This section resumes that review and takes it up to the present, describing the development of both the income statement and the quality standards that underlie accrual accounting. This review is short, though a great deal has happened in the last 30 years in particular. See the references at the end of the chapter for some sources of further reading.[1]

As businesses grew in size and complexity, the demand for information on financial performance increased. The static picture presented by the balance sheet was not good enough for the emerging stock markets, for the increasingly large group of nonowner professional managers, or for governments that wished to evaluate (and tax!) businesses' performance (to mention just a few of the groups interested in evaluating performance). The income statement came into its own as a central part of financial reporting in the last hundred years, and its measurement of financial performance is central to economic activity and performance evaluation in most of the world.

Modern financial accounting as practised in Canada is the result of many economic, social, and political forces operating in Canada, Great Britain, and the United States over the last 200 years. Canadian financial accounting is not much different from British and American accounting, though details do vary among the three countries. This is so because the economic and other forces have behaved similarly in the three countries. Canadian practice has its roots in 19th-century Great Britain,[2] but in the 20th century it has become more strongly influenced by developments in the United States, as that country has risen in economic prominence. Recently, business and commercial activities have become more international, so influences on Canadian financial accounting may become more international too.

DEVELOPMENTS IN THE 19TH CENTURY[3]

Up to the early 19th century most business enterprises were formed for specific ventures, were financed by a few wealthy owners, and were disbanded when the ventures were completed. The sharing of profits among the owners of the enterprise or venture took place at the end, when all of the assets were sold, the liabilities were paid off, and the net amount remaining was distributed among the owners. When, as industrialization increased, large industrial plants began replacing short-term ventures as the major form of business enterprise, the traditional method of financing and profit sharing was no longer acceptable. The large cost of constructing and maintaining these more capital-intensive enterprises was often more than a few owners could afford, and the long life of the assets made it unsatisfactory to wait for the winding up of the enterprise to share profits.

Various pieces of companies' legislation were introduced in Britain in the 1830s, 1840s, and 1850s. This legislation allowed companies to sell shares in stock markets (which, because the initial issuing of shares provides capital, that is to say, equity funds for the companies, are also called **capital markets**).

The legislation also provided a major feature of corporations: liability of the corporation's owners to the corporation's creditors was, and still is, limited to the amount of the owners' equity in the corporation. The justification for the limited liability feature was that individual investors could not always be aware of the actions of the directors they elected or the managers who were in turn engaged by the directors. Therefore, investors should not be liable for any more than the amount of money they invested in the enterprise.

Limited liability of its owners and an existence separate from its owners largely define the corporation. Modern laws and business practices complicate the operation of capital markets and can reduce the protection of limited liability, but the idea that a corporation is a "legal person," able to act on its own and survive changes in owners, is still central to business and to much of the rest of our lives.

The problem of how to ensure fair calculation and sharing of ownership interests led legislators to require that a corporation present its balance sheet annually to its shareholders and that an auditor be present to report to the shareholders on the validity of that financial statement. Legislation also required that any annual payments to shareholders should not come out of the sale of, or by decreasing the value of, a corporation's long-term capital assets. Such payments should be made out of monies earned yearly from these assets after all yearly debts are paid. We can think of "monies earned yearly" as revenues, and "yearly debts" as expenses, so this meant, roughly, that payments to shareholders should come out of yearly income. This is close to the dividend requirement placed on most corporations today (dividends can normally only be paid out of net income). Corporations began to compute income in separate statements or schedules, so that they could demonstrate that they had performed well enough to permit the distribution of dividends or the issuing of more shares.

From an accounting perspective, the problem was that there were no accounting theories or conventions to help illustrate and define the responses to demands for better performance and other financial information. There was no nationally organized association of accountants in Britain until the end of the 19th century (although the Accountants' Society of Edinburgh received a royal charter in 1854, an event that led to the term "chartered accountant"). Accounting methods developed situation by situation, with no overall plan or concepts throughout this period.

The beginning of the 20th century saw accountants little further ahead than they were at the beginning of the 19th as far as having some larger set of theories or principles upon which to base their profession. Some model financial statements and examples from legislation were being used, and income statements were becoming established, but it was becoming necessary to establish a rational basis, that is, principles, for preparing financial statements and for extending the principles to new settings, as business and commercial activity continued to increase.

Toward the end of the 19th century, several British court cases had established that accountants and auditors had to decide what were proper and fair financial statements, and could not expect courts and legislatures to decide for them. A prominent accountant, Ernest Cooper, voiced his concern a hundred years ago, in 1894: "... the already sufficient responsibilities and anxieties of an Auditor will be extended beyond those known of any trade or profession."[4]

Accounting was on its way to formulating the professional rights, responsibilities, and criteria for competence, as had the already established professions of law, engineering, and medicine.

DEVELOPMENTS IN THE 20TH CENTURY[5]

In the 20th century, Canadian accounting practice began to develop more independently from that in Britain, but it also came under the stronger influence of events in the United States. Canada's federal system of government, different from the more centralized one in Britain, meant that legislation affecting accounting and professional accounting associations in Canada had strong provincial as well as national influences. As an example, in the early part of this century, Ontario led the rest of the country in introducing legislation that affected accounting methods. Today, the Ontario Securities Commission is the most important regulator of capital markets in Canada and therefore has great influence on the accounting used by corporations whose shares are traded on stock exchanges (especially the Toronto Stock Exchange, the country's largest). There is no national securities commission in Canada, while in the United States, the national Securities and Exchange Commission plays an even more dominant regulatory role there than does the Ontario Securities Commission in Canada.

By 1920, legislation in Canada had established mandatory reporting of the financial position of incorporated companies (corporations) and had begun to set requirements for the contents of the income statement. The income statement became important both because income tax legislation passed in 1917 established rules for calculating revenues and expenses, and because the growing amount of equity investment in Canadian industry put pressure on for better performance measures and for more financial disclosure in general. Another reason for the income statement's growing prominence was the increased investment in Canadian industry by investors from the United States, which created a demand, similar to that in the United States, for disclosure of how net incomes, and therefore the dividends declared on the basis of the incomes, were calculated.

There was, and often still is, considerable resistance by management to increased income statement disclosure, such as of the amounts of important revenues and expenses, because of a fear that competitors and others not necessarily friendly to the company will use the information to the company's detriment. This fear is likely stronger than the fear of disclosing the balance sheet's position information, because the income statement's performance information can be used to judge the company's market share (revenue as a percentage of the industry's revenue), sales margins or markups, and other such competitively sensitive factors.

Though these pressures for more disclosure existed, the general prosperity in North America during the 1920s prevented serious concern about companies' financial disclosure. The 1929 stock market crash and ensuing Great Depression permanently changed this. From the 1930s onward, accounting practices, like many aspects of companies' financial and productive operations, attracted great, and often critical, attention from legislators and the public. The U.S. Securities and Exchange Commission was established in the mid-1930s, and securities commissions were also established in some of Canada's provinces. Their impact has steadily increased in the period since the Second World War.

REGULATION OF FINANCIAL ACCOUNTING: ACCOUNTING STANDARDS

Professional associations of accountants began to develop more rigorous accounting standards and auditing standards for their members to follow, and legislation began to require companies to adhere to these standards. In Canada, the Dominion Association of Chartered Accountants (now called the Canadian Institute of Chartered Accountants or the CICA) presented briefs to Parliament on accounting issues, issued bulletins making suggestions on financial accounting and auditing standards, and in the late 1960s began to issue official standards in the ***CICA Handbook***. *Handbook* standards are given considerable authority by company legislation and securities commissions' regulations and will be referred to frequently in this book. Having a detailed set of accounting standards with legal authority is quite a recent phenomenon in Canada, as it is in many parts of the world.

In the United States, the American Institute of Accountants (now called the American Institute of Certified Public Accountants or the AICPA) also began to issue pronouncements on financial accounting and auditing. The AICPA still issues auditing standards, but in the early 1970s its financial accounting standard-setting body, the Accounting Principles Board, was replaced by a new body set up to be independent of the AICPA: the Financial Accounting Standards Board (FASB). The Securities and Exchange Commission (SEC) generally supports the FASB's position as financial accounting standard setter for the United States, which gives the FASB great influence in accounting throughout much of the world, including Canada. There has been quite a proliferation of accounting standards in the United States, with over 100 separate FASB standards (many of those very long and complex) and many SEC pronouncements issued over the last 20 or so years.

There are many other voices in the setting of financial accounting standards and in the development of financial accounting, as you will see in this book. There is, for example, legislation requiring particular accounting methods for some sensitive companies, such as banks and trust companies. Standard-setting activities are also carried out by other associations, such as the Canadian Certified General Accountants' Association, and courts often establish precedents in accounting issues as in other areas. There is much activity at the international level, such as that of the International Federation of Accountants; and the International Accounting Standards Committee, founded in 1973, has published a large number of international financial accounting standards. These standards have so far been less binding than such national standards as those issued by the CICA or the FASB, but there is great interest in harmonizing standards so that investors, managers, and other interested parties will be able to rely on the content and quality of financial statements no matter where in the world the statements originate.[6]

The 20th century has seen great growth in business and commercial activity, in stock markets and other capital markets, in international trade, in governments, in the sophistication of managers and investors, and in the communication links among them all. At any hour of the day, there is a major stock market open somewhere, with investors from all over the world trading on it. Business activity is truly a 24-hour-a-day, 365-day-a-year affair, with information about business activities flowing throughout the world via electronic, paper, and other media. Financial accounting is being continually shaped by all this activity. The basic double-entry model of financial accounting has endured for hundreds of years, but the way that model is applied and the supplementary information associated with it have developed far beyond Pacioli's description. Financial accounting's measures of financial position and performance are central to national and international economies and political structures, and financial accounting and its standards themselves are economically and politically powerful institutions in society.

Financial accounting is continuously evolving as the nation and the world evolve. (Management accounting and other aspects of accounting beyond this book's scope also continue to evolve.) This is not to say that every change is for the better, any more than it is in other human endeavours, but rather to emphasize that financial accounting is an organic, evolving discipline: the best prediction we can make about balance sheets and income statements is that they will not be exactly the same in the future as they are now. This book attempts to develop in you an understanding of how financial accounting got to where it is and what the pressures on it are. This understanding will help you to keep in mind that financial accounting is not cast in stone and will equip you to deal with the changes that are sure to come.

HOW'S YOUR UNDERSTANDING

Here are two questions you should be able to answer, based on what you have just read:

1. Describe the user demands that furthered the development of the income statement.
2. Why do we have accounting standards and who issues them?

3.3 INTRODUCTION TO THE INCOME AND RETAINED EARNINGS STATEMENTS

A business exists over a period of time. If the owners and managers are successful, it may prosper for a long time. The Hudson's Bay Company is such a business: incorporated in 1670, it is more than 300 years old! Suppose a measure of the company's financial performance were desired for comparison to other companies, for assessing income tax, for help in deciding how much to sell the company for, or for many other reasons we will come to. How could such performance be measured?

Well, we might measure the company's financial performance by closing it down, selling off all its assets, paying off all its liabilities, and seeing how much is left for the owners. Good performance would be indicated if the money left for the owners plus the amounts they withdrew over the years was greater than the amount they put in when they founded the company, perhaps adjusted for inflation over that time and for the owners' costs of raising the money they put in. But killing the business to measure how well it has been doing is a little drastic! Waiting until it dies of natural causes seems hardly a better solution: the Hudson's Bay Company has outlasted many generations of owners and managers, and the Ford Motor Company has outlasted a number of Ford family members. It would be more useful to measure performance over selected shorter periods of time: annually, every three months (quarterly), or on a monthly basis. People could then make their decisions about investing in the company or getting out, and hiring managers or firing them, when they wanted to do so.

THE INCOME STATEMENT

This is where the income statement comes in. This statement uses accrual accounting to measure financial performance over a period of time, usually a year, three months, or one month, coming up with the "bottom line" net income for the period, calculated as revenues minus expenses. Remember the income statement for Gurjit's jewellery business in Section 1.4 of Chapter 1:

Revenue	
($4,350 collected plus $310 still to be received)	$4,660
Expenses	
($1,670 paid minus $280 goods still on hand plus $85 unpaid plus $120 amortization)	1,595
Accrual income based on the information provided	$3,065

This simple income statement illustrates the form of all business income statements as they are done in North America and much of the rest of the world:

Net Income for the period = Revenue(s) – Expenses for the period

Gurjit's income statement shows no income tax on that income. Her business is a proprietorship, and any income tax is her personal responsibility. The income statements of corporations, which are responsible for their own income taxes, do have income tax deducted as one of the expenses. The phrase **net income** is usually used to refer to the amount left after the income tax. Net income is based on accrual accounting, so it is a measure of economic performance, not cash income (remember the different cash income calculation we did for Gurjit's jewellery business back in Section 1.4).

REVENUES AND EXPENSES

If net income is the difference between revenues and expenses, what are these two kinds of performance measures?

Revenues are *increases in the company's wealth arising from the provision of services or sales of goods to customers.* Wealth increases because customers:

- pay cash;
- promise to pay cash (such promises are called **accounts receivable**); or, more rarely,
- pay with other forms of wealth, such as by providing other assets to the company or forgiving debts owed by the company.

So, if, *in return for services or goods*, a customer paid $1,000 in cash, another customer promised to pay $1,000 later, another gave the company $1,000 in equipment, or another forgave a $1,000 debt the company had owed the customer, these would each be called a revenue of $1,000.

Expenses are the opposite of revenues. They are decreases *in the company's wealth that are incurred in order to earn revenue*. Wealth decreases because operating costs have to be borne; customers have to be given the goods they have paid for; long-term assets wear out as they are used to earn revenue; and liabilities may be incurred as part of the process.

So, if, *as part of its attempt to earn revenues*, the company paid $600 in rent, or the goods bought by a customer cost the company $600 to provide, or the building depreciated by $600, or the company promised to pay an employee $600 in wages later on, each of these would be called an expense of $600.

Both revenues and expenses are measured following the concepts of accrual accounting, therefore, they represent increases or decreases in wealth, whether or not cash receipts or payments occur at the same time. As net income is the difference between revenues and expenses, it represents the net *inflow of wealth* to the company during the period. The reporting of net income means that the company has become wealthier during the period. If net income is negative, that is, if revenues are less than expenses, it is instead called **net loss** and represents a net *outflow of wealth*. In this case, the company has become less wealthy.

Expenses include all the costs of earning the revenues, including income and other taxes, but they do *not* include payment of returns (withdrawals by proprietors or partners, or dividends to shareholders of corporations). Payments or promises of payment of returns to owners (such as when a corporation's board of directors *declares* [promises] a dividend), are considered to be *distributions* of net income to owners. The undistributed remainder is kept in the company as retained earnings.

THE RETAINED EARNINGS STATEMENT

The **statement of retained earnings** shows what has been done with the period's income. Retained earnings is the sum of past net incomes, measured since the company began, minus dividends declared (even if not yet paid) to owners since the beginning. The statement of retained earnings updates retained earnings from the end of the preceding period (year, quarter, month, or whatever), which is also the beginning of the present period, to the end of the present period:

Retained earnings at end of period	=	**Retained earnings at beginning of period** **+ Net income (or – Net loss)* for the period** **– Dividends declared during the period**

* Net income is the figure shown on the income statement for the same period. If the company performed badly, the income could be negative (expenses greater than revenues, producing a net loss instead), and in that case, the net loss is deducted from the beginning retained earnings. If things get really bad, retained earnings can also be negative (losses having overwhelmed incomes), in which case the negative retained earnings figure is called a **deficit**.

The statement of retained earnings, therefore, shows that the net income for the period is part of the retained earnings at the end of the period, by showing that the income is part of the *change* in retained earnings over the period covered by the income statement. The usual format of the retained earnings statement is:

Start with retained earnings, beginning of period (end of previous period)	$ XXXX
Add net income for the period	XXXX
Deduct dividends declared during the period	(XXXX)
Equals retained earnings, end of period	$ XXXX

You might be interested to know that you can, *if you have the past records*, go back year by year, figuring out how much income was added to retained earnings each year and how much in dividends was deducted. You could go all the way back to the first day of the company, when there had not yet been any income and therefore not yet any retained earnings. Retained earnings is therefore like an onion: you can keep peeling away each year's layer until you have peeled it all away and are back to zero. You can similarly peel away each year's transactions in every balance sheet account, for example, you can trace all the changes in cash back to the very beginning. For this reason, the balance sheet can be said to reflect everything that has ever been recorded in the accounts: it is the accumulation of everything that happened from when the company began until now. Accounting really is a historical information system!

In a corporation, the board of directors is the senior level of management, operating the company on behalf of the owners. When the board declares a dividend, the amount is deducted from retained earnings then. At that point, the company has a liability to the owners, which it pays off by sending the owners the promised cash, or, in some cases called **stock dividends**, sending the owners more shares of the company. This involves two principles of financial accounting: (1) transactions with owners, of which the main example is dividends, are shown on the statement of retained earnings and not on the income statement, so that the net income can be measured without considering such transactions; and (2) owners can be creditors too, if they are owed dividends or have lent the company money in addition to the shares they bought.

CONNECTING THE INCOME STATEMENT TO THE BALANCE SHEET

The balance sheet shows all assets, liabilities, and owners' equity accounts as at a point in time. Usually the balance sheet is comparative, showing the accounts at both the beginning of the income statement's period (that is, the end of the previous period) and at the end of the income statement's period, and therefore showing both the beginning retained earnings and the ending retained earnings.

Assets at beginning = Liabilities + Equity (including retained earnings) at beginning

Assets at end = Liabilities + Equity (including retained earnings) at end

***Change* in Assets = *Change* in Liabilities + *Change* in Equity (including retained earnings)**

Using some illustrative numbers:

Beginning:	$1,200 Assets	=	$750 Liabilities + $450 Equity
End:	$1,450 Assets	=	$900 Liabilities + $550 Equity
Changes:	$ 250 Assets	=	$150 Liabilities + $100 Equity

The equity at the beginning might be $200 in share capital and $250 in retained earnings. If there is no change in contributed capital, the equity change comes entirely from a retained earnings change, which, for example, might be made up of $175 in net income minus $75 in dividends declared.

Therefore, the beginning and ending balance sheets define the financial position at the beginning and end of the period over which the income statement measures performance. The net income is part of the change in retained earnings, which in turn is part of the change in the balance sheet over that period. The statement of retained earnings therefore "knits" the income statement and the balance sheet together by showing that the net income is part of the change in the balance sheet over the period. (Accountants refer to this knitting together as the **articulation** of the income statement and the balance sheet.) Income is part of the change in retained earnings for the period, therefore:

Income is part of the equity component of the balance sheet equation.

Make sure you understand how this works:

- A *revenue* increases wealth, so it either increases assets or decreases liabilities, and therefore increases equity;
- An *expense* decreases wealth, so it either decreases assets or increases liabilities, and therefore decreases equity;
- Positive net income has the overall effect of increasing assets and/or decreasing liabilities, and therefore increases equity (a net loss, which is negative net income, does the opposite).

Therefore the balance sheet and income statement articulate in two complementary ways:

- When the revenue or expense is recorded, the income statement is affected, and so is/are one or more balance sheet asset and/or liability accounts;
- The income statement's resulting net income affects the balance sheet retained earnings account.

AN EXAMPLE OF INCOME STATEMENT AND BALANCE SHEET ARTICULATION

Bratwurst Inc. had the following balance sheet at the end of 1994 (beginning of 1995): Assets, $5,000; Liabilities, $3,000; Equity, $2,000.

- The beginning equity figure was made up of the owners' invested share capital of $500 plus retained earnings accumulated to the end of 1994 of $1,500. (That $1,500 was therefore the sum of all the net incomes the company had ever had up to the end of 1994 minus all the dividends ever declared to owners up to that point.)
- During 1995, the company had revenues of $11,000 and expenses of $10,000, and declared dividends to owners of $300.
- At the end of 1995, the company had assets of $5,900, liabilities of $3,200, and equity of $2,700, made up of the owners' invested share capital of $500 plus retained earnings of $2,200.

Exhibit 3.1 shows the three financial statements reporting all this:

Exhibit 3.1

Bratwurst Inc.
Income Statement for 1995

Revenues	$11,000
Expenses (including income tax)	10,000
Net income for 1995	$ 1,000

Bratwurst Inc.
Statement of Retained Earnings for 1995

Retained earnings, beginning of 1995 (end of 1994)	$1,500
Add net income for 1995 (from income statement)	1,000
	$2,500
Deduct dividends declared during 1995	300
Retained earnings, end of 1995	$2,200

Bratwurst Inc.
Balance Sheets at Beginning and End of 1995

Assets			Liabilities and Equity		
	End	Begin		End	Begin
Assets	$5,900	$5,000	Liabilities	$3,200	$3,000
			Owners' equity:		
			Share capital	500	500
			Retained earnings*	2,200	1,500
Total	$5,900	$5,000	Total	$5,900	$5,000

*From Statement of Retained Earnings.

You can see from this example that

- the income statement's bottom line is transferred to the statement of retained earnings, and
- the retained earnings statement's bottom line is transferred to the balance sheet,
- showing that the three statements tie together (articulate) through retained earnings.

In addition,

- balance sheet asset and/or liability accounts also have to change to reflect the wealth changes that revenues and expenses involve. These changes keep the balance sheet in balance with the change in retained earnings.

This is true for all companies, not just simple ones like Bratwurst Inc.

The Bratwurst example shows that the income and retained earnings statements could be said to be detailed explanations of the change in the balance sheet retained earnings figure. But the balance sheet could instead have had the following format under the retained earnings part of owners' equity:

Retained earnings:	
Beginning balance	$ 1,500
Add revenues	11,000
	$12,500
Deduct expenses	10,000
	$ 2,500
Deduct dividends declared	300
Ending balance	$ 2,200

The information is there, but putting all this on the balance sheet would make it rather cluttered, and there would hardly be room to provide any details about the various revenues, expenses, and dividends. Also, the concept of income as a measure of performance would be obscured. Therefore, the income and retained earnings statements were developed to provide the detailed performance measure demanded by users of the information without complicating the balance sheet.

HOW'S YOUR UNDERSTANDING

Here are two questions you should be able to answer, based on what you have just read:

1. In financial accounting, what is a revenue and what is an expense?
2. Suppose Bratwurst Inc.'s accounting records showed the following for the next year, 1996: Revenues earned, $14,200; Cash collected from customers, $13,800; Expenses incurred, $12,900; Expenses paid in cash, $11,200; Dividends declared, $600; and Dividends paid in cash, $500. (Remember, retained earnings equalled $2,200 at the end of 1995.) What were Bratwurst's net income for 1996 and its retained earnings as at the end of 1996? (You should get $1,300 and $2,900.)

3.4 A CLOSER LOOK AT INCOME AND RETAINED EARNINGS STATEMENTS' CONTENT

Social and economic forces have helped to produce an income statement that is more complex than the simple Bratwurst Inc. example we saw earlier. More representative of the modern income statement and the associated statement of retained earnings are those of Dominion Textiles Inc. reprinted in Exhibit 3.2. Dominion Textiles is a Montreal-based but international producer of textiles and fabrics. Founded in 1905, it produces and markets textiles and related products in more than 50 countries on all five continents and, according to its 1993 annual report, is the world's largest producer of denim. It produces denim for your pants, your shirt, and even your chair.

Exhibit 3.2

DOMINION TEXTILE INC.

Consolidated Statements of Income for the years ended 30 June

(in thousands of dollars)	**1993**	**1992**	**1991**
Sales	**$1,335,203**	$1,373,038	$1,271,368
Cost of Sales	**(1,062,282)**	(1,146,359)	(1,140,644)
Selling and administrative expenses	**(144,688)**	(140,724)	(145,769)
Income (loss) from operations	**128,233**	85,955	(15,045)
Interest expense, net	**(61,576)**	(68,548)	(60,199)
Income (loss) from operations after interest	**66,657**	17,407	(75,244)
Share in net income of associated companies	**6,900**	5,462	4,327
Restructuring and other non-recurring charges	**—**	(75,000)	(67,968)
Other expense, net	**(4,868)**	(2,986)	(1,360)
Income (loss) before income taxes	**68,689**	(55,117)	(140,245)
Income taxes (credits)	**35,320**	14,881	(16,264)
Minority interest	**3,035**	4,825	4,846
Net income (loss)	**$ 30,334**	$ (74,823)	$ (128,827)
Net earnings (loss) per common share	**$ 0.68**	$ (2.31)	$ (4.07)

Consolidated Statements of Retained Earnings (Deficit) for the years ended 30 June

(in thousands of dollars)	**1993**	**1992**	**1991**
Balance at beginning	**$(100,715)**	$ (20,728)	$ 120,469
Net income (loss)	**30,334**	(74,823)	(128,827)
	(70,381)	(95,551)	(8,358)
Dividends —			
Cumulative First Preferred	**4**	4	4
Second Preferred — Series C	**302**	443	654
Second Preferred — Series D	**3,617**	3,629	3,625
Second Preferred — Series E	**1,088**	1,088	1,088
Common			
$0.22 per share in 1991	**—**	—	6,999
	5,011	5,164	12,370
Share issue expenses	**2,456**	—	—
Balance at end	**$ (77,848)**	$(100,715)	$ (20,728)

See notes to consolidated financial statements. *(Not included)*

REPRODUCED COURTESY OF DOMINION TEXTILE INCORPORATED, ANNUAL REPORT, JUNE 30, 1993.

Among the things you may notice as you review the two statements are:

1. The statements cover a *period of time* (years ending June 30 in this case), not a point in time as the balance sheet does. Like the Paychex, Inc. balance sheet in Chapter 2, these statements are *comparative*, in this case for three years. They also are shown in thousands of dollars.
2. As for balance sheets, extensive explanatory notes are referred to on the income statements and appended to them. The notes are not attached here; the content of such notes is important, however, so some comments are made about that below and further attention will be paid to it in later chapters.
3. The upper part of the income statement generally contains the ordinary revenues, along with the ordinary expenses incurred to earn those revenues. Often, "operating income," which is the difference between ordinary revenues and expenses, is reported. Dominion reported income from operations of $128,233 thousand ($128 million) in 1993, quite an improvement over the loss from operations suffered in 1991.
4. Further down the income statement are often a host of additions and subtractions for items thought to be separate from the ordinary or operating performance. Some of these are quite complicated: in an introductory book like this one, only a general understanding of them can be developed. For now, note the following:
   a. Interest expense (net of interest income) is often shown below operating income, as Dominion does, because interest is thought to be related to the company's financial structure (need to borrow to finance assets), rather than necessarily to the level of revenue. Disclosure of the amount of interest expense is helpful in financial statement analysis, as we will see in later chapters.
   b. Amortization and depreciation expense is also usually disclosed separately on the income statement. Dominion does not do this, but does disclose it elsewhere in the financial statements. In 1993, for example, this expense totalled $65,733 thousand, so that amount is included in the cost of sales (**cost of goods sold** expense) and selling and administrative expenses.
   c. Income tax is levied on corporations' income because they are legally separate from their owners. Such tax is usually a percentage of income before income tax (though there are many complications). If income is negative (a loss), that sort of percentage calculation can produce a tax refund (often called a tax credit), though again there are many complications. You might say that the government shares the income or the loss, though this does not always work as you might expect: you will see that Dominion had income tax expense of $14,881 thousand in 1992 even though there was a loss before income tax that year. The expense (or revenue if there was a loss before income tax) is shown separately near the bottom of the income statement. In 1993, Dominion's income tax expense was $35,320 thousand on income before income tax of $68,689 thousand, for an income tax rate of about 51%. A note to the financial statements disclosed that $18,843 thousand of this tax was payable currently, and the $16,477 thousand remainder was deferred until future years. (This latter amount is called **deferred income tax expense** and will be examined further later. The liability that accumulates deferred income tax is usually shown among the noncurrent liabilities, because payment is unlikely to be needed for several years, and

may even be postponed indefinitely. It is not a debt because the company pays the tax it owes each year: the deferred income tax liability is rather an estimate of likely future tax based on various present assumptions.) The term **net income** is usually reserved for the figure that appears after the income tax line, so it means income net of income tax.

d. Dominion is a group of companies. Therefore, consolidated revenues and expenses are aggregations of the revenues and expenses of a large number of companies in which Dominion has voting control, directly or indirectly, through other companies in the group. We will see more about this in Chapter 5. Note for now two income statement items that reflect the fact that Dominion does not fully own all the companies in the group.

   One of these is "minority interest," $3,035 thousand in 1993. This is a deduction from income, an expense reflecting the share of income earned by consolidated companies that is attributed to owners other than Dominion. For example, if Dominion owns 80% of a company the revenues and expenses of which are included in the consolidated figures, 20% of that company's net income is deducted as a minority interest expense, so that the consolidated net income includes only Dominion's 80% share. So 100% of such a company's revenues and expenses are included in the consolidated revenues and expenses, but only 80% of its net income is included in the consolidated net income. The account that accumulates the minority's (or noncontrolling shareholders') interests in incomes over the years is usually included in noncurrent liabilities, because it represents a long-term obligation of the majority owners to safeguard the minority's share of their company's equity. However it is not a debt, because no payment of that interest to the minority has been promised.

   The second item is "share in net income of associated companies." This is the opposite of the minority interest situation. These companies are not majority owned by Dominion, so their revenues and expenses are not included in the consolidated revenues and expenses. The $6,900 thousand income in 1993 is Dominion's share of those companies' net incomes. So if Dominion owned 30% of such a company, the only effect of that ownership in the consolidated income statement is that 30% of the company's net income is included in the $6,900 thousand figure.

e. Sometimes major events happen that are not typical of normal business operations for the company. To help users of the income statement estimate trends and make predictions, such events are disclosed separately so that users can figure out what the net income would have been without them. There are two main kinds of such nontypical events.

   The first kind is major decisions taken by management to restructure operations or divest the company of unprofitable parts. You might see large expenses with descriptions such as "write-down of investments" or "discontinued operations." Sometimes these can be positive, too, for example, if management decided to sell off a division that was profitable, the income (revenues minus expenses) of that division might be shown as income from discontinued operations (and not included in general revenues and expenses), so that the user could see what the company might be like without that division. You can see that Dominion had major restructuring expenses in 1992 and 1991 ($75,000 thousand in 1992 alone), but none in 1993.

The second kind is major events that happen to the company but are quite beyond its control, dependent on nature or on decisions by outsiders. These are called **extraordinary items** and are shown on the income statement just above the net income line. Because they are shown after the income tax expense line, they have their own income tax expense included with them. Dominion has not had any of these items in the three years from 1991 to 1993.

5. The net income (or net loss) is carried to the statement of retained earnings, to be accumulated with past years' incomes and losses. You can see that, while Dominion had a net income in 1993, it had losses in prior years, and its losses have been so great that they have exceeded prior years' incomes, producing a deficit (negative retained earnings) of $100,715 thousand at the beginning of the 1993 year. A corporation that has a net loss and/or a deficit does not usually declare dividends, as you can imagine! However, you will see that Dominion has declared dividends on its preferred shares—that is because such shares are almost like debt. They have a right to dividends even if the common shareholders get none.

6. Ending retained earnings equals the beginning figure, plus net income, minus dividends declared, plus or minus some other items. There are three main kinds of these other items that you might see in a statement of retained earnings. The first two do not appear in the Dominion statements, but the third does.

   a. The first kind is called **prior period adjustments**. These are revenues or expenses that came in or went out this year, but related specifically to prior years. They are put on the statement of retained earnings to avoid confusing this year's net income number with them. (If they are small they are usually just buried in this year's results, so you will only see the fairly rare large cases.) An example is a lawsuit filed against the company six years ago and finally settled this year. The payout by the company really relates to six years ago, not this year, so it will appear as a deduction from retained earnings (which, after all, is where the income from six years ago is) on the statement of retained earnings.

   b. The second kind is adjustments or corrections to past years' income calculations that were determined this year but are retroactive to the past. These can arise from the discovery of plain errors not noticed before, or from changes in accounting methods or policies made this year, but affecting prior years. An example of an error would be a mistake in calculating revenue and accounts receivable discovered this year when the customer complained about being over-billed. An example of a policy change would be choosing a different amortization method for the factory that results in greater amortization starting five years ago when the factory was purchased. Like prior period adjustments, these error corrections and retroactive policy changes are listed in the statement of retained earnings only if they are large; otherwise they are just lumped in with this year's revenues and expenses.

   c. The third kind is transactions with the shareholders beyond declaring dividends. Dominion had "share issue expenses" of $2,456 thousand in 1993, for example. Such "expenses" are not put on the income statement because they relate to raising equity capital, not to the day-to-day business operations that the income statement's revenues and expenses are meant to include.

HOW'S YOUR UNDERSTANDING

Here are two questions you should be able to answer, based on what you have just read:

1. What is the usual general format of the income statement and what assistance to users is intended from that format?
2. Why are prior period adjustments and corrections of past years' accounting errors included on the statement of retained earnings rather than being added to or subtracted from this year's revenues and expenses on the income statement?

3.5 ACCOUNTS

So far we have seen three financial statements: the balance sheet, the income statement, and the statement of retained earnings. The three financial statements are all prepared from the underlying **accounts**, which have been recorded using the double-entry system so that the sum of the dollars in all the debit accounts equals the sum in all the credit accounts. But what is an account exactly? Let us use the following working definition: *an account is a record of the dollar amounts comprising a particular asset, liability, equity, revenue, or expense*. The net effect of these amounts is a debit or credit and is called the account's balance.

Below are some examples of how account balances are calculated. The particular format of accounts varies. Originally, accounts were just pages in hand-written ledgers (the "books") showing each account's beginning balance and then listing all the debit and credit entries posted to it, updating the balance after each entry. Some instructors use a short-hand version of this called a "T-account," useful to illustrate the effects of entries. In a T-account, all the debits (including the beginning balance if that was a debit) are listed on the left side of the T and all the credits (including the beginning balance if a credit) are listed on the right side, and then the new balance is calculated by adding up all the debits and then all the credits and determining the difference between the two sums. Modern computerized accounting systems can produce accounts in various formats thought to be useful, but they all use the arithmetic illustrated below.

a. If the enterprise's cash began at $500 and there was a receipt of $400 and one of $750, and a payment of $300 and one of $525, the Cash asset account would show a balance of $825 (a debit because there is a positive balance in this asset account).

   Cash = $500DR + $400DR + $750DR – $300CR – $525CR = $825DR

b. If share capital began at $1,000 and more shares were sold for $400 (which, let's say, caused the cash receipt above), the Share capital equity account would show a balance of $1,400 (a credit because there is a positive balance in this equity account).

   Share capital = $1,000CR + $400CR = $1,400CR

c. If amounts owing to trade creditors began at $950 and a creditor was paid $300 (the first payment above), the Accounts payable liability account would show a balance of $650 (a credit because there is a positive balance in this liability account).

   Accounts payable = $950CR – $300DR = $650CR

d. If a cash sale (say the first sale of the year) was made for $750 (the second cash receipt above), an account with a name like Sales revenue would show an amount of $750 (a credit because the balance is positive and, as we saw earlier in the chapter, revenue is part of income, which is part of retained earnings, which is an equity, therefore having a credit balance when positive).

   Sales revenue (part of equity) = $0CR + $750CR = $750CR

e. If a $525 cash payment was made for the first month's rent for the year (the second cash payment above), an account with a name like Rent expense would show an amount of $525 (a debit because expenses reduce income and so have a negative effect on retained earnings, which is an equity account that therefore is credited with positive amounts and debited with negative ones).

   Rent expense (part of equity) = $0DR + $525DR = $525DR

Balance sheet accounts continue indefinitely, as long as events happen that affect them. Income statement accounts and the Dividends declared account, however, are used to record only one period's revenues, expenses, and dividends at a time. When the period ends, the balances in those accounts are transferred to the equity account Retained earnings on the balance sheet, so that those accounts may start out the next period fresh, with zero balances. This transfer of the revenue, expense, and dividend account balances to retained earnings is called **closing**.

The figures on the financial statements may be made up of various individual account balances. The financial statements are summary documents and do not show all the details of the accounting system that underlies them. For example, a balance sheet may show "Accounts receivable $145,290," which turns out to be the sum of four account balances:

- Accounts receivable from customers, $129,300, plus
- Loans to employees, $5,000, plus
- Travel advances, $3,860, plus
- Due from associated company, $7,130.

As a second example, an income statement may show "Sales revenue $329,540," which is the sum of two account balances: Sales on credit, $301,420; and Cash sales, $28,120.

3.6 DEBITS AND CREDITS, REVENUES AND EXPENSES

In Section 2.7, we saw how entries and accounts were used to record events as transactions in the double-entry accounting system. The CappuMania Inc. example there was limited to balance sheet accounts. Let's expand the example to bring in income statement accounts and to close those to retained earnings, so that the articulation of the income statement and balance sheet accounts may be illustrated. After this example, in Section 3.7, we will do an example of pulling a set of financial statements together from a set of accounts.

We left CappuMania with the following list of account balances (trial balance) at April 1, 1995:

Account names	**Account balances**	
	Debits	**Credits**
Cash	3,200	
Inventory of unsold food	800	
Inventory of supplies	2,350	
Equipment cost	9,200	
Accumulated amortization		1,500
Owing to suppliers (Accounts payable)		1,550
Sales and other taxes owing		100
Loan to buy equipment		3,900
Share capital contributed		4,100
Retained earnings		4,400
	15,550	15,550

To keep the example uncluttered, we will group all the company's activities for the year ended March 31, 1996, into the following summary list:

a. *First, the economic events to be accrued:*

1. Revenue for 1996 was $89,740. The coffee bar does mostly cash business, so of this, $85,250 was in cash and the rest was on credit.
2. General expenses for 1996, not including depreciation or income tax, totalled $67,230. Most of the expenses were on credit, for coffee supplies and so on, so of this, only $2,120 was in cash.
3. At the end of the year, it turned out that unsold food on hand cost $550 and supplies on hand cost $1,740. Therefore, the Food inventory account has to be reduced by $250 ($800 – $550) and the Supplies inventory account has to be reduced by $610 ($2,350 – $1,740). Using up these inventories is part of the cost of earning revenue, so these reductions will be included in the company's general expenses.
4. Amortization expense for the year was $2,380.
5. The company's income tax expense for 1996 was estimated as $4,460. (It is estimated because until the income tax authorities issue a formal assessment of tax, the company does not know for sure what its tax will be for the year.)
6. The company's board of directors declared a dividend of $1,000.

b. *Cash inflows and outflows by March 31, 1996, not already mentioned:*

7. Collections of the revenue on credit totalled $3,330.
8. Payments to suppliers totalled $59,420.
9. The company paid $3,000 toward its income tax.
10. Only $800 of the dividend had been paid.

Now we can do entries to record these activities. To help you understand the entries, remember that, because income is a part of retained earnings, which is an equity account and therefore a *credit* account on the balance sheet, anything that helps income is a credit. *A revenue is therefore a credit balance account.* Conversely, anything that hurts income reduces retained earnings and equity, and is therefore a debit. *An expense is therefore a debit balance account.* When dividends are declared, they are deducted from retained earnings, therefore such deductions are *debits* because they reduce equity. All this produces the following table of double-entry accounting's debits and credits:

Debits	Credits
Increases in assets	Decreases in assets
Decreases in liabilities	Increases in liabilities
Decreases in equity:	Increases in equity:
Dividends declared	Contributed capital
Expenses	Revenues

Here are the entries for the ten items given on the previous page:

1. Revenue		
CR Revenue (equity increased)		89,740
DR Cash (assets increased)	85,250	
DR Accounts receivable (assets increased)	4,490	
2. General expenses		
DR General expenses (equity decreased)	67,230	
CR Cash (assets decreased)		2,120
CR Accounts payable (liabilities increased)		65,110
3. Using up of inventories		
CR Inventory of unsold food (assets decreased)		250
DR General expenses (equity decreased)	250	
CR Inventory of supplies (assets decreased)		610
DR General expenses (equity decreased)	610	
4. Amortization of equipment		
DR Amortization expense (equity decreased)	2,380	
CR Accumulated amortization (assets decreased)		2,380
5. Estimated income tax expense		
DR Income tax expense (equity decreased)	4,460	
CR Sales and other taxes owing (liabilities increased)		4,460
6. Dividend declared		
DR Retained earnings (equity decreased)	1,000	
CR Dividend payable (liabilities increased)		1,000
7. Collections of accounts receivable		
DR Cash (assets increased)	3,330	
CR Accounts receivable (assets decreased)		3,330

continued next page

8. Payments of accounts payable		
CR Cash (assets decreased)		59,420
DR Accounts payable (liabilities decreased)	59,420	
9. Payments toward income tax		
CR Cash (assets decreased)		3,000
DR Sales and other taxes owing (liabilities decreased)	3,000	
10. Payment toward dividend		
CR Cash (assets decreased)		800
DR Dividend payable (liabilities decreased)	800	

We can post these ten entries to the company's accounts, using the spreadsheet basis we had in Section 2.8. The resulting spreadsheet is shown in Exhibit 3.3. Note that the April 1, 1995, figures, which is what we ended with in Section

EXHIBIT 3.3

	A	B	C	D	E	F
1		CappuMania Inc. Example, in Spreadsheet Form (Continued)				
2						
3			April 1/95	Events and	Events and	March 31/96
4			Trial balance	Transactions *	Transactions *	Trial balance
5			Debit or credit	Debits	Credits	Debit or credit
6						
7	Cash		3200	(1) 85250	(2) -2120	26440
8				(7) 3330	(8) -59420	
9					(9) -3000	
10					(10) -800	
11	*Accounts receivable*		0	(1) 4490	(7) -3330	1160
12	Inventory of unsold food		800		(3) -250	550
13	Inventory of supplies		2350		(3) -610	1740
14	Equipment cost		9200			9200
15	Accumulated amortization		-1500		(4) -2380	-3880
16	Accounts payable		-1550	(8) 59420	(2) -65110	-7240
17	Sales and other taxes owing		-100	(9) 3000	(5) -4460	-1560
18	*Dividend payable*		0	(10) 800	(6) -1000	-200
19	Loan to buy equipment		-3900			-3900
20	Share capital contributed		-4100			-4100
21	Retained earnings		-4400	(6) 1000		-3400
22	*Revenue*		0		(1) -89740	-89740
23	*General expenses*		0	(2) 67230		68090
24				(3) 250		
25				(3) 610		
26	*Amortization expense*		0	(4) 2380		2380
27	*Income tax expense*		0	(5) 4460		4460
28						
29		Totals	0	232220	-232220	0
30						
31						
32						
33						
34						
35						

* The numbers in brackets have been added to the spreadsheet printout to refer to the 10 events and transactions described in the text.

2.7, are now in the first column, the starting figures. (We could have continued by adding our new columns (now columns D, E, and F) as columns G, H, and I to the right of the ending column F in Section 2.7, but that would have produced a cluttered example.) Some new accounts (such as accounts receivable and revenue) are needed to record the entries: the titles of these are shown in italics.

You can see that everything is still in balance. The sums of the debits and credits in the ten entries are $232,220, and the March 31, 1996 accounts add up to zero (remember that, arbitrarily, debits are shown as positive amounts and credits as negative ones). To highlight the calculation of income from the expanded set of accounts, a second version of the spreadsheet is shown in Exhibit 3.4. It is the same as in Exhibit 3.3, except that the balance sheet accounts and the income statement accounts are now separately subtotalled. You will see that income (the difference between the revenue and expense accounts) equals $14,810. It is a credit, which is what equity is. You will also note that, without the income statement accounts, the balance sheet accounts are out of balance by the same $14,810. We will do something about that shortly.

Now, let's prepare the company's income statement for the year (see Exhibit 3.5).

EXHIBIT 3.4

	A	B	C	D	E	F
38		**CappuMania Inc. Example, in Spreadsheet Form (Continued)**				
39		**(With subtotals to show income calculation)**				
40						
41			April 1/95	Events and	Events and	March 31/96
42			Trial balance	Transactions	Transactions	Trial balance
43			Debit or credit	Debits	Credits	Debit or credit
44						
45	Cash		3200	85250	-2120	26440
46				3330	-59420	
47					-3000	
48					-800	
49	*Accounts receivable*		0	4490	-3330	1160
50	Inventory of unsold food		800		-250	550
51	Inventory of supplies		2350		-610	1740
52	Equipment cost		9200			9200
53	Accumulated amortization		-1500		-2380	-3880
54	Accounts payable		-1550	59420	-65110	-7240
55	Sales and other taxes owing		-100	3000	-4460	-1560
56	*Dividend payable*		0	800	-1000	-200
57	Loan to buy equipment		-3900			-3900
58	Share capital contributed		-4100			-4100
59	Retained earnings		-4400	1000		-3400
60	**Balance sheet subtotals**		**0**	**157290**	**-142480**	**14810**
61	*Revenue*		0		-89740	-89740
62	*General expenses*		0	67230		68090
63				250		
64				610		
65	*Amortization expense*		0	2380		2380
66	*Income tax expense*		0	4460		4460
67	**Inc. stmnt. subtotals**		**0**	**74930**	**-89740**	**-14810**
68						
69		Totals	0	232220	-232220	0

Exhibit 3.5

CappuMania Inc.
Income Statement for the Year Ended
March 31, 1996

Revenue		$89,740
Expenses:		
General	$68,090	
Amortization	2,380	70,470
Income before income tax		$19,270
Estimated income tax expense		4,460
Net income for the year		$14,810

Before going on to the statement of retained earnings and the balance sheet, let's see how accountants close the revenue and expense accounts. The idea here is to transfer balances from those accounts to retained earnings, so that the income is transferred to retained earnings and the revenue and expense accounts are reset at zero and can then be used to record revenue and expenses for the next year (1997). The closing entry also illustrates how amounts can be moved around from account to account, to group accounts together or otherwise rearrange balances in a desired way. To close the revenue and expense accounts, each account with a credit balance is debited by that amount, and each account with a debit balance is credited by that amount. This brings all those accounts to zero:

DR Revenue	89,740	
CR General expenses		68,090
CR Amortization expense		2,380
CR Income tax expense		4,460
CR Retained earnings (the net income)		14,810

This entry is posted to the accounts in the next spreadsheet (Exhibit 3.6) showing the closing amounts in bold italics. You will see that all the revenue and expense accounts have a zero balance now, and retained earnings now has a balance of $18,210. The March 31, 1996, balance sheet figures are now in balance, as you can see from the balance sheet subtotals line.

Now we can prepare the other two financial statements (see Exhibit 3.7 on page 97).

Well, there you have it! This example has illustrated how accounting accumulates information about activities and how the financial statements are prepared from the accounts that are produced as the information is accumulated. You can see how the three financial statements fit together (articulate) because they are all based on the double-entry accounting system:

- A set of accounts is created which is in balance (sum of all the debit account balances = sum of all the credit account balances);
- From these accounts are produced:
  - the income statement, the bottom line net income of which is transferred to

Exhibit 3.6

	A	B	C	D	E	F
70		**CappuMania Inc. Example, in Spreadsheet Form (Continued)**				
71		**(With transfer ("closing") of income to retained earnings)**				
72						
73			April 1/95	Events and	Events and	March 31/96
74			Trial balance	Transactions	Transactions	Trial balance
75			Debit or credit	Debits	Credits	Debit or credit
76						
77	Cash		3200	85250	-2120	26440
78				3330	-59420	
79					0000	
80					-800	
81	*Accounts receivable*		0	4490	-3330	1160
82	Inventory of unsold food		800		-250	550
83	Inventory of supplies		2350		-610	1740
84	Equipment cost		9200			9200
85	Accumulated amortization		-1500		-2380	-3880
86	Accounts payable		-1550	59420	-65110	-7240
87	Sales and other taxes owing		-100	3000	-4460	-1560
88	*Dividend payable*		0	800	-1000	-200
89	Loan to buy equipment		-3900			-3900
90	Share capital contributed		-4100			-4100
91	Retained earnings		-4400	1000	***-14810***	-18210
92	**Balance sheet subtotals**		**0**	**157290**	**-157290**	**0**
93	*Revenue*		0	***89740***	-89740	0
94	*General expenses*		0	67230	***-68090***	0
95				250		
96				610		
97	*Amortiztion expense*		0	2380	***-2380***	0
98	*Income tax expense*		0	4460	***-4460***	0
99	**Inc. stmnt. subtotals**		**0**	**164670**	**-164670**	**0**
100						
101		Totals	0	321960	-321960	0

- the statement of retained earnings, the bottom line ending retained earnings of which is transferred to
- the balance sheet, which summarizes all the accounts.

Activities affecting income therefore affect the balance sheet through the double-entry system. Looking back at the entries above, for example:

- Entry 1 increased the balance sheet's assets and increased revenue on the income statement (thereby also increasing income, which is transferred to retained earnings, therefore increasing equity, which keeps the balance sheet in balance);
- Entry 2 decreased the balance sheet's assets and increased its liabilities and increased expenses on the income statement (thereby also decreasing income, therefore decreasing equity, which keeps the balance sheet in balance).

We will see this sort of relationship among the financial statements many times. It is the basis of one of the most important *uses* of financial statements: analyzing the financial statements in order to evaluate financial performance and financial position.

Exhibit 3.7

CappuMania Inc.
Statement of Retained Earnings
for the Year Ended March 31, 1996

Retained earnings, beginning of year	$ 4,400
Add net income for the year, per income statement	14,810
	$19,210
Deduct dividend declared during the year	1,000
Retained earnings, end of year	$18,210

CappuMania Inc.
Balance Sheet as at March 31, 1996

Assets		Liabilities and Shareholders' Equity	
Current assets:		**Current liabilities:**	
Cash	$26,440	Accounts payable	$ 7,240
Accounts receivable	1,160	Sales and other taxes owing	1,560
Inventory of unsold food	550	Dividend payable	200
Inventory of supplies	1,740		$ 9,000
	$29,890	**Noncurrent liabilities:**	
		Loan to buy equipment	3,900
Noncurrent assets:			$12,900
Equipment cost	$ 9,200		
Accumulated		**Shareholders' equity:**	
amortization	(3,880)	Share capital contributed	$ 4,100
	$ 5,320	Retained earnings	18,210
			$22,310
	$35,210		$35,210

HOW'S YOUR UNDERSTANDING

Here are two questions you should be able to answer, based on what you have just read:

1. At the end of 1994, Hinton Hats Ltd. had retained earnings of $29,490. During 1995, it had revenue of $112,350, general expenses of $91,170, amortization expense of $6,210, and income tax expense of $3,420. Dividends of $5,000 were declared during 1995. At the end of 1995, the company's accounts were closed, in preparation for 1996. After closing, what were the balances in the following accounts: Revenue, General expenses, Amortization expense, Income tax expense, and Retained earnings? (You should get $0, $0, $0, $0 and $36,040.)
2. The company's first event in 1996 was to pay $1,200 cash for the rent on its store for the first month of 1996. What did this event do to: assets, liabilities, income for 1996, retained earnings, equity? (You should get down $1,200, no effect, down $1,200, down $1,200, down $1,200.)

3.7 ANOTHER PREPARATION ILLUSTRATION

Having a solid understanding of how the financial statements reflect, through the accounts, the activities of the enterprise is very important to your understanding of accounting. Therefore, this section presents another example of preparation of financial statements, using a more intuitive approach rather than writing out entries as above.

The income and retained earnings statements report on performance over a period of time. As we saw with the Bratwurst Inc. and CappuMania Inc. examples, one balance sheet can be prepared at the beginning of that period, and another at the end. A sequence that will help you keep things straight is, therefore:

1. **Balance sheet at the beginning of the period**
2. **Income statement for the period**
3. **Retained earnings statement for the period**
4. **Balance sheet at the end of the period**

The Flashy Fashions example given below will further illustrate several things, among them:

- How the income and retained earnings statements are prepared from the accounts;
- How the accrual basis of calculating net income works;
- How the accounts themselves reflect business events; and
- How the above sequence connects (articulates) the beginning and ending balance sheets to the other two statements.

Flashy Fashions Inc. is a small company in a coastal town. It rents its premises and its sales are all on credit (customers do not pay cash when they get the goods, but rather pay later, when billed, so a sale produces an account receivable until the cash is paid). It has only three expenses: cost of goods sold, rent, and income tax. **Cost of goods sold**, often abbreviated as **COGS**, is what the company pays to acquire and prepare for sale the goods that customers buy. It is not the same thing as sales revenue, but is rather an expense the company incurs in order to *get* sales revenue.

At the end of its previous fiscal year, September 30, 1994, Flashy's balance sheet was as shown in Exhibit 3.8. During the year ended September 30, 1995, the following information was recorded in the company's accounts:

Exhibit 3.8

Flashy Fashions Inc.
Balance Sheet as at September 30, 1994

Assets		**Equities**	
Current assets:		Current liabilities:	
Cash	$ 800	Purchases payable	$ 600
Accounts receivable	400	Rent payable	300
Inventory	900	Shareholders' equity:	
		Share capital	500
		Retained earnings	700
	$2,100		$2,100

After these nine items, the company's accounts showed the following balances:

1. Revenue from credit sales, $10,000;
2. Collections from customers, $9,600;
3. Purchases of inventory for sale, $6,100;
4. Payments to suppliers, $6,300;
5. Cost of goods sold, $6,400;
6. Rent charged by the landlord, $2,400;
7. Rent paid to the landlord, $2,900;
8. Income tax payable for the year, $350;
9. Cash dividends declared and paid to the shareholders, $450.

	Debits	Credits
Cash ($800 + $9,600 – $6,300 – $2,900 – $450)	$ 750	
Accounts receivable ($400 + $10,000 – $9,600)	800	
Inventory ($900 + $6,100 – $6,400)	600	
Purchases payable ($600 + $6,100 – $6,300)		$ 400
Dividends payable ($450 – $450)		0
Rent payable ($300 + $2,400 – $2,900)	200	
Income tax payable (owing for this year)		350
Share capital (no change)		500
Retained earnings (not changed yet by closing)		700
Dividends declared	450	
Revenue from credit sales		10,000
Cost of goods sold expense	6,400	
Rent expense	2,400	
Income tax expense	350	
	$11,950	$11,950

Before we prepare financial statements, let's be sure you understand what happened in the accounts between 1994 and 1995:

a. Cash went up because of collections and down because of payments to suppliers, the landlord, and the shareholders.

b. Accounts receivable went up because of credit sales revenue and down because of collections.

c. Inventory went up because of purchases and down because the cost of goods sold was transferred to an expense account to recognize the value given up when the customers took the goods away.

d. Purchases payable went up because of purchases and down because of payments to suppliers.

e. Dividends payable went up when the dividends were declared and down when they were paid.

f. Rent payable went up because of bills from the landlord and down because of payments to the landlord. During the year, the landlord was paid more than had been billed, so rent payable reversed its sign: it's now a debit (prepaid rent). (Many accounts can be debits *or* credits, depending on temporary circumstances like overpaying. Even cash can be a credit: if you write too many cheques you can end up with an overdraft, in which case you have negative cash because you owe the bank instead of having money in the bank.)

g. Income tax payable went up from zero because the company owes tax on its income for this year (it did not owe any at the end of last year).

Now let's prepare the accrual basis financial statements using the sequence suggested earlier. First, the income statement (Exhibit 3.9):

Exhibit 3.9

Flashy Fashions Inc.
Income Statement
for the Year Ended September 30, 1995

Revenue		$10,000
Operating expenses:		
Cost of goods sold	$ 6,400	
Rent	2,400	8,800
Income before income tax		$ 1,200
Income tax expense		350
Net income for the year		$ 850

So, the accrual basis income is $850. This is not the change in cash but is rather a measure of economic events, not all of which are settled in cash during the year.

Other events summarized on the statement are:

- Customers promised to pay $10,000. That is the accrual basis revenue, not whatever was collected ($9,600).
- Customers took goods that had cost Flashy $6,400. That is the accrual basis COGS expense, not whatever was purchased ($6,100).
- Rent of $2,400 was billed. That is the accrual basis expense, not whatever was paid to the landlord ($2,900).
- Income tax of $350 is due on the income. That is the accrual basis expense, even though no tax has yet been paid for the year.

Note that dividends are not shown on the income statement. These are considered a *distribution* of income, not an expense of producing the income. Dividends are on the statement of retained earnings (Exhibit 3.10).

Exhibit 3.10

Flashy Fashions Inc.
Statement of Retained Earnings
for the Year Ended September 30, 1995

Beginning balance (September 30, 1994)	$ 700
Add net income for the year, as shown in the income statement	850
	$1,550
Deduct dividends declared	(450)
Ending balance (September 30, 1995)	$1,100

The retained earnings statement serves as a transition from the income statement to the balance sheet. We can see this in two ways. First, we can close the income statement accounts and dividends to retained earnings and *after that* list the post-closing accounts:

Post-closing List of Accounts (Trial Balance)

	Debits	Credits
Cash	$ 750	
Accounts receivable	800	
Inventory	600	
Purchases payable		$ 400
Rent payable (now prepaid)	200	
Income tax payable		350
Share capital		500
Retained earnings ($700 + $10,000 – $6,400 – $2,400 – $350 – $450)		1,100
	$2,350	$2,350

The accounts still balance, but now retained earnings contains all the information in the income and retained earnings statements. It is an accumulation of all the incomes (revenues minus expenses) minus all the dividends since the company began.

Second, we can prepare comparative balance sheets at the ends of 1995 and 1994 (Exhibit 3.11).

The 1995 balance sheet account balances consist of the 1994 balances plus or minus cash transactions *and* plus or minus revenues and expenses. (For example, 1995 accounts receivable equal the 1994 balance plus 1995 revenue minus 1995 cash collections.) As was emphasized at the end of the CappuMania example in Section 3.6, this demonstrates an essential feature of accrual accounting and the balanced double-entry system: *the calculation of income implies the calculation of balance sheet values, and vice versa*. The income statement and the balance sheet are intimately, and necessarily, related:

Exhibit 3.11

Flashy Fashions Inc.
Balance Sheet as at September 30, 1995
(with Comparative Figures for September 30, 1994)

	1995	1994
Assets		
Current assets:		
Cash	$ 750	$ 800
Accounts receivable	800	400
Inventory	600	900
Prepaid rent	200	–
	$2,350	$2,100
Liabilities and Equity		
Current liabilities:		
Purchases payable	$ 400	$ 600
Rent payable	–	300
Income tax payable	350	0
	$ 750	$ 900
Shareholders' equity:		
Share capital	$ 500	$ 500
Retained earnings	1,100	700
	$1,600	$1,200
	$2,350	$2,100

one always implies the other. You can see from the Flashy Fashions calculations and the CappuMania entries that whenever income is affected (via a change to a revenue or expense account), the balance sheet is affected by the same amount. This point is one of the most important in understanding financial accounting, and we will encounter it frequently.

HOW'S YOUR UNDERSTANDING

Here are two questions you should be able to answer, based on what you have just read:

1. Garf Ltd. had accounts receivable at the beginning of the year of $5,290. During the year, it had revenue from sales on credit of $39,620 and collected $41,080 from its customers. What balance did the company's Accounts receivable account show at the end of the year? ($3,830)
2. Garf Ltd.'s net income for this year was $2,940, and it declared $900 in dividends to its shareholders during the year. Retained earnings were $7,410 at the beginning of the year. What are retained earnings at the end of the year, *after closing*? ($9,450)

3.8 CAPITAL MARKETS, MANAGERS, AND PERFORMANCE EVALUATION

Section 2.9 noted that managers have to pay attention to the balance sheet, not only because it provides information useful to them, but also because others outside the enterprise pay attention to it and use it in their evaluation of managers' performances. That is at least as true for the income statement, especially where capital markets, such as stock markets, are concerned. Managers of large, publicly traded companies are under constant pressure because of the spotlight on earnings (net income) and its components. Business and social observers often comment that this spotlight is too intense, that there is more to managerial performance than the income statement shows and that the income statement is doubtful as a measure because it reflects the limitations of accrual-based, double-entry accounting. Nevertheless, the spotlight is there.

An indication of the importance placed on the bottom line can be found in almost any issue of a financial newspaper, such as the *Globe and Mail*, the *Financial Post*, or the *Wall Street Journal*, in their regular announcements of corporations' annual and/or quarterly earnings. Exhibit 3.12 is a sample of such announcements from a set of about 25 reported by the *Globe and Mail* on a single day.

Exhibit 3.12

CANADIAN CORPORATE REPORTS

HALLMARK TECHNOLOGIES

Year to Dec. 31, 1993		**Year ago**
Revenue	$ 19,164,269	$ 15,361,951
Pre-tax Income	2,328,465	169,333

TORONTO-DOMINION BANK

3 months to Jan. 31, 1994		**Year ago**
Revenue	$940,000,000	$741,000,000
Net profit	168,000,000	al.000,000
Net profit/share	0.52	a(0.02)
Loan loss prvsn	113,000,000	150,000,000
Total assets	92.4-billion	81.0-billion

a. Includes an after-tax restructuring charge of $79-million. Preferred-share dividends were $10-million vs $8-million.

TRIMAC LTD.

3 months to Dec. 31, 1993		**Year ago**
Revenue	$172,727,000	$140,778,000
Prof. cont. ops.	11,107,000	5,310,000
Prof. disc. ops	(62,000)	(98,000)
Net profit	11,045,000	5,212,000
Cont. ops./share	0.29	0.14
Disc. ops./share	(0.01)	nil
Net profit/share	0.28	0.14

Year to Dec. 31, 1993		**Year ago**
Revenue	$618,803,000	$476,055,000
Prof. cont. ops.	27,720,000	a27,236,000
Prof. disc. ops.	(340,000)	(413,000)
Net profit	27,380,000	a26,823,000
Cont. ops./share	0.70	a0.73
Disc. ops./share	(0.01)	(0.01)
Net profit/share	0.69	a0.72

a. Includes 41 cents a share of gains related to the sale of 2 million shares of Chauvco Resources Ltd. and dilution gains relating to share issues by Chauvco in which Trimac didn't participate at its pro-rata share.

SOURCE: *GLOBE AND MAIL*, 25 FEBRUARY 1994.

These announcements presumably are meant to focus on the crucial bits of information. You can see quite a variation, from Hallmark Technologies' brevity to the longer, footnoted data about the Toronto-Dominion Bank and the pair of quarterly and annual announcements about Trimac. The footnotes alert the reader about complications, such as the bank's restructuring charge. Many figures are converted to per-share data (roughly these are the income statement figure divided by the number of common shares issued by the corporation). Per-share amounts are thought to be helpful to the user who owns or is thinking of buying a particular number of shares and wonders what portion of the corporation's results can be related to that number of shares. If you own n shares of Trimac, you can say that your shares earned $\$0.69n$ in 1993, $\$0.70n$ from continuing operations minus $\$0.01n$ from discontinued operations.

Balance sheet and cash management data are sometimes included in such announcements, but the emphasis is on earnings (income, profit). There is almost never any data about nonfinancial performance, longer-term issues (except sometimes the trend in earnings per share), or other aspects of managers' efforts. This is not to say that such other factors are not considered at some point, but when announcements tend to stress earnings, other things can be overlooked.

Stock market traders pay particular attention to the factors that produce good, or poor, earnings. Stock market prices and earnings are positively correlated: when earnings go up, share prices tend to be going up too, because investors want to buy the shares; and when earnings go down, share prices tend also to be going down, because investors want to sell them. What seems to be happening is that investors learn about things like good (or poor) management decisions and the attractiveness of the shares is increased or decreased accordingly. When the financial statements are produced and announcements like those above are made from them, the statements will also have reflected the same things, the same management decisions. Therefore, share prices on the stock market will change when investors get news about the corporation that changes the shares' attractiveness. If this news comes out before the financial statements and the above announcements (which is usually the case, especially for well-known corporations that are frequently in the news), then the share prices will already have changed in the way you would expect from the announcements. If the announcement was not expected (surprisingly good or bad results), the share prices will change then, because the announcement is the news. In either case, stock market prices and earnings announcements tend to end up moving in the same direction and so are correlated.

We can conclude that the performance factors measured by accrual accounting are similar to the factors share buyers and sellers are assessing when they decide to try to buy, or sell, a corporation's shares. Managers of corporations with traded shares are therefore keenly aware of accounting's income measurement, because accounting is tracking factors investors are concerned about, and if the investors do not learn about these factors from other sources, they will certainly learn about them from the accounting statements.

It is harder to tell if the income statement is as important for managers of smaller or private companies, the shares of which are not traded and about which there is less news in general, but there is no reason to think the importance is not comparable. Managers and owner–managers of smaller companies are at least as concerned as managers of larger companies are about management bonuses, income tax, and other effects of the figures in the income statement, and the kind of changes in confidence that change stock market prices are likely to be present for smaller companies too. Managers of many companies, especially but not only larger corporations, go to great lengths to explain their performance to investors and to people on whom investors rely, such as stock market analysts and business journalists. So, in conclusion, every manager should be conversant with how her or his performance is measured in the income statement, because a lot of other people are.

3.9 ACCOUNTING RESEARCH: MEASURING PERFORMANCE

Determining income is one of the most important tasks of accounting—to many people, it is the most important. Income and its revenue and expense components are financial accounting's measure of an enterprise's economic performance over a period of time. (Cash performance is measured in a separate but related way, as Chapter 4 will show.) Given the importance of income, it is not surprising that much accounting research has focused on it. Here are just two of the results of such research:

1. The way of measuring income developed by accountants over the centuries, and now pretty well defined by various accepted accounting standards and methods, is not easy to connect to economic theory about performance. There is certainly a relationship, but it is both complex and subtle. For example, accounting treats debt-holders differently from equity holders: interest on debts is deducted as an expense in calculating income, but dividends to owners are not. Yet both groups have invested in the company, they both are concerned about its ability to give them the return they expect. It is not easy to determine how best to measure performance so as to provide both groups with comparable information, nor is it clear that accounting's distinction between interest and dividends is always meaningful economically. Another example of the complexity is in the value of accrual income (versus other measures of performance, such as cash flow). In economics and finance, evaluations of performance, risk, and returns to investors depend on a host of factors (such as economy-wide interest rates, inflation, and overall stock market movements) that are difficult to tie to accounting's measurement of an individual company's performance. Accrual accounting's measurement of economic performance is not universally accepted, and though the accounting measure of income does correlate with such economic indicators as stock prices, it is not at all the same.[7] Examining the relationship between accounting income and economic indicators is a major area of accounting research, which we will encounter again later in this book.
2. Accrual accounting requires that judgments and estimates be made in computing income. We will see many examples of this as we go along. An interesting field of research examines **income smoothing** and has found that many companies' senior managers choose accounting policies and methods that have the effect of making their reported accounting income

look smoother over time than it might otherwise be, and usually smoother than income measured on a cash basis, without the use of accrual accounting. "Smooth" here means that income goes up and down less than it might, so that if you plotted a company's income over time, the year-to-year variations would be smaller than they would otherwise be. Accrual accounting is generally a smoother measure of income than cash income is, because cash receipts and payments depend on all sorts of factors beyond the economic performance accrual accounting tries to track.

When managers do make accounting choices that produce a smoother income, such choices are not necessarily motivated by a wish to mislead—there may be income tax and other good reasons for such choices—but the idea behind smoothing is that managers would prefer the smoother trend of earnings shown in column B below to the trend in column A, even though the total income over the five years is the same and both columns show an increasing trend.

	A (original)	B (smoother)
Income for 1987	$ 1,800,000	$ 4,150,000
Income for 1988	6,570,000	4,310,000
Income for 1989	2,650,000	4,570,000
Income for 1990	8,230,000	4,820,000
Income for 1991	3,620,000	5,020,000
Sum over the 5 years	$22,870,000	$22,870,000

These data are presented in graph form in Figure 3.1. The main reason for wanting to show a smoother trend in earnings seems to be that the smoother trend may make it appear that management has a firm hold on the company, that it is competent and in control of events. The less smooth trend implies more risk, more variation. So if managers are held accountable to owners for keeping risk down, they may prefer the smoother trend.

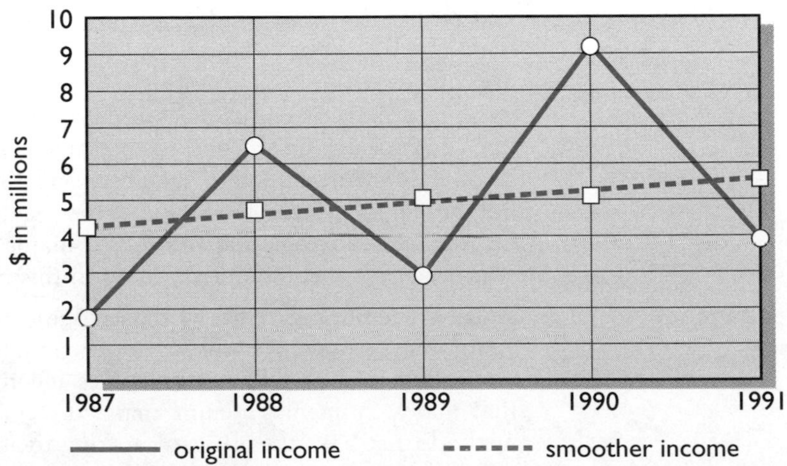

FIGURE 3.1

Counter-smoothing accounting choices have also been observed. An example is the so-called **Big Bath**, in which a company having a bad year (poor earnings or even a loss) chooses accounting methods that make the results look even worse. Managers apparently think that they are going to be in trouble anyway, and so decide they might as well clean up the accounting records. A new president may also want to blame the previous president for past trouble, and so want to clear the accounts of some assets the previous president thought valuable but the new president doubts. This produces a terrible year as far as the accounting numbers go, but increases the chances that in future years, accounting results will be better than would happen without the Bath. An example would be that of writing off the cost of an investment in a factory that the company no longer wishes to operate, rather than keeping the cost on the balance sheet and amortizing it in the future. This leaves less cost to be amortized in the future, and so should mean that future incomes will be higher than they would be otherwise because of lower future amortization expenses.[8]

3.10 CONTINUING DEMONSTRATION CASE

INSTALMENT 3

Data for Instalment 3

In Instalment 2 this beginning balance sheet (Exhibit 3.13) was developed for the fledgling company:

Exhibit 3.13

Mato Inc.
Balance Sheet as at March 1, 1994

Assets		**Liabilities and Shareholders' Equity**	
Current assets:		Current liabilities:	
Cash	$130,000	Account payable	$ 1,100
Noncurrent assets:		Loan payable	15,000
Automobile (at cost)	10,000	Shareholders' equity:	
Incorporation costs	1,100	Share capital	125,000
Total	$141,100		$141,100

During the first six months of the company's existence, life was hectic for Mavis and Tomas. The main pressure was to get set up and get goods out to retailers in time for the heavy selling season from July to December. Mavis regretted several times not having started earlier, because it took much more time to make arrangements with suppliers and retailers and get goods delivered than she had expected. The first six months did generate some revenues, but the period was largely one of building.

Some important events in the six months to August 31, 1994, took place.

- The warehouse space was occupied in early March, and the renovations ("leasehold improvements," consisting of partitions, shelving, and other fixtures) were completed in early June, a month later than had been desired.

- A computer was bought to handle the company's accounting, purchases, sales, inventory, and customer relations records. Software packages suitable to these tasks were also purchased.
- Tomas quit his bank job and began to work full-time for the company in July, after having devoted most of his evenings and weekends to the company since March.
- Mavis travelled both around the region, to talk to retail boutique owners and line up orders, and out of the region to meet with suppliers. The company ran up large phone bills in connection with all the business development activity, but that had been anticipated in the business plan.
- In mid-August, an employee was hired to maintain all the records and help Mavis organize her activities.

Tomas recorded amortization on the physical and nonphysical assets, improvements to leased premises, and computer software as follows: car, leasehold improvements, computer, and software: 1/2 year × 20% of cost; other equipment and furniture: 1/4 year × 10% of cost. As of August 31, 1994, the company's accounts showed the following balances ("accum. amort." is accumulated amortization):

Debit balance accounts		**Credit balance accounts**	
Cash	$4,507	Bank loan	$ 75,000
Accounts receivable	18,723	Accounts payable	45,616
Inventory	73,614	Loan payable	15,000
Automobile	10,000	Share capital	125,000
Leasehold improvements	63,964	Revenues	42,674
Equipment and furniture	29,740	Accum. amort.—auto	1,000
Computer	14,900	Accum. amort.—leasehold imp.	6,396
Software	4,800	Accum. amort.—equip.	744
Incorporation costs	1,100	Accum. amort.—computer	1,490
Cost of goods sold expense	28,202	Accum. amort.—software	480
Salary—Mavis	15,000		$313,400
Salary—Tomas	9,280		
Salary—other	1,200		
Travel expense	8,726		
Telephone expense	2,461		
Rent expense	12,000		
Utilities expense	1,629		
Office and general expenses	3,444		
Amort. expense—auto	1,000		
Amort. expense—leasehold imp.	6,396		
Amort. expense—equipment	744		
Amort. expense—computer	1,490		
Amort. expense—software	480		
	$313,400		

A board of directors' meeting was scheduled for early September 1994 to review the results for the first six months and make plans for the future. Some financial statements were therefore prepared from the above account balances.

Results for Instalment 3

Exhibit 3.14 shows the statement of income and retained earnings (deficit), and Exhibit 3.15 provides the comparative balance sheet for the company's first six months.

Exhibit 3.14

Mato Inc.
Statement of Income and Deficit
for the Six Months Ended August 31, 1994

Revenues		$42,674
Cost of goods sold		28,202
Gross profit		$14,472
Operating expenses:		
Salaries	$25,480	
Travel	8,726	
Telephone	2,461	
Rent	12,000	
Utilities	1,629	
Office and general	3,444	
Amortization	10,110	63,850
Net loss for the six months (no tax)		$49,378
Deficit as at August 31, 1994		$49,378

The two entrepreneurs were certainly not very happy with these results. They had expected to lose money in the start-up period, but not this much! The loss was 40% of the share capital, so the company could not sustain losses at this level for long. Working capital was negative: current liabilities exceeded current assets by nearly $40,000. Tomas was sure the bank would be nervous, and both he and Mavis expected the board of directors, meeting to be a difficult one. They began to prepare a report to the board, including a plan for improvements to be made in the next period.

Exhibit 3.15

Mato Inc.
Balance Sheets as at August 31 and March 1, 1994

Assets	August	March	Liabilities and Shareholders' Equity	August	March
Current assets:			Current liabilities:		
Cash	$ 4,507	$130,000	Bank loan	$ 75,000	$ 0
Receivables	$ 18,723	0	Payables	45,616	1,100
Inventory	73,614	0	Loan payable	15,000	15,000
	$ 96,844	$130,000		$135,616	$ 16,100
Noncurrent assets:			Shareholders' equity:		
Equip. cost	$ 54,640	$ 10,000	Share capital	$125,000	$125,000
Equip. acc. amort.	(3,234)	0	Deficit	(49,378)	0
Leasehold (net)*	57,568	0		$ 75,622	$125,000
Software (net)**	4,320	0			
Incorp. costs	1,100	1,100			
	$114,394	$ 11,100			
TOTAL	$211,238	$141,100	TOTAL	$211,238	$141,100

* Net book value of leasehold improvements = $63,964 cost – $6,396 accumulated amortization.
** Net book value of software = $4,800 – $480 accumulated amortization.

3.11 HOMEWORK AND DISCUSSION TO DEVELOP UNDERSTANDING

PROBLEM 3.1* Define terms

Define the following terms in your own words:

- Revenue;
- Expense;
- Net income;
- Dividend;
- Retained earnings;
- Owners' equity.

PROBLEM 3.2* Basic balance sheet, income, and retained earnings ideas

Labott's Bottlery Ltd. had the following recent balance sheet:

Labott's Bottlery Ltd.
Balance Sheet as at September 30, 1994

Cash	$1,642	Mortgage	$1,000
Inventory	1,480	Share capital	3,000
Land	2,100	Retained earnings	1,222
	$5,222		$5,222

These questions start you out in Chapter 2 and take you into Chapter 3, to help you think of accounting in an integrated way, not just as a set of disconnected chapter-by-chapter subjects.

1. Why is "land" on the balance sheet, and what does it represent?
2. On October 5, 1994, the company borrowed $2,410 from the bank and used the money immediately to buy more land. What was the total dollar figure of the company's assets after this point?
3. Why did the company not just use the $3,000 share capital to buy more land instead of borrowing from the bank?
4. Explain how "retained earnings" comes to be on the balance sheet and what it represents.
5. For the year ended September 30, 1994, the company's revenues were $10,116, and its expenses (including income tax) were $9,881. What was its net income for the year?
6. During the year ended September 30, 1994, the company declared dividends of $120. Considering this and point 5, what was the balance in retained earnings at the *beginning* of that year (October 1, 1993)?
7. If the 1994 expenses were $11,600 instead of the figure in point 5, and the company did not declare any dividends, what would the retained earnings be at September 30, 1994?
8. The answer to point 7 is a negative number, which would be a debit. Would you think such a debit should be shown with the assets on the left side of the company's balance sheet? Why or why not?

PROBLEM 3.3* Prepare a simple set of financial statements from accounts

Following are account balances of Arctic Limo Services Ltd. Prepare a 1995 income statement, a 1995 statement of retained earnings, and comparative 1994 and 1995 balance sheets. State any assumptions you feel are necessary.

	September 30, 1995 Debit (Credit)	September 30, 1994 Debit (Credit)
Accumulated amortization	$(30,000)	$(20,000)
Cash on hand	2,000	4,000
Dividends declared	80,000	
Due from Lucky Eddie		1,000
Due to Amalgamated Loansharks		(10,000)
Income tax expense	35,000	
Limousines amortization expense	10,000	
Limousines cost	90,000	60,000
Long-term limousine financing	(50,000)	(30,000)
Other expenses	70,000	
Retained earnings	(4,000)	(4,000)
Revenue	(300,000)	
Share capital	(1,000)	(1,000)
Wages expense	100,000	
Wages payable	(2,000)	
	$ 0	$ 0

PROBLEM 3.4* Explain terms in nontechnical language

Explain the following in nontechnical language that a business person who has not read this text would understand:

1. What is net income as it is meant in financial accounting?
2. Why is net income part of owners' equity?
3. If net income is part of owners' equity, why is it necessary to have a separate income statement? Why not just report net income on the balance sheet?
4. Why are dividends to shareholders not considered to be an expense in calculating net income? Employee wages are considered an expense, as is the cost of products delivered to customers, and shareholders must be kept happy, as must employees and customers.

PROBLEM 3.5* Prepare financial statements from transactions

At the end of last year, Fergama Productions Inc., a company in the movie industry, had the following balance sheet accounts (in no particular order):

Cash	23,415	Share capital	20,000
Accounts payable	37,778	Office equipment cost	24,486
Accum. amortization	11,134	Accounts receivable	89,455
Retained earnings	51,434	Inventory of supplies	10,240
Long-term loan payable	15,000	Taxes payable	12,250

During this year, the company's activities resulted in the following:

a Revenue, all on credit, totalled $216,459.

b. Production expenses totalled $156,320, $11,287 of which were paid in cash and the rest charged.

c. Amortization on the office equipment came to $2,680 for the year.

d. The company bought, on credit, new supplies costing $8,657, and used up supplies costing $12,984 during the year.

e. Income tax expense for the year was estimated to be $12,319.

f. The board of directors declared a dividend of $25,000.

g. Collections from customers totalled $235,260.

h. Payments to suppliers totalled $172,276.

i. Payments of taxes totalled $18,400.

j. A $5,000 payment was made on the long-term loan.

k. The dividend was paid in cash to shareholders.

1. To get you started, prepare a balance sheet for Fergama Productions Inc. as at the end of the last year.
2. Record the activities for this year using accounting entries and post those entries to accounts (using paper or a computer spreadsheet).
3. Prepare a trial balance of your accounts to show that it is in balance (if you are using a computer spreadsheet, it should do this for you).
4. From those accounts, prepare the following financial statements:
   - Income statement for this year;
   - Statement of retained earnings for this year;
   - Balance sheet at the end of this year (it would be useful to prepare a comparative balance sheet for this year and last year together).
5. Comment on what the three financial statements show about the company's performance for this year and financial position at the end of this year. Would you say the company is better off than it was last year?

PROBLEM 3.6 Examples of related development of business and accounting

This book so far has emphasized that financial accounting is not an intellectual island, complete unto itself. Rather, it has developed along with business and society over the centuries, both responding to and, in turn, influencing changes in business and society. Give two examples of this parallel development.

PROBLEM 3.7 Questions about accounting asked by a business person

Jeanette is an electrical engineer and has been working for a large company in its technical electronics area for several years. She has decided to go into business for herself, offering electronics design and general consulting to other companies. To prepare for this, she has raised the necessary capital and has been reading books on business management and talking to business people about running a business. She learns that you are taking a financial accounting course and says, "Maybe you can help me understand some of the peculiarities of accounting!" You protest that you have just started your course, but she asks you to try to answer her questions anyway. Provide brief answers, in plain English without using jargon, to the following questions she has asked you:

1. Everyone says they will be interested to see if my company can make a profit. How will the accountants measure my profit? I know it's done on the income statement, but I really don't understand what that statement includes or doesn't include.
2. One reason I can see for wanting a good profit is that it will put money in the bank. But someone told me that accrual accounting doesn't depend on money in the bank for its measure of profit. What does that mean?
3. One of the books I've read says that a company's accounting will use the double-entry system and said that that means the balance sheets and income statements all fit together. How does that work?
4. One person told me to keep my company's accounting income low to save income tax. Another person said to keep it high to attract other investors and soothe creditors. Why is there any choice? I thought that financial accounting just reported the facts!
5. There was an odd phrase in one book. It talked about "closing the accounts" at the end of the year. How do you close accounts, and why bother?

PROBLEM 3.8 Examples of and reasons for the income statement's format

1. Give three examples of how the income statement differentiates between current operating results and events that are not part of operations.
2. Why is the income statement formatted in this way?

PROBLEM 3.9 Prepare financial statements from accounts

1. Looking at the list of accounts of Geewhiz Productions, at November 30, 1995, that follow in no particular order, decide which ones are income statement accounts.
2. Calculate net income based on your answer to #1.
3. Calculate ending retained earnings based on your answer to #2.
4. Prepare the following financial statements, demonstrating that your answers to #2 and #3 are correct:

   a. Income statement for the year ended November 30, 1995;

   b. Statement of retained earnings for the year ended on that date;

   c. Balance sheet at November 30, 1995.
5. Comment briefly on what the financial statements show about the company's performance for the 1995 year and financial position at November 30, 1995.

Salaries expense	$ 71,000DR	Dividends declared	$ 11,000DR
Income tax payable	2,800CR	Accumulated amortization	94,000CR
Land	63,000DR	Cash in bank	18,000DR
Employee benefits expense	13,100DR	Income tax expense	6,900DR
Tax deductions payable	5,400CR	Credit sales revenue	346,200CR
Accounts receivable	16,400DR	Inventory on hand	68,000DR
Cash sales revenue	21,600CR	Prepaid insurance	2,400DR
Dividends payable	5,500CR	Beginning retained earnings	92,800CR
Amortization expense	26,700DR	Accounts payable	41,000CR
Cost of goods sold	161,600DR	Interest income	1,700CR
Insurance expense	11,200DR	Building	243,000DR
Share capital	200,000CR	Trucks and equipment	182,500DR
Office expenses	31,100DR	Salaries payable	4,100CR
Mortgage payable	114,000CR	Miscellaneous expenses	8,200DR
Bank loan owing	21,800CR	Interest expense	16,800DR
	$ 23,000DR		$ 23,000CR

PROBLEM 3.10 Discuss comments on importance of accounting information

Accounting is important to the extent people rely on accounting information in making decisions that are important to them. Below are various comments on the importance of accounting information. Discuss briefly why each comment may be valid, or invalid.

1. Double-entry accounting's arithmetically correct measure of financial performance is important in creating trust in the information.
2. The income statement's segregation of activities into revenues and expenses is important to interpreting net income (revenue minus expenses).
3. The statement of retained earnings is important in indicating to shareholders how much cash is available for paying dividends.
4. Effort by some top managers to smooth accounting income or to otherwise alter the way it measures performance is evidence of its importance.
5. The accounts underlying financial statements are important to the way the statements measure financial performance and position.
6. Understanding how accrual accounting reflects economic activities is important to interpreting the financial statements.

PROBLEM 3.11 Prepare month-end financial statements from accounts

Matilda Jamison runs a successful second-hand clothing shop, Waltzing Matilda's Boutique Ltd. She buys quality new and used clothes from several sources and then sells them at reasonable prices. To establish her business, Matilda invested $1,500 of her savings and her mother contributed $500. Both received shares in the company in return for their investment, so the company's share capital is $2,000. The company also took out a $3,000 bank loan.

Matilda rents retail space in a shopping mall on a monthly basis at $200 per month. She pays rent in advance for a six-month period (in other words, $1,200 twice a year) on January 1 and July 1 of every year. The company owns the display units, racks, shelving, and hangers she uses in her business, which cost $2,400 in total. She expects these items to last for five years and has, therefore, amortized them by $480 per year ($2,400/5 years = $480 per year). The resulting accumulated depreciation is included on the balance sheet. The insurance policy is an annual policy purchased January 1 for $1,200.

Matilda pays her employees for work done from the 1st to the 15th of each month, on or about the 20th of each month. As a result, half of the wages earned by employees during the month has been paid (that earned from the 1st to the 15th of the month) and the remaining half is still payable. The company's income tax rate is 20%. Matilda closes her accounts monthly, so revenue and expense accounts contain only one month's data at a time.

	Resources	Sources
Balance sheet accounts as at April 30, 1995:		
Cash	$ 780	
Accounts receivable	1,300	
Inventory of unsold goods	10,000	
Office supplies on hand	500	
Prepaid insurance	800	
Prepaid rent	400	
Shelving/hangers/display units	2,400	
Accumulated depreciation	(1,120)	
Bank loan		$ 3,000
Accounts payable		2,800
Wages payable		500
Taxes payable		1,200
Share capital		2,000
Retained earnings March 31, 1995		4,360
Income Statement accounts for April 1995:		
Revenue		7,000
Cost of goods sold		(3,500)
Wages		(1,000)
Insurance		(100)
Rent		(200)
Janitor and miscellaneous		(580)
Office supplies used		(50)
Interest		(30)
Depreciation		(40)
Income tax		(300)
	$15,060	$15,060

From the account balances at the end of April 1995 (shown on the previous page), prepare income and retained earnings statements for Waltzing Matilda's Boutique Ltd. for the month of April 1995 and a balance sheet as at April 30, 1995. Notes to the statements are not necessary.

PROBLEM 3.12 Income and retained earnings format with special items

The accounts for Prentice Retail Ltd. for last year included the following (in alphabetical order):

Cost of settling lawsuit that began four years ago	DR	$ 62,340
Correction of error in previous year's income	CR	2,430
Dividends declared	DR	87,000
Income tax expense	DR	121,315
Income tax saved by deducting cost of lawsuit	CR	23,895
Loss on expropriation of land by municipality	DR	14,210
Operating expenses	DR	1,689,260
Miscellaneous revenue from investments	CR	23,570
Retained earnings, beginning of year	CR	354,290
Revenue from sales	CR	2,111,480

Prepare an income statement and statement of retained earnings for the company for last year, in as good a form as you can with the information provided.

PROBLEM 3.13 Identify items as revenues or expenses

State whether or not, and why, each of the following items is likely to be a revenue or expense *for this year* of the company indicated:

Company	Item
1. Noranda Inc.	Cost of advertising for new employees
2. Canadian Utilities Ltd.	Collection of old accounts from customers who had skipped town and were tracked down by a collection agency
3. Royal Bank of Canada	Cost of renovating its main Winnipeg branch
4. T. Eaton Co. Ltd.	Increased value of the land under Eaton's department stores
5. Wendy's Restaurants	Food sold to customers who paid with their VISA cards
6. Pacific Furniture Mart	Money paid by customers in advance on special furniture orders
7. The Bay	A lawsuit by a customer who fell down the escalator and was injured
8. Northern Gold Mines Ltd.	Cost of issuing new shares to raise funds for exploration
9. XXX Escort Agency	Bribes paid to try to avoid having employees arrested for prostitution

10. Grand Centre Ltd.	Income taxes paid in France
11. Advanced Management Ltd.	Special good-performance bonuses promised this year but not to be paid until next year
12. Advanced Management Ltd.	Special dividend to owners, all of whom are also employees
13. Sears Inc.	Decreased value of the land under some of its inner-city locations
14. Procter & Gamble Inc.	Cost of scientific research aimed at developing new products
15. General Motors Inc.	Estimated amount of money needed to provide pensions to this year's employees when they retire
16. Hattie's Handbags Ltd.	Goods lost to shoplifting
17. Hattie's Handbags Ltd.	Salary of floorwalker who tries to catch shoplifters
18. PCL Construction Ltd.	Contract payments to be received over the next five years for construction work on a large bridge project

PROBLEM 3.14 Prepare a monthly income statement

(Challenging) Mr. Laing runs a small bakery. It produces only sourdough bread, which he sells for $1 per loaf. During the month of May 1995 Mr. Laing was able to sell 600 loaves of bread, 400 for which the customers paid cash and 200 which were bought on credit. The cost to Mr. Laing to produce the bread is $0.50 per loaf (this includes the cost of flour, shortening, electricity to run the ovens, and plastic bags for wrapping the bread). Early in April, one of Mr. Laing's bread mixers had broken. His friend, Andrea Reed, repaired the machine and charged him only for the cost of the replacement part, $40. This $40 was a debt, therefore, before May began. Andrea and Mr. Laing agreed to settle the $40 debt on a noncash basis. Mr. Laing was to provide Andrea with two loaves of bread, valued at the retail price of $1 per loaf, per week starting on May 1, until the debt was settled. Also, Mr. Laing was thinking of expanding. He hired a marketing student for $150 to do some customer interviews in May to find a feasible method of increasing sales. He agreed to pay the $150 at the end of June, even though the work would be done in May.

With this information, produce an income statement for Mr. Laing's bakery for May.

PROBLEM 3.15 Income statement from partial information

(Challenging) A list of some events that occurred during the month of September at Tune-Craft Instruments, Ltd. follows. Review the list of events and decide whether each event is a revenue or an expense for Tune-Craft for September. Build a *partial* income statement for September from these revenues and expenses, putting in any important account titles you would expect to see on the income statement even if the information you would need to come up with dollar figures is lacking. The result will therefore be an outline of the September income statement, including whatever numbers you can determine so far.

Date	Event
Sept. 2	Cash sales, $300.
5	Cheque received and recorded as revenue in August deposited in bank, $500.
8	Sale on account to M. Green, $650.
8	Showroom is painted. Tune-Craft will be billed $250.
9	Cash sales, $150.
11	Collection on outstanding account from customer R. Bowles, $75.
14	Instruments purchased for inventory, $1,500. One-third is paid in cash, the rest is on account.
17	Collection from customer M. Green, $300.
18	A utility bill is paid, $65.
20	Sales of $550 cash; $200 on account.
23	Office furniture is purchased, $710. Tune-Craft pays nothing down, no payments until six months from now.
24	Common shares are issued for cash, $2,000.
25	Cash sales, $275.
30	Two employees receive cheques for month of September totalling $1,800. One of the employees also receives a cheque for overtime

PROBLEM 3.16 Income smoothing and ethics

(Challenging)

1. Section 3.9 referred to income smoothing as a way of manipulating a company's net income in order to create a desired impression of management's capability and performance. Other kinds of income manipulation by management have also been alleged. Do you think it is ethical for management to manipulate the figures by which its performance is measured? Why or why not?
2. The usual answer to #1 is that such behaviour is unethical. Can you think of any circumstances under which such manipulation of income would be ethical? Putting it another way, are there any people, other than management, whose interests would be served by such behaviour?

PROBLEM 3.17 Reasons for and value of accounting standards

(Challenging)

During a speech to a business club, an accounting professor, who was describing the benefits of business competition, remarked:

> Over the last 200 years, there has been a large increase in the regulation of financial accounting by professional associations and government agencies. This has led to a large political component in the setting of financial accounting standards: accounting thus has to respond to the concerns of the time, rather than being objective and stable. This sort of thing is part of what has made measuring each company's financial performance quite complicated and expensive. In my opinion, financial accounting costs a company more than it is worth to the company.

Exercise your knowledge of the world, as well as of accounting, by answering the following questions briefly. There are not any definitive answers to these questions, but the issues are important. You might like to redo this question at the end of the course and see how your thinking has changed.

1. Why do you think society appears to desire that financial accounting be regulated—that there be standards a company has to follow in its financial accounting?
2. Is it possible that a company's financial accounting may cost more than that company feels it is worth, but be worthwhile doing anyway?
3. Should accounting standards be set as part of society's political processes, or should such standards be stable and uninfluenced by changes in society?
4. If the professor is right in saying that financial accounting and its standards are complicated and expensive, why do they not prevent such questionable phenomena as income smoothing and the Big Bath?

PROBLEM 3.18 Income calculation without dollars

(Challenging) A year has elapsed since you solved the argument between Bob and Doug, the shepherds (Problem 2.16). After studying your solution, Doug and Bob grudgingly accepted your opinion as to their relative wealths at the end of last year. The passage of time has not diminished their penchant for argument, however. Now they are arguing about who had the largest income for the year just ended.

Doug points out that the number of sheep that he personally owns at year end exceeds his personal holdings at the beginning of the year by 80, whereas Bob's increase was only 20. Bob replies that his increase would have been 60, had he not traded 40 sheep during the year for 10 acres of additional land. Besides, he points out, he exchanged 18 sheep during the year for food and clothing items, whereas Doug exchanged only 7 for such purposes. The food and clothing have been pretty much used up by the end of the year.

Bob is happy because his wife made 5 coats during the year (fulfilling the orders she had at the beginning of the year) and received 25 goats for them. She managed to obtain orders for another 5 coats (again for 25 goats)—orders on which she has not yet begun to work. Doug points out that he took to making his own lunches this year; therefore, he does not owe Ted anything now. Doug was very unhappy one day last year when he discovered that his ox had died of a mysterious illness. Both men are thankful, however, that none of the other animals died or was lost.

Except for the matters reported above, each man's holdings at the end of the current year are the same as his holdings at the end of last year. Provide advice to the two men as to who had the higher income for the year.[9]

PROBLEM 3.19 General or user-specific income statements?

(Challenging) Write a paragraph giving your considered views on the following question: do the accrual basis and the standard content and format of the income statement provide useful information to all people who are interested in companies' financial performance, or should there be different kinds of income statements prepared to suit the needs of different kinds of users?

PROBLEM 3.20 Propose research on the use of the income statement

(Challenging) One of the vexing problems in accounting research is to understand how income statements' measures of performance are used by people in their decision-making.

There are so many different kinds of users (investors, managers, taxation authorities, creditors, etc.) and so many different kinds of decisions (whether to buy, hold or sell shares, whether to reward or fire managers, whether to assess various kinds of taxes, etc.), that getting a clear picture of the use of income statements is a challenge for researchers.

Choose any user of financial statements you like and any kind of decision that user might be making, and suggest how research might be done to understand how the income statement is used by that user and what components of the statement are important to that decision.

PROBLEM 3.21 Prepare income statement from transactions

(Challenging)

(This problem follows from Problem 2.19, PastaPastaPasta Inc. You should review that problem before doing this one, but it is not necessary to have answered that problem in detail before attempting this one.)

Below are events that happened to Tanya's new company during its first six months of operation. From these events, prepare an income statement for the first six months. (If you did Problem 2.19, you could also go on to record the events and prepare a balance sheet at the end of the six months.)

1. Customers took away pasta, sauces, cookware, etc. for which they promised to pay $87,340. By the end of the six months, Tanya had collected $78,670 of this, had taken back $420 of defective merchandise (which she had to just throw away), and had given up on collecting $510. She expected the $7,740 remainder to be collected within a month or two.
2. Tanya purchased $32,990 of food and pasta-making supplies and $19,320 of cookware for resale. By the end of the six months, she had paid the suppliers $47,550 toward these purchases and those owing at the end of the preparatory time described in Problem 2.19.
3. The pasta and sauces taken by customers cost Tanya $31,840 to make, so at the end of the six months, $5,870 of food and pasta-making supplies were still on hand. The cookware and other equipment taken by customers cost Tanya $9,110 to buy, so at the end of the six months, $14,120 of goods for resale were still on hand.
4. Tanya estimated the following for the six months: amortization on equipment, $3,950; amortization of improvements to rented space, $450; amortization of minivan, $750. She was not sure what to do about the recipes, because they had shown themselves to be very valuable, or the incorporation costs, because the company should last many years. She thought perhaps each could be amortized at 10% of cost per year.
5. The company paid $8,000 in rent during the six months. The landlord was charging $2,000 per month, and was concerned that, while at the beginning of the period, the company had paid $2,000 in advance, it had fallen behind by $2,000 by the end. Tanya promised to pay the rent more promptly in the future.
6. The company paid the first $7,050 instalment on the equipment liability, plus $1,410 interest on the total debt at 8% per annum. The second instalment would be due in another year.
7. The $2,500 bank loan was paid off, including $80 in interest.

8. In consultation with the other owners, Tanya set her monthly salary at $2,100. She took only $8,000 of that in cash. The company paid $950 more to Revenue Canada as income tax deductions and still owed $190 for such deductions. Tanya decided to take the remaining $3,460 in a few months, when she wanted to go on a holiday.
9. Other expenses for the six months came to $6,440, all but $760 having been paid by the end of the period.
10. Tanya's accountant said that the company did not yet owe any income tax, but that there would likely be a small tax liability by the end of the year. The accountant estimated that about $1,500 would be owed for the first six months' income.
11. Everyone agreed that no dividends to owners should be declared yet, but the hope was that about $3,000 of the first six months' income would eventually be paid as dividends.

CASE 3A Interpret a real income statement

In Case 2A, the 1993 balance sheet of TSC Shannock Corporation was presented. The company is a Burnaby, B.C. distributor of pre-recorded video cassettes, audio cassettes, compact discs, laser discs, and similar items. The following are the company's 1993 statements of income and retained earnings plus an excerpt from management's discussion of the results in the 1993 annual report.

What does this information tell you about how management performed in earning a return for the owners of the company? What aspects of the company's performance are not covered at all, or not very clearly, as far as you can tell? What questions would you like to ask management if you were considering making a significant investment in the company?

TSC SHANNOCK CORPORATION

STATEMENTS OF INCOME

Years ended May 31, 1993 and 1992

	1993	1992
Sales	$55,980,637	$51,179,956
Cost of goods sold	49,021,187	44,537,203
	6,959,450	**6,642,753**
Expenses		
General and administrative	4,409,025	3,416,689
Selling	1,600,003	1,613,975
Depreciation and amortization	315,722	211,586
Interest	31,372	22,719
	6,356,122	**5,264,969**
Income from operations	603,328	1,377,784
Interest and other income	144,957	177,331
Income before income taxes	748,285	1,555,115
Income taxes (Note 6)	354,304	705,000
Net Income	**$ 393,981**	**$ 850,115**
Income per common share	$ 0.13	$ 0.32

STATEMENT OF RETAINED EARNINGS

Years ended May 31, 1993 and 1992

	1993	1992
Retained Earnings (Deficit), beginning of year	$ 808,069	$ (42,046)
Net Income	393,981	850,115
Retained Earnings, end of year	**$1,202,050**	**$808,069**

See accompanying Notes To Financial Statements. (*Not included*)

Results of Operations

(Excerpt from Management's "Discussion & Analysis of Financial Condition and Results of Operations")

Operating Results Review

Operating Revenues for 1993 totalled $55.9 million, up $4.8 million or 9.3% from 1992 revenues of $51.1 million. The Company has achieved strong sales growth due in large parts to an improvement in market share combined with a stronger sell-through video market. Growth in the sell-through video market continues, with unit sales more than doubling over the past five years. The success of sell-through video is due as much to the number of available titles as to the shorter periods between theater and video release dates. The Company manages its inventory in having the proper selection for the customer. Shannock carries between 10,000 and 13,000 title selections. Shannock continues to sustain the video catalogue business in sell-through product.

The market for movies and other pre-recorded video cassettes has enlarged in direct response to the rapid penetration of video cassette recorders into homes. The video sell-through market is a relatively new business that has been growing at an annual rate of approximately 25%. The video sell-through market has also been stimulated by the lowering of prices by the movie studios. Shannock is outpacing the growth rate in the video sell-through market. Sales in this category represent 42.7% of total sales. Sales growth also resulted from the addition of new product lines which Shannock's Division SMA has secured the exclusive rights in Canada.

The pre-recorded audio market has grown an average of 7.9% annually since 1970. Shannock's audio products in the past 3 years have exceeded the average annual growth rate by 4.4%. The CD market has also grown significantly over the last few years. Sales of pre-recorded music are driven by new technology and/or new releases. This year Shannock still showed a slight increase of 2.9% in music sales in spite of the loss of Woodwards.

Income

Total gross profit for the year was $6.9 million or 12.4% of sales, a decrease from 12.9% achieved in 1992, due to difficulties experienced, and increased pressure being placed on the company's gross margin during 1993. This pressure continues due to intense competition competing for market share and pricing on blockbuster titles. The Company earned income from operations of $603 thousand compared to $1.3 million before tax the same period last year. These results reflect the year end write off of the unsecured Woodwards accounts receivable. In January the Company announced the reserve of $513 thousand for Woodwards. This reserve was reduced to $304 thousand at year end, as a result of the final settlement with Woodwards.

Subsequent to the year end the Company has been paid for all monies owed based on 100 cents on the dollar for all consignment product and $0.37 cents on the unsecured accounts receivable.

Net Income for the year was $393 thousand, ($0.13 per share) as compared to $850 thousand ($0.32 per share) for the prior year.

Expenses

Total operating expenses of $6.3 million increased by $1 million or 20% from 1992. This increase includes non-recurring expenses such as the Woodwards reserve and related legal and administration costs.

General, Administrative and Overhead Costs
General and administrative costs are up 29% over the previous year. One of the major increases was the Woodwards reserve. Increases in overhead, selling, and marketing costs were required as well as investments in staff and other resources that helped the Company achieve and support its rapid growth. Other increases in operating expenses include a $104 thousand increase in depreciation expense from 1992.

The increase reflects net capital spending for the year and the implementation of depreciation rates for changes to the estimated useful lives of computer leases.

Total expenses as a percentage of sales were 11.3% for 1993 and 10.3% for 1992.

CASE 3B Interpret a real income statement

Several excerpts from the 1993 annual report of Magna International Inc., an Ontario-based multinational corporation specializing in technologically advanced automotive components, assemblies, and systems, follow. Assuming you are an investor in Magna, examine this information, identify any other things you'd like to know, and discuss the company's performance in 1993.

MANAGEMENT'S DISCUSSION AND ANALYSIS OF RESULTS OF OPERATIONS AND FINANCIAL CONDITION

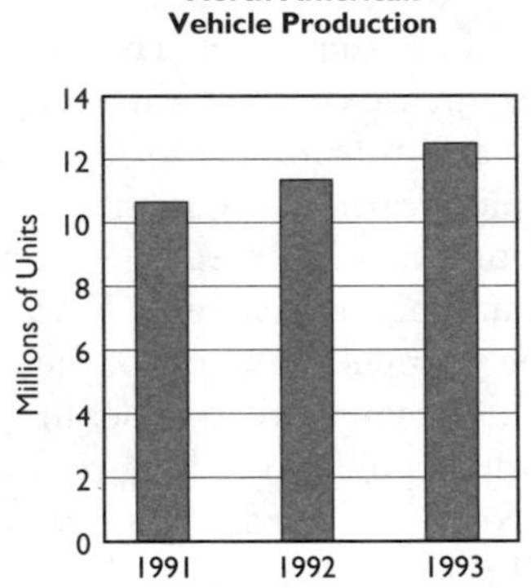

Managed
Sales

Canadian $ Billions

0 1 2 3 4

1991 1992 1993

Results of Operations

Overview: Operating income before income taxes and minority interest of $219.9 million in fiscal 1993 was $55.1 million higher than the fiscal 1992 level of $164.8. This 33% improvement over fiscal 1992 was primarily achieved as a result of higher sales, a reduction in interest expense of approximately $33 million and a significant improvement in income from equity investments.

Sales: The Company's consolidated sales increased to $2,606.7 million for fiscal 1993 compared to $2,358.8 million for fiscal 1992. This reflects an increase in production sales of approximately 11% compared to fiscal 1992, attributable to a 9% increase in North American vehicle production to 12.5 million units for fiscal 1993 and a 2% improvement in the Company's average production content per vehicle. Included in consolidated sales are tooling sales which, in fiscal 1993 were $192 million, compared to $190 million in fiscal 1992, reflecting continued new vehicle launches by original equipment manufacturers (OEM) customers. Sales by joint venture companies totalled $671.5 million for fiscal 1993, bringing managed sales to approximately $3.3 billion.

Substantially all of the Company's revenues are generated from sales of automotive components, assemblies, parts and tooling to North American OEMs. During fiscal 1993, approximately 45% of the Company's sales were in respect of products supplied for inclusion in five vehicle body types (including approximately 23% supplied for the Chrysler minivans).

While both North American vehicle production and sales in fiscal 1993 and the Company's average production content per vehicle were higher than in fiscal 1992, there can be no certainty of the level of North American vehicle production or the Company's average production content per vehicle in fiscal 1994. The Company's sales and profitability are directly affected by such levels of production and average production content per vehicle.

Facilities: The Company has 67 manufacturing facilities, 62 in North America and 5 in Europe, 9 of which are joint venture operations. During fiscal 1993, the Company commenced production at its first Mexican manufacturing facility, commenced development of a facility in South Carolina and acquired two manufacturing facilities from joint venture partners.

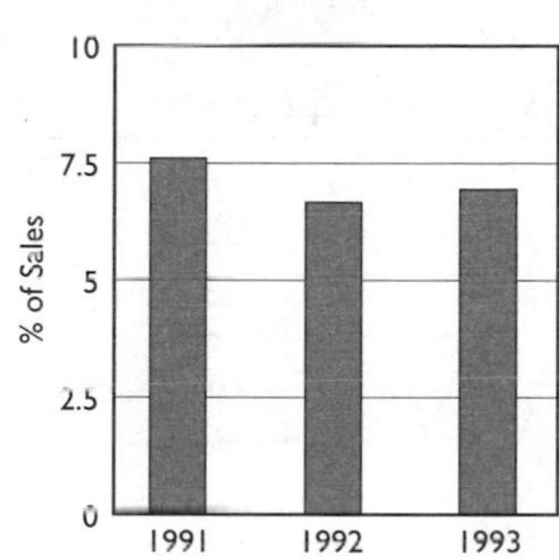

Gross Margin: Gross margin as a percentage of sales declined approximately 0.8% to 19.3% for fiscal 1993 as compared to 20.1% for fiscal 1992, reflecting major new program launch costs, the start-up of the new Mexican manufacturing facility and continued customer pricing pressure, offset partially by higher rates of capacity utilization and improved operating efficiencies.

The competitive environment within the automotive industry has caused OEMs to increase pressure on suppliers for price concessions. While the Company believes that it is, and will remain, competitive, there can be no assurance that the Company will continue to be successful in offsetting required price concessions through cost reductions.

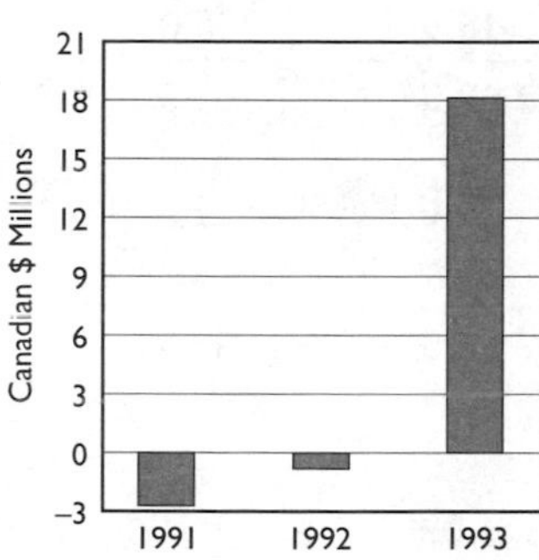

S, G & A: Selling, general and administrative expenses increased by $23.2 million in fiscal 1993 to $179.2 million, as compared to fiscal 1992. The increase is attributable to the higher level of sales activity in fiscal 1993 and retirement and severance costs of approximately $11.3 million incurred in fiscal 1993. Selling, general and administrative expenses, as a percentage of sales, excluding retirement and severance costs, decreased by 0.2% to 6.4% in fiscal 1993, reflecting the effect of spending controls previously put in place by the Company.

Interest Expense: Interest expense in fiscal 1993 decreased by approximately 66% from fiscal 1992 levels, primarily as a result of declining debt levels and a reduction in the average cost of borrowing. Total interest expense for fiscal 1993 amounted to $17.2 million compared to total interest expense for fiscal 1992 of $49.9 million.

Equity Income: Income from equity accounted joint ventures and investments for fiscal 1993 was $18.3 million, an improvement of $19.1 million over the $0.8 million of equity losses for fiscal 1992. Increased sales, the elimination of start-up losses and continued operating improvements at joint ventures contributed to the improvement in results.

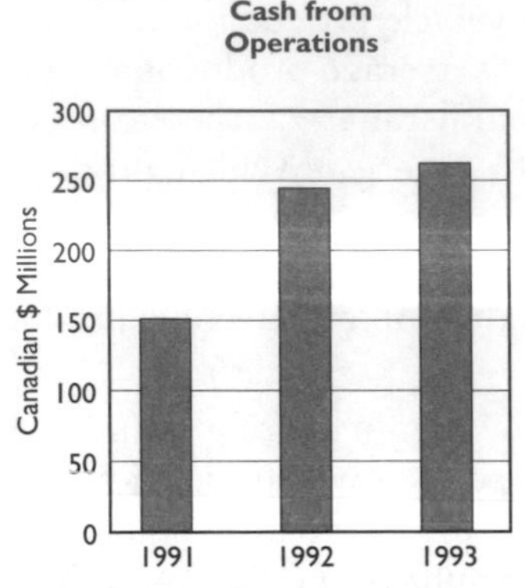

Income Taxes: The Company's effective income tax rate, before equity income, of approximately 31% in fiscal 1993 was consistent with fiscal 1992 and lower than the statutory tax rate primarily as a result of the reduction in the income tax provision in fiscal 1993 of $16.8 million ($17.3 million in 1992) due to the benefit of certain losses incurred by subsidiary companies in prior years. Since such losses have been substantially utilized, the Company expects no similar reduction in fiscal 1994 and expects to return in such year to an effective income tax rate, before equity income, approximately equal to the Canadian statutory rate of 36%.

CONSOLIDATED STATEMENTS OF INCOME AND RETAINED EARNINGS (DEFICIT)

[Canadian dollars in millions, except per share figures] **Years ended July 31**

	Note	**1993**	1992	1991
Sales		**$2,606.7**	$2,358.8	$2,017.2
Cost of goods sold		**2,104.2**	1,884.9	1,622.4
Depreciation and amortization		**104.5**	102.4	105.3
Selling, general and administrative	13	**179.2**	156.0	154.3
Interest	7	**17.2**	49.9	82.3
Equity (income) loss	4	**(18.3)**	0.8	2.7
Income before income taxes and minority interest		**219.9**	164.8	50.2
Income taxes	6	**60.6**	49.8	27.0
Minority interest		**18.9**	17.0	6.7
Net income		**140.4**	98.0	16.5
Retained earnings (deficit), beginning of year		**48.9**	(35.0)	(51.5)
		189.3	63.0	(35.0)
Dividends on Class A Subordinate Voting and Class B Shares		**25.0**	7.4	
Share issue expenses [net of related income taxes]			6.7	
Retained earnings (deficit), end of year		**$ 164.3**	$ 48.9$	(35.0)
Earnings per Class A Subordinate Voting or Class B Share:				
Basic		**$ 3.09**	$ 2.91	$ 0.59
Fully diluted		**$ 2.55**	$ 2.08	$ 0.58
Cash dividends paid per Class A Subordinate Voting or Class B Share		**$ 0.55**	$ 0.20	$ Nil
Average number of Class A Subordinate Voting Shares and Class B Shares outstanding during the year [in millions]:				
Basic		**45.4**	33.6	27.8
Fully diluted		**58.6**	52.4	29.0

See accompanying notes (*Not included*)

CONSOLIDATED BALANCE SHEETS

Incorporated under the laws of Ontario

[Canadian dollars in millions] **As at July 31**

	Note	**1993**	1992
ASSETS			
Current assets:			
Cash		**$ 105.0**	$ 51.6
Accounts receivable		**314.6**	255.7
Inventories	3	**187.1**	172.3
Prepaid expenses and other		**19.9**	20.6
		626.6	500.2
Investments	4,14	**103.9**	80.3
Fixed assets	5	**736.7**	751.7
Goodwill	4	**21.3**	17.8
Other assets	14	**62.6**	51.4
		$ 1551.1	$1,401.4
LIABILITIES AND SHAREHOLDERS' EQUITY			
Current liabilities:			
Bank indebtedness	7		$ 70.4
Accounts payable		**$ 301.1**	233.3
Accrued salaries and wages		**47.1**	41.2
Other liabilities		**70.8**	48.2
Income taxes payable	6	**11.4**	10.9
Long-term debt due within one year	7	**7.6**	9.3
		438.0	413.3
Long-term debt	7	**30.1**	80.5
Convertible subordinated bonds and debentures	8	**64.7**	165.2
Deferred income taxes	6	**90.8**	81.9
Minority interest	9	**83.1**	70.2
Shareholders' equity.			
Capital stock	9		
Class A Subordinate Voting Shares [issued: 1993 – 48,807,924; 1992 – 38,755,717]		**668.0**	544.6
Class B Shares [convertible into Class A Subordinate Voting Shares] issued: 1993 – 1,128,009; 1992 – 1,288,584]		**1.3**	1.5
Retained earnings		**164.3**	48.9
Currency translation adjustment	10	**10.8**	(4.7)
		844.4	590.3
		$1,551.1	$1,401.4

See accompanying notes. (*Not included*)

REPRODUCED COURTESY OF MAGNA INTERNATIONAL INCORPORATION, ANNUAL REPORT, JULY 31, 1993.

NOTES

1. Information about the history of accounting and business is published in many places. A variety of professional and academic journals have shown an interest in such material, and there is a journal devoted specifically to it: the *Accounting Historians Journal*. A large amount of Canadian material is collected in George Murphy (ed.), *A History of Canadian Accounting Thought and Practice*, New York: Garland Publishing Inc., 1993). See also the references below.
2. George Murphy, "Corporate Reporting Practices in Canada: 1900–1970," *The Academy of Accounting Historians, Working Paper Series*, vol 1. (The Academy of Accounting Historians, 1979).
3. Some of the ideas in this section were developed with reference to Ross Skinner's *Accounting Standards in Evolution* (Toronto: Holt, Rinehart and Winston, 1987). For a comprehensive treatment of the development of accounting standards, see Part 1 of Skinner's book.
4. Ibid., 23.
5. Some of the ideas in this section were developed by reference to Murphy, "Corporate Reporting Practices."
6. For an indication of the variety of sources of Canadian financial accounting standards, see Christina S.R. Drummond and Alister K. Mason, *Guide to Accounting Pronouncements & Sources*, 3rd ed. (Toronto: Canadian Institute of Chartered Accountants, 1992). For an indication of the variety of bases for financial statements in the world, see *The Spicer & Oppenheim Guide to Financial Statements Around the World* (New York: John Wiley & Sons, 1989). For a brief background on international financial accounting standards, see the interview, "Setting New Standards," *CGA Magazine* (February 1991), 36–43.
7. For more information on the accounting concepts of income and its similarities to and differences from economic concepts, see writings from the 1960s, 1970s, and early 1980s by such authors as E.O. Edwards, P.W. Bell, R.J. Chambers, and R.R. Sterling. Intermediate and advanced financial accounting texts usually have chapters on "income measurement" or "income theory." See also Kenneth W. Lemke, "Asset Valuation and Income Theory," *The Accounting Review*, January 1966, 32–41.
8. For more on income smoothing, see Joshua Ronen and Simcha Sadan, *Smoothing Income Numbers: Objectives, Means, and Implications* (Reading, Mass.: Addison–Wesley, 1981). Smoothing and other apparent manipulations of income figures have often been the subject of articles in business magazines such as *Forbes*, *Fortune*, and *Business Week*. For critical and very readable commentaries on income manipulation, see a series of articles and books by Abraham Briloff, including *Unaccountable Accounting* (New York: Harper & Row, 1972).
9. Adapted from *Accounting Education: Problems and Prospects* (Sarasota, Fla: American Accounting Association, 1974).

The Cash Flow Statement's Analysis of Cash Flow

4.1 Chapter Overview

Evaluating the enterprise's cash management is so important that the result of this analysis, called the **cash flow statement** or **statement of changes in financial position (SCFP)**, is normally included as part of the set of statements. (As noted in Chapter 2, the balance sheet is also called the *statement of financial position*. The cash flow statement is developed by comparing balance sheets from the beginning and end of the period, so it is called the statement of *changes* in financial position.) The cash flow statement is *derived from these changes* and from some additional information; *it is not based on the accounts in the way the other three statements are*. It is, therefore, a major example of *analysis* of the statements: financial statement analysis is an important part of the later chapters of this book.

In this chapter you will learn:

Use concepts: how a broader interpretation of performance than that measured by the income statement has led to a demand for information about how cash has been obtained and used;

Preparation concepts: how the accrual-based financial statements (particularly the balance sheet) you have already studied can be reworked to produce an insightful analysis of cash flows;

Preparation techniques: how, by classifying financial statement accounts into standard categories, accountants can facilitate analysis of those statements—the usefulness of this technique is illustrated by cash flow analysis;

Use techniques: skill in analyzing financial accounting information, developed further in later chapters, is begun with cash flow information.

4.2 The Purpose of Cash Flow Analysis

Performance in generating additional wealth for the enterprise, as measured by the accrual accounting-based income statement, is very important to managers, investors, tax authorities, and many others. But the world is a complex place, and there is more to performance than generating accrual income. An additional important aspect of performance is managing the inflow and outflow of cash so that the enterprise has enough cash to pay its bills, finance its growth, and keep its borrowing under control. This will not be a surprise to you—everyone has to worry about cash flow, about how much cash is available, and where needed additional cash will come from.

No business enterprise can survive without cash. (Nor can other organizations, such as governments, as we have seen in recent years with governments struggling to raise enough cash from taxes and other charges to meet their financial and social obligations.) Employees, suppliers, and tax authorities must be paid, loans must be repaid, and assets must be kept up to date. Many new and established firms have had positive net income figures, yet have still run out of cash and gone bankrupt. Thus it is important for present and potential investors and creditors to have information about a firm's cash inflows and outflows and its resulting cash position. Can the firm meet all its debts and obligations as they fall due, an ability commonly referred to as **solvency**, and does it have enough cash and short term assets now to cover its immediate debts and obligations, a condition commonly called **liquidity**? Enterprises can get into difficulty by not managing their cash properly. On the other hand, some enterprises seem to have rather a lot of cash, raising questions about why they are so well off and what is being done with the cash. Keeping a large supply of cash lying around idle is no way to earn a return for owners: the cash should be put to work by making investments, improving the buildings and equipment, attracting new customers, or paying off interest-bearing debt.

The cash situation can be obscured somewhat by accrual accounting. Let's take an extreme example. Suppose a company has revenue of $1,000 but it is all on credit, and none of the customers have paid yet. In order to generate the revenue, the company has expenses of $700, and they all have to be paid soon. The accrual income will be the revenue minus the expenses, or $300. Looks good: a 30% return on revenue. But the company is in trouble: it has no cash to pay its expenses; instead, it has $1,000 of accounts receivable, which cannot be used to pay expenses unless the customers pay or some other way is found to get cash for the receivables. The company is likely to want to borrow money from a bank or other lender to provide it the needed cash: how much should it borrow? Should it hound the customers for payment? Should it beg its creditors for more time to pay the $700 in expenses? How will it be able to afford a planned new machine to keep its product quality competitive? All these questions are about the management of cash, and they are not easy to answer by examining the accrual accounting income statement.

To assist with such questions, the fourth major financial statement has been developed. The cash flow statement (statement of changes in financial position or SCFP) provides information about a firm's generation and use of cash and highly liquid short-term assets, and, therefore, assists in evaluating the firm's financial viability. The SCFP's analysis of cash flows provides different information from the income statement's summary of accrual-based performance does.

In the example of Gurjit's jewellery business in Chapter 1, it was shown that accrual income is not the same as cash income. Some revenues and expenses do not involve an inflow or outflow of cash in the present period. The example of uncollected revenue has already been mentioned. Amortization (depreciation) is another example here: the cash flow happened when the asset was acquired, so the amortization expense does not involve any current cash flow.

Even cash income is not a complete measure of what has happened to cash. Certain inflows of cash (such as those resulting from getting a bank loan or issuing shares) or outflows of cash (such as dividends or a purchase of land) are not part of the day-to-day process of generating revenue and incurring expenses, so they would not be covered even by a cash income measure. They reflect management decisions beyond generation of income in the current period, though they may well tell us something about what ability to generate income the firm might have in the future.

The purpose of the analysis of cash flow is therefore twofold:

- To produce a measure of performance that is based on day-to-day cash flow, cash generated by ordinary business activities, instead of accrual accounting. This measure, which we have called **cash income** and which the SCFP calls **cash from operations**, does not imply that accrual income is invalid; rather, it provides a different perspective on performance and so enhances the information for users.
- To incorporate other nonoperating cash inflows and outflows, such as from investing in new assets, selling off old ones, borrowing or repaying debts, obtaining new capital from owners, or paying dividends to the owners. By including these nonoperating cash flows, the SCFP can provide a complete description of how the firm's cash was managed during the period. It can tell the full story of why the firm has more, or less, cash at the end of the period than it had at the beginning.

With all this information, the user can evaluate management's strategy for managing cash and make a better judgment of the company's liquidity, solvency, risk, and opportunities than could be made just from the balance sheet, income statement, and statement of retained earnings.

4.3 THE BASIC IDEA: ANALYSIS OF BALANCE SHEET CHANGES

The balance sheet is the *statement of financial position*. The cash flow statement is the *statement of changes in financial position* (SCFP). This chapter will show you how to construct a cash flow analysis based simply on the changes from one period's balance sheet to the next. There are other methods used by accountants, which can handle any degree of complexity. But for this introductory book, we will keep the analysis at a fairly basic level, so that you will get practice in analyzing and interpreting financial statement information. Many complexities accountants have to deal with will be left out or just mentioned in passing.

To show you how the analysis works, let's take the very simple balance sheet in Exhibit 4.1 and calculate the changes in it.

Exhibit 4.1

Simplistic Enterprises Ltd.
Balance Sheets for 1995 and 1994, with Changes Calculated

	1995	1994	Change
Assets			
Current assets:			
Cash	$150	$130	$20
Accounts receivable	200	160	40
Noncurrent assets:			
Building cost	500	420	80
Accumulated amortization*	(180)	(130)	(50)
	$670	$580	$90
Liabilities and Equity			
Current liabilities:			
Accounts payable	$120	$ 90	$30
Noncurrent liabilities:			
Mortgage debt	240	265	(25)
Equity:			
Share capital issued	100	85	15
Retained earnings**	210	140	70
	$670	$580	$90

* The change in accumulated amortization is due to $50 in amortization expense deducted in determining 1995 accrual income.

** The change in retained earnings is due to the 1995 net income of $70 having been added to the 1994 balance.

The SCFP is just a rearrangement of the balance sheet changes, focusing on their cash effects. The format is to list all the changes in the *noncash* balance sheet accounts and sum them up to equal the change in cash. The logic is as follows:

	Effect on cash during 1995
Operating activities (*day-to-day activities*):	
Change in retained earnings due to net income for 1995 (more income should mean more cash, other things being equal)	$ 70
Add back change in accumulated amortization (this expense reduced income but did not reduce cash so the cash income was really higher than $70)	50
Deduct change in accounts receivable (the receivables are higher, so some of the 1995 net income is from revenue that has not yet been collected, hence cash income was lower because of that)	(40)

continued next page

Add change in accounts payable (the payables are higher, so some of the 1995 net income is from expenses that have not yet been paid for, saving cash for now and meaning cash income was higher because of that)	30
Cash generated from operations (cash income)	$110
Investing activities (*changes in noncurrent assets*):	
Building cost is higher by $80, so it appears cash was used to increase the investment in the building	(80)
Financing activities (*changes in noncurrent debts and capital*):	
Mortgage debt is $25 lower, so it appears cash was used to repay some of the mortgage	(25)
Share capital is $15 higher, so it appears cash was obtained by issuing more shares	15
Total change in cash for 1995	$ 20
Proof: Cash at the end of 1994	130
Cash at the end of 1995	$150

The cash flow statement is an insightful analysis. Just by rearranging the balance sheet changes from one period to the next (1994 to 1995), we have produced several pieces of information:

- Day-to-day operations produced $110 of cash, more than the $70 accrual net income.
- Accrual income is reduced, compared to cash income, by deducting noncash expenses such as amortization. These expenses are quite proper for calculating net income, but they have to be ignored (added back to net income) if we are to calculate cash income.
- Cash income would have been even higher if accounts receivable had not risen, because the rise represents revenue included in accrual income but not yet received from customers. (We might ask why the receivables are rising: is the company not paying sufficient attention to collecting from customers, or is it having to give customers more time to pay in order to get business, or are some customers in trouble?)
- On the other hand, cash outflow was reduced, and cash income therefore increased, because accounts payable also rose. If you do not pay your own bills, you save cash. (This does not mean not paying bills is a good idea: we are just analyzing what happened to cash, not yet making judgments about the appropriateness of what happened. But you can see that disclosing the information at least allows users to make judgments they probably could not make if they were ignorant of what happened.)
- Investing and financing activities also affected cash. Cash was reduced $80 by investing more in the building, reduced by $25 by paying some of the mortgage, and increased $15 by getting more cash from shareholders. These activities help us to understand what happened to cash, and they give us some clues as to management's strategy in maintaining and financing the company's assets. In this case, the company relied

on internal financing in 1995: the building investment was paid for out of cash from operations. The company did not have to borrow to do that, in fact it had enough cash to reduce the mortgage. Some cash was obtained from the owners, but the $15 here was a small amount compared to the $110 from operations.

The steps in producing the basic cash flow analysis in the SCFP are therefore:

1. Calculate the *change* in *every* balance sheet account.
2. Arrange the changes to *every* account *except cash* under the SCFP's headings of Operations, Investing, and Financing.
3. Specify each change as being positive or negative in its effect on cash, either directly or through the correction to net income it implies.
4. Add and subtract all the effects on cash and calculate the total change in cash for the period.
5. Prove that the total change equals the change in the cash account.

You should be able to do step 3 intuitively, by reasoning of the sort outlined in the example above. There is a simple pair of ideas you can apply to keep the directions of various changes' effects on cash straight:

Acquiring assets costs cash.
Going into debt and raising share capital produce cash.

These should make sense. They can be extended into the following rules:

Increases in noncash assets (debits)	Decrease cash
Decreases in noncash assets (credits)	Increase cash
Increases in noncash liabilities and equity (credits)	Increase cash
Decreases in noncash liabilities and equity (debits)	Decrease cash

Stating the rules a different way:

Credit changes in noncash balance sheet accounts (liabilities and equity up or assets down) are shown as increases in cash on the SCFP.

Debit changes in non-cash balance sheet accounts (assets up or liabilities and equity down) are shown as decreases in cash on the SCFP.

Make sure you understand all this before you go on. More examples will be shown as the chapter proceeds, but they are all based on the simplified method described in this section.

HOW'S YOUR UNDERSTANDING

Here are two questions you should be able to answer, based on the material you have just read:

1. Why is the analysis of cash flow important?
2. Horizon Inc. has the following balance sheet changes. Calculate cash from operations, investing, and financing cash flows, and determine the total change in cash for the year. Noncash current assets up $4,320; cost of noncurrent assets up $18,930; accumulated amortization up (credit) $9,360; noncash current liabilities up $2,110; noncurrent debts up $7,000; share capital up $5,500; retained earnings up $3,920 due to net income. (Cash from operations = $3,920 + $9,360 – $4,320 + $2,110 = positive $11,070. Cash from investing = negative $18,930. Cash from financing = $7,000 + $5,500 = positive $12,500. Total cash up $11,070 – $18,930 + $12,500 = $4,640.)

4.4 EXTENDING THE BASIC CASH FLOW ANALYSIS

There are a few more things you will need to know in order to cope with the SCFP of a real company.

1. *Balance sheets and SCFPs are summarized statements.* When you see a company's balance sheet, it is a summary of perhaps hundreds of accounts. If you tried to reconstruct the company's SCFP, you probably would not get the same figures under the various SCFP categories, because you are working with summarized figures and the accountants who prepared the SCFP had access to all the original accounts and could organize them in ways you cannot know about. The purpose of this chapter is to show you enough so that you can prepare a simple SCFP and understand by extension what the information in a real company's SCFP means. You will be able to do an approximate reconstruction of the real SCFP, but unless you are very lucky, you will not be able to reconstruct it exactly. This is not due to any lack of ability on your part, but rather to lack of sufficiently detailed information.
2. *Cash usually is not just cash, but rather,* ***cash and cash equivalents.*** If you have some extra cash you do not need for a short time, you may invest that in an investment certificate at a bank, or buy some shares on the stock market, just to earn a little return from the cash until you need it. Therefore, "cash" on the SCFP includes cash on hand plus temporary investments of cash (called "cash equivalent assets"). On the other hand, you may have a very short-term loan from the bank, or a bank overdraft, which has to be paid before you can apply your cash to any other uses. Such "cash equivalent liabilities" are considered to be negative cash. So the SCFP does not show the total change in cash, but rather the total change in cash and cash equivalents, calculated in the following manner:

   Cash and cash equivalents, beginning of period:
   Cash and cash equivalent assets – cash equivalent liabilities

   Cash and cash equivalents, end of period:
   Cash and cash equivalent assets – cash equivalent liabilities

   The phrase cash and cash equivalents may be used, or just the word cash. The user is supposed to know that cash may include several items. Each company has to determine what to include in cash and cash equivalents. Usually the company will state its definition at the bottom of the SCFP, to assist users. All other balance sheet changes are used to calculate the Operations, Investing, and Financing figures.
3. *Paying dividends reduces cash.* In the Simplistic Enterprises example in Exhibit 4.1, the change in retained earnings was entirely due to net income. That is unlikely to be true in general, because as we know from studying the statement of retained earnings, many companies pay dividends to their shareholders. Therefore, the change in retained earnings on the balance sheet should be separated into two items: increase due to net income and decrease due to dividends.

   There is a complication here that you should be aware of. The change in retained earnings reflects dividends declared, whether paid or not. To get to the cash flow effect on the SCFP, the dividends declared figure is adjusted by including the change in the dividends payable account in current liabilities. For example, if a dividend of $1,000 was declared and dividends payable increased by $300, the cash spent on dividends would be shown as $700. The dividends payable change is therefore not included in Operations with other noncash current liability changes.

Where should dividends paid be shown on the SCFP? Some companies show them as a separate category and some include them with Financing. You might feel they should be part of Operations. Just watch for them, wherever they are on the SCFP!

4. *Not all noncurrent liability changes involve cash.* In the Simplistic Enterprises example, the noncurrent liability was a mortgage debt. This sort of liability produces cash at the beginning and requires cash to repay it. No problem there. But there are several noncurrent liabilities that are estimates of long-term obligations and that are created by debiting an expense and crediting the liability. They may be paid in cash, but they do not arise from borrowing cash, and therefore they are not shown in the Financing section of the SCFP, but rather in the Operations section as add-backs to income. Just like amortization expense, they reduce income when recorded, but involve no cash at that point and so have to be added back to get to the cash income. Therefore, changes in noncurrent liabilities such as the following are shown in Operations, not in Financing:
   - Deferred income tax liability (created through deferred income tax expense);
   - Pension, warranties, and similar liabilities (created through various expenses);
   - Minority (noncontrolling) interest liability (created through the ex-pense deducting the minority owners' share of consolidated income).
5. *The SCFP may reflect standard assumptions.* An important example is that changes in noncurrent assets, noncurrent liabilities, and invested capital are *assumed* to involve cash flows. For example, if land is acquired at a cost of $1,000, the SCFP shows that as a cash outflow in the investing activities category. If it turns out that the land was financed by cash from borrowing long term, the $1,000 borrowed will also show as a cash inflow in the financing activities category. But the SCFP will not necessarily connect the two, because each was derived by separately calculating the changes in the particular balance sheet account (land or noncurrent debt). The presumption is that the cash from the borrowing was put in the bank, and then, as a separate event, cash was spent on the land.

   The SCFP can show the same totals even if no cash was ever involved, for example if the land was acquired just by a promise to pay later, with no cash inflow or outflow. (You can see that conceptually this is the same thing as if cash had come in from the borrowing promise and out for the land.) This procedure, called "grossing up" by accountants, is thought to provide maximum information, because the SCFP shows the effects of all changes in noncurrent assets, noncurrent liabilities, and invested capital, so the user can see everything that happened.
6. *Focus on balance sheet changes.* The cash flow analysis method used here requires that you allocate every balance sheet change to one of the SCFP categories. If you do not do that, it will not work. The amounts you put on the

SCFP must be the changes in the balance sheet, or if you use other figures derived from the income statement or the notes, these other figures must still add up to the balance sheet changes. Here is an example:

Balance sheet changes: Equipment cost is up $17,000;
Accumulated amortization is up $4,300;
Net change in the two accounts is $12,700.

With just this information, we would expect the SCFP to show:
Amortization added back to income in Operations, $4,300;
Addition to equipment deducted from cash in Investing, $17,000;
Net effect of the two on total cash, negative $12,700.

Further information obtained from the company:
A piece of equipment (cost $9,000) was sold;
The accumulated amortization on that piece was $5,300;
Therefore, its book value was $3,700;
It was sold for $2,000;
Therefore, there was a loss on sale of $1,700 (included in general expenses on the income statement);
Its cost and accumulated amortization were removed from the accounts;
Therefore, the cost of new assets must have been $26,000 because that minus $9,000 equals the change in cost;
Also, amortization expense must have been $9,600, because that minus $5,300 equals the change in accumulated amortization.

With this added information, we can show on the SCFP:
Amortization added back to income in Operations, $9,600;
Loss on sale added back to income in Operations, $1,700;
Addition to equipment deducted from cash in Investing, $26,000;
Proceeds from sale of equipment added to cash in Investing, $2,000;
Net effect of the four on total cash, negative $12,700.

We have replaced the original two SCFP items with four, and have therefore made the SCFP more informative. The original two items were not wrong, they were all we could do with the information we had. The purpose of this long example is just to reassure you that you can produce a serviceable, rudimentary SCFP from the balance sheet changes you have, and to caution you that if you try to improve on that rudimentary version, make sure your "better" figures add up to the rudimentary ones you are replacing. The example also points out two more items you will see on many SCFPs:

- Losses on sale added to net income (and gains on sale subtracted) in the Operations section. This is explained further in Section 10.6 (the reason is that losses are adjustments to amortization and, since amortization is added back, so are they. Gains are adjustments to amortization too, but in the opposite direction);
- Proceeds from disposals of noncurrent assets shown as increases in cash in the Investing section.

7. *There are usually some other complications.* Many companies will have balance sheet accounts whose changes are hard to understand or do not

seem to fit anywhere on the SCFP. Usually they are not large and so do not disturb the overall interpretation of the SCFP. You will not go far wrong if you just plunk them arbitrarily in Operations, Investing, or Financing, or even create a separate SCFP category for them. Just use the rule at the end of Section 4.3:

> Credit changes in noncash balance sheet accounts (liabilities and equity up or assets down) are shown as increases in cash on the SCFP.
>
> Debit changes in noncash balance sheet accounts (assets up or liabilities and equity down) are shown as decreases in cash on the SCFP.

8. *Cash flow analysis follows from the balance sheet categorization.* The SCFP categorizes balance sheet changes in accordance with their placement in the balance sheet. Retained earnings changes go to Operations (income) and Dividends; noncash working capital changes, accumulated amortization changes, and some noncurrent liability changes go to Operations; noncurrent asset cost changes go to Investing; and noncurrent debt changes and share capital changes go to Financing.

   The SCFP thus follows the other financial statements in that the placement of the figures in it is supposed to provide information in addition to the figures themselves. **Classified financial statements** are an important way of adding information to the double-entry accounting records. The double-entry system creates accounts, but it is in the classifying of the accounts into the set of financial statements that the accountant creates the meaning, the message, from the accounts. For example, if the accountant thinks that the bank loan is a cash equivalent current liability, the balance sheet will have a different meaning than if the bank loan is included with noncurrent liabilities, the SCFP will show the loan as part of cash instead of as a source of cash in Financing, and comparisons such as the working capital ratio will be different.

HOW'S YOUR UNDERSTANDING

Here are two questions you should be able to answer, based on the material you have just read:

1. If all you know is that the change in accumulated depreciation is $4,000 and that the depreciation expense on the income statement is $5,000, which figure do you add back to income in the Operations section of the SCFP? ($4,000)
2. Trangar Ltd. has cash on hand of $21,674 but, according to its SCFP, it has negative cash and cash equivalents of $17,031. How is this possible? (It must have cash equivalent liabilities greater than the sum of cash and cash equivalent assets.)

4.5 THE CASH FLOW STATEMENT

To summarize the previous two sections, the SCFP is composed of six basic parts:

1. *Cash generated from operations*: cash brought in by day-to-day income-generating activities, through transactions with customers, employees, suppliers, governments, and other parties represented in the enterprise's revenues and expenses, and in the current assets and current liabilities. This "operating cash flow" is the same thing as the cash income calculated in the example of Gurjit's jewellery business in Chapter 1, Section 1.4. It is a measure of performance that focuses on collections and payments, *without considering the accruals* that are the basis of the income statement's way of measuring performance. It could be derived directly from the records of cash transactions, but instead it is derived more simply by just taking the net income figure and *eliminating the effects of the accruals*. In principle, this produces exactly the same result.
2. *Cash used to pay dividends*: cash paid to owners as dividends. This is the dividends declared during the year, minus any part not yet paid, plus any past years' dividends paid this year. So, like cash from operations, this is dividends declared adjusted to remove the accruals for unpaid dividends.
3. *Cash used in investing activities*: cash paid to acquire long-term assets, minus cash proceeds obtained by selling off such assets.
4. *Cash obtained from financing activities*: cash obtained from long-term borrowing (noncurrent liabilities) and issuing of share capital (equity), minus cash used to repay any such borrowing or redeem shares.
5. *Net total change in cash and cash equivalents*: the bottom line of the SCFP, equalling the net total of the above four categories.
6. *Reconciliation of cash and cash equivalents (CCE)*: a summary table to report how the enterprise has defined CCE and to show that the net total of the four cash flow categories equals the change in CCE for the year.

Each of these parts has been described above as they usually exist, but it is not uncommon, especially for enterprises that are in trouble, for some to have the opposite sign to that indicated. If cash from operations is negative, it is called something like "cash used by operations"; if more cash is obtained by selling off assets than is spent acquiring more, that category is called something like "cash obtained by investing activities"; and cash from financing activities and even cash and cash equivalents itself can also be negative. Also, companies often separate net income into that from continuing and that from discontinued operations and may also separate investing and financing activities the same way. The idea is to provide useful information, though sometimes the result is a little complex to read!

Exhibit 4.2 provides an example of the SCFP's format, with rather long explanations of items. Most companies use very short explanations, but the figures are usually arranged in the following order.

Exhibit 4.2

Northscape Engine Rebuilders Inc.
Statement of Changes in Financial Position
for the Year Ended March 31, 1996

Cash and equivalents generated from operations:		
Net income for the year (usually the first item on the SCFP)		$1,695
Adjustments to remove accruals for noncash expenses (or revenues) arising from noncurrent asset changes, such as amortization expense, and expense-based noncurrent liability changes, such as pension expense		845
Adjustments to remove accruals for uncollected revenues, revenues received in advance, prepaid expenses, and unpaid expenses, represented by changes in noncash working capital accounts (current assets and current liabilities)		535
Cash generated from operations		$3,075
Dividends paid (declared dividends adjusted for changes in dividends payable)		(600)
Cash used in investing activities:		
Noncurrent asset changes (cost of additional assets acquired minus proceeds from any disposals)		(3,155)
Cash produced in financing activities:		
Noncurrent debt changes	$(490)	
Invested capital changes	300	(190)
Net change in cash and cash equivalents for the year		$ (870)
Reconciliation of cash and cash equivalents change:		
Cash plus term deposits minus demand loan, beginning of year		$ 582
Cash plus term deposits minus demand loan, end of year		$ (288)

Here are some comments about Northscape's SCFP to illustrate the value of the cash flow analysis:

1. The company had a $1,695 positive net income for the year, but its cash and cash equivalents (CCE) went *down* by $870. So, in terms of its income performance, the company had a positive year, but in terms of cash flow performance, the company had a negative year.
2. CCE went from positive $582 to negative $288 during the year. So, at the beginning of the year, there was net cash on hand, but by the end of the year, the company actually had negative cash. The company has spent more cash than there was!
3. The company defines CCE in the most common way: cash on hand plus term deposits (temporary investments), minus demand loan owing to the bank. There is negative CCE by the end of the year, because the bank loan must be bigger than cash and term deposits put together.

4. Accrual accounting procedures made the net income of $1,695 smaller than the cash actually generated from operations of $3,075. This is a common difference, because accrual accounting provides for expenses such as amortization, which reduce income but do not reduce cash, and for unpaid expenses that are reflected, for example, in accounts payable, which again reduce income but do not reduce cash until they are paid. The 1996 SCFP shows that the net effects of the two kinds of accruals on the net income were $845 and $535, totalling $1,380, which is 81% of the net income figure. Cash income (cash generated from operations) is 181% of net income, rather a significant difference! (Because of amortization in particular, it is normal that cash income is higher than net income, so you should be very cautious of a company that shows the opposite, especially if cash income is negative when net income is positive. It might be that the company is accruing too much in uncollected revenues, or failing to accrue enough unpaid expenses.)
5. The company's poor cash performance for the year is a result of paying dividends of $600, spending $3,155 on noncurrent assets (equipment, buildings, etc.), and paying off noncurrent liabilities by $490. These cash flows totalled much more than the $3,075 cash inflow from operations and the $300 raised from issuing new equity. Though the cash outflows might have happened for good business reasons, they nevertheless were not adequately financed and left the company's cash position much weaker.

HOW'S YOUR UNDERSTANDING

Here are two questions you should be able to answer, based on what you have just read:

1. Broomby Ltd.'s net income is much larger than cash from operations. Why might this indicate a problem?
2. Alliance Inc.'s SCFP shows that the investing activities used twice as much cash as had been generated by operations. Because the company had not borrowed much, the result was a large decline in CCE. Does this indicate a problem?

4.6 A FURTHER EXAMPLE OF PREPARING THE SCFP

Let's do another example. Exhibit 4.3 illustrates how the SCFP can be prepared straightforwardly from the changes in the balance sheet from the beginning to the end of the period. The SCFP category to which the account change is assigned is shown to the right of the "Change" column.

Exhibit 4.3

Tamarack Systems Inc.
Balance Sheets for 1996 and 1995, with Changes Calculated

	1996	1995	Change	
Assets				
Current assets:				
Cash	$ 16,064	$ 12,440	$ 3,624	CCE
Temporary investments	0	65,000	(65,000)	CCE
Accounts receivable	220,668	143,962	76,706	OP
Inventories	176,962	187,777	(10,815)	OP
Prepaid expenses	9,004	14,321	(5,317)	OP
Total current assets	$422,698	$423,500	$ (802)	
Noncurrent assets:				
Land cost	$ 82,500	$ 75,000	$ 7,500	INV
Building cost	600,898	420,984	179,914	INV
Accumulated amortization	(243,224)	(173,320)	(69,904)	OP
Net total noncurrent assets	$440,174	$322,664	$117,510	
Totals	$862,872	$746,164	$116,708	
Liabilities and Equity				
Current liabilities:				
Demand bank loan	$ 64,900	$ 43,200	$ 21,700	CCE
Accounts payable	199,853	163,866	35,987	OP
Income taxes payable	17,228	16,090	1,138	OP
Dividends payable	0	6,000	(6,000)	DIV
Current portion of bonds payable	22,000	20,000	2,000	FNC
Total current liabilities	$303,981	$249,156	$ 54,825	
Noncurrent liabilities:				
Bonds payable	$213,000	$235,000	$ (22,000)	FNC
Provision for warranty costs	8,925	11,850	(2,925)	OP
Deferred income tax	43,439	38,923	4,516	OP
Total noncurrent liabilities	$265,364	$285,773	$ (20,409)	
Equity:				
Share capital issued	$150,000	$100,000	$ 50,000	FNC
Retained earnings	143,527	111,235	32,292	OP,DIV
Total equity	$293,527	$211,235	$ 82,292	
Totals	$862,872	$746,164	$116,708	

Further information:

1. The change in retained earnings is composed of net income $56,292 minus dividends declared of $24,000.
2. Cash and equivalents are defined as cash plus temporary investments minus demand bank loan.
3. Current and noncurrent portions of the bonds payable will be included together in the Financing section of the SCFP.

Using the categorizations indicated above for the changes, we get the SCFP shown in Exhibit 4.4. Every account change is shown below, so you can trace each back to the balance sheet changes. Most companies would group changes together to make a less detailed SCFP.

Exhibit 4.4

Tamarack Systems Inc.
Statement of Changes in Financial Position for 1996

Operations		
Net income for the year		$ 56,292
Adjustments for noncash expenses:		
Amortization of building	$ 69,904	
Warranty provision	(2,925)	
Deferred income tax	4,516	71,495
Adjustments for changes in noncash working capital:		
Accounts receivable	$(76,706)	
Inventories	10,815	
Prepaid expenses	5,317	
Accounts payable	35,987	
Income taxes payable	1,138	(23,449)
Cash from operations		$104,338
Dividends Paid		
Dividends declared	$(24,000)	
Adjustment for change in dividends payable	(6,000)	(30,000)
Investing Activities		
Additions to land	$ (7,500)	
Additions to building	(179,914)	(187,414)
Financing Activities		
Repayment of bonds ($22,000 – $2,000)	$(20,000)	
Share capital issued	50,000	30,000
Net Total Change in Cash and Equivalents		$ (83,076)
Cash and equivalents—beginning of year ($12,440 + $65,000 – $43,200)		34,240
Cash and equivalents—end of year ($16,064 + $0 – $64,900)		$ (48,836)

From this cash-focused summary of balance sheet changes, we can make several observations:

- The company's total cash flow was strongly negative for the year;
- Cash from operations was almost twice accrual net income;
- Cash from operations has been severely reduced by a large rise in accounts receivable (uncollected revenue);
- Operations were the major source of cash during the year—there was no new borrowing and the issue of shares brought in only half the cash that operations did;
- The major use of cash was additions to noncurrent assets;
- The company's CCE reversed from $34,240 to a cash deficit of $48,836.

We do not know the reasons for the effects shown in the SCFP, but we certainly do know several things we might like to ask management about. In particular, we might like to know how management proposes to get cash back onto the positive side.

HOW'S YOUR UNDERSTANDING

Here are two questions you should be able to answer, based on what you have just read:

1. How does an SCFP explain what happened to cash and cash equivalents during the year?
2. The following changes occurred in Bradee Ltd.'s accounts during the past year: noncash current assets increased by $270; cost of noncurrent assets increased by $600; accumulated amortization increased by $250; noncash current liabilities increased by $340; warranty provision in noncurrent liabilities increased by $80; non-current debts decreased by $120; share capital increased by $200; net income was $475; and $215 in dividends were paid. Calculate the change in cash and cash equivalents for the year. ($475 + $250 + $80 + $340 – $270 – $215 – $600 – $120 + $200 = $140 increase)

4.7 INTERPRETING A COMPANY'S CASH FLOW STATEMENT

The recent consolidated statement of cash flows for an American company, Tyson Foods, Inc. (Exhibit 4.5), provides a good example of the cash flow analysis we have been developing. You will note that it is comparative for three years, and that the three years vary a great deal in the details of their cash flows. A great deal of information is provided about various financing and investing activities. There is no explanation of what cash and cash equivalents includes, but on the balance sheet there is a current asset called cash and cash equivalents that has the same amount shown at the bottom of the cash flow statement, so the company does not categorize any liabilities as part of cash and cash equivalents.

Exhibit 4.5

Consolidated Statements of Cash Flows
Tyson Foods, Inc.

Three Years Ended October 2, 1993			*(In thousands)*
	1993	**1992**	**1991**
CASH FLOWS FROM OPERATING ACTIVITIES			
Net income	**$180,334**	$160,534	$145,498
Adjustments to reconcile net income to cash provided by operating activities:			
Depreciation	**145,756**	119,363	106,630
Amortization	**30,753**	29,502	29,201
Deferred income taxes	**5,378**	17,883	3,784
Loss on dispositions of property and equipment	**695**	218	816
(Increase) decrease in accounts receivable	**35,344**	(25,259)	(3,810)
(Increase) decrease in inventories	**(66,909)**	10,606	(14,238)
Increase (decrease) in trade accounts payable	**(41,001)**	7,414	(6,396)
Net change in other current assets and liabilities	**18,052**	(54,381)	35,589
Cash Provided by Operating Activities	**308,402**	265,880	297,074
CASH FLOWS FROM INVESTING ACTIVITIES			
Net cash paid for acquisitions	**(43,377)**		
Additions to property, plant, and equipment	**(225,305)**	(107,990)	(213,576)
Proceeds from sale of property, plant, and equipment	**7,387**	6,615	15,294
Net change in other assets and liabilities	**(41,393)**	(3,309)	(7,424)
Cash Used for Investing Activities	**(302,688)**	(104,684)	(205,706)
CASH FLOWS FROM FINANCING ACTIVITIES			
Net increase (decrease) in notes payable	**(29,200)**	(10,000)	10,000
Proceeds from long-term debt	**977,421**	131,941	155,500
Repayments of long-term debt	**(954,497)**	(278,694)	(246,642)
Dividends and other	**(4,951)**	(2,836)	(1,716)
Cash Used for Financing Activities	**(11,227)**	(159,589)	(82,858)
Increase (Decrease) in Cash	**(5,513)**	1,607	8,510
Cash and Cash Equivalents at Beginning of Year	**27,060**	25,453	16,943
Cash and Cash Equivalents at End of Year	**$ 21,547**	$ 27,060	$ 25,453

See accompanying notes. *(Not included)*

REPRODUCED COURTESY OF TYSON FOODS INCORPORATED, ANNUAL REPORT, OCTOBER 2, 1993.

Let's see some of the things Tyson's cash flow statement tells us.

- The company's cash from operations is very large in relation to its other cash flows. This allows the company to finance most of its activities from such internally generated cash, rather than having to borrow or issue more share capital.
- The company does not keep much cash on hand relative to its annual flow. Cash from operations has been about, or more than, 10 times cash on hand in each of the three years.
- Interesting changes are suggested in the company's relationship with its customers and suppliers. Accounts receivable had been increasing each year in 1991 and 1992, but were significantly decreased in 1993. (It turns out that new arrangements were made to sell accounts receivable continuously to a bank, speeding up the company's receipt of cash.) Inventories rose quite a lot in 1993 and accounts payable were paid off faster: these two items reduced cash from operations by more than $100 million.
- The company acquired more noncurrent assets, including some other food companies (poultry, seafood, and pork processors) during 1993, adding those companies' assets (and liabilities) into Tyson's as part of consolidating the companies together. Those acquisitions cost more than $250 million in 1993, more than twice what was spent in 1992, and more than was spent in 1991. Such acquisitions have been Tyson's major use of the cash it generates from operations.
- These acquisitions help the company keep its assets renewed as they lose their value through use. The sum of the company's amortization and depreciation for the year gives an indication of that lost value, which is only about $80 million less than the spending on noncurrent assets.
- Tyson did a major refinancing of its long-term debt during 1993, trying to take advantage of financial market changes such as interest rate reductions. The company has a large amount of "revolving" prearranged credit lines and other flexible arrangements, so it was able to rearrange its debts. You can see that though nearly a billion dollars was rearranged, the net amount of additional borrowing was small.
- The company does not pay much in dividends. Dividends are so small they are lumped with "other" in the Financing section of the cash flow statement. This is presumably part of the company's internal financing strategy: retained earnings is the largest single account on the right side of the company's 1993 balance sheet.
- Net total cash flow (increase [decrease] in cash) is small compared to the size of the Operating, Investing, and Financing flows. The company appears to be doing a careful job of balancing incoming and outgoing cash flows.

You may have more observations about Tyson's cash flow statement. Keep thinking about cash, investing and financing, and the financial statement analysis material in Chapter 9 will add more ideas about analyzing and interpreting cash flows.

HOW'S YOUR UNDERSTANDING

Here are two questions you should be able to answer, based on what you have just read:

1. It was stated above that Tyson Foods relies on internal financing of its investing activities. How can you tell?
2. Comparison of which figures on the SCFP gives an indication of whether a company appears to be renewing its assets as they lose their value through use?

4.8 EXAMPLE FINANCIAL STATEMENTS

Much of the accountant's work in preparing financial statements is in classifying the information: putting the accounts in the appropriate categories in the statements. The category selected is important because it tells us a great deal about the account. For example, cash classified as a current asset tells us that the cash is available for use; cash classified as a noncurrent asset tells us that the cash is *not* available, that it is restricted in some way. As another example, a revenue included with operating revenue is ordinary, but one included with nonoperating revenues and expenses is something out of the ordinary.

This book includes many example financial statements to help you get used to their contents and formats. We have already seen several general examples plus some of the statements of real companies: Paychex, Inc., Dominion Textile Inc., and Tyson Foods, Inc. End-of-chapter cases have included excerpts from the statements of Intrawest Corporation (Case 1B), TSC Shannock Corporation (Cases 2A and 3A), the CBC (Case 2B), and Magna International Inc. (Case 3B). More such examples will appear as the book proceeds; for example, the full set of 1993 financial statements for Microsoft Corporation is in Case 4A at the end of this chapter.

In addition, the complete financial statements and notes of The North West Company Inc. are at the back of the book. These statements will be thoroughly analyzed in Chapter 9, but in the meantime will serve as further examples for your reference.

4.9 CASH FLOW AND THE MANAGER

Managers are responsible not only for earning income for the company, but also for managing cash so that bills can be paid on time, excess borrowing and interest costs can be avoided, and the company's liquidity and solvency can be generally protected. Effectively employing available cash so that it does not remain idle, earning nothing, is also important. Cash flow and income are generally positively correlated (good performance tends to move them both up, and poor performance tends to move them both down), and over a long enough time (years), they are almost the same. But in the short run their relationship can be complex, as these two examples illustrate:

1. A few years ago, Quebec increased gasoline taxes to a higher rate than that in Ontario. This caused immediate problems for Quebec gas stations near the Ontario border: driving a few kilometres to buy gas in Ontario

made a big difference in the price, unless a Quebec gas station owner decided to "swallow" the difference in tax. A CBC reporter interviewed a Quebec owner and asked, "What are the implications of this for your long-run profitability?" The owner said, "Unless I can get some cash in in the short run, there isn't going to be a long run!"

2. A problem new businesses can have is to grow too fast. Often the product demand and the entrepreneurial enthusiasm are high: the business was founded in the hope that people would want the product or service, and it is exciting to everyone when they do! The income statements of such businesses often show high profits (net incomes), but the SCFP and the balance sheet may tell a different story. In the enthusiasm of making sales and satisfying customers, inventory levels often get too high (making sure there is something for everyone on hand) and collections from customers often lag (receivables get too high as the entrepreneur concentrates on the pleasures of selling rather than the nuisance of collecting). The SCFP deducts the increases in inventories and receivables from accrual-basis net income, and may show that operating cash flows are small or even negative. When this happens, you do not need an SCFP to know you are in trouble: your bank balance tells you that! But the SCFP reports the whole story to others, so that they can see what you have accomplished in obtaining and using cash in your operating, financing, and investing activities. You then have to be prepared to explain such activities to users of the financial statements.

The SCFP provides a measure of managerial performance in managing cash, so smart managers must be aware of how their efforts are reflected in it, just as they are aware of the income statement and balance sheet measures of performance and position.

4.10 ACCOUNTING RESEARCH: INCOME OR CASH FLOW?

This chapter has presented the SCFP as an important addition to the set of financial statements, providing cash flow information in addition to the income statement's accrual income information and the balance sheet's static "position" information. Is there any evidence that this extra information is useful? Does it affect anyone's decisions?

Researching this question has been difficult. One reason, already mentioned in Section 4.9, is that for most companies, income (in the income statement) and cash provided by operations (in the SCFP) are quite highly correlated, so their effects are difficult to separate. They can be separated for companies that do not keep income and cash flow correlated by managing both income and cash flow well, but such companies are usually not around long enough to be studied very deeply! Another reason is that the response, for example by stock markets, to earnings information is quite strong—so strong that it may swamp the effects of the added SCFP information.

Finally, because the SCFP is produced by a reworking of the balance sheet changes, you could argue that theoretically it cannot contain much added information. New information would have to come from the format and descriptions of the SCFP or from splitting up changes in balance sheet accounts (for example, cash instead of noncash changes) in ways that were not apparent from just looking at the balance sheets. The existence of added information in the SCFP is plausible because, as noted earlier in this chapter, you can seldom exactly reproduce a company's SCFP on your own: it reflects detailed knowledge of the accounts you cannot get from the fairly summarized balance sheet.

What is the research evidence on the value of the SCFP? Well, this issue has begun to be studied only recently, mostly in connection with public companies' share price changes (buy and sell decisions by investors). Most research so far defines cash flow simply as net income plus amortization (depreciation) expense. This of course is only a part of the SCFP information, a part that can be calculated easily without an SCFP, because depreciation expense is on the income statement. Such research usually finds that share prices do respond a little to the added information. While most of the share price response is to the earnings (accrual net income) figure, some response to the cash flow information has also been found. This is quite preliminary, however, and much work still needs to be done on the cash flow question. But the information does seem useful because evidence of some effect has been found for only part of the SCFP's contents in only one kind of decision.[1]

4.11 CONTINUING DEMONSTRATION CASE

INSTALMENT 4

Data for Instalment 4

In order to prepare for the board of directors' meeting, Tomas thought it would be a good idea to be able to explain what had happened to the company's cash during the first six months. As a reference, Exhibit 4.6 shows the comparative balance sheet we saw in Instalment 3:

Exhibit 4.6

Mato Inc.
Balance Sheets as at August 31 and March 1, 1994

Assets	**August**	**March**	**Liabilities and Shareholders' Equity**	**August**	**March**
Current assets:			Current Liabilities:		
Cash	$ 4,507	$130,000	Bank loan	$ 75,000	$ 0
Receivables	18,723	0	Payables	45,616	1,100
Inventory	73,614	0	Loan Payable	15,000	15,000
	$ 96,844	$130,000		$135,616	$ 16,100
Noncurrent assets:			Shareholders' equity:		
Equip. cost	$ 54,640	$ 10,000	Share capital	$125,000	$125,000
Accum. amort.	(3,234)	0	Deficit	(49,378)	0
Leasehold (net)	57,568	0		$ 75,622	$125,000
Software (net)	4,320	0			
Incorp. cost	1,100	1,100			
	$114,394	$ 11,100			
TOTAL	$211,238	$141,100	TOTAL	$211,238	$141,100

Tomas decided that for his cash analysis, he would define cash and cash equivalents as cash minus bank loan, because the bank loan was a demand loan. He began his analysis by identifying the changes in financial position since March 1, which resulted in the following analysis:

Changes in Financial Position
between March 1 and August 31, 1994

Changes in Assets		Changes in Liabilities and Equity	
Cash	$ (125,493)	Bank loan	$75,000
Receivables	18,723	Payables	44,516
Inventory	73,614	Loan payable	0
Equipment cost	44,640*	Share capital	0
Accum. amort.	(3,234)	Deficit	(49,378)
Leasehold cost	63,964		
Accum. amort.	(6,396)		
Software cost	4,800		
Accum. amort	(480)		
Incorp. costs	0		
	$ 70,138		$70,138

*Computer, $14,900; other equipment and furniture, $29,740.

Results for Instalment 4

Tomas then wrote down all the categories of the statement of changes in financial position and filled in the appropriate figures, producing the statement shown in Exhibit 4.7.

(The SCFP is shown in more detail than might be done in practice, so that you can trace every figure from the balance sheet change analysis above to the SCFP. Make sure you do this, to improve your understanding of the derivation of the SCFP.)

Exhibit 4.7

Mato Inc.
Statement of Changes in Financial Position
for the Six Months Ended August 31, 1994

Operations:		
Net loss for the six months		$(49,378)
Add back amortization for the period ($3,234 + $6,396 + $480)		10,110
		$(39,268)
Changes in noncash working capital accounts:		
Increase in accounts receivable	$(18,723)	
Increase in inventory	(73,614)	
Increase in accounts payable	44,516	(47,821)
Cash *used* in operations		$(87,089)

Exhibit 4.7 continued

Dividends paid		0
Investing activities:		
Equipment, computer and furniture acquired	$(44,640)	
Leasehold improvements made	(63,964)	
Software acquired	(4,800)	(113,404)
Financing activities		0
Decrease in cash during the six months		$(200,493)
Cash on hand, March 1, 1994		130,000
Cash and equivalents, August 31, 1994*		$ (70,493)
*Cash and equivalents, August 31, 1994:		
Cash on hand	$ 4,507	
Demand bank loan	(75,000)	
	$(70,493)	

The SCFP shows that the dramatic decline in cash has two causes.

- First, day-to-day operations produced a cash loss of $87,089. This was a combination of expenses exceeding revenues and the build-up of current assets, especially inventory. The increase in accounts payable helped to finance this, but even after, in essence, borrowing from suppliers, the company still fell far behind in its cash flow.
- Second, noncurrent asset acquisitions cost $113,404 in cash.

The net result is that a healthy cash balance of $130,000 six months ago was turned into a negative cash balance of $70,493. The company clearly has to get on top of its cash problems quickly.

HOMEWORK AND DISCUSSION TO DEVELOP UNDERSTANDING

PROBLEM 4.1* Basic questions about cash management and the SCFP

Answer the following questions briefly:

1. Why is managing cash flow important?
2. Can a company have a good net income and little cash generated from operations in the same year? If it can, how does this happen?
3. Why is cash generated from operations usually larger than net income?
4. What are cash and cash equivalents?

PROBLEM 4.2* Prepare the example SCFP shown in Section 4.5

In Section 4.5, the 1996 SCFP of Northscape Engine Rebuilders Inc. was presented as an example. Below are the company's balance sheets for 1996 and 1995. Use them to derive the SCFP in Section 4.5. The 1996 statements of income and retained earnings are provided as well, in case you find them useful.

Northscape Engine Rebuilders Inc.
Balance Sheets as at March 31, 1996 and 1995

Assets	1996	1995	Liabilities and Equity	1996	1995
Current assets:			Current Liabilities:		
Cash and bank	$ 512	$ 382	Demand loan	$ 1,000	$ 800
Term deposits	200	1,000	Payables	4,691	3,887
Receivables	3,145	2,690		$ 5,691	$ 4,687
Inventories	5,420	5,606	Noncurrent liabilities:		
	$ 9,277	$ 9,678	Mortgages	$ 7,105	$ 7,595
Noncurrent assets:			Shareholders' equity:		
Asset cost	$15,641	$12,486	Share capital	$ 2,300	$ 2,000
Accum. amort.	(6,066)	(5,221)	Retained earnings	3,756	2,661
	$ 9,575	$ 7,265		$ 6,056	$ 4,661
	$18,852	$16,943		$18,852	$16,943

Income Statement
for the Year Ended March 31, 1996

Operating revenue		$14,689
Operating expenses:		
Amortization	$ 845	
Other expenses	11,160	12,005
		$ 2,684
Income tax expense		989
Net income for 1996		$ 1,695

Statement of Retained Earnings
for the Year Ended March 31, 1996

Beginning balance	$ 2,661
Add net income for 1992	1,695
	$ 4,356
Deduct dividends declared	600
Ending balance	$ 3,756

PROBLEM 4.3* **SCFP basics plus some "what if" questions**

1. What does the cash flow information in the SCFP tell you that you cannot get directly, if at all, from the income statement and balance sheet?
2. Beta Company's SCFP showed the following figures: Cash generated from operations, $127,976; Dividends paid, $40,000; Cash used in investing activities, $238,040; and Cash obtained in financing activities, $147,000. What was the net change in the company's cash and cash equivalents for the year?
3. Indicate the effect on Beta Company's SCFP of each of the following events, *if they had occurred during the year*:
   a. What if a new truck was purchased at a cost of $38,950, and of this, $10,000 was paid in cash and the remainder was borrowed long term?
   b. What if the company had sold a machine that had a book value of $3,220 for $4,100 cash?

c. What if collections of accounts receivable had been $6,000 less than actually happened?
d. What if the company had declared an additional dividend of $15,000, but had not paid any of it by the end of the year?
e. What if the company borrowed $25,000 from the bank as a demand loan?

PROBLEM 4.4* Interpret a real company's SCFP

Get a company's annual report (perhaps from the library), or use the set of financial statements for The North West Company Inc. at the back of the book, and refer to the cash flow statement.

1. What are the differences in title and format of the company's cash flow statement from those this chapter has said are usual for an SCFP? Do you like the company's variations or not?
2. Figure out which number is cash provided by operations and compare that to the net income figure on the income statement. What accounts for the difference?
3. What does the company define as cash and cash equivalents?
4. What has each of the following done to (i) working capital and (ii) cash during the last year?
   a. changes in accounts receivable and payable
   b. changes in inventories
   c. amortization and similar expenses
5. Your answer to 4 (c) should have been that amortization and similar expenses have *no* effect on working capital or cash. Why then are they added back to income on the SCFP?
6. Write a paragraph summarizing the major causes of the change in cash and cash equivalents experienced by the company during the year. What major activities seem to have been going on?

PROBLEM 4.5* Effects on SCFP of unpaid dividends and building disposal

1. You have just prepared an SCFP for Frogmorton Corp., and it works out to the correct change in cash and cash equivalents. You then discover that included in the current liabilities is an account for dividends payable that you had not realized was there. Explain why the cash from operations and dividends paid figures on your SCFP are incorrect and why the total change in CCE on your SCFP is correct in spite of your error.
2. You are struggling with the SCFP for Magdalen Inc. You know that the net total change in noncurrent assets over the year is an increase of $459,200 and that amortization expense for the year was $236,100. You then learn that during the year, the company sold a building for $200,000. The building had cost $840,000 and there was accumulated amortization on it of $650,000 at the date of sale.
   a. Calculate the apparent amount spent on acquisitions of noncurrent assets during the year.
   b. Calculate the gain or loss on the sale of the building.

c. Specify the adjustments to income in the operations section of the SCFP arising from noncurrent assets.

d. Specify the figures in the investing activities section of the SCFP.

PROBLEM 4.6 Explain what the SCFP tells about a company

Explain to your uncle (who has never studied accounting) what the statement of changes in financial position tells him about a company he owns shares in.

PROBLEM 4.7 Prepare and explain basic SCFP from balance sheet changes

Another student has been having an awful time trying to prepare a cash flow statement (SCFP) for Greenplace Restaurants Inc. for the 1995 fiscal year. You go over to help and find the disorganized list of balance sheet changes below. About all that can be said for it is that it does balance out to zero, so the student has managed to identify all the changes from 1994.

1. Take the list below and prepare an SCFP for Greenplace for the 1995 fiscal year. (To do this, you will have to start by defining which accounts are to be considered as cash and cash equivalents.)
2. Explain what your SCFP reveals about the company's 1995 cash management.

List of Balance Sheet Changes for Greenplace Restaurants Inc. for Fiscal Year 1995

	Direction	Debit	Credit
Trade payables	Up		$ 54,240
Accumulated amortization	Up		67,300
Cash in bank	Up	$ 4,328	
Receivables	Down		34,984
Demand loan	Up		35,400
Inventories	Up	53,202	
Net income	Positive		87,345
Dividends declared and paid	Positive	30,000	
Prepaid expenses	Up	12,540	
Buildings, equip.	Up	295,631	
Mortgage payable	Up		65,000
Taxes payable	Down	13,568	
Share capital	Up		50,000
Term deposits	Down		15,000
Sums of changes		$409,269	$409,269

PROBLEM 4.8 Prepare and interpret a basic SCFP from financial statements

1. Prepare a statement of changes in financial position from the following financial statements of Fuzzy Wuzzy Wines Ltd.:

Balance Sheets as at August 31, 1995 and 1994

Assets			**Liabilities and Equity**		
	1995	1994		1995	1994
Current assets:			Current Liabilities:		
Cash	$ 80	$ 175	Demand loan	$ 140	$ 100
Term deposits	0	150	Payables	$ 425	$ 200
Receivables	520	350		$ 565	$ 300
Inventories	340	250	Noncurrent liabilities:		
	$ 940	$ 925	Long-term loans	225	400
Noncurrent assets:				$ 790	$ 700
Factory cost	$1,450	$ 925	Shareholders' equity:		
Accum. deprec.	(475)	(350)	Share capital	$ 700	$ 500
	$ 975	$ 575	Retained earnings	425	300
				$1,125	$ 800
	$1,915	$1,500		$1,915	$1,500

Statement of Income and Retained Earnings
for the Year Ended August 31, 1995

Revenue		$3,000
Expenses:		
Amortization	$ 125	
General	2,450	2,575
Income before income tax		$ 425
Income tax expense		190
Net income for the year		$ 235
Retained earnings—beginning of year		300
Dividends declared and paid		(110)
Retained earnings—end of year		$ 425

2. Comment on what your SCFP tells you about the company's cash management during the year ended August 31, 1995. If you were a shareholder in Fuzzy Wuzzy, would you be happy with management's performance?

PROBLEM 4.9 Interpret a simple SCFP and answer two "what if" questions

A high school friend of yours, Natasha Wheeler, is currently in second-year fine arts and, in addition to many other talents, happens also to have an entrepreneurial flair. For the last two summers, she has operated a bicycle rental business near a local park. Last year (1994), even though the business was just getting started, she made enough money to pay for tuition and get herself through the school year. Encouraged by this initial success, she bought several more bikes this year (1995) and constructed a movable shed out of which she operated her business and serviced the bikes.

Business was even better this summer, but Natasha is confused. While her business income was great, there is no cash for her to withdraw. She does not know how she will pay for tuition this year, not to mention living expenses.

Knowing that you are taking an accounting course, she comes to you for help. She realizes that you cannot lend her any money, but maybe you can explain what is going on with her business.

1. Using the statement of changes in financial position, explain to Natasha how it is possible that the income statement can show a profit, while there is no cash for her to withdraw from the business. Explain to her where all the cash went.
2. In order to pay her tuition and keep a roof over her head, Natasha decides that she will have to borrow another $4,000 from her parents, who will not expect her to repay the money in the near future, and another $2,000 from the bank, which is looking very carefully at Natasha's cash position (*and* at her very saleable bicycles) and expecting to be repaid as soon as possible. What effect will these two events have on the statement of changes in financial position?

Wheeler's Bicycle Rental Ltd.
Statement of Changes in Financial Position
for the Year Ended August 31, 1995
with Comparative Figures for 1994

	1995	1994
Operations:		
Net income	$ 9,000	$ 5,500
Add back depreciation expense	3,000	1,000
Cash from operations	$ 12,000	$ 6,500
Dividend paid	–	(5,500)
Investing:		
Purchases of bikes	(15,000)	(5,000)
Purchase of shed	(5,000)	–
Financing:		
Bank loan	7,000	–
Loan from parents	–	3,000
Share capital issued	–	2,000
(Decrease) or increase in cash	$ (1,000)	$ 1,000
Cash balance—beginning of year	1,000	0
Cash balance—end of year	$ 0	$ 1,000

PROBLEM 4.10 Prepare a more complex SCFP

(Challenging) Below are two lists of Johnson Feeds Ltd.'s accounts in alphabetical order within the balance sheet and the income statement: the post-closing account balances at the end of 1994 and the pre-closing balances at the end of 1995. From that information, define cash and cash equivalents in a way that makes sense to you and then prepare an SCFP for 1995, in standard format. State any assumptions you need to make.

Account	1995	1994
Accounts payable	84,500	94,400
Accounts receivable	93,900	86,700
Accumulated amortization—building	136,800	123,800
Accumulated amortization—equipment*	77,400	68,200
Bank loan to buy equipment	43,000	0
Building—cost	268,400	261,300
Cash in bank	17,300	13,200
Cash on hand	1,600	1,500
Current income tax liability	2,200	3,100
Equipment—cost*	161,400	114,600
Deferred income tax liability**	26,200	24,500
Demand bank loan from line of credit	63,200	54,100
Inventory of feed and supplies	124,500	118,600
Investment in associated company	25,000	0
Investment in marketable securities	0	18,000
Land	80,000	80,000
Loan from shareholder	30,000	35,000
Mortgage on building and land, due 1999	128,800	143,500
Pension liability***	32,100	23,600
Prepaid insurance	300	1,400
Retained earnings****	87,100	97,100
Share capital	38,000	28,000
Cost of goods sold expense	356,700	
Amortization expense—building	13,000	
Amortization expense—equipment	12,800	
Income tax expense—current	7,700	
Income tax expense—deferred**	1,700	
Gain on sale of equipment*	400	
General expenses	163,900	
Interest expense	15,400	
Pension expense***	8,500	
Revenue	602,400	

Notes

*During the year, a piece of equipment that had cost $5,200 and had accumulated amortization of $3,600 was sold for $2,000. Its cost and accumulated amortization were removed from the cost and accumulated amortization accounts.

**The change in deferred income tax liability was entirely due to the amount of deferred income tax expense estimated for the year.

***The change in pension liability was entirely due to the amount of pension expense estimated for the year. No employees have yet retired so there has not yet been any payment of pensions.

****A dividend of $10,000 was declared and paid during the year.

PROBLEM 4.11 Why pay attention to the cash flow statement?

(Challenging) A senior financial executive for a large public company remarked to a stock market analyst: "I don't know why you people worry so much about what is in our cash flow statement. Managing cash flow is our responsibility as managers; it involves paying close attention to cash on a daily basis. Why don't you pay attention to our income performance and just forget about cash flow? We'll look after that!"

Respond to the executive's comments. You do not have to agree or disagree entirely.

PROBLEM 4.12 Why not just have cash basis accounting?

(Challenging) A business commentator made the following remark during a discussion of the financial performance of a large, but struggling, company. "These accountants are something to behold! They spend lots of money to create complicated financial statements, especially income statements, that use what they call 'accrual' accounting, and come up with an income number they expect us to take seriously. Then they spend a whole lot more money creating cash flow statements, which are just as complicated as the other statements, and that take away all the accruals and supposedly return us to the cash income number we would have had anyway, if they hadn't bothered with accrual accounting in the first place! Nice work! You get paid to create a dubious income measure and then more money to uncreate it. What kind of idiots do they take the business community for? Why don't they just give us the cash income and leave it at that? We can understand that, and it would make a simple income statement and no need for a cash flow statement to just cancel out the income number, as we have now."

If you were an accountant involved in the discussion and everyone turned to you to hear what you would say in response to the commentator, what would you say?

PROBLEM 4.13 Use a SCFP to derive an ending balance sheet

(Challenging) This chapter has emphasized that the SCFP is prepared from differences between the balance sheet at the end of the period and that at the beginning. To test your understanding of how this works, derive the balance sheet of TGIF Industries Ltd. at the end of 1995 from the two statements given below: the balance sheet at the end of 1994 and the SCFP for 1995. When you have done that, prepare some comments on what the company's cash management strategy seemed to be for 1995, and whether that left the company financially stronger or weaker at the end of 1995 than at the end of 1994.

TGIF Industries Ltd.
Balance Sheet at December 31, 1994
(in thousands of dollars)

Assets	1994	Liabilities and Equity	1994
Current assets		*Current liabilities*	
Cash on hand	$ 19	Demand bank loan	$2,205
Cash in bank	238	Other bank indebtedness	840
Accounts receivable	2,868	Accounts payable, accruals	1,948
Inventories	2,916	Income, other taxes payable	213
Prepaid expenses	184		$5,206
	$6,225		

continued next page

		Noncurrent liabilities	
Noncurrent assets		Mortgage payable	$ 516
Land cost	$ 416	Loans from shareholders	600
Automotive equipment cost	892	Other long-term loans	318
Buildings cost	2,411	Deferred income tax	248
Equipment cost	1,020	Estimated pension liability	163
	$ 4,739		$ 1,845
Accumulated amortization	863	*Shareholders' equity*	
	$ 3,876	Share capital	$ 1,000
Investments, cost	740	Retained earnings	2,790
	$ 4,616		$ 3,790
TOTAL	$10,841	TOTAL	$10,841

TGIF Industries Ltd.
Statement of Changes in Financial Position
for the Year Ended December 31, 1995
(in thousands of dollars)

Operations:		
Net income for the year		$ 614
Add expenses (deduct revenues) not involving cash:		
Amortization expense	$ 291	
Loss on sale of investments	85	
Deferred income tax expense	68	
Estimated pension expense	53	
Gain on sale of land	(210)	
Gain on sale of building	(38)	249
Add (deduct) effects of changes in noncash working capital:		
Accounts receivable	$ 1,134	
Inventories	647	
Prepaid expenses	37	
Other bank indebtedness	(360)	
Accounts payable, accruals	(587)	
Income, other taxes payable	(14)	857
Cash generated by operations		$ 1,720
Dividends paid		(40)
Investing activities:		
Proceeds from sales of long-term assets:		
Investments (cost $560)	$ 475	
Land (cost $80)	290	
Building (cost $890)	514	
Cost of acquisitions of long-term assets:		
New building	(1,670)	
New equipment	(643)	(1,034)

continued next page

Financing activities:		
Payments on mortgage	$ (103)	
Additional loans from shareholders	250	
Debenture debt issued	300	
Payments of other long-term loans	(71)	
Payments of employee pensions	(43)	
Share capital issued	250	580
Increase in cash and cash equivalents		$1,226
Reconciliation of changes in cash and cash equivalents:		
Increase in cash on hand	$ 6	
Decrease in cash in bank	(17)	
Increase in term deposits asset	100	
Decrease in demand bank loan	1,137	
Increase in cash and cash equivalents	$1,226	

PROBLEM 4.14 Prepare a SCFP from summarized information

(Challenging) Here are the summarized 1996 and 1995 balance sheets for Saint John Enterprises Inc., showing the changes calculated by subtracting 1995 from 1996. Using them and the additional information below, prepare the SCFP for 1996.

	1996	1995	Changes
Cash equivalent assets	$ 17,400	$ 14,300	$3,100
Other current assets	164,100	123,500	40,600
Noncurrent assets, net	319,800	286,200	33,600
	$501,300	$424,000	$77,300
Cash equivalent liabilities	$ 11,200	$ 9,100	$ 2,100
Other current liabilities	117,900	90,600	27,300
Noncurrent liabilities	174,800	175,300	(500)
Share capital	80,000	60,000	20,000
Retained earnings	117,400	89,000	28,400
	$501,300	$424,000	$77,300

Additional information:

- The 1996 net income was $38,400.
- Dividends declared during the year were $10,000.
- $1,500 of the dividends are still unpaid at the end of 1996 (there had been none unpaid at the end of 1995).
- There was an expense in 1996 for deferred income tax, recorded by increasing the noncurrent income tax liability by $8,800.
- Some of the noncurrent liabilities were paid off during the year.
- During the year, the company sold for $8,400 a truck that cost $25,000 and had accumulated amortization of $17,300. There was thus a gain on sale of

$700 (proceeds of $8,400 – book value of $7,700 ($25,000 – $17,300). The gain on sale was part of the net income for the year.

- Amortization expense for the year, shown on the income statement and added to the accumulated amortization account on the balance sheet (thereby reducing the net figure for noncurrent assets), was $37,700.
- Acquisitions of noncurrent assets came to $79,000 for the year.

PROBLEM 4.15 Prepare and comment on a more complex SCFP

(Challenging) Using the following comparative balance sheets and additional information for Prairie Products Inc., prepare an SCFP for the year ended November 30, 1995. (*Note*: depending on your assumptions, different SCFPs are quite possible!) Comment on what your SCFP shows about the company's cash management for 1995.

Prairie Products Inc.
Balance Sheet at November 30, 1995
with 1994 Figures for Comparison
(in thousands of dollars)

Assets	**1995**	**1994**	**Liabilities and Equity**	**1995**	**1994**
Current assets			*Current liabilities*		
Cash	$ 31	$ 38	Demand bank loan	$ 25	$ 30
Marketable securities	100	200	Accounts payable	195	284
Accounts receivable	281	315	Taxes payable	34	20
Inventories	321	239	Dividends payable	20	30
Prepaid expenses	12	18		$ 274	$ 364
	$ 745	$ 810	*Noncurrent liabilities*		
Noncurrent assets			Mortgage payable	$ 240	$ 280
Land cost	$ 182	$ 70	Bonds payable	200	0
Buildings cost	761	493	Deferred income tax	138	111
Equipment cost	643	510	Warranty liability	126	118
	$1,586	$1,073		$ 704	$ 509
Accum. amortization	631	569	*Shareholders' equity*		
	$ 955	$ 504	Share capital	$ 600	$ 450
Investments, cost	365	438	Retained earnings	487	429
	$1,320	$ 942		$1,087	$ 879
TOTAL	$2,065	$1,752	TOTAL	$2,065	$1,752

Additional information (all figures are in thousands of dollars):

a. During 1995, net income was $98 and dividends of $40 were declared.

b. During the year, a building was sold for $42 that had cost $110 and had accumulated amortization of $56. The loss was deducted on the income statement.

c. Amortization expense for the year was $118.

d. During the year, one of the noncurrent investments, which had cost \$73, was sold for \$102. The gain was included in income.

e. The change in deferred income tax liability was entirely due to the deferred portion of income tax expense.

f. The change in warranty liability was composed of warranty expense of \$23 minus payouts on warranties of \$15.

g. It has been determined that the bank loan is really not payable on demand, but has an agreed repayment schedule extending over the year 1996. Therefore, it should not be considered a cash equivalent liability.

PROBLEM 4.16 "What if" questions involving the SCFP

(Challenging)

By making certain business decisions or choosing the location of items in their financial statements, companies may be able to alter the "story" the SCFP tells. For each action or choice below, explain what effect (if any) would result in the SCFP for the present year (including the cash and cash equivalents figures put at the bottom of the SCFP) if the action or choice happened.

1. Company A decides to borrow \$100,000 in a demand bank loan instead of as a long-term loan.
2. Company B decides to classify \$50,000 of its accounts receivable as long-term assets instead of current assets.
3. Company C decides to buy land for \$500,000, arranging for 100% long-term debt financing instead of by issuing new share capital.
4. Company D decides to increase its depreciation expense for this year by \$75,000.
5. Company E decides to declare a \$40,000 dividend to shareholders payable immediately in cash.
6. Company F decides to donate \$25,000 to the Poor Accountants' League (which donation will be included with business expenses).

PROBLEM 4.17 Interpret trends in cash management

(Challenging)

Apex Accessories Inc. makes, imports, and sells various goods for the fashion trade, including costume jewellery, belts and other leather goods, hats, and many kinds of apparel. The business is both seasonal and very unstable, with products coming and going as fashions and availability from foreign suppliers change. During a very interesting "business issues" TV program about the fashion industry, some of Apex's financial results were displayed in an on-screen table, while a narrator gushed about the marvellous management the company had. Here is that table:

Year	Year-end total assets	Year-end total bank borrowing	Net income for the year	Year's cash flow from operations
1986	$24,400,000	$8,300,000	$2,100,000	$3,200,000
1987	29,100,000	9,600,000	2,400,000	3,900,000
1988	28,500,000	8,900,000	2,300,000	3,200,000
1989	34,700,000	10,300,000	2,600,000	2,500,000
1990	37,800,000	12,000,000	2,800,000	2,200,000
1991	35,400,000	14,100,000	3,000,000	1,800,000
1992	37,000,000	14,200,000	3,100,000	3,800,000
1993	39,600,000	15,200,000	3,300,000	3,400,000
1994	43,000,000	16,400,000	3,200,000	2,800,000
1995	45,700,000	18,500,000	3,400,000	1,900,000

1. Which column of figures do you suppose the narrator was referring to when gushing about the "marvellous management"?
2. Provide as many comments as you can about the company's results. Do you think the management is marvellous?
3. For this particular company (which is listed on a stock exchange), would you expect market traders to respond much to the cash flow information once they know the net income figures? Put another way, do you think the cash flow information has any added value to the net income information?

PROBLEM 4.18 Ethics of cash flow manipulation

(Challenging) There is an interesting ethical issue behind the very reason the cash flow statement is thought by some people to have advantages over the income statement. The reason is that people are often mistrustful of the income statement, because they feel its accrual accounting methods can be used to manipulate net income as a measure of performance, and think that the cash flow figures are more "real." For example, a company might claim large revenues, not yet collected, that make its income higher (via the entry DR Accounts receivable, CR Revenue), but if the cash has not been collected, the increase in accounts receivable will be deducted from net income on the SCFP, and the lack of "real" cash inflow will be apparent because cash from operations will be lower than would be expected from the income number. Thus, it is thought, the SCFP's cash from operations figure is more believable than net income and even, if it is too different from net income, will unmask manipulations of the net income.

The ethical issue is that it is possible to manipulate the cash flow figures too. For example, a company might accelerate or delay receivables collections in order to change the cash flow figures, whether or not the net income is also being manipulated. There may be a difference from manipulating net income, because changing cash flow figures requires real actions, affecting customers or suppliers or employees, so there are real consequences, such as irritating customers or having to offer inducements for early payment. Nevertheless, it can be done.

It seems that most people would feel that altering the accruals just to make net income better (or worse, or smoother) is ethically questionable. even if it is understandable because of the way management is evaluated and rewarded. But is altering the cash flow ethically questionable? Is there an ethical problem if management decides to put pressure on customers to accelerate collections and improve the company's cash position? Sounds like good management, not like manipulation.

Suggest two or three ways, not included above, by which operating, investing, or financing cash flows could be altered from their normal levels. For each, discuss whether, or under what conditions, you would think there is an ethical problem in such alteration.

PROBLEM 4.16 Prepare a full set of statements, including SCFP

(Challenging) Grandin Ltd. manufactures a single product and has revenue from related service activities. The company had been growing slowly but steadily until this year (1996), when revenue, especially from services, increased substantially.

The company's bookkeeper was part way through preparing the 1996 and 1995 financial statements and asked you for help in completing them. When you went to the company's offices you got the information below. Assume these figures are correct.

1. Prepare a set of statements, including a comparative balance sheet, income statement, and statement of retained earnings for 1996 and 1995.
2. Define "cash and cash equivalents" for Grandin.
3. Prepare a 1996 SCFP in the usual format. Note that the 1995 balance sheet is relevant to this task, but that the 1995 income and retained earnings statements are not, because they are for a period prior to the beginning of 1996.

	1996		1995	
Account Name	**Debit**	**Credit**	**Debit**	**Credit**
Accounts payable		$ 12,300		$ 8,900
Accounts receivable	$ 44,200		$ 21,300	
Accumulated amortization		36,000		32,000
Administrative expenses	14,600		11,900	
Bank loan—current		29,000		19,000
Cash	4,700		5,400	
Cost of goods sold	103,190		71,650	
Current income tax expense	5,200		3,000	
Deferred income tax expense	250		500	
Deferred income tax liability		4,350		4,100
Amortization	4,000		5,800	
Dividends paid	4,000		6,000	
Equipment	87,000		87,000	
Equipment financing		20,000		24,000
Income taxes payable		2,200		1,000
Interest expense	4,800		3,900	
Inventory	42,500		37,000	
Packaging and shipping expense	8,100		7,500	
Prepaid expenses	2,100		800	
Retained earnings—opening		37,500		33,300

continued next page

Revenue—product sales		163,290		116,250
Revenue—service		73,700		32,600
Service wage expense	69,500		28,200	
Share capital		25,000		25,000
Utilities expense	9,200		6,200	
	$403,340	$403,340	$296,150	$296,150

CASE 4A Comment on Microsoft's cash flow and financial condition

Microsoft Corporation is the world's largest computer software company, headquartered in the Seattle suburb of Bellevue, Washington. The 1993 financial statements (without notes) follow. Comment on the company's 1993 income and cash flow performance and on its resulting financial condition.

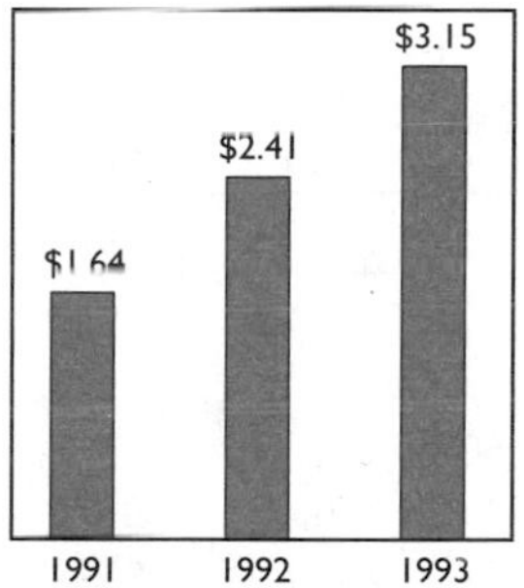

MICROSOFT CORPORATION

INCOME STATEMENT

(In millions, except earnings per share)	**Year Ended June 30**		
	1993	**1992**	**1991**
Net revenues	$3,753	$2,759	$1,843
Cost of revenues	633	467	362
Gross profit	3,120	2,292	1,481
Operating expenses:			
Research and development	470	352	235
Sales and marketing	1,205	854	534
General and administrative	119	90	62
Total operating expenses	1,794	1,296	831
Operating income	1,326	996	650
Interest income—net	82	56	37
Other	(7)	(11)	(16)
Income before income taxes	1,401	1,041	671
Provision for income taxes	448	333	208
Net income	$ 953	$ 708	$ 463
Earnings per share	$ 3.15	$ 2.41	$ 1.64
Weighted average shares outstanding	303	294	282

See accompanying notes. *(Not included)*

MICROSOFT CORPORATION
BALANCE SHEETS

(In millions)	June 30	
	1993	1992
Assets		
Current assets:		
Cash and short-term investments	$2,290	$1,345
Accounts receivable—net of allowances of $76 and $57	338	270
Inventories	127	86
Other	95	69
Total current assets	2,850	1,770
Property, plant, and equipment—net	867	767
Other assets	88	103
Total assets	$3,805	$2,640
Liabilities and stockholders' equity		
Current liabilities:		
Accounts payable	$ 239	$ 196
Accrued compensation	86	62
Income taxes payable	127	73
Other	111	116
Total current liabilities	563	447
Commitments and contingencies	—	—
Stockholders' equity:		
Common stock and paid-in capital—shares authorized 500; issued and outstanding 282 and 272	1,086	657
Retained earnings	2,156	1,536
Total stockholders' equity	3,242	2,193
Total liabilities and stockholders' equity	$3,805	$2,640

See accompanying notes. *(Not included)*

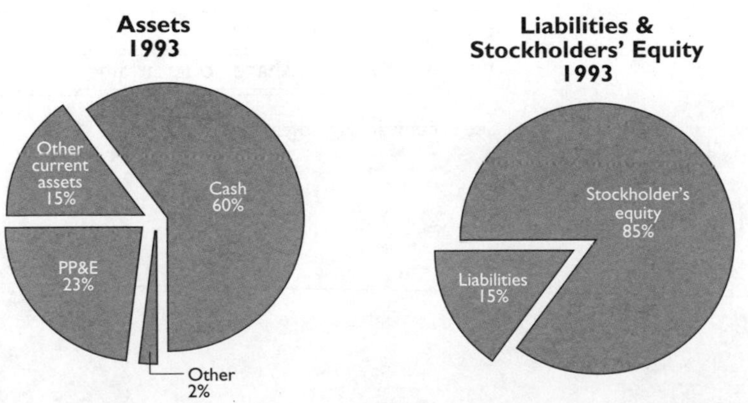

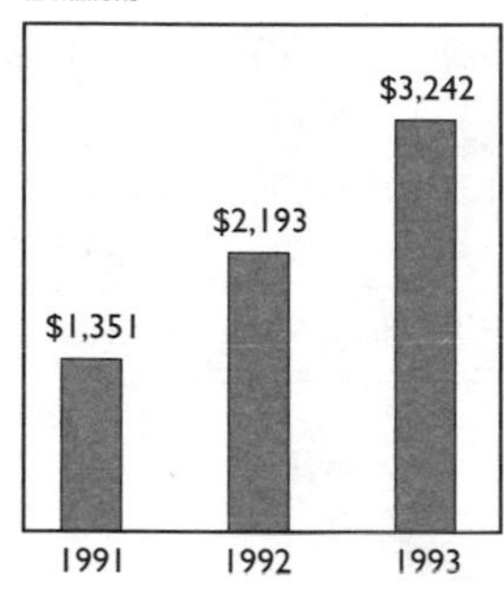

MICROSOFT CORPORATION
STATEMENTS OF STOCKHOLDERS' EQUITY

(In millions)	Year Ended June 30		
	1993	**1992**	**1991**
Common stock and paid-in capital			
Balance, beginning of year	$ 657	$ 395	$ 220
Common stock issued	229	135	95
Common stock repurchased	(7)	(3)	(5)
Stock option income tax benefits	207	130	85
Balance, end of year	1,086	657	395
Retained earnings			
Balance, beginning of year	1,536	956	699
Common stock repurchased	(243)	(132)	(192)
Net income	953	708	463
Translation adjustment	(90)	4	(14)
Balance, end of year	2,156	1,536	956
Total stockholders' equity	$3,242	$2,193	$1,351

See accompanying notes. *(Not included)*

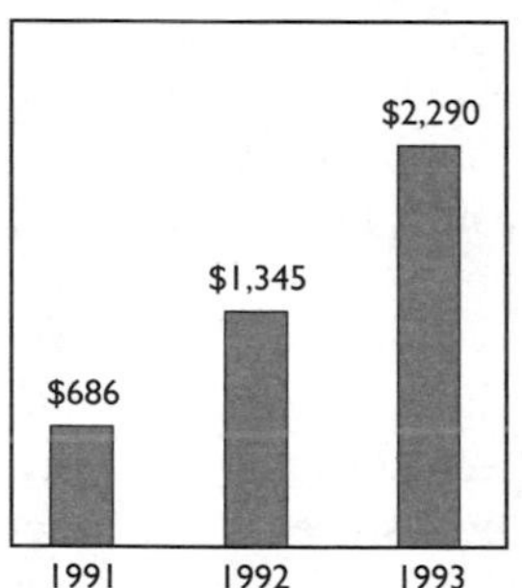

MICROSOFT CORPORATION
CASH FLOWS STATEMENTS

(In millions)	Year Ended June 30		
	1993	**1992**	**1991**
Cash flows from operations			
Net income	$ 953	$ 708	$463
Depreciation and amortization	151	112	76
Current liabilities	177	167	107
Accounts receivable	(121)	(33)	(65)
Inventories	(51)	(40)	8
Other current assets	(35)	(18)	(18)
Net cash from operations	1,074	896	571
Cash flows from financing			
Common stock issued	229	135	95
Common stock repurchased	(250)	(135)	(197)
Stock option income tax benefits	207	130	85
Net cash from financing	186	130	(17)
Cash flows used for investments			
Additions to property, plant, and equipment	(236)	(317)	(264)
Other assets	(17)	(41)	(40)

continued next page

CASH FLOWS STATEMENTS CONTINUED			
Short-term investments	(723)	(284)	(77)
Net cash used for investments	(976)	(642)	(381)
Net change in cash and equivalents	284	384	173
Effect of exchange rates	(62)	(10)	(2)
Cash and equivalents, beginning of year	791	417	246
Cash and equivalents, end of year	1,013	791	417
Short-term investments	1,277	554	269
Cash and short-term investments	$2,290	$1,345	$686

See accompanying notes. (*Not included*)

REPRODUCED COURTESY OF MICROSOFT, ANNUAL REPORT, JUNE 30, 1993.

CASE 4B Discuss the article on cash flow effects and the SCFP

Discuss the author's claims for the importance of cash flow assessment, criticisms of the SCFP, and proposals for improvement in it and in the income statement. Are any other points about cash flow and/or the strengths and weaknesses of the SCFP raised in your mind by the article?

COMPANIES IN CONVALESCENCE

Small changes to the financial statements can reveal a patient's chance of recovery

Despite the oversupply of headlines shouting to the contrary, not all companies are desperately ill. Indeed, a whole new category of company has appeared on the scene, one that consists of firms in various stages of recovery from the trauma of recession. They are, so to speak, the convalescents, and at the moment one can find plenty of them in the *Survey of Industrials* and in every lending officer's loan portfolio.

When companies emerge from a bad bout with the recession, cash flow (both as a measure of returning health and a major function of the business) counts more than book profits. The reason is simple: With bank lines stretched taut and sales hard to come by, the critical question is whether the debt can be properly serviced. And debt service is obviously a function of cash flow, not book profits.

Unfortunately, standard financial statements do not focus enough attention on the ramifications of cash flow. This is partly because it is a long-standing habit of financial statement readers to pay close attention to net profits and not much else. Such habits are easy to confirm. Simply note where the media place emphasis: Revenue, net income and debt are the usual topics covered in the business press.

Cash flow is also neglected, in part, because of changes made in 1985 to the statement that ought to tell us all about cash, "The statement of changes in financial position" (*CICA Handbook* Section 1540, also known as the "cash flow statement"). One item in particular, changes in noncash working capital, has been confusing accountants and non-accountants ever since its introduction. As it stands, the statement fails to answer the most important question of all: Is the company generating cash or consuming it? The current form of presentation may actually conceal significant improvement or deterioration in operations. For example, if the sales of a convalescing company improve, the welcome and inevitable increase in inventories and receivables appears in an unfavourable light as a use of cash. The opposite also applies. If sales decline, the consequential liquidation of inventories and receivables appears

BALANCE SHEET

Assets	
Current	$2,000,000
Fixed, net	3,000,000
Total assets	$5,000,000
Liabilities	
Current	
Bank	$2,000,000
Payables	1,000,000
Total current	$3,000,000
Term debt	$1,500,000
Total liabilities	$4,500,000
Equity	500,000
Total liabilities and equity	$5,000,000

INCOME STATEMENT

Sales	$5,000,000
Gross margin	1,500,000
Operating expenses	1,700,000
Net profit (Loss)	$(200,000)

REVISED INCOME STATEMENT

Sales	$5,000,000
Gross margin	1,500,000
Operating expense	1,000,000
EBIDT (Earnings before interest, depreciation and taxes)	500,000
Depreciation	370,000
Interest	330,000
Net income (Loss)	$ (200,000)

as a contribution to cash—even though the decline in sales may be catastrophic.

Another drawback to the present format is that EBIDT, "earnings before interest, depreciation and taxes," is not reported anywhere within the statements as a separate line item. Yet IBIDT is a prime measure of the profitability of operating the business, as opposed to managing the balance sheet or financing the business.

In many companies, the assets produce comfortable returns which are then destroyed or greatly reduced by the interest spawned by excessive debt. Keeping the results of these two functions (operations and financing) separate is, I submit, essential to real understanding.

EBIDT is fundamental to assessing the stress that debt places on a company. From EBIDT, the reader may readily (1) gain a sense of how protracted the stress is likely to be, (2) estimate the worth of the assets on an earnings basis, and (3) consider what resources will be available for expansion in due course.

Because of the undue attention paid by most readers to the bottom line, changes should be made to both the statement of cash flow and to the income statement. For the statement of cash flow, two changes are in order. First, "Changes in noncash working capital" should become the last item on the statement. This removes it from the operating section where, as already mentioned, it frequently emits misleading signals. Second, the beginning entry in the section "Cash flow from operations" should be changed from net income or loss to EBIDT. This item can be picked up readily by the reader from the income statement and will reinforce attention on this critical element of the financial statements. Interest would then be deducted as a separate line item.

In the income statement, operating profit is usually a line item, net of depreciation and amortization. Especially in smaller companies, depreciation and amortization may (albeit with a line of their own) be buried within the list of operating expenses. If, instead of this presentation, EBIDT became a mandatory disclosure, it would provide a much-needed focal point on the statement.

These are small changes, but their effect is to enhance the ordinary reader's comprehension of the company. Consider the example shown on the previous page. It begins with a typical balance sheet that has taken a turn for the worse. Obviously, the company is far from healthy. The debt ratio is nine to one. The current ratio is .66. Each ratio is badly out of line.

The income statement looks just as bad. Together, they offer a major dose of pessimism.

Now consider what happens when this statement is modified to isolate interest and depreciation.

A glance at the income statement reveals that the company, despite a serious book loss, is actually generating a substantial $500,000 in cash. The impact of the statement is clearly greater. Interest-bearing debt out of the $4,500,000 of total liabilities is $3,500,000. This is the critical liability. A little calculation indicates just how powerful cash flow—as opposed to book profits—can be. The company will continue to show a loss, but in five years virtually $1,000,000 will come off the interest-carrying debt. This would not restore the company to full health, but at least management would be sleeping a little easier at night.

Naturally, capital expenditures would have to be severely restricted throughout the recovery period (bearing in mind that a company can seldom avoid all capital spending). Nevertheless, revealing the power of the cash flow to those concerned with the patient may be considered important therapy. In some cases, it may be the difference between life and death.

SOURCE: IVAN KILPATRICK, "COMPANIES IN CONVALESCENCE," *CA MAGAZINE* (APRIL) 1993, 18–19.

NOTE

1. For more information on the "cash flow" research results, see W.H. Beaver, *Financial Reporting: An Accounting Revolution*, 2nd ed. (Englewood Cliffs, N.J.: Prentice–Hall, 1989), 116; or P.A. Griffin, ed., *Usefulness to Investors and Creditors of Information Provided by Financial Reporting*, 2nd ed. (Stamford, Conn.: Financial Accounting Standards Board, 1987), 144–45. Accounting research journals such as *The Accounting Review, Contemporary Accounting Research, Journal of Accounting and Economics*, and *Journal of Accounting Research* occasionally have articles examining cash flow or comparing cash flow to accrual net income.

Financial Reporting, Accounting Principles, and Auditing

5.1 Chapter Overview

You have now seen the four financial statements forming the standard set that is the main product of financial accounting. To round out your understanding of the statements, this chapter introduces you to the system of principles and rules that govern the way the financial statement figures are calculated and presented: **generally accepted accounting principles** (GAAP). Three topics will be connected to GAAP: the **annual report** issued by larger companies, containing the set of financial statements and much more; the presence of an **auditors' report** to add credibility to the financial statements; and examples of specific accounting principles for balance sheet values, corporate groups, and not-for-profit organizations.

To provide a foundation for the rest of the book, in this chapter you will learn:

Use concepts: more about how the demand for regularity and quality in the preparation and presentation of financial statements arises from the concerns of the wide variety of people who rely on them in their decision-making;

Preparation concepts: what the important concepts are behind determining the numbers in the financial statements and the general set of written standards and general practices called GAAP, and how these concepts and standards have developed to meet the demand for good accounting information;

Preparation techniques: how to apply GAAP to the problem of which numbers to report for assets and other financial statement items, so that the results will be credible and fair, including how to understand combined financial statements for corporate groups;

Use techniques: an understanding of how GAAP have been applied in producing financial statements; this provides a basis for the use-oriented analysis emphasized in later chapters.

5.2 The Annual Report and the Set of Financial Statements

Financial reporting is important for many organizations. All incorporated companies, and most other legally constituted organizations, are required to prepare a set of financial statements at least annually, explaining their financial performance and position. **Public companies**, which are those whose shares are traded on a stock exchange or in more informal "over-the-counter" markets, usually also issue some interim or quarterly financial information, especially on the subject of earnings. Most proprietorships and partnerships also prepare annual financial statements, at their bankers' request or for inclusion with the proprietor's or partners' income tax returns, even if there are no other reasons for doing so.

The standard set of financial statements has five components:

1. Balance sheet (statement of financial position);
2. Income statement;
3. Statement of retained earnings;
4. Statement of changes in financial position (cash flow statement);
5. Notes to the financial statements.

A sixth item accompanies the financial statements and notes: the **auditors' report** on the fairness of the set. The contents of the statements and its notes are the responsibility of management, and the auditors' report consists of the auditors' opinion about those statements and notes. You should be skeptical of financial statements that have not been audited or those whose audit report is not attached.

Public companies and other organizations include their set of financial statements in a much larger **annual report**. This report usually contains (in approximately the following order):

1. Summary data on the company's performance for the year, usually in a graphical or other easy-to-read form, and comparisons going back five or ten years;
2. A letter to the shareholders from the company's chief executive officer, who is usually its president or chairperson of the board of directors;
3. An often extensive "management discussion and analysis," including a description of the economic, financial, and other factors behind the company's business, usually broken down by its main products or departments;
4. A short section explaining that the financial statements and the general internal control of the business are the responsibility of management;
5. The set of financial statements and the auditors' report;
6. Various details about the company's legal status, names of its directors and officers, and other information the company thinks is important.

In an article about the annual report, a leading Canadian accountant commented:

> Although recent years have ushered in many changes in corporate financial reporting...the annual report remains the centrepiece of the whole reporting process....The world of financial reporting is changing. Recognition of users' needs has expanded such reporting far beyond the financial statements.[1]

Many people besides the company's accountants and the external auditors are involved in preparing the annual report. The top managers set its tone, and advertising and public relations staff design its presentation, often using photos and attractive graphs. Overall, the annual report can be quite a fancy document, and 50 or more pages long! Here are some comments about annual reports:

> At one time, annual reports were little more than a collection of financial numbers in a stapled booklet. Today, they've become full-blown magazine efforts, with...as much information and pizzazz as they can pack between two covers...[reflecting] the image the firm wants to project.[2]

> [People] want more, more, more [information]. But some things don't change, such as the need for honest, candid interpretation of company performance presented in such a way the average person can understand it.[3]

> Annual reports—the yearly report card, photo album, and corporate promo in one. Some trumpet the successes of the 12 months past, real or not. Others just trumpet.[4]

> McDonald's is serving up something new to its stockholders—a McVideo annual report.... Its yearly printed narrative on the company's performance will be shipped to shareholders with a 17-minute video cassette.... Shareholders who prefer their annual reports the traditional way can flip through a written version that includes a transcript of the video.[5]

If you have not seen an annual report, you might find it interesting to browse through one. Most libraries have some examples, and most public companies will make theirs available on request. At the back of this book are the complete 1994 financial statements and notes of The North West Company Inc., plus the auditors' report, a summary of management's responsibility for the financial statements, and a multi-year summary of the financial statements. All these are taken from the company's 1994 annual report. The financial highlights section of that report is in the next section.

5.3 ACCOUNTING PRINCIPLES AND THE USE OF ACCOUNTING INFORMATION

Financial accounting has a surprisingly large set of concepts and principles to guide accountants in preparing financial statements, auditors in verifying them, and users in interpreting them. A very large amount has been written about the conceptual and theoretical side of accounting, and as we saw near the end of Section 3.2 of Chapter 3, several groups are involved in setting financial accounting standards and otherwise regulating accounting information.

All this material occupies many metres of library shelves and much space in computer databases. This section will give you a glimpse of the conceptual structure behind financial accounting, by focusing on some concepts of particular value to the users of accounting information. These concepts have been deduced by accountants, researchers, and standard-setters from logic and observation of good practices, and they are used to guide everyone who prepares, audits, uses, and studies financial accounting.

A phrase often used in respect to accounting's conceptual structure is **generally accepted accounting principles (GAAP)**. GAAP are the rules, standards, and usual practices that companies are expected to follow in preparing their financial statements. They are a combination of the authoritative standards issued by accounting standard-setters (such as the CICA Accounting Standards Board in Canada and the Financial Accounting Standards Board in the United States) and the accepted ways of doing accounting that are not included in such standards. Year by year, the set of authoritative standards gets larger, but the world continues to increase in complexity, so the standards never are extensive enough to include everything. Probably they should not try to cover everything, even if the standard-setters could catch up to every problem: then financial accounting would become just a boring, inflexible collection of rules.

The development of GAAP can be traced back to the evolution of financial accounting, as well as to the efforts of standard-setting bodies that attempted to improve accounting principles and practices by increasing the authoritative, documented part of GAAP. Until this century was well along, authoritative accounting standards did not exist. As noted in Chapter 3, the catalyst that produced increased financial disclosure and brought more rules governing it was the stock market crash of 1929. Poor **financial reporting** and **disclosure** were seen as contributing to the crash. It was argued that had investors been better informed, they could have made sounder financial decisions, thus preventing the stock market collapse and its harmful economic and social consequences. Canadian GAAP grew out of:

1. Legislation governing the incorporation of Canadian companies, which made incorporation contingent upon greater financial disclosure;
2. The establishment by provincial governments of provincial securities commissions, with their rules requiring companies trading on provincial stock markets to file audited financial statements; and
3. The development of independent professional accounting bodies, such as the Canadian Institute of Chartered Accountants, which has taken upon itself the job of determining financial accounting standards for Canada that auditors and others could use to evaluate the appropriateness of financial statements.

In Canada, the main source of the authoritative part of GAAP is the ***CICA Handbook***, a looseleaf package hundreds of pages long (quite a handful!) that is continuously updated to reflect the standard-setters' judgments about how to deal with ever-changing circumstances. The *Handbook* consists of various discussions of accounting (and auditing) topics, accompanied by "Recommendations" on what to do in those cases that the standard-setters have resolved. If the *Handbook*'s recommendation on a particular issue is not followed, that is likely to be seen as not following GAAP; however, the *Handbook* recognizes that its recommendations cannot cover everything and that there may even be circumstances where following them would be misleading. Therefore, accountants and auditors must exercise their professional judgment about each accounting issue: they cannot just ignore the *Handbook*, but neither can they just follow it if it does not apply appropriately to the issue. The overriding criterion is that the financial statements should present the company's financial affairs *fairly*. **Fairness** is a fundamental criterion in judging whether financial statements do, or should, follow GAAP: we will see it again shortly.

Well, let's bring all this down to earth. The "Financial Highlights" section of the 1994 annual report of The North West Company Inc. is shown in Exhibit 5.1. The company operates retail stores across northern Canada and

Exhibit 5.1

(in thousands)	*52 weeks ended January 29, 1994*	*53 weeks ended January 30, 1993*	*52 weeks ended January 25, 1992*
Results for the Year			
Sales and other revenue	$548,679	$472,710	$410,879
Earnings from continuing operations before interest and income taxes and unusual items	38,054	33,371	32,054
Earnings from operations	17,162	14,954	12,923
Financial Position			
Total assets	$331,055	$298,412	$242,214
Shareholders' equity	147,652	135,346	94,132
Per share ($)			
Fully diluted earnings for the year	1.06	1.05	0.93
Cash dividends	0.36	0.36	0.32
Shareholders' equity	9.13	8.41	6.88
Financial Ratios			
Return on net assets from continuing operations*	14.9%	16.2%	17.2%
Return on average equity	12.3%	14.6%	14.9%

*Pre-tax earnings plus interest as a percent of average net assets employed.

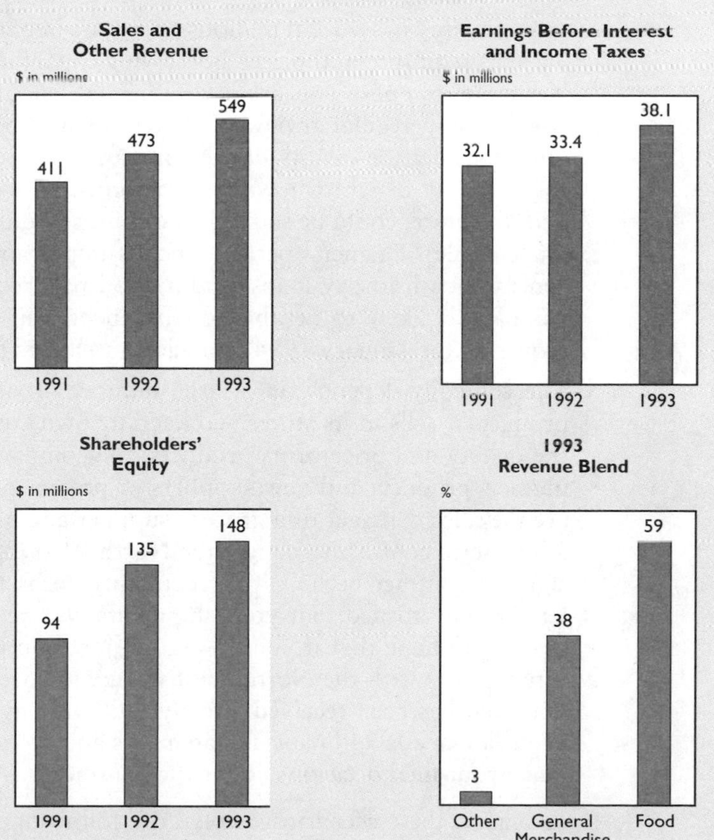

REPRODUCED COURTESY OF THE NORTH WEST COMPANY, ANNUAL REPORT, JANUARY 29, 1994.

Alaska. Appendix A includes the complete 1994 financial statements from the 1994 annual report, plus other information about the company. You might find it useful to read the "Profile" at the front of that material now.

INFORMATION USE SCENARIOS

Let's consider some possible users of the financial statements summarized in these highlights:

a. The company's **board of directors** manages the company on behalf of the shareholders. One function of the board that involves the financial statements is hiring the company's top operating management, especially the president and chief executive officer (CEO). Suppose you are a member of the board and are preparing for a discussion at the next board meeting. The board evaluates the CEO's performance continuously, which is its responsibility. The January 1994 financial statements have been provided to the board prior to the meeting, and will be a major input to this evaluation.

b. The company's shares are listed (that is, can be bought and sold) on the Toronto and Winnipeg stock exchanges. Suppose you are a financial analyst for a Canadian investment dealer and are preparing a report projecting future earnings and making recommendations about whether the company's shares are worthwhile to buy, or to keep if already held, or instead should be sold. You have the January 1994 financial statements and will use them as support to your report.

c. The company has several millions of dollars in bank borrowing and has lines of credit (pre-authorized borrowing capability) for millions of dollars more. Suppose you are a commercial lending officer for a bank, conducting a regular review of the company's borrowing status. You must consider the quality of the company's financial performance and assets (many of which have been assigned as security on bank loans and, therefore, could be seized if the company didn't pay its loans back on schedule). Financial performance is important because net income generates cash to pay loans, and a good past record suggests that the company is likely to be able to earn income in the future. You have requested the January 1994 financial statements to use in your review.

d. The company depends on a large number of suppliers to obtain the products it sells in its stores. To keep its own customers satisfied with the quality and price of its products, the company is always considering new products and new suppliers of present products. Suppose you are the sales manager of a grocery supplier and are considering signing a long-term contract to supply the North West Company. You want to sign the contract because your company needs the business, but you have to be satisfied that your shipments will be paid for. More positively, you hope that if you do a good job, you will have an opportunity to grow with the North West Company. Most of the information you need has been received already, but you have obtained the North West January 1994 financial statements and are reviewing them as you make your final decisions about the contract.

In summary, these scenarios involve the following reasons for using the January 1994 financial statements of the North West Company Inc.:

a. Evaluation of the CEO's performance by a member of the board of directors;
b. Preparation of "buy," "sell" or "hold" recommendations by a financial analyst;
c. Review of the company's borrowing status by a bank lending officer;
d. Development of a supply contract with the company by a grocery supplier's sales manager.

These scenarios have been chosen to add to your insight into the use of financial accounting information. They are not complete. In all cases, the financial statements would be only part of the set of information used in the decision-making. Also, there are many other uses of financial statements, some of which might make different demands on the quality of the information than are discussed here.

DEMANDS ON THE QUALITY OF FINANCIAL ACCOUNTING INFORMATION

Let's think about what the users in these scenarios might reasonably expect of the financial statements. You'll see that important accounting concepts and principles arise. Those are described in italics below.

1. The financial statements should not be deliberately misleading. The bank loans officer would want to feel confident that the statements were not prepared in such a way as to make the company appear to be a better lending risk than it is. The board of directors similarly would want the statements to provide an objective portrayal of the CEO's performance in running the company.

   *This is the criterion of **fairness**. It is so important that the auditors' report refers to it explicitly. The auditors state their opinion that the financial statements "present fairly" the company's financial position and results. There is sufficient flexibility and judgment involved in financial accounting, so that the auditors cannot say that the statements are* correct, *but they can testify to their fairness. A very important fairness-related criterion for choosing accrual accounting methods is **matching**: revenues and expenses should be determined using compatible methods so that the net income (which is revenues minus expenses) makes sense. Matching is central to many accounting methods, including those for income tax, inventory and cost of goods sold, amortization, pensions, and warranties. We will see it again in Chapters 7 and 10 especially.*

2. Preparing financial statements, like any other activity, costs money and takes time. Most people would be satisfied if the statements were fair as to the important things and would not mind a few minor errors in them, especially if preventing small errors cost the company money (reducing the company's income and cash flow) or delayed the release of the statements. The grocery sales manager would not want to wait for the statements while North West's accountants changed the cost of the company's inventory of unsold string (part of the multi-million-dollar balance sheet inventory account) to \$1,199 from \$1,189.

   *This is the criterion of **materiality** (significance). Financial statements are supposed to be materially fair, so that users can be confident that the state-*

ments do not contain major errors. Materiality is also explicitly mentioned in the auditors' report: the auditors say that the statements present fairly, "in all material respects," or words to that effect. Just what is or is not material is a matter of judgment and has been the subject of considerable research and study by accountants and auditors. Usually, people judge materiality by considering the size of a possible error compared to the net income or the total assets. For example, an accountant or auditor might judge that an error over 5% of net income or 1% of total assets is material and a smaller one is not. But, as you might expect, the materiality judgment depends on any particular uses of the information that are expected, and on whether the error seems to be a unique random problem or part of a repeated pattern of mistakes, or even fraud.

3. The criteria of fairness and materiality imply some standard against which an accounting method or number can be judged. The financial analyst would like to know that North West's financial statements were materially fair, given accepted current methods. In the income statement, for example, sales revenue should mean what a knowledgeable analyst or other user would expect for such a company. The company is actually a group of companies, so its financial statements are consolidated, and it would be reasonable to expect that the company's method of calculating consolidated figures was proper.

   This is where GAAP come in. To assure the users that accepted methods have been followed, the auditors' report also says that the auditors' opinion is that the statements have been prepared in accordance with generally accepted accounting principles. This does not mean that one particular method has been followed: GAAP often include several acceptable methods, depending on the circumstances. Therefore, the auditors are saying that the company's accounting methods and the resulting figures are appropriate to its circumstances.

4. If accounting information is to tell people about the economic forces affecting the company and the business arrangements the company has made to deal with those forces, it should connect to such important underlying phenomena. A financial statement that is fair would also thus agree with these phenomena, and the auditors should be able to trace the accounting back to the phenomena to verify that the accounting does agree. The board of directors should be able to assume that the company's figure for sales revenue is supported by sales invoices, cash records, shipping records, and other evidence of actual sales.

   This is the criterion of ***reliability****. The financial statements should report the economic substance of events happening to the company, the numbers should be verifiable back to evidence of such events, and the numbers should measure the events neutrally, neither overstating nor understating their impact. (****Verifiability*** *involves being able to reconstruct the accounting numbers by checking evidence, identifying assumptions and estimates, and re-doing calculations.) The* CICA Handbook *observes that, in addition to this, it is prudent to be cautious when estimating uncertain amounts, such as future collections and the value of unsold inventory. This leads to another criterion,* ***conservatism****. This often-controversial criterion states that under uncertainty, assets, revenues, and income should* *not be overstated and liabilities, expenses, and losses should not be understated. Conservatism should involve being careful, not deliberately biasing important numbers, but just where prudence ends and bias begins is a matter of judgment.*

5. The previous criteria indicate that the financial statements necessarily reflect judgment on the part of the preparers. Also, the figures in the statements are summaries of many accounts: for example, "accounts receivable" and "long-term debt" may include dozens or thousands of different customers or creditors. The bank loan officer may want to know what sort of long-term debts the company has, so that those may be evaluated against the bank borrowing by the company. The bank would not want other creditors to interfere with the company's ability to pay the bank back. The financial analyst may want to know if the company has made commitments to issue more shares (such as in a plan to motivate senior management by issuing shares to them cheaply if they perform well), because those might reduce the equity of anyone buying the shares now.

   This raises the principle of ***disclosure****. The financial statements include a large number of notes and account descriptions intended to make it clear to the reader which important accounting methods have been followed (especially if those methods are not what might be expected) and to provide supplementary information on debts, share capital, commitments, lawsuits, and other things thought to be helpful, or necessary, in understanding the statements. Disclosure beyond the accounting figures is increasingly extensive: many pages of notes often accompany the set of statements, and companies disclose additional information to taxation authorities, to securities regulators (such as the Ontario Securities Commission and the U.S. Securities and Exchange Commission), and to important other parties who have a reason to get the information (such as the bank loan officer and the financial analyst).*

6. The banker and the financial analyst are also involved with other companies. They would like to be able to compare North West's financial statements to those of similar companies, such as other retail chains. It may be difficult to be sure that a company is performing well or badly in an absolute sense, but it can always be compared to others, as long as the financial statements have been prepared in a comparable way.

   You will not be surprised that this principle is called ***comparability****. It will be important when we review techniques for financial statement analysis in Chapter 9.*

7. The banker, the analyst, and the board of directors' member will also want to study the trend in financial performance and position over time. Is the net income improving over time, or deteriorating? How about liquidity? Or the ratio of debt to equity financing? As noted in Chapter 3, it is important to know if significant events have happened to make comparisons over time difficult or even impossible. It is also important to know if the company has changed its accounting methods over time, because such changes may affect the comparability of the accounting figures from year to year.

Keeping the same accounting methods over time is called **consistency**. *Until recently, the auditors' report said specifically whether the financial statements were prepared consistently, but now it is presumed that if the company is following GAAP, that includes using consistent methods or else telling the reader of the statements what the effects of changes in accounting methods are (if they are material).*

TRADEOFFS AMONG ACCOUNTING PRINCIPLES

If you think about the criteria and principles mentioned above (fairness, matching, materiality, conformance with GAAP, reliability, verifiability, conservatism, disclosure, comparability, and consistency), you may see that they do not always fit together well. Five examples:

- Conservatism is often argued to be a bias that interferes with fairness.
- As mentioned already, the *CICA Handbook* recognizes that conformance with GAAP may not mean fairness, if the circumstances are unusual.
- If some other companies with which a company is likely to be compared (such as others in its industry) change their accounting methods, the company has to decide whether to change its methods too for the sake of comparability, even though that means inconsistency in its own figures over time.
- Similarly, when a new or revised accounting standard is issued by the CICA or FASB, following the new standard (that is, conforming with GAAP as they now exist) will mean inconsistency over time for all companies that did not previously use the approved new method.
- It has been argued that it does not matter a great deal if a company's revenues and expenses are not properly matched, as long as the problem is disclosed. The idea is that users of the company's financial statements can adjust the results to improve the match, as long as the relevant information is available. (Some people agree with this idea, but most do not, partly because it is difficult to make such adjustments. Later chapters of this book have more about the "effects analysis" skill that such adjustments require. You can decide then if it is reasonable to expect users of financial statements to be able to do it!)

You might feel that GAAP are not very well constructed if such problems can happen. Others have certainly criticized GAAP for being inadequate and inconsistent. Many studies have been done to try to remove problems, including a multi-million-dollar study for the FASB called the "Conceptual Framework Project." That project was launched in the mid-1970s and was largely abandoned 10 years later. It appears that one framework, one way of thinking about financial statements, cannot deal with all the conflicting interests and priorities of the many users, preparers, and auditors. The inherent struggle and competition among people in our economic system tends to rule out single solutions, no matter how internally logical they may be, and the result is the rather imperfect but also flexible set of principles that make up GAAP. You might say there is something for everyone in GAAP, but not everything for anyone!

Here is an example of a trade-off that simply cannot be avoided.

- It would seem sensible that the more reliable the accounting information is, the better. You get more reliable information by being very careful about how you prepare it, checking it carefully, having the auditors come in and verify it, maybe even waiting until some major uncertainties are resolved, so you do not have to guess about them.
- It also seems sensible that decision makers need information relevant to their decisions when they are making the decisions. This means that information should be timely: people should not have to wait for the information they need. **Decision relevance** and **timeliness** are two more concepts behind GAAP, not mentioned above.

So, let's take the example of a company trying to report on its liability for pensions to employees. It has thousands of employees, who will retire at various times over the next 40 years, if they do not quit, die, or get fired first. The pension paid will depend on how much the employees earn before they retire, and that is not known yet for most of them—the younger ones' earnings are all in the future, and who knows what the future holds? The pension also depends on how long the employees live after they retire and on whether they will have surviving spouses to be supported as long as they will live. The company is trying to put aside enough money to cover all these pensions and will earn interest on the money saved for this purpose, so the amount of money required now depends on how much interest will be earned on it over the years before the employees retire.

How is that for a mass of uncertainty? Any number you come up with for the pension liability will be based on all sorts of estimates of unknown future events. So to get a liability figure that is at all reliable, you really have to wait 20 or 30 years until most of the employees have retired. You can always expect to get reliability by just waiting a while, even years, to see how things turn out. But waiting 20 or 30 years will hardly provide timely information, relevant to decisions like those being made by the board of directors, investment analyst, banker, and supplier mentioned above. Such decisions require the best information we can come up with now, even if it is necessarily based on estimates and assumptions. Therefore, there is almost never a solution that produces both the most reliable and the most timely, relevant accounting information. As time passes, reliability rises and timely relevance falls, so we have to try to find some mid-point where there is enough of both, but not as much as we would like of either.

SUMMARY

This section has illustrated decision settings using accounting information and identified some accounting principles that respond to those settings. There are many more principles, some of which will be mentioned as this book proceeds, but be sure you understand the ones described above and collected together in Exhibit 5.2 on the next page.

Exhibit 5.2

◆ fairness	◆ matching	◆ materiality
◆ conformance with GAAP	◆ reliability	◆ verifiability
◆ conservatism	◆ disclosure	◆ comparability
◆ consistency	◆ decision relevance	◆ timeliness

HOW'S YOUR UNDERSTANDING

Here are two questions you should be able to answer, based on what you have just read:

1. You have just opened the annual report of The North West Company Inc. and found that the auditors' report says that it is the auditors' opinion that the financial statements have been prepared in accordance with generally accepted accounting principles. What concepts of information value would the auditors have assumed as part of GAAP?
2. Can accounting numbers such as those in North West's financial statements and highlights be relevant, fair, and conservative all at once?

5.4 THE EXTERNAL AUDITORS' REPORT

Several references to the auditors were made above. The auditors' report is normally a routine statement by the auditors that says they find the statements to be fair. But if it is not routine, the auditors are trying to tell the users something they think is important. The auditors' report may be qualified in some way, indicating that the auditors have some concern about the statements; in extreme cases, the report may even "deny" the fairness of the statements, saying that the auditors have some very serious objection. (Often, smaller companies have something less than a full audit done. In such a case, instead of an auditors' report, there will be a letter from an accountant or accounting firm stating that somewhat less has been done: read such a letter carefully so that you know how much assurance the accountants are offering.)

Before we turn to some examples of applying GAAP to financial statement preparation and use, it will be useful to point out a few things about the auditors' role in financial reporting. (In the discussion below, the auditor will be referred to in the singular for simplicity. Most of the time, auditors are members of public accounting firms of auditors and related professionals, and so are often referred to in the plural, as the title of this section does.)

External auditing refers to the evaluation of an organization's financial statements by an auditor who is supposed to be unconnected with, and so, independent of, the management of the organization. The role of the external auditor has two fundamental parts:

- To have an independent, unbiased, and professional perspective; and
- To render a competent opinion on the fairness of the financial statements (given GAAP, as discussed in Section 5.3).

Many companies, governments, and other organizations also have *internal auditors*. Such auditors work within the organization and help management operate the organization. Their work is not dealt with in this book.

Let's begin with independence and professionalism. Auditors are members of professional associations, such as the Canadian Institute of Chartered Accountants and the corresponding provincial institutes, and, in the United States, the American Institute of Certified Public Accountants and corresponding state societies. Other professional accounting associations also have auditing components, such as the Certified General Accountants' Association of Canada and the Society of Management Accountants of Canada.

A fundamental objective of these professional associations is to protect society by ensuring the professionalism and independence of the external auditors who belong to them. Protecting society should be consistent with protecting the association's members' professional reputations. To this end, there are complex rules of professional ethics that prohibit the external auditor from having a financial interest, directly and in most indirect ways as well, in the client companies or other organizations being audited. These rules and similar ones related to other relationships between the auditor and the client are intended to ensure that the auditor has no personal interest in whether the financial statements report one kind of performance or another. In other words, the auditor should be an unbiased, professionally sceptical reviewer of the financial statements and not someone who wants the result to turn out one way or another.

Maintaining this independence is not easy because the auditors are business entrepreneurs themselves and their clients pay them for doing the audit. The idea is that independence is maintained because the auditor is appointed by, and reports to, the shareholders, not management. Since the financial statements are reports on management's stewardship performance, the auditor is presumed to be working for the shareholders in verifying management's reports. In practice, however, external auditors must have a close working relationship with client management.

Also, managers are in a strong position to recommend a change in auditor if the relationship is not to their liking. Maintaining independence under these circumstances is difficult and is complicated further by the fact that auditing (public accounting) firms offer nonauditing services, the revenue for which may exceed the fee for doing the audit. It is also complicated by the fact that if users of financial statements suffer losses, they can, and often do, sue the auditor, so the auditor must be very careful not to be compromised by the relationship with management.

The second part of the auditor's role is to render a competent opinion on the financial statements. If you refer to an audit report such as that for The North West Company Inc. at the back of this book, you will see that it says the auditors have reached an opinion as to the fairness of the financial statements, evaluated with reference to GAAP. It is an opinion, not a guarantee, nor does it say that the company has performed well or badly. It simply says that the performance and the position have been measured and presented in a generally accepted and unbiased way.

Given the complexity of accounting, auditing, and business in general, the auditor's opinion is fundamentally a professional judgment. The auditor must be competent but, in addition, must weigh all sorts of factors in determining whether the overall result is fair. Concerned about the quality of their judgment, auditing firms in North America have sponsored a great deal of research into the professional judgment of auditors.

An auditor tends to focus on issues that could have a significant effect on the financial statements (the materiality criterion), because it is considered by most people to be uneconomical to have the auditor concern herself or himself with the many small errors and irregularities that may crop up during the year. Auditors plan their work so that they have a reasonable likelihood of detecting material misstatements and errors. This criterion has been claimed by auditors to apply to fraud and misrepresentation by management or employees, and so only those instances of fraud that are large enough to materially affect the overall financial information should be caught by the external auditors. For a large company, one with a net income of $100,000,000 or more, that would have to be a very large case of fraud indeed—in the millions of dollars. In practice, however, many client companies wish their external auditors to assist them in protecting and controlling cash and other assets subject to theft or misappropriation, so the auditors often spend significantly more time verifying cash and other such assets than would be warranted by the size of such assets in the financial statements.

The external auditors' report on The North West Company Inc. accompanies the financial statements at the back of this book. The form and content of the auditors' report changes every few years, as auditors rethink how best to communicate with the users of financial statements. Because the auditors are formally reporting to the owners of the company, not to management, the report is usually specifically addressed to the owners (the shareholders). The latest standard version of the auditors' report has three paragraphs:

1. The first identifies the company and the set of statements and their date and states that they are the responsibility of management and that the auditors' responsibility is to express an opinion on them.
2. The second paragraph outlines what the auditors did to enable them to express an opinion, stating in particular that they followed generally accepted auditing procedures in assessing the accounting principles and estimates used by management.
3. The third paragraph states what the auditors' opinion is concerning the fairness of and adherence to generally accepted accounting principles of the statements (or, if there are problems, the lack thereof).

You should expect to find most auditors' reports to be worded pretty well the same. This sounds boring, but there is a purpose: any non-standard wording is likely to be a warning to anyone planning to use the financial statements in decision-making. For example, the first paragraph should cover all the statements you plan to use, prepared as of the date you expect. The second paragraph should say that the auditors followed **generally accepted auditing standards (GAAS)**. Any problems here, or restrictions on the evidence the auditors were able to examine, will be noted by the auditors and could be significant to you. The third paragraph should say that the auditors' opinion is that the statements are fair, in accordance with GAAP. There are three main exceptions to this *clean opinion*: a *qualified opinion*, when the auditors are generally satisfied except for a specified problem in doing their work or a specified departure from GAAP in the statements; an *adverse opinion*, when the auditors say that their opinion is that the financial statements are not presented fairly in accordance with GAAP; and *denial of an opinion*, when the auditors are unable to express an opinion either way because of a limitation in the work the auditors were able to do.

HOW'S YOUR UNDERSTANDING

Here are two questions you should be able to answer, based on what you have just read:

1. The external auditor's report on Alcan Aluminum Ltd. refers to "generally accepted auditing standards." Why is the auditor referring to GAAS?
2. The president of a small company recently said, "We need to have an external auditor for our financial statements so we can guarantee their accuracy to our bank." Will that be the result if an auditor is appointed?

5.5 THE NATURE OF A PROFESSION AND PROFESSIONAL ETHICS

Many of the people involved in financial accounting consider themselves to be professionals. Evolving systems of standards, such as GAAP and GAAS, work reasonably well partly because professionals, who are both expert and ethical, are involved. Ethical behaviour comes from personal standards plus various written-down codes of ethical conduct. Those who may be tempted not to be ethical know that severe penalties, including fines and even imprisonment, can result from unethical behaviour.

For many people today, there is strong concern about being professional. There are, however, certain occupations that have established status as the professions. In today's world some groups that have this status are physicians, lawyers, engineers, architects, and professional accountants.

Part of the reason these groups stand out is that entry into each of them requires a post-secondary education, including training and examination by practitioners, and members are bound by a code of conduct or professional ethics. Members of each professional group usually enjoy a monopoly in their particular area of expertise. Associations of architects, physicians, engineers, lawyers, and other members of legally recognized professions can all prevent people from calling themselves members of their particular professions and practising in that capacity. Such groups have to convince the public (as represented by governments, for example) that they have expertise and appropriate codes of ethical conduct, but also that entrance to their area of expertise should be regulated for the public good.

The provincial institutes of chartered accountants have the right to train students in that province to prepare them to write the national exam to become a Chartered Accountant (CA). There are two other accounting designations also generally protected in Canada: CGA (Certified General Accountant) and CMA (Certified Management Accountant). These two groups have provincial and national associations as do CAs, and they compete to a degree with CAs for clients. There are sometimes conflicts among the three bodies of accountants, particularly over the right to act as an external auditor. CAs can do so in every province, but CMAs and CGAs have more restricted rights. Federal laws also affect this; for example, banks must still be audited by CAs. In general, the larger the company the more likely a CA will be the auditor.

Plain, uncertified accountants do not enjoy the same powers or privileges that members of the above professions do. You, your friend, or anyone can all call yourselves "accountants." There are no restrictions preventing you or anyone else from advertising in the paper, yellow pages, or any other publication to attract clients. However, if you want to call yourself a CA, CGA, or CMA, you must meet various requirements, for they are professional designations protected by provincial law, as are other professional designations. For professional accountants, there are both powers and restrictions (for example, advertising must meet certain standards of content and decorum).

The rights that a particular profession enjoys come in return for promises made about the quality and ethics of its members' work. If a professional accountant has not lived up to the standards of conduct held by the profession, he or she can be reprimanded or expelled by the profession and/or sued in court. (Anyone can be sued, of course, but professionals are usually held to a higher standard of performance than are non-professionals.)

All told, being in a profession has many advantages (including service to society, monopoly over an area of work, collegial support, social prestige, and good pay), but one must remember that in return there is the social responsibility of discharging one's duties competently and in accordance with the profession's code of ethics. Professional codes of ethics involve not only behaving in a professional manner (for example, with integrity and objectivity), but also maintaining the level of expertise required in order to perform skilfully. This involves following procedures (often as set out in documents like the *CICA Handbook*) that will, or should, ensure that high standards of work and performance are met, and exercising informed judgment.

Here are examples of ethical problems that may be faced by professional accountants. What would you, as a member of society or as someone who may rely on accounting information or auditors' reports, think would be appropriate ethical behaviour in each case?

- Mary works for a public accounting firm and is part of the team doing the external audit of Westward Industries Inc. Staff at Westward are all very friendly, and Mary is offered the chance to buy one of the company's high-quality sound systems for only about half the usual price. Should she accept the deal?
- Karim is also on the Westward external audit team. He is a member of a bowling league. During a game, he hears a member of another team boast of cheating Westward systematically by overbilling on printing invoices. Should he tell Westward?
- Joan and Henry fall in love and decide to marry. Both are professional accountants: Joan is the chief accountant of Westward, responsible for preparing all the company's financial statements, and Henry is a partner of the public accounting firm and is in charge of the external audit of the company. Should Henry turn the audit over to another partner,

or perhaps even ask the accounting firm to resign as auditor (because as a partner, he shares in the firm's income from all audits)?

- Michel is another member of the Westward external audit team. During some audit tests, he discovers that Westward engaged in some business activities that appear to be illegal. Breaking that particular law can bring large fines and even jail terms. Should Michel go to the police?
- Erin works for the same public accounting firm. During the audit of Basic Electronics Ltd., she discovers that an employee of Basic is overcharging Westward by applying too high a mark-up to services contracted with Westward. Documents indicate that Basic's management is aware of this and is happy to be getting away with it, because it has a material effect on Basic's income. Should she tell the management of Basic that she knows what they are doing? Should she tell Henry, the partner responsible for the Westward audit? Should she tell Westward?
- Giorgio is a partner of the same public accounting firm. For years, his father has owned a few shares of Westward, among a whole portfolio of shares of many companies. His father has just died and willed all the shares to Giorgio. Should he sell the Westward shares?

Well, we could go on for some time. One of the more interesting and challenging aspects of being a professional is dealing with such ethical issues. Some of these examples do not have clear answers, but here are some ideas:

- The external auditors are supposed to be independent scrutineers of their clients' financial affairs. Mary should probably not accept the deal, unless it is available to anyone who turns up at a retail store, because accepting it would undermine her independence. Being friendly with clients is fine, but auditors also have to maintain some distance from clients to protect their independence and integrity.
- Karim should tell Westward what he heard and suggest they look into their printing costs. When doing their work, auditors acquire much confidential information about their clients and must be very careful about how they use it. In this case, the information was not acquired under circumstances of confidentiality. He may find himself in court over the issue, however, so he may need to seek legal advice before speaking to Westward.
- Henry needs to take some action to remove himself from the job of auditing his wife's work, to protect both her and his integrity. The public accounting firm probably has rules about such relationships, which likely involve transferring the job to another partner and keeping Henry entirely ignorant of the work on the Westward audit. The firm might have to resign the audit (this would likely be expected in the United States, for example); Westward might even ask it to do so to protect the credibility of its audited financial statements.
- Michel's situation is very complex. There is a mixture of confidentially acquired information and a duty to society. Much more has to be known before any advice could be offered to Michel. At the very least, Michel and the public accounting firm would have to get legal advice immediately. The board of directors of most large companies has an

audit committee to give the auditors a way to bring criticisms of management to the board's attention. Michel's firm would likely raise this with Westward's audit committee.

- Erin's is another very complex situation. Erin is responsible for protecting the confidentiality of her client, Basic, and would be in trouble if she told another company what she learned on the audit. But her firm is responsible to both clients. Again, she and the firm would need immediate legal advice.
- Most public accounting firms have rules prohibiting members of the firm from having an interest in any clients audited by the firm. Giorgio would probably have to sell his shares of Westward.

Behaving ethically requires sound thinking and sensitivity to complexity. If you would like to read some suggestions for a way of thinking your way through ethical problems, see the report by Ponemon and Gabhart in the notes at the end of this chapter[6] or the framework included in Case 5C, also at the end of this chapter.

HOW'S YOUR UNDERSTANDING

Here are two questions you should be able to answer, based on what you have just read:

1. Why do professional accountants have to abide by codes of ethics, and what difference might that make to the users of their services?
2. What ethical issues do you see in the following situation? During the audit of Westward Industries Inc., Sonya discovered that an accounting clerk, needing money for a child's operation, had temporarily taken some cash collected from customers. The clerk had returned the money a short time later, before anyone had known it was missing, and was otherwise a very competent and valued employee. The company's controls over cash have since been tightened, and it is unlikely that the clerk would be able to repeat the theft. Sonya is the only person, other than the clerk, who knows about the theft.

5.6 APPLYING GENERALLY ACCEPTED ACCOUNTING PRINCIPLES

You have seen that financial accounting has developed over hundreds of years and that in the 20th century there has been an increase in the regulation and standardization of financial statements and other financial disclosures. But financial accounting is by no means completely rule-bound and regulated. There are many accounting methods that are not covered by specific rules but are so well accepted that they are taken for granted as proper, and there are many problems that no rules seem likely to settle and that must be solved using the professional judgment of managers, accountants, and auditors. GAAP are mostly stable, so that people can get used to what to expect, yet they are not fixed. They change as demands for information change and as new solutions are developed. They are "generally accepted," but not always easy to tie down, because they are flexible enough to be tailored to the circumstances of particular companies and other organizations. They are often controversial because people feel they are too flexible, or not flexible enough, or too detailed, or not specific enough. Their combination of technicality and judgment makes them both interesting and frustrating to learn about.

It is all very well to know that GAAP exist, but how do you know when and how to apply them? The answer is that this requires significant expertise in today's world of complicated businesses, complicated governments, and complicated accounting. Basically, you have to get to know what GAAP are for the kind of company or financial statement item you are concerned about. This can require both a lot of reading of published standards, texts, and other material, consultation with others, and a lot of experience in making it all work. You have already learned many parts of GAAP, as you learned about the set of financial statements. The rest of this book will show you many more aspects of GAAP in order to get your interpretive expertise started.

The following sections of this chapter offer examples of the application of GAAP to particular financial accounting issues.

- Section 5.7 examines the general question of how to determine the values (figures) used on the balance sheet.
- Section 5.8 goes on to explain how to figure out the cost of specific assets.
- Section 5.9 gives an example of the effects of possible asset valuations other than cost, just to illustrate why the choice of valuation method might make a significant difference to the financial statements.
- Section 5.10 provides examples of solutions to a difficult accounting problem: how to account for *groups* of companies. Many of the financial statements you will see, and certainly those of most large companies, are really those of groups of companies, and if you are to interpret them intelligently, you should know something about how they have been put together.
- Section 5.11 reviews the usual contents of the notes to the financial statements. The notes often take many more pages than the financial statements do.
- Section 5.12 has brief comments on and an illustration of governmental and not-for-profit accounting. This book focuses on accounting for businesses, but financial accounting, GAAP, and standards are also important for other kinds of organizations.

5.7 BALANCE SHEET VALUATION AND MEASUREMENT

When we look at financial information, such as The North West Company's, what do the numbers, the numeric values assigned to assets and liabilities, mean? The **asset valuation** (or, more generally, **balance sheet valuation**) question is both complex and controversial. You may intuitively think that the assets should be valued at what they are worth, but what does that mean? There are five basic methods often suggested for **measuring** (valuing) assets and liabilities:

- Historical cost;
- Price-level-adjusted historical cost;
- Current or market value;
- Value in use; and
- Liquidation value.

As you read the description below of each measurement and valuation method, think about which one you believe is appropriate, and in which circumstances. There is much variety and judgment within generally accepted accounting principles, so no one method, even the main one (historical cost), is considered best in all circumstances.

Balance sheet valuation is often controversial, partly because of a concern that the values should be useful in people's decision-making and a suspicion that historical cost values are not as useful as those that look more to the future. Would you drive your car looking only in the rearview mirror to see where you have been and not look out the front window to see where you are going? One worry is that historical cost valuation, the most common method, leaves financial statements too much a history, when there are equally important needs to recognize changes in market conditions and to predict the future when making decisions.

Two controversies will serve as examples. For asset valuation, one issue is whether market values may actually be better than historical cost, at least in some cases, such as for the financial and monetary assets of banks and similar financial institutions. For liability valuation, an issue is whether obligations due well into the future, such as warranty obligations, should be valued at the "present value" of the likely future payments (future cash flows minus interest lost by waiting for the money), rather than just at the estimated future cash outflow itself, as is done now.[7]

Now let's turn to the five balance sheet valuation methods.

HISTORICAL COST

Historical cost, otherwise known as acquisition cost, values assets at the amount of the payments made or promised to acquire the assets, and values liabilities at the amounts of any associated promises. These amounts can generally be found by referring to transactional evidence, such as invoices, receipts, or contracts. The ability to document the cost (remember "verifiability" in Section 5.3 above) is a major reason historical cost is the usual valuation method for most assets and liabilities. Another principal reason is that an enterprise will rarely purchase assets or make promises for more than the enterprise believes them to be worth. If you believe that an asset will provide you with \$10,000 worth of productive capacity, you will not rationally pay or promise more than \$10,000 for it. Under this method an asset valued at historical cost is valued at its expected lowest, or most conservative (Section 5.3 again), value of future benefits at the date of acquisition. In most cases, GAAP imply the use of historical costs, unless some other valuation basis is more appropriate and is specifically disclosed in the financial statements (Section 1500 of the *CICA Handbook* recommends such disclosure unless the basis is "self-evident").

Some additional points in connection with this method are worth noting.

- At the point of acquisition, historical cost = market value = value in use, in most cases. (We assume that rational people would pay only what the asset is worth to them in the future in their business and that in general such use valuation would therefore tend to determine the market value of the asset.)
- Much of the criticism of historical cost has to do with time issues. That a piece of land was purchased 10 years ago for $50,000 has little meaning today. Is the land worth $200,000 or $100? That is something you do not know with historical cost.
- If an asset's market value later falls below its original cost, the asset may be written down to the market value. This violation of strict historical cost accounting is very much part of generally accepted accounting principles, largely because of conservatism. It is behind two important accounting phenomena: "writing down" of unproductive assets, and the "lower of cost or market" rule used in valuing inventories and some other current assets. We will see more about these later in the book.
- The income statement and some associated balance sheet accounts, such as accumulated amortization or prepaid expenses, have more to do with measuring income than with valuing assets or liabilities on the balance sheet. It has been said that many of the assets on the balance sheet (especially the less liquid ones) are, because historical cost is used, valued not so much as assets but as "costs waiting to be deducted from revenue in the future" or "unexpired costs." While this residual view of such assets is quite consistent with the income measurement and consistency provisions of GAAP, it is opposed by some accountants, who feel that asset values should represent something more meaningful than just unexpired costs, that they should, for example, represent more current value using current prices.

Concerns over how assets are valued using historical cost have led people to suggest alternative methods for valuing assets and liabilities on the balance sheet. Some of the more popular alternatives are shown below.

PRICE-LEVEL-ADJUSTED HISTORICAL COST

This approach adjusts for changes in the value or purchasing power of the dollar (the measuring unit), rather than for changes in the values of particular assets. The historical cost values of the assets and liabilities are adjusted for changes in the value of the dollar (using economy-wide indices such as the Consumer Price Index) since the assets were acquired or liabilities were incurred. Though this is a venerable idea, first proposed early in this century, and has been used by some companies (for example, the Philips electronics company in the Netherlands) and by some countries that had high inflation (Brazil for one), it has not found much favour in North America. One reason for its lack of popularity is that if historical cost is unsatisfactory compared to current values, adjusting the cost for inflation still leaves it unsatisfactory, only now less understandable.

CURRENT OR MARKET VALUE

This approach records the individual assets and liabilities at their current particular market value. It focuses on the individual values of the balance sheet items, not on changes in the dollar itself, as price-level-adjusted accounting does. It assumes that value is market determined and that income should be measured using changes over time in market values. The argument is that if, for example, your house's market worth is greater today than yesterday, you have made money on it today, even if you have not sold it. If its market worth is less, you have lost money on it, even if you have not sold it. This method has been the subject of much writing and experimentation in the United States and Canada and has some theoretical attraction in economics and finance, but it does not seem likely to replace historical cost as the most popular method.

Current value accounting can use either, or a mixture of, input or output values:

a. *Input market value*, or entry value, refers to the amount it would cost to bring the asset into the company if it were not now in, usually measured by estimating "replacement cost" to purchase it again or "reproduction cost" to make it again. The same idea holds for the hypothetical reborrowing of liabilities;

b. *Output market value*, or exit value, is the amount an asset is worth if sold now (in other words, its "net realizable value") or the amount that a liability could be paid off at now, usually measured by quoted prices, appraisals, and similar estimates.

VALUE IN USE

This approach considers that value flows from the way the company will use the asset to generate future cash flows (cash generated from revenues net of expenses). Value in use is usually estimated by calculating the "net present value" of future cash inflows (the cash flows minus lost interest implied by waiting for the cash) expected to be generated by the asset, or cash outflows it will make unnecessary. For example, a machine might be valued according to the products that it will make and that will be sold. Modern theories of finance and management accounting presume that value in use, measured by net present value, is an appropriate method for managerial decisions about asset acquisition and financing, and many people presume it underlies market values, but the approach has been little used in producing financial accounting numbers.

LIQUIDATION VALUE

Liquidation value is like output market value, but used on a "going out of business, sell it for what you can" basis. It is the value that the company's assets would bring upon being sold and that liabilities would be paid off for, if the whole company went out of business. It is used when the company is *not* felt to be a **going concern**, that is, if its continued viability cannot be assumed. Therefore, the reader of financial statements prepared on the historical cost basis should be entitled to presume that the company in question is a going concern. This presumption is an important part of financial accounting, but every year it turns out to be wrong for some companies that unexpectedly fail.

Such bad outcomes remind us that good judgment is required in selecting the balance sheet valuation basis, as with other aspects of financial accounting. A judgment that a company is a going concern and so should use historical cost accounting will turn out to have been wrong if the company fails. On the other hand, a judgment that it is *not* a going concern might be self-fulfilling: it might panic creditors and investors, and spark a failure no one wants.

HOW'S YOUR UNDERSTANDING

Here are two questions you should be able to answer, based on what you have just read:

1. The owner of Staely Industries Inc. is grumbling about the limitations of historical cost accounting for valuing the company's assets and liabilities. Tell the owner what other valuation or measurement methods can be used and what each does that the historical cost basis does not do.
2. What are some reasons that other valuation methods than historical cost have not replaced it in general use?

5.8 THE COST OF AN ASSET: THE BASIC COMPONENTS

The basic premise of historical cost valuation is to use the cost, at acquisition, of an asset to value it on the balance sheet. On the surface, this looks simple. You buy a truck for $25,000 and value the truck on the balance sheet at $25,000. However, there is often more to the cost of an asset than just the simple invoice cost or direct cost. For example, when you purchase a big computerized manufacturing machine, it may cost you $500,000 for the actual machine. But, in order to use the machine, certain environmental conditions must exist, such as temperature control, a raised floor for wiring, and a fire protection system. Therefore, a section of the factory must be renovated to meet these specifications.

These costs, known as installation costs, are a good example of expenditures that are a component of the asset's cost. Overall, the **cost** of an asset includes all those costs required to *make it suitable for its intended purpose*. That can sometimes be difficult to determine. For example, suppose an enterprise constructs a specialized new manufacturing machine, using some of its regular employees and resources. The cost of such assets, which an enterprise constructs for itself rather than buying finished, will obviously include the cost of raw materials and labour needed to make them. But should the interest on monies borrowed to finance the project be included? It is a matter of judgment and depends on the situation. Sometimes interest is included in the cost of such assets; most of the time it is not. Enterprises often have policies for how to determine whether expenditures, such as interest, are included in assets' costs. These policies are designed to ensure consistency in calculating cost, to fit the accounting to the enterprise's particular circumstances, and to meet other criteria such as conservatism. Because of conservatism, most enterprises do not include interest on borrowed funds in the cost of assets, but some do, such as electric utilities, which borrow money over the several years it takes to construct power plants.

Inventory is another asset for which costing can be difficult. Purchased inventory can be straightforward. It is basically the invoice cost plus transportation, storage, and handling costs. Manufactured inventory, on the other hand, requires some decisions. As with other assets constructed by the enterprise, the cost of raw materials and direct labour are usually included. But what about overhead? Overhead costs are those that are indirectly related to the production process, such as accountants' and supervisors' salaries, and building operating costs, including electricity, rent, depreciation, and insurance. Most manufacturing companies include some or all of such costs when they are calculating the cost of unsold manufactured goods.

Deciding what to include in an asset's cost can make quite a difference to the enterprise's balance sheet and income statement. Suppose Gondola Inc. has spent $100,000 this year on supervisors' salaries in connection with setting up a new mountain gondola ride in the Rockies. If that cost is just deducted from revenue as an expense this year, that will reduce income and income tax expense. But if the cost is added to the gondola ride asset instead, total assets will be higher, and this year's income and income tax expense will be higher too. Over the next several years, incomes and income tax expenses will be lower because of higher amortization (depreciation) on the higher asset cost. So, aside from accounting appropriately and fairly for the asset, the decision about how to handle the supervisors' salaries will affect income, assets and income tax expenses this year and in several future years. This decision is often called the **capitalizing** vs. **expensing** choice (including the expenditure with the assets vs. deducting as an expense in the current year), and we will see it several times in this book.

In summary, the components of the cost of an asset include all those costs that are required to make it suitable for the purpose intended, whether it be making a computer usable in the information-gathering process or bringing inventory into saleable condition. Some common components of the cost of an asset are listed in Exhibit 5.3.

In the years following acquisition, the question of whether the asset cost should be changed will crop up again when repairs must be made. When a major repair or apparent improvement in the asset is done, the question to ask yourself is whether the asset's productivity or efficiency has been improved, or its useful life extended. If so, there has been a **betterment** of the asset and the cost of that should be capitalized (added to the cost of the asset). If not, the cost should just be charged to expense, such as an account called repairs and maintenance expense.

HOW'S YOUR UNDERSTANDING

Here are two questions you should be able to answer, based on what you have just read:

1. Magnus Fabricators Ltd. has just constructed a new factory building, using company employees and equipment for most of the work. The company's accountant has said that "various costs must be capitalized to produce an appropriate balance sheet figure for the building's cost." What does the accountant mean and what sorts of costs are likely meant?
2. How does a company determine when to stop adding expenditures to the cost of a new building and instead to add those expenditures to repairs and maintenance expense?

Exhibit 5.3

Common Components of Asset Cost

a. Inventory

- Raw materials costs;
- Labour costs;
- Storage costs;
- Handling costs prior to sale;
- Indirect overhead costs of production, such as heat, power, and supervisors' salaries.

b. Land

- Purchase price, including real estate agent commissions;
- Costs of obtaining clear title, such as legal fees and title searches;
- Costs of clearing, removing unwanted structures, draining, and landscaping.

c. Building (purchased)

- Purchase price;
- Renovation or upgrading costs to make it suitable for the intended use;
- Initial painting and decoration.

d. Building (self-constructed)

- Materials costs;
- Labour costs;
- Excavating, surveying, engineering, and design costs;
- Insurance while constructing the building;
- Perhaps some overhead costs and even financing costs incurred during construction.

e. Purchased Equipment

- Purchase price, including taxes;
- Transportation costs;
- Installation costs;
- Testing costs;
- Overhauls that extend equipment's life or increase its value (betterments).

f. Leasehold Improvements on Rented Property

- Materials costs, labour costs, and other costs to construct the improvements;
- Initial painting and decoration of the rented premises.

5.9 AN EXAMPLE OF THE EFFECTS OF ACCOUNTING CONCEPTS AND GAAP

Historical cost is the backbone of GAAP, used because it is thought to be fair, accurate in representing economic transactions, and verifiable, among other things. But there are methods other than historical cost, as Section 5.7 showed. Maybe one of these would be more relevant, or more comparable to the methods of other companies, than historical cost. What would be the effects on the balance sheet, income statement, and cash flow statement of using one of the alternative balance sheet valuation methods instead of historical cost?

Let's look at a realistic and relevant example. Canada has many companies that specialize in acquiring and developing real estate for office buildings, shopping centres, industrial plants, housing developments, and many other uses. Trizec, Cadillac Fairview, Bramalea, Oxford, Cambridge, Carma, Princeton, Triple-Five, and Markborough are only a few examples of such companies. As you probably know, real estate values are highly variable, with frequent booms and busts. Consider two real estate development companies operating in the Toronto market. Let's call them Oxbridge and Bramview:

- Oxbridge has undeveloped land, bought during a downturn in the Toronto real estate market, that cost \$5,000,000 and has an estimated current market (output) value of \$8,000,000. The company's net income has been about \$700,000 per year in the last few years.
- Bramview also has undeveloped land, comparable to Oxbridge's except bought during an overheated period of the Toronto market at a cost of \$11,000,000. Its estimated current market value is also \$8,000,000, and the company's net income has also been about \$700,000 per year.

An initial question is whether historical cost is an appropriate asset valuation basis for these companies. The two pieces of land are about the same, but the companies' balance sheets certainly do not look the same:

- Oxbridge: Undeveloped land, at cost \$5,000,000
- Bramview: Undeveloped land, at cost \$11,000,000

Also, Oxbridge will show a higher ratio of net income to total assets, indicating apparently stronger performance than Bramview, because its total assets will be lower than Bramview's. Now, we could argue that this is as it should be, that Bramview has not really done as well because too much was paid for the land, in hindsight. But another argument is that since the two pieces of land are comparable economic assets, net income should be related to the economic value (e.g., market value) of the assets, not to costs that depend on historical happenstance rather than currently relevant economic conditions.

Conceptually, then, let's consider the idea of changing both companies' balance sheet valuations for the land to current market value. Using the concepts from earlier in this chapter, what might be some pros and cons of this idea?

Pros:
- More relevant valuation for users in assessing company's value;
- More useful in comparing companies with similar economic assets;

- Fairer way of relating performance (income) to the economic value that managers are managing on behalf of owners;
- More timely data than the "obsolete" cost figures;
- Not costly to implement (unless real estate appraisers have to be paid);
- Understandable to users who know something about real estate.

Cons:
- Less reliable numbers because based on estimated selling value of land that has not been sold;
- Less consistent balance sheet values because real estate values tend to vary a great deal over time;
- Not transaction based and therefore not verifiable;
- Not conservative in the long run because land values have tended to rise over time, especially as measured in dollars subject to inflation;
- Not a generally accepted procedure, so users accustomed to GAAP would have to adjust their performance evaluation methods and rewrite contracts, such as for lending agreements and management compensation, that depend on financial statement information;
- No effect on cash flow directly or through income tax, because the land has not been sold, so there might be doubt that moving the financial statement numbers around in the absence of real economic effects would be very helpful to anyone.

Well, you can probably add more pros and cons. But you should see that the accounting concepts are useful in figuring out what would be the appropriate accounting procedure to use.

We have not considered the significance (materiality) of the idea to the companies' financial statements, nor even how the idea might be implemented. Here are some possibilities (all ignoring income tax considerations):

1. Any difference between current market value and the value on the companies' balance sheets (cost, so far) could be just included in the current year's net income:
   - Oxbridge's land asset would be debited $3,000,000 to bring it up to the $8,000,000 market value, and the credit would go to an income statement account like Other revenue, raising current year's income by more than 400% to $3,700,000;
   - Bramview's land asset would be credited $3,000,000 to bring it down to the $8,000,000 market value, and the debit would go to an income statement account like Other expense, changing current year's income to a *loss* of $2,300,000 (more than three times the current income).
2. The difference could be put directly into retained earnings. Oxbridge's retained earnings would rise $3,000,000, and Bramview's would fall $3,000,000. Oxbridge would appear more able to pay a dividend, Bramview would appear less able. As would also happen with method (1), this could paradoxically hurt Oxbridge more than Bramview, because the accounting change could produce pressure from shareholders for increased dividends, even though there is no additional cash to pay such dividends.

3. The difference could be put into owners' equity but not into retained earnings, by creating a new equity account called something like Unrealized changes in asset valuations. This would increase Oxbridge's equity by $3,000,000 with a new credit balance account, but would decrease Bramview's equity by $3,000,000 with a new debit balance account. Since it would not be part of retained earnings, the new account might not affect the owners' demand for dividends, thus avoiding the implication that the valuation change is similar to the kinds of events behind the revenues and expenses that form net income and retained earnings. (Some methods of implementing current value and price-level-adjusted accounting that have been developed, and adopted by a few companies and countries, have used such an Unrealized gains and/or losses account.)
4. Perhaps the principle of conservatism should be invoked, whereby one of the above methods (most likely the first) would be followed only when the market value is less than the present balance sheet value. In this case, only Bramview would adjust its figures, because its cost is higher than current market value. Though the companies' accounting would still show different figures for the same sort of land, using "lower of cost or market" would be conservative, so users could rely on the balance sheet values not being overstated relative to current conditions. This might be done particularly if a decline in market value indicated a permanent or long-term impairment in the land's value.
5. Perhaps the historical cost numbers should not be changed, but each company could disclose the current market value of the land on its balance sheet or in a note:

    - Oxbridge: Undeveloped land (current market value estimated at $8,000,000), at cost $5,000,000;
    - Bramview: Undeveloped land (current market value estimated at $8,000,000), at cost $11,000,000.

    This method provides users with information about the market values, but does not presume what they mean, as the other methods do. Users probably can make intelligent use of information as long as they know about it (that is, if it is disclosed). With full information and "what if" analytical skill, they can adjust the financial statements to reflect the information in whatever way they consider relevant to their needs.

Because any change from historical cost in the absence of actually selling the land would not affect cash flow (no proceeds) and, we will assume, would not affect income tax either, there is no net effect on the cash flow statement (SCFP). Cash from operations would not be affected, nor would any of the other SCFP categories. Net income at the top of the SCFP might change, but the change would be cancelled out by adding back any reduction of income, or subtracting any gain, because the items would be noncash items.

You can see that not only do accounting concepts make a difference in evaluating ideas, they can make quite a difference to the figures in the financial statements (with the important exception of the SCFP) and, therefore, to how the statements are interpreted and used. As we have seen before, any method that changes balance sheet numbers will correspondingly affect the income statement numbers and retained earnings, unless an unusual method, such as (3) above, is used to confine the effects to the balance sheet. So people argue not only about the effects on the balance sheet, but also about the effects on the income statement—often primarily about the effects on the income statement. Right now, the most likely method of giving financial statement users information about something like the Oxbridge–Bramview situation is method (4), keeping historical cost in the financial statements unless the asset's long-term value has been impaired.

HOW'S YOUR UNDERSTANDING

Here are two questions you should be able to answer, based on what you have just read:

1. Greyhurst Land Development Inc. has large landholdings. The company's president said recently that historical cost valuation for the company's land is correct according to GAAP but is nevertheless inappropriate for the company. Is this possible?
2. Greyhurst's president is considering revaluing the company's land on its balance sheet, to reflect current real estate market values that are much lower than the cost of the land. What might such a revaluation do to the company's assets, owners' equity, and net income?

5.10 INTERCORPORATE INVESTMENTS AND CORPORATE GROUPS

Modern business organizations, especially large ones, are often groups of separately incorporated companies. You will have heard terms like "merger," "takeover," "parent," and "subsidiary": these all come from the phenomenon of grouping corporations together. General Motors, John Labatt, Noranda, Sears, Royal Bank, and Nestlé are examples of organizations that are actually made up of several, even hundreds, of companies. Such groups are linked in many ways, including:

- By formal ownership of all or parts of each member by one or more of the group (General Motors owns General Motors of Canada, General Motors Acceptance Corporation, Saturn, Opel, and many other companies forming the General Motors group);
- By the business relationships that provide the rationale for forming the group in the first place (General Motors of Canada makes certain lines of cars or trucks sold by other companies in the group and financed by General Motors Acceptance, if customers wish); and
- By internal patterns of performance reporting, motivation, and promotion that encourage managers and other employees to feel part of the larger group (the president of General Motors of Canada may have been promoted from another company in the group and may be promoted to yet another, if he or she does well in the Canadian operation).

Most of the financial statements included in published annual reports are **consolidated**, that is, really those of groups of companies. Accounting for corporate groups is a complicated part of financial accounting and is covered in detail in the authoritative financial accounting standards of CICA and FASB. This book only introduces you to the main principles behind it and shows you how to apply the principles to do some basic calculations.

KINDS OF INTERCORPORATE INVESTMENTS

Corporations invest in other corporations in many ways. Six common ways of such investment are: (1) temporary use of cash, (2) long-term passive investment, (3) long-term active investment, (4) joint venture, (5) acquisition, and (6) merger (for more information see Exhibit 5.4).

Exhibit 5.4

Nature and Intent of the Investment	Place on the Investing Company's Balance Sheet	Accounting Method
1. Temporary use of cash	Marketable securities	Lower of cost or market
2. Long-term passive	Noncurrent assets	Cost investment
3. Long-term active	Noncurrent assets	Equity basis investment
4. Joint venture	Noncurrent assets	Equity basis
5. Acquisition	Combined balance sheets	Purchase method consolidation
6. Merger	Combined balance sheets	Pooling of interests consolidation

1. Temporary Use of Cash

a. *Temporary Investments and Marketable Securities*

Temporary investments are held primarily to put extra cash to work. They include stocks, bonds, commercial paper (such as notes issued by financial companies), government bonds and treasury bills, and investment certificates and term deposits in banks. Not all of these are really *intercorporate* investments, in that there may not be any ownership or business relationship connecting the holder of the security to the issuer.

Because there is no intention to hold such investments for long or to try to influence the operations or policies of the organizations that issued the securities, such investments are included in current assets. The very short-term ones are usually considered part of cash and equivalents. The investments are valued at the lower of cost or market (net realizable value), because the reader of the balance sheet should be able to assume that the value shown is not higher than what would be obtained by selling the investments. Dividends and interest from such investments are usually also included in nonoperating revenues. If the investments are **marketable securities** having a quoted market value, such as shares in public companies, that value is usually disclosed if it is different from the amount at which they are valued on the balance sheet.

Financial Reporting in Canada 1993, a survey of Canadian companies conducted by the CICA, which will be referred to frequently in this book, reports that in 1992, 103 of 300 companies surveyed reported temporary investments, 83 of these combining such investments with cash. Twenty-three of the 103 reported cost as the valuation, 11 reported lower of cost or market, and 69 did not say specifically what basis of valuation they were using.[8] Presumably they were using lower of cost or market. Such lack of disclosure is an example of an apparent assumption that the reader of the financial statements should be sufficiently knowledgeable about financial accounting to know what basis is used if it is not specified. Developing your knowledge about GAAP bases is one of this book's main objectives.

b. *Example of Effects of Accounting Method*

Wildrose Inc. has temporary investments costing \$520,000. Suppose the investments' market values slipped to \$484,000 on the balance sheet date. What would happen to income if the company followed the lower of cost or market rule? Suppose instead that the investments' market values went up to \$585,000 on the balance sheet date. How much better off would the company appear to be if it could avoid accounting conservatism and report the investments at market value instead of lower of cost or market?

In the first case, the company should write the investments down to \$484,000.

- The difference, \$36,000, would be included as an expense (probably a nonoperating one) and the write-down would reduce income tax expense if the write-down were a tax-deductible expense. Net income would go down by \$36,000 minus any tax saving. The working capital would be reduced by the write-down, also minus any reduction in income tax payable.
- If, as is likely, the investments were considered to be a cash equivalent asset, the write-down would reduce cash and, through the reduction in net income, also reduce cash generated by operations on the SCFP. If the investments were considered to be a noncash current asset, the write-down would not affect cash or cash generated by operations (it would be added back on the SCFP as a noncash expense).

In the second case, the company's current assets would be \$65,000 higher, and net income and working capital would be higher by that amount less any income tax estimated on the increase in value. If it cannot show the investments at market value, the company may still get the message across by disclosing the market value, which the *CICA Handbook* recommends. Then readers of the financial statements can do this sort of effects analysis if they wish.

2. Long-Term Passive Investment

The accounting for long-term intercorporate investments depends on the *intention* behind and *control* involved in the ownership, which relate to the proportion of the issuing organization's voting shares held. If the proportion is low (the *CICA Handbook*, Section 3050, suggests less than 20% as a guideline), the investing company is usually presumed not to be interested in exercising, or able to exercise, significant influence on the issuing organization.

For such an investment, the accounting is simple:

- The investment asset is valued at cost and is shown among the noncurrent assets. (The lower of cost or market value rule is not considered relevant because there is no intention to sell the investment.)
- Revenue from the investment (interest if bonds, dividends if shares) is included with nonoperating other revenue when it is received.

3. Long-Term Active Investment

a. *Significant Influence but Not Control*

When the investing company exercises some influence but does not have voting control (that is, it has more than the 20% voting interest suggested above but not more than 50%), the **equity basis** of accounting is used. Under this basis, the investing company includes in its income statement and balance sheet its share of earnings by the investee company, because it has influenced that company's performance.

Under the equity basis:

- The investment asset is still valued initially at cost, as it was for passive investments (the method for which we will call the **cost basis**).
- As the investee company earns income (or incurs losses), the asset is increased for the investing company's share of that income (or decreased for its share of losses) and that share is included in the investing company's income. This is an accrual of income the investing company is entitled to, so it is taking credit for its share of the investee's income (increase in retained earnings). Nonoperating Other revenue is credited with this share and the Investment asset account is debited, so the asset account is treated like an account receivable for the accrued income.
- When the investee company pays a dividend, the investing company receives some of the accrued income as its share of the dividend, so the dividend received is deducted from the investment asset account, just as collection of an account receivable would be deducted from the account receivable asset. The dividend is not called income by the investing company because the income has already been accrued; instead, the dividend is deducted from the investment asset because it is considered a return of some of the money invested.
- There are some other more complicated features of equity basis accounting we will not get into.

Financial Reporting in Canada 1993 reports that 169 of the 300 companies surveyed had long-term investments in 1992. Of these, 28 used the cost basis, 49 used the equity basis, 20 did not say what basis they used, and the rest had a variety of investments and used various mixtures of cost and equity bases.[9]

b. *A Cost and Equity Basis Example*

This is a summary of how the two methods work (ignoring complexities):

	Cost basis	Equity basis
Initial carrying value of the investor's intercorporate investment asset	Original cost	Original cost
Investor's share of income earned by investee	Nothing done	Add to asset and to other revenue
Investor's share of dividend paid by investee	Add to cash and to other revenue	Add to cash and deduct from investment asset
Resulting balance sheet value of the investor's intercorporate investment asset	Just original cost	Original cost plus accrued income share minus share of dividends paid

Here is an example. Grand Ltd. acquired investments in two other companies on January 1, 1995. These acquisitions are (a) and (b) in the list below; events (c) to (e) also took place in 1995.

a. 60,000 shares (15% of the voting interest) in A Ltd. were purchased for $1,800,000 cash. Because this is to be a fairly passive long-term investment, Grand will account for it using the *cost basis*.
b. 145,000 shares (29% of the voting interest) in B. Ltd. were purchased for $4,640,000 cash. Since Grand intends to participate in the management of B Ltd., Grand will account for it using the *equity basis*.
c. On June 30, both investee companies announced their earnings per share for the first six months of 1991: $2 per share for A Ltd. and $2.10 per share for B Ltd.
d. On December 10, both investee companies paid dividends to shareholders: $1.50 per share for A Ltd. and $1.60 per share for B Ltd.
e. On December 31, both investee companies announced their earnings per share for 1995: $3.40 per share ($1.40 additional since June 30) for A Ltd. and $3.90 per share ($1.80 additional since June 30) for B Ltd.

The effects of items (a) to (e) on the financial statements of Grand Ltd. at the end of 1995 are:

Investment in A Ltd. (Cost Basis)

a. Long-term investment asset starts out at the purchase price of $1,800,000 (cash reduced by same amount).
b. (Concerns only B Ltd.)
c. Earnings announcement is ignored for accounting purposes.
d. Cash received and dividend revenue are recorded for $90,000 (60,000 shares × $1.50).
e. Earnings announcement is ignored for accounting purposes.

Using the cost basis, Grand Ltd.'s financial statements as of December 31, 1995, will therefore include for A Ltd.:

Investment in A Ltd. (noncurrent asset)	$1,800,000
Dividend revenue (in Other revenue)	$ 90,000

Investment in B Ltd. (Equity Basis)

a. (Concerns only A Ltd.)

b. Long-term investment asset starts out at the purchase price of $4,640,000, the same as if the cost basis were used.

c. Upon earnings announcement, both investment revenue and investment asset are increased by $304,500 (145,000 shares × $2.10).

d. Cash is increased by, and investment asset is reduced by, $232,000 (145,000 shares × $1.60): the dividend is therefore deemed to be a return to Grand Ltd. of some of its investment.

e. Upon earnings announcement, both investment revenue and investment asset are increased by $261,000 (145,000 shares × $1.80).

Using the equity basis, Grand Ltd.'s financial statements as of December 31, 1995, will therefore include for B Ltd.:

Investment in B Ltd. (noncurrent asset) ($4,640,000 + $304,500 – $232,000 + $261,000)	$4,973,500
Investment revenue (in Other revenue) ($304,500 + $261,000)	$ 565,500

HOW'S YOUR UNDERSTANDING

Here are two questions you should be able to answer, based on what you have just read:

1. If Gretel Ltd. buys a noncontrolling number of shares of Hansel Inc. for $460,000, what are the criteria by which management of Gretel should decide if the investment is to be accounted for on the cost basis or the equity basis?
2. During the year, Gretel receives a $45,000 dividend from Hansel. At the end of the year, Hansel reports a net income. If Gretel's proportion of the Hansel voting shares is applied to Hansel's net income, the resulting figure is $78,500. What income from its investment in Hansel will Gretel report if it is using the cost basis? The equity basis? What is the "Investment in Hansel" asset on Gretel's books at the end of the year on the cost basis? The equity basis? ($45,000; $78,500; $460,000; $493,500)

4. Joint venture

A **joint venture** is a partnership between the investing company and other investors, usually formed to conduct exploration (such as in the oil and gas industry), develop new products, or pool resources in some other way. It is common in international business. Here, the investing company does not have control, but it does have significant influence on the joint venture because of the partnership arrangement and the business arrangements among the joint venture and the partner investors.

Joint ventures use the equity basis of accounting, unless the venture's earnings are unlikely to accrue to the investing company, in which case the cost basis is used. Sometimes "proportionate consolidation," in which the investing company's shares of the venture's assets and liabilities are combined with its assets and liabilities, is used. We will not examine this method in this book.

5. Acquisition

a. *Purchase Method*

Frequently, one corporation acquires more than 50% of the voting shares of another, becoming the majority owner of the other. This is done for many reasons, including to operate the two companies jointly and gain the benefits of such coordination. As long as voting control is held, the investing company can gain many benefits without having to own *all* the shares of the other, though it may well do so. Financial accounting uses a technique called **consolidation** to present the two companies as one economic entity, almost as if they were one company. The controlling company (the "**parent**") and the controlled company (the **subsidiary**) are not equal, because the parent is in control, so Canadian GAAP prescribe the "**purchase method**" of accounting for this business combination. A merger, where both companies really do join and there is no acquisition of one by the other, is dealt with in part 6 below. In Canada, acquisitions are very common and mergers are very rare, so if you see a set of consolidated financial statements, the purchase method is almost certain to be the accounting method used.

Consolidation is imaginary: there is no *legal*, consolidated entity. Rather, it is legally a group of separate companies with connected ownership. The idea is to present the group of companies as if it were a single entity. This method is thought to represent the economic and business circumstances more faithfully than would reporting separate statements for all the legally separate companies and leaving the user to try to add them together.

Consolidation uses a simple idea: to prepare the financial statements of a group of companies, put the balance sheets, income statements, and other statements for all the companies side by side and, mostly, add them up. The consolidated balance sheet's cash figure would be the sum of all of the companies' cash figures, the consolidated income statement's cost of goods sold expense figure would be the sum of their cost of goods sold figures, and so on. To apply this simple idea to the complexities of modern businesses, a quite complicated set of GAAP for consolidation has arisen. In this book, the complexities will be left out in favour of a focus on three main issues in consolidation accounting:

- What to do if the parent company owns less than 100% of the subsidiary's voting shares;
- Determining the asset and liability values that are to be added together; and
- Determining any "goodwill" arising from the acquisition price paid by the parent.

b. *Three Basic Concepts in Purchase Method Consolidation*

i. Noncontrolling (minority) interest

This arises if the parent owns less than 100% of the subsidiary and equals the percentage of the voting shares *not owned* by the parent times the subsidiary's shareholders' equity at the date of acquisition, adjusted for changes since that date. For example, if P Inc. bought 75% of the voting shares of S Ltd. on January 3, 1995, when S Ltd.'s shareholders' equity equalled $300,000, then the noncontrolling interest would equal 25% of that, or $75,000. This amount is shown as a liability on the consolidated balance sheet, representing the part of the joint consolidated entity's equity *not* owned by the parent company's shareholders. It represents someone else's equity in the group, so it is not included with the consolidated equity. It is not a debt of the consolidated entity, because it need not be paid—you could think of it as an acknowledgement that the consolidated entity has an obligation to the minority owners of S Ltd., who did not sell their shares to P Inc.

Over time, the noncontrolling interest liability is accounted for similarly to the way the investment asset was in the equity method above. The liability is increased (and consolidated net income is decreased) each year by the minority owners' share of the subsidiary's net income, and it is decreased (and consolidated cash is decreased) whenever the minority owners receive a dividend. So if the parent company succeeds in getting the subsidiary to earn income, some of that income is credited to the minority owners, and when the minority owners are paid a dividend, the liability is reduced just as any liability would be.

ii. Balance sheet asset and liability values

The idea of consolidation is just to add the accounts together: the parent's accounts receivable are added to the subsidiary's accounts receivable, the land is added to the land, the accounts payable are added to the accounts payable, and so on. But two changes to the parent's and subsidiary's balance sheets are made before that is done.

The first change is that any intercompany balances are ignored. If S Ltd. owes P. Inc. $40,000, for example, that would be on S Ltd.'s balance sheet as an account payable and on P Inc.'s balance sheet as an account receivable. If the consolidated balance sheet is to represent the two companies as if they were one entity, then this $40,000 amount is an internal matter to that entity: it is not owed to or receivable from anyone outside the entity, so it is not like the other accounts payable and accounts receivable. Therefore it is just left out of the consolidated figures. (Intercompany sales and expenses, such as management fees, are also left out of the income statement, and any profit made by one company in dealing with the other is left out as well. Eliminating these can be complex.)

The account for the parent company's investment in the subsidiary is also an intercompany account, so it too is ignored in the consolidation. Another intercompany amount left out is the parent's share of the subsidiary's shareholders' equity. It is what the parent bought, so it is included in the parent's investment account and therefore is not part of the consolidated equity external to the consolidated entity. The part of the subsidiary's equity *not* bought is transferred to a liability (as noted above), so the result is that *none* of the subsidiary's equity at the date of acquisition is included in consolidated equity. Consolidated equity at date of acquisition equals just the parent's equity alone.

The second change is to recognize that the parent company may have had a different value in mind for various of the subsidiary's assets and liabilities when it acquired the subsidiary from the amounts shown for those on the subsidiary's balance sheet. Because a transaction did happen (the parent bought shares of the subsidiary), the historical cost basis of accounting requires that any revised values at that date be taken into account. These are called the *fair values* at that date. However, because the minority owners did not sell, there was not a transaction for their share of the subsidiary's assets and liabilities, so their share is not taken into account. We know what the parent paid for what it got; we do not know what might have been paid for what it did not buy (the minority's share). Therefore, at the date of acquisition, each of the subsidiary's assets and liabilities is added into the consolidated figures using the following formula:

Amount used in consolidation calculation = Book value in subsidiary's balance sheet + Parent's share of subsidiary × (Fair value – subsidiary's book value)

For example, if the subsidiary's land was on its balance sheet at a value (presumably cost) of $120,000, but the parent's evaluation indicated its fair value was $180,000 and the parent bought 85% of the subsidiary, that land would be included in the consolidated figures at a value of $171,000 [$120,000 + .85 ($180,000 – $120,000)]. Therefore, the consolidated figures do not fully revalue the subsidiary's assets and liabilities: the minority owners' share of such revaluation is left out because they did not sell. (Any revaluations of assets and liabilities that are done may affect future consolidated income; for example, if the subsidiary's buildings and equipment are increased in value in the consolidation, then the consolidated amortization expense will have to be increased too, in order to take that into account. This is another complication we will not take any further!)

iii. Goodwill arising on consolidation

What if P Inc. paid more for the shares of S Ltd. than the sum of the fair values of S Ltd.'s assets minus its liabilities? This indicates that P Inc. is buying something else *not on* S Ltd.'s balance sheet, something in addition to all the individual parts of S Ltd. This something is called **goodwill**, or goodwill arising on consolidation. It might represent good managers, a good location, faithful customers, economies of scale with the parent, reduced competition, or other factors the parent company took into account in agreeing to a price for the subsidiary's shares.

Goodwill asset = Cost of parent's investment – Parent's portion of (fair values of subsidiary's assets – fair values of its liabilities)

For example, if Very Big Inc. paid $1,200,000 for 80% of the voting shares of Not So Big Ltd., and at that date Very Big evaluated Not So Big's assets to be worth $4,300,000 and its liabilities to be

$3,000,000, then consolidated goodwill at date of acquisition would be $160,000 [$1,200,000 – .80 ($4,300,000 – $3,000,000)].

Goodwill is shown among the noncurrent assets on the consolidated balance sheet, and it is amortized over time by charges against consolidated income (goodwill amortization expense).

Two wrinkles regarding goodwill might as well be mentioned. First, if the difference is negative (investment cost is *less* than the parent's portion of the net sum of the fair values), you might expect this to be called "badwill" and to be shown on the consolidated balance sheet too. But under GAAP, it is assumed that there was something wrong with the subsidiary's assets for this to happen, so the fair values are reduced in the consolidation calculation until the parent's portion exactly equals the purchase price. The result is that goodwill (or badwill) is zero. Second, if the subsidiary already had goodwill, that is wrapped into the new goodwill figure and not carried forward separately.

To summarize, the consolidated balance sheet at date of acquisition includes:

- The parent company's balance sheet figures;
- The subsidiary's assets and liabilities, revalued to reflect the parent's portion of any increases and decreases to fair values;
- Any noncontrolling (minority) interest in the subsidiary's equity;
- Any consolidated goodwill.

The consolidated balance sheet does *not* include:

- The parent's account for investment in subsidiary;
- The subsidiary's shareholders' equity;
- Any other intercompany asset and liability accounts.

c. *An Example of Consolidation at Date of Acquisition*

ABC Company purchased 80% of XYZ Company's voting shares for $500,000. We have the following information for XYZ as at the date of acquisition (no intercompany receivables or payables existed at that date):

XYZ Data	Book Values	Fair Values
Cash	$ 45,000	$ 45,000
Accounts receivable	75,000	60,000
Inventory	100,000	120,000
Property and equipment (net)	200,000	300,000
	$420,000	$525,000
Accounts payable	$ 90,000	95,000
Common shares	50,000	
Retained earnings	280,000	
	$420,000	
Sum of fair values of net assets		$430,000

continued next page

Goodwill Arising on Consolidation

ABC paid $500,000 for 80% of $430,000 (the identifiable fair values):

Purchase price	$500,000
Minus acquired fair value (80% x $430,000)	344,000
Goodwill	$156,000

Noncontrolling Interest

ABC purchased only 80% of XYZ. Therefore, the other 20% is the owners' equity of the noncontrolling owners. It is 20% of the book value of XYZ's owners' equity at date of acquisition, or 20% × ($50,000 + $280,000) = $66,000.

Consolidated Figures for ABC

See Exhibit 5.5.

Exhibit 5.5

	Balance Sheet Book Values as at Date of Acquisition		**Adjust 80% of FV–BV* of XYZ**	**Include Goodwill and Non-controlling Interest**	**Consolidated Balance Sheet**
	ABC	**XYZ**			
Cash	$ 175,000	$ 45,000	$ 0		$ 220,000
Receivables	425,000	75,000	(12,000)		488,000
Inventory	660,000	100,000	16,000		776,000
Investment in XYZ	500,000	—		Ignore	—
Property & equipment	1,700,000	200,000	80,000		1,980,000
Consolidated goodwill	—	—		$156,000	156,000
	$3,460,000	$420,000			$3,620,000
Payables	$ 730,000	$ 90,000	$ 4,000		$ 824,000
Long-term debt	850,000	0	0		850,000
Consolidated noncontrolling interest	—	—		$ 66,000	66,000
Common shares	100,000	50,000		ABC only	100,000
Retained earnings	1,780,000	280,000		ABC only	1,780,000
	$3,460,000	$420,000			$3,620,000

* FV – BV = Item's fair value – Its value on XYZ's balance sheet

d. *A Comment on Consolidated Net Income After Acquisition*
Consolidated net income is the sum of the incomes earned since acquisition, with adjustments to remove intercompany balances and any subsidiary's noncontrolling owners' interest in the income earned by the subsidiary and to reflect amortization of goodwill, among other things. The calculation is as follows:

Start with the sum of the parent's and the subsidiaries' incomes	$ XXXX
Subtract	
a. Any profits earned by any of the companies on intercompany sales	(XXXX)
b. Any income from the subsidiaries *already included* in the parent's or other subsidiaries' accounts through use of the equity method of accounting on the companies' individual financial statements (these are intercompany amounts too)	(XXXX)
c. Any extra amortization and other expenses resulting from adjusting subsidiaries' assets and liabilities to fair values in the consolidation	(XXXX)
d. Any noncontrolling owners' share of the net income earned by the subsidiary of which they remain part owners (roughly equal to the noncontrolling ownership percentage multiplied by the subsidiary's net income)	(XXXX)
e. Amortization of any goodwill arising on consolidation	(XXXX)
The result is consolidated net income	$(XXXX)

You can see that consolidated net income will be less than the sum of the individual companies' net incomes, perhaps substantially less if goodwill is large or there are significant minority interests.

6. Merger

When there is a real merger of two similarly sized corporations, in which neither can be said to be buying the other, the **pooling of interests method** of consolidation is used. Such a merger can be recognized by an exchange of shares (rather than by one company paying cash for the shares of the other), by the continuance of the management of both companies, and by other evidence that the two companies are continuing in a joint enterprise. In a pooling of interests, the consolidated financial statements are prepared simply by adding the accounts together. Assets equal the sum of the balance sheet assets of the two companies, as do liabilities, and equity is the sum of the equities. There is no revaluation of any of the balance sheet accounts, and the special consolidation accounts, "noncontrolling (minority) interest" and "goodwill," do not arise.

In Canada, the conditions under which GAAP prescribe the pooling of interests method very rarely occur. The method was abused during a big merger boom in the late 1960s and early 1970s, and financial accounting standards have since been written largely to prevent its use. Instead, the purchase method is the one you will see virtually all the time.

HOW'S YOUR UNDERSTANDING

Here are two questions you should be able to answer, based on what you have just read:

1. On January 1, 1996, Supersix Inc. bought 75% of the voting shares of Weaknees Ltd. for $231,000 cash. At that date, Weaknees's balance sheet showed assets of $784,000 and liabilities of $697,000. Supersix assessed the fair values of Weaknees's assets to be $800,000 and its liabilities to be $690,000 at acquisition date. Why do noncontrolling (minority) interest and goodwill appear on Supersix's consolidated balance sheet, and what were the figures for those items at acquisition date? ($21,750; $148,500)
2. At the same date, Supersix's balance sheet showed assets of $56,782,000 and liabilities of $45,329,000. What would be the consolidated equity of Supersix after consolidating Weaknees? ($11,453,000)

5.11 NOTES AND OTHER SUPPLEMENTARY INFORMATION

The four standard financial statements are not enough to transmit all the information felt to be needed by users of the statements. Therefore, GAAP require that a variety of supplementary narrative and tabular data be appended to the statements. Companies may add more if they wish, but GAAP provide that at a minimum, certain added pieces are sufficiently important that they are considered an integral part of the statements and are covered by the auditor's report (list 1 below).

Here are outlines of the kinds of information typically covered by the notes and supplementary disclosures. See the financial statements of The North West Company at the back of the book for examples.

1. *Normally Required by Authoritative Standards*
   a. A description of the company's significant accounting policies, understanding of which is necessary in interpreting the statements' figures (usually the first note following the statements);
   b. Backup details on any statement figures needing further explanation, typically the amortization figures, long-term debts, share capital, pension liability, and any accounts unusually calculated or very significant for the particular company;
   c. Information on some things not included in the figures, such as "contingent" (potentially possible) liabilities, purchase commitments, lawsuits, relationships with associated companies or persons, significant "subsequent" events since the official balance sheet date (for example, a major fire);
   d. Analysis of revenues and contributions to income of any significant product-line or geographical "segments" of the company's business (for example, contribution of a lumber product line vs. a food line, or operations in Canada vs. the United States).
2. *Also Pretty Much Part of GAAP, Especially for Larger Companies*
   a. Comparative income and balance sheet figures going back at least five years, often ten. If a company changes any important accounting poli-

   cy, it has to go back and change such trend analyses to keep past figures comparable;
   b. An explanation of the different responsibilities of management and the external auditors for the financial information and of management's responsibility to maintain control over the company's assets;
   c. A "management discussion and analysis" of the decisions and results for the year.
3. *Still Largely Voluntary*
   a. Graphs and other pictorial supplements;
   b. Details of employment contracts, product specifications, business policies, donations, business objectives, and other such details;
   c. Lists of subsidiary and associated companies, senior managers, and office addresses;
   d. Reports on pollution control, human resource management, trade with unpopular countries, and other socially sensitive information.

5.12 A NOTE ON GOVERNMENTAL AND NOT-FOR-PROFIT ACCOUNTING

This book emphasizes business organizations, because they provide quite enough complexity for an introductory study of financial statements! But there are many other kinds of organizations that produce financial statements, and because these organizations are often structured as they are for particular reasons, their accounting must adapt to their legal, organizational, and financial peculiarities. Two common nonbusiness organizations are governments and not-for-profit organizations.

GOVERNMENTS

Governments represent people but do not have owners, nor are they created to earn income or retain earnings. Therefore, government financial statements differ from those of business in many ways, including:

- No owners' equity section (usually just a "fund balance" that indicates assets minus liabilities);
- No income statement (instead, a statement of revenues and expenditures, using only partial accruals, for short-term receivables and payables, and related to authorized budgets and other rules set by legislatures);
- No or little amortization (because income measurement is not a goal);
- Lack of provision for long-term obligations such as civil servant and taxpayer pension plans (the cost of which governments appear to expect to meet out of future tax revenues);
- Lack of consolidation, because various special funds require separate accounting and legislator scrutiny.

NOT-FOR-PROFIT ORGANIZATIONS

An enormous range of organizations, including private clubs, charities such as the Red Cross, sports teams, universities, political parties, research units, the Girl Guides, churches, and unions, are classified as not-for-profit (or nonprofit) organizations. The members of such organizations do not own them as do owners of businesses and do not have a right to a share of any equity (assets minus liabilities), nor are members usually as oriented to making income, because most such organizations are created to perform a specific service or other function. Some of the accounting methods used by these organizations are similar to those of governments, but many such organizations, especially those close to being businesses, use fairly complete accrual accounting, including amortization.

To give you an example of the accounting for not-for-profit organizations, reprinted as Exhibit 5.6 without notes, is the March 31, 1993, balance sheet of Glenrose Rehabilitation Hospital, an Edmonton, Alberta, hospital that helps people incapacitated by illness, accident, or genetic problems. You will see many similarities between this balance sheet and the business balance sheets this book has focused on. You will also see some differences, such as:

- No long-term debt (because long-term assets have been provided by government grants);
- Some government grants for operating and capital purposes have not yet been spent for the specified purposes, so the unspent parts are shown as liabilities;
- No share capital or other owners' contributions, because Glenrose does not have owners as do private companies, but instead receives funds from governments and various donors;
- The equity section of the balance sheet is separated by origin of the equity: some is due to accumulation of greater operating revenues than operating costs (similar to the retained earnings of a private business), some has been produced by donations and other special funding sources that require Glenrose to spend the money only on designated purposes (the "Discretionary fund surplus" and "Trust fund"), and most has been provided by government grants to construct capital assets;
- Equity in capital assets (building, equipment, etc.) equals the book value of the capital assets, so that equity is reduced each year by the same amount as the amortization and depreciation on the capital assets.

Keeping various designated funds separate and accounting operations separate from other activities requires accounting methods that can be more complex than those used by private businesses. Amortization and other accrual accounting procedures can also be more complex. The trend, encouraged by the *CICA Handbook*, is to bring the accounting for such organizations as much as possible under the same GAAP structure as that applying to businesses, without removing such important features as keeping designated funds separate and without obscuring the fair reporting of nonprofit activities by reporting them as if they were intended to generate profit.

Exhibit 5.6

Glenrose Rehabilitation Hospital
Balance Sheet
as at March 31, 1993

	1993	1992
Assets		
Current:		
Cash	$ —	$2,640,627
Short term deposits	10,191,211	7,888,050
Accounts receivable *(Note 4)*	1,381,917	1,414,271
Inventories	281,207	309,288
Accrued interest	115,296	133,592
Prepaid expenses and deposits	2,307	2,123
Long-term deposits	1,848,612	810,950
Capital assets (Note 5)	63,780,936	66,168,973
	$77,601,486	$79,367,874
Liabilities and Equity		
Liabilities:		
Current:		
Bank indebtedness	$ 264,971	$ —
Accounts payable and accrued liabilities *(Note 6)*	4,363,520	4,596,978
Deferred designated operating grants *(Note 7)*	11,951	196,132
Deferred capital grants *(Note 8)*	510,130	3,099,148
Construction holdbacks	—	36,908
	5,150,572	7,929,166
Equity:		
Operating surplus	4,518,206	2,379,127
Discretionary fund surplus	3,624,491	2,441,495
Trust fund	527,281	449,113
	8,669,978	5,269,735
Equity in capital assets	63,780,936	66,168,973
	72,450,914	71,438,708
	$77,601,486	$79,367,874

The accompanying notes are part of these financial statements. *(Not included)*

5.13 MANAGERS AND FINANCIAL ACCOUNTING STANDARDS

Managers may be interested in accounting standards for several reasons. On the positive side, standards should:

1. Make reporting managers' performance clearer;
2. Make for easier comparisons with other companies;
3. Reduce the costs of accounting (each company would not have to work through and invent accounting methods on its own);
4. Increase the company's credibility to important users of financial statements in general; and
5. Help to evaluate the conceptual and numerical effects of accounting choices and business decisions managers may have to make (as we saw in the land accounting example in Section 5.9).

On the negative side:

1. Standards may specify general methods that do not work well for or even mismeasure some specific companies or situations;
2. Not all managers may wish to be measured clearly or to have their company's performance easily comparable to that of other companies;
3. Some complex standards may be quite costly to follow for some companies; and
4. New standards may cause difficulty for loan agreements, bonus plans, or other arrangements that depend on accounting information and that were agreed to prior to the implementation of the new standards.

With reasons like these, it should be no surprise that the top management of many companies (and of the firms of auditors who have the companies as clients) take accounting standards very seriously. Many companies seek to influence accounting standards through lobbying standard-setters (such as CICA or FASB), lobbying securities commissions and other government agencies, doing their own studies of the effects of proposed standards, looking around for audit firms that will help them avoid the negative effects they fear, and even launching lawsuits.[10]

5.14 ACCOUNTING RESEARCH: PROFESSIONAL JUDGMENT AND STANDARDS

The following passages are quoted from a research study, titled *Professional Judgment in Financial Reporting*, to outline the connection between accounting standards and the judgment and decision-making of professional accountants and managers who prepare financial statements and audit them.[11]

> The exercise of professional judgment by those preparing and auditing financial accounting information is at the core of financial reporting. Without the flexibility and the intelligence provided by professional judgment, the complex system of financial accounting procedures, standards

> and rules would be ponderous, unresponsive, insensitive: in short, unworkable. Financial reporting, as it operates in Canada and elsewhere, requires professional judgment at many levels, in a host of circumstances, and by a variety of skilled and experienced professionals.
>
> It is one of financial accounting's paradoxes that, though the reported information is largely numerical, has a factual, dispassionate character, and is supported by systematic accounting procedures, the messages it conveys have been shaped, often perhaps determined, by an extensive professional judgment process. There is evidence, in this study and in other research, that two experienced accountants may well make different judgments based on the same situation, the same information, and thus may produce or attest to different accounting results in that situation.

The research study drew several conclusions from an examination of the relationship between professional judgment and professional standards, including:

1. The relationship between professional judgment and professional standards is crucial to understanding the value and quality of professional judgment in financial reporting.
2. Standards are useful in reducing the risks implied by imperfect human judgment, in transmitting professional wisdom on common judgment problems efficiently, and in coping with the subjectivity and complexity of accrual accounting and with the continually changing environment.
3. Professional judgment is also important to the effective operation of standards. It is needed in determining the specific applicability of general standards, in making required estimates and evaluating materiality, and in ensuring that the financial statements reflect the economic substance of events. It also assists in the evolution and adaptation of standards as conditions change.
4. Standards affect the nature of, and demand for, professional judgment by limiting alternatives and clarifying judgment criteria, but also by being occasionally unclear, contradictory, or otherwise imperfect.
5. The judgment/standards relationship is important, not only to preparers and auditors, but also to the users of the resulting information.

Chapter 5 of the same study reviews several reasons for having professional standards, some of which are to reduce the risk of judgment error, to set down the best thinking about solutions, to increase efficiency in solving problems, and to cope with the complexities of business and of accounting's accrual methods of reflecting business complexities.

In their summary, the authors commented:

> The relationship between professional judgment and professional standards is close and is in most respects mutually supportive. Improvements in standards will improve professional judgment, and vice versa, and preparers, auditors and users of accounting information all have an important stake in an effective professional judgment/standards relationship.

5.15 CONTINUING DEMONSTRATION CASE

INSTALMENT 5

Data for Instalment 5

The preparation of the standard set of financial statements for Mato Inc. to August 31, 1994, has been illustrated. We left Mavis Janer and Tomas Brot preparing for the board of directors' meeting and thinking about how to get their company out of trouble. As they reviewed their financial statements, Mavis and Tomas had some questions about their accounting. They are not accountants, remember, and are anxious to get on with running the business. Here, then, are some of their questions:

a. Should they hire an accountant to "do their books" so they will not be responsible for that job?

b. Do their financial statements have to follow the *CICA Handbook*'s standards?

c. What things, if any, in the financial statements will require policy decisions by them as the owners/managers?

d. Should their company appoint an external auditor?

Results for Instalment 5

a. Hiring an accountant is really a matter of preference and money. If they do not want to do the job and feel strongly enough about it to want to pay someone else, and can afford to do so, they should go ahead. Their new employee may be able to do what is needed, with the help of the software they already have. However, this does not absolve them of their ultimate managerial responsibility for the accounting and financial statements.

b. No, their statements do not have to follow the *Handbook*. The *Handbook* is a guide, not law. However, their company is incorporated and the statute under which it is incorporated will require that annual financial statements be prepared following accepted principles. The statute may even state or imply that the *Handbook* is the source of what is acceptable. Also, groups of people such as their bankers, the other investors, prospective purchasers of their business, income tax authorities, and external auditors may object to their financial statements if they diverge much from the guidelines in the *Handbook*.

c. From the financial statements in Instalments 3 and 4, some possible financial accounting issues are:

   - Amortization seems to be calculated in a simple way. While this is not a bad thing, the simple calculations may not provide figures that are useful in evaluating the performance of this particular business.
   - Inventory is getting large. If the customers are boutique retailers who are likely to be sensitive to seasonal and other changes in demand, the company may have to deal with obsolete or out-of-style inventory items and may need an accounting policy for valuing such items (reducing their value to some estimate of market value).
   - The balance sheet does not say much about the company's authorized and issued share capital, such as the number of shares or rights of shareholders. A note to the statements giving this information would be a good idea (and expected by GAAP).

- The company may have made commitments to purchase various items, such as those intended for the Christmas season. Users of the financial statements might like to know about any such commitments.
- The company is operating in leased premises and has spent a large amount of money to improve those premises. Users of the financial statements may find some information about the lease useful, especially its term and any renewal privileges.
- Users of the financial statements might like more information about the loan made by Tomas's father, such as confirmation of the fact that it is repayable on demand, as it appears to be (and so may be more like the bank loan than it now seems) and what interest is payable on the loan, if any.
- The income statement shows no interest expense at all, yet there is a significant bank loan. There appears either to be an error or an unrecorded liability. (Or perhaps interest has been paid and is included in the office and general expenses.)
- It is likely that the bank can seize the inventory and accounts receivable to collect on its loan: this and other security on the bank loan should be disclosed.
- It is common to disclose salaries paid to directors and officers (in other words, those of Mavis and Tomas) separately from other salaries.

d. There is probably little need to have their financial statements audited at this point. Auditing does cost money! However, they will have to satisfy the income tax authorities, their banker, and the other investors as to the credibility of their financial statements, so they should keep careful records and look into hiring an outside accountant to at least review the financial statements and report that no substantial errors appear to have been made. (There are several levels of external help, including simple advice, a more substantial review, and even a full audit.)

HOMEWORK AND DISCUSSION TO DEVELOP UNDERSTANDING

PROBLEM 5.1* Connections among the financial statements

Why should the set of financial statements that is included in the annual report be interpreted as a set? Putting it another way, does the income statement tell you anything about the balance sheet, does the balance sheet tell you anything about the cash flow statement, etc.?

PROBLEM 5.2* Identify some accounting concepts and principles

Identify the accounting concepts or principles that relate to each of the following sentences and explain what effect the concepts or principles have on financial statements:

1. Users of financial statements should be able to believe that the numbers represent real events.
2. Financial statements should avoid undue optimism about the future.

3. It is hard to say absolutely that a company is performing well or badly, but you can evaluate its relative performance.
4. Financial accounting should be helpful both in understanding the past and looking ahead to the future.
5. The content of financial statements should not depend on who prepares them.

PROBLEM 5.3* Reasons for and difficulty of auditor independence

Auditors play an important role in the financial reporting system, and their independence from their clients is an essential feature of this system.

1. Why is such independence considered necessary?
2. Why is it difficult to maintain?

PROBLEM 5.4* Explain the effects of changing from non-GAAP to GAAP

The president of a small local company has been advised by a newly hired accountant that the company's balance sheet valuation methods are not quite appropriate. One example is that the company has been valuing inventories at cost, whereas GAAP normally require that the lower of cost or market be used for such a current asset. Explain as carefully as you can what would be the effect on the company's balance sheet, income statement, and cash flow statement if the accounting for inventory were changed to the GAAP basis.

PROBLEM 5.5* Cost vs. equity basis for nonconsolidated investment

China Sports Ltd. purchased 40% of the voting shares of Brassy Ltd. at the beginning of this year for $4,100,000. During the year, Brassy earned net income of $600,000 and paid dividends of $250,000. China Sports, which has been accounting for its investment in Brassy on the cost basis, has income of $800,000 for this year. If the equity basis were used instead, what would China Sports Ltd.'s income be?

PROBLEM 5.6* Basic consolidation calculations and balance sheet

Seeking to expand its markets, Big Ltd. recently purchased 80% of the voting shares of Piddling Ltd. for $10,800,000. At the date of the acquisition, Piddling had assets of $14,600,000, liabilities of $8,200,000, and equity of $6,400,000. By the best estimate Big could make at the date of acquisition, the fair market value of Piddling's assets was $16,100,000 and that of its liabilities was $8,300,000.

1. Calculate the goodwill on consolidation as of the acquisition date.
2. Calculate the noncontrolling (minority) interest as of the acquisition date.
3. Complete the consolidated balance sheet figures below.

Account	Big Ltd.	Piddling Ltd.	Consolidated
General assets	$105,000,000	$14,600,000	$
Investment in Piddling	10,800,000		
Goodwill			
General liability	83,700,000	8,200,000	
Noncontrolling interest			
Equity	32,100,000	6,400,000	

PROBLEM 5.7 Is disclosure enough if GAAP are not followed?

Section 1500, paragraph .06 of the *CICA Handbook* recommends:

> Where the accounting treatment or statement presentation does not follow the recommendations in this Handbook, the practice used should be explained in notes to the financial statements with an indication of the reason why the recommendation concerned was not followed.

Does paragraph .06 mean that a company is free to use whatever accounting treatment or statement presentation it likes, as long as the notes to the financial statements explain the situation? Why or why not?

PROBLEM 5.8 Which GAAP principles apply and how are they applied?

You happen to be walking past your boss's office and you hear her exclaim, "These generally accepted accounting principles give me a headache! How can I figure out which ones apply to my business and decide how to apply them?" Wanting to impress your boss, you rush into her office and blurt out some answers to the questions. What do you say?

PROBLEM 5.9 Is historical cost accounting irrelevant to decision-making?

Argue both for and against the following proposition: historical cost accounting is irrelevant to users' decision-making.

PROBLEM 5.10 Is having no GAAP worse than the present GAAP complexity?

Write a paragraph or two discussing the following topic: The only thing worse than the large and complex set of practices, standards, and theories that make up GAAP would be if there were no such thing as GAAP.

PROBLEM 5.11 Contents of a normal set of financial statements

Your friend John operates a successful small business. He recently came to you, saying, "I went to the bank to borrow some money for my business, but the banker said that before the bank would consider a loan, I had to submit a 'proper' set of financial statements. I'm not sure what that includes!" After wondering to yourself how your friend ever got this far in business, you explained what components normally comprise a set of financial statements and described what each of them does.

Outline what you said to John.

PROBLEM 5.12 Usefulness of accounting concepts and principles

Harold is a hard-driving, impatient business executive. You work for him and can feel the grey hair sprouting on your head from all the pressure. One day, he returns from a lunch meeting with his accountant and says, "That accountant told me that there are accounting concepts and principles that tell me important things about why my financial statements are useful, why they are worth all the money they cost to produce and audit. I'm not convinced."

Choose any five of the concepts and principles listed at the end of Section 5.3 and explain to Harold why those five are useful. Make your explanations brief and to the point: Harold hates long-winded answers!

PROBLEM 5.13 Can one criterion of materiality suit different users?

The president of a public corporation recently commented:

> Our auditor says that our financial statements present fairly our financial position and the results of our operations. I challenged him as to how he determined such fairness. He replied that fairness means that the financial statements are not misstated in amounts that would be considered material, that is, significant.
>
> I believe that there is some confusion with this materiality concept, since different users of our financial statements may have different ideas as to what is material. For example, bankers, institutional investors, small investors, and tax assessors all have different perceptions of materiality.

Discuss the issues raised by the president.

PROBLEM 5.14 Purpose, value, and limitations of the auditor's report

1. What purpose is served by the external auditor of a corporation?
2. Review the auditor's report included with the financial statements of any company you like. What is the report telling you?
3. To an investor, what value has been added to the financial statements by the auditor's report? Why?
4. Suggest some limitations on the value of the auditor's report that an investor should be aware of.

PROBLEM 5.15 Determine asset costs from various possible components

Determine the costs of land and building that would appear on the balance sheet of Smith Co. Ltd., based on the following information:

Purchase price of plant site	$ 175,000
Building materials (includes $10,000 in materials wasted due to worker inexperience)	700,000
Machinery installation charges	40,000
Grading and draining plant site	20,000
Labour costs of construction (Smith Co. used its own workers to build the plant rather than laying them off because business was slack. However, the labour to build the plant cost $40,000 more than outside contractors would have charged, due to inside workers' inexperience and inefficiency.)	500,000
Machinery purchase cost	1,000,000
Machinery delivery charges	10,000
Parking lot grading and paving	60,000
Replacement of building windows shot out by vandals before production start-up	7,000
Architect's fees	40,000

PROBLEM 5.16 Conceptual components of asset cost

The new accountant for Mactaggart Industries is wondering how to calculate the cost of a new machine the company just installed. Explain briefly whether or not you think each of the following items should be part of the machine's cost, and why:

a. The invoice price of the machine;
b. Sales tax paid on the machine;
c. Shipping charges to get the machine to the company's factory;
d. The cost of the factory manager's trip to the machine manufacturer's plant to choose the machine;
e. The cost of painting the machine light green, as other machines in the factory are painted;
f. Estimated revenue lost because the machine was late arriving;
g. The cost of substandard products made while the factory personnel were learning how to operate the machine (all thrown away so as not to damage the company's reputation for quality products);
h. Interest cost on the bank loan used to finance the machine's purchase;
i. The cost of moving three other machines in the factory to make room for the new one.

PROBLEM 5.17 Effects of asset accounting change to market from cost

Beauport Inc. owns several parcels of land in the Montreal area. The area has been subject to wide swings in real estate values, and the president is doubtful that the historical cost basis is appropriate for accounting for the company's land and buildings. Give short but careful answers to the following questions asked by the president:

1. If we changed to market values for the real estate instead of cost, would that make our balance sheet look better, or worse?
2. Similarly for income, would using market value instead of cost make us look more profitable, or less?
3. Does it matter what we do, as long as we disclose both cost and market value somewhere in our financial statements?

PROBLEM 5.18 Equity and cost bases of accounting for an investment

Baxter Investments Inc. owns 23% of the voting shares of Bluebird Hotel Ltd. It bought them last year for $1,500,000, and, since then, Bluebird has reported net income of $400,000 and declared dividends totalling $160,000. Baxter accounts for its investment in Bluebird on the equity basis.

1. Give the figures for:
   a. The revenue Baxter will have recognized from its investment since acquisition.
   b. The present balance in the company's balance sheet account for investment in Bluebird Hotel Ltd.
2. Give the same figures requested in question 1 if Baxter accounted for its investment on the cost basis.

PROBLEM 5.19 Basic questions about temporary investments

1. Many companies have temporary investments on their balance sheets. How do these investments differ from:

a. cash?
b. intercorporate investments accounted for on the equity basis?

2. Why, in spite of 1 (a), are such investments often included in cash and cash equivalents for purposes of deriving the SCFP's cash flow information?
3. Why are such investments valued at the lower of cost or market?

PROBLEM 5.20 Equity basis of accounting vs. consolidation

Accounting for intercorporate investments is subject to GAAP. Apply your knowledge of GAAP to the following situation:

International Newspapers Ltd. owns 45% of the voting shares of Nomad Printers Ltd. It acquired the shares several years ago for $10,000,000. Nomad lost money for some years after acquisition but has recently begun to be profitable: since International acquired its shares, Nomad has had losses totalling $790,000 and incomes totalling $940,000, for a total net income since acquisition of $150,000. Last year, Nomad paid its first dividend, $100,000.

1. International accounts for its investment in Nomad on the equity basis. What does this mean?
2. What is the present figure for Investment in Nomad on the balance sheet of International?
3. What difference would it make to the balance sheet of International if the Nomad investment were consolidated instead?
4. Suppose that International had bought 65% of the Nomad voting shares for its $10,000,000 and that at that date the following values existed for Nomad: book value of assets, $18,000,000; sum of fair values of assets, $19,000,000; book value of liabilities, $7,000,000; sum of fair values of liabilities, $10,000,000. Calculate the goodwill that would have been shown on the consolidated balance sheet of International if the Nomad investment had been consolidated at that date.

PROBLEM 5.21 Basic consolidated figures

Fat Furniture has decided to purchase 65% of Banana Appliances Ltd. for $43,000,000 in cash. The two companies' balance sheets as at acquisition date are (in millions of dollars):

Assets	**Fat**	**Banana**	**Liabilities and Equity**	**Fat**	**Banana**
Cash equivalent assets	$112	$10	Cash equivalent liabilities	$128	$ 0
Other current assets	304	45	Other current liabilities	160	10
Noncurrent assets (net)	432	25	Noncurrent liabilities	272	15
			Share capital	160	15
			Ret. earnings	128	40
	$848	$80		$848	$80

Fat Furniture has evaluated all of Banana's assets and liabilities as having fair value equal to book value except for its noncurrent assets, which Fat Furniture believes have a fair value of $33 million.

1. Calculate the consolidated goodwill that would appear on the consolidated balance sheet at acquisition date.
2. Calculate the following consolidated figures as at acquisition date:
   a. Consolidated total assets;
   b. Consolidated owners' equity;
   c. Consolidated total liabilities.

PROBLEM 5.22 Goodwill amount and reasons; later consolidated income

White Knight Acquisitions Ltd. recently purchased a 70% interest in Premier Publications, a small magazine wholesaler. Premier's balance sheet on the date of acquisition appears below.

Assets		Liabilities and Equity	
Cash	$ 10,000	Liabilities	$102,000
Accounts receivable (net)	55,000	Owners' equity	108,000
Inventory	70,000		
Fixed assets (net)	75,000		
	$210,000		$210,000

Premier's receivables have an adequate provision for doubtful accounts. Inventories are carried at cost and current replacement value is about $70,000. Land with a book value of $20,000 has a market value of $29,000. In the purchase agreement, White Knight assumed all of Premier's liabilities. Before the sale was final, the then owners of Premier were allowed to withdraw all cash from the company as a dividend.

1. If White Knight paid $104,000 (in addition to the $102,000 to pay the liabilities) for its interest in Premier Publications, what was the amount of purchased goodwill? (Hint: all White Knight got for its money were receivables, inventories, and fixed assets.)
2. Why would White Knight have been willing to pay this amount for goodwill?
3. Assume that in the year following the acquisition, Premier made a net income of $14,000. Therefore, decide whether the following statement is true or false and tell why: To record Premier's earnings, the consolidated retained earnings of White Knight Acquisitions will be increased by $14,000.

PROBLEM 5.23 Answer conceptual questions on consolidation

Chromium Furniture Ltd. wishes to expand operations by acquiring other furniture manufacturers and associated businesses. In relation to this, the president is curious about accounting methods for groups of companies. Answer briefly the following four questions the president has asked:

1. Why does a subsidiary have to be consolidated with the parent's accounts?
2. Why doesn't consolidating a newly acquired subsidiary affect consolidated retained earnings? (After all, the subsidiary has retained earnings too.)
3. Since it is the sum of more than one company, won't a consolidated balance sheet present a stronger financial picture than the parent's unconsolidated balance sheet does?
4. What does "Goodwill on consolidation" on the consolidated balance sheet mean?

PROBLEM 5.24 Explain consolidation for acquisition vs. merger

You are the newly appointed assistant to the president of Hollywood Horror Inc., a movie producer. While you are at lunch with the president and another executive high up in another producing company (Pasadena Productions), the subject of a possible merger of the two companies, or perhaps a purchase of Pasadena by Hollywood, comes up. The president turns to you and says, "What accounting difference will it make if we buy Pasadena outright, or if we just buy a controlling interest, or if we and they exchange shares and merge the two companies?" What is your answer?

PROBLEM 5.25 Business GAAP for governments and nonprofit groups

1. Do you think governments should follow the same GAAP that business enterprises follow in their financial accounting? Why or why not?
2. Do you think not-for-profit organizations should follow the same GAAP that business enterprises do? Why or why not?

PROBLEM 5.26 Answer accounting questions from the treasurer of a club

Roy has just been elected treasurer of Club Ped, a bicycle touring club, and has been handed the club's accounting records by the previous treasurer. The club accounts for its revenue on the accrual basis, but records expenditures from cash, not accrual expenses. Roy has taken a course in business accounting, but feels his accounting skills are quite modest and he is nervous about the accounting he will be responsible for as treasurer. Answer the following questions Roy has asked you:

1. "Will I have to follow GAAP in doing the club's financial statements?"
2. "The club has not had an income statement, but has had a 'statement of revenue and expenditure' that shows how much revenue excess (or deficit) is left over each year. Why is there no income statement as a business would have?"
3. "The club members are concerned about several things—like the number of members we have, the sources of grants we've received, and the success of various bicycle tours we've taken. Can I include these sorts of things in the financial statements?"
4. "Do we have to have the financial statements audited?"

PROBLEM 5.27 Should small businesses have different GAAP?

(Challenging) Several authors have addressed the question of whether small business enterprises should have their own set of GAAP rather than be required to comply with all the recommendations presently in the *CICA Handbook*. The writers reason that many current accounting principles seem to be geared to large businesses and that small ones should not be asked to implement recommendations that are irrelevant or that do not justify their costs through greater benefits.[12]

1. Give the arguments for having one set of GAAP for all sizes of businesses.
2. Now argue for small businesses having their own set of GAAP.

PROBLEM 5.28 Is accounting neutral?

(Challenging)

A speaker at a recent conference stated:

> Many groups, including governments, financial institutions, investors, and corporations in various industries, argue that their interests are affected by present and proposed accounting pronouncements. The sometimes contradictory interests of these groups are recognized by the accounting profession. However, accounting is neutral and is not influenced by the self-interest of any one group.[13]

Discuss the above quotation.

PROBLEM 5.29 Current values rather than usual GAAP?

(Challenging)

1. Some business people persist in thinking that a balance sheet measures a business's current value either as to assets or as to net worth (equity). Explain why they are wrong.
2. Suggest as many ways as you can of providing just what the above people want. Feel free to ignore GAAP in your answer.
3. When methods of replacing traditional asset valuation methods with current values have been tried, they have generally been rejected by the very people (owners, stock markets, and managers) they were intended to help. Why has this been so?

PROBLEM 5.30 The need for independent and objective auditors

(Challenging)

1. Discuss the major factors in today's society that have made the need for independent audits much greater than it was 25 years ago.
2. Give examples of cases where there is conflict of interest between preparers of financial statements and users of them.
3. Why are independence and an objective state of mind essential in an auditor? Are they necessary in all professions?

PROBLEM 5.31 What if top managers disagree with GAAP?

(Challenging)

Should top managers be held responsible for their companies' accounting if authoritative standards prescribe accounting methods they disagree with? Why or why not?

PROBLEM 5.32 Threats to an auditor's independence

(Challenging)

Pat is the partner on the audit of Hardwood Emporium Ltd. Comment on whether or not, and why, each of the following may be a threat to Pat's independence.

1. Pat and the chief financial officer of Hardwood Emporium play golf together every few weeks.
2. During the audit, Pat notices that the company has a serious problem with its computer system. Pat's accounting firm is then hired by Hardwood Emporium to do a major redesign of the system, for a large fee.
3. As part of the completion of the audit, Pat works with the company to determine its likely income tax liability for the year, including helping to prepare the company's income tax returns. Pat bills the company for the tax advice separately from the audit fee.
4. Pat's former assistant on the Hardwood Emporium audit is hired by the company as the chief financial accountant, responsible for preparing all the company's financial statements.
5. Pat is asked to submit a bid on the next year's Hardwood Emporium audit fee, in competition with several other accounting firms. Pat decides to submit a very low bid because the income from tax and consulting services would make up for the lower audit revenue.

PROBLEM 5.33 Prepare a full set of statements under GAAP

(Challenging)

Macro Ltd. services personal computers. Don Debit, the company's accountant, has compiled the following list of balances in the accounts of Macro Ltd. at January 31, 1996, the company's year-end.

Macro Ltd.
List of Account Balances, January 31, 1996

Accounts payable	$ 40,000
Accounts receivable	48,000
Accumulated depreciation—building	6,000
Bank loan	100,000
Building	86,000
Cash	30,000
Depreciation on building for the year	6,000
Dividends declared	20,000
Dividends payable	5,000
General expenses	170,000
Investments	16,000
Income tax expense	3,000
Interest on bank loan for the year	12,000
Land	50,000
Service fee revenues	213,000
Share capital	15,000
Shareholders' loan	60,000
Repair supplies used during year	38,000
Retained earnings	25,000
Gain on sale of plant and equipment	15,000

Here is additional information about some of these figures:

1. Accounts payable will be paid in February 1996 except for $5,000, which will be paid February 1, 1997.
2. Accounts receivable will be collected in February or March 1996.
3. The bank loan is payable in yearly payments of $20,000, which are to be made December 31 of each year for the next five years. Interest on the loan has been paid up to January 31, 1996.
4. A dividend of $20,000 was declared on January 31, 1996, and $15,000 was paid to the shareholders on the same day. The balance will be paid on December 31, 1996.
5. "Investments" were purchased just before the year-end and consist of the following:

8% term deposits, due in April 1996	$ 4,000
Investment in shares of ABC Ltd.	12,000
	$16,000

   The shares of ABC Ltd. are not publicly traded. so there is no ready market for them. Macro Ltd. owns 3% of ABC Ltd.'s shares.
6. The shareholders' loan is due on demand, but no repayment is expected to be made in the upcoming year. This loan is unsecured.
7. The land and building are recorded at estimated market value, based on an appraisal done on January 2, 1996. The land had cost $40,000; the building had cost $96,000.
8. The bank loan is secured by a first mortgage on the land and building.
9. Of the cash, $5,000 is held in trust, as part of the terms of a recent sales agreement with a customer.
10. "General expenses" includes $50,000 of a bad debt expense that was due to the bankruptcy of a major customer during the year.
11. "Income tax expense" includes $1,000 of tax related to the sale of plant and equipment during the year.
12. "Service fee revenues" includes $20,000 of revenue that should have been recorded in the prior year.

Prepare a properly classified balance sheet, income statement, and statement of retained earnings from the above information for the year ended January 31, 1996, as well as any notes to the financial statements that you feel are necessary to satisfy user needs and disclosure requirements under GAAP. If it is helpful, assume a prospective creditor such as a bank will use the financial statements.

PROBLEM 5.34 Discuss materiality, fairness, and conservatism

(Challenging) Some of the criteria involved in justifying the accounting method and the disclosure choices are troublesome to many people. Using the following opinions as starters, discuss the theoretical, social, and ethical merits of each of the criteria commented on:

1. *Materiality*

   "Using materiality as a criterion implies that some accountant has the arrogance to suppose that he or she can judge on behalf of all sorts of other people what information those people should or shouldn't have."

2. *Fairness*
   "Fairness seems to be an empty assurance. It refers to the financial statements being not misleading, but wouldn't it be more useful to go back to earlier times and ask the auditors to state whether the statements are correct?"
3. *Conservatism*
   "Conservatism benefits the potential investor or lender to the disadvantage of the present owners and managers. How can accountants who think seriously about the value of objective, independent information consider conservatism as an even remotely legitimate factor in choosing the numbers to report?"

PROBLEM 5.35 Applicability of ethics to manager and auditor

(Challenging)

1. Should a senior financial manager who works for a company and who is a professional accountant have to meet the same standards of professional ethics as does a colleague who is an external auditor in public practice? Why or why not?
2. Should codes of professional ethics prohibit external auditors from offering other services to audit clients, such as tax advice or financing advice? Why or why not?

PROBLEM 5.36 How to write down some assets

(Challenging)

Management of Apex Angora Inc., a major clothing manufacturer and retailer, wants to reduce the values of several assets on the company's balance sheet to recognize that severe business problems affecting the company's industry have reduced the assets' values. The assets in question include some inventory, some store buildings and land, and some manufacturing equipment specialized for making certain lines of clothing that are no longer selling well. The assets' write-down would be accomplished by crediting the asset accounts, but there is argument within the company about what to debit. Discuss briefly each of the following places to put the debit, advanced by various members of management (ignore income tax):

1. Use the debit to reduce share capital, because the company's troubles have reduced its value on the stock market.
2. Use the debit to reduce retained earnings directly, as a prior period adjustment that does not affect the income statement, because the assets' values have been declining for several years.
3. Add the debit to cost of goods sold for the year, because this sort of thing happens often enough to companies that it might as well be considered a cost of doing business.
4. Put the debit below the "income after income tax" line on the income statement as an extraordinary item, because it is very large for this company and management certainly hopes it will not happen again.
5. Put the debit below the "income after income tax" line on the income statement as a "discontinued operations" item, because the company is getting out of whole product lines.

PROBLEM 5.37 Various intercorporate investment questions

(Challenging) Tundra Industries has decided on a policy of growth through acquisition. During the last several years, it has purchased shares in several other companies:

Woodland Forestry Ltd. (65% owned)
Lac La Biche Developments Inc. (10% owned)
Arizona Meat Packing Corp. (30% owned)
Computer Control Services Ltd. (100% owned)

1. GAAP provide different methods of accounting for investments in companies such as those in which Tundra has shares, relative to the percentage of the voting interest held.
   a. Why are different methods provided?
   b. If Arizona Meat Packing reports a net income of $600,000 and declares dividends of $150,000 in a given year, what should Tundra show on its income statement for that year as its income from investment in Arizona?
2. Tundra recently bought its shares in Woodland for $200,000 cash. At that date, Woodland's shareholders' equity was: share capital, $50,000 and retained earnings, $110,000. Tundra's consolidated figures (*not including Woodland*) were: share capital, $2,600,000 and retained earnings, $4,900,000. Tundra will consolidate Woodland in its financial statements. At the date of acquisition that would be:
   a. The consolidated liability for minority interest in Woodland;
   b. Consolidated shareholders' equity.
3. If Woodland makes $50,000 of net income in any year, will that increase consolidated net income by $50,000? By less? By more? Explain briefly.
4. Consolidated financial statements add companies' figures together because they have joint ownership, not because they are necessarily similar. The companies Tundra owns, for example, are not much alike. Do you think this makes sense? Why?

PROBLEM 5.38 Goodwill and consolidated net income

(Challenging) Northern Supermarkets Inc. is increasing the vertical integration of its operations by buying out suppliers. On July 1, 1995, Northern purchased 70% of the common shares of Green Acres Farms, an Alabama supplier of asparagus, celery, and other produce. Green Acres is itself a bit of a conglomerate because it has extensive landholdings in Atlanta and Dallas, and owns dairies in Wisconsin and Ontario.

On July 1, 1995, Green Acres's balance sheet showed a net book value of $112,800,000. The aggregate net fair value of individual assets and liabilities was $161,000,000 as at that date. Northern paid $154,000,000 ($25,000,000 cash, the rest newly issued shares of Northern) for its investment in Green Acres.

It is now March 31, 1996, the end of Northern's fiscal year. For Northern, it has been a good year. Green Acres has also done well, reporting a net income of $33,000,000 during the nine months ended March 31, 1996, and declaring $15,000,000 in dividends during that period. On a nonconsolidated basis, Northern's investment in Green Acres stood at $166,600,000 at March 31, 1996, and its net income for the year was $74,200,000.

1. What accounting method is Northern using for its investment in Green Acres? How can you tell?

2. Two figures that may appear on the consolidated balance sheet of Northern and Green Acres are "Goodwill arising on consolidation" and "Minority interest liability." Why are the fair values of Green Acres's individual assets relevant for calculating the former but not the latter?
3. Calculate consolidated net income for the year ended March 31, 1996, as well as you can, with the data provided.

PROBLEM 5.39 Equity accounting, consolidation, segments

(Challenging) One of Vast Inc.'s investments in partly owned businesses is the Red Robin Baseball Club, of which Vast owns 45% and for which Vast accounts on the equity basis. The Robins have been losing money for years. Vast originally invested $20,000,000 in the club. The club lost $8,000,000 in the year ended April 30, 1995 (Vast's share of the loss would be $3,600,000), bringing its total accumulated losses by April 30, 1995, to $18,000,000 (Vast's share of which would be $8,100,000). Needless to say, the Robins have paid no dividends to their owners, having had losses all along.

1. The investment in the Robins is accounted for on the equity basis. What does this mean?
2. What is the book value of Vast's investment in the Robins as at April 30, 1995, on the equity basis?
3. What difference would it make to Vast's financial statements if the Robins investment were consolidated instead of being accounted for on the equity basis?
4. Vast's annual report includes information on both industry and geographic segments. What information does this supplementary data provide that the consolidated financial statements do not, and how might it change a decision on the part of a user?

PROBLEM 5.40 Accounting effects of a business acquisition

(Challenging) Suppose that, to spread its business risk, a major brewing company decides to buy into the retail furniture business by acquiring a controlling interest in a national chain that sells furniture, appliances, and related goods at discount prices. Changing its usual policy of 100% ownership, the brewer acquires a 60% voting interest. On January 1, 1996, the brewer pays $54,000,000 cash for 60% of the chain's voting shares. At that date, the chain's balance sheet shows:

Cash	$ 2,000,000	Demand bank loan	$14,000,000
Other current assets	53,000,000	Other current liab.	26,000,000
Noncurrent assets	38,000,000	Noncurrent liab.	20,000,000
Less accum. amort.	(6,000,000)	Shareholders' equity	27,000,000
	$87,000,000		$87,000,000

The brewer's evaluation is that the fair values at January 1, 1996, are the same as the book value for all of the chain's assets and liabilities except land; it is on the chain's books at a cost of $4,000,000, but the brewer's evaluation is that its fair value is $7,000,000 at January 1, 1996.

The furniture chain is expected to report a substantial net income for the four months, January 1, 1996, to April 30, 1996 (the brewer's year-end), so the brewery managers are pleased with their decision to get into the furniture retailing business.

1. The brewer owns more than 50% of the furniture chain, so it should be consolidated with the brewer's other companies in preparing financial statements. But the chain is quite different from the brewer's other activities, so would it make sense to add apples in with oranges? Comment on this question.
2. Calculate the consolidated goodwill (if any) arising as at January 1, 1996, from the purchase of the furniture chain.
3. Evaluate each of the following items, stating assumptions or reasons if you wish. If the furniture chain were consolidated with the brewer as of January 1, 1996, what would happen on *that* date to:

	Would Go Up	**Would Go Down**	**No Effect**	**Not Possible to Tell**
a. Consolidated total assets				
b. Consolidated shareholders' equity				
c. Consolidated net income since May 1, 1995				

4. Looking ahead to the consolidated income for the year ended April 30, 1996, will the furniture chain's expected substantial net income contribute significantly to the brewer's consolidated net income? Comment on this question.

PROBLEM 5.41 Accounting for merger vs. acquisition

(Challenging)

Winnipeg Merchandisers Ltd. and Red River Stores Ltd. are considering some form of business combination. Three alternatives are being studied: a full merger, accomplished by an exchange of shares; purchase of all the voting shares of Red River by Winnipeg; and purchase of 75% of the voting shares of Red River by Winnipeg. Management of the two companies wants to know what the combined company's consolidated balance sheet would look like, based on their present financial information. (The final figures will depend on the actual date of the combination.) Here are the two companies' balance sheets as at a recent date:

	Winnipeg Book Values	**Red River Book Values**	**Red River Fair Values**
Assets			
Current assets	$1,124,645	$1,005,789	$1,104,311
Noncurrent assets	3,678,872	2,890,003	3,040,722
Liabilities and Equity			
Current liabilities	1,076,554	879,321	899,321
Shareholders' equity	3,726,963	3,016,471	

If there is a merger, a new company, Winnipeg–Red River, will issue one share in itself in return for each share in either Winnipeg or Red River. If Winnipeg purchases all of Red River's voting shares, it is willing to pay $3,400,000, which it will finance by borrowing against the values of its and Red River's assets. If Winnipeg purchases only 75% of the voting shares, it is willing to pay only $2,400,000, because the remaining block of 25% would be held by a single person who might interfere with Winnipeg's plans for the combined company. If there is a merger, that person plans to sell all shares owned and move to another city.

1. Present the consolidated balance sheet under each of the three combinations being considered:
   a. Full merger;
   b. 100% purchase of Red River by Winnipeg; and
   c. 75% purchase of Red River by Winnipeg.
2. Write a brief report to the managements of the two companies, explaining carefully, and avoiding accounting jargon:
   a. Specifically, what are the differences in the consolidated balance sheets under the three combinations and why do those differences exist; and
   b. Which of the three balance sheets, in your opinion, would be the strongest.

CASE 5A Extend GAAP to cover environmental reports?

COMPANIES RUSH TO COME CLEAN

Trend to producing annual environmental reports picks up speed

A handful of Canadian companies are coming clean with annual environmental reports, joining a movement one international survey calls a small stampede.

Like annual financial reports, environmental reports allow shareholders, employees and customers to judge a company's performance and its future prospects.

"Investors have always been able to see the correlation between good management and good corporate citizenship," says Bill Davis, director of the Task Force on the Churches and Corporate Responsibility. "An environmental report sets some of that in the public domain."

While these reports are eagerly read by investors, customers and environmentalists, the practice remains in its infancy.

"We're sort of grappling and feeling our way along as to what information is needed and whether or not that information is going to be audited," says Nola Buhr, a doctoral candidate at the University of Western Ontario business school in London, Ont., who has studied environmental reporting.

But the early success of environmental reports by Monsanto Co. of St. Louis and Norway's Norsk Hydro AS "has been followed by a small stampede, with growing numbers of companies in all regions producing their own reports," says Coming Clean, a recent international survey of such reports sponsored in part by the International Institute of Sustainable Development in Winnipeg and Deloitte Touche Tohmatsu International.

Canadian Pacific Forest Products Ltd.'s second environmental annual report discusses each of its operations, with the support of charts and figures to track progress.

With the exception of the Thunder Bay complex, most of the Montreal-based company's mills reduced total suspended solids in their effluent last year. The amount of suspended particles emitted into the air was also reduced at most operations, but not at its newsprint plant in Dalhousie, N.B.

CP Forest's report not only will help its executives reassure shareholders at the company's annual meeting in Vancouver tomorrow that they are taking environmental issues seriously, but it also will help shareholders appreciate the challenges the company faces.

CP Forest, a unit of Canadian Pacific Ltd., has not been a lone pioneer in this area. Noranda Forest Inc. produced its third annual environmental report this year and Shell Canada Inc. will soon release its second.

As far back as the 1960s, companies set aside sections in their annual reports to discuss the environment, but the rush to publish separate environmental reports began after 1989.

"Some people say it was the Exxon Valdez," Ms. Buhr says.

The huge oil spill off the Alaska coast in March, 1989, probably served to focus executives' attention on several factors, including tougher government regulations, a growing environmental movement and lenders' increasing worries about liability for polluted sites.

"Today, financial institutions are becoming as critically interested in the environmental performance of assets where they have some involvement as lenders as they are of the financial performance of the company that manages those assets," says Jack MacLeod, who retired as chief executive of Calgary-based Shell Canada in January.

In addition to lenders and shareholders, companies are targeting customers and employees as crucial audiences for environmental reports.

A positive report can be used as a competitive advantage in marketing a company's products or as a morale builder for its staff.

But the growing use of environmental reports among competitors is forcing companies to support their statements of good intentions with more substantive data.

"The honeymoon period, in which early reports were welcomed more for the fact that they had been produced than because of what they said, will soon end," the Coming Clean report states.

As a result, more companies are delivering the bad news with the good in their reports. For example, Noranda Forest, a unit of Toronto-based Noranda Inc., says in its latest report that the amount of timberland it hasn't satisfactorily regenerated climbed to 3,250 hectares last year from 1,600 hectares a year earlier.

"We took a warts-and-all approach," says John Roberts, Noranda Forest's vice-president of environment. "You don't want to get into a whitewashing situation where your report looks like just more pablum."

Companies deciding to produce an environmental report should approach it almost like a marketing process, says Barry McDougall, director of environmental services at Deloitte & Touche in Ottawa.

The report's audience should be determined and the type of information they want identified and then delivered. The company should also follow up the report with surveys to determine if the report satisfied the needs of the audience and then make any necessary changes.

"[Companies] should not worry about failing the first time or not meeting all the expectations the first time, because this is an emerging field and it's not going to be easy," says Randy Billing, co-director of Ernst & Young's environmental practice.

The Goal

A good environmental report should show shareholders their company has the following:

- An environmental policy.
- A senior executive responsible for the company's environmental performance.
- A committee at the board level charged with overseeing environmental issues.
- Environmental performance goals or targets.
- Hard data indicating whether or not the company is in compliance with governmental regulations, and is progressing toward its stated goals.
- Estimated costs of any environmental liabilities such as polluted sites.
- An awareness of pending environmental legislation and its impact on operations.
- On-going reviews of environmental performance at its various facilities.
- Independent verification of its report, if affordable.
- A willingness to discuss its environmental successes and failures.

SOURCE: CASEY MAHOOD, "COMPANIES RUSH TO COME CLEAN," *GLOBE AND MAIL*, APRIL 26, 1993, B1.

Do you think the kinds of accounting concepts and standards this chapter has illustrated as being part of GAAP can or should apply to companies' environmental reports? Discuss the pros and cons of such an expansion and interpretation of GAAP, given the reasons you think companies would want to produce environmental reports and people would want to get them.

CASE 5B Should GAAP be tightened up?

Over coffee one morning, some accountants were discussing an editorial from the *Financial Post* criticizing GAAP. Here is the editorial.

IT'S TIME TO NARROW THE GAAP GAP

Financial reporting in Canada is just not good enough. There is too much deliberate, legally sanctioned, holier-than-thou confusion. It's pleasantly called the GAAP gap.

The Ontario Securities Commission is scrutinizing one side of the reporting issue—getting the company to put out the "facts." And hopefully, public companies will soon become liable for continually good disclosure.

But good reporting also embraces the way in which the so-called "facts" are colored, or spun, on the way out of the company's mouth. And that's the notorious GAAP gap.

GAAP stands for Generally Accepted Accounting Principles. Every public company must report according to GAAP, by law.

Well, GAAP is too elastic. Like a child's balloon, a company can make its earnings or assets grow bigger or smaller under GAAP, provided its accountants blow or suck hard enough.

In other words, public companies can adopt a careful, conservative approach to financial reporting or one that's freewheeling. It's up to them.

Well, this won't do. The accounting profession and the regulators must narrow the GAAP gap, so that investors can understand what's going on in companies into which they put their precious savings.

Here are some examples of companies riding horses through the GAAP gap. In all cases, the company's accounting falls within GAAP's legal limits.

A trust company conglomerate reports a $16-million profit, which could also be interpreted as a $12-million loss.

A holding company suddenly reclassifies some short-term investments as long term, raising a morass of valuation and liquidity issues.

A beverage company capitalizes some of its expenses, controversially. This practice maximizes assets and profits at the same time.

Some companies account for subsidiaries by cost accounting, which does not recognize the subsidiaries' losses, when they could use equity accounting, which does.

Another company has used slower depreciation schedules than the rest of its industry without explaining why. And so it goes on.

When confronted with these cases, the accounting profession argues, loftily, that GAAP must be elastic enough to allow for the reporting of unusual situations.

Well, some regulators paint a darker picture. Too many company accountants have become rule oriented, they say. When challenges about a loose presentation, the accountant often replies: "Show me where it says I can't do that?"

Well, if the accountants are becoming rule-oriented, give them tighter rules, within GAAP. That's the answer.

Investors are too often led into confusion through the GAAP gap. It must be narrowed.

SOURCE: "IT'S TIME TO NARROW THE GAAP GAP," *FINANCIAL POST*, JANUARY 29–31, 1994, S1.

Here are some comments the accountants made. What do you think?

"Those journalists are always after accountants and auditors. Don't they realize that we are professionals and exercise our judgment carefully, so that there were undoubtedly circumstances that made the editorial's examples sensible to the accountants and auditors involved? Even if they were not sensible, they are only a few examples—what about some examples of all the times the accountants and auditors did the right thing? Not newsworthy, I guess."

"Don't be too hard on the media. They're an important part of the workings of GAAP—after all, we find out that way if what we do really *is* generally accepted! Remember some of the media attention that led to improvements in accounting? Like the trouble over pooling of interests consolidation, and poor accounting by governments and non-profit organizations?"

"You know, the editorial does make me wonder just what advantage GAAP provide society. I remember an editorial somewhere after a plane crash, where the claim was that air regulations weren't strong enough to prevent crashes, and the counter-claim was that anytime you take off in an aluminum tube that is heavier than air, you're taking a chance and sooner or later someone will crash, regulations or not. Investing in businesses and managing them is at least as risky as flying, and people shouldn't expect GAAP to remove that risk. People need to become familiar with accounting principles and with the companies they invest in, so they can tell if something is amiss."

"I'll bet you could make an argument that having flexible GAAP to permit companies to tell their financial stories to the public in ways that fit those companies is cheaper for society in the long run than trying to control every accounting number with detailed rules. The rules would cost so much in accounting time, computers, and paper to administer that the cost of a few bad apples in the accounting barrel would be small in comparison."

"The editorial makes a good point about the dark side of the rules. If you have detailed rules, the accountants and auditors just turn into rule followers rather than professionals. You could extend that argument to say that GAAP are already too detailed."

"That's not what the editorial means. It is saying that accountants view rules as constraints, preventing them from doing things, not as guides to appropriate behaviour. It says that the accountants seem to think that unless a rule exists, they can do anything, so I think it means that the accountants don't exercise professional judgment at all."

CASE 5B Discuss ethics of an accounting manager's behaviour

Discuss the ethical issues involved in the situation described below. If it is helpful to you, a suggested framework for ethical decision-making follows the situation.[14]

Leslie was chief accountant for a municipality. The job included responsibility for the municipality's computer systems, which are mostly used for financial records such as tax billings and collections, budgets, operating expenditures, payrolls, and services such as parks and swimming pools, but also are used by the police, fire department, welfare office, and other municipal operations. Recent budget pressures and technological developments have created some information system challenges, so the municipal Council set up a task force to respond to the challenges and put Leslie in charge. The task force was specifically directed to find ways to save money that the municipality desperately needed elsewhere, in particular for services to several kinds of disadvantaged citizens.

Leslie was recently fired by Council for "insubordination and incompetence" resulting from the task force's work. Two problems were especially irritating to Council.

1. The task force developed an integrated computer system for recording and responding to emergency calls. The system would connect the emergency response system to tax records and other information about citizens, to discourage abuse and ensure that the municipality billed people for all services provided. Considerable financial benefit to the municipality would result, but at the cost of delays in responding to emergency calls and substantially reduced privacy for callers. Leslie was concerned about these costs, because delays could cost lives and loss of privacy might discourage needy people from calling. However, a meeting of the task force with the Finance Committee of Council, chaired by the mayor, resulted in instructions to Leslie to disregard those concerns because the efficiencies gained would allow other needy people to be helped with the funds saved. Leslie was not satisfied with this, feeling that the impact on emergency response was too high a price to pay, and as the person responsible for computer systems and head of the task force, wrote a confidential memo to the mayor stating that the Finance Committee's instructions were inappropriate and giving careful reasons. Someone leaked the memo to the local media, with sensational results that were quite embarrassing to Council.
2. As Council investigated the first problem, a second one came to light. Earlier in the task force's work, a list of abuses of municipal resources and services had been developed, so that the new system could be designed to reduce or eliminate them. The list included such things as people avoiding property taxes on home improvements, plowing and cleaning streets of important citizens first, people making multiple welfare claims, municipal employees taking unauthorized holiday leaves, sending several ambulances to one emergency call because of duplications in recording calls, senior citizens receiving more than authorized discounts on recreation fees, and gifts by some contractors to municipal employees who send business their way. In the interests of task force efficiency, because not everything could be solved at once, Leslie had shortened the list and asked the task force to focus only on the remaining abuses. Leslie had thought a lot about which abuses to keep on the list and had eliminated several that potentially involved large dollars but seemed to Leslie to be socially acceptable, like the seniors' discounts. Council members questioned Leslie's judgment on these issues and criticized Leslie for presuming to make the eliminations in the first place.

A FRAMEWORK FOR ETHICAL DECISION-MAKING ETHICS SHAREWARE

I. Identify the problem.

A. State the case briefly, with as many of the relevant facts and circumstances as you can gather within the decision time available. While accuracy is important, there can be a trade-off between gathering more information and letting morally significant options disappear.

B. What decisions have to be made? Remember that there may be more than one decision-maker and that their interactions can be important.

C. By whom? Who are the relevant decision-makers?

II. Specify feasible alternatives.

State the live options at each stage of decision-making for each decision-maker. You then should ask what the likely consequences are of various decisions. Here, you should remember to take into account good or bad consequences not just for yourself, your company or clients, but for all affected persons.

III. Use your ethical resources to identify morally significant factors in each alternative.

A. Principles. Remember that these principles provide a general direction and are not rules to be mechanically applied.

[1] Would be disregarding someone's autonomy? Would I be exploiting others or treating them paternalistically? Have promises been made? Are there legitimate expectations on the part of others because I am a business or professional person?

[2] Would I be harming someone to whom I have a general or specific obligation as a professional or as a human being?

[3] Should I be preventing harm, removing harm, or even providing positive benefits to others?

[4] Am I acting justly or fairly?

What would a good person do in these circumstances?

B. Policies and other source materials, professional norms such as company policy, legal precedents, and wisdom from your religious or cultural tradition.

C. Contextual features of the case that seem important such as the past history of relationships with various parties.

D. Personal judgements: yours, your associates, and trusted friends or advisors can be invaluable. Of course in talking a tough decision over with others you have to respect client and employer confidentiality. Discussion with others is particularly important when other decision-makers are involved, such as, your employer, co-workers, clients, or partners.

Experienced co-workers can be helpful. Some forward-looking companies have ethics committees or ombudsmen to provide advice. Discussion with a good friend or advisor can also help you by listening and offering their good advice.

IV. Propose and test possible resolutions.

A. Perform a sensitivity analysis. Consider your choice critically: which factors would have to change to get you to alter your decision?

B. Think about the effect of each choice upon the choices of other responsible parties. Are you making it easier or harder for them to do the right thing? Are you setting a good example?

C. Ask yourself what would a virtuous professional—one with integrity and experience—do in these circumstances?

D. Formulate your choice as a general maxim for all similar cases?

E. Are you still satisfied with your choice? If you are still satisfied, then go with your choice. If not, consider the factors that make you uncomfortable with a view to coming up with a new general rule with which you are satisfied.

V. Make your choice and live with it.

This means accepting responsibility for your choice. It also means accepting the possibility that you might be wrong or that you will make a less than optimal decision. The object is to make a good choice with the information available, not to make a perfect choice.

SOURCE: MICHAEL MCDONALD, "A FRAMEWORK FOR ETHICAL DECISION-MAKING ETHICS SOFTWARE."

NOTES

1. G.D. Trites, "Read It in the Annual Report," *CA Magazine*, December 1990, 45–48.
2. B. Gates, "Reports Deliver Message with Style and Pizzazz," *Financial Post*, November 27, 1990, 17.
3. S. Noakes (quoting P. Creighton), "Reports Gain New Prominence," *Financial Post*, December 2, 1993, 16.
4. G.M. Kang, "It's Corporate America's Spring Hornblowing Festival," *Business Week*, April 12, 1993, 31.
5. News item from Reuter, "McDonald's Serves Up Annual Report Video," *Financial Post*, April 13, 1993, 7.
6. L.A. Ponemon and D.R.L. Gabhart, *Ethical Reasoning in Accounting and Auditing* (Vancouver: CGA-Canada Research Foundation, 1993).
7. For comments on the idea of using market values for such items as loans and securities held by banks and other financial institutions, see, for example, Kevin G. Salwen and Robin G. Blumenthal, "SEC Starts a Revolution in Accounting," *Globe and Mail*, October 15, 1990, B8; and Dana W. Linden, "If Life Is Volatile, Account for It," *Forbes*, November 12, 1990, 114–15. For studies of how to value long-term liabilities, see, for example, J. Alex Milburn, *Incorporating the Time Value of Money within Financial Accounting* (Toronto: Canadian Institute of Chartered Accountants, 1988) and the FASB's discussion memorandum, *Present Value-Based Measurements in Accounting* (Stanford, Conn.: Financial Accounting Standards Board, December 7, 1990).
8. *Financial Reporting in Canada 1993* (Toronto: Canadian Institute of Chartered Accountants, 1993), 88.
9. Ibid., 97.
10. R.L. Watts and J.L. Zimmerman, *Positive Accounting Theory* (Englewood Cliffs, N.J.: Prentice–Hall, 1986), especially Chapters 7–10, examines management's interest in accounting standards and disclosure, and documents many instances of that interest.
11. M. Gibbins and A.K. Mason, *Professional Judgment in Financial Reporting* (Toronto: Canadian Institute of Chartered Accountants, 1988). Excerpts are from Chapter 1, 1–2, Chapter 5, 36, and the Executive Summary, xvi.
12. Adapted from the 1979 National CA Uniform Final (Qualifying) Examination. By permission of The Canadian Institute of Chartered Accountants, Toronto, Canada.
13. Adapted from the 1984 National CA Uniform (Qualifying) Examination. By permission of the Canadian Institute of Chartered Accountants Toronto, Canada.
14. The framework for ethical decision-making was developed by Michael McDonald, Centre for Applied Ethics, University of British Columbia, and is used with permission. Case 5A is based on a real case suggested by Dr. McDonald.

Recordkeeping and Control

6.1 Chapter Overview

This chapter emphasizes the very basic parts of accounting: the **recordkeeping** (**bookkeeping**) procedures and **internal control** considerations that form the records on which accounting information is built. Recordkeeping was introduced in the first few chapters of this book; now we will examine it in some depth. In the next chapter, Chapter 7, we will see how accrual accounting methods are built onto the underlying transactional recordkeeping system.

In this chapter you'll learn:

Use concepts: what management's responsibilities are for keeping complete and accurate accounting records, and for maintaining control over the enterprise's assets, plus the value of good records for everyone;

Preparation concepts: how accounting's transactions-based recordkeeping system works to produce good records, providing an objective and verifiable means of recording business events, and a good basis for internal control over assets;

Preparation techniques: basic "debit and credit" skills in preparing financial accounting information via the bookkeeping procedures involved in the creation of the transactional records, the source documents, journal entries, ledgers, and other items in the recordkeeping process, and the basic techniques for providing control over two important assets: cash and inventory;

Use techniques: some insight into the usefulness of various procedures and their role in producing the information that appears in the financial statements, as well as in providing information for tax, insurance, and other purposes, such as fraud prevention.

6.2 The Importance of Good Records

Complete and accurate records are important: they provide the observations and the history of the enterprise. Without knowing what has happened, investors and managers cannot make plans for the future, evaluate alternatives properly, or learn from past actions. In today's complex business environment, especially since enterprises have become very large, the number of events (or **transactions**, as we will call them) is much too great for anyone to keep track of without keeping accurate records (written or, these days, mostly computer records). Records provide the basis for extrapolations into the future, information for evaluating and rewarding performance, and a basis for internal control over the existence and quality of an enterprise's assets. Internal control, furthermore, not only provides systematic protection from theft and loss, but also documentation for legal and insurance purposes. Recordkeeping, however, does cost money, and therefore records should be worth their cost. How complex and sophisticated to make one's records is a business decision, as are such decisions as how to price or market one's product.

Here is what the Royal Bank of Canada had to say about the topic in a booklet prepared for people starting a business:

> Establishing a good system for keeping your books and papers in order is imperative and will save you much time and effort when your business is going full throttle. Not only will thorough accounts help you fulfil your recordkeeping obligations under Canada's tax laws, but they can also serve as a vital tool for managing your business. With well-designed accounts formulated specifically for your business, you can keep tabs on the results of your operations. You can compare actual performance with your original plans and monitor how well you're doing by comparing your financial and operational ratios with those of similar businesses. Knowing what is happening—and what isn't—in time to do something about it can mean the difference between success and failure.[1]

The booklet suggests several examples of how records are useful. These include meeting legal requirements, preparing marketing and business plans, measuring and analyzing performance, insurance, and management control.

6.3 FINANCIAL ACCOUNTING'S TRANSACTIONAL FILTER

Information systems such as accounting filter and prepare information; they select observations from the world, collect those results into data banks, and organize and summarize the data to produce specific kinds of information. Two of the main reasons for this filtering and summarizing are:

- People cannot cope with masses of raw, unorganized observations; and
- It is economically efficient to have one person or system organize data into information on behalf of various users or one user at various times.

An everyday example of the first reason is the daily newspaper: the editors group stories and features, so that you know where to look for what you want. There's a sports section, an entertainment section, a page for letters to the editor, and so on. The daily paper is also an example of the second reason: while no newspaper contains exactly what you want, it gets close enough to what most people want, so that it can be published at a low cost compared to what it would cost you to hire reporters to get information just for you. In order to make this work, every information system has to be choosy: it has to filter all the available data and pick what is relevant to its purpose. You don't expect the newspaper to contain glossy reproductions of Rembrandt paintings suitable for framing or to print the grades you got in your university courses: you go to other information sources for such things.

An **information system** such as financial accounting is inherently limited. It can report only what its sensors pick up as it seeks out data or filters data from the mass of ongoing events. No information system tells you "the truth," and certainly not "the whole truth," because it can only pass along information based on what it has been designed or permitted to gather as data.[2] Figure 6.1 represents the situation:

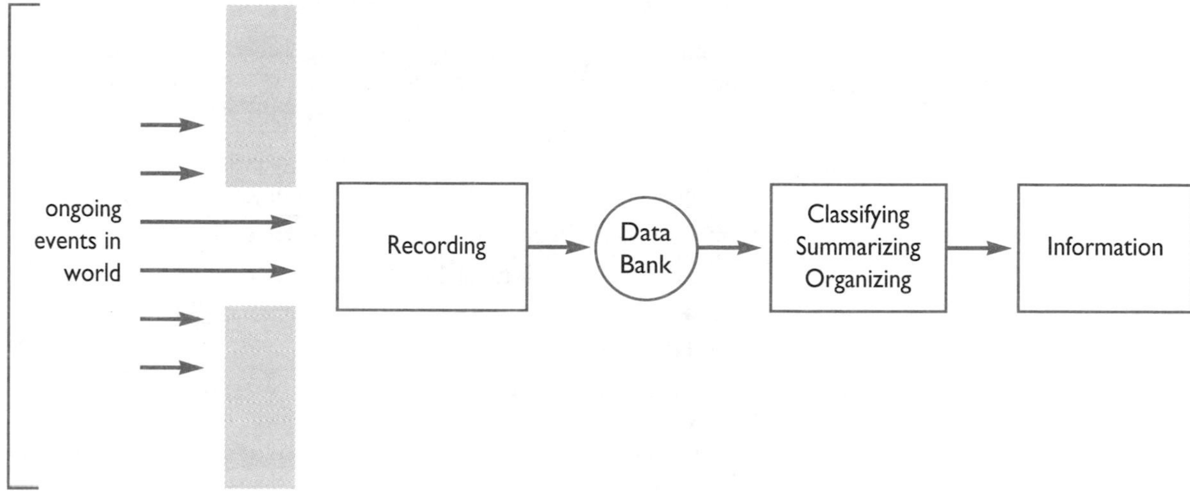

FIGURE 6.1

- The gap in the wall is the system's filter or "window on the world."
- Once a piece of raw data is admitted, recording activity takes place and it is stored in a bank of data (in accounting: stored in manual or computerized accounts, ledgers, journals ("the books"), and supporting records).
- The data in this bank are then organized to produce usable information (in accounting: financial statements and reports).

In accounting, we generally refer to the left part of the diagram, the data recording and some routine classifying and summarizing, as "bookkeeping." We refer to the right part, the turning of data into information for users, as "accounting" or "reporting." Financial accounting information is contained in the system's final product, the financial statements and notes.

Accounting reports are based on, and are limited by, the data collected. Therefore, if you are to understand the reports, you have to understand how accounting filters, notices, and chooses events to record into its data bank. Financial accounting's filter, its window on the world, is the **transaction**. Generally, if an event is a transaction, it is recorded into financial accounting's database; if it is not, the routine accounting system ignores the event. (We'll see in Chapter 7 that one of the reasons for accrual accounting techniques is to provide for events or even nonevent data that the transaction-based record-keeping system has ignored or treated improperly.)

The following are examples of accounting transactions. They should be recorded routinely by the accounting system:

a. The payroll department issues a cheque to pay an employee;
b. A customer pays, in cash, an account owing since last month and gets a receipt;

c. A sales clerk prepares an invoice for a customer, for the sale of goods the customer is taking with her and promises to pay for;

d. The head cashier deposits the day's receipts into the bank;

e. The stockroom receives a shipment of spare parts for the delivery trucks, along with an invoice from the parts supplier.

The following are examples of events that are not accounting transactions and that will therefore not be recorded routinely by the accounting system:

i. The president of the company breaks her leg while skiing;

ii. The credit department manager decides that a particular customer is probably never going to pay the account the customer owes;

iii. The main warehouse burns to the ground overnight;

iv. A customer orders a machine to be delivered next month;

v. Real estate reports indicate the company's land has gone up in value by 14% since last year.

What distinguishes accounting transactions from the sorts of events in the second list, all of which may be important economically, but are not routinely recorded by the accounting system? In order to qualify as a financial accounting transaction, an event must normally have *all four* of the following characteristics:

1. *Exchange*: the event must involve an exchange of goods, money, financial instruments (such as cheques or bonds), or other items of economic value;
2. *External*: the exchange must be between the enterprise being accounted for and someone outside the company;
3. *Evidence*: there must be some documentation of what has happened (on paper or electronically recorded);
4. *Dollars*: the event must be measurable in dollars or the currency unit relevant in the country where the transaction happens.

These characteristics indicate the value of financial accounting information.

- First, they are linked to the legal concept of completing a contract by giving or receiving consideration in return for the goods or services that change hands. The transactional basis of financial accounting thus has roots in the fundamental legal processes by which society and business operate. It is no accident that accounting recognizes as transactions events that have a broader legal and business importance too.
- Second, they constitute a large part of the underlying rationale for the historical cost basis of accounting, which is firmly founded on the transaction. If a transaction has *happened*, it should be in the accounting system and in the financial statements. It is history. If it has not yet happened, it is not yet the same sort of legal event and will not yet be in the historical accounting system.
- Third, the characteristics of the transaction provide the basis on which the records can be verified (audited) later as part of the process of ensuring that the accounting information is credible. Events that do not have these characteristics would be difficult to verify later, and therefore inevitably lack credibility as measures of financial performance or position.

Let's look at the events from the first list above and see that they fit the set of transaction characteristics:

	Exchange	External party	Evidence	Dollars
a.	money	employee	cheque	cheque
b.	money	customer	receipt	cash
c.	goods, promise	customer	invoice	price
d.	money	bank	deposit slip	cash
e.	goods, promise	supplier	invoice	price

The events in the second list lack several characteristics, especially that of being an economic exchange. (Event (iv), for example, is not yet an exchange because the machine hasn't yet been delivered.)

What if an accountant is not satisfied with the set of data recorded by an accounting system and wishes to adjust that data to reflect some event he or she thinks is important in measuring financial performance or position? This can be done by recording special alterations to the data bank called **adjustments** or **adjusting journal entries,** which introduce new data or alter the recording of previous data. Deciding whether to make such adjustments and determining the dollar amounts to use in them require expertise and good judgment, since they involve events that are not exchanges, are not accompanied by normal evidence, or are not readily measurable in dollars. Items (ii) and (iii) in the second list above are examples of events that are normally handled via adjusting entries; item (v) is an example that is *not* normally adjusted for, as we saw in Chapter 5. You'll see much more about adjustments in Chapter 7's coverage of accrual accounting.

Most of this book involves the accounting (right-hand) side of the earlier information system diagram: deciding on adjustments, deciding on reporting format, making supplementary notes, and other such activities. Don't forget that the basic transactional recording system underlies the whole process, and the preceding clear definition of what is and isn't a transaction gives the accounting system much of its valuable objectivity.

6.4 RECORDING TRANSACTIONS: DOUBLE-ENTRY BOOKKEEPING

Chapter 2 introduced basic ideas about how debits and credits make the financial accounting system work and keep the balance sheet equation in balance. In this section, we will go into the bookkeeping methods in more detail. ("Bookkeeper" and "bookkeeping" are the only words in English with three consecutive double letters!)

In a transaction, there is an exchange. The genius, and that's the right word, of double-entry bookkeeping is that it records two aspects of the exchange at once, from the point of view of the enterprise whose records are being created:

a. *What has happened to the enterprise's resources (assets).*
(Assets are the enterprise's wealth, so you can think of this as the reason the enterprise engaged in the transaction: gaining some resources or, if necessary, giving some up.)

b. *What the "story" was for the resource change.*
(Was the resource, say cash, gained because it was: provided by a customer, borrowed, obtained by selling or collecting another asset, or provided by an owner? Was the resource, say cash, lost because it was: given to a supplier or employee, used to reduce a debt, used to obtain another asset, or given to an owner as a dividend?)

As you will remember from the earlier material, the system used for recording transactions uses the familiar debits and credits:

Increases in assets are debits	Increases in liabilities and/or equity are credits (revenues and income increase equity and are therefore credits)
Debits =	Credits
Decreases in assets are credits	Decreases in liabilities and/or equity are debits (expenses and dividends decrease equity and are therefore debits).
Credits =	Debits

An interesting aspect of a transaction is that, because it is an exchange, both parties to the exchange would record it, each from that party's point of view. If Enterprise A gains cash for services provided to Enterprise B, A would record an increase in cash (a debit) and a revenue (an increase in equity, a credit), while Enterprise B would record a decrease in cash (a credit) and an expense (a decrease in equity, a debit). Both enterprises benefit from the exchange: Enterprise A gets cash in exchange for the service, and Enterprise B gets the value of the service, in exchange for the cash.

Here are examples of some exchanges and of how both parties would record the two aspects of each. The tradition of recording the debits first in an entry is sometimes disregarded here, so that you can see the parallels between Party A's and Party B's records.

Party A			**Party B**		
1. Bob borrows $1,000 cash from the bank			**The bank lends Bob $1,000 cash**		
Bob's records:			The bank's records:		
Debit Cash	$1,000		*Credit* Cash		$1,000
Credit Loan payable		$1,000	*Debit* Loan receivable	$1,000	
To record bank loan.			To record loan to Bob.		
2. Jan pays a $500 phone bill recorded earlier			**The phone company receives the $500 cash**		
Jan's records:			The phone company's records:		
Credit Cash		$ 500	*Debit* Cash	$ 500	
Debit Accounts payable	$ 500		*Credit* Accounts receivable		$ 500
To record payment of phone bill.			To record receipt of cash from Jan.		

3. Helen pays George $400 for legal advice			**George collects $400 from Helen for legal advice**		
Helen's records:			George's records:		
Debit Legal expense	$400		*Credit* Revenue		$400
Credit Cash		$400	*Debit* Cash	$400	
To record payment for legal advice.			To record receipt of cash for legal advice.		

These are simple examples, but they illustrate several features of the bookkeeping system, including:

a. The *double-entry* records shown, with something *debited* and something *credited*, are called **journal entries**. A journal entry can list as many accounts as are needed to record the transaction, but each journal entry must be recorded so that the sum of the debits equals the sum of the credits for that entry. If not, the balance sheet equation will not be maintained (the books will not balance).

b. It is traditional for the debits to be listed first in each journal entry and for the debits to be written to the left and the credits to the right. Neither of these is arithmetically necessary, but keeping a consistent style helps keep the records understandable.

c. It is also traditional to write a short explanation below each entry, as a memorandum of what the recorded transaction was about. Again, this is not necessary but helps to make the record understandable.

d. Every journal entry should also be dated and is usually numbered so that there is no doubt when the transaction was recorded. (This is not done in the examples above.) The date can have important legal and tax implications, and, of course, it is necessary to know to which fiscal period a transaction belongs when financial statements are being prepared.

e. There's a saying that "Every person's debit is another person's credit." You can see that in each of the examples above. Bob's debit (increase) in cash goes with the bank's credit (decrease) in cash. The bank's cash has become Bob's. Helen's debit for legal expenses goes with George's credit for revenue. George's revenue is Helen's expense. These reflect the exchange that lies behind the accounting concept of a transaction.

f. The examples above illustrate various types of transactions:

   - Bob is acquiring an asset, cash, and the story, financing of the asset, is that it is from a bank loan (assets up, liabilities up).
   - The bank is rearranging its assets, losing cash but gaining a receivable (assets up, assets down).
   - Jan is losing cash, and the story is that a debt is being reduced (assets down, liabilities down).
   - The phone company is rearranging its assets, gaining cash but losing a receivable (assets up, assets down).
   - Helen is losing cash, and the story is that an expense has been incurred, reducing her income and therefore her equity (assets down, equity down).

- George is gaining cash, and the story is that he has earned revenue, increasing his income and therefore his equity (assets up, equity up).

Enterprises with many transactions to record, which are most enterprises, do not create a separate journal entry for each transaction, but instead use special records for each general kind of transaction, such as a sales record, a cash receipts record, a cheque record. A company could list only cash receipts debits in one record, and only cash sales revenue credits in another record. The books (the balance sheet) will balance only if the two records have the same totals, so, keeping them separate may be a useful *internal control*. The people maintaining the two records have to be very careful or their records will not have the same totals. (More will be said about such special records later.)

Many bookkeeping systems are computerized. These systems may or may not produce records that look like the preceding examples, but they have the same arithmetical objective of keeping all the debits equal to all the credits. We saw spreadsheet printout examples in Chapters 2 and 3, but spreadsheets are a little cumbersome for handling large numbers of transactions, so most enterprises use special accounting software.

Here is an example of a more complex transaction, which also gives a way goodwill can arise as an asset other than the "goodwill on consolidation" case examined in Chapter 5. On December 14, 1995, Sorhem Inc. acquired a healthy, operating business upon the retirement of its owner, Rex Johnston.

- The agreed price was $523,000; but since Sorhem was a little short on cash, it financed the purchase by borrowing $150,000 from the bank and the seller agreed to wait for some years to be paid part of the price, therefore holding a long-term mortgage on the land and building of $178,000.
- Sorhem, therefore, had to pay only $195,000 of its own cash (total payment equalling $345,000 including the borrowed cash).
- Sorhem acquired the following, at values agreed to by it and Johnston: Accounts receivable, $57,000; Inventory, $112,000; Land, $105,000; Building, $194,000; Equipment, $87,000; Accounts payable that Sorhem will pay, $69,000.
- The sum of these values (subtracting the payable) is $486,000. The price of $523,000 is $37,000 greater than that, so Sorhem will call that difference goodwill due to the business's health, good location, and loyal customers.

The following journal entry records this transaction in the accounts of Sorhem Ltd.:

December 14, 1995		Debits	Credits
DR Accounts receivable	(current asset)	57,000	
DR Inventory	(current asset)	112,000	
DR Land	(noncurrent asset)	105,000	
DR Building	(noncurrent asset)	194,000	
DR Equipment	(noncurrent asset)	87,000	
CR Accounts payable	(current liability)		69,000

December 14, 1995, continued		Debits	Credits
DR Goodwill	(noncurrent asset)	37,000	
DR Cash	(current asset)	150,000	
CR Cash	(current asset)		345,000
CR Bank loan	(current liability)		150,000
CR Mortgage payable	(noncurrent liability)		178,000
To record the purchase of Rex Johnston's business.			

Quite a long journal entry!

- It meets the arithmetic requirement: the sum of the debits equals the sum of the credits ($742,000).
- It uses whatever account names make sense to record the transaction (different companies or bookkeepers could well have named the accounts differently).
- Debits are abbreviated DR, and credits as CR, as is customary.
- As is also customary, dollar signs are omitted.

HOW'S YOUR UNDERSTANDING

Here are two questions you should be able to answer, based on what you have just read:

1. How do you know what kinds of business events are reflected in a company's bookkeeping records?
2. Record the following event in the accounts of Whatzis Inc. The company bought a large truck, costing $89,000, by putting down $20,000 in cash and financing (borrowing) the rest from the truck dealer's finance company. (DR Truck asset 89,000, CR Cash asset 20,000, CR Truck Loan liability 69,000)

6.5 MORE ABOUT ACCOUNTS

Accounts are summaries of the recorded transactions. Therefore, the account balance reports the net effect of all the transactions recorded that specify that

CASH IN BANK

Date	Description	Entry No.	Debits	Credits	Balance
Dec. 1/95	First deposit	1	10,000		10,000
Dec. 2	Deposit	3	1,146		11,146
Dec. 2	Cheque	7		678	10,468
Dec. 2	Cheque	8		2,341	8,127

account. The Cash in Bank account for a company might look like this:

You see the idea. Each account is really just a convenient summary of the entries affecting it.

For demonstration and analysis purposes, accountants and accounting instructors often use a simplified version of an account called a "T-account," which includes only the debits and credits columns of the account, without calculating the balance after every entry. A T-account version of the above example would look like this:

CASH IN BANK	
10,000	678
1,146	2,341
11,146	3,019
8,127	

6.6 ACCOUNTING'S "BOOKS" AND RECORDS

SUMMARY OF ACCOUNTING'S PROCEDURES

The general steps followed in coming up with a set of audited financial statements are:

1. Record transactions.
2. Summarize the transactions by posting them to accounts.
3. Choose accounting policies to be followed consistently in reporting performance and position (more about specific important policies is in Chapters 7 and 10).
4. In accordance with those policies, make end-of-period accruals, corrections, and other adjustments (examples will be given in Chapter 7).
5. Prepare the balance sheet, income statement, and retained earnings statement from the accounts.
6. Prepare the SCFP from the other three statements and additional information about changes in noncurrent assets and liabilities and owners' equity.
7. Prepare the accounting policy notes and other footnote disclosures, and add comparative figures for last year.
8. Have the full set of statements and notes audited (usually, the auditing process begins earlier, before the year-end and before the statements have been prepared).
9. Append the auditors' report to the set of statements and notes and have the balance sheet signed as approved by the board of directors.
10. Release the statements, notes, and auditors' report as a set.
11. Somewhere after step 5, close the income, dividends. and retained earnings adjustments accounts to retained earnings to make all those accounts' balances zero in preparation for next year's step 1 (the balance sheet accounts continue into the next year and so are not closed).

THE UNDERLYING ACCOUNTING SYSTEM

This section summarizes some of the mechanics of the accounting system behind steps 1 and 2 above, to show you how transactions are summarized into accounts—the preliminary material for the financial statements. Keep in mind, though, that this is a basic description: we have to leave a lot of things out in order to keep the portrayal clear. These days, for many companies, many of the "books" referred to below are actually electronic records in computer systems.

a. Source documents and the transactional cycle

Accounting recordkeeping depends upon sets of documents to show that transactions have occurred. Such documents are kept so that the accounting records can be checked and verified to correct errors, permit auditing, be used in case of dispute, and support income tax claims and other legal actions. The transactions themselves reflect various events in operating the business. Here are some examples from a real company, Barcol Doors Ltd.

1. Barcol sells products that it buys from other companies. Ordering the kinds of products customers will want is an important early step. Ordering is not an accounting transaction, so orders are not recorded in the accounts, but documenting and keeping track of them is very important to Barcol, so it uses "purchase order" forms for this. Figure 6.2 provides an example. You'll see that it is dated and prenumbered, so that it may be followed up in case of problems, and the items ordered are listed in detail so they can be checked against what actually arrives from the supplier.

BARCOL DOORS
Your Door Specialists Since 1952
15104 - 118 AVENUE, EDMONTON, ALBERTA T5V 1B8
TELEPHONE (403) 452 - 7140 FAX (403) 451 - 0724

PURCHASE ORDER
14124

DATE: MAR. 2/94
TERMS: ☑ Net 30 ☐
CONFIRMATION ONLY ☐
ORDER PLACED WITH: FAX
DATE ORDERED: MAR. 2/94

STEELCRAFT

PLEASE SHIP THE FOLLOWING MATERIALS SUBJECT TO CONDITIONS SHOWN ON THIS ORDER.

SHIP TO BARCOL VIA ☑ TRUCK ☐ PICK-UP ☐ COURIER ☐ MAIL ☐ UPS SHIPMENT REQUIRED

QUANTITY	DESCRIPTION	DATE REC'D	QUAN. REC'D	AMT.PAID
1	8'X7' - 24 GA.INSUL., 2" HDWE, 4'-6" HI-LIFT, SOLID SHAFT			
1	10'X10' - 24 GA.INSUL., 3" HDWE.			
1	20'X14' - 24 GA.INSUL., 5-24"X12" THERMOLITES, 3" HDWE.,			
	11ga. hinges, 100 000 cycle springs, H.D. Bearings,			
14	8'X9' - 24 GA INSUL., 1-18"X5" THERMOLITE - LH SIDE FROM INSIDE			
	3" HDWE. F.V.L. LIFT HANDLES STEP PLATES AT N/C AS PER D.E.			
2	8'X12' - 24 GA.INSUL., 1-18"X5" THERMOLITE - LH SIDE FROM INSIDE			
	3" HDWE., 4'-6' HI-LIFT, LIFT HANDLES/STEP PLATES AT N/C			
	[CONTRACTOR/job name			
	job number]			

1. ALL INVOICES MUST BE RENDERED IN DUPLICATE.
2. Acknowledge receipt of order with shipping date.
3. Delivery Slip must accompany all shipments.
4. Bill of Lading or Express Receipt must accompany Invoice.
5. No changes or alterations without consent of Purchasing Agent.

BARCOL DOOR LTD.
PURCHASING AGENT

TO SUPPLIER

FIGURE 6.2

REPRODUCED COURTESY OF BARCOL DOORS.

2. When ordered items arrive, they are checked against purchase orders and the supplier's packing slips, to ensure all is proper. When Barcol accepts a delivery, this is an accounting transaction, and a purchases record is created to support the transaction *debit Inventory asset and credit Accounts payable liability*. Returns of goods to suppliers are recorded as well, in just the opposite way: *credit Inventory and debit Accounts payable*. Figure 6.3 provides an example of Barcol's record with a supplier it uses regularly: you'll see that five sets of returns were made from previous shipments and then one large purchase was recorded. You'll also see that the company expects to receive a $53.69 discount by paying the account on time.

100			XYZ MANUFACTURING		Mar 4 94
DM33418	Jan 28 94		315.65–	0.00	315.65–
DM33420	Jan 28 94		450.00–	0.00	450.00–
DM33421	Jan 28 94		599.20–	0.00	599.20–
DM33422	Jan 28 94		203.30–	0.00	203.30–
DM33423	Jan 28 94		385.20–	0.00	385.20–
28292	Feb 10 94		2,872.42	53.69	2,818.73
			919.07	53.69	865.38

FIGURE 6.3 REPRODUCED COURTESY OF BARCOL DOORS.

3. When Barcol pays the supplier, a cheque is written and a copy of that is the source document for recording the transaction *debit Accounts payable and credit Cash (Bank)*. In this case, Barcol takes the discount, so the cheque is for less than the amount owed; the difference is *debited to Accounts payable and credited to Cash discounts received*, an "other revenue" account. Figure 6.4 shows Barcol's cheque. You'll see it is dated, prenumbered, and has other details to allow reference later in case of problems.

BARCOL DOORS
Your Door Specialists Since 1952
15104 - 118 AVENUE, EDMONTON, ALBERTA T5V 1B8

CANADIAN IMPERIAL BANK OF COMMERCE
14310 - 111 AVE., EDMONTON, ALBERTA

17400

CHEQUE NO.	CHEQUE DATE	VENDOR NO.
17400	Mar 4 94	100

CHEQUE AMOUNT
$865.38

**************** Eight Hundred Sixty-Five and 38/100 ****************

PAY TO THE ORDER OF
XYZ MANUFACTURING
322 MAIN STREET EAST
EDMONTON, ALBERTA
T5T 5T5

PER ____________
PER ____________

⑆04959⑈010⑆ 13⑈02213⑈

FIGURE 6.4 REPRODUCED COURTESY OF BARCOL DOORS.

4. Selling the products is what Barcol is in business to do. When a sale is made, a sales invoice is prepared, specifying various useful details. A copy of this invoice supports the transaction *debit Accounts receivable and credit Sales revenue*. (Through the company's computerized inventory sys-

tem, the sales invoice also supports recording the cost of the goods taken by the customer, *debit Cost of goods sold expense and credit Inventory.*) Figure 6.5 provides an example of an invoice. You can see there is $49.98 sales tax on the total, so the invoice also supports a *debit to Accounts receivable and a credit to Sales tax payable* for the tax, which is not part of Barcol's revenue, but instead is collected on behalf of the government.

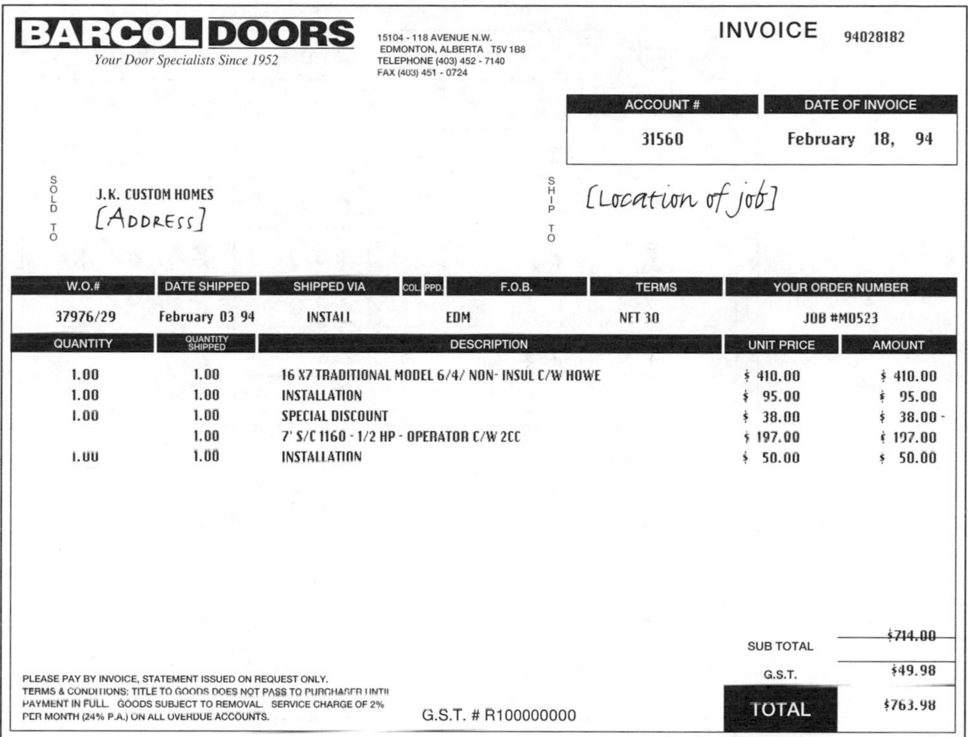

BARCOL DOORS
Your Door Specialists Since 1952

15104 - 118 AVENUE N.W.
EDMONTON, ALBERTA T5V 1B8
TELEPHONE (403) 452 - 7140
FAX (403) 451 - 0724

INVOICE 94028182

ACCOUNT #	DATE OF INVOICE
31560	February 18, 94

SOLD TO: J.K. CUSTOM HOMES [ADDRESS]

SHIP TO: [Location of job]

W.O.#	DATE SHIPPED	SHIPPED VIA	COL.	PPD.	F.O.B.	TERMS	YOUR ORDER NUMBER
37976/29	February 03 94	INSTALL			EDM	NET 30	JOB #M0523

QUANTITY	QUANTITY SHIPPED	DESCRIPTION	UNIT PRICE	AMOUNT
1.00	1.00	16 X7 TRADITIONAL MODEL 6/4/ NON- INSUL C/W HOWE	$ 410.00	$ 410.00
1.00	1.00	INSTALLATION	$ 95.00	$ 95.00
1.00	1.00	SPECIAL DISCOUNT	$ 38.00	$ 38.00 -
	1.00	7' S/C 1160 - 1/2 HP - OPERATOR C/W 2CC	$ 197.00	$ 197.00
1.00	1.00	INSTALLATION	$ 50.00	$ 50.00
			SUB TOTAL	$714.00
			G.S.T.	$49.98
			TOTAL	$763.98

PLEASE PAY BY INVOICE, STATEMENT ISSUED ON REQUEST ONLY.
TERMS & CONDITIONS: TITLE TO GOODS DOES NOT PASS TO PURCHASER UNTIL PAYMENT IN FULL. GOODS SUBJECT TO REMOVAL. SERVICE CHARGE OF 2% PER MONTH (24% P.A.) ON ALL OVERDUE ACCOUNTS.

G.S.T. # R100000000

FIGURE 6.5 REPRODUCED COURTESY OF BARCOL DOORS.

5. Collecting from customers is the last event we will illustrate. When a customer pays Barcol, the payment is listed in the day's collections. That list is the source document to support the transaction *debit Cash (Bank) and credit Accounts receivable.* It also supports the bank deposit made that day, so that if there are problems, someone can start with the monthly bank statement and trace the deposits shown on it back to the payments by individual customers. Figure 6.6 shows the list of collections for February 14, 1994.

Barcol uses more kinds of documents. There are many kinds of documents used by various companies. Each company adapts documents to its own needs, especially to provide legal evidence and support accounting transactions records.

b. Books of original entry

Based on source documents, accounting transactions are recorded. Because this is when the business event first is recorded by the accounting system, these

ACCOUNTS RECEIVABLE OPEN ITEM PAYMENTS

DATE

02	94

AMOUNT RECEIVED		DAY	ACCOUNT NUMBER	REFERENCE	A/R DISTR. AMT. (CREDIT)	
2264	12	14	855	1096/4263	2264	12
56	71		10982	6943	56	71
56	71		12018	7379	56	71
363	67		14440	7334/43	363	67
223	63		14430	7369/35	223	63
836	74		16285	7425/7430 2347	836	74
64	20		16750	7543	64	20
245	57		17545	7160	245	57
393	72		17626	6946	393	72
145	52		18458	7419	145	52
247	17		20334	7342/CN	247	17
1328	15		20333	7882	1328	15
22	47		21229	7676	22	47
461	28		24015	7550	461	28
178	75		25550	7800	178	75
850	65		29820	DEC	850	65
113	70		29822	7463	113	70
279	27		35914	7394	279	27
62	06		33435	6753	62	06
742	82		37480	6953	742	82
4962	03		36956	OCT/NOV	4962	03
13898	94			TOTAL	13898	94

FIGURE 6.6

basic transactional records are often called "books of original entry." Typically, transactions of a similar nature are grouped together and separate special records are used to record frequent routine transactions. Some examples of special records are:

- A sales journal, listing all sales in sales invoice order;
- A cash receipts journal, listing payments received from customers (Barcol's collections list is a form of this);
- A cheque register or cash disbursement journal, recording all cheques issued, in cheque number order. Companies usually have separate cheque registers (and bank accounts) for major areas, such as payment of accounts payable, general payroll, executive payroll, and dividend payments.

Each company will also have a "general journal," used mainly to originate journal entries for transactions that are not provided for in separate bookkeeping records, such as those described above. The general journal is also used for accruals and other adjustments (as later chapters will illustrate).

c. Ledgers

Ledgers are books (or computer records) having a separate page or account code for each individual account referred to in the books of original entry. Each area or page contains a summary of all the transactions relating to that particular account and therefore "posted" to it.

General ledger—the collection of all the asset, liability, equity, revenue, and expense accounts, summarizing the entire operations of the business. The general ledger is the backbone of the accounting system and is the basis on which the balance sheet, retained earnings statement, and income statement are prepared. The ledger may be a "book" or it may be space on a computer disk. Many companies now keep their records on the computer and print out information only as they require it. A trial balance of all the general ledger accounts and their balances is prepared periodically (such as at the end of each month) in order to demonstrate that the ledger is in balance. (A listing of just the account names without balances is called a "chart of accounts.")

Special (or subsidiary) ledgers—accounts receivable and accounts payable ledgers are two examples of specialized ledgers. For instance, if a company extends credit to its customers, it may want to keep a separate ledger account for each account (customer). These ledgers are balanced by making sure that their accounts add up to the same amount as is shown in the relevant general ledger account (for example, the accounts receivable "control" account should have the same balance as the list of customers' individual accounts).

6.7 AN EXAMPLE: NORTHERN STAR THEATRE COMPANY

Recordkeeping examples were used in prior chapters without exactly calling them that. Therefore, to help you tie down your knowledge, let's examine a specific example and follow the business events from transactions through to the financial statements. We will go part way with the example now and will finish it, including the financial statements, in Chapter 7.

A group of aspiring actors from Saskatchewan decided to form a theatre company to perform in Canada's various "fringe" and other summer festivals. Here are events that happened to Northern Star Theatre Company in its first production, presented at the Edmonton Fringe Theatre Festival in 1994:

1. The theatre company (really, an informal partnership) was formed in November 1993 (the 5th), and a bank account was arranged for in the company's name. Six actors each agreed to put $500 into the company, but not until the money was needed.
2. The company applied in December 1993 for a place in the August 1994 Fringe, paying a fee of $400. Each actor paid $75 of the agreed amount to provide the money for the fee.
3. The Fringe notified the company in January 1994 that it had been accepted and allocated seven performances.
4. The company would have to pay a royalty to the play's author after the performances. The details were agreed with the author in March 1994.
5. Rehearsals began in March, and costumes and other props costing $470 were purchased. To pay for those items, each of the actors paid $100 more of the agreed amount, except one, Fred, who was broke at the time but promised to pay soon.
6. In early August, one of the actors, Elaine, drove out to Edmonton to see the venue and settle some staging details. The trip cost $290 in gas and other expenses, all of which the company reimbursed after collecting another $100 from each member of the company except Fred, who was still broke in July.
7. In mid-August, the six actors drove to Edmonton, a few days ahead of their performance date. They stayed with friends and spent the time constructing a set for the play and gathering up other props. The set and props cost $610 in materials to construct, all of which was promised to be paid as soon as the play was over. The cost of the car gas and motels along the way was $190, and the members who had paid for such expenses were also promised repayment after the play was over.
8. The play opened to a moderately enthusiastic audience. The Fringe collected $960 ($8×120 seats) and turned $897 over to the company that day after deducting $63 in sales tax. The money was deposited in the company's bank account using an Edmonton branch of the bank.

We'll now work through how these simple events are recorded (if at all) and accumulated in a very simple accounting system. Note that though this system is much simpler than those large companies would have, it probably is all the company needs at this stage in its existence. It is important to match the accounting system to the needed level of sophistication.

Step 1: Source Documents

The six aspiring actors, who kept their other jobs, had a lot to plan and prepare, without worrying about accounting. But they knew they had to keep track of things, so one of them kept a box for all the company's documents. For the above events, the following items were in the box the morning after the first performance:

1. A bank account agreement signed by the bank and two of the actor–partners on behalf of the company was in the box, along with unused cheques and deposit slips for the account. As to the agreement to put in $500 each, there was only the corner of a place mat from a Saskatoon restaurant, where they had all met to celebrate their plan. The place mat fragment had the names of the six and of the company and the number $500, but no signatures by anyone.
2. A bank statement showing the $450 deposit and the $400 cheque was in the box, along with the processed cheque itself and a receipt from the Fringe for the $400 fee.
3. The Fringe's notification of acceptance was in the box.
4. A scribbled note about the phone call making the royalty agreement with the author was in the box.
5. Processed cheques and bills for the $470 were in the box, along with a bank statement showing the deposit of the $500 and the $470 in cheques. There was also a note that "Fred has yet to pay his $100."
6. A bank statement showing the deposit of the $500 and the $290 cheque was in the box, along with the processed cheque and various bills supporting the $290 travel cost. Another note said "Fred still broke."
7. Bills for the $610 in props and the $190 in travel expenses were in the box.
8. A receipt for the deposit of the $897 was in the box. A "front-of-house" report showing the $897 was also in the box.

Step 2: Recording the Transactions in a Journal

A general journal to record the transactions is shown in Exhibit 6.1 below. Exact dates would be necessary, but only the months were given above and they are used below. (Journals and ledgers are recorded to the penny, but we will ignore cents here.)

Exhibit 6.1

Northern Star Theatre Company
General Journal

No.	Date	Description	Debits	Credits
1.	Nov. 93	No transaction so no entry		
2a.	Dec. 93	Cash (Bank)	450	
		Partners' capital		450
		Initial contributions by partners: 6 × $75, per bank records.		
2b.	Dec. 93	Performance fees expense	400	
		Cash (Bank)		400
		Fee paid to Edmonton Fringe to apply for a performance venue in 1994.		
3.	Jan. 94	No transaction so no entry		

Exhibit 6.1 continued

4.	Mar. 94	No transaction so no entry		
5a.	Mar. 94	Cash (Bank)	500	
		Partners' capital		500
		Further contributions by five partners: 5 × $100. (No contribution from Fred.)		
5b.	Mar. 94	Costumes and props expense	470	
		Cash (Bank)		470
		Costumes and props purchased in North Battleford, per suppliers' bills.		
6a.	Jul. 94	Cash (Bank)	500	
		Partners' capital		500
		Further contributions by five partners: 5 × $100. (No contribution from Fred.)		
6b.	Jul. 94	Travel expense	290	
		Cash (Bank)		290
		Reimbursement to Elaine for her trip to Edmonton to check out the venue.		
7a.	Aug. 94	Travel expense	190	
		Accounts payable		190
		Recording the liability to those partners who spent money getting the group to Edmonton for the Fringe.		
7b.	Aug. 94	Costumes and props expense	610	
		Accounts payable		610
		Recording the liability to various people for sets and props constructed in Edmonton.		
8.	Aug. 94	Cash (Bank)	897	
		Performance revenue		897
		Gate receipts for the first night.		

Let's stop at this point. We can pick up other necessary items in Chapter 7, when this example is continued.

Step 3: Posting (Summarizing) Journal Entries in Ledger

The recorded transactions, posted to general ledger accounts, are shown in Exhibit 6.2. The accounts are listed in the order in which they arose in the entries, not necessarily in balance sheet or income statement order.

Exhibit 6.2

Northern Star Theatre Company
General Ledger

Cash (Bank)

Date	Entry	Debit	Credit	Balance
Dec. 93	2a	450		450 DR
Dec. 93	2b		400	50 DR
Mar. 94	5a	500		550 DR
Mar. 94	5b		470	80 DR
Jul. 94	6a	500		580 DR
Jul. 94	6b		290	290 DR
Aug. 94	8	897		1,187 DR

Partners' Capital

Date	Entry	Debit	Credit	Balance
Dec. 93	2a		450	450 CR
Mar. 94	5a		500	950 CR
Jul. 94	6a		500	1,450 CR

Performance Fees Expense

Date	Entry	Debit	Credit	Balance
Dec. 93	2b	400		400 DR

Costumes and Props Expense

Date	Entry	Debit	Credit	Balance
Mar. 94	5b	470		470 DR
Aug. 94	7b	610		1,080 DR

Travel Expense

Date	Entry	Debit	Credit	Balance
Jul. 94	6b	290		290 DR
Aug. 94	7a	190		480 DR

Accounts Payable

Date	Entry	Debit	Credit	Balance
Aug. 94	7a		190	190 CR
Aug. 94	7b		610	800 CR

Performance Revenue

Date	Entry	Debit	Credit	Balance
Aug. 94	8		897	897 CR

Step 4: Trial Balance to See if Ledger Balances

Exhibit 6.3

Northern Star Theatre Company
General Ledger Trial Balance, mid-August 1994

Account	Debit	Credit
Cash (Bank)	1,187	
Partners' capital		1,450
Performance fees expense	400	
Costumes and props expense	1,000	
Travel expense	480	
Accounts payable		800
Performance revenue		897
TOTALS	3,147	3,147

So the ledger balances!

This is enough for now. The purpose was to demonstrate how the account balances used to prepare the financial statements arise from the underlying transactions and documents, and Step 4 above got us to some account balances. In Chapter 7, we will extend this example to illustrate accruals and adjustments.

HOW'S YOUR UNDERSTANDING

Here are two questions you should be able to answer, based on what you have just read:

1. You are the owner of a business. Your bookkeeper has just given you the month-end trial balance of the business's accounts. What are the main records you would expect to have been used in coming up with that list of account balances?
2. Your bookkeeper rushes into your office to apologize for the fact that posting the cash sales journal to the general ledger has been accidentally forgotten for that month. The journal showed that cash received for cash sales during the month was $6,782. Which ledger accounts would be incorrect because of the error, and by how much? (Cash would be too low by $6,782, as would Revenue.)

6.8 INTERNAL CONTROL

Recordkeeping has more value than just providing the data bank for the preparation of financial statements. An appropriate recordkeeping system for any organization is one that can be used to keep track of resources, thus discouraging misappropriation of the organization's property or inefficient use of resources and helping management safeguard assets, yet is not overly cumbersome or bureaucratic. Records also help management meet its responsibility to run the enterprise effectively and generally to control what is going on. Such **internal control** is not only a matter of recordkeeping; physical protection, insurance, and proper supervision of employees are also important to internal control. The Barcol Doors documents in Section 6.6 were part of the company's internal control system: they were numbered and dated, and contained several details that could be used to follow up if problems arose.

This is a brief introduction to an interesting area of management responsibility that accountants and auditors consider part of their area of expertise, and it serves to demonstrate that recordkeeping and accounting in general have more purposes than just preparing financial statements. The *CICA Handbook* (paragraph 5200.05) defines internal control as:

> Internal control comprises the plan of organization and all the co-ordinate systems established by the management of an enterprise to assist in achieving management's objective of ensuring, as far as practical, the orderly and efficient conduct of its business, including the safeguarding of assets, the reliability of accounting records and the timely preparation of reliable financial information.[3]

MAIN COMPONENTS OF INTERNAL CONTROL

As the *CICA Handbook* excerpt above points out, internal control is a responsibility of management. Here are some ways that management can establish proper control over the enterprise's affairs:

1. *Run the enterprise competently*. Looking after the enterprise's assets and making sure various activities, including recordkeeping, are done well is just part of being a good manager. A well-run enterprise has a climate of efficiency and records that cross-check each other, as well as competent managers who are likely to realize quickly when something is going wrong. Having a good internal control system contributes to the profitability and efficiency that good managers seek.
2. *Maintain effective records*. Having a comprehensive, connected set of records, as was illustrated for Barcol Doors in Section 6.6, provides an early warning system and helps to motivate good performance by everyone, because the records provide routine monitoring and act as the basis for hourly pay, performance appraisals, bonuses, and other parts of the motivation system. Records also provide an audit trail of events that can be traced back to identify the causes of problems. An effective recordkeeping system goes well beyond accounting transactions (we saw the example of Barcol's purchase order system), but accounting records are likely to be at the heart of it. Many modern organizations have integrated their accounting and other records into a decision-oriented **management information system** that can be used to support a wide range of management decisions and evaluations.
3. *Use the records to act and learn*. It is an unfortunate fact of life in many organizations that many records seem to be maintained just for the sake of doing that. We all have chafed at bureaucratic form-filling and having to prepare multiple copies of things for no apparently good reason. If

management allows records to grow of their own accord, money is wasted and, perhaps equally important, people in the organization learn that the records don't matter, that mistakes and worse will not be acted upon or corrected. This can seriously undermine the ability of the recordkeeping to do its control job, and is likely to produce records that are useless for managers to learn from events, because the records either have too many errors or have become irrelevant to the organization's current needs.

4. *Separate recordkeeping from handling assets.* An effective way of providing security over assets like cash, accounts receivable, and inventories is to have records showing how much of each asset is supposed to be on hand at any time. But if the person who physically handles the asset (say, cash) also keeps the records of it, then errors or fraud can be hidden by altering the records. Accountants call separation of recordkeeping from handling assets "segregation of duties." One person collects the cash, and another person maintains the cash records. So if one or the other makes a mistake, a difference will arise between the count of cash on hand and what the record shows should be on hand. This difference then can be investigated and the cause corrected. Segregation of duties can also be used within the recordkeeping system, for example one person can maintain the general ledger, with the total accounts receivable account, and another can maintain the accounts receivable subsidiary ledger, with the detailed list of customer accounts. It is hard for smaller enterprises with few employees to spread the jobs around enough to segregate all the important tasks, but it should be done as much as is sensible. If segregation of duties doesn't exist, the boss needs to keep a close eye on important assets, such as cash and inventories.
5. *Adequately pay and motivate employees.* A more positive side of internal control is to pay and reward people for their efforts on behalf of the enterprise, so that they try to do a good job and are not tempted to subvert recordkeeping and other control systems. Disgruntled employees may not care if things go wrong or may even take some pleasure when the enterprise suffers losses. As may already have occurred to you, the control provided by segregation of duties is destroyed if the people involved "collude" (work together) to cover up errors or fraud, and while such actions can never be wholly prevented, their probability is reduced if people feel good about the enterprise.
6. *Carry insurance on assets.* Like anything else, internal control has to be worth its cost. It is probably worth the cost to have a careful control system for the main part of the enterprise's activities, for example buying and selling goods, but there will be some unusual circumstances that are not anticipated or for which setting up elaborate controls doesn't seem worthwhile. Some events, such as earthquakes or fires, may be entirely or mostly beyond management's control. So it makes sense to protect the owners' investment by carrying insurance for some events against which internal control systems cannot provide adequate protection. There is a side benefit of insurance: insurance companies tend to want to know a lot about how the enterprise is protecting and managing its assets, and satisfying the insurance company about this can result in improvements in controls.

7. *Physically protect sensitive assets.* This control method is rather obvious, but it's easy to overlook too. Sensitive assets, such as cash, inventories, and tools, should be behind lock and key, kept in particular storage areas, or otherwise protected from unauthorized or casual access. Many enterprises are sloppy about access to their inventories in particular and sometimes protection is a good idea for assets you might not think of. For example, many manufacturers produce scrap as a by-product, and the scrap can be very valuable. One Canadian manufacturer put its scrap in the backyard and found out later that thousands of dollars worth had been lifted over the back fence and sold on the scrap market.

There is much more to internal control. Designing effective control systems requires an understanding of management's objectives, a sensitivity to the cost–benefit balance needed between tight but costly controls and loose but cheap controls, knowledge of computer systems and other recordkeeping methods, and considerable insight into the subtleties of human motivation and behaviour. It also requires some common sense: complete protection is not possible, and tying the enterprise up in red tape in order to try to get complete protection is *not* what a good internal control system does. Let's turn now to examples of internal controls in two major areas, cash and inventories.

HOW'S YOUR UNDERSTANDING

Here are two questions you should be able to answer, based on what you have just read:

1. What should a good internal control system do?
2. What are some components of an internal control system?

6.9 INTERNAL CONTROL OF CASH

Cash is the asset usually most susceptible to theft because of its liquid and generally anonymous nature.

A real case: Mike, a junior auditor in a northern town, was assigned to do a surprise count of the cash on hand at a local clothing store. The cash counted was short as compared to what was expected, based on the auditors' projections of cash from sales and bank deposit records. Mike was accused by the store's accounting clerk of stealing the cash himself while counting it, and he had to call the police from the store and insist that they search him and so demonstrate that he had not stolen it. It turned out that the accounting clerk had been stealing cash and covering up the thefts by changing the sales records—a classic case of poor internal control through lack of segregation of duties, because the clerk had access to both the cash and the records of the cash. The theft was discovered only because Mike's surprise cash count referred to sales records that the clerk had not yet altered to cover up the shortage. The clerk was fired and promised to make restitution, though it was difficult to tell how much had been taken because sales records had been altered for several years. The owner of the store was quite critical of the auditors for "not preventing the loss," but the auditors showed that they had indeed warned the owner, who had said that it would be too expensive to employ someone else to keep the sales records or control the cash.

For cash sales, one of the common controls is to have locked-in sales registers or other carefully controlled records. Registers (such as you would see at any supermarket) usually print a consecutive number on the locked-in tape for each transaction. The access key is kept by a single person, perhaps a supervisor who balances cash to sale records. The proceeds that should have been received will be recorded on the tape. The person who keeps the key should count the cash with the cashier, compare it to the sales proceeds, and check that the tape numbers are consecutive from one person's shift to that of the next person. If this sort of system is to work, there has to be no collusion between the people controlling the cash and checking the records—often collusion is difficult to prevent, so having yet another person provide overall monitoring of the process is a good idea.

A real case: A large company established a "petty cash" fund in its front office to be used to pay for small purchases, such as office supplies and courier charges. The receptionist was given a fund of $1,000, in cash, and when most of that was spent, submitted all the receipts in an envelope and was refunded the cash spent, to bring the petty cash fund back up to $1,000. The internal control therefore was that, at any time, the receptionist should have cash on hand plus receipts for payments totalling $1,000. What the company did not know was that the receptionist was involved with the delivery driver from the store from which the company got most of its office supplies, and nearly all invoices from that company paid through petty cash were inflated. The company paid far more than it should have for the supplies, but no one knew because the people who got the supplies did not see the invoices, which were kept by the receptionist as evidence of cash payouts. The people who reimbursed the receptionist had not seen the office supplies and so did not know the invoices were inflated. The thefts and the collusion between the receptionist and driver were discovered long after the two had moved to another city: someone noticed that office supplies costs were lower than they used to be! The company has no good idea of how much was stolen, but it probably exceeded $10,000 over the years.

Another way to control cash from sales is to have multi-copied, prenumbered sales invoices, as Barcol Doors has. The invoice copies are then removed by one person: for cash sales, the amounts are cross-checked to cash records, and for credit sales, the amounts are cross-checked to accounts receivable records. Any gaps in the invoices' numerical continuity are investigated. For this control to work, supervisors must ensure that an invoice is prepared for each sales transaction. An additional control is to regularly check inventory and compare it with the sales records. This should prevent, or at least detect, someone selling inventory and pocketing the cash.

Take, for example, the Mayfield Pro Shop, which accumulated $10,000 in sales at the end of a month according to the invoice copies in the locked box.

If the inventory at the start of the month was worth $25,000 and at the end of the month was worth $14,000 (based on the retail price of the goods), the shop should have sold $11,000 worth of goods. The $1,000 difference could be due to one of the following:

1. Someone could have kept $1,000 worth of cash from sales and not written any invoices for those sales.
2. Someone could have shoplifted $1,000 worth of goods.
3. The inventory could be inaccurate, or other errors could have occurred.

Thus, there could be other reasons for shortfalls besides theft by employees, but keeping track of cash and inventory together is one method of highlighting the possibilities and investigating them.

These examples of cash-control problems are presented to illustrate that accounting records have a variety of uses beyond preparing financial statements. The examples are *not* intended to suggest that employees or customers are crooks, but to show that management must be prudent in meeting its responsibility of good stewardship in taking care of the owners' assets. Part of that responsibility lies in not putting employees or others in such poorly controlled situations that they are tempted to steal, and paying people with responsibility for cash well enough that they do not start thinking of themselves as underpaid and therefore deserving of more money from the company!

A real case: An armoured truck company had developed a good business picking up cash from supermarkets and other stores and delivering it to banks. The company trusted its employees and had never had problems. Usually the trucks were staffed by two people, a driver and a second person who rode in the back. The two had to sign various forms and, in a sense, they kept an eye on each other so no one got tempted: there was often a million dollars or more in unmarked, untraceable cash in the truck. Sometimes, though, one of the two people was sick, or on vacation, or called away on some errand for the company, and there would be just one person to drive the truck and collect the money. On one day like that, there was a particularly large amount of money in the truck, and the driver, apparently on impulse, just took it and departed for foreign parts!

6.10 INVENTORY CONTROL

This chapter has emphasized the importance of keeping accurate records to provide information to both internal and external users. Many of the records kept have to do with the control of inventory. Inventory control is an important issue for management because a high percentage of working capital may be tied up in inventory. Inventory may be perishable or become obsolete if held too long, and, due to the physical attributes of some types of inventory, there may be a great potential for theft.

Several different inventory control systems may be used, depending on the nature of the inventory and the objectives of management. The methods explained below are the three most commonly used by business. Each provides a different amount of information at a different cost. It is important to note that the choice of inventory control system is a *recordkeeping* choice as opposed to a *reporting* choice: management is simply deciding how to record the inventory. How inventory is reported on the financial statements will be dealt with in Chapter 10.

THE PERPETUAL ACCOUNTING CONTROL METHOD

When an order of inventory items is received, the quantity received is added to the quantity recorded as being already on hand. When items are sold, they are deducted from the recorded quantity. Therefore, the perpetual method shows how many items are supposed to be on hand at any time:

- Take the quantity on hand at the beginning of the period;
- Add the quantity purchased during the period;
- Deduct the quantity sold during the period;
- Equals the quantity that should be on hand at the end of the period.

If a physical count of the inventory fails to show that quantity, the company knows that some have been lost or stolen, or that there has been an error in the records.

If the cost of items is included in the count along with the quantity, the perpetual record can be used to estimate the total cost of inventory at any time, without having to bother counting and pricing everything.

Beginning inventory cost (support with physical count if desired)
+ Cost of purchases of inventory (records)
– Cost of inventory sold (records)
= Ending inventory cost (support with physical count if desired)

THE RETAIL ACCOUNTING CONTROL METHOD

This is like the perpetual method, except that records are based on selling prices of goods rather than just quantities or costs. A department or branch is charged with the total selling value (sales price times quantity) of all items for sale delivered to it. Revenue from sales is then deducted from this total value as the items are sold. This ties inventory control to cash control, as in the Mayfield Pro Shop example in Section 6.9. At any point in time, the department or branch should have inventory, plus cash from sales made since the last revenue report, plus records of sales on credit or via credit cards, equal to the current total retail value:

- Start with the retail price of all goods delivered to the department;
- Deduct the department's sales (connected to cash and credit card control procedures);
- Difference equals inventory that should be on hand, priced at retail.

If a physical count, with items priced at retail, fails to show the expected total retail value, the company knows that some items have been lost or stolen, or that there has been an error in the records. Total cost of the inventory can be estimated at any time by deducting the average markup from the current total retail value. The retail method is, however, a little complicated in practice because of the need to keep track of markdowns, returned goods, special sale prices, and other price adjustments if the method is to work accurately.

THE PERIODIC COUNT METHOD

When goods are bought, they are put on the shelf or in the storeroom, and when they are sold or used, they are taken off the shelf or out of the storeroom. With the above two control systems, records are kept of these movements, to provide expected quantities or values on hand. But if complete records of such inventory changes are not kept, the enterprise does not have records to indicate what should be on hand. The only way to tell what is on hand is to go and count it. Because this sort of counting tends to be done only periodically, when an inventory figure is needed for financial statements or insurance purposes, this *lack of* accounting control is called the "periodic" method. While there may be other features of internal control present, such as physical protection and insurance, it lacks the parallel recordkeeping that gives the above two methods their value. There is no way to reconcile counts to records in order to discover errors, but it is simple and cheap to operate because no continuing records are kept. Recordkeeping does cost money!

Beginning inventory (count)
\+ Purchases (records)
– Ending inventory (count)
= Inventory sold (deduced)

Because what has been sold is deduced rather than known from records, you can see that it might not all have been sold. Some could have been lost, stolen, evaporated, etc. So under the periodic method, cost of goods sold expense (cost of counted beginning inventory + cost of purchases – cost of counted ending inventory) includes all these other possibilities.

INVENTORY AND CASH CONTROL: CAR DEALERS AND COFFEE SHOPS

The perpetual method can be costly in terms of recordkeeping. (So can the similar retail method, though probably sales records have to be kept anyway, so the extra cost of the inventory control may not be large.) Management must pay someone to record, sort, and compile the information. What type of business uses a perpetual system? The local car dealership is a good example of one. Cars are expensive—therefore a large investment must be made if a good supply is to be on hand for customers to choose from. The high value of cars and the need to keep track for licence and insurance purposes means that serial numbers and other identification information is easily available and usually recorded in various places. Automobiles have a high risk of becoming obsolete because consumer preferences change, and the cost of theft is high even if only one car is stolen. Because of the relatively small quantity of cars sold by most dealerships, recordkeeping costs are not high.

A local coffee counter we'll call HotCaf is another example enterprise using perpetual inventory control. Here is what HotCaf does to control its coffee inventory. With this system, HotCaf always knows how much coffee it should have on hand.[4]

1. When coffee beans are received from the warehouse, both the price and amount of each type of bean are recorded.
2. Coffee beans are removed from the bins for grinding in standard amounts. This is recorded on "Daily Usage Sheets."

3. The coffee is apportioned by weight into filters and brewed as needed.
4. At the point of sale, the amount for each cup sold is rung into the computerized cash register. This provides a record of the number of cups sold, and, because supervisors know how many cups each pot makes and how many grams of coffee are needed per pot, the amount of coffee used can be, and is, computed and recorded at the end of every day. Sales are also recorded at this time.

Another interesting aspect of inventory control at HotCaf is its connection with cash control. Cash control is provided by means of the cash register and the coffee cups. The cash register is computerized and has a separate code for each item of merchandise sold at the counter. Thus, the cash register also provides a type of inventory control whenever a sale is rung in. A sale implies removal of that item from inventory. To make sure that all sales are recorded on the cash register, HotCaf reconciles coffee sales to the number of cups sold. This is accomplished by keeping daily track of the amount of unused cups on hand. Every morning and every night a physical count of the cups is done. All the spoiled cups (usually ones with dirt or holes in them) are put aside and counted at the end of the day to provide a more accurate reconciliation with the amount recorded on the cash register. The reconciliation looks something like this:

Cups: Number of cups on hand at beginning of day
+ Number of new cups received from the warehouse that day
– Number on hand at end of day
– Number of spoiled cups on hand
= Number of cups used for sales

Sales: Number of cups used for sales
× Selling price per cup
= Expected coffee sales revenue for the day

The expected sales figure as per the coffee cup method is then compared to the cash register record and to the physical amount of coffee remaining on hand. The coffee used for the day's sales can then be calculated and recorded, and any missing coffee inventory or cash can be identified.

As an example of the variety of problems that can come up, HotCaf's neat control system has recently been complicated by the increasingly popular practice of customers bringing their own cups! Recordkeeping, like other aspects of accounting, has to change to meet changing circumstances.

INVENTORY CONTROL JOURNAL ENTRIES: BRANSWORTH LTD.

Bransworth Ltd. uses a perpetual accounting control system for its inventory. It has the following data for a recent period:

Beginning accounts receivable	$ 40,000	Beginning inventory	$ 23,000
Purchases during period (all cash)	114,000	Sales (all credit)	150,000
Cash collected in period	115,000	Ending inventory count	28,000

The company's markup is 50% on cost (that is, selling price is 150% of cost). Just to make it easier, we'll assume all sales, purchases, and collections were in single transactions. Here are summary journal entries for the company's system:

a. Purchases	DR Inventory asset	114,000	
	CR Cash		114,000
	Purchases during the period.		
b. Sales	DR Accounts receivable	150,000	
	CR Sales revenue		150,000
	Sales on credit during the period.		
c. Cost of goods sold	DR Cost of goods sold expense	100,000	
	CR Inventory asset		100,000
	COGS expense: $150,000 revenue minus 50% markup on cost.		
d. Count adjustment	DR Inventory shortage expense	9,000	
	CR Inventory asset		9,000
	Shortage: record indicates inventory should be $23,000 + $114,000 – $100,000 = $37,000, but only $28,000 is on hand.		
e. Collections	DR Cash	115,000	
	CR Accounts receivable		115,000
	Customer collections during the period.		

Let's review two accounts here, to ensure you see how the accounting figures help with the control:

The inventory account:	Beginning cost balance	$ 23,000
	Purchases	114,000
	Cost of goods sold	(100,000)
	Expected balance on hand	37,000
The count showed less than expected on hand	Adjustment for loss	(9,000)
	Revised ending cost balance	$ 28,000

(If the company did not have its perpetual control system [that is, if it used the periodic count method], we'd have the $23,000 from the beginning, plus the $114,000 purchased, less the $28,000 counted at the end, for an apparent cost of goods sold of $109,000. You can see that, had we had the perpetual records, we'd know that this figure is actually the sum of $100,000 cost of goods really sold and $9,000 shortage. Both methods have the same revenue and the same total expense, $109,000; they differ in the information they provide management about what is going on.)

The accounts receivable account:	Beginning	$ 40,000
	Sales	150,000
	Collections	(115,000)
	Ending balance	$ 75,000

We can check with the customers or otherwise verify that this amount really is a collectible asset.

Cash control follows from this, too. The collections figure from the accounts receivable account is part of the deposits to cash, so it becomes part of the record-based control system for cash.

HOW'S YOUR UNDERSTANDING

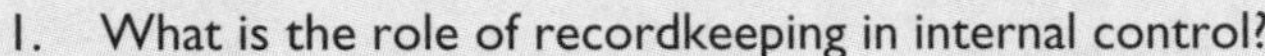

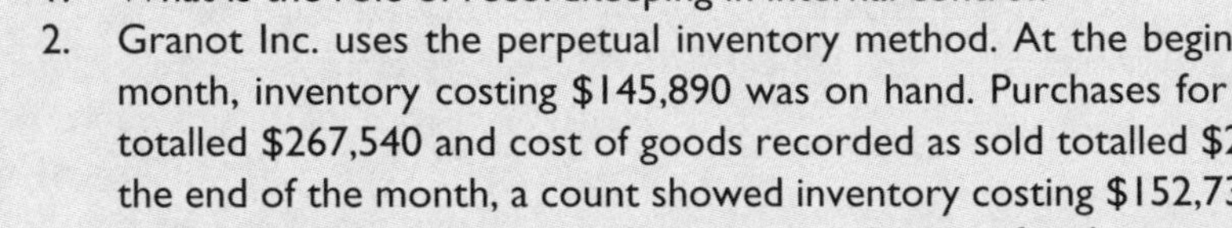

Here are two questions you should be able to answer, based on what you have just read:

1. What is the role of recordkeeping in internal control?
2. Granot Inc. uses the perpetual inventory method. At the beginning of the month, inventory costing $145,890 was on hand. Purchases for the month totalled $267,540 and cost of goods recorded as sold totalled $258,310. At the end of the month, a count showed inventory costing $152,730 to be on hand. What, if anything, was the inventory shortage for the month? ($2,390)

6.11 MANAGERS, BOOKKEEPING, AND CONTROL

Not many managers think of recordkeeping as a breathtaking topic. This chapter has demonstrated, however, that it is an important topic for managers, primarily for two reasons:

1. Bookkeeping and associated recordkeeping provide the underlying data on which accounting's information is built. To a large extent, management decision-making and evaluations of management performance depend on accounting information. Such decisions and evaluations may be constrained by the nature of the underlying data. For example, if certain events are not recognized as transactions by the bookkeeping system, they may not be reflected in the financial statements either. Frustration with the limitations implied by this often leads top managers to want to override the routine transactional system with special adjustments and accruals (Chapters 7 and 10 elaborate), but because such action has a manipulative ring to it, it is often ineffective in convincing users, and management's frustration remains.
2. Bookkeeping and associated recordkeeping provide the data and systems used in meeting management's important responsibility to safeguard assets and generally keep the business under control. Management's internal control responsibilities are becoming more and more prominent, and there is a brief acknowledgment of that in most annual reports. For example, the annual report for The North West Company has a section titled

"Management's Responsibility for Financial Statements" (reprinted with the financial statements at the back of this book), which points out, among other things:

> In order to meet its responsibility and ensure integrity of financial reporting, management maintains accounting systems and appropriate internal controls and an internal audit function designed to provide reasonable assurance that assets are safeguarded, transactions are authorized and recorded and that the financial records are reliable.

6.12 ACCOUNTING RESEARCH: PREDICTION OR CONTROL?

We have so far identified several different uses for financial accounting information, including:

a. Evaluation of management's performance, for the purpose of deciding whether to reward or punish managers;
b. Prediction of future performance, for the purpose of deciding whether to invest in or lend to the company (Chapters 8 and 9 will emphasize this);
c. Division of the company's returns (incomes) into portions for various parties: management bonuses, income taxes, dividends to owners, and so on;
d. Maintenance of internal control over assets and such day-to-day activities as making sales, collecting cash, and incurring expenses.

This section reports a research gap, rather than a result! While there have been significant degrees of attention paid to management control in management accounting research, there has been virtually no research on the control aspects and functions of financial accounting (bookkeeping or financial statements). Most financial accounting research has focused on prediction and associated performance evaluation, and a great deal has been learned about that (as Chapters 8 and 9 will demonstrate). But little has been published about the control side: accounting's effectiveness in that area, the costs of control information, control information's relationship with other managerial information, or other such issues. Perhaps someone reading this will do research to help fill the gap!

6.13 CONTINUING DEMONSTRATION CASE

INSTALMENT 6

Data for Instalment 6

The following trial balance of Mato Inc.'s general ledger at August 31, 1994, was reported in Instalment 3 (Chapter 3):

Debit balance accounts		Credit balance accounts	
Cash	$ 4,507	Bank loan	$ 75,000
Accounts receivable	18,723	Accounts payable	45,616
Inventory	73,614	Loan payable	15,000
Automobile	10,000	Share capital	125,000
Leasehold improvements	63,964	Revenue	42,674
Equipment and furniture	29,740	Accum. amort.—auto.	1,000
Computer	14,900	Accum. amort.—leasehold imp.	6,396
Software	4,800	Accum. amort.—equip.	744
Incorporation costs	1,100	Accum. amort.—computer	1,490
Cost of goods sold expense	28,202	Accum. amort.—software	480
Salary—Mavis	15,000		$313,400
Salary—Tomas	9,280		
Salary—other	1,200		
Travel expense	8,726		
Phone expense	2,461		
Rent expense	12,000		
Utilities expense	1,629		
Office and general expenses	3,444		
Amort. expense—auto	1,000		
Amort. expense—leasehold imp.	6,396		
Amort. expense—equipment	744		
Amort. expense—computer	1,490		
Amort. expense—software	480		
	$313,400		

Alarmed by the company's loss for the six months ($49,378 per Instalment 3) and negative cash generation (decrease in cash of $200,493 per Instalment 4), Mavis and Tomas took strong action over the next six months. They put extra effort into sales, pressed the boutiques for collection as much as they could without damaging their new relationships with these customers, reduced inventory levels, and generally tried to run "a lean shop," as Tomas put it.

Here are events for the six months ended February 28, 1995, grouped and identified for later reference:

a. Revenue for the six months totalled $184,982, all on credit.

b. Collections from customers during the six months were $189,996.

c. Purchases for the six months were $71,004, all on credit. (With its computerized inventory system, the company uses the perpetual method of inventory control.)

d. Payments to suppliers during the six months came to $81,276. (To conserve cash, the company continued to rely on the patience of its suppliers more than Tomas liked. But doing so did save interest expense, because the suppliers did not charge interest while the bank did!)

e. Cost of goods sold for the six months was $110,565.

f. An inventory count on February 28, 1995, revealed inventory on hand costing $33,612.

g. Tomas decided to combine the three salary expense accounts into one, effective September 1, 1994.

h. Salaries for the six months to February 28, 1995, totalled $42,000. The company had paid all of this, except that it owed the government $2,284 in income tax and other deductions, and the employees $2,358 in net salaries at the end of February.

i. Various operating expenses for the six months were: travel, $1,376; phone, $1,553; rent, $12,000; utilities, $1,956; office and general expenses, $2,489. All of these were paid by February 29, except for $1,312.

j. The company bought further necessary equipment at a cost of $2,650 cash on November 3, 1994.

k. The company's bank loan rose and fell during the period. A total of $32,000 in further borrowing was incurred, and $59,500 was repaid.

l. Bank loan interest of $4,814 was paid during the six months (including a portion for the period prior to August 31, 1994, that had not been included in the accounts to that date).

m. Unfortunately (personally and financially), Tomas's father's health had deteriorated over the autumn and so he requested that his loan be repaid. The company did that on December 15, 1994, including interest of $1,425.

The employee (mentioned in an earlier instalment) had been hired in August and looked after the bookkeeping for the company. The above events were made up of hundreds of individual transactions recorded by the employee, but they are summarized by the journal entries that follow. See if you can do them before you look at the results!

Results for Instalment 6

Journal entries for the period September 1, 1994, to February 28, 1995, follow, corresponding with the events listed previously. To save clutter, they are not accompanied by explanations or DR and CR indications, other than in the placement of the figures (the debits to the left). Since they are summary entries, their dates are also omitted.

	Debit	Credit
a. Accounts receivable	184,982	
Revenue		184,982
b. Cash	189,996	
Accounts receivable		189,996
c. Inventory	71,004	
Accounts payable		71,004
d. Accounts payable	81,276	
Cash		81,276
e. Cost of goods sold expense	110,565	
Inventory		110,565
f. Inventory shortage expense	441	
Inventory		441
($73,614 + $71,004 – $110,565 – $33,612)		
g. Salaries Expense	25,480	
Salary—Mavis		15,000
Salary—Tomas		9,280
Salary—Other		1,200
h. Salaries expense	42,000	
Deductions payable		2,284
Salaries payable		2,358
Cash (deduced)		37,358
i. Travel expense	1,376	
Phone expense	1,553	
Rent expense	12,000	
Utilities expense	1,956	
Office and general expense	2,489	
Accounts payable		1,312
Cash (deduced)		18,062
j. Equipment and furniture	2,650	
Cash		2,650
k. Cash	32,000	
Bank loan		32,000
Bank loan	59,500	
Cash		59,500
l. Interest expense	4,814	
Cash		4,814
m. Loan payable	15,000	
Interest expense	1,425	
Cash		16,425

Posting of these journal entries results in the following general ledger account balances at February 28, 1995 (arranged in balance sheet order, as is usually, but certainly not always, done). Credits are shown in brackets.

Account	Balance Aug. 31/94	Transactions for period to February 29, 1995	Balance Feb. 28/95
Cash	4,507	189,996 (81,276) (37,358) (18,062) (2,650) 32,000 (59,500) (4,814) (16,425)	6,418
Accounts receivable	18,723	184,982 (189,996)	13,709
Inventory	73,614	71,004 (110,565) (441)	33,612
Automobile	10,000	0	10,000
Accum. amort.—auto	(1,000)	0	(1,000)
Leasehold improvements	63,964	0	63,964
Accum. amort.—leasehold imp.	(6,396)	0	(6,396)
Equipment and furniture	29,740	2,650	32,390
Accum. amort.—equip.	(744)	0	(744)
Computer	14,900	0	14,900
Accum. amort.—computer	(1,490)	0	(1,490)
Software	4,800	0	4,800
Accum. amort.—software	(480)	0	(480)
Incorporation cost	1,100	0	1,100
Bank loan	(75,000)	(32,000) 59,500	(47,500)
Accounts payable	(45,616)	(71,004) 81,276 (1,312)	(36,656)
Deductions payable	0	(2,284)	(2,284)
Salaries payable	0	(2,358)	(2,358)
Loan payable	(15,000)	15,000	0
Share capital	(125,000)	0	(125,000)
Revenue	(42,674)	(184,982)	(227,656)
Cost of goods sold expense	28,202	110,565	138,767
Salary—Mavis	15,000	(15,000)	0
Salary—Tomas	9,280	(9,280)	0
Salary—other	1,200	(1,200)	0
Salaries expense	0	25,480 42,000	67,480
Travel expense	8,726	1,376	10,102
Phone expense	2,461	1,553	4,014
Rent expense	12,000	12,000	24,000
Utilities expense	1,629	1,956	3,585
Office and general expense	3,444	2,489	5,933
Interest expense	0	4,814 1,425	6,239
Inventory shortage expense	0	441	441
Amortization expense—auto.	1,000	0	1,000
Amortization expense—leasehold	6,396	0	6,396
Amortization expense—equipment	744	0	744
Amortization expense—computer	1,490	0	1,490
Amortization expense—software	480	0	480
Net Sums	0		0

HOMEWORK AND DISCUSSION TO DEVELOP UNDERSTANDING

PROBLEM 6.1* Users and financial statements vs. detailed data

Financial statements are highly summarized documents, representing thousands of transactions. Financial newspapers and commentators produce information about companies that is even more summarized. Why would users accept, or even prefer, summarized information to detailed data? How important is it for the user to understand the procedures and assumptions behind such summarizations?

PROBLEM 6.2* Journal entries for simple transactions

The events listed below all took place on *December 15*, 1995. Provide the journal entry necessary to record each event in the accounts of Company A for the year ended December 31, 1995. If no entry is required, indicate that and give reasons. In most cases an assumption is not necessary. If you feel an assumption is necessary, however, state it.

a. A new general manager is hired at an annual salary of $60,000.

b. Company A receives a bill for $200 from a newspaper for an advertisement to be run on December 31, 1995. Payment is not due for 60 days.

c. A bond is purchased by Company A for $2,000 cash. The bond will have a maturity value of $2,500 in three years because interest will accumulate.

d. A landscaper agrees to improve land owned by Company A. The agreed price for the work is $700.

e. An order for $900 of merchandise is received from a customer along with a cash deposit of $300.

f. A $600 insurance premium for coverage over the period from December 1, 1995, to November 30, 1996, is paid in cash.

PROBLEM 6.3* Journal entry for a business acquisition

Big Ideas Inc. decided to buy parts of the business of a competitor, which was cutting back operations. For a price of $4,200,000 (a $1,000,000 down payment and the rest in four equal annual instalments plus interest at 12% per annum), Big Ideas got inventory it valued at $280,000, land it valued at $1,500,000, a retail store building it valued at $1,800,000, furniture and equipment it valued at $470,000, and some dealership rights it valued at $40,000. Big Ideas also agreed to pay a bank loan of $130,000 secured by the inventory.

Write a journal entry to record Big Ideas Inc.'s purchase.

PROBLEM 6.4* Periodic and perpetual inventory control calculations

You are the senior accountant for a shoe wholesaler that uses the periodic inventory method. You have determined the following information from your company's records, which you assume are correct:

a. Inventory of $246,720 was on hand at the start of the year.

b. Purchases for the year totalled $1,690,000. Of this, $1,412,000 was purchased on account, that is, accounts payable was credited for this amount at the time of the purchase.

c. The ending balance in accounts payable was $47,500 higher than the opening balance.

d. A year-end inventory count revealed inventory of $324,800.

1. Calculate cost of goods sold according to the periodic inventory method.
2. Assume now that your company uses the perpetual method of inventory control, and that your records show that $1,548,325 of inventory (at cost) was sold during the year. What is the adjustment needed to correct the records, given the inventory count in item (d) above? What might the need for this adjustment indicate about company operations?
3. If the perpetual method generally provides more control over inventory for management, why don't all companies use it?

PROBLEM 6.5* Journal entries for a small new business

Graham Cline, a second-year university student, was tired of low-paying, temporary summer work. He decided to go into business by setting up a company, Graham Cline Inc., to sell hot dogs in city parks over the summer.

The company commenced operations on January 1, 1995, and completed its first year of operations on December 31, 1995. During the year the following events occurred:

a. On January 1, 1995, the company issued 100 shares to Graham at $1 each. In addition, Graham's father lent the company $5,000. The loan has no repayment terms and is not interest bearing.

b. On January 1, 1995, Graham Cline Inc. negotiated a contract with a local butcher shop to store its supplies in a refrigerated locker. Looking to the future, the company signed a two-year agreement that would expire December 31, 1996. The agreement called for payments of $120 on January 1, 1995, and $130 on January 1, 1996.

c. On June 1, 1995, Graham Cline Inc. purchased food for the summer for cash, consisting of 500 dozen buns at $1 per dozen and 500 dozen wieners at $3 per dozen.

d. On June 1, 1995, Graham Cline Inc. purchased two portable hot dog stands from a retiring vendor for $300 each. The company agreed to pay the former owner $100 at the purchase date, and the balance plus interest at 10% per year on December 31, 1995. The company also incurred an expense of $60 for fixing up the hot dog stands. The economic value of the stands will be "used up" by the end of the first summer and, therefore, costs related to them are all expenses for 1995.

e. During the year, sales for Graham Cline Inc. totalled $7,000.

f. The company hired another student to run one of the hot dog stands. The student was paid $800 per month for the three months she worked for the company (June through August).

Other information, not yet recorded in the accounts, is as follows:

g. The inventory at December 31, 1995, consisted of:

Buns	10 dozen
Wieners	10 dozen

h. The company's income tax rate is 20%. It paid its taxes owing on December 31, 1995.

i. All contractual commitments of the company have been satisfied up to December 31, 1995.

j. On December 31, 1995, the company declared and paid a dividend of $5 per share.

1. Prepare journal entries to record the foregoing events in the records of Graham Cline Inc. for the year ended December 31, 1995.
2. Prepare a balance sheet as at December 31, 1995, and statements of income and retained earnings for the year ended December 31, 1995.
3. Has Graham been successful at his venture? Would you recommend that he continue his operations next summer? Consider qualitative aspects as well as the financial statements you prepared.

PROBLEM 6.6 Explain the value of recordkeeping to a business person

At a recent Student Accounting Club wine and cheese party, local business people mixed with students. One small business entrepreneur was heard to say, "All that financial accounting information you students learn about is not relevant to me. I just started up my business. I only have five employees: four people in the shop building the product and one person in shipping/receiving. I'm out on calls, drumming up business so I have my finger on the real pulse of the firm—that's sales. My brother pays the bills and does up the payroll every two weeks. Once in a while I write cheques too. It's all simple and smooth; so, why add a lot of time-consuming, costly recordkeeping to it all? All those books and financial statements are fine for the big public companies. I can do without the complications."

Prepare an appropriate response to the businessman.

PROBLEM 6.7 Recordkeeping differences in large vs. small businesses

Identify some differences you might expect to find between the transaction filters and accounting books and records of a large corporation and those of a corner store run by one person.

PROBLEM 6.8 Double-entry transactional records: strength and weakness

In a flight of accounting passion, Professor Lump exclaimed, "The double-entry transactional recording system is financial accounting's greatest strength and its greatest weakness!" Lump went on to explain this odd comment. Write down what the professor probably said in explanation.

PROBLEM 6.9 Identify whether or not events are accounting transactions

The following events happened at the Guzzle Beer Corporation. For each, indicate whether or not it is an accounting transaction for Guzzle Beer Corp. and state, in five or ten words, why.

a. A large tank containing beer mixture broke, and all of the mixture spilled.

b. A major shareholder sold 50,000 shares on the stock exchange.

c. The corporation paid $60,000,000 for a Mexican brewery.

d. An invoice for next week's TV advertising arrived.

e. A pub took delivery of its weekly shipment of Guzzle Beer.

PROBLEM 6.10 Necessary source documents and purpose of trial balance

1. Make a list of the source documents you expect would be needed to back up the transactional records in an accounting system and describe in ten words or so why each document would be useful.
2. Why does the bookkeeper (or the computer system) produce a trial balance of the general ledger regularly?

PROBLEM 6.11 Evaluate statements about accounting and recordkeeping

State whether or not you agree with each of the statements below and, in a few words, tell why.

a. Land is classified as a long-term asset on the balance sheet.

b. Generally accepted accounting principles (GAAP) are specified in laws passed by governments.

c. If an event satisfies all four of the transaction criteria, you can be sure it will be recorded by the entity's accounting system.

d. Purchases and sales by investors of existing issued shares of a company listed on the Toronto Stock Exchange are not accounting transactions in the company's records.

e. The perpetual method of accounting for inventory provides better internal control than the periodic method.

f. A properly designed system of internal control over cash should prevent employee theft of cash.

PROBLEM 6.12 Explain nature and purpose of internal control to a manager

A friend, Janet, has accepted a job as president of a local company. During a meeting you attended, an accountant mentioned to Janet that she would be responsible for internal control of the company. When the accountant left the room, Janet turned to you and asked, "What is internal control and why should I care about it?" Answer Janet's question, using clear language without technical jargon.

PROBLEM 6.13 Identify source documents; make journal and ledger entries

The following six transactions happened to a new business, Josie's Socks:

a. Josie, a young entrepreneur, decided that there was a lucrative business opportunity at the first annual Snowflake Festival: selling woollen socks. (Record cold weather was expected.) She approached the Colossal Bank for a very short-term loan of $2,000 and received the loan in return for pledging her car as security.

b. She bought 200 pairs of socks at Sock Shop Inc. for $3 a pair.

c. She obtained a vendor's licence from the municipality for $65, paid in advance.
d. She rented a booth for six days at $25 a day and paid in advance.
e. She had a sign to advertise her wares made by a local graphics firm at a cost of $140. She hasn't paid for it yet.
f. She sold all of the 200 pairs of socks for $5.40 a pair cash during the first two days of the Festival (February 15 and 16).

1. Indicate the source document(s) you'd expect Josie to have as evidence of each transaction and in support of her accounting records.
2. Write a journal entry to record the transaction.
3. Post the transactions to a simple set of general ledger accounts.
4. Prepare a trial balance of the ledger to demonstrate that it is in balance.

PROBLEM 6.14 Identify transactions and write journal entries for them

The following events happened today at Billowy Balloons, Inc., a sightseeing and advertising company featuring large hot-air balloons. For each event listed below, state whether or not it is an accounting transaction for Billowy and why. If it is an accounting transaction, write a journal entry to record it.

a. The president, despondent over poor sales performance, jumped out of a balloon from 1,000 feet up. The president's salary was $75,000 per year.
b. The president's widow immediately sued the company for $500,000, stating that job-related stress caused him to jump.
c. The company agreed with the barn owner that after the funeral it would pay $10,000 to repair the barn roof that the president had fallen through.
d. Learning about the president's action, shareholder Jumpy John sold his shares, which had cost him $20,000, to Happy Harry for $18,000.
e. Learning about the president's action and concerned about its possible effects on the company's share price, the board of directors declared a dividend of $25,000, to be paid in two weeks as a shareholder morale booster.

PROBLEM 6.15 Identify transactions and write journal entries for them

The following events took place on February 1, 1996. For each event, give the journal entry (if any) that should be made to record the transaction in the account of Smith Ltd. Indicate clearly where in the financial statements you think the accounts involved belong. State any assumptions you feel are necessary.

a. The company purchased supplies to be used immediately. The purchase price of the supplies was $5,000. Only $2,000 was paid in cash, on delivery. The balance is due in 30 days.
b. The company decided to rent a service vehicle for $4,800 per year. A rental contract was signed February 1, 1996, to take effect March 1, 1996. Smith Ltd. paid $400 cash to the rental company on February 1, 1996, which represented the rent for March 1996.
c. Some of Smith's repairmen were not busy on February 1. The manager had them paint the inside of a storage room. Assume the repairmen's salaries of $300 were paid in cash at the end of the day.

d. A shareholder sold her car to the company. The vehicle cost her $15,000 two years ago. An equivalent used vehicle would have been worth about $8,000 on February 1, 1996. No cash changed hands, but the shareholder expects the company to pay her for the car eventually.

e. An invoice for $5,000 was received, relating to repairs and maintenance work done in December 1995. The company's year end is December 31. This expense was not recorded in the 1995 financial statements.

PROBLEM 6.16 Identify transactions and write journal entries for them

Southward Stores Ltd. is a general merchandise retailer operating in the suburbs. During a recent month, the events listed below happened. For each event, decide if it is an accounting transaction. If it is an accounting transaction, state briefly why and record it in journal entry form. Indicate where in the financial statements you wish each account to appear. If it is not an accounting transaction, state briefly why it is not.

a. Southward borrowed $500,000 from the Great Pacific Bank (Canada). Payment is due in three years, but the loan can be called on ten days' notice if Southward fails to make any of the monthly interest payments, which begin next month.

b. The retailer ordered inventory for resale costing $300,000, to be delivered in 40 days, and sent a deposit of $10,000 with the order.

c. The company renewed its lease on the store premises, signing an agreement which provided that, beginning in three months, the monthly rent would rise from $21,000 to $23,000.

d. Southward was charged with unfair pricing of its main line of merchandise. News of this sent the company's shares (listed on a stock exchange) down in price from $10 to $8.50 each. The company has 1,000,000 shares outstanding, all publicly traded.

e. The company declared a dividend of $0.50 cents per share, to be paid in one week, on each of its 1,000,000 outstanding shares. This news sent the company's shares up by $0.40 each on the stock exchange.

PROBLEM 6.17 Calculations for perpetual vs. periodic inventory

Razzmatazz Ltd. uses a perpetual inventory control system. The following data are available:

Inventory on hand at beginning of year (100,000 units at $5 cost each)	$ 500,000
Purchases for the year (850,000 units at $5 cost each)	$4,250,000
Sales for the year (865,000 units at $11 price each)	$9,515,000
Inventory on hand at end of the year (70,000 units at $5 cost each)	$ 350,000

1. Calculate the cost of goods sold expense for the year, based on the company's perpetual inventory system.
2. If the company had been using the periodic inventory method, what would the cost of goods sold expense for the year have been?
3. A perpetual system costs money to operate. Is it likely to be worthwhile for Razzmatazz?

PROBLEM 6.18 Reconstruct journal entries from T-accounts

Sanderson Electronics is a new retail store that sells mainly small parts, such as switches, circuit boards, and wire. Sanderson's ledger accounts are shown below in T-account form, with entries made for the first month of business.

Cash	
(a) 30,000	(c) 1,200
(f) 1,300	(h) 1,000
(g) 650	(j) 560

Accounts Receivable	
(e) 900	(g) 650
(f) 1,400	

Prepaid Supplies	
(i) 300	

Equipment	
(c) 3,600	

Inventory	
(b) 5,000	(e) 540
	(f) 1,620

Accounts Payable	
(h) 1,000	(b) 5,000
	(d) 700

Notes Payable	
(j) 500	(c) 2,400

Common Shares	
	(a) 30,000

Sales Revenue	
	(e) 900
	(f) 2,700

Supplies Expense	
(d) 700	(i) 300

Interest Expense	
(j) 60	

Cost of Goods Sold	
(e) 540	
(f) 1,620	

For each of the transactions from (a) to (j), write the general journal entry that was used to post the accounts, including an explanation of the entry.

PROBLEM 6.19 Identify cash control problems

(Challenging)

Many companies put a great amount of effort into controlling their cash, both that on hand and in banks, often more than for any other asset.

1. Why do you think such great effort is required to control cash?
2. List the control problems you'd expect in each of the following cases. To answer, try to visualize how the cash would probably flow into and out of the company and its bank accounts:
   a. Cash collected at the sales counter of the local fast-food outlet;
   b. Wages being paid to construction employees working on a large highway project;
   c. Donations to the Heart Fund being collected by door-to-door volunteer canvassers;
   d. Money deposited into parking meters owned by your municipality;

e. Cash provided to the receptionist at the main entrance of a large company, to be used to pay for deliveries, buy emergency supplies, and other such minor things.

PROBLEM 6.20 Recordkeeping and control needs of a business

(Challenging) You've probably patronized coffee counters like HotCaf (Section 6.10) that are part of a chain. Think about another such business and its recordkeeping and control requirements and answer the following questions:

1. Describe the business and indicate what external factors the company should monitor in order to plan and control its operations.
2. From the point of view of the company's owner, what are the control problems that financial accounting information may assist in solving? What effect would growth have on such control problems?
3. How might the increasing use of computer technology affect the choice of inventory control method by this company?
4. How might the company's accounting records assist it in such areas as obtaining insurance, obeying laws regarding treatment of its employees, and paying its income taxes?

PROBLEM 6.21 Is a new control system worth its cost?

(Challenging) Company X is thinking about putting in a new inventory control system at an annual operating cost of $480,000. The company's average cost of financing its assets is 8%. The control system would reduce average inventories by 25% from the present level of $2,000,000 without affecting revenue ($10,000,000 per year) and would affect other items as follows:

Various losses on inventory	Now	With new system
Theft or loss of inventory items	1% of revenue	negligible
Items made unsaleable due to style changes	8% of revenue	3% of revenue
Items made unsaleable due to deterioration	5% of revenue	no change

Would the new control system be worth its cost?

PROBLEM 6.22 Do an income statement from accounts and events

(Challenging) To diversify his activities, hockey player Knuckles Gronsky opened a boutique for children's sportswear. He incorporated a company under the name Gronsky's Great Things Ltd., and the boutique opened for business on September 1, 1994.

Account balances and other information for the year ended August 31, 1995, for Gronsky's company follow. From this information, prepare an income statement (only) for the year ended August 31, 1995.

Cash	2,600
Accounts receivable	3,500
Inventory of clothing (after fire)	30,000
Sales revenue	240,000
Wage and salary expense	27,500
Rent paid in advance	2,000
Furniture and fixtures	15,500
Accumulated amortization	3,000
Tax expense	7,000
Loan payable	8,000
Accounts payable	23,000
Investment in Number One Ltd.	10,000
Inventory sold (Cost of goods sold)	100,000
Supplies purchased	14,500
Rent expense	24,000
Capital from shareholder	15,000
Amortization expense	3,000
Costs associated with incorporation	1,900
Interest paid on loan	500
General operating expenses	5,000
Dividends payable	2,000
Dividends declared	4,000
Loss due to storage room fire	40,000

The following information will explain some of the preceding items:

a. On August 20, 1995, someone started a fire in the storage room and burnt $40,000 worth of inventory. There will be no insurance claim on this loss.

b. The loan is payable in yearly payments of $2,000 plus interest. Payments are to be made on August 31 each year over the next four years. The payment and interest for August 31, 1995, are already reflected in the preceding balances.

c. The investment is shares in Number One Ltd., a private company. Gronsky has no intention of selling the shares in the immediate future.

d. On August 30, 1995, the board of directors declared dividends of $4,000, $2,000 of which were paid on August 31, 1995, and the remaining $2,000 of which were payable September 12, 1995.

e. The clothing inventory is kept on a perpetual basis, whereas supplies are included in expenses immediately when purchased. At August 31, 1995, supplies were counted and $9,000 remained on hand. The count has *not* been reflected in the preceding balances.

PROBLEM 6.23 Journal entries for a complex transaction

(Challenging)

In September 1995, Knuckles Gronsky (from Problem 6.22) flew to Northburg for the annual general meeting of his children's wear boutique company, Gronsky's

Great Things Ltd. After having waited in vain to be picked up by a friend at the airport, Gronsky decided that since he was in Northburg so often on business, he needed a vehicle for ready transportation. He immediately went to Country Ford and decided on a red convertible. The list price was $25,000, but the salesperson said if Gronsky took it that day he could have it for $23,000. (This was still above Country Ford's cost of $18,000 for the car.)

Gronsky knew from Country Ford's advertisements that the car dealership would match any down payment to a maximum of $1,000 by reducing the price accordingly. He reminded the salesperson of the down payment offer and took advantage of it by plunking down a crumpled $1,000 bill. In addition, Gronsky negotiated a deal whereby he would pay for only half the price of the car (the $1,000 down plus $10,000 more) and do five television commercials in the coming year for Country Ford, instead of paying the $11,000 balance of the price. At this point, the deal being struck, Gronsky phoned North Bank and obtained a demand loan to cover the $10,000 balance of the cash part of the purchase. After being assured that the funds would immediately be put in his account, he wrote a cheque for the car and drove off with the top up because it was –35°C.

1. Write a journal entry for Country Ford, which uses the perpetual inventory system, to record the sale of the car. Make it clear exactly where each account goes in the financial statements. (Ignore any income taxes and sales commissions that might arise.)
2. From Gronsky's point of view, would the car purchase be recorded in the accounts of Gronsky's Great Things Ltd. or be treated as a personal purchase by Gronsky? State your opinion and give reasons for it.
3. Write a journal entry to record the car purchase in either Gronsky or his company's accounts, depending on which you chose in Part 2. Follow the same directions and assumptions as in Part 1.

PROBLEM 6.24 Entries and statements for a used car business

(Challenging)

You've decided to take a job as a part-time accountant, working for a friend of yours, John Rogers, who operates a used car lot called Honest John's Used Cars Ltd. John's records consist primarily of a cheque book and a bank deposit book. He uses a cheque to pay for every purchase and always describes the purchase on the cheque stub, which remains in the cheque book. He also describes each deposit on the duplicate deposit slip, which he keeps.

John likes having things simple. He rents a small lot with a furnished sales office for $1,000 per month (including utilities). He carries no parts and provides no service on cars. His company's share capital is $50, so most of the owner's investment is retained earnings. The company has no employees except him (he gets a monthly salary of $3,000). At January 31, 1996, he had a $20,000 operating loan that carried interest at 12% (1% per month) and was payable on demand. All interest had been paid up to January 31, 1996. His inventory of unsold cars (all of which the company paid cash for) at January 31, 1996, was as follows:

Unsold Cars on Hand—January 31, 1996	Purchase Price
1992 Ford	$ 4,500
1990 Volkswagen	4,000
1989 Oldsmobile	5,000
1990 Camaro	7,500
1991 Mazda	4,800
1989 Toyota	6,200
	$32,000

John has assured you that all cash and cheques received in February 1996 were deposited in the bank. His receipts and disbursements for that month were as follows:

Cheques written during February (from cheque stubs)

Cheque #	Date	Description (Paid to, etc.)	Amount
51	Feb. 1/96	XL Property Management—Rent for February and March 1996	$ 2,000
52	Feb. 4/96	XL Property Management—Alterations to sales office	4,000
53	Feb. 10/96	Jack Yee—Purchase of 1991 Chrysler, paid in full	6,500
54	Feb. 15/96	John Rogers—Salary for February 1996	3,000
55	Feb. 22/96	Skyline Auto Auctions—Purchase of 3 cars (1989 Lincoln—$8,500; 1992 Nissan—$6,000; 1990 Honda —$4,500)	19,000
56	Feb. 29/96	Royal Bank—Payment of February interest in full	200
		Total Cash Disbursements	$34,700

Cash and cheques received in February (from duplicate bank deposit slips)

Date	Description (Received from, etc.)	Amount
Feb. 6/96	Tim Boychuk—Sale of Camaro, paid in full	$10,000
Feb. 12/96	Bob Scott—Sale of Oldsmobile, paid in full	7,400
Feb. 19/96	Downtown Dodge Used Cars—Sale of Mazda and Ford, paid in full	10,300
Feb. 29/96	Additional operating loan from bank	5,000
	Total Cash Receipts	$32,700

John has informed you that no other cars were purchased or sold during February and that no amounts are owed by or to him at January 31 or February 29, 1996. You also learned that the balance in his bank account on January 31, 1996, was $6,800. *Ignore sales taxes throughout this problem.*

1. Prepare a balance sheet for Honest John's Used Cars Ltd. as at January 31, 1996. (Deduce the retained earnings from the other account balances.)
2. Record the February 1996 transactions in journal entry form.
3. Post these transactions to the general ledger of Honest John's Used Cars Ltd.
4. Prepare a balance sheet as at February 29, 1996, and statements of income and retained earnings for the company for the one-month period ended February 29, 1996.
5. Make up a list of unsold cars at February 29, 1996, and their purchase prices. The total of these amounts should agree with the inventory account in your general ledger and balance sheet as at February 29, 1996.
6. Compare the company's net income for the month of February with the change in the bank account balance between January 31, 1996, and February 29, 1996. Why are these amounts different?
7. What are some advantages of John's having monthly financial statements? (In the past John has prepared one set of statements each year for income tax purposes.)
8. Would you be willing to provide an audit opinion on the above statements? In other words, based on what you know of John's recordkeeping methods and internal control, would you express a written opinion that the financial statements present fairly the results of operations for the month of February? Why or why not?

CASE 6A Records and internal control for Harvey's and Swiss Chalet

The 1993 annual report of Cara Operations Limited contained the following "Corporate Profile":

CARA OPERATIONS LIMITED

Cara Operations Limited is a leader in the food services industry and in the retailing and commercial distribution of office products/furniture.

Family style dining is offered at Swiss Chalet and Steak & Burger Restaurants throughout Canada and in certain Florida and New York State cities. Fast food, featuring charbroiled hamburgers and chicken is served at Harvey's and Harvey's Plus, while Hershel's offers delicatessen fare. Home delivery service for charbroiled chicken and ribs is offered through Swiss Chalet.

The Airport Services Division provides catering and ancillary services to major Canadian and International airlines through flight kitchens and commissaries across Canada. It also operates restaurants, gift stores and newsstands at airports, hotels and railway stations.

Office products and furniture are offered through Grand & Toy retail outlets and commercial distritution centres in many major cities in Canada.

Beaver Foods Limited is the country's largest most diverse, Canadian-owned contract catering company providing service to corporate and government cafeterias, high schools, colleges, universities, hospitals, nursing homes, institutions and remote resource camps across Canada. Beaver provides these services along with its divisions —

Les Services Alimentaires CVC Inc., Nutricare and CVC Sevices.

Summit Food Distributors Inc. is a full-line wholesale food distribution company operating primarily in Southern Ontario and the Ottawa Valley area through its locations in London, Ottawa and Fingal. Summit services a wide cross section of clients including institutions, healthcare, universities and restaurants.

Further information about the Harvey's and Swiss Chalet divisions was provided in the "Management Discussion and Analysis" section of the annual report:

Harvey's Sales 1992–1993

Percentage sales by meal period

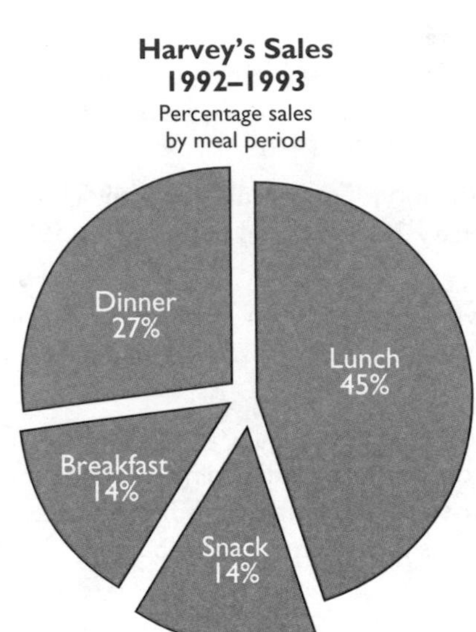

DIVISIONAL PERFORMANCE

Harvey's

The Harvey's division performed well in what remains a challenging recession with aggressive ongoing competitive activity. Despite this, Harvey's gained market share and solidified its number two market position. Real sales growth and prudent cost management ensured that franchisee profitability was protected. Innovative promotional campaigns such as Breakfast Specials and Pennyfries Specials, the latter involving french fries for a penny with the purchase of one of Harvey's specialty sandwiches, helped to promote business growth. Divisional performance was maintained at the same pace as last year.

The development of the Harvey's Plus concept (which also serves Swiss Chalet chicken) continues to be a major initiative through the conversion of existing Harvey's units and new unit growth. In the past year, Harvey's and Harvey's Plus aggressively pursued unit development in the non-traditional sector (universities, airports, and retail centres). The size of these Harvey's restaurants was scaled down to fit the needs of these specialized facilities. This initiative provides enormous opportunity to capitalize on the Harvey's brand awareness.

Harvey's continues to focus on promoting the customized service aspect of its business. Freshly prepared charbroiled products are promptly topped with a generous choice of garnishes by friendly staff. As part of the effort to continuously improve customer service levels, Harvey's continued to focus on staff training. Toward this end, a second Training Centre dedicated to Quebec operations was opened in Montreal this past year.

Harvey's will address changing consumer values through research, menu development, focus on dinner, and new product introductions. This year, Harvey's is well positioned for aggressive growth with a tailored approach for each market segment, in both the traditional and non-traditional sectors, to ensure consumer needs continue to be met. Plans for the international launch of Harvey's and/or Swiss Chalet are proceeding smoothly. The initial focus is on the Czech Republic, where discussions with potential investor-operators, the identification of prime locations, and the planning of operating logistics have all progressed very well. Cara expects to have one or two prototype stores operating in the Czech Republic early in 1994.

Swiss Chalet Sales
1992–1993
Percentage sales
by type of service

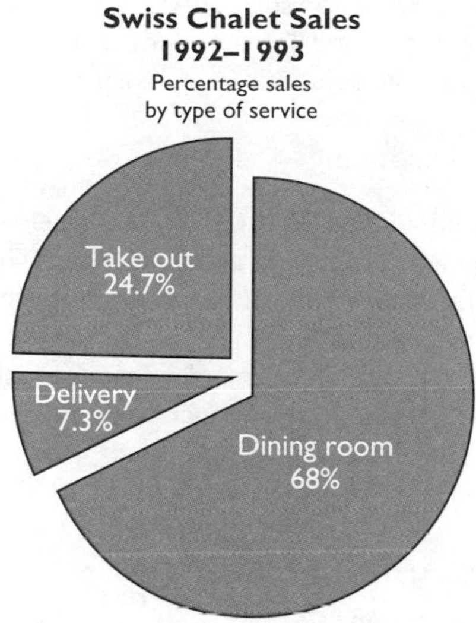

Swiss Chalet

"Back to Basics" has been the focus at Swiss Chalet during the past year as the Division responded to the hard realities of an increasingly tight economy and a very competitive hospitality industry. Despite the continuing recession, sales grew by 1% over the prior year, but Divisional operating profit declined slightly. At the franchisee level, extra training and improved controls allowed operators to improve their profit over the previous year.

Swiss Chalet has reaffirmed its traditional mission with renewed focus on service. Responding to the expectations of a more discerning guest, whose concerns today run far deeper than just a restaurant visit, presents a significant challenge for Swiss Chalet. Many initiatives during 1992-1993 were designed to meet these expectations by building on our strengths. Swiss Chalet has invested more time, effort and dollars than ever before to ensure that the Division is in touch with our guests' perceptions and evaluations of our concept. This information has allowed the development of strategic plans that will enable Swiss Chalet to build upon its solid foundation by further fostering value and service.

During the year, the Division continued the process of upgrading restaurants to a very popular new contemporary design. New attitudinal training programs are under way strengthening the emphasis on hospitable service to ensure continued satisfaction of loyal guests and to be aggressive with our major competitors, thereby fostering the growth of our customer base.

We have successfully launched three new Swiss Chalet restaurants in the past year. Three joint venture take-out locations were closed due to the prohibitive cost of lease renewals, while a fourth location closed at Commerce Court, Toronto, due to mall redevelopment, and was replaced with a Harvey's Plus. National promotions were well received. This, coupled with the continued expansion and refinement of the home delivery program into Quebec and Alberta, allowed Swiss Chalet sales to marginally exceed prior year's, despite the significant sales reduction that the industry has experienced. Swiss Chalet will further continue to expand the home delivery service in 1993-1994. New products were researched and successfully introduced including marinated chicken breast and warm chicken salad amandine to enhance menu variety. As outlined in the discussion of the Harvey's division, Swiss Chalet is working closely with Harvey's on the initial international expansion of a Harvey's and/or Swiss Chalet store.

The strength of the Swiss Chalet concept was never as evident as it is today. With the backing of operators and front line staff, Swiss Chalet will adapt to change, invest in training and excel at guest satisfaction to continue improving sales and profitability.

Discuss how the Harvey's and Swiss Chalet divisions do their business, then suggest (a) the kinds of transactions that would occur for such businesses and the recordkeeping that would be appropriate for them, and (b) the kinds of internal control problems that seem likely and some possible solutions for those problems.

CASE 6B Consider the cost of accounting an recordkeeping

An article from *Business Week*, "A Day of Reckoning for Bean Counters," is below. Discuss the article's perspective on the *cost* of accounting and recordkeeping. (The article mentions "T&E": that's travel and entertainment expense claims. Also, the article considers accounting and recordkeeping to be part of the "finance function" in a business: not everyone would put it that way, but it's a reminder that accounting and financial statements are part of the business's overall financial management and control activity.)

A DAY OF RECKONING FOR BEAN COUNTERS

Now, finance departments are hearing the axman's footsteps

When Union Carbide Corp. spun off its industrial-gases business two years ago, that prompted a companywide restructuring designed to pare some $400 million in costs. For Chief Financial Officer John K. Wulff, the exercise proved eye-opening. He decided to find out how the chemical company's costs of performing such simple finance functions as cutting checks, posting entries in accounting ledgers, and reviewing travel and expense reports compared with those of other large companies.

His conclusion? Carbide was a high-cost operation. It spent $9.45 to process a single invoice. Other companies spent an average of $8, with the best performers under $1. A journal entry cost Wulff's people $16.22—about 10 times what other large industrial companies were spending. Carbide did do some things well, with T&E forms being processed at half the average $20 cost of comparative companies. 'But, overall, Carbide's performance left a lot of room for improvement. "I knew our costs were high," says Wulff. "But in certain areas, like general accounting, I was a little surprised."

Since then, Wulff has been aggressively reducing the costs of Carbide's finance operation. Some 200 positions have been eliminated, saving more than $20 million.

"SHARED SERVICES." Carbide's experience, and that of some other big American companies taking similar measures, offers surprising lessons. Carbide has spent much of its recent history redesigning manufacturing operations, managing inventories more closely, and speeding up product-development cycles. But these very same companies—zealous in their ability to cut the cost of making products—had allowed their backroom bean counters to grow very flabby. Now, though, CFOs are giving finance the same makeover that manufacturing and marketing received in the late 1980s. Companies as diverse as Johnson & Johnson and General Electric Co. are finding they can cut overhead by a third or better with new ways to bill customers, pay employees, and process checks. "This is going to be the agenda at every company within the next five years," says consultant Robert W. Gunn, who has helped such companies as Hewlett Packard, Shell, and U S West reengineer their finance shops.

In many ways, the changes afoot parallel what has happened on the shop floor. GE is using the very same techniques of mapping work processes that it uses to speed up production of appliances to increase the output of accounting clerks. But in other ways, the trend is counter to the latest dogma from management consultants. Leading-edge companies that are actively trying to push decision-making to the lowest point are just as quickly centralizing their finance functions into one or two regional data centers under a system known as "shared services." Instead of each business unit having its own CFO and accounting operations, the businesses in effect become "customers" of a centralized finance function. "Once we got control of these functions, we could reengineer them," says Walt Hazelton, manager of accounting service operations for Xerox Corp.

IMPACT. That's exactly what happened at GE. Its far-flung businesses once used 34 different payroll systems. But over the past five years, GE has transferred work from five different regional accounting centers to one megacenter in Fort Myers, Fla. Along the way, the number of finance-department workers has fallen by 40%, to 600. "They do the work differently," says Robert Frigo, manager of GE's Financial Services Operation. "There's much more use of electronic media and local-area-network technology." And with fewer workers, notes Frigo, come fewer supervisors.

Johnson & Johnson CFO Clark H. Johnson slays he saw the light in the 1980s when the company participated in a benchmarking study. The survey found most large companies spent about 2.3% of their annual sales on finance-department overhead. "We were at 2.8%, and that kind of woke us up," says Johnson.

Armed with the data, J&J began a consolidation that combines regional data centers and undertook the use of uniform ledgers and accounts-payable systems. "We had 100 manufacturing locations with 106 payroll people," says Johnson. "We're now doing our payroll of 40,000 people with 28 people." All told, J&J slashed its finance-department head count by a third, or 600 positions, even as sales increased 30%.

The cuts had a bottom-line impact. Johnson says that in the past four years, the company has reduced its worldwide finance budget by $84 million. To accommodate the downsizing, Johnson says the company used early retirement programs and tried to move affected workers to other jobs in the company. And Johnson cut back sharply on his use of temporary workers brought in to manage the paperwork overload.

The effort encouraged Johnson to push even harder for savings. Once, it took J&J 26 days to close its books. Now, it's down to 7 days. "My target is 2 days," says Johnson. "It's really computerization as well as different attitudes." Johnson has also eliminated monthly closings, going to quarterly instead, and reduced much of the paperwork associated with a huge finance staff. "We were producing too much paper that no one has time to use," he says.

At Ford Motor Co., what began as an attempt in the mid-1980s to cut costs by 20% in its accounts-payable department soon led to a wholesale reworking of the company's procurement system. In the old days, Ford would order a part, and when the supplier shipped it, accounts-payable clerks would attempt to match the purchasing order with a form produced at the receiving dock and reconcile that with the vendor's invoice. When all three agreed, payment was made to the vendor. Armies of clerical workers were spending hours chasing missing forms.

Nowadays, a clerk orders a part, enters the order into an electronic data base, and then awaits shipment. When the part comes in, a worker in receiving checks the data base to make sure the part has been ordered and then approves it, at the same time prompting the computer to automatically issue payment to the vendor.

ENTRENCHED. The changes at Ford, J&J, GE and other companies have led to byproducts other than reduced costs and shrinking staffs. GE's Frigo says the goal is to get finance people integrally involved in overall business strategy. Instead of just checking T&E reports for errors, workers can now develop information about company spending practices that lead to better deals with vendors. "It's more than just paying the bills," says Frigo. "We're trying to push the focus from processing transactions to adding value."

But change is slow in coming in some companies, where the finance function is often a protected fiefdom. While outfits such as GE and Xerox are pacesetters, many companies are barely dealing with the growing costs of their finance units. "I would say most people are groping," says Patrick J. Keating, a business professor at San Jose State University who has studied the issue. "Most finance people are so entrenched, they can't even visualize where they are trying to go."

That's a shame. Consultant Gunn says finance staffs in large companies average nearly 5% of the total employment and in some cases account for more than 10% of the company's payroll—

which creates major opportunities for big savings. Companies that seize those opportunities could get a big leg up on global competitors, especially since reengineering of back-office operations is something that American companies are far further along on than overseas companies. "I think it's what is going to beat the Japanese," says Gunn.

That may be carrying it too far. But it's still an incentive that any American company can appreciate.

NOTES

1. Royal Bank of Canada, "Starting Out Right," *Your Business Matters* series, 1990, 37. Reprinted by permission of the Royal Bank of Canada.
2. For a more complete depiction of an accounting system that incorporates the user's decision-making, see Robert H. Crandall, "Information Economics and Accounting Theory," *The Accounting Review*, July 1969, 457–66.
3. *CICA Handbook*, Paragraph 5200.05 (Toronto: Canadian Institute of Chartered Accountants, version in effect at December 31, 1993). Reprinted by permission of The Canadian Institute of Chartered Accountants, Toronto, Canada.
4. Discussions with management of an Edmonton, Alberta, chain of coffee counters were very helpful in developing the description of HotCaf's cash and inventory control system.

Revenue and Expense Recognition in Accrual Accounting

7.1 Chapter Overview

This chapter addresses the demand for timely information and the problems encountered in trying to carve essentially continuous business events up into reporting periods. The **accrual accounting** approach better approximates the economic process of earning income than does the transactional information in the bookkeeping records. Accrual accounting transforms the information from the records into the reports (financial statements) that are demanded by decision makers. The general techniques of **revenue recognition** and **expense recognition** form the core of this chapter. Comparisons to cash measures are made at several points.

In this chapter you'll learn:

Use concepts: how users' demand for relevant information about business performance involves both the timeliness and the economic substance of the information;

Preparation concepts: how accrual accounting works to make the accounting reports reflect economic information more complex than that usually embodied in the recorded transactions, by tracking important "streams" of events (revenue generation, expense incurrence, and asset changes) through **recognition** and **matching**, two of the most important concepts in modern financial accounting;

Preparation techniques: how to implement recognition and matching by **accrual** and **deferral** entries to **cut off** the continuous streams of events at the beginning and end of the reporting period, so as to produce meaningful income and financial position measurement;

Use techniques: how to evaluate the results of revenue and expense recognition methods and do simple "what if" analysis, as a foundation for the financial statement analysis and other use techniques of Chapters 8, 9, and 10.

7.2 What Is Accrual Accounting?

Accrual accounting is the dominant form of financial accounting in the world today. This chapter builds on the foundation laid in earlier chapters and on the introduction in Section 1.4; it explains why accrual accounting exists and distinguishes the accrual basis from cash basis accounting.

Accrual accounting exists because cash flow information is simply not complete enough to assess financial performance or financial position. Keeping track of cash flow is crucial for business success, but it is not enough. We have to go beyond cash flow to assess economic performance more broadly and to assess noncash resources and obligations. We do this even though it forces us to make estimates, judgments, and other accounting choices that, in turn, make the results less precise than we would wish, and more subjective than transaction-based cash flow figures.

Let's imagine the following conversation between a student and a relative who is also a professional accountant:

> *Accountant:* Well, you spent the summer working at High-Class Boutique. How did you do?
>
> *Student:* I had a great time. Met some great people, learned a lot about retailing, and so decided to major in marketing.
>
> *Accountant:* No, I meant how did you do financially?
>
> *Student:* Let's see. I received $4,260 over the four months. I have $2,330 left in the bank; so, I guess I must have spent $1,930. Gee, $2,330 doesn't seem much for a summer's work! But the Boutique still owes me for my last week of work.
>
> *Accountant:* What did you spend the $1,930 on?
>
> *Student:* I blew some of the money on burgers and evening entertainment, and on that trip to the lake. But also, I bought a good set of clothes for the fall term, and I have the answering machine, and the fancy calculator I got so that I might be able to pass accounting.
>
> *Accountant:* Don't forget you have to pay your Uncle Al back the money he lent you in May. That's in your bank account too. You promised to pay him, plus interest, at the end of the summer. And then there's your university tuition for next year. And didn't you say once that you owed a friend something for gas for that trip to the lake?
>
> *Student:* I don't think we should count the tuition because it doesn't really apply until I register. Although I guess that *is* why I was working. Now I'm not sure if I had a good summer or not!

This example illustrates many of the issues accrual accounting tries to deal with, including:

1. The more you think about it, the more complex measuring performance and position seems to be, and the less satisfactory cash by itself seems to be as a measure.
2. Some of what is earned may not yet have been received in cash (payment for the last week of work).
3. Similarly, some costs incurred may not yet have been paid (the gas for the lake trip).
4. Some cash payments result in resources still having economic value at the end of the period (the answering machine, the calculator, and maybe the clothes).
5. Some cash receipts result in obligations still outstanding at the end of the period (Uncle Al's loan).

6. The longer-term resources may have deteriorated during the period (not all the clothes purchased during the summer will still be valuable because fashions change, and the answering machine and calculator are now used items).
7. Obligations may build up during the period (the interest on Uncle Al's loan).
8. There is often doubt about whether some things should be included in measuring performance for a given period or position at a given point in time (the university tuition).
9. Generally, how do we relate the *timing* of cash flows to the period we're concerned with? Most of the above items involve cash flows sooner or later; the awkward cases are usually those for which the period when the cash moves and the period for which we're measuring performance don't match.

Think of accrual accounting as an attempt to measure economic performance and financial position in a more complex way than just using cash. There is *always* a trade-off here: the closer to cash, the more precise the measure, but also the more limited and less informative. This is the same trade-off between reliability and timely decision relevance that was mentioned in Section 5.3. The more accountants try to make the financial statements economically relevant, the more they must include estimates and other sources of imprecision or error.

7.3 CONCEPTUAL FOUNDATION OF ACCRUAL ACCOUNTING

Accrual accounting is based on the idea that events, estimates, and judgments important to the measurement of financial performance and position should be **recognized** by entries in the accounts (and therefore reflected in the financial statements), *whether or not* they have yet, or already, been **realized** by cash received or paid out. To slightly oversimplify, we might say that the objective is to recognize economic flows in addition to cash flows. To clarify this idea, we will focus on revenue and expense recognition, but connections will also be drawn with balance sheet valuation (Chapter 5) and cash flow measurement (Chapter 4).

Let's build the accrual accounting approach from some basics. These four cornerstones have come up already in this book, but we'll give them brief definitions again and then build from there:

- **Revenues** are *inflows* of economic resources from customers. We might say that earning revenues is the reason a company is in business.
- **Expenses** are *outflows* of economic resources to employees, suppliers, taxation authorities, and others, resulting from business activities to generate revenue and serve customers. We might say that incurring expenses is the cost of earning revenues.
- **Net income** is the *difference* between revenues and expenses over a period of time, such as a month, a quarter, or a year. We might say that net income is the measure of success in generating more revenues than it costs to do so.

- **Matching** is the *logic* of income measurement, ensuring that revenues and expenses are measured comparably, so that deducting the expenses from the revenues to calculate net income produces a meaningful result. We might say that matching ties accrual accounting together into a coherent system.

Note some features of these cornerstones:

- Revenues and expenses refer to inflows and outflows of economic resources. These flows may be represented by the kinds of events recognized by the transactional recordkeeping system described in Chapter 6, but they may also involve other phenomena. In particular, they may involve phenomena that arise before or after cash changes hands, as well as at the point of the cash flow.
- Net income is dependent on how revenues and expenses are measured, and really is not well defined by accounting separately from revenues and expenses. Accountants don't, or shouldn't, choose the income number first and then force revenues and expenses to result in that, but instead measure revenues and expenses as best they can and let net income be whatever the difference is between properly measured revenues and expenses.
- Matching involves trying to line up measures of economic inflows with those of economic outflows. It is logical, but not the only logic one could imagine applying. For example, if revenues are overestimated and then expenses are overestimated to match, the net income figure may be more or less all right because the overestimations may roughly cancel out, but the figures for revenues and expenses will be misleading, as will any balance sheet accounts related to them, such as accounts receivable and accounts payable. If the method of recognizing revenue is poor, it hardly makes sense to argue for a poor expense recognition method for the sake of matching. So, many other criteria enter into revenue and expense recognition and income measurement to fine tune the system and ensure that the matched measures are sensible. Examples of such criteria are fairness, comparability, consistency, conservatism, and other concepts we saw in Chapter 5, plus various detailed methods for determining how much revenue has been earned and how much expense has been incurred, which we will see in this chapter.

A Conceptual System for Accrual Income Measurement

Accrual accounting's purpose is to extend the measurement of financial performance and position by recognizing phenomena *prior* to and *subsequent to* cash flows, as well as *at the point of* cash flows (which cash basis accounting already does). We need a system, therefore, that covers the following categories:

	Revenues	Expenses
◆ Recognition of resource inflow or outflow prior to cash inflow or outflow	A	B
◆ Cash flow:		
■ Cash inflow or outflow related to prior recognition, see above	a	b
■ Cash inflow or outflow for cash revenues and expenses	C	D
■ Cash inflow or outflow related to subsequent recognition, see below	e	f
◆ Recognition of resource inflow or outflow subsequent to cash inflow or outflow	E	F

Accrual accounting derives its value from categories A, B, E, and F. These allow measurement of performance and position to be spread out in time: A and B extend the time horizon out prior to the cash flow, and E and F extend the time horizon out subsequent to the cash flow. Categories C and D are already there in the cash basis of accounting, so the *accrual method* includes the cash basis. It just does more. Categories a and b record the collection of revenues recognized in A and the payment of expenses recognized in B. Categories e and f record the collection of cash to be later recognized as revenue in E and the payment of cash to be later recognized as expense in F. Categories a, b, e, and f are important because sooner or later nearly all events involve cash flows, but they are shown in lower case letters because, in accrual accounting, they are secondary to the time dimension accrual accounting adds through A, B, E, and F.

EXAMPLE JOURNAL ENTRIES TO IMPLEMENT THE ACCRUAL FRAMEWORK

The following example journal entries in Exhibit 7.1 may help you think about what is going on. As you review them, try to think about the general accrual accounting framework they represent. They are not the only examples that could be listed, and a key to understanding what accrual accounting does is to think about what is going on in concept, so that you can choose or understand a journal entry or financial statement item that you might not have seen before but that does the kind of job required in that category.

Exhibit 7.1

	Revenues	Expenses
Recognition of resource inflow or outflow prior to cash inflow or outflow		
Categories A and B	DR Accounts receivable CR Revenue	DR Wages expense CR Wages payable
Category B		DR Warranty expense CR Warranty liability
Category B		DR Income tax expense CR Income tax liability
Cash inflow (collections) or outflow (payments) related to prior recognition (above)		
Categories a and b	DR Cash CR Accounts receivable	DR Wages payable CR Cash
Category b		DR Warranty liability CR Cash
Category b		DR Income tax liability CR Cash
Cash inflow or outflow for cash revenues and expenses		
Categories C and D	DR Cash CR Revenue	DR Donations expense CR Cash
Categories C and D	DR Cash CR Dividend revenue	DR Office supplies expense CR Cash
Cash inflow (deposits) or outflow (acquisitions) related to subsequent recognition (below)		
Categories e and f	DR Cash CR Customer deposits liability	DR Building asset CR Cash
Categories e and f	DR Cash CR Deferred revenue liability	DR Inventory asset CR Cash
Category f		DR Prepaid Insurance asset CR Cash
Recognition of resource inflow or outflow subsequent to cash inflow or outflow		
Categories E and F	DR Customer deposits liability CR Revenue	DR Amortization expense CR Accumulated amortization
Categories E and F	DR Deferred revenue liability CR Revenue	DR Cost of goods sold expense CR Inventory asset
Category F		DR Insurance expense CR Prepaid insurance asset

Here are some things to notice about the accrual accounting framework that these sorts of journal entries implement.

1. The "recognition" journal entries are the ones that create the revenues and expenses that are used in measuring income:
    - Category A recognizes revenues not yet collected;
    - Category B recognizes expenses not yet paid;
    - Category C recognizes cash revenues;
    - Category D recognizes cash expenses;
    - Category E recognizes revenues earned after the cash was received;
    - Category F recognizes expenses incurred after the cash was paid.

    These are the only categories of journal entries that involve revenues and expenses. Categories a, b, e, and f involve balance sheet accounts only, and so do not affect the calculation of income.

2. You can say that accrual accounting makes much of the balance sheet into a sort of "holding area" for incomplete revenue and expense events:
    - Category a completes the revenue event begun in Category A;
    - Category b completes the expense event begun in Category B;
    - Category E completes the revenue event begun in Category e;
    - Category F completes the expense event begun in Category f.

3. You can see how accrual accounting spreads out these events over time by comparing the upper-case and lower-case entry categories:
    - Categories A and a: the accounts receivable created in A are removed (collected) in a, so that the net effect of A and a is the same as C. Cash is eventually received for the revenue.
    - Categories B and b: the liabilities created in B are removed (paid) in b, so that the net effect of B and b is the same as D. Cash is eventually paid for the expense.
    - Categories e and E: the liabilities created in e when cash is received before revenue is earned are removed in E when the revenue is recognized as being earned, so that the net effect of e and E is the same as C. Revenue is eventually earned for the cash received.
    - Categories f and F: the assets created in f when the cash is paid out are removed in F (by amortization or other charges to expense as the assets are consumed), so that the net effect of f and F is the same as D. Expense is eventually recognized for the cash paid out.

4. There are complications, but the general pattern behind accrual accounting's revenue and expense recognition system is:
    - Recognition of revenue prior to cash collection is done by creating an asset account (accounts receivable, usually), which stands in for the economic value gained until the cash has been collected.
    - Recognition of expense prior to cash payment is done by creating a liability account (current, such as accounts, wages, or tax payable, or noncurrent, such as pensions, warranties, or deferred taxes liabilities), which stands in for the economic value lost until the cash is paid.

- Recognition of revenue after cash collection is provided for by creating a liability account (customer deposits or deferred revenue), which represents the commitment to the customer until the economic value is gained by providing the goods or services the customer has paid for.
- Recognition of expense after cash payment is provided for by creating an asset account (a noncash current asset or noncurrent asset), which represents the available resource until the economic value is lost by consuming the asset. (Assets can be acquired by promises to pay, not just by cash, so Category f journal entries might credit accounts payable, mortgage payable, or other liabilities rather than cash. But you can see that the "asset" side of entries in Category f still represents resources that are to be consumed later. Accrual accounting recognizes the expense when the consumption happens, not when the asset is acquired, no matter how it is acquired.)

5. Not all cash flows involve revenues or expenses. Such flows have to be included in the accounts but, since they do not affect income, they are limited to balance sheet accounts. Categories a, b, e, and f are examples, but these have some connection with revenues and expenses. There are other events even farther removed from the income calculation. Some examples of these are: receipt of cash from an issue of share capital, disbursement of cash to pay a dividend, disbursement of cash to make a mortgage payment, disbursement of cash to pay for an investment in another company, and receipt of cash from a bank loan. Sometimes these sorts of cash flows are called "nonoperating" receipts and disbursements, though that phrase is also often used for some events, such as receipts of progress payments on long-term construction contracts or disbursements for asset acquisitions, that we might put into Categories e and f.

The various categories set out above were used just to help you think about what is going on, and see that there is a pattern behind the great variety of entries used in accrual accounting. For instance, the following are all examples of asset consumption, recognized via the sort of entries in Category F:

- Reduction in the economic value of a building (credit accumulated amortization, debit amortization expense);
- Reduction in inventory as goods are sold (credit inventory asset, debit cost of goods sold expense);
- Reduction in supplies asset as supplies are used (credit supplies inventory, debit supplies expense);
- Reduction of prepaid insurance asset as the coverage is used (credit prepaid insurance asset, debit insurance expense);
- Reduction in accounts receivable when customers fail to pay their accounts (credit accounts receivable, debit bad debts expense (more about this later in this chapter));
- Reduction in consolidated goodwill as time passes since the subsidiary was acquired (credit goodwill asset, debit goodwill amortization expense).

Entries that are essentially opposite those in Category F are sometimes used to **capitalize** expenses. In such a case, it is believed that the expense account inappropriately contains an amount that should have been recognized as an asset instead. The entry to capitalize an expense is, therefore, to debit an asset and credit an expense. Two examples are: to capitalize amounts charged to machine maintenance that actually produced a better machine (debit machine asset, credit maintenance expense); and to capitalize interest paid on a loan obtained to finance a major construction project (debit factory asset, credit interest expense). Capitalizing expenses is often controversial because doing so reduces expenses and so increases income, so most companies do this only when there is clear evidence that it is appropriate.

Think about the pattern rather than trying to memorize details like the identification letters used for the categories. Don't try to memorize what category A is, for example; instead, remember how accrual accounting recognizes revenue when it is earned before the cash is collected.

HOW'S YOUR UNDERSTANDING

Here are two questions you should be able to answer, based on what you have just read:

1. How do accrual accounting entries work to separate the earning of revenue from the receipt of cash? Is it always necessary to separate them, or can they happen at the same time?
2. In what way can it be said that amortization expense and cost of goods sold expense are examples of the same thing?

7.4 ACCRUAL ACCOUNTING ADJUSTMENTS

The transactional records provide the foundation of the financial accounting system. In order to implement the accrual accounting system outlined above, such records usually require **adjustments**. Three main kinds of adjustments are needed:

a. Correction of errors discovered in the transactional record.

b. Implementation of routine accruals, such as those indicated in Section 7.3: revenues earned but not yet collected, expenses incurred but not yet paid, cash received from customers prior to the related revenues having been earned, and consumption of assets. The degree to which accrual adjustments are needed in any accounting system depends on the sophistication of the system: sophisticated accounting systems may go beyond the transactional records and routinely include many adjustments that for simpler systems are made at year-end in a special set of journal entries. Many large companies have monthly accruals for interest expenses and other expenses as they build up, and monthly allowances for depreciation and other consumptions of assets. Many small companies don't bother until annual financial statements are needed.

c. Recognition of nonroutine events or estimates needed to bring the financial statements into line with what management (or the auditors) believe is the economic and business substance of the enterprise's performance and position. Examples here could include reducing the balance sheet figure for ("writing down") assets whose economic value has been impaired due to changes in market value or poor management, changing the way warranties are accounted for as a result of lawsuits about product quality, and re-estimating income tax liability on the basis of recently announced tax law revisions.

Accrual accounting adjustments follow the same double-entry format as do the transactional records:

Some account or accounts must be debited; and
Some account or accounts must be credited; and
The sum of the debits must equal the sum of the credits.

Accountants call such adjustments **adjusting journal entries**. They are just the same as any other journal entries, except that they do not involve cash (except to correct errors). Their purpose is to *augment* the transaction-based (especially cash-based) figures, to add to the story told by the transactional records. They implement accrual accounting.

The objective of accrual accounting is to improve the measurement of financial performance and position. However, because different choices can be made about what accounts need to be adjusted and by how much, accrual accounting can be a mechanism for manipulating results and producing misleading reports. Therefore, the auditors give particular attention to the kinds of accrual adjustments a company makes, and most of the criticism of financial reporting is directed at subjective accrual adjustments, made using judgment, rather than at the more objective, verifiable transactional records. In spite of the subjectivity and criticism, most accountants believe the accrual accounting basis to be superior to the cash basis, because it provides a more complete record that is also more representative of economic performance than the cash basis. Not everyone agrees with this; in particular, modern finance theory puts more emphasis on cash flow than on accrual accounting's income measure. Chapter 8 has more on this.

AN EXAMPLE: NORTHERN STAR THEATRE COMPANY II

The mechanics of adjusting and correcting entries are not difficult. They involve the same asset, liability, and owners' equity accounts (including revenues and expenses) that have become familiar to you by now. To illustrate how they work and carry them through to the resulting financial statements, let's continue with the example of the six aspiring actors at the Edmonton Fringe, begun in Section 6.7, where we saw how some basic recordkeeping was done. Now we will make accrual accounting adjustments to augment the records.

We left Northern Star Theatre at the end of Step 4 of the accounting process. We'll begin by showing the result of that step again (see Exhibit 7.2).

Exhibit 7.2

Northern Star Theatre Company
General Ledger Trial Balance, mid-August 1994

Account	Debit	Credit
Cash (Bank)	1,187	
Partners' capital		1,450
Performance fees expense	400	
Costumes and props expense	1,080	
Travel expense	480	
Accounts payable		800
Performance revenue		897
TOTALS	3,147	3,147

It was agreed that a set of financial statements would be a good idea, as soon as the Fringe production was over. A date of August 26, 1994, was selected for the financial statements.

Before the production ended, there were only three more cash transactions (continuing the numbering started in Section 6.7):

9. A local printing shop was paid $320 for printing programs and brochures describing the theatre company, to be handed out as people entered the venue to see the play and to be used generally to promote the play. These were available and used the first night, but were not paid for until two days later
10. $525 of the amounts owing for props and set materials were paid.
11. The play was a moderate success. The audience was small after an initial bad review, but more people came to later performances. Total revenue for the remaining performances was $4,840. The group was not invited to perform at any of the "after the Fringe" events, so August 26 turned out to be as good a date as any for taking financial stock of the company.

Step 5: Accruals and Adjustments

Several things required decisions and adjustments in order to prepare the August 26 financial statements. Continuing the above numbering sequence, these were:

12. The play's writer was owed her royalty, which had been agreed at $450.
13. Additional travel expenses for getting back to North Battleford, to be reimbursed to various members of the group, totalled $215.
14. $1,080 had been spent on costumes and props. The group estimated that costumes and props costing about $420 were not reusable, but that the rest were reusable and would last on average about five engagements, including the just-finished Fringe as one of the five. The actors agreed to keep going, and therefore agreed that the costumes and props could be accounted for on a **going concern** basis, that is, assuming there would continue to be a theatre company and, therefore, that the usable costumes and props had some future value.

15. There were some programs and brochures left over. The programs were pretty well useless, but the brochures describing the company could be used to seek future engagements and generally advertise. Brochures costing about $80 were thought still to be useful.
16. After talking to the bank, one of the actors estimated that, to August 26, about $20 in interest would have been earned by the money in the bank account. This wasn't much, but everyone wanted to see an accurate set of financial statements, so this was deemed **material** (significant) enough to be included.
17. The actors agreed that they would share any income or loss equally. The one who was broke said that rather than pay any cash in he would transfer to the other members, out of his share of the income, the $200 he had not paid in, to settle his obligation.

Here are journal entries to *record* the three additional cash transactions and to adjust the accounts to *recognize* the effects of the additional information.

Exhibit 7.3

Northern Star Theatre Company
General Journal

No.	Date	Description	Debits	Credits
9.	Aug. 94	Programs and brochures expense	320	
		Cash (Bank)		320
		Programs and brochures to be handed out at performances.		
10.	Aug. 94	Accounts payable	525	
		Cash (Bank)		525
		Some of what is owed for materials for set and props.		
11.	Aug. 94	Cash (Bank)	4,840	
		Performance revenue		4,840
		Gate receipts for the remaining performances.		
12.	Aug. 94	Royalties expense	450	
		Accounts payable		450
		Royalty owed to author.		
13.	Aug. 94	Travel expense	215	
		Accounts payable		215
		Expenses for getting back to North Battleford.		
14a.	Aug. 94	Costumes and props asset	660	
		Costumes and props expense		660
		Capitalizing the cost of the costumes and props having future value.		
14b.	Aug. 94	Amortization expense	132	
		Accumulated amortization		132
		Amortization of costumes and props assets: 1/5 of cost for the Edmonton Fringe engagement.		

Exhibit 7.3 continued

15.	Aug. 94	Brochures inventory	80	
		Programs and brochures expense		80
		Recognizing the inventory of usable brochures still on hand, at cost.		
16.	Aug. 94	Interest receivable	20	
		Interest revenue		20
		Estimated interest earned by the bank account to August 26, 1994.		
17.	Aug. 94	Partners' capital (Fred)	200	
		Partners' capital (Others)		200
		Transfer from Fred to the other partners to make up for the $200 in cash not paid in by Fred as originally agreed. *(Note that this entry has no effect on the summary figures in the financial statements, but is written to recognize an economic event, Fred's agreement to settle his obligation by transferring some of his capital to the other partners. That is important to the partners. The effects of the entry are on the details of partners' balances within the capital account, not on the account's total.)*		

Step 6: Posting the Remaining Transactions and the Accrual Adjustments

These entries have to be posted, just as the ones in Section 6.7 were. Do that and see if you agree with the August 26 trial balance below.

Step 7: Another Trial Balance

Exhibit 7.4 shows a trial balance at August 26, 1994, using the original accounts from Step 4 and the additional accounts required by the entries in Step 5. The members decided to rearrange the posted ledger accounts into the order in which they would appear in the financial statements, to help everyone understand the eventual statements.

If you have trouble getting any of these account balances, here are the calculations for some, beginning with the mid-August trial balance:

Cash = $1,187 – $320 – $525 + $4,840 = $5,182
Accounts payable = $800 – $525 + $450 + $215 = $940
Performance revenue = $897 + $4,840 = $5,737
Costumes and props expense = $1,080 – $660 = $420
Travel expense = $480 + $215 = $695

Exhibit 7.4

Northern Star Theatre Company
General Ledger Trial Balance, August 26, 1994

Account	**Debit**	**Credit**
Cash (Bank)	5,182	
Interest receivable	20	
Brochures inventory	80	
Costumes and props	660	
Accumulated amortization		132
Accounts payable		940
Partners' capital		1,450
Performance revenue		5,737
Amortization expense	132	
Costumes and props expense	420	
Performance fees expense	400	
Programs and brochures expense	240	
Royalties expense	450	
Travel expense	695	
Interest revenue		20
TOTALS	8,279	8,279

The financial statements to be drawn up at August 26 are "interim" ones: they are not year-end statements, so the accounts for the year are not closed at this point. *If they were*, the entry would be:

DR Performance revenue	5,737	
CR Amortization expense		132
CR Costumes and props expense		420
CR Performance fees expense		400
CR Programs and brochures expense		240
CR Royalties expense		450
CR Travel expense		695
DR Interest revenue	20	
CR Partners' capital		3,420

So far, the company has an income of $3,420. In the details of the partners' capital, the $3,420 would be allocated to the partners under the agreement among the six actors, so each would be allocated one sixth, $570. Like the retained earnings of a corporation, the earnings of this partnership will not necessarily all be withdrawn by the partners, and to August 26, none of the partners has withdrawn any. The financial statements in Exhibits 7.5, 7.6, and 7.7 reflect this.

Step 8: The August 26 Financial Statements

Exhibit 7.5

Northern Star Theatre Company
Income Statement for the Period
November 5, 1993, to August 26, 1994

Performance revenue		$5,737
Expenses:		
Amortization of costumes and props	$132	
Costumes and props not reusable	420	
Performance fees	400	
Programs and brochures	240	
Royalties	450	
Travel	695	2,337
Operating income		$3,400
Other income (bank interest)		20
Partnership income for the period *(Note 1)*		$3,420

Northern Star Theatre Company
Statement of Partners' Capital for the Period
November 5, 1993, to August 26, 1994

Beginning capital	$ 0
Capital contributed during the period	1,450
Income for the period, per income statement	3,420
Withdrawals during the period	0
Capital at end of the period *(Note 2)*	$4,870

Exhibit 7.6

Northern Star Theatre Company
Balance Sheet at August 26, 1994

Assets		
Current assets:		
Cash in bank	$5,182	
Bank interest receivable	20	
Inventory of brochures	80	$5,282
Noncurrent assets:		
Costumes and props, at cost	$ 660	
Less accumulated amortization	132	528
TOTAL		$5,810
Liabilities and Capital		
Current liabilities:		
Accounts payable		$ 940
Partners' capital *(Note 2)*		4,870
TOTAL		$5,810

Exhibit 7.7

Northern Star Theatre Company
Cash Flow Statement
for the Period November 5, 1993,
to August 26, 1994

Operations:	
Partnership income for the period	$3,420
Add back amortization expense	132
Increase in interest receivable and inventory	(100)
Increase in accounts payable	940
Cash from operations	$4,392
Investing activities:	
Costumes and props	(660)
Financing activities:	
Contributions by partners	1,450
Cash provided during the period and on hand at its end	$5,182

Northern Star Theatre Company
Notes to the August 26, 1994, Financial Statements

1. The company is an unincorporated partnership of six actors who share incomes and losses equally. No provisions have been made in the financial statements for salaries to the partners or for such personal expenses as income taxes.
2. At August 26, 1994, the six partners' capital accounts are:

	Part. A	Part. B	Part. C	Part. D	Part. E	Part. F	Total
Contributed	$275	$275	$275	$275	$275	$ 75	$1,450
Transfer	40	40	40	40	40	(200)	0
Income	570	570	570	570	570	570	$3,420
Capital	$885	$885	$885	$885	$885	$445	$4,870

HOW'S YOUR UNDERSTANDING

Here are two questions you should be able to answer, based on what you have just read:

1. Brazza Ltd. management wishes to recognize $12,000 revenue that it believes has been earned on a contract it has with a customer. No revenue for the contract has yet been collected from the customer or previously recognized. What journal entry would accomplish management's wish? (DR Accounts receivable 12,000; CR Revenue 12,000)
2. Brazza Ltd. management also wishes to recognize that, because the company this year began to offer a warranty with its products, it incurs an expense for future estimated warranty service costs each time it makes a sale. Management estimates that for the sales recorded so far this year, the warranty costs will be $3,200. What journal entry would accomplish this? (DR Warranty expense 3,200; CR Liability for estimated warranty costs 3,200)

7.5 AN EXAMPLE OF CASH BASIS VS. ACCRUAL BASIS FIGURES

To help you see how accrual accounting works by augmenting records of cash receipts and disbursements, here is an example that builds on the income measurement and cash flow content of prior chapters (ignoring income tax for now).

Information for Goblin Consulting Ltd. for this year is:

Cash in bank, end of last year		$ 2,800
Cash receipts:		
Collections on last year's revenue	$ 1,600	
Collections on this year's revenue	75,200	
Deposit received on next year's revenue	1,000	
Long-term debt issued	6,000	
Sale of old equipment (proceeds)	500	$84,300
		$87,100
Cash disbursements:		
Payment of last year's expenses	$ 900	
Payment of this year's expenses	61,300	
Advance payment on next year's expenses	2,200	
Payments on long-term debt	3,000	
Purchase of new equipment	14,000	81,400
Cash in bank, end of this year		$ 5,700
Increase in cash during the year ($5,700 – $2,800)		$ 2,900
Additional information:		
Equipment amortization for this year	$ 3,100	
Uncollected revenue at the end of this year	2,500	
Unpaid expenses at the end of this year	1,700	
Book value of old equipment at date of sale	300	
Gain on sale of equipment (proceeds – book value = $500 – $300)	200	

If we did a cash basis income statement for this year, we would get something like this:

Operating receipts ($1,600 + $75,200 + $1,000)	$77,800
Operating expenditures ($900 + $61,300 + $2,200)	64,400
Cash income for this year	$13,400

There are also:

- Nonoperating receipts of $6,500 ($6,000 debt + $500 proceeds); and
- Nonoperating expenditures of $17,000 ($3,000 debt payments + $14,000 new equipment).

If we added and subtracted those from $14,600, we'd get the total increase in cash during the year of $2,900:

Cash income	$13,400
Nonoperating receipts	6,500
Less nonoperating expenditures	(17,000)
Increase in cash during the year	$ 2,900

In contrast, the accrual basis income statement for this year would look like this, recognizing *this year's* earned revenues and incurred expenses:

Revenue ($75,200 cash sales + $2,500 uncollected)		$77,700
Expenses:		
General ($61,300 paid + $1,700 unpaid)	$63,000	
Amortization (specified above)	3,100	66,100
Operating income		$11,600
Gain on sale of equipment (calculated above)		200
Income for this year		$11,800

Because both cash flow and accrual figures are important, we want people to be able to understand how they are related to each other, and how they differ. That is what the statement of changes in financial position (cash flow statement) is for. Here's what the SCFP for this year would look like:

Operations:		
Income for the year (accrual basis)		$11,800
Add back noncash expense (amortization)		3,100
Deduct back gain on sale (cash is in "proceeds" below)		(200)
		$14,700
Changes in noncash working capital accounts:		
Accounts receivable (up $2,500 – $1,600)	$ (900)	
Prepaid expenses ($2,200 now, none last year)	(2,200)	
Deferred revenue ($1,000 now, none last year)	1,000	
Accounts payable (up $1,700 – $900)	800	(1,300)
Cash from operations		$13,400
Investing:		
Purchases of new equipment	$(14,000)	
Proceeds from equipment sale	500	$(13,500)
Financing:		
Issue of long-term debt	$ 6,000	
Repayment of long-term debt	(3,000)	3,000
Increase in cash for this year		$ 2,900
Cash at beginning of this year		2,800
Cash at end of this year		$ 5,700

You can see that the SCFP's $13,400 "cash from operations" figure (which is derived from the $11,800 accrual basis income) is what you'd have as your cash income had you done the income statement on the cash basis. So the SCFP reconciles the two ways of calculating income. The SCFP also provides the rest of the information (investing, financing, and dividends, if any) to allow you to see the total effects on cash for the year.

Therefore, with the accrual basis income statement *plus* the SCFP, you get the broader economic measure of performance that accrual accounting provides, as well as cash flow information with which to evaluate the company's cash management. The set of financial statements provides an integrated, mutually reinforcing package of information.

HOW'S YOUR UNDERSTANDING

Here are two questions you should be able to answer, based on what you have just read:

1. The owner of Frenzied Productions Inc. was looking at the company's income statement and said, "I understand this statement was prepared using accrual accounting. What does accrual accounting try to do and why isn't it good enough just to report my company's cash receipts and disbursements?" Briefly answer the owner's question.
2. In 1995, Frenzied collected $53,430 from customers for sales made in 1994 and $421,780 for sales made in 1995. In 1996, it collected $46,710 from customers for sales made in 1995. At that point, all 1994 and 1995 sales had been collected. What were the operating cash receipts for 1995 and the accrual accounting revenue for 1995? ($475,210; $468,490)

7.6 THE FISCAL PERIOD

Financial statements all have a time dimension. Balance sheets are prepared as at specific points in time and the other three statements cover specified periods of time. Business and other economic activities go on continuously, so if the financial statements are to be at, or begin and end at, particular dates, financial accounting must somehow find a way to separate all those activities into periods.

Here's an example of the problem. Quantum Inc. earns its revenue through a series of projects, done one at a time. Cash inflows (receipts) for revenues happen once or twice during each project, and cash outflows (disbursements) for expenses happen about a month after expenses are incurred. Projects affecting 1995 were:

	Revenues	Expenses
Project #39		
Work began on the project		Nov. 94
Some cash received from the customer	Dec. 94	
Disbursements for expenses began		Dec. 94
Work completed on the project		Feb. 95

continued next page

	Revenues	Expenses
Disbursements for expenses ended		Mar. 95
Remaining cash received from the customer	Apr. 95	
Project #40		
Work began on the project		Mar. 95
Disbursements for expenses began		Apr. 95
All cash received from the customer	Sep. 95	
Work completed on the project		Oct. 95
Disbursements for expenses ended		Nov. 95
Project #41		
Some cash received from the customer	Nov. 95	
Work began on the project		Nov. 95
Disbursements for expenses began		Dec. 95
Work completed on the project		Mar. 96
Disbursements for expenses ended		Apr. 96
Remaining cash received from the customer	Apr. 96	

Well, if we are to calculate net income for 1995 using accrual accounting, we can use the various categories of entries set out in Section 7.3. We can recognize revenues and expenses before or after cash inflows and outflows. But how do we actually do that? We need to find a way to **cut off** the accounting records of what are continuous activities, so that 1995 can be separated from 1994 and 1996. The 1995 net income is a measure of the economic value added by the projects *during that year*, and by the matching criterion that measure is produced by calculating the increase in resources (revenues) minus the decrease in resources (expenses), determined using comparable methods so that their difference is a meaningful income figure.

Let's try to do this project by project.

- Project #40 seems easiest. All the revenue was earned and collected in 1995. All the expenses were earned and paid in 1995.
- Project #39 is more awkward. There were two cash inflows, Dec. 94 and Apr. 95. If the Dec. 94 inflow was *less* than the amount of revenue earned by the end of the year, then there should be a Dec. 31/94 account receivable created for the rest of the revenue earned but not collected. However, if the Dec. 94 inflow was *greater* than the amount of revenue earned by the end of the year, then there should be a Dec. 31/94 deferred revenue liability created for the unearned portion. For the expenses, there are two problems. First, the expenses incurred in December would not be paid until January, so a Dec. 31/94 account payable should be created for those. Second, the amount of expenses recognized in 1994 should *match* the revenue recognized for 1994, so that their difference is meaningful.
- Project #41 has the same sort of awkwardness as #39, except it has to be cut off properly at the end of 1995.
- So 1995 revenues, expenses, and resulting net income will be a combination of the part of Project #39's revenues and expenses *not* recognized in 1994, all of Project #40's revenues and expenses, and the part

of Project #41's revenues and expenses recognized in 1995. You can see that *both* the cut-off at the end of 1994 and the one at the end of 1995 have to be appropriate if the 1995 revenues, expenses, and net income are to be fair. Because of this, the 1995 results involve estimates on Projects #39 and #41 that also affect the fairness of the results for 1994 and 1996. The revenues and expenses for those projects have to be properly **allocated** among the years they involve, and the results for all those years will be affected by the quality of the allocations.

Making effective cutoffs for revenues and expenses is a major problem for accrual accounting. Much effort is put into determining whether revenues are placed in the appropriate years, whether there are bills outstanding for expenses that should be taken into account, whether inventories of goods and supplies are actually on hand, and so on. It is generally harder to do this, the larger and less frequent an enterprise's revenue and expense transactions are, and easier therefore for enterprises that have many short and simple transactions. But even there it can be difficult to keep track of just where the enterprise stands, if there are thousands of transactions in process across a year end.

When should the fiscal (accounting) year begin and end? Companies have an initial choice, but once they make it, reasons of habit and legal and tax rules usually force them to stay with that choice indefinitely. They may select a fiscal year end that is a relatively quiet time, so that there aren't many unfinished transactions in process and the revenue and expense cutoffs can be made more cleanly. However, in practice, most companies select December 31 as their fiscal year end. *Financial Reporting in Canada 1993* reported that 63% of the companies it surveyed (and 61% of the U.S. companies in a similar survey) chose December 31, with no more than 6% choosing any other month end.[1]

The following article outlines the reasons some U.S. companies have fiscal year ends other than December 31.

LET'S GET FISCAL

Most companies end their business years in December, but many actually don't. That could well save them money.

Old timers at Campbell Soup Co. still remember the days when the firm lived and died by the tomato. Every August the streets of Camden, N.J. ran red when the crop reached the factory, or so the reminiscence goes.

Today, of course, tomato soup is only a tiny fraction of Campbell's $3.3 billion in sales. But the corporation's fiscal year still ends on July 31—just before the harvest comes in, when the tomato inventory is at its lowest.

An isolated anachronism? Hardly. Look closely and you find that natural business cycles are the source of many noncalendar fiscal years. According to the American Institute of Certified Public Accountants, 37% of the merchandising and industrial companies it surveys don't close their books on Dec. 31—a fact that plagues statisticians and analysts who yearn for comparability.

There are good reasons for going against the herd. For starters, you can save a few bucks. Public accounting firms work around the clock from January to April preparing both annual reports and tax returns. Naturally, they charge full freight, not to mention overtime. But there's also an off-season for auditors. Hire accountants in June or after, for example, and firms may cut prices, perhaps by 15%.

For small companies just starting out, this can be a great place to cut cost. According to James Pitts, Data General's corporate controller, that's one reason so many young high-tech companies have odd fiscal years. "They adopt their year at the whim of the accounting firms," he explains. "The accountants don't want to add to their year-end crunch, so they will quote you a lower audit fee."

Producing an annual report in the off-season can also mean getting better service—from accountants, of course, but also from printers, lawyers and even the SEC. Answers to disclosure questions may come more rapidly during slack periods. An odd year-end can also increase investor attention. Analysts who scramble to keep up with annual reports in March are more likely to lavish time on those that arrive in August.

So, if a company can save money and headaches, why aren't fiscal years spread evenly from January to December? William Chatlos, a New Jersey-based consultant who proselytized for the so-called natural fiscal year in the Sixties, thinks it's just institutional inertia and insecurity. "Companies ignore the advantages and have had this knee-jerk reaction to the fear of baffling analysts," he explains.

The advantages of non-December year-ends are compelling to Chatlos. He tells the story of a New York bearing company that switched, and ended up cutting costs and avoiding the discomfort of taking inventory in freezing temperatures. "When it comes to natural fiscal years," says Chatlos, "the corporate community is just being silly."

Ironically, many of the companies that chose their off-calendar fiscal years did so, not for reasons of cost-cutting and convenience, but because of history. In some cases the original, historical reasons still apply, in others they don't. A few of the more prominent off-calendar operators:

- *Retailers* Companies like Associated Dry Goods, Federated Department Stores and Kmart wrap up the fiscal year in January, the true finish to the Christmas season. The holiday shopping season, after all, spills over into the new year, when a flurry of sales and returns adds the final touches to revenue and profit figures.
- *Food companies* Corporations that started as simple grain-milling operations often end their fiscal years in May or June, just before or after the winter grain crops are harvested. Pillsbury, General Mills and Quaker Oats all have such late spring or early summer closings.
- *Energy* Ashland Oil still ends the year in September, a reminder of the old seasonal pause when the then-tiny company would start refining less gasoline for cars and churn out more heating oil for homes. Natural gas companies are also likely to close the books in September, since the "heating year," which generates the bulk of sales, starts in October and goes through to April. The American Gas Association, in fact, says that some members are gradually switching to September-end fiscal years.
- *Automobile suppliers* During the first half of the century, Armstrong Rubber, Dayco and Firestone found their natural business years ended in September or October. That was after heavy spring and summer driving, when inventories were at their lowest, most manageable point. The same for Deere & Co. and International Harvester. Their farm equipment sold briskly right through the harvest. Then sales slowed until spring.
- *Tobacco* Dibrell Brothers and Universal Leaf Tobacco, major processors for the cigarette industry, start their years July 1. That's just before the American farmers haul in their fresh leaf to the annual auctions, and after last year's crop has finally been cured and packed in casks. Far easier to count casks for inventory than comb through a warehouse full of loose tobacco.

Regardless of the reasons for odd fiscal years, this much is certain for many firms. The business calendar quickly becomes engraved in stone. Procter & Gamble, for example, closes its books at the end of June. No one remembers why. Is a change likely? Not on your life.

SOURCE: CHRISTOPHER POWER, "LET'S GET FISCAL," *FORBES*, APRIL 30, 1984, 102–103. REPRINTED BY SPECIAL PERMISSION OF *FORBES* MAGAZINE, APRIL 30, 1984.

7.7 REVENUE RECOGNITION

ACCURACY VS. DECISION RELEVANCE

It can be said that income over the life of an enterprise is easy to determine. At the end of the enterprise's life, all expenses have resulted in cash outflows and all the revenue earned has resulted in cash inflows. There is no need for estimates; the results are known with certainty. Income for the life of the firm is simply the difference between the total cash contributed to the business by the owners and the total cash withdrawn by the owners plus any cash remaining at the end.

The difficulty in reporting income periodically, which is how economic decision makers require information about the operations of a firm, is that of finding a way to put the essentially continuous operations of a firm into discrete time periods. The result is that income determined earlier, so that it is relevant for evaluating the enterprise's performance over shorter decision periods, is unavoidably subject to estimates and judgments because the whole story is never known until the end, but no-one wants to wait for the end.

We are back to the ever-present trade-off between accuracy and relevance in income measurement. If revenues and expenses are recognized earlier, so that they are more relevant for decision making, then they will not be as accurate as they would be if recognition were delayed until later, when outcomes of the various economic activities are better known. Figure 7.1 illustrates the trade-off.

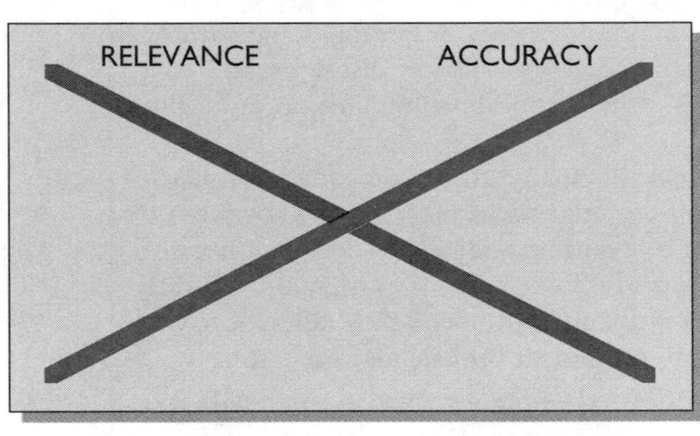

FIGURE 7.1

CRITICAL EVENT SIMPLIFICATION

If we are to describe the firm's operations for a given period by calculating the income for that period, we must define a means by which to measure the amount of income that can be attributed to that period. We accomplish this by:

- Defining how much revenue can be *recognized* in that period; and then
- Matching to that revenue the expenses which were incurred to generate the revenue.

Income, the value added by the activities of the firm, is just the difference between the recognized revenue and the recognized expenses.

But what are the revenues, or the expenses, for a period? From an economic and business point of view, income is earned by a wide variety of actions taken by the firm. There is a whole sequence of activities intended to help generate income, which therefore generate revenue and incur expenses, including, for example:

- Organizing the firm in the first place;
- Building the factory;
- Buying or making inventory;
- Advertising;
- Selling;
- Delivering to customer;
- Billing;
- Collecting cash; and
- Providing warranty service.

Revenue recognition is important because, by the matching criterion, expense recognition and therefore income measurement should correspond with the revenue. This gets rather messy in practice, as you might imagine, for example because some expenses are only indirectly related to revenue, being incurred as time passes (such as interest) or as other business decisions are made by management (such as donations, research and development, or maintenance). But for simplicity, let's assume that revenue recognition is the primary driver of income measurement.

How should we recognize revenue when there is such a series of activities as those listed above? Recognize it a bit at a time as each activity is carried out? This would approximate the economic process underlying the business. This would be relevant, all right, but by the same token it would be very subjective and imprecise, because it is difficult to say what each activity actually adds. How do you tell, when the company is just being organized, what revenue that form of organization will help to generate, for example? It would also be expensive to implement, with armies of accountants scurrying about measuring minute value changes generated by the various activities and writing masses of journal entries to recognize each value change.

Instead, for greater objectivity and verifiability and less accounting cost, accountants usually choose one activity in the sort of sequence above as the **critical event** in the revenue generation sequence that can be readily documented, and recognize all of the revenue at that point. This is a simplification, because clearly some revenue could have been recognized when earlier activities were carried out, and probably some should be recognized when later activities take place. In theory, revenue is under-recognized prior to that point and over-recognized after it. For some companies, such as those building big projects like power stations or pipelines, or project-based companies such as Quantum Inc. in Section 7.6, it is worthwhile estimating revenue at several points along the way, but for most the simplification of the critical event is followed. *The most common critical event used is the point of delivery of the goods or services to the customer.*

CRITERIA FOR REVENUE RECOGNITION

Revenue recognition, then, becomes the first step in determining income for the period. The revenue recognition criteria discussed below have been formulated for the purpose of making sure that revenue will be recognized only when there is objective evidence that revenue has indeed been earned. The following four criteria must normally *all* be met in order that revenue may be recognized. For most firms, the activity nearest to fitting these criteria is chosen as the critical event. However, as we'll see, there are exceptions (as usual!).

1. All or substantially all of the goods or services to be provided to customers have been provided or performed.
2. Most of the costs to generate the revenue have been incurred, and those remaining can be measured with reasonable accuracy.
3. The amount of the revenue can be reasonably measured in dollar terms.
4. Cash, a promise of cash (a receivable), or other asset that can be measured with reasonable precision has been received.

Although the above criteria seem fairly clear, there are still many judgments to be made about when the criteria are met. For instance, how should "substantially all of the services…have been performed" be defined? Is it when 100% of the services have been performed? 90%? 80%? To deal with such problems, there are several points in the revenue-earning process at which revenue is commonly recognized, though as noted above, point of sale or delivery is the most common. We'll see those points below.

To recognize the earning of revenue when the critical event has taken place, we make the following recognition entry (Categories A, C, and/or E of the framework in Section 7.3):

DR Cash or Accounts receivable		
or Deferred revenue liability	XXXX	
CR Revenue		XXXX

Let's take a closer look at the four most commonly used methods of revenue recognition and a fifth very conservative method:

1. At Point of Sale or Delivery

For most retail, service, and manufacturing businesses, revenue is recognized when the product or service is sold. "Sold" is usually defined as being when the goods or services have been shipped to the purchaser, when legal title passes to the purchaser.

- At that point substantially all of the service has been performed, terms and price have been set, and cash has been received, or it is at least reasonably certain that it will be received.
- Even though there is some risk involved in extending credit, this can usually be adequately estimated and deducted from the gross revenue by way of the bad debts expense account (see Section 7.9).

- Another risk at the point of sale is the possibility of returns and the likely service obligation under the warranties for the product or service sold. Again, this can usually be adequately estimated and recognized as an expense of the business and matched against the revenue of that period.

Point of sale or delivery is so common a revenue recognition method that most companies do not mention in their financial statements that they are using it. You are expected to assume it is the one being used if you are not told otherwise, as you probably would be if any of the other four methods below were used.

2. During Production

Sometimes the earnings process extends well beyond one fiscal period, as is the case in building construction, road building, ship building, and other lengthy processes. In such situations, if a firm waited until the point of delivery to recognize revenue, it might report no revenue for one or more years, and then, when the project was complete, would report all the revenue. This would distort the performance picture of the firm for the duration of the project: some years with no revenue, then one year with huge revenue, even though the firm was working faithfully on the contract all along. There are not likely many projects going on at once (few, anyway, in comparison to the number of hamburgers making up a burger bar's revenue), and projects include enough documentation that the value added can usually be estimated and verified. Therefore, in an attempt to provide users with useful information and reflect the economics of what is happening, revenue may be recognized during production. (With matching, this also means recognizing expenses and therefore income during production.) A typical description of this is the following from the 1992 annual report of United Dominion Industries: "For financial statement purposes, income on construction projects is recognized on the percentage-of-completion basis. Provisions for anticipated losses on uncompleted contracts are made in the period in which such losses are first determinable."[2] This is a conservative policy: if a project looks as if it will make money (project revenues greater than expenses), a portion of that income is recognized in the period in which the portion seems to have been earned, but if a project looks as if it will lose money (project revenues less than expenses), the whole anticipated loss is recognized right away.

Percentage of completion is the most common method of recognizing revenue during production. This method entails determining what proportion of the project has been completed during the year and recognizing that proportion of total expected revenue, expenses (costs), and, therefore, income. Often this is done by measuring the proportion of expected total costs incurred during the period. In order to recognize revenue in this manner, total costs must be reasonably determinable, the contract price (total revenue) must be reasonably certain, and there must be reasonable assurance of payment. The frequent use of the word "reasonable" here shows that a lot of judgment is required in using this method!

Let's assume Greenway Construction had a large, three-year project with total revenue of $4,000,000 and total costs of $3,400,000. (Prior to expense recognition, project costs are charged to an inventory account for costs of construction in process. Like other inventories, this account holds costs until they are matched to revenues.) Total income for the project over the three years was therefore $600,000. The project was 20% completed at the end of the first year, 65% completed at the end of the second year, and 100% completed at the end of the third year. Ignoring complications that arise when revenues and costs do not work out as expected, here are journal entries to implement percentage of completion revenue (and matched expense) recognition during production. (For presentation purposes, all amounts are in thousands of dollars.)

	Year 1		Year 2		Year 3	
Percentage of contract done in the year	20%			45%		35%
Revenue recognition:						
DR Accounts receivable	800		1,800		1,400	
CR Revenue		800		1,800		1,400
Percentage earned each year.						
Expense recognition:						
DR Cost of goods sold expense	680		1,530		1,190	
CR Construction in process inventory		680		1,530		1,190
Percentage matched to revenue.						
Resulting income each year	$120		$270		$210	

You can see the *timing* effect of accrual accounting here. The annual entries have the effect of spreading the $600,000 project income out over the three years: 20% to the first year, 45% to the second, 35% to the third.

3. Completion of Production

In the percentage-of-completion method, revenue is recognized as the work proceeds. It is also possible to wait until the work is all done and recognize the revenue then. This is like the point-of-sale method, except if the work took a long time, perhaps several accounting periods, then it is very conservative because no revenue would be recognized for a long time, then all of it at once. In the Greenway Construction example above, if revenue and the associated expenses were recognized on the completion of production, the project income would be:

- $0 in Year 1;
- $0 in Year 2; and
- $600,000 in Year 3.

Compared to the percentage of completion method, income would be:

- $120,000 *lower* in Year 1;
- $270,000 *lower* in Year 2; and
- $390,000 *higher* in Year 3.

So if the company wanted to know "what if" it changed to the completion of production (or "completed contract") method, there's the answer, ignoring income tax.

If there is no customer yet, but the production is done, is that a legitimate time to recognize revenue? Only under very limited circumstances is that appropriate, such as when there are ready or guaranteed markets for the product, stable prices, and minimal marketing costs. Historically, revenue from gold mines was recognized at this point; producers could expect to sell all they produced since there was a world price for gold and Western governments provided a ready market. This is no longer the case, and today almost the only time revenue is recognized at time of completion is in agricultural concerns that produce within government quotas.

4. When Cash Is Received

If there is serious doubt as to the collectibility of cash from a revenue-generating transaction, revenue recognition is delayed until the collection has taken place. This does not mean that any time a business extends credit to a customer, revenue recognition is delayed; this is only the case when the risk is great and the amount collectible cannot be reasonably determined, or is not sufficiently predictable.

For example, certain real estate transactions that are speculative in nature and/or for which the collection of cash is contingent upon some future condition (such as the purchasers of a shopping mall successfully leasing a certain percentage of the space) will not be recognized as revenue until the cash is received.

Another example of revenue recognition at time of collection is the "instalment sales" method. When the majority of the revenue will come in over a long series of instalments, and there is substantial uncertainty that a given customer will actually make all the payments, the revenue is recognized in stages as the cash comes in. The instalment sales method has some complexities, but in principle it is just a way of recognizing revenue on a cash received basis.

5. At Some Point After Cash Has Been Received

Revenue recognition methods 1, 2, and 3 use accrual accounting, while 4 uses the cash basis for recognizing revenue. It is also possible to *defer* recognition for some time after the cash has been collected. Even though cash has been received, all revenue may not be recognized immediately because of some circumstance, such as a guaranteed deposit refund policy or a policy of "satisfaction guaranteed or money back." A current liability account (Deferred revenue) is credited when the cash is collected:

DR Cash
CR Deferred revenue or Deposits received liability

Revenue will be recognized at a point in the future, normally after the refund time has expired or the required after-delivery service has been performed:

DR Deferred revenue or Deposits received liability
CR Revenue

(You'll recognize this pair of entries as Categories e and E of Section 7.3.)

7.8 EXPENSE RECOGNITION AND MATCHING

According to the "matching" criterion, expense recognition should be timed to match the revenue recognition method. The journal entries for doing this were described in earlier sections, and various ways of accomplishing the required expense recognition will be examined later, especially in Chapter 10. The basic idea is that expense accounts should be debited in parallel to the crediting of revenue accounts. In practice, this is done quite routinely for most expenses. When expenses such as wages, interest, heat, property taxes, or advertising are incurred, they are recognized as expenses on the assumption that they were incurred to help earn revenues in the same period. Sometimes this assumption is a bit strained; for example, advertising may stimulate revenue over more than the current period, but the subjectivity of estimating multi-period effects and the simplicity of just expensing such costs when incurred lead most companies to just expense them, matching them to current revenues.

There are cases, however, when the accounting has to be more refined. We saw above an example of expense recognition matching to the revenue recognized during production. Just to help you see the potential accrual accounting offers for fine tuning revenue and expense recognition, here's another example, from the growing field of franchising.

WonderBurgers Ltd. is a franchisor, which means it sells the right to sell its products in particular geographic areas. For example, a franchisee might pay $25,000 for the right to set up a WonderBurgers fast-food restaurant in Sudbury, and no one else would be able to use the WonderBurgers name in Sudbury.

Let's suppose that the management of WonderBurgers estimates that it takes three years for a franchise to become viable and knows that during that time it will have to provide a lot of help. Suppose the sort of schedule of cash flows and economic activity that WonderBurgers has experienced for a typical $25,000 franchise fee is much like the one shown below. The "percent-of-fee-earned" amounts could have been determined by how much revenue was collected or how much support cost was spent, but because of the kinds of effort the company and its franchisees go through in getting a franchise going, management has worked out a general policy of recognizing 40% of the revenue in the first year of a franchise and 30% in each of the next two years. (It's a lot like the percentage of completion method we saw above, which is no accident. Franchise accounting is a form of the percentage of completion method.)

Year	Cash Paid by Franchisee	Cash Cost to Help Franchisee	Percent of Fee Earned
1	$15,000	$4,000	40%
2	5,000	3,000	30%
3	5,000	1,000	30%
	$25,000	$8,000	100%

Using management's estimates of percent of fee earned as the basis of revenue recognition, the revenue recognized from the franchise sale would be:

- Year 1, $10,000 (40%); and
- Years 2 and 3, $7,500 each (30% each).

According to the matching criterion, the expense of helping the franchisee should be recognized on the same schedule, so the expense recognized would be:

- Year 1, $3,200 (40%); and
- Years 2 and 3, $2,400 each (30% each).

This matching process means that the income from the contract follows the same pattern. The total expected income is $17,000 ($25,000 minus $8,000), and the matching process produces an income pattern of:

- Year 1, $6,800 (40% of $17,000, which is $10,000 revenue recognized minus $3,200 expense recognized); and
- Years 2 and 3, $5,100 (30% of $17,000 each, which is $7,500 revenue minus $2,400 expense).

The resulting income schedule and differences between accrual basis and cash basis income are below.

	Accrual Basis Income			Cash Basis Income		
	(a)	(b)	(c)	(d)	(e)	(f)
Year	Revenue	Expense	Income	Received	Spent	Income
1	$10,000	$3,200	$ 6,800	$15,000	$4,000	$11,000
2	7,500	2,400	5,100	5,000	3,000	2,000
3	7,500	2,400	5,100	5,000	1,000	4,000
	$25,000	$8,000	$17,000	$25,000	$8,000	$17,000

	Difference		
Year	(a)–(d)	(b)–(e)	(c)–(f)
1	$(5,000)	$(800)	$(4,200)
2	2,500	(600)	3,100
3	2,500	1,400	1,100
	0	0	0

You can see the point again about accrual accounting being a matter of timing. Both the accrual and the cash basis get to the same point, $17,000 income over the three years, but they take different routes to get there. In Year 1, the accrual income is $4,200 less than the net cash inflow of $11,000, but in Years 2 and 3, the accrual income is greater than the net cash inflows. The statement of changes in financial position reconciles the two methods, as usual.

All methods of managing the accounts so that the accrual income can be different from the cash flow involve creating balance sheet accounts to hold the differences until they disappear. Accounts for doing this have names like accounts receivable, inventory, contract work in process, deferred revenue liability, and accounts payable. The details of their workings are often complicated, and each company has its own system.

HOW'S YOUR UNDERSTANDING

Here are two questions you should be able to answer, based on what you have just read:

1. Why is revenue recognition not always so simple as just debiting accounts receivable and crediting revenue at the point of sale?
2. In 1995, Flimsy Construction Ltd. has recognized 38% of the total expected revenue from a contract to build a garage onto Professor Blotz's house. The total contract price is $43,000, and Flimsy expects its costs for the contract to be $29,500. Costs so far have been in line with expectations. How much contract expense should Flimsy recognize for 1995 and what would be the resulting contract income for 1995? ($11,210, $5,130)

7.9 ACCOUNTS RECEIVABLE

TRADE ACCOUNTS RECEIVABLE

Most accounts receivable are *recognized but uncollected revenue*, created by the accrual accounting entry: DR Accounts receivable, CR Revenue. Such receivables arise from the company's day-to-day business activities and so are often called "trade" receivables. They are included in current assets because they're usually expected to be collected within one year. Any interest charged to slow payers is added to the balance by an entry like this: DR Accounts receivable, CR Interest revenue (nonoperating revenue).

VALUATION OF ACCOUNTS RECEIVABLE

Like other current assets, receivables are valued on the balance sheet at the lower of cost or market. "Cost" here is the original transaction value of the sale that gave rise to the receivable, plus any subsequent interest charges. "Market" is the amount expected to be collected (the cash value of the receivable, if you like). There's often collection uncertainty, and many times companies experience difficulties in collection, especially as time passes after the sale. So, if the collectible amount is now expected to be lower than originally anticipated, the receivable must be reduced to an estimated collectible amount. The method for doing this by subtracting an allowance for doubtful accounts from the accounts receivable balance is described in Section 7.11.

The estimated collectible amount is the net of accounts receivable minus the allowance, so the allowance functions to adjust the net value down to the lower of cost (original value) and market (current estimated collectible amount). On the balance sheet, accounts receivable are valued at this net amount; most companies do not disclose either the original value or the allowance, just the net. They probably don't want competitors to know what proportion of their accounts receivable are in trouble! *Financial Reporting in Canada 1993* indicates that, in 1992, only 25 of the 300 companies surveyed disclosed the amount of the allowance.[3]

OTHER RECEIVABLES

There are two other main kinds of receivables. If large, these are shown separately from trade receivables. But if not, they are usually just lumped in with the trade receivables. *Financial Reporting in Canada 1993* reports that, in 1992, only 87 of the 295 companies that had receivables broke them down and reported them in more than one figure.[4]

- The first kind is "notes" receivable. These are supported by a signed contract between buyer and seller that specifies a payment schedule, an interest rate, and often other legal details. Such notes are often used for large and/or long-term receivables, such as sales of automobiles, houses, or appliances, and loans by banks and finance companies. Notes are shown at "present value" (only interest that has built up so far is included in the asset, not future interest). An "allowance for doubtful notes" is used if necessary.
- The second kind is loans to employees, officers, and shareholders, loans to associated companies, tax refunds the company is waiting for, expense advances not yet accounted for by employees, and other receivables *not* arising from revenue transactions. They are accounted for and valued much as normal trade receivables and notes receivable are, but because some may arise from peculiar circumstances, companies often disclose the reasons for them and explain other circumstances about them.

7.10 PREPAID AND ACCRUED EXPENSES

Prepaid expenses are assets that arise because an expenditure has been made, but there is still value extending into the future. They are usually classified as current assets because the future value usually continues only into the next year. But sometimes the value extends beyond a year, and the company may then appropriately show a noncurrent prepaid expense (that is, if it is a significant enough amount to warrant such classification). Prepaid expenses arise whenever the payment schedule for an expense doesn't match the company's fiscal period, such as for annual insurance premiums when the policy date is not the fiscal year end, or property taxes that are based on the municipality's tax assessment schedule rather than on the company's fiscal period.

Prepaid expenses are not assets in the same way as are receivables (to be collected in cash) or inventories (to be sold for cash). They arise from accrual accounting, in cases where the expense recognition follows the cash flow. As was indicated earlier in this chapter, this is conceptually the same reason inventories and fixed assets are on the balance sheet: something of value exists and therefore its cost should not yet be deducted as an expense. Here, the value is in the fact that, having spent the money already, the company will not have to spend it in the next period. So, prepaid expenses do not necessarily have any market value, but they have an economic value because future resources will not have to be expended.

Accrued expenses are liabilities, usually current, that arise from exactly the same timing problem as do prepaid expenses, but in their case the cash flow happens *after* the economic value has been obtained. For example, Argosy Ltd. has a June 30 fiscal year end and pays property taxes to the local municipality. Property taxes apply to the calendar year:

- *Prepaid* property taxes at June 30, 1994, arise if property taxes for calendar 1994 are paid in June, before the end of the fiscal year;
- *Accrued* property taxes at June 30, 1994, arise if property taxes for calendar 1994 are not paid until July, after the fiscal year end.

Therefore, accrued expenses and prepaid expenses are just opposite sides of the same coin, reflecting a mismatch between the cash payment and the use of the economic value. They arise as accrual accounting tries to arrange the expenses to reflect economic use rather than cash flow. They are assets or liabilities depending on how the cash flow and the expense recognition happen to mismatch, so you often see similar kinds of items as prepaid expense assets and as accrued expense liabilities, or even as an asset one year and a liability the next. Common examples include insurance, property taxes, sales commissions, interest, licences, and current income taxes (payable if owing, or refundable if overpaid). Similarly, sometimes liabilities arise when customers overpay their accounts receivable, and assets arise when the company overpays its accounts payable.

Here is an example. Day and Night Inc. has ten local corner stores that are part of a national chain. Each year, it pays a franchise fee to the chain for use of the chain's logo and other rights during the *calendar* year. No matter when the fee is paid, its economic value applies to the calendar year. The company's *fiscal* year end is September 30, however. The situation is shown in the top panel of Figure 7.2 below. It's the kind of mismatch of periods that gives rise to prepaid and accrued expenses.

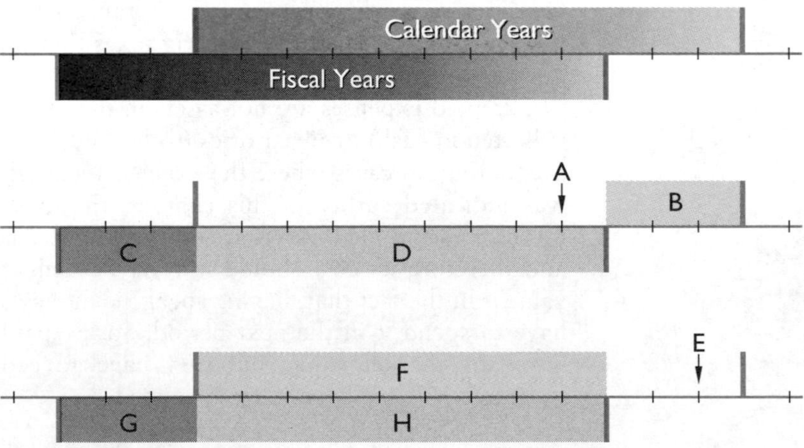

FIGURE 7.2

Let's consider the effects of two different payment dates.

1. The company pays the annual fee on August 31 every year (point A on the middle panel of the figure).
   - At September 30, the fiscal year end, the fee for the calendar year has been paid, so there is a prepaid expense asset for the three months of the calendar year remaining (space B on the middle panel).
   - Expense for each fiscal year includes 3/12 of the previous year's fee (prepaid at the end of last year: space C on the middle panel) plus 9/12 of the current year's fee (the portion *not* prepaid at the end of this year, space D on the middle panel).
2. The company pays the annual fee on November 30 every year (point E on the bottom panel of the figure).
   - At September 30, the fiscal year end, no fee for the current calendar year has yet been paid, so there will be an accrued expense liability for 9/12 of the fee for the current calendar year (space F on the lower panel).
   - Expense for each fiscal year includes 3/12 of the previous year's fee (the part *not* accrued at the end of last year: space G on the lower panel) plus 9/12 of the current year's fee (the part accrued at the end of this year: space H on the lower panel).

Accrual accounting has used a prepaid expense asset in the first case and an accrued expense liability in the second case to produce the same calculation of expense: 3/12 of last year's fee plus 9/12 of this year's (spaces C and D are the same as G and H). The happenstance of the payment date does not affect the expense. The asset or liability accounts arise as a consequence of accrual accounting's method of measuring expenses (and therefore income) properly.

HOW'S YOUR UNDERSTANDING

Here are two questions you should be able to answer based on what you have just read:

1. What other kinds of receivables besides uncollected revenue might be included in a company's balance sheet figure for accounts receivable?
2. Mah Stores Inc. pays its insurance premium in advance every year on September 30 for the year beginning that date. This year, the premium (paid last September) was $5,280 and next year it is estimated to be $5,400. If the company's fiscal year end is July 31, what is the prepaid insurance asset or accrued insurance liability at this July 31? If the company failed to pay its premium for next year until November 1, what would be the prepaid insurance asset or accrued insurance liability on its quarterly balance sheet at October 31? [Asset, $880 (2/12 x $5,280); Liability $450 (1/12 × $5,400)].

7.11 CONTRA ACCOUNTS

Contra accounts are a common method of managing accrual accounts. In financial accounting, contra accounts are used to accumulate amounts that will be deducted from asset, liability, or even owners' equity accounts. Why are they needed in these situations? How are they used? This section answers both questions.

Why do we need to keep these amounts separate from the accounts from which they are deducted? The reason most often cited is to provide better and more useful information by not mixing these deductions in with the accounts from which they are to be deducted. Thus, both the original accounts and the deductions are shown in the accounts and can be examined separately. We'll see below why this is useful.

Contra accounts are used mostly for expense recognition, but there are other versions, which we will not go into. Here we will focus only on the primary uses of contra accounts: accumulating amortization (depreciation) and allowing for doubtful accounts receivable.

ACCUMULATED AMORTIZATION (DEPRECIATION)

Contra accounts are used to accumulate **amortization** on fixed assets, such as buildings and equipment. The terminology is changing here: until recently, such amortization was called **depreciation** and the word amortization was used for intangible assets, such as goodwill, leasehold improvements, and patents. Many companies still use the word depreciation, and call the contra account accumulated depreciation.

In the case of amortization (depreciation), a contra account is created when the periodic expense for using the asset is recognized. For example, the annual depreciation charge of $100,000 on a building would be recognized this way, as we've seen already several times:

DR Amortization expense	100,000	
CR Accumulated amortization		100,000

The debit is an expense account in the income statement. The credit is a contra asset account. The credit side of the journal entry could have been to the asset account "Building." Instead the contra account is used, so that by leaving the asset cost account alone, the balance sheet presents the acquisition cost of the asset along with the accumulated amount of expense that has previously been recognized. Showing both of these items allows users to make a rough guess as to how long the asset has been in service. Remember that *accumulated amortization* on the balance sheet is the amount of amortization *accumulated over the life of the asset* to date, whereas the amount of amortization charged *this year* (to match the revenues the asset consumption is presumed to have helped generate) can be determined from the *amortization expense account* in the income statement and/or the amortization added back to income on the SCFP.

Let's look at a simple example involving the dog pound's purchase of a new truck to catch strays. If the truck cost $50,000 and an annual amortization expense of $8,000 was determined, the annual journal entry to recognize amortization would be:

DR Amortization expense		8,000
CR Accumulated amortization	8,000	

On the balance sheet, the asset account for the truck's cost would continue to show a balance of $50,000, but each year the accumulated amortization contra asset account would increase by $8,000. Deducting accumulated amortization from the long-term asset account leaves a figure known as the **net book value.** So, we would have:

	Cost	Accumulated Amortization Contra	Net Book Value
Date of purchase	$50,000	$ 0	$50,000
End of first year	50,000	8,000	42,000
End of second year	50,000	16,000	34,000

If the truck were sold at any time, the cost would be removed from the ledger, but so would the contra account. *The contra is meaningful only in comparison to the cost*, and when the truck is gone neither account is needed any more. Suppose the truck was sold for $37,000 at the end of the second year. Then we would have the following entry:

DR Cash (the proceeds)	37,000	
CR Truck asset (removing the cost)		50,000
DR Truck accumulated amortization (removing the contra)	16,000	
CR Gain on sale of truck (an "other revenue" account in the income statement)		3,000

The gain on sale is just the difference between the proceeds and the net book value at the date of sale.

- If the proceeds had been $29,000 instead, the debit to cash would have been $29,000 and there would have been a debit to loss on sale (an "other expense" account in the income statement) for $5,000, the difference between the proceeds and the net book value.
- Let's suppose that at the end of the second year the truck was used to pick up a particularly ornery bunch of dogs, which turned out to have a highly contagious disease. The truck had to be junked, and the insurance company refused to pay anything because such a risk was not contemplated when the insurance was written. Now we have what accountants call a "write-off": a disposal without proceeds. The journal entry would still credit cost for $50,000 and debit the contra for $16,000, and there would now be a $34,000 debit to a loss on disposal or write-off expense account (still an "other expense" account on the income statement, or perhaps in some circumstances an extraordinary item). The whole net book value is said to have been written off. You can see that gains, losses, and write-offs are all just variations on the same theme:

  Proceeds greater than 0 and greater than net book value: Gain on sale
  Proceeds greater than 0 and equal to net book value: No gain or loss
  Proceeds greater than 0 and less than net book value: Loss on sale
  Proceeds equal 0 and so less than net book value: Write-off

When nonphysical assets, such as goodwill, patents, and franchise fees paid, are amortized, the accumulated amortization is often just deducted from the asset cost on the balance sheet, not shown separately (or disclosed in a footnote) as it is for physical assets' accumulated amortization. However, for purposes of internal control (keeping track of asset costs), there may well be an accumulated amortization account in the ledger, which is deducted from the asset cost account when the balance sheet is being prepared. Gains, losses, and write-offs on such assets are calculated just as for the physical assets illustrated above.

Enterprises may have hundreds of ledger accounts, kept separate for internal control purposes, which are aggregated into the relatively few figures on the balance sheet. We now turn to an example account that is typically kept separate in the ledger but *not* shown separately on the balance sheet.

DOUBTFUL ACCOUNTS RECEIVABLE

Now, let's look at the other most common use of contra accounts, the **allowance for doubtful accounts.** When a company sells to a customer on account, there will always be some risk that the customer will fail to pay. Therefore, a portion of the sales on account will be doubtful, and that portion should be deducted from revenue on the income statement in the period of sale to match the expense (resulting from the probable failure to collect) to the revenue recognized that period. Let's assume that the company determines, by past experience or current evidence of customers' troubles, that about $500 of sales on account will likely not be paid. The journal entry to *recognize* the expense is:

DR Bad debts expense	500	
CR Allowance for doubtful accounts		500

The credit in this entry is again to a contra asset account, just as it was for amortization. (That account was in the noncurrent assets section of the balance sheet, while this one is in the current assets section.) The reason for not deducting the amount directly from the accounts receivable asset is that even after the usual collection time has passed, the company may still try to collect on the accounts and therefore doesn't want to alter the accounts receivable amount. The list of individual accounts should have the same total as that of the accounts receivable account for control reasons, and so the account should not be changed just because collection is doubtful.

The main difference between this situation and that of amortization is that only the net amount of the accounts receivable less the allowance for doubtful accounts is disclosed on the balance sheet This contra account is deemed to be less useful for readers of the balance sheet than the accumulated amortization contra account, and perhaps more sensitive if disclosed. Also, the income statement always discloses the amortization expense but seldom discloses the bad debts expense, which is just included with other expenses somewhere.

Eventually, after pursuing a nonpaying customer for months, a company may decide to write the account off. Another journal entry is then needed. Suppose the account in question equals $100 (it was one of the risky ones contemplated when the allowance was created above), then the write-off entry is:

DR Allowance for doubtful accounts	100	
CR Accounts receivable		100

This entry eliminates the account from the books of the company completely, but you'll notice that it does not affect expenses (or, therefore, income): that effect was created when the allowance and expense were *recognized* earlier. The power to write off an account is usually quite tightly controlled and great care is taken to keep track of payments received. The reason should be fairly obvious: if you write an account off it is no longer on the books anywhere, and then, if the deadbeat customer pays, the person who receives the money could simply keep it and no one else in the company would know.

You'll note that this write-off is handled differently from the noncurrent asset write-offs described above. The reason is that the allowance for doubtful accounts is considered to apply to the whole list of accounts receivable, in aggregate. We don't necessarily know *which* specific accounts receivable were allowed for: for example, the $500 allowance for doubtful accounts was probably based on an average experience, such as that, say, 15% of accounts over 40 days old will not be collected. We don't need to know *which* accounts in order to make such an allowance for the aggregate risk being taken. There was a contra accumulated amortization for each building or truck, but there is no particular contra for each account receivable, so both the account receivable asset and an equal amount of the allowance for doubtful accounts contra are just eliminated in the above bad debt write-off. It's like assuming that the written-off receivable had been 100% allowed for.

Bad debt write-offs can throw the system off if they are large enough. For example, in the above case, what if a customer account for $800 had to be written off? That's more than there is in the allowance! There are methods for adjusting the allowance to take such problems into account, but this book will not include them beyond the next little example.

Here is a final example of the use and effect of an allowance for doubtful accounts contra.

- Jellyroll Sweets Inc. sells confections to retail stores. At the end of 1994, it had accounts receivable of $53,000 and an allowance for doubtful accounts of $3,100. *Therefore, the estimated collectible amount of the accounts receivable was $49,900 at the end of 1994.*
- During 1995, the company had credit sales of $432,800 and collected $417,400 from customers. Therefore, at the end of 1995, the accounts receivable stood at $68,400 ($53,000 + $432,800 – $417,400).
- At that point, the sales manager went through the list of accounts receivable and determined that accounts totalling $1,200 were pretty much hopeless and should be written off, and furthermore that an aggregate allowance at the end of 1995 of $4,200 was required.

Here are journal entries to accomplish what is needed:

Write off the bad ones:

DR Allowance for doubtful accounts	1,200	
CR Accounts receivable		1,200

Allow for the doubtful ones:

DR Bad debts expense	2,300	
CR Allowance for doubtful accounts		2,300
(Balance in allowance = $3,100 – $1,200	= $1,900	
Allowance needed at the end of 1995	= $4,200	
Additional allowance = $4,200 – $1,900	= $2,300)	

The accounts receivable balance is now $67,200 ($68,400 – $1,200) and the contra balance is $4,200.

- Therefore, the estimated collectible value of the accounts receivable (the net balance sheet value) is $63,000 at the end of 1995.
- Bad debts expense for 1995 is $2,300.
- The write-off of the hopeless ones cleaned them out of the list of receivables, but did not affect either income or the net balance sheet value. You can see this by redoing the second entry above with no first entry (that is, no write-off of the hopeless ones).
- If none had been written off, the allowance balance would still be the $3,100 from last year.
- But now the allowance needed would be $4,200 for the doubtful ones and $1,200 for the hopeless ones (still in the receivables), totalling $5,400.
- Subtracting the $3,100 from that total leaves $2,300, so the second journal entry and, therefore, the bad debts expense would be the same!
- Now the accounts receivable would be $68,400, and the allowance would be $5,400. So, the estimated collectible amount of the accounts receivable (the net balance sheet value) would still be $63,000.

The purposes of contra accounts are, like most other things in accounting, to provide useful information to the readers of financial statements and/or to assist in accounting's internal control functions.

7.12 A Procedural Review

By this time, you should be "thinking double-entry": aware that when one account is affected, another must be too. Consider the following examples:

a. *Revenue cycle*

Recognition:	DR Accounts receivable
	CR Revenue
Collection:	DR Cash
	CR Accounts receivable

b. *Doubtful account cycle*

Allowance:	DR Bad debts expense
	CR Allowance for doubtful accounts
Write-off:	DR Allowance for doubtful accounts
	CR Accounts receivable

c. *Purchases cycle (perpetual method)*

Purchase:	DR Inventory
	CR Accounts payable
Payment:	DR Accounts payable
	CR Cash
Recognition:	DR Cost of goods sold expense
	CR Inventory

d. *Capitalization/amortization/disposal cycle*

Acquisition:	DR Noncurrent asset
	CR Cash or liability account
or Capitalization:	DR Noncurrent asset
	CR Expense
Amortization with a contra account:	
	DR Amortization expense
	CR Accumulated amortization contra
or Amortization without a contra account:	
	DR Amortization expense
	CR Noncurrent asset account
Disposal:	DR Cash (proceeds)
	CR Noncurrent asset (cost)
	DR Accumulated amortization contra
	CR or DR Gain or loss on sale

HOW'S YOUR UNDERSTANDING

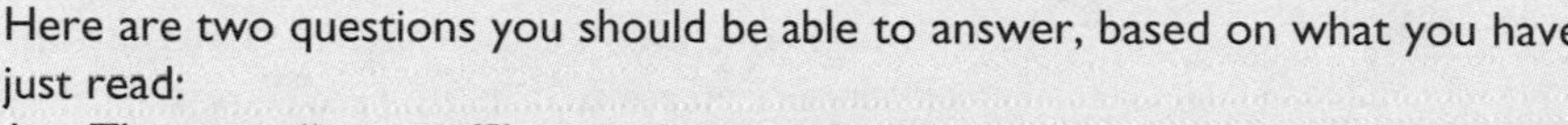
Here are two questions you should be able to answer, based on what you have just read:

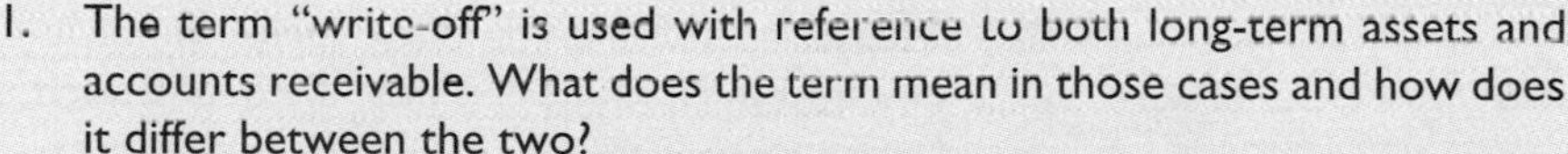
1. The term "write-off" is used with reference to both long-term assets and accounts receivable. What does the term mean in those cases and how does it differ between the two?

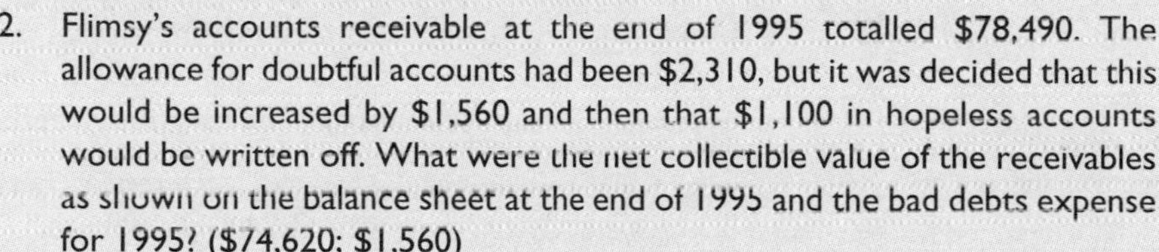
2. Flimsy's accounts receivable at the end of 1995 totalled $78,490. The allowance for doubtful accounts had been $2,310, but it was decided that this would be increased by $1,560 and then that $1,100 in hopeless accounts would be written off. What were the net collectible value of the receivables as shown on the balance sheet at the end of 1995 and the bad debts expense for 1995? ($74,620; $1,560)

7.13 RECOGNITION OF INCOME TAX EXPENSE

In Canada, as in most countries, tax is assessed by governments on income earned. For this book's introduction to financial accounting, you do not have to know how to calculate income tax; that is a very complicated matter for most corporations and many individuals. But there are some things you should be aware of:

- A major use of financial statements is for the assessment of income tax. In every country, province, or state that has income tax, the tax laws specify how the tax is to be calculated, and the rules often diverge significantly from generally accepted accounting principles. However, the GAAP-based financial statements (especially the income statement) are part of the evidence used in determining tax, and many tax jurisdictions start with those in assessing income tax, making adjustments to them only as specified in the law.

- Most corporations, and individuals, pay income tax at a substantial rate on their before-tax income, therefore net income (after income tax) is likely to be much less than the operating income because of the subtraction of a third or more in income tax expense.
- Because income tax expense is a major item on the income statement, there are accrual accounting principles involved in determining it, just as there are for revenue and the other expenses on the income statement.

Recognizing income tax expense is awkward because:

a. The income tax expense should be recognized in a way that matches recognition of revenue and other expenses, so that the expense makes sense by comparison to the other items in the income statement. *Therefore the income tax expense on the income statement should be recognized according to the matching criterion and other features of GAAP.*

b. But the income tax laws, not GAAP, specify how income tax is to be assessed and paid. *Therefore the income tax liability on the balance sheet should be determined according to the income tax laws.*

c. Though the income tax payable calculation starts with revenues and expenses determined using GAAP, it has many differences with GAAP. Therefore, the income tax expense determined in (a) is unlikely to be equal to the income tax payable determined in (b). If you debit income tax expense from (a) and credit income tax payable from (b), the journal entry will not balance! Income tax accounting provides a way to balance the entry by making use of the difference between the income tax laws and the company's accounting methods.

There are two general kinds of differences between the income tax law and accounting methods under GAAP.

1. Some are permanent differences; for example, there may be a kind of revenue included in the income statement that is not subject to tax (such as dividends from already-taxed associated companies), or an expense that is not deductible in determining tax.
2. Some, on the other hand, are timing differences, in which the tax law and the accounting method both eventually agree, but one is temporarily ahead of the other. For example, if an expense is deducted from revenue in this year's income statement but in next year's tax return, because of some provision in the tax law, the difference is only temporary because by the end of next year it will have been deducted in both calculations.

Timing differences give rise to **deferred income tax,** which is an attempt to reflect the effects of income tax occurring in different years in the financial statements. Deferred income tax arises when the income tax expense and the income tax payable are not equal:

a. GAAP state that the income statement's income tax *expense* should be matched to the revenue and other expenses shown on the income statement, whether or not the same amount of income tax is payable that year, as long as it will be payable (or was payable) in some other year;

b. The income tax *payable* (which would be on the balance sheet, either as a liability or a reduction in cash if paid) depends on what the tax laws say is to be paid this year, even if the income statement includes the revenue or expense in some other year.

If the amount in (a) is not equal to that in (b), there is a problem in recording the income tax expense. Deferred income tax is the account used to hold the temporary difference and keep the accounts in balance. Let's say that for a particular company, the amount in (a), to match revenues, has been determined to be $45,000, while the amount payable for the year, (b), is $32,000 according to the company's income tax return.

DR Income tax expense	45,000	
CR Income tax payable liability		32,000
CR Deferred income tax liability (to balance the entry: $45,000 – $32,000)		13,000

The entry illustrates several points about income tax accounting.

1. For most companies most of the time, tax expense recognized is greater than tax payable, so deferred income tax is the sum of credits like that above. Deferred income tax is included in the liability section of the balance sheet, where other credit balance accounts are placed. Though it is among the liabilities, it is not a debt: it is not owed to anyone. After all, the government is being paid the currently payable tax each year, which is all that it requires. The deferred tax liability is a consequence of accrual accounting's attempt to match expenses with revenues, rather than an attempt to estimate a debt. But since it is typically a credit balance, it ends up on the liabilities section of the balance sheet, usually just above owners' equity, because it is not like other liabilities.
2. The deferred income tax liability rises and falls as the difference between tax expense and tax payable changes each year. The amount credited or debited to deferred income tax is whatever is needed to balance the journal entry. It is possible for the accumulated balance to become a debit (tax expenses recognized having accumulated to less than the taxes payable), in which case deferred income tax would be placed among the assets. *Financial Reporting in Canada 1993* reports that of the 300 companies surveyed in 1992:

   180 showed deferred income tax as a noncurrent liability;
   19 showed it as a current liability or had some in both current and noncurrent liabilities;
   25 showed it as a noncurrent asset;
   4 showed it as a current asset or had some in both current and noncurrent assets;
   29 showed it in both liabilities and assets (because the difference between expense and payable had components going in opposite directions); and
   43 did not mention a deferred income tax liability or asset.[5]
3. You can partition the $45,000 income tax expense into two parts: the $32,000 currently payable and the $13,000 deferred. You will often see

this sort of presentation of the income tax expense on the income statement:

Income tax expense:	
Current portion	$32,000
Deferred portion	13,000
Total expense	$45,000

Therefore, the journal entry above can also just as easily be written in the two parts:

DR Income tax expense—current portion	32,000	
CR Income tax payable		32,000
DR Income tax expense—deferred portion	13,000	
CR Deferred income tax liability		13,000

4. The deferred portion of the income tax expense and the deferred income tax liability arise *only* from the temporary (timing) differences between the company's accounting under GAAP and the income tax laws. The deferred income tax liability or asset therefore will, in principle, eventually become zero when the temporary difference goes away. To ensure that temporary differences are all that lie behind the deferred income tax liability or asset, any *permanent* differences between the accounting statements and the income tax law are not reflected in the income tax expense. The current portion of the expense is the amount the tax law specifies, and the deferred portion is based only on temporary timing differences and so ignores permanent differences. If the company has revenues not taxable at all or expenses not deductible in determining income tax, then the total income tax expense will be different from what you might expect if you know the tax rate such companies are expected to pay, but that is right: the company does not pay income tax at that rate because it has revenues or expenses not subject to that rate. For example, if a company that you'd expect to pay tax at a 45% rate has substantial nontaxed revenues (such as dividends from associated companies), the effective tax rate on its overall income might only be 35%: that's a combination of 45% on most of its income and 0% on some. GAAP require a footnote disclosing the components of any significant variation from the expected (statutory) income tax rate. Many companies include a calculation of the effective tax rate (35% in the example above) after leaving out the permanent differences.

   The main temporary difference that arises is due to amortization:

   - The company can determine its amortization expense each year in whatever way makes sense for measuring its income, as long as that method is within GAAP.
   - But, in computing its income tax, the company must follow tax rules for computing amortization. In Canada, tax amortization has another name: **capital cost allowance** (CCA).
   - Amortization and CCA both eventually allow the asset's cost to be written off as an expense, but they may do so on a different schedule. The difference is temporary (lasting only as long as the asset's life), so it is a timing difference and will affect deferred income tax.

For example, a company may have only one automobile, costing $30,000, that it amortizes over ten years at $3,000 per year because it will be scrapped as worthless after ten years. CCA for tax purposes may be based on a formula applying a 15% rate to the cost in the first year and a 30% rate to the undepreciated (unamortized) cost remaining each year after that. This sort of "declining balance" CCA is generally required in Canada. The CCA would be:

- 15% of $30,000 = $4,500 in the first year;
- 30% of ($30,000 – $4,500) = $7,650 in the second year;
- 30% of ($30,000 – $4,500 – $7,650) = $5,355 in the third year; and so on.

CCA in the tenth year would be whatever the remaining undepreciated cost is at that point, assuming that the automobile is junked for no cash and was the only automobile the company had. (If there are other automobiles the situation is more complex to calculate because of the tax law that applies, but the principle that the difference is a temporary timing one remains.) The result would be the following differences:

Year	Amortization	CCA	Difference
1	$ 3,000	$ 4,500	$ (1,500)
2	3,000	7,650	(4,650)
3	3,000	5,355	(2,355)
4	3,000	3,749	(749)
5	3,000	2,624	376
6	3,000	1,837	1,163
7	3,000	1,286	1,714
8	3,000	900	2,100
9	3,000	630	2,370
10	3,000	1,469	1,531
	$30,000	$30,000	$ 0

You can see that the timing difference is temporary because, after ten years, the amortization and the CCA both equal the original cost of the automobile. This neat comparison gets muddied in practice by changes in tax laws and rates, buying new assets, selling old ones before they are used up, and other complications, but the idea of temporary timing differences still applies.

Let's look at an example of computing deferred income tax that has both permanent and timing differences. The example is that of Prolox Inc., which has an expected (statutory) income tax rate of 38%.

- For the year 1995, its income statement showed income before income tax of $120,000.
- Included in that were a nontaxable revenue of $4,000, a nondeductible expense of $2,500, and amortization expense of $89,400.
- Capital cost allowance on the company's depreciable assets for 1995 came to $114,700.

a. The company's income tax expense, calculated to match its other income statement items, would be 38% of its income statement income before tax, not including permanent differences. This would be:

38% of ($120,000 – $4,000 + $2,500)
= 38% of $118,500
= $45,030

You'll note that $45,030 is 37.525% of the $120,000 accounting income. The company might disclose this effective tax rate in its income tax footnote.

b. The company's income tax payable would be 38% of taxable income, which would be:

38% of $118,500 plus $89,400 amortization (not allowed for tax purposes) minus $114,700 (CCA is deductible instead of the amortization expense)
= 38% of $93,200
= $35,416

c. The deferred income tax for the year would be 38% of the temporary timing difference between the income statement's income (adjusted for permanent differences) and the taxable income, which is:

38% of $118,500 – $93,200
= 38% of $25,300
= $9,614

(Note that the $25,300 timing difference is equal to the difference between amortization and CCA, the only items temporarily different this year.) The following journal entry recognizes the income tax expense:

DR Income tax expense (current portion)	35,416	
CR Income tax payable liability		35,416
DR Income tax expense (deferred portion)	9,614	
CR Deferred income tax liability		9,614

- The deferred and current portions of the income tax expense add up to $45,030, which is the income tax expense previously calculated as matching the rest of the income statement.
- Income tax payable would be a current liability, because the government expects to be paid soon.
- The deferred income tax liability is noncurrent in this case, because it usually takes several years for the temporary differences to change signs (in the previous example, this did not happen until the fifth year). When the differences do change signs, the deferred part of the income tax expense becomes a credit, and there is a debit to the deferred part of the income tax liability, which therefore begins to shrink.

This has been a small sampling of the effects of the income tax system on financial statements. The purpose has been to demonstrate such effects and also to acquaint you with a major item on the financial statements. Income tax expense is often a large expense, and deferred income tax liability is often a large liability. Other taxes, such as sales and excise taxes, may also affect the financial statements, but the most visible and significant effects are those caused by income tax.

As we'll see further in Chapter 8, income tax also complicates any analysis of the effects on income of various methods of revenue and expense recognition. Any income the company makes is likely to be taxed, and losses may be deductible for tax purposes (that is, reduce the income tax payable on other income). Therefore, any conclusions about effects have to consider income tax: you might get a different response from your boss if you said a certain accounting change would increase income by $10,000, but the company would have to find $4,000 to pay the income tax on the increase, from the response you would get if you forgot to mention the tax effect!

HOW'S YOUR UNDERSTANDING

Here are two questions you should be able to answer, based on what you have just read:

1. Deferred income tax usually appears in the noncurrent liability section of the balance sheet. Is it a debt? If yes, to whom is it owed? If no, why is it among the liabilities?
2. Last year, Kite Ltd. owed $32,118 in income tax, but if you applied its tax rate to its income statement's "income before income tax," you would get $43,786. There were no permanent differences between Kite's accounting and the income tax law. What was Kite's income tax expense for last year, and what, if any, portion of that was deferred income tax? ($43,786; $11,668)

7.14 MANAGERS AND THE ECONOMIC ASSUMPTIONS OF ACCRUAL ACCOUNTING

Accrual accounting's purpose is to move beyond cash flows toward a broader economic concept of earnings and financial position. From a manager's point of view, this has several important implications:

- As a more inclusive way of measuring performance and position, accrual accounting should reflect more of what a manager is trying to do than cash flow can. This should make accrual accounting attractive to managers who want to be evaluated fairly and who are interested in comparing their companies to others.
- This attractiveness depends on how complete accrual accounting is in representing managers' performance. Here there is a limitation that often frustrates managers: accrual accounting, based on the historical transaction base of recordkeeping, is better suited to measuring past performance than to looking into the future, as managers are inclined to do.
- Accounting runs into a fundamental problem here. While managers' expectations are a main reason for their actions, accounting cannot observe their expectations, but only their actions. (Expectations are not observable in general, so this is not just a problem for accounting.) So, accounting reports the results of actions, not the reasons for them (except by implication). Managers may therefore feel that the accounting statements are incomplete because they miss the "why" behind the revenues, expenses, assets, and liabilities.

- To many people, earnings should be defined as changes in the value of the company. Economic earnings can be defined as increase in value.[6] Value changes are a function of performance, but also of expectations and of the market prices for assets and whole companies. The evidence-based accounting procedures for revenue recognition, expense recognition, and matching them to measure income may not relate very well to economic concepts of earnings, or to managers' struggle to increase the value of their companies.
- Accrual accounting's procedures require evidence to support entries and conservatism in estimating the effects of future events (provide for expected losses, but not for expected gains until they occur). To managers seeking an even-handed evaluation of their performance, accounting may seem overly sceptical about the future and downwardly biased in its measures. Accrual accounting goes beyond cash flows, and managers may wish that it went further, to recognize their optimism about the future more than it does.
- The criteria as to when and how to recognize revenues and expenses are inescapably judgmental and, therefore, to many managers' tastes, are both arbitrary and subjective. Earlier chapters have suggested that some managers may be motivated to manipulate the accounting results, and accrual accounting procedures can be a way of doing that, but it should also be said that many managers find accrual accounting too loose and flexible and would prefer less estimation and subjectivity. Prudence and conservatism are traits of many managers, not just of accountants and auditors!
- Modern finance theory, which is influential in the evaluations by financial markets, banks, and takeover specialists, makes much of cash flows (especially discounted expected future cash flows, to be examined in Chapter 8) but, as we have seen, cash flow does not necessarily connect well to accrual accounting's earnings figure. This connection is worse the shorter the period (for example, cash flow and accrual income are probably similar over a ten-year period, but unlikely to be similar over a month). However, because of the generally high level of error in forecasting future earnings and cash flows, the differences between them may not matter much in making evaluations based on expectations. For example, amortization is a major part of the difference between current earnings and cash flow, but looking into the future, the amortization may be taken as a rough measure of how much cash the company should put into replacement of assets as they wear out.

Another reason, therefore, for managers to take financial accounting seriously is so that they can know when the accounting measures seem appropriate and when not. Accrual accounting has many advantages and is very widely used, but managers should not accept it uncritically.

7.15 ACCOUNTING RESEARCH: DOES ACCRUAL ACCOUNTING MAKE A DIFFERENCE?

Section 4.10 asked whether cash flow (SCFP) information makes a difference in the presence of accrual accounting income information and concluded that it did, somewhat. Asking whether accrual accounting makes a difference is "the other side of the coin." There is also an implied reference to the alternative economic measure of value changes. Modern finance methods measure much of current value by discounting expected future cash flows, so the economic measure can be tied to cash flows. Does accrual accounting matter? Briefly, here are some research results:

> Accrual accounting can be viewed as one potentially cost-effective compromise between merely reporting cash flows and a more ambitious system of fuller disclosure.[7]
>
> There is a significant, positive correlation between (share) price changes and earnings changes. ... It is not a simple one-to-one relationship. ... Prices behave as if earnings contain a [temporary, random] component.[8]
>
> Price changes appear to be more highly correlated with earnings changes than with changes in "cash flow."[9]
>
> The research provides clear evidence that investors and creditors can use accounting information to predict many phenomena of interest. Statistical models have effectively used accounting numbers and ratios to make predictions in the following areas: (a) enterprise failure and financial distress, (b) judgments by [corporate bond] rating agencies, (c) trade credit and lending decisions, (d) corporate restructurings (mostly mergers and acquisitions), and (e) audit qualifications [objections by auditors]. Empirical analysis of the link between accounting earnings and future cash flows remains limited. However, recent evidence indicates that reported accrual earnings correlate well with *future* cash dividend distributions, the present value [discounted future value] of which partially explains the market value of firms' equity.[10]

The conclusion is that, for all its difficulties, accrual accounting is a valuable and significant financial measurement system. Exactly why and how its value is produced, and whether it is as cost-effective as it could or should be, are not clear. The study of the value of accrual accounting information is one of the largest and most active areas of accounting research, so stay tuned for more results!

7.16 CONTINUING DEMONSTRATION CASE

INSTALMENT 7

Data for Instalment 7

After recording the transactions to February 28, 1995, in Instalment 6, the trial balance of Mato Inc.'s general ledger was (credits are bracketed):

Cash	6,418	Share capital	(125,000)
Accounts receivable	13,709	Revenue	(227,656)
Inventory	33,612	Cost of goods sold expense	138,767
Automobile	10,000	Salary—Mavis	0
Accumulated amortization —auto	(1,000)	Salary—Tomas	0
Leasehold improvements	63,964	Salary—Other	0
Accumulated amortization —leasehold	(6,396)	Salaries expense	67,480
Equipment and furniture	32,390	Travel expense	10,102
Accumulated amortization —equipment	(744)	Phone expense	4,014
Computer	14,900	Rent expense	24,000
Accumulated amortization —computer	(1,490)	Utilities expense	3,585
Software	4,800	Office and general expense	5,933
Accumulated amortization —software	(480)	Interest expense	6,239
Incorporation cost	1,100	Inventory shortage expense	441
Bank loan	(47,500)	Amortization expense—auto.	1,000
Accounts payable	(36,656)	Amortization expense—leasehold	6,396
Deductions payable	(2,284)	Amortization expense—equipment	744
Salaries payable	(2,358)	Amortization expense—computer	1,490
Loan payable	0	Amortization expense—software	480

It was time to prepare the financial statements for the year ended February 28, 1995. Before that could be done, the following adjustments had to be made:

a. Based on the amortization calculations made during the first six months, the amounts for the second six months would be:
   - ◆ Car, leasehold improvements, computer, and software: 1/2 year × 20% of cost;
   - ◆ Equipment and furniture: 1/2 year × 10% of cost.

   The expenses for the second six months would therefore be: car, \$1,000; leasehold improvements, \$6,396; computer, \$1,490; software, \$480; equipment and furniture, \$1,620.

b. Estimated unpaid bank loan interest to February 28 was \$230.

c. Unfortunately, some of the boutique customers had run into financial difficulty. One customer who owed \$894 had gone bankrupt and other accounts totalling \$1,542 were doubtful.

d. Tomas had been getting some accounting assistance from a local public accountant. No bill had yet been received for this help, but Tomas estimated that the company owed about \$280 at the end of February.

e. It turned out that included in the revenue figure was a deposit of \$500 made by a customer on a special order from Africa that had not yet arrived.

f. Included in the office and general expenses was an insurance policy costing \$1,050, good for two years from March 1, 1994.

g. Mavis and Tomas decided that they should pay the company back about $200 for Mavis and $425 for Tomas for personal use of the company automobile. Automobile expenses were included in the travel expense account.

h. Mavis was concerned that the accounts receivable list "didn't look right," as she put it. Upon checking, she discovered that shipments totalling $2,231 in revenue had been made in late January and early February, but had not yet been billed. The cost of the goods shipped had been correctly removed from the inventory account and charged to cost of goods sold.

Results for Instalment 7

Adjusting journal entries at February 28, 1995, to take the above information into account:

	Debit	Credit
a. Amortization expense—auto.	1,000	
Accumulated amortization—auto.		1,000
Amortization expense—leasehold	6,396	
Accumulated amortization—leasehold		6,396
Amortization expense—computer	1,490	
Accumulated amortization—computer		1,490
Amortization expense—software	480	
Accumulated amortization—software		480
Amortization expense—equipment and furniture	1,620	
Accumulated amortization—equipment and furniture		1,620
b. Interest expense	230	
Accounts Payable		230
c. Bad debts expense	2,436	
Allowance for doubtful accounts		2,436
($894 + $1,542 = $2,436)		
Allowance for doubtful accounts	894	
Accounts receivable		894
d. Office and general expenses	280	
Accounts payable		280
e. Revenue	500	
Deferred revenue liability		500
f. Prepaid insurance	525	
Office and general expense		525
($1,050 over two years = $525 per year)		
g. Accounts receivable	625	
Travel expense		625
($200 + $425 = $625)		
h. Accounts receivable	2,231	
Revenue		2,231

After posting the adjusting journal entries to the trial balance given earlier, the following final February 28, 1995, account balances were produced (credits are bracketed as usual):

Cash	6,418	Deferred revenue liability	(500)
Accounts receivable	15,671	Share capital	(125,000)
Allowance for doubtful accounts	(1,542)	Revenue	(229,387)
Inventory	33,612	Cost of goods sold expense	138,767
Prepaid insurance	525	Bad debts expense	2,136
Automobile	10,000	Salary—Mavis	0
Accumulated amortization —auto	(2,000)	Salary—Tomas	0
Leasehold improvements	63,964	Salary—other	0
Accumulated amortization —leasehold	(12,792)	Salaries expense	67,480
Equipment and furniture	32,390	Travel expense	9,477
Accumulated amortization —equipment	(2,364)	Phone expense	4,014
Computer	14,900	Rent expense	24,000
Accumulated amortization —computer	(2,980)	Utilities expense	3,585
Software	4,800	Office and general expense	5,688
Accumulated amortization —software	(960)	Interest expense	6,469
Incorporation cost	1,100	Inventory shortage expense	441
Bank loan	(47,500)	Amortization expense—auto	2,000
Accounts payable	(37,166)	Amortization expense —leasehold	12,792
Deductions payable	(2,284)	Amortization expense —equipment	2,364
Salaries payable	(2,358)	Amortization expense —computer	2,980
Loan payable	0	Amortization expense —software	960
	71,434		(71,434)

That's enough for now! The financial statements prepared from this trial balance are presented in Instalment 8.

HOMEWORK AND DISCUSSION TO DEVELOP UNDERSTANDING

PROBLEM 7.1* Explain how revenues and expenses differ from cash flows

1. Explain the difference between a revenue and a cash receipt.
2. Give examples of items that are revenue of a given period but not receipts of that period, items that are receipts but not revenue, and items that are both revenue and receipts.
3. Explain the difference between an expense and a cash disbursement.
4. Give examples of items that are expenses of a given period but not disbursements of that period, items that are disbursements but not expenses, and items that are both expenses and disbursements.

PROBLEM 7.2* Adjusting journal entries

It is the end of International Fabrics Inc.'s fiscal year. You are working on the company's financial statements, and have discovered the following items. For each item:

1. State whether or not the item requires that an adjustment be made in the company's accounts according to the principles of accrual accounting; and
2. If the answer to part 1 is yes, write a journal entry to adjust the company's accounts.
   a. $3,200 of sales made on account just before the end of the fiscal year were not recorded until the beginning of the next year.
   b. The cost of goods sold for those sales, totalling $1,900, has not yet been recognized. The company uses a perpetual inventory system.
   c. During the year, deposits of $5,300 were made by customers on special orders and were credited to the deposit liability account. Deposits of $1,400 are still being held, but all the other special orders have been completed and the customers have paid the rest of the price for those orders (those payments are included in sales revenue).
   d. Maintenance expenses seemed rather high, and on investigation it turned out that an addition to the company's store, constructed over a period of several months at a cost of $62,320, had been included in the maintenance expenses.
   e. Just before the year end, the company was sued by a customer whose expensive curtains lost their colour as soon as they were exposed to sunlight. The lawsuit was for $4,300 to replace the curtains and $50,000 in pain and suffering damages. Legal advice indicates that the curtains should be replaced (which would cost the company about what it is being sued for) but that the customer will not succeed with the pain and suffering damages.
   f. The company's auditors sent a bill for $2,350 for the year's audit work.
   g. Effective just before the year end, the company agreed to buy an automobile from a major shareholder for $17,220.
   h. At the beginning of the year, the company had paid $2,000 for the exclusive right to distribute in Canada fabrics made by Silk Dreams Inc. of Pennsylvania. The exclusive distributorship is for a period of four years.

PROBLEM 7.3* Calculate accrual net income from various accounts

Pottery Galore Ltd. has just finished its 1995 fiscal year. From the following data, calculate net income for 1995:

Collections from customers during 1995	$174,320
Accounts receivable, end of 1994	11,380
Accounts receivable, end of 1995	9,440
Allowance for doubtful accounts, end of 1994	890
Allowance for doubtful accounts, end of 1995	1,130
Bad debts written off during 1995	520
Payments to suppliers and employees during 1995	165,690
Accounts and wages payable, end of 1994	12,770
Accounts and wages payable, end of 1995	15,510
Inventory of unsold goods, end of 1994	21,340
Inventory of unsold goods, end of 1995	24,650
Bank loan, end of 1995	12,000
(The loan was taken out a month before the end of 1995 at an interest rate of 8%. No interest has yet been paid.)	
Income tax payable, end of 1995 (none end of 1994)	2,340
Income tax paid during 1995	3,400
Deferred income tax liability, end of 1995 (none end of 1994)	1,230

PROBLEM 7.4* Revenue and expense recognition for a franchisor

The Pie Place, Inc. (TPP) was started in 1994 to franchise a chain of fast-food outlets that would sell only pies: meat, mince, pecan, sugar, and the like. A specialty was to be "pi-pie," a recipe made from various roots (ginger, ginseng, etc.) and invented by Janet Randolph, the founder and owner of TPP.

Janet has divided each major city into population sectors of about 200,000 each and plans to sell one franchise per sector. For smaller cities, franchises will cover rural areas as well. The franchises will be good for ten years, renewable for at least two more ten-year periods, and will sell for $20,000 each. Each franchisee must pay TPP $5,000 down in cash, pay the remainder in three equal annual instalments (with no interest charges), and agree to buy various ingredients from TPP. In return, TPP will provide expert advice (Janet's), recipes, help with locating and constructing the food outlet, management training, and some national advertising. (Most advertising costs will be charged back to the franchises on a pro rata basis.)

Here are data for TPP's first year, ended August 31, 1995:

Franchise agreements signed	28
Down payments received	26
Fast-food outlets opened	18
Franchise-related costs	$230,000
Other general expenses	$55,000

One of the franchises has already gone out of business (having paid only the initial $5,000), two others of those that have opened do not look as if they are going to make it, and one of the unopened franchises looks as if it will never get going.

1. List as many methods as you can think of for recognizing revenue from franchise sales.
2. Rank those methods from least conservative to most conservative.

3. List as many methods as you can think of for recognizing expenses from franchise-related costs.
4. Match each expense recognition method to the revenue recognition method that seems most appropriate.
5. Compare the income before tax for 1995 that would be produced by two or three of the more reasonable matched methods of recognizing revenue and expense.
6. Choose a matched method that you think would be most appropriate for TPP.
7. Draft an "accounting policy" footnote describing your chosen revenue/expense recognition method for TPP's August 31, 1995, financial statements.

PROBLEM 7.5* Calculate income tax expense and deferred tax liability

At the end of 1995, Henrik Inc. had deferred income tax liability of $329,612 and retained earnings of $3,949,286. For 1996, the company's income statement showed income before tax of $648,960 and amortization expense of $1,149,612. Inspection of the company's income tax records showed that in 1996, $29,650 of its revenue was not subject to income tax, and its capital cost allowance was $1,493,114. The company's income tax rate for 1996 was 32%. The company paid no dividends in 1996.

Calculate the following:

a. Current portion of income tax expense for 1996.
b. Deferred portion of income tax expense for 1996.
c. Net income for 1996.
d. Deferred income tax liability at the end of 1996.
e. Retained earnings at the end of 1996.

PROBLEM 7.6 Simple accrual revenue calculation

A weekly newspaper began operations on July 1 and collected payments for 1,000 one-year subscriptions at $5.20 each in the first three days of that month. Editions were published on July 7, 14, 21, and 28. How much revenue should the newspaper recognize in its accounts in July?

PROBLEM 7.7 Simple accrual expense questions

Prior to its opening, the Novelty Shop arranged for telephone service. The telephone company, the shop's owner was told, bills the customer for each month's service at the end of the month, and no deposit or installation fee is required.

1. Did the installation of the telephone increase the assets of the Novelty Shop? Did it result in an expense at the time of installation?
2. If the monthly service charge is $21, how will this affect the computation of income for the first two weeks?
3. What would be the effect on assets and income if the service charge for the first month were paid in advance at the beginning of the month?
4. What would be the effect on assets and income if an installation charge of $10 were paid at the beginning of the month?

PROBLEM 7.8 Discuss the basis of accrual accounting

Discuss the following:

1. Speaking positively, it might be said that accrual accounting improves on the cash flow information. Speaking negatively, it might be said that accrual accounting messes up the picture by introducing noncash flow factors. Whether or not you like the result they achieve, how do accrual accounting entries work to alter the cash flow story?
2. Why can it be said that timing is at the centre of accrual accounting?

PROBLEM 7.9 Explain why accrual accounting diverges from cash flow

Respond, in point form, to the following complaint by a business person:

> I find modern financial accounting really annoying. The basis of financial strength is the availability and use of real resources, like cash and machinery, yet accrual accounting produces an income measure that is deliberately different from the cash return earned by the business. Why is this so? Why should accrual accounting diverge from the measurement of cash flow?

PROBLEM 7.10 Examine some accrual accounting phenomena

1. On December 31, the end of the accounting period of Ultra Corp, the company accountant is about to make some adjustments. Describe a set of circumstances where, in making the typical year-end adjustments:
   a. An expense is debited and a liability is credited.
   b. An expense is debited and an asset contra account is credited.
   c. An asset is debited and revenue is credited.
   d. A liability is debited and revenue is credited.
2. A business executive remarked, "Accountants use a dual standard for measuring assets. Some are on the balance sheet because they have real future economic value. Others are there only because they're left over from the income measurement process...sort of expenses waiting to be deducted. Similarly with liabilities: some are really owed but some are just leftovers of the accrual accounting process for measuring income."

Discuss the remark, citing examples of assets and liabilities that might fit the executive's four categories.

PROBLEM 7.11 Managers and accrual accounting

Now that you are a famous business person, you are frequently asked to make after-dinner speeches on business topics. Without thinking about it too much, you agreed to make a speech on accrual accounting to a class of graduating business students. Now you have to think of something to say, and you have decided to title your talk, "Why managers like me like accrual accounting and why we worry about it." List the topics you plan to talk about under this heading.

PROBLEM 7.12 Simple adjusting entries, followed by financial statements

(This is a continuation of the Josie's Socks situation, in Problem 6.13.) The trial balance for Josie's sock business at the end of her second day in business was determined in Problem 6.13. If you didn't do that problem, here is the trial balance:

Account	Debit	Credit
Cash (Bank)	2,265	
Bank loan		2,000
Inventory of socks	600	
Business expenses	355	
Accounts payable		140
Sales revenue		1,080
TOTALS	3,220	3,220

One of Josie's last sales on her second day in business was to her bank loans officer, who was interested in seeing a set of financial statements for those two days. Since Josie was more than delighted with the results of her first business endeavour (she planned to go out that night and buy several hundred more pairs of socks if she could find a supplier), she had immediately undertaken the task of making up a set of financial statements. Upon examination of the ledger and trial balance (completed as part of Problem 6.13), Josie noticed several problems about which she would have to make decisions before doing the financial statements.

a. Although she had recorded the sale of the socks in the journal, she hadn't recorded the corresponding entry for the reduction in her inventory. All the socks had been sold, but there was still an inventory asset account.

b. She decided that the rent still had future benefit to her—remember, she had paid for six days, so there were four left.

c. She felt that the sign had been recorded in the wrong account—it also had future value and, therefore, wasn't just an expense (though it had blown down twice and so had deteriorated, Josie estimated, by 10%.)

d. She estimated that the unpaid interest on the bank loan was $5.

1. Write journal entries to recognize the additional information in Josie's accounts.
2. Prepare another trial balance to make sure your accounts are in balance.
3. From the trial balance and the other information above and in Problem 6.13, prepare a full set of financial statements for Josie's Socks for the first two days of business. Include the SCFP and any notes you think would be appropriate.

PROBLEM 7.13 Calculation of accrual income from cash records

Mike Stammer is a private investigator. He keeps his accounting records on a cash basis and has produced the following income statement, *as he calls it*.

Mike Stammer Income Statement for the Year Ended June 30, 1995	
Fees collected in cash	$85,000
Less cash expenses	34,600
Net income	$50,400

An examination of Mike's records shows these balances at the beginning and end of fiscal 1995:

	July 1, 1994	June 30, 1995
Fees receivable	$10,350	$ 3,900
Client deposits on continuing investigations	—	1,200
Accrued expenses	3,490	5,250
Prepaid expenses	1,700	2,500

1. a. What amount of the fees Mike collected in 1995 were received for investigations he actually completed in 1994?
   b. What amount of the fees received in 1995 will he earn in 1996?
   c. How much in fees did he earn in 1995 but not collect?
2. a. What amount of the expenses Mike paid in 1995 should be matched with his efforts in 1994 or 1996?
   b. What amount of expenses paid in previous years should be matched with revenues Mike earned in 1995?
3. Use your answers to Questions 1 and 2 to prepare an accrual basis income statement for Mike Stammer for the year ended June 30, 1995.
4. Add or subtract whichever adjustments to the cash income statement are necessary to reconcile Mike's $50,400 "income" to your figure.
5. Compare the two income statements. Why might Mike Stammer (or others using his financial information) prefer to use the cash basis of accounting? Why might he (or others) prefer the accrual basis?

PROBLEM 7.14 Write adjusting journal entries

Write an adjusting journal entry, if required, for each of the following items, which have been encountered during preparation of Ajax Sales Inc.'s January 31, 1995, financial statements.

1. A pile of sales invoices totalling $3,124 has yet to be recorded.
2. A customer had paid a deposit of $500 on a special order, which has not yet arrived. The deposit was included in the sales amount for the day it was paid.
3. The company has a $123,000 bank loan owing. Interest at 8% was last paid 23 days before the end of the year.
4. The year-end inventory count showed that goods costing $87,943 were on hand. The inventory account (perpetual system) showed a balance of $89,221 on the same day.

5. At the end of January, the account for advances to employees for travel expenses had a balance of $3,200. Expense accounts received after that date showed that employees had spent $1,823 of this by the end of January.
6. The credit manager decided to write off some hopeless accounts receivable totalling $320.
7. After a study of the company's employee pensions, it was decided that an additional $38,940 should be accrued for pensions earned during the year. This amount would be paid to the pension fund trustee in March 1995.
8. A court case involving another company showed that one of the company's patents was worthless, so management decided to write the patent off. It was on the accounts at a cost of $74,500 and there was accumulated amortization of $42,100 against it.
9. A search of cheque payments during February turned up $5,430 of payments that related to expenses incurred before the end of January.
10. The board of directors declared a $150,000 dividend January 25, to be paid in mid-February 1995.

PROBLEM 7.15 Adjusting journal entries

The accountant for Chewie Crusts Ltd., a bakery specializing in pizza crusts for the fast-food trade, is working on the year-end accounting for the company. For each item below, decide what (if anything) needs to be done and prepare any journal entry needed to implement your decision. Use whatever account titles you like, but be clear where on the statements the accounts would be located and write clear explanations for your entries. This is the company's first year of existence.

1. The company paid $1,120 for cleaning and office supplies, all of which have been expensed. The accountant discovered that another $114 is owing but not recorded and that supplies costing $382 are still on hand and usable at the end of the year.
2. The company's sales are all on credit because its customers are restaurants, stores, and institutions, such as hospitals. All cash collections have been recorded as sales revenue. The accountant added up the customers' bills still not collected and got a total of $11,621.
3. All purchases of flour and other raw materials have been expensed, and there is no significant inventory of finished products at the end of the year because each night's production is shipped in the morning to ensure maximum freshness. However, usable raw materials costing $6,210 are on hand at the end of the year.
4. Purchases of small tools and parts (still on hand) totalling $238 were charged to expenses during the year.
5. The accountant found an unpaid invoice for $900 for advertising services on behalf of the company. The advertising campaign had been planned and advertising contracts signed before the year end, but the campaign took place just after the year end.
6. The president of the company suggested that $2,316 directly spent on repairs and maintenance, plus 50% to allow for heat, light, and other costs incurred during the repairs, be capitalized to recognize the creation of valuable equipment and fixtures. This is unusual for the company, but the repairs were so

good that the useful life of the assets involved had been extended by several years more than expected originally.

7. Employees are paid just after the end of each week. At the end of the year, employees were owed $1,802, and tax and other deductions of $481 still had to be remitted on these unpaid wages.
8. All payments on the company's building mortgage had been made on time. Since the last payment, $187 of mortgage interest (the accountant's estimate) had accumulated, but the next regular payment was not due for ten days.
9. The company's board of directors declared a dividend of $14,000 to shareholders. The board meeting to declare the dividend was held three days before the year end, but the dividend was explicitly not to be paid until two months after the year end.
10. The general manager's employment contract specifies that at the end of the third month of each year, she is to be paid a bonus of 8% of the company's pre-tax and pre-bonus income. The accountant calculated the first year's pre-tax income, after all accruals and adjustments, to be $38,226.

PROBLEM 7.16 Likely revenue recognition policies for various cases

When is a sale a sale? When does the accounting system recognize revenue as having been earned? Indicate what you think would be the revenue recognition policy in each of the following cases. Remember to think of whether the general criteria for revenue recognition have been met, the concept of a "critical event" for revenues recognized all at once, and the proportionate recognition that is available for revenue earned over several accounting periods.

a. HotCaf's coffee counter (from Chapter 6);
b. Alcatraz Development Inc.'s housing subdivisions in eastern cities;
c. Northwestern Utilities' sales of natural gas to businesses and residences;
d. *Maclean's* magazine subscription sales;
e. The Stratford Festival's ticket sales;
f. The Big Warehouse's instalment sales of appliances and furniture;
g. Bow Valley Resource Services Ltd.'s revenue from drilling oil wells on others' property;
h. Imperial Oil's revenue from oil production on its own land;
i. Potter Henny Glover's revenue from sales of pottery on consignment through local craft shops;
j. CBC-TV's revenues from advertising on sports programs;
k. Fiberglas Canada's revenues from sales of manufactured products;
l. Computer Wizard Shop's sales of microcomputer software;
m. Eaton's revenue from clothing sales (some people pay cash; some charge on their Eaton's cards; some charge on other credit cards; and some return their purchases after deciding they don't like them);
n. Your university or college's revenue from student tuition fees;
o. The Canadian Red Cross's revenues from donations;
p. Western Greenhouses's revenues from contract landscaping work for homeowners.

PROBLEM 7.17 Choose suitable revenue recognition policies

In each of the following independent cases below, indicate when you think the company in question should recognize revenue. Support your decision with reference to the generally accepted criteria for revenue recognition.

a. Alaska Gold Co. mines and refines gold. The company waits to sell the gold until it feels the market price is favourable. The company can, if it wishes, sell its entire inventory of gold at any time at the prevailing market price.
b. Crazy Freddie sells cheap, ugly furniture on the instalment plan. His customers take delivery of the furniture after making a down payment. In the course of the past year, Crazy Freddie has had to repossess over 50% of the furniture that he sold, due to customers defaulting on payments.
c. Tom and Mark's Construction Co. undertakes long-term construction contracts. The company only accepts contracts that will pay a fixed fee. Costs can be estimated with reasonable accuracy, and there has never been a problem collecting from customers.
d. Cecily Cedric Co. is a toy manufacturer, producing toys that are shipped to various retail customers upon receipt of their purchase order. Sales are billed after shipment. The company estimates that approximately 2% of credit sales prove to be uncollectible.

PROBLEM 7.18 Interpret expense recognition footnotes

Read the following excerpts from past annual reports, and explain what is going on and why the companies have the policies described.

Key Anarcon Mines Limited, 1983
Development and administrative expenditures amounting to $3,417,537 at December 31, 1983, have been deferred with the intention they be amortized by charges against income from future mining operations. Realization of this income is dependent on the known ore body, and the additional reserves which may be developed...becoming economic within the framework of metallurgical recoveries, metal prices, and other operating costs.

Bow Valley Resource Services Ltd., 1983
Costs relating to specific development projects that...are technically feasible and have a clearly defined future market are capitalized [then] amortized over periods not exceeding the [project's] estimated revenue-generating life...If a project is subsequently determined not...feasible or commercially viable...the capitalized costs are [then] charged to income.

PROBLEM 7.19 Recommend revenue and expense recognition policy

Gary Slapstick Promotions Inc. (G.S.P.I.) acquired the rights to use the names of a number of hockey players on life-sized stuffed dolls it purchases from a toy manufacturer. The dolls are marketed through mail-order advertisements in the TV-listings inserts of large newspapers. When an order is received (with a money order, cheque, or credit card number), G.S.P.I. contacts the toy manufacturer. The toy manufacturer is responsible for manufacturing and shipping the doll to the lucky boy or girl. G.S.P.I. is notified at the time of shipment. The customer has the option of returning the doll within two weeks of the day it is received. G.S.P.I. pays the toy manufacturer within 30 days after delivery. Response to the dolls this Christmas has been overwhelming. In fact, the toy manufacturer is working extra shifts to try and keep up with the demand.

1. Identify three points in time that G.S.P.I. could recognize revenue on the dolls. Which would you recommend? Why?
2. Identify two different points in time that the toy manufacturer could recognize revenue on the dolls.
3. Discuss how G.S.P.I. should account for its payments to hockey players for the right to use their names. (Assume that each player is paid a lump sum initially and a royalty on each doll sold that uses his name.)

PROBLEM 7.20 Builder's revenues, expenses, and assets

A builder formed a construction company in September. After several months' effort, the company completed a residence at a total cost of $70,000 and advertised it for sale. By December 31, the company had received three offers: one of $78,000 cash; another of $83,000, to be paid in monthly instalments over 20 years at 10% annual interest; and another of $50,000 cash plus a residential lot worth $31,000. The builder decided to wait for a higher offer, which he seemed certain to get.

1. What was the amount of the construction company's revenue for the year?
2. How much were its expenses?
3. In what form, if any, were its assets on December 31?
4. Taking each offer separately, assume the offers were accepted and calculate the amount of revenue and expense for the four-month period ended December 31 in each case. Assume that for each situation the sale closed December 26.

PROBLEM 7.21 Franchise revenue amounts and policies

Pickin Chicken Inc. (PC) and Country Delight Ltd. (CD) both sell franchises for their chicken restaurants. The purchaser of the franchise (the franchisee) receives the right to use PC's and CD's products and benefit from national training and advertising programs for ten years. The buyers agree to pay $50,000 for a franchise. Of this amount, $20,000 is paid upon signing the agreement and the remainder is payable in five equal annual instalments of $6,000 each.

Pickin Chicken recognizes all franchise revenue when franchise agreements are signed. Country Delight recognizes franchise revenue as cash is received. In 1993 the companies each sold eight franchises. In 1994 they each sold five. In 1995 and 1996 neither company sold a franchise.

1. Determine the amount of franchise revenue recognized by each company in 1993, 1994, 1995, and 1996.
2. Do you think that revenue should be recognized when the franchise agreement is signed, when cash is received, or over the life of the franchise agreement? Why? Fully support your answer.

PROBLEM 7.22 Calculate bad debt allowance and expense

Windhook Technologies Ltd. has been having difficulty collecting its accounts receivable. For the year 1995, the company made provisions for bad debts of $43,000, bringing the balance in the allowance for doubtful accounts to $71,000. At the end of 1995, accounts receivable equalled $415,000. When the year-end audit was being done, it was decided that a further $54,000 of accounts receivable were doubtful and that $36,000 of accounts receivable previously deemed doubtful should be written off altogether.

Calculate the following:

a. Bad debts expense for 1995;

b. Allowance for doubtful accounts at the end of 1995;

c. Estimated collectible value of accounts receivable at the end of 1995.

PROBLEM 7.23 Discuss ways of accounting for bad debt risk

When revenue for credit (noncash) sales is recognized by debiting accounts receivable and crediting revenue, there is clearly a risk (a business risk) that some of the customers will not pay for the goods or services they have received. Discuss the advantages and disadvantages of each of the ways of accounting for this risk outlined below.

1. Wait until there is clear evidence that the receivable will not be collected and then just write it off to expense by crediting accounts receivable and debiting bad debts expense.
2. When accounts begin to look doubtful, either because of specific evidence or because statistical analysis shows a decline in likelihood of collectibility of accounts as they get older, create an allowance against the receivable asset (reducing it to the estimated collectible value) by crediting allowance for doubtful accounts and debiting bad debts expense. When specific accounts clearly have become uncollectible, they can then be eliminated from the accounts by crediting accounts receivable and debiting the allowance.
3. As credit sales are made, estimate the risk being taken (for example, by statistical analysis of collection patterns) and create an immediate recognition of the risk by crediting allowance for doubtful accounts and debiting bad debts expense. When specific accounts clearly have become uncollectible, they can be eliminated from the accounts as in Question 2.

PROBLEM 7.24 Are deferred income taxes funds owing to governments?

A number of years ago, considerable controversy was created when a Canadian political party referred to companies with deferred tax liabilities showing on their balance sheets as "corporate welfare bums." It was contended that these deferred tax liabilities represented billions of dollars of unpaid taxes owing to the federal and provincial governments of Canada by corporations, which would likely never be collected.

Discuss the contention.

PROBLEM 7.25 Explain the purpose and nature of deferred tax accounts

George picked up the financial statements of a company he owns shares in and noticed the following two accounts, which he didn't understand:

Deferred portion of income tax expense	$19,749,200
Deferred income tax liability	$86,293,500

Explain to George the purpose of deferred income tax accounting and what the two figures he didn't understand mean.

PROBLEM 7.26 Journal entry for income tax payable and deferred tax

For 1995, Great World Air Inc. had income before income tax of $23,960 (in thousands of dollars). Other 1995 figures, also in thousands of dollars, were: amortization expense, $34,211; nondeductible expense, $814; and capital cost allowance, $37,578. The company's income tax rate for 1995 was 36%.

1. Write a journal entry to record the company's 1995 income tax expense. Show your calculations.
2. Based on your answer to Question 1, what was the company's net income for 1995?

PROBLEM 7.27 Journal entry to correct tax accounts

(Challenging) The accountant for Zorp Corp. recorded the company's 1996 income tax payable as 30% of the $142,000 income before income tax, according to the income statement. But, because 1996 capital cost allowance was larger than 1996 amortization, taxable income was only $116,000. Also, the income tax rate should have been 25%.

Record a journal entry to correct the accountant's work. Show your calculations.

PROBLEM 7.28 Conversion from cash to accrual basis

(Challenging) Temporary Help Ltd. is a company offering specialized personal services (for example, secretarial assistance, delivery of advertising, errands, shopping for gifts). The company's accounts have been kept on a cash basis, but its banker has asked that the accounting be changed to the accrual basis. Income for 1995 on the cash basis was $147,000. Using the following figures (note the order of the years), calculate the company's 1995 income on the accrual basis:

	Assets		Liabilities	
	1995	**1994**	**1995**	**1994**
Cash basis:				
Current	$ 98,000	$ 56,000	$35,000	$35,000
Noncurrent	—	—	—	—
Accrual basis:				
Current	182,000	112,000	70,000	49,000
Noncurrent	21,000	28,000	14,000	—

PROBLEM 7.29 Accounting vs. economic view of revenue

(Challenging) An economist might argue that revenue is created or earned continuously by a wide variety of the firm's activities (such as production, sales, delivery), yet the accountant in a typical case selects only one of these steps (the "critical event") to signal the time at which all revenues are to be recognized.

a. Assuming that the economist's view is correct, under what circumstances would the accountant's method lead to an undistorted measure of periodic income? In other words, under what conditions will the opinion that income is continuously earned agree with income as determined by accountants?
b. What are the obstacles to the practical implementation of the economist's view as the basis for accounting income determination?

PROBLEM 7.30 Explain accrual concepts to a business person

(Challenging) A business person you know has just received the financial statements of a company in which that person owns shares. Answer the following questions asked by the person. Try to answer without jargon and use examples that will make your answers clear.

1. I've been told that these accrual accounting numbers are "mainly a matter of timing." What does that mean?
2. I see the company has a note in its financial statements describing its "revenue recognition" method. Why would I want to know that?
3. I know from my business experience that sometimes you collect cash sooner or later than you expect. Customers may have cash, or not, for all sorts of reasons that have nothing to do with you. I understand that accrual accounting takes this into account so that it doesn't matter when cash is collected, you get the same revenue figure anyway. Is this true?
4. I understand that accountants try to be sure that revenues and expenses "match" each other so that the income you get by subtracting expenses from revenues makes sense. Seems quite appropriate. But what effect, if any, does this matching procedure have on the balance sheet figures?

PROBLEM 7.31 Is accrual accounting a tool of management?

(Challenging) A professor said recently that accrual accounting was invented because managers wanted something they could manipulate to their own purposes more than was possible with transactions-based, cash-based data. Accrual accounting, the professor continued, is a tool of management and has driven accounting away from the goal of producing information that is representative of any real phenomena and toward fanciful reports largely devoid of real meaning.

1. What do you think of the professor's views? Are there any better reasons for accrual accounting?
2. The professor said that academics and practitioners tend to differ in their responses to his views. What do you think the differences would be?
3. If the professor is right, what does that say about the dictum that management bears the responsibility for providing financial information about an enterprise?

PROBLEM 7.32 Income on various revenue recognition bases

(Challenging) The Latanae Company produces a single product at a cost of $6 each, all of which is paid in cash when the unit is produced. Selling expenses of $3 a unit are paid at the time of shipment. The sale price is $10 a unit; all sales are on account. No customer defaults are expected, and no costs are incurred at the time of collection.

During 1994, the company produced 100,000 units, shipped 76,000 units, and collected $600,000 from customers. During 1995, it produced 80,000 units, shipped 90,000 units, and collected $950,000 from customers.

1. Ignoring income tax for now, determine the amount of income that would be reported for each of these two years,
   a. If revenue and expense are recognized at the time of production.
   b. If revenue and expense are recognized at the time of shipment.
   c. If revenue and expense are recognized at the time of collection.
2. Would the asset total shown on the December 31, 1995, balance sheet be affected by the choice among the three recognition bases used in Question 1? What would be the amount of any such difference?
3. Re-do Question 1, assuming that the company's income tax rate is 30%.

PROBLEM 7.33 Cost capitalization, rental income issues

(Challenging) A company stops accumulating costs (capitalizing) in a long-term asset account (for example, a building asset), and begins charging expenditures to expense and computing amortization expense on the asset when the asset is put into service and begins to earn revenue. This is usually fairly straightforward, but consider the following.

A company owns an office building that is scheduled to be completely finished on September 1, 1995. As of July 1, 1995, construction costs totalled $3,000,000, including interest on construction financing of $150,000 ($10,000 from April 1, 1995, to July 1, 1995). The first tenant moved in on April 1, 1995, followed by several others. At July 1, 1995, approximately 40% of the space had been rented. Projections indicate that 70% of the office space needs to be rented before the building will be profitable. Unfortunately, the vacancy rate is extremely high for office space in this area of town due to a recent economic downturn. Average occupancy is 60% in other office buildings nearby, with no expectation of improvement for at least three years. To date, rent of $50,000 has been paid by the tenants, in addition to expenses amounting to $10,000 to reimburse the company for some of the utilities, janitorial, and other common-area costs of the building that total $25,000 from April 1 to July 1, 1995. The rental revenue, common-area costs, and common-area cost reimbursements have been netted and capitalized, reducing the construction costs to date by $35,000 in total ($50,000 + $10,000 – $25,000).

As well, the construction costs to date include $100,000 paid to these tenants by the company to cover some of their leasehold improvements (alterations the tenants had to make to their office space to make it suitable for their use—interior walls, painting, carpeting). These payments to the tenants were inducements to lure them away from their old premises in other nearby buildings and into signing long-term rental agreements (five years) with the company.

1. Is the company "correct" in capitalizing some or all of the above items? Why or why not?

2. When might be an appropriate time to record cash receipts and disbursements related strictly to rental activity as income statement items, rather than balance sheet items (that is, to recognize revenues and expenses)?

PROBLEM 7.34 Real company's revenue, expense recognition

(Challenging)

Using the financial statements of any company you are interested in, or, instead, those of The North West Company Inc. at the end of this book, write a comprehensive review of the company's revenue and expense recognition policies. Cover such points as:

a. What the nature of the company's business is and how it earns its revenue and incurs its expenses;
b. What the company's financial statements and notes disclose about its important revenue and expense recognition policies;
c. Based on (a) and (b) and on your own thinking about the company, the appropriateness of the company's revenue and expense policies and what questions or concerns you have about them;
d. What the company's cash flow statement (SCFP) tells you about how close the company's accrual net income is to cash income.

PROBLEM 7.35 Comprehensive revenue and expense issues

(Challenging)

CompCom Inc. is engaged in developing a computerized scheduling, shipping, maintenance, and operations system for the North American trucking industry, which has been "loosened up" by deregulation.

CompCom has spent the last five years conducting systems development work and this year (ended November 30, 1995) sold its first systems. Initial funding of $2,500,000 came from the founder, who invested $1,250,000 for shares and $1,250,000 in the form of a loan. In the past, the company was not very concerned about accounting issues and financial statements, but now it is seeking external financing and is required to prepare financial statements to obtain this financing.

It is now December 19, 1995. The president is very concerned about how the company's results for the year ended November 30, 1995, will appear to investors. He understands that GAAP allow choices to be made regarding accounting policies and is interested in the choices available for the following two issues:

- Costs totalling $2,500,000 have been incurred evenly over the last five years in developing systems. Of these costs, $1,000,000 relate to failed efforts on a system that was found this year to be unmarketable. The rest of the costs are attributable to the development of a system that is currently being sold. The company expects to be able to sell the system for five years before it becomes technologically obsolete, becoming more obsolete (therefore, harder to market) as the five years progress. Right now, the company anticipates selling the system as follows:

Fiscal year ended Nov. 30, 1995	2 systems already sold
Fiscal year ended Nov. 30, 1996	4 systems expected to be sold
Fiscal year ended Nov. 30, 1997	3 systems expected to be sold
Fiscal year ended Nov. 30, 1998	2 systems expected to be sold
Fiscal year ended Nov. 30, 1999	1 system expected to be sold

◆ Sales commenced in the last half of 1995. Each sales contract is priced to provide a $250,000 margin over estimated contract costs. Sales arise as follows: a contract is negotiated covering the services to be provided; a nonreturnable deposit of 10% of the negotiated price is required before work commences; as work continues, regular billings are made at specific stages of completion of the system. To November 30, 1995, the following sales have occurred:

Sold to	Total Contract Price	Deposit	Contract Billings So Far	Cash Rec'd Including Deposit	Completed So Far	Cash Paid for Costs So Far
Co. A	$2,000,000	$200,000	$750,000	$600,000	40%	$500,000
Co. B	2,250,000	225,000	Nil	225,000	Nil	Nil
	$4,250,000	$425,000	$750,000	$825,000		$500,000

Prior to making any accounting decisions involved in the above issues, the company's account balances at November 30, 1995, are:

	Debit	Credit
Cash	$ 325,000	
Contract costs paid	500,000	
Contract receipts		$ 825,000
Development costs	2,500,000	
Share capital		1,250,000
Shareholder loan		1,250,000
	$3,325,000	$3,325,000

The following additional information is relevant:

a. All but $200,000 of the costs to date have been paid in cash, and the only cash inflow this year has been from contract deposits and billings.

b. The company is still in the development stage and is not required to pay income tax for 1995 or prior years.

c. The founding shareholder's loan is interest-free and due on demand, but the shareholder has signed a letter confirming that he will not withdraw the funds over the course of the next year.

Given all of the above information, answer the following:

1. Suggest two different methods of recognizing revenue from sales of the systems. (No calculations are needed—just describe the methods.)
2. Choose a revenue recognition method for CompCom and state why you prefer it.
3. Based on the method you chose in Question 1, calculate the company's revenue and contract cost expense for the year ended November 30, 1995.

4. The president wants to capitalize the development costs. How much would you recommend be capitalized, and why?
5. Explain to the president why amortization of any such development cost asset is necessary.
6. Choose a method of amortizing the development cost asset that makes sense to you and calculate the amortization expense for 1995 and the accumulated amortization at November 30, 1995.
7. Based on your answers to the previous parts, prepare an income statement and statement of retained earnings for 1995 and a balance sheet as at November 30, 1995, with appropriate notes.
8. If you're not exhausted, also prepare a statement of changes in financial position for 1995.

CASE 7A Revenue and expense recognition in the computer industry

With the help of the article "How IBM played the numbers game" from *The Globe and Mail,* discuss the problems of accounting for revenues and expenses in the volatile computer industry, where change is constant and the future is especially hard to predict.

HOW IBM PLAYED THE NUMBERS GAME

Bold accounting called "prudent"

To all outward appearances, International Business Machines Corp. ran into trouble with startling speed.

Even its harshest critics have been stunned by its nearly $5-billion (U.S.) of losses last year, its first layoffs in half a century and an unprecedented purge of top executives. Its stock has lost more than $70-billion in market value since it peaked in 1987. And the crisis has sparked a once unthinkable move: IBM has turned to an outsider, Louis Gerstner, to rescue it.

Now, considerable evidence suggests that IBM may have helped delay its day of reckoning with some surprisingly aggressive accounting moves. The moves didn't violate any laws or cause the company's fundamental business problems. Some, although not all, of the moves were fully disclosed to the public.

But some finance experts say that just as IBM's business started to sour, its accounting became markedly less conservative. "Since the mid–1980s, IBM has been borrowing from the future to bolster today's profits," says Thornton O'glove, a frequently critical San Francisco accounting expert and former publisher of the Quality of Earnings newsletter.

Although IBM doesn't dispute any of the facts about the accounting changes, it takes strong issue with the conclusion by some experts that it was stretching to makes its numbers look better, while pushing possible bad news into the future.

In a 22-page response to questions, it writes: "When our accounting policies and practices are compared with others in our industry or other major corporations, they cannot be shown, even with perfect hindsight, to be other than thoughtful and prudent."

The evidence of the aggressive accounting comes on several fronts.:

IBM's former chief outside auditor, Price Waterhouse's Donald Chandler, wrote IBM a blistering 20-point memo in November, 1988, suggesting the company was reporting revenue it might never get. For example, he criticized IBM for booking revenue when its products were shipped to dealers who could return them and sometimes even to its own warehouses—a far more aggressive approach than many companies take.

IBM calls the Chandler memo part of the normal give-and-take between a company and an auditor with a flair for peppery language. The company says it has improved its procedures in response to some of his concerns but hasn't changed its general accounting philosophy and many of the practices at issue.

Mr. Chandler, who retired last year, at first declined to comment when reached at home. Later, in a statement released by IBM, he said his work with the company was "totally open and frank." Of his specific criticisms, he cautioned, "it's absolutely vital that they not be taken out of context." He said every "significant" matter he raised was "satisfactorily resolved" and noted that he consistently blessed IBM's financial statements with clean audit opinions.

In his memo to Michael Van Vranken, then IBM's controller, Mr. Chandler's fundamental complaint was that IBM was rushing to record revenue on its books as soon as it shipped a product, even for sales with escape hatches that could reduce the revenue IBM ultimately received.

IBM defends its continuing practice of booking revenue as soon as it ships a product and says it makes allowances for returns. "The earnings process is substantially complete upon shipment," IBM contends, adding: "Price Waterhouse was, and continues to be, in full agreement." Price Waterhouse's current lead partner for auditing IBM, Kenneth Doyle, says IBM's terms with dealers weren't as lenient as Mr. Chandler believed.

IBM isn't the only company that books revenue upon shipment. But many of its high-tech rivals are more conservative.

"We just don't put it on the floor, then say we can book it," says a spokesman for Amdahl Corp., IBM's leading rival in mainframe computers. "It has to be turned over by our field engineering group. They have to check the machine out, and make sure it's up and running. That's the point we actually take credit for the revenue."

IBM concedes that it sometimes books revenue when it ships a product to its own warehouses—for "temporary in-transit storage" en route to a customer. But it says it does so only when "installation at the customer" is "expected within 30 days." In part because of the Chandler memo, IBM says it cut that period from 45 days previously.

Mr. Chandler also found "very troubling" IBM's handling of "price protection"—its term for assuring customers that if it later cut prices, they would owe only the reduced price. He said IBM was booking full revenue as soon as it shipped its products despite "ample evidence" that it would later cut prices and thus receive less money. IBM says Mr. Chandler wasn't giving it enough credit for its broad allowance for "revenue adjustments," which was "based on historical experience and was applied to all revenue."

In 1982, IBM asked Merrill Lynch to perform a rare, inventive piece of financial surgery that directly affected its profits, although few shareholders or analysts ever heard of it. Experts say that in the arcane area of lease financing, IBM exploited accounting rules in a troubling way.

When companies lease out equipment, they can account for it as an "operating" or a "sales-type" lease. An operating lease is conservative; revenues go on the books as they actually flow in each year. A sales-type lease is more liberal; all the revenue that will ever come in is recorded in the first year.

To restrain revenue-hungry companies, the Financial Accounting Standards Board has extensive rules, running more than 100 pages, about sales-type leases. IBM's accountants zeroed in on a formula in paragraph 7D: add up all the lease payments, plus the value of the computer when the lease expires. If the total is 90 per cent of the computer's value today, the lease can be considered a sales-type one.

In the hotly competitive market, IBM was offering terms that didn't add up to the 90-per-cent mark. Merrill's solution: it sold IBM "7D insurance" guaranteeing a certain value of the computer at the end of the lease—enough to push IBM over 90 per cent.

IBM says its deal with Merrill lasted until 1990. Today, IBM uses an offshore 7D insurer it won't identify. Price Waterhouse's Mr. Doyle won't say how much IBM revenue is affected by 7D insurance, but he calls it "not material"—accounting parlance for 5 per cent of revenue or less.

In hindsight, 1984 was almost precisely when the computer industry dynamics began to turn against IBM. The personal computer boom was just starting to erode the role of IBM's mighty mainframes in office work. IBM's return on equity hit a peak of 26.5 per cent that year—before plunging to 9.6 per cent by 1989 and disappearing amid losses in 1991 and 1992.

Footnotes in IBM's 1984 annual report show that was when it began overhauling its accounting tactics to spread the costs of factories and other investments far into the future, instead of recording them in the short term. IBM also reduced the estimated cost of its retirement plans, which then would take a smaller chunk out of each year's earnings.

The accounting changes themselves were standard practice at many companies and hardly a secret; IBM's annual report disclosed them.

Mr. O'glove, the auditing expert, calculates that in 1984, the accounting changes were responsible for 26 per cent of IBM's profit gain. That year, profit surged $1.73 a share to $10.77; so that 26 per cent amounts to 45 cents a share. In 1985, profit fell 10 cents a share, but without the accounting changes, Mr. O'glove says, it would have dropped 86 cents.

"It was just the beginning of the slide that many other financial analysts missed in the mid- and late-1980s because they continued to believe that IBM was following conservative accounting as it did in the early part of the decade."

Although IBM has never specified how much the accounting changes affected its earnings, it says Mr. O'glove's numbers are "way off." It also cites a 1985 accountants' survey showing that 70 per cent of U.S. companies were spreading investment costs into the future, just as IBM did. And as for lowering its retirement plan costs, IBM says its financial advisers predicted the plans' invested assets would start earning a higher return—and thus the cost to the company would drop. "We strongly disagree that our actions were anything but appropriate."

SOURCE: M.W. MILLER AND L. BERTON, "HOW IBM PLAYED THE NUMBERS GAME," *THE GLOBE AND MAIL*, APRIL 10, 1993, B1, B4 (FROM *THE WALL STREET JOURNAL*. REPRINTED BY PERMISSION OF *THE WALL STREET JOURNAL*

CASE 7B Revenue and expense recognition by a restauranteur

Using the following article, "Scott's serves up lean profit" from *The Globe and Mail*, discuss the problems of recognizing revenues and expenses in the volatile restaurant and fast-food industry. Consider Scott's Hospitality Inc.'s attempt to diversify out of that industry in your discussion.

SCOTT'S SERVES UP LEAN PROFIT

$31-million writedown hurts fast-food, hotel and transportation conglomerate

At last year's lavish annual meeting of Scott's Hospitality Inc., shareholders stuffed themselves with mounds of Chinese food, pizza and fried chicken. Yesterday, they sipped coffee and nibbled on muffins.

"We didn't have much cause for celebration this year," chairman Giles Meikle said in explaining the company's new-found austerity.

Until recently, shareholders of the fast-food, hotel and transportation conglomerate could pretty much count on two things: Steadily rising profit, and a filling lunch once a year. Now, neither is assured.

Toronto-based Scott's scraped by with a profit of $7,000 in fiscal 1993 after a writedown of $31.3-million for discontinued operations. Black's Photography chain was sold to Fuji Photo Film Canada Inc. in June, and Scott's has earmarked a number of smaller, non-strategic assets for sale.

While shedding operations to reduce debt, Scott's has curtailed spending as it seeks to emerge from the recession as a leaner, more focused company. It projects capital expenditures of just $80-million this year, down from a peak of $217-million in 1991 and $139.3-million last year.

"Scott's is determined to live within its means," said John Lacey, president and chief executive of the company that dishes up more than 250,000 meals a day through its stable of fast-food restaurants. They include Manchu Wok in North America, Kentucky Fried Chicken in Canada and Perfect Pizza in Britain.

With fast-food sales hurt by intense competition and heavy discounting, Scott's is fighting back by introducing one-number home delivery at its three major chains and aggressively marketing new products. At KFC, a revitalization program is under way that will see the addition of more cash registers, extra seating and drive-thrus at some locations.

Scott's KFC chain will soon begin market research for a non-fried chicken, Rotisserie Gold, launched recently in the United States and targeted at health-conscious consumers. Management can only hope it is a bigger success than Caribbean chicken, which was pulled from stores this year.

Meanwhile, Manchu Wok is experiencing growing pains. Though still in its infancy, the Chinese food chain was forced to close a small number of U.S. restaurants last year, resulting in a $1.3-million provision. Potential franchisees aren't exactly beating down the door. Many are unable to get start-up loans, according to Scott's, which has joined with a U.S. bank to develop a financing package for would-be restaurateurs.

Still, there are signs that the current year is shaping up better for Scott's than the one just passed. Results released yesterday show that first-quarter sales rose to $203-million from $191.6-million a year earlier—a 6-per-cent gain. Profit for the three months to July 31 was ahead 11 per cent to $8.7-million from $7.9-million.

Leading the recovery is Scott's hotel business in Britain, which posted an operating profit of $1.6-million after losing $1.9-million in the year-earlier first quarter. Hotel revenue edged up to $27.2-million from $26.2-million, as occupancy rates rose.

All but two of Scott's businesses reported higher operating earnings. The exceptions were Perfect Pizza, which absorbed start-up costs for the one-number delivery system, and the transportation division, which recorded lower gains on the sale of used buses.

While the company is constantly reviewing its operations for sale candidates, Mr. Lacey said Scott's would also entertain potential acquisitions, possibly in the hotel or transportation business.

SCOTT'S HOSPITALITY

Year to April 30	1993	1992
Sales, million	$785.3	$748.1
Profit, million	0	$ 53.3
Share profit	0	$ 0.90

Divisions (% of '92 sales):

Food services (50%): 400 Kentucky Fried Chicken restaurants in Central Canada
Manchu Wok restaurants in Canada and the United States
Perfect Pizza chain in Britain

Hotels (11%): 15 hotels in Britain

Transportation (25%): 6,000 school business in Canada and the United States

Photography (14%): Sold Black's 210-store chain

Share price on the TSE

Yesterday's close: $28, up $1; 52-week high: $30; 52-week low: $8

SOURCE: J. HEINZL, "SCOTT'S SERVES UP LEAN PROFIT," *THE GLOBE AND MAIL*, SEPTEMBER 9, 1993, B1.

CASE 7C Discuss accruals for health care costs and their effects.

In the United States, as in Canada, there has been great concern over health costs. Until 1993, most American companies provided health benefits to employees after their retirement, but did not show the expected costs of such benefits as liabilities or expenses. Beginning in 1993, companies providing such benefits were required by the Financial Accounting Standards Board to accrue expected costs, roughly by the following sort of journal entry:

CR Health Benefits Liability	Expected cost of promises made to current and past employees, taking uncertainties such as death rates and interest rates into account.
DR Health Benefits Expense	Expected cost of promises made this year.
DR Special Expense	Expected cost of promises made in past years (may be deducted from income all at once or bit by bit over several years: "amortized").

For some companies the expected cost of the promises is huge, in the billions of dollars, enough to produce huge losses in the 1993 income statement and even to wipe out most of retained earnings. Two effects of the FASB's attempts to improve accrual accounting for retirees' health care costs are apparent:

1. Many companies suffered huge losses in 1993 and/or will have large charges against income for years as they build up the liability year by year (amortize it);
2. Many companies are cutting back on their promises to employees for after-retirement health care to avoid such huge charges in the future, so the accounting standard is not just measuring the cost of health benefits, it is also changing them.

Discuss the issue of including accruals for such obligations as future health care costs in present financial statements, using as background the following article from Business Week, November 22, 1992.

HONEST BALANCE SHEETS, BROKEN PROMISES

Now that FASB requires retiree's health costs to be counted, companies are slashing them

Accounting rules, an abstract realm known to few, have introduced a harsh new reality into Clifford Davis' retirement. Navistar International Corp., where Davis worked as a maintenance man for 32 years, has long picked up the medical bills for its 40,000 pensioners. But starting Jan. 1, an accounting-rule change requires many large companies to include on their balance sheets immense sums for these even-more-costly health benefits.

So the Chicago-based truckmaker wants to cut back its two-decade-old plan, forcing Davis and fellow retirees on fixed incomes to fork over a hefty chunk of money for their coverage. Money-losing Navistar says it will go bust if former workers don't pick up part of their health costs. Yet Davis, who lives in a trailer in McCordsville, Ind., and is not yet 65, contends that he would have to shell out 25% of his monthly $1,400 pension check. Says Davis: "I can't afford to pay."

Lots of other corporations are axing or curtailing retiree health benefits (table), hoping to minimize the financial broadside of the so-called 106 rule, as well as curb runaway health costs in general. The rule was adopted in 1990 by the Financial Accounting Standards Board, the overseer of U.S. accounting criteria. As FASB sees it, failing to recognize the steadily growing health-care liability misleads investors about a company's financial condition.

Some large companies with strong balance sheets that can afford the hit are simply taking a one-time earnings and net worth write-off. But others, often less robust outfits like Navistar, are finding ways to circumvent the full force of 106 at their retirees' expense.

McDonnell Douglas Corp. is replacing its health plan for white-collar retirees by giving each a one-time payment of $18,000, using surplus pension-fund money. This will halve the St. Louis plane-maker's liability under the FASB rule, to $700 million. But after 1996, most bets are that payments to new retirees will be eliminated. According to a survey by the consulting firm A. Foster Higgins & Co., almost two-thirds of U.S. companies will have scaled back or eliminated the benefits by next year. "Employers are backpedaling like crazy from their commitments to workers," complains Clare Hushbeck, a senior analyst at the American Association of Retired Persons.

Certainly, retirees are the easiest target: They can't strike or quit for another job. Management "is picking on a group that can fight back the least," says Jerry Feldscher, a pensioner at Unisys Corp., which intends to phase out its plan entirely by 1995.

Retirees slammed with health-care cuts do have an option. Many are fighting back in court, although too few cases have been decided to discern a trend. Thus far, the key legal issue is how explicit the company has been in promising medical benefits. As a result, most employers steer away from cutting programs for union retirees because those plans are usually written into labor contracts. General Motors Corp., for instance, imposed 80% reimbursement limits on white-collar pensioners' bills but left United Auto Workers retirees alone.

MISCALCULATION. Navistar is bolder. Aiming to save 71% on retiree health-care costs, it tried to ram through the benefits reduction for both union and nonunion pensioners. But the UAW launched a legal counterstrike that threatened to tie the company up in court for years. As a compromise, the union and the truck manufacturer have agreed to reopen their contract now, a year before the pact expires, to negotiate health issues.

Retiree health plans first came into vogue in the late 1960s and early 1970s, after medicare was enacted. The idea was that the plans would take care of areas not covered by the federal medical program for the elderly: prescription drugs, home nursing care, and hospital stays beyond 90 days. "They thought the cost to supplement medicare would be small," says Richard Ostuw, a vice-president at consultant Towers Perrin Foster & Crosby. Wrong. For the past few years, the cost of corporate retiree health plans has been surging at a 15% annual clip.

Employers have two unappetizing choices under the new rule. They can either amortize the cost of the benefits over 20 years or take the entire charge to earnings in the first year. IBM took its $2.6 billion earnings hit in the first quarter of 1991. Analyst Philip C. Rueppel of Sanford C. Bernstein & Co. says Big Blue wanted to show that the rule "wouldn't be a big deal for them." Despite rocky times, IBM has not announced any benefit reductions.

But the most vulnerable companies are waiting until the last possible minute to reveal how they will stomach the 106 rule. Consider the desperate situation at GM: a potential charge ranging from $16 billion to $24 billion. The carmaker plans to say how it will handle the problem in February. Most analysts expect it to spread the shock over 20 years. After all, the higher figure would gobble up most of GM's net worth. The auto giant, which is mired in red ink as well as unfunded pension liabilities, could much more easily withstand the slow nibbling of amortization, at $800 million to $1.2 billion per year.

'SOFT NUMBER.' Saving the day, of course, would be some form of national health insurance to bridge the gaps left by medicare. President-elect Bill Clinton wants to widen the availability of health-care coverage, and the Democratic-controlled Congress seems receptive to the notion. Whether the legislative process will get to the plight of corporate retirees is an open question. Still, McDonnell Douglas hopes that by 1996, when its $18,000 subsidies to retirees will likely end, some government measure will be in place. "We don't know what will happen by then, but we can hope," says spokeswoman Barbara Anderson.

Meanwhile, the FASB rule will drag down corporate performance across the board in 1993. Shearson Lehman Brothers Inc. figures that without the rule, Standard & Poor's 500-stock-index companies would enjoy a 17% boost in earnings per share next year. With it, the S&P 500 may climb only 10%. On the plus side, no money for health-care liabilities need be immediately diverted from operations or capital spending. "This is the ultimate soft number," says Solomon Samson, S&P's managing director for corporate finance.

Eventually, though, affected companies must come up with cold cash. That's why, bean-counting contrivance or no, the rule has led companies to limit the liability by slicing retiree health plans. And that's how the abstract art of accounting has a real and painful impact.

HANDLING THE HEALTH-CARE HITS

Company	Charge to earnings Millions of dollars
General Motors Likely 20-year phase-in. Will announce plans in February. Has imposed health-care reimbursement limits for white-collar retirees.	$16,000–24,000
Hewlett-Packard Taking charge-off now. Looking at making retirees pick up more of medical tab in 1994	544
McDonnell Douglas Currently taking hit. Ending company subsidy of health care. Until 1996, nonunion retirees will get $18,000 each to fund care. Program may not continue after that	700
Navistar Phasing in charge-off over 20 years. Tried to make retirees pick up part of medical expenses, but union thwarted move in court. Now negotiating with union	2,500
Unisys Hit, being taken now, will be offset by tax savings. Phasing out subsidy of health plan by 1995, when nonunion retirees will have to foot their entire insurance bill	170

Data: Company Reports

NOTES

1. *Financial Reporting in Canada 1993* (Toronto: Canadian Institute of Chartered Accountants, 1993), 2.
2. United Dominion Industries, "Notes to Consolidated Financial Statements," in 1992 annual report.
3. *Financial Reporting in Canada 1993*, 90.
4. Ibid.
5. Ibid., 132.
6. Thomas R. Dyckman and Dale Morse, *Efficient Capital Markets and Accounting: A Critical Analysis*, 2nd ed. (Englewood Cliffs, N.J.: Prentice–Hall, 1986), 49–50.
7. W.H. Beaver, *Financial Reporting: An Accounting Revolution*, 2nd ed. (Englewood Cliffs, N.J.: Prentice–Hall, 1989), 8. Reprinted by permission of Prentice–Hall Inc.
8. Ibid., 105. Reprinted by permission of Prentice–Hall Inc.
9. Ibid., 105. Reprinted by permission of Prentice–Hall Inc.
10. P.A. Griffin, ed., *Usefulness to Investors and Creditors of Information Provided by Financial Reporting*, 2nd ed. (Stamford, Conn.: Financial Accounting Standards Board, 1987), 14. Copyright by Financial Accounting Standards Board, 401 Merritt 7, P.O. Box 5116, Norwalk, Connecticut, 06856–5116, U.S.A. Reprinted with permission. Copies of the document are available from the FASB.

Prelude to Financial Accounting Analysis

8.1 Chapter Overview

Previous chapters have developed an understanding of the financial statements and how they are prepared using transaction records and accrual accounting. Chapters 9 and 10 will describe techniques for the analysis of financial statements and of the effects of accounting policy choices made by management in preparing those statements. This chapter is a bridge to those analytical chapters. It expands the description of the roles of financial accounting so that analysis and policy choice may be understood in context. As has been emphasized already, financial accounting does not exist in a vacuum: it plays a role in the world—in fact it plays many roles. To help make learning about analysis and policy choice meaningful, this chapter adds some perspective and depth to understanding those roles.

In this chapter you'll learn:

Use concepts: how, broadly speaking, **stock markets** and other **capital markets** and financial **contracts** work, and the roles of information in these contexts;

Preparation concepts: the roles of accounting in meeting the demands of markets and contracts;

Preparation techniques: little new material here, enabling you, in this breathing space, to consolidate the understanding of preparation developed in previous chapters, but there is a short procedural review, and the continuing case provides a further illustration of pulling the financial statements together;

Use techniques: how to do **"what if" effects analysis** of accounting data, and how to do simple **discounted cash flow** or **present value** analysis.

8.2 The Social Setting of Financial Accounting

We already know that financial accounting has been shaped by the development of business and society and that it has many functions, including:

- It helps stock market investors decide whether to buy, sell, or hold shares of companies.
- It helps managers run enterprises on behalf of owners.
- It provides basic financial records for the purposes of internal control, insurance, and fraud prevention.

- It is used by governments in monitoring the actions of enterprises and in assessing taxes, such as income tax and sales taxes.

We could go on for some time listing major and minor functions of financial accounting. Whole books can be, and have been, written about each of the many functions! And, though we will focus on business firms because the ideas in this chapter are most fully worked out for them, don't forget that there are many other organizations that use, and are affected by, accounting.

The centre of our interest in this book, financial accounting for the enterprise, operates within and serves a complex social setting. It seeks to monitor and report on financial events initiated by or happening to the enterprise. These events come from and in turn affect the social setting, so the accounting is not passive: it tells us what is going on, but in doing so it affects our decisions and actions and, therefore, also affects what is going on.

The social setting is composed of many people. There are at least three parties directly concerned with what financial accounting says about the enterprise:

- the owners (shareholders of a corporation, for example);
- the managers, who are running the company on behalf of the owners; and
- the auditors, who are employed by the owners to evaluate the accounting reports presented by the managers.

These parties have relationships among each other, as well as with financial accounting.

- Managers, for example, may work for a company throughout their careers and, therefore, may have as much a feeling of ownership as do shareholders who may, through buying and selling shares on the stock market, be part-owners of the company for only a few months before moving on to another investment.
- In smaller companies, managers and owners may be the same people.
- The auditors are formally appointed by the owners, for example, at the annual shareholders' meeting, but they work with the managers on a day-to-day basis and may also offer advice on tax, accounting, and other topics of practical interest to managers, which are separate from the knowledge they use in their role as auditors.

In addition to these three central parties, and often hard to distinguish from them, is a host of other groups, companies, institutions, and parties interested in, or having an influence on, the company's financial accounting. Some of these others are:

- stock markets (where shareholders may buy and sell their shares);
- other capital markets, such as bond markets;
- stock-market regulators, such as stock exchanges and securities commissions;
- governments;
- employees;
- creditors;

- competitors;
- potential owners, creditors, employees or competitors;
- the accounting professions; and
- society in general.

As we have already seen, these parties do not share the same interest in the company's accounting and may even be in competition or conflict with each other. Most will be in the same country as the company and its management, but, increasingly, companies and other enterprises are operating internationally. So, the other groups interested in, and affecting, the company's financial accounting may be all over the planet.

8.3 CAPITAL MARKETS

STOCK MARKETS AND OTHER MARKETS FOR FINANCIAL CAPITAL

As business corporations developed, ownership rights in them were sold more and more broadly. The owners (shareholders) began to invest in several businesses at once and to buy and sell their shares from and to each other. To facilitate such buying and selling ("trading") of shares among **investors**, stock markets organized as **stock exchanges** developed. Today there are many such exchanges, including the major international ones in New York, London, Tokyo, Paris, and Toronto, as well as regional exchanges, such as those in Montreal, Vancouver, and Calgary. There are also "over-the-counter" markets and other alternatives to the major exchanges. Brokers, investment banks, market analysts, and others conduct, assist in, and advise on trading.

Trading goes on in more than just shares of companies. There is also trading of rights (using terms such as "warrant" or "options") to buy or sell shares in the future, to convert from one kind of share to another, to receive dividends, and to perform a wide variety of other future actions. New rights and financial instruments to convey such rights are being invented and traded all the time. Special markets have been developed for some of these, such as an options exchange in Chicago, but many are traded on regular stock exchanges. Corporate and government bonds are also traded, and there is such a variety of financial instruments that the distinction between ownership shares, creditorship bonds, and other rights and instruments is often blurred. For example, some bonds carry the right to be converted into shares at the option of the holder.

Many exchanges and over-the-counter markets use computerized trading systems for the listed companies whose shares and other **securities** (the usual general name for all these shares, bonds, and other financial instruments) trade on the exchanges and other markets, and, increasingly, investors can buy or sell securities pretty well 24 hours a day somewhere in the world. Taken together, all these exchanges, markets, and buying and selling activities are usually called **capital markets**. They include both share (stock) trading and trading of all the other securities that corporations and governments use to finance their assets.

It is important to emphasize that these markets operate quite separately from the organizations that initially issue the securities.

- For example, when a company decides to issue some bonds or shares, these securities are offered to the market(s), and the company receives the proceeds of the initial sale of them (less commissions to brokers and others involved). After that, however, the company ceases to be a direct participant. Investors buy the securities from each other and sell them to each other with no participation from the company.
- Investors may even act in the face of opposition from the company. For example, an investor may try to get enough shares together to get voting control of the company (a "takeover"). There is always a risk for so-called public companies (companies whose shares members of the public are able to buy or sell from each other without permission of the companies) that the markets will behave in ways the companies do not like.
- There are other examples of investors acting in ways not desired by the company. One is that the company may announce a new management team that it expects will improve the company's performance, only to see the price of its shares fall because the people buying and selling the shares do not like the new team and more people want to sell their shares than want to buy them, producing a fall in the share price.
- The markets often create new securities out of the ones the company initially issued and then trade those. For example, a share may carry the right to buy another share in the future. That right may be bought and sold separately on the market, so that you could own the share without any such right, or the right without any such share. You might even be able to buy an "option" consisting of a bet as to whether the share price will rise or fall in the next month or year, or buy a bet as to the overall price of the market's shares in the future. (Overall price measures, such as the Dow Jones Average or the Toronto Stock Exchange Index, are closely watched by many people.)

To prepare you for financial accounting analysis, five particular aspects of capital markets are outlined in this section. These are:

- The way securities are traded and security prices are established;
- The role of information (such as accounting reports) in such a market;
- The idea of a "risky return";
- The fact that markets are "aggregates"; and
- The concept of "market informational efficiency."

These aspects, among many others, are dealt with in **capital market theory**. This theory is very down-to-earth and incorporates much practical knowledge of how markets work. It has been a powerful impetus to economics, finance, and accounting research, and to changes in the way capital markets are operated.[1]

SECURITY TRADING AND SECURITY PRICES

Capital markets work about the same as any market. People trade (buy and sell) what they own for something else, usually money or a promise of it.

- There are people who own securities, such as shares of the Royal Bank of Canada. Some of these will be willing to sell their shares, if the price is right. If no one was willing to sell at any price, there would be no trading!

- There are people who don't own the securities, but who are willing to buy them from the above people, if the price is right. If no one was willing to buy at any price, there would be no trading! Let's call the first group the sellers and the second group the buyers. Suppose we had the following list of possible prices of Royal Bank shares:

Price	Sellers' Willingness to Sell	Buyers' Willingness to Buy
$31	Everyone would sell	No one would buy
$30	Most would sell	A few would buy
$29	Half would sell	Half would buy
$28	Some would sell	Most would buy
$27	None would sell	All would buy

You'll recognize from this hypothetical list of prices that we have a supply curve and a demand curve. Capital market prices are set by the interaction between those wanting to sell and those wanting to buy. At a price of $31, there'd be lots of shares for sale but no buyers; at a price of $27, there'd be lots of buyers but no sellers. Each day's market price for the shares is set by the balance between people willing to buy and people willing to sell:

- If there are more sellers than buyers, the price will fall, roughly down to the level at which there is an equal number of buyers and sellers (or at least, shares demanded and shares for sale); and
- If there are more buyers than sellers, the price will rise, roughly up to the level at which there is an equal number of sellers and buyers (or shares for sale and shares demanded).

In the above example, we'd expect the buyers and sellers to agree to trade (buy and sell) at a price around $29. So if we looked up the Royal Bank's shares in the newspaper's listing of Toronto Stock Exchange prices (the Royal Bank is listed on the TSE), we'd expect to see today's price to be about $29. But the daily price is set by the pressures of supply and demand, so it will vary depending on how many buyers and sellers make offers to buy or sell, and, therefore, it will vary around $29 as those pressures vary.

ROLE OF INFORMATION IN A CAPITAL MARKET

Why would the pressures of supply and demand vary? Broadly speaking, there are three kinds of reasons that are of interest in accounting analysis:

1. Noninformation-based trading. The circumstances of some buyers and sellers may require them to sell, or even buy, almost regardless of anything to do with the particular company whose shares are being traded. An owner of some shares may die and the estate may have to sell the shares in order to distribute the money to the beneficiaries of the owner's will. Or an "institutional" investor, such as a pension plan, may need some cash to pay pensions or other payments. Or a person may win a lottery and buy shares in a mutual fund (an investment consisting of a sample of shares of

many companies), so that the mutual fund in turn has to buy some shares. Therefore, some trading is likely to be occurring continuously for reasons of raising or spending available cash. Such trading is referred to as "liquidity trading."

2. General information-based trading. Companies whose shares are traded are part of a general economic system, and some general events may change people's views on the wisdom of investing in anything and so cause changes in all or most shares traded on an exchange. The share price of companies such as the Royal Bank may therefore change along with the rest. Examples of such general events are changes in national interest rates, announcements of trends such as inflation or consumer confidence, wars, illness or death of important people, and elections that change the party in power. If the Canadian federal government announced a new special tax on corporations' incomes, we might expect pretty well every company's share price to fall, including the Royal Bank's, because investors would see this as hurting every company's future incomes and, therefore, the returns investors would get from owning shares in any company. Market-wide price changes coming from the economic system are often called "systematic" effects. It is not clear theoretically why general information generates trades, because if all companies are affected, why bother to trade? Some of the trades may happen because investors think some companies will be hurt or helped more than others, and some investors may be getting out of that market altogether, such as by selling their shares and buying gold or real estate.
3. Specific information-based trading. Information specifically about the Royal Bank's future prospects may also cause changes in the willingness of people to buy or sell its shares. For example, if the bank announces that it is going to buy another bank, some people may like that idea (and, wanting to buy, increase the demand for shares) and other people may dislike the idea (and, wanting to sell, increase the supply of shares). If most people think the Royal's buying the other bank is a good idea, the share price will rise; if most people think it is a bad idea, the share price will fall. This phenomenon, in which share prices reflect people's evaluation of the impact or meaning of an event on the wisdom of holding a company's shares, is very important to understanding share prices and accounting's information role. We can say that the stock market "prices" the information, in that the change in the trading price of the shares (up, down, or not at all) is a measure of the value of the information to the market. Harking back to the accounting concepts of Chapter 5, we might say that in a stock market sense, *decision-relevant information* is *material* to the market if knowing about it changes, or would change, a security's market price or, perhaps, would prompt trading (buying and selling) even if the net effect on price were zero.

A great amount of analysis and research in accounting, finance, and economics uses this idea to measure the apparent value of all sorts of company-specific information, such as the bank's annual announcement of its net income ("earnings announcement"), announcements of changes in management, and news about other events initiated by or affecting the company. (Presuming that change in stock market prices is a measure of information value requires some faith in the market system as a social good and confidence in the market's ability to respond appropriately ["efficiently"] to information.)

RETURN AND RISK

The return you earn by owning a security (a share or bond) is the sum of:

- the cash you get (from dividends or interest payments) plus
- the change (hopefully an increase) in the market price of the security.

So, you get a cash return plus a holding gain or "capital gain" (or loss).

Capital market theory develops much of its power from analyzing the nature of these two kinds of returns, particularly the second kind. If the security you own varies in market price, that variation is, according to the theory, a measure of the *risk* from owning the security, since price could go up or down. Risk is calculated as the variance or standard deviation of the prices around the average price, or trend in average price, of that security. A risky security, therefore, is one whose price varies all over the place. As described above, a security's price may vary because the whole stock market or bond market is going up or down, or because of information specific to that security or to the company issuing the security. So, analytically, the risk is separated into:

- *systematic risk*: the portion of the security's variation that relates to or correlates with variation in the overall market; and
- *unsystematic risk*: the security's own residual variation not related to the market. "Beta" (a term coming from the mathematical model used to relate a firm's returns to those of the market overall) is a measure of the security's relationship to overall market variations. Securities can be classified according to this relationship: a *low beta* security's prices vary less than overall market prices do, while a *high beta* security's prices vary more than the market.

Risk can be controlled to some extent by holding a variety of securities having different betas. More will be said about this in the section Aggregates below.

A natural question at this point might be, "Does accounting information (especially income or cash flow) help to predict security prices and, therefore, risks and returns?" Market prices are pretty hard to predict, period. Therefore, accounting information isn't much help, but neither is anything else. However, accounting information can be helpful indirectly. When important events that do affect security prices are also represented in the accounting information (perhaps later on, since accounting reports come out only quarterly or annually), then the accounting information will indirectly be predictive too. It depends on how well accounting does represent the original event: it seems that if phenomena reported in the accounting information have a clear economic meaning (such as when they represent an impact on cash or risk), they do have some incremental predictive value.

After the fact, however, it is clear that accounting information (especially earnings) does correlate highly with market prices. The longer the accounting–price relationship is measured, ordinarily the better it is: accounting earnings, for example, usually correlate better with stock prices over several years than over a few months. Accounting does relate to whatever affects markets, though calling the shots in advance is hard!

AGGREGATES

Securities markets involve aggregate behaviour. Capital market theory proposes that a sensible investor will invest in a group of securities termed a *portfolio*. By choosing a group with various individual betas (risk measured by variation in returns), the investor can assemble a portfolio with whatever overall risk the investor wishes. Generally, a portfolio is less risky than any individual security because, by adding together a group of securities with different unsystematic risks, the unique variations in each partially cancel each other out. When one's price goes up, another's may go down. Thus, a portfolio is a way of diversifying away the unsystematic risk.

Portfolio thinking has become pervasive in the investment community. Most research on the impact of accounting information presumes that investors have portfolios of securities, and companies' accounting for their *own* investments (marketable securities and pension funds, for example) increasingly makes the same presumption.

MARKET INFORMATIONAL EFFICIENCY

Efficiency of information use means that markets respond so quickly and smoothly to information that, once the information becomes public, its effects are immediately reflected in prices through the trading of securities. People who think the information implies that they should buy do so, from people who think they should sell. This fast response means that if the market is efficient, you can't use publicly available information (such as public financial statements everyone can read) to "beat" the market; by the time you have the information and can act, the market will already have reacted to the information and produced a new trading price that reflects that. You, as an individual trader, don't have the power to do much about the price that the overall sum of buys and sells has produced, so, unless you can trade on your information before anyone else knows it, you will find that the price already reflects the value of the information. If everyone gets an accounting report at the same time, probably only those traders nimble enough to act immediately will be able to take advantage of any news in the report. (More comments on whether accounting reports are likely to be news are below.)

Capital markets operate on information, but they do so in light of expectations already formed, in accordance with what was already known. Therefore, the markets tend to respond to new information only if it is *unexpected*. The argument can be made that for an efficient capital market, only the unexpected portion of earnings (or of any other such item or announcement) is information to the market. The market will not respond much to financial results that are exactly as everyone expected. There always is *some* response, though, because various market traders have different expectations and beliefs—these differences make the markets work!

Research indicates that some markets (for example, the New York Stock Exchange) are quite efficient with respect to publicly available information, but many people don't believe these findings. The research is by no means conclusive, and the behaviour of many markets is not well understood (the Alberta Stock Exchange, for example, has been studied much less than the New York Stock Exchange). Because informational efficiency is a difficult phenomenon to demonstrate conclusively, it is often called a hypothesis about how markets work: the **efficient market hypothesis**.

Securities commissions, such as the U.S. Securities and Exchange Commission, the Ontario Securities Commission, the Alberta Securities Commission, and the Commission des valeurs mobilières du Québec are responsible for ensuring that securities trading is as fair as possible. One problem securities commissions worry about is so-called "asymmetric information": some market traders know more than others do about a security and, therefore, potentially take advantage of the more ignorant traders. If you know that bad things are ahead, you sell to people who don't know that the price will fall when everyone learns about the bad things, or if you know that good things are ahead, you buy from people who don't know their shares are worth more than they think. A major role of financial accounting is to reduce information asymmetries by producing information that informs everyone.

An example of the effects of asymmetric information is that people on the "inside" of the company might use their private knowledge to take advantage of other investors. Such insiders can buy or sell before other investors learn about something and, therefore, before the market can reach a new price based on the information. If you were a senior executive of the Royal Bank, and you knew that tomorrow the company will release an unexpectedly poor earnings report that will cause the share price to fall, you could sell out today to share buyers who are ignorant of what you know. Securities commissions require that any significant information be released quickly and to everyone at once, and they keep an eye on insider trading.

Accounting standards, requirements that companies release significant information as soon as it is known, and other efforts to remove information asymmetries probably assist the markets to behave fairly, in that prices will be set by buyers and sellers all equally knowledgeable about the company. However, even if someone less knowledgeable is being unfairly taken advantage of, the market will still be efficient in that its prices will still reflect whatever the various people know.

8.4 CORPORATE DISCLOSURE

Financial statements are one of the ways that companies disclose information about themselves to outsiders. Securities markets certainly pay attention to financial accounting information, but in a world in which many people buy and sell bonds, shares, and options several times a day, quarterly or annual financial statements are only helpful infrequently. Much of the information in the financial statements leaks out over the year, in press releases, announcements, and official information filings with securities commissions or stock exchanges. For example, the audit of a company's December 31 financial statements may be completed in February and the financial statements printed and issued in May, but throughout the prior year there will have been announcements about important events, of quarterly per-share-earnings figures and, as early as January (before the audit has been completed), the final earnings per share for the year. Not surprisingly, accounting research shows that stock price changes generally happen before the official earnings reports are released, and this is more likely to happen for larger firms, about which there tends to be more information available between accounting reports.

There is, therefore, a continual flow of financial statement-related and other significant information from public companies to securities markets. The general idea is that information should be released as soon as it is known, so that general market traders are not disadvantaged compared to insiders. This helps to keep the system fair for all, but also it should assist the market's pricing system to reflect informed evaluations of companies' prospects, so that the market prices are consistent with society's overall interest in appropriate allocation of economic resources.

The following excerpt from an article by an officer of the Toronto Stock Exchange describes the situation.

CORPORATE DISCLOSURE

Equal access to information cornerstone of TSE policy

It is a cornerstone policy of the Toronto Stock Exchange that all persons investing in securities listed on the Exchange have equal access to information that may affect their investment decisions. Public confidence in the integrity of the Exchange as a securities market requires timely disclosure of material information concerning the business and affairs of companies listed on the Exchange, thereby placing all participants in the market on an equal footing.

Material information is any information relating to the business and affairs of the company that results in or would reasonably be expected to result in a significant change in the market price or value of any of the company's listed securities.

Material information consists of both material facts and material changes relating to the business and affairs of a listed company.

In addition to material information, trading on the Exchange is sometimes affected by the existence of rumors and speculation. Where this is the case, the Exchange may require that an announcement be made by the company whether such rumors and speculation are factual or not.

It is the responsibility of each listed company to determine what information is material according to this definition in the context of the company's own affairs. The materiality of information varies from one company to another according to the size of its profits, assets and capitalization, the nature of its operations and many other factors. An event that is "significant" or "major" in the context of a smaller company's business and affairs is often not material to a large company. The company itself is in the best position to apply the definition of material information to its own unique circumstances. The Exchange recognizes that decisions on disclosure require careful subjective judgments, and encourages listed companies to consult the Market Surveillance Section when in doubt as to whether disclosure should be made.

Disclosure Must Be Immediate

A listed company is required to disclose material information concerning its business affairs forthwith upon the information becoming known to management, or in the case of information previously known, forthwith upon it becoming apparent that the information is material. Immediate release of information is necessary to ensure that it is promptly available to all investors and to reduce the risk of persons with access to the information from acting upon undisclosed information.

Unusual trading marked by significant changes in the price or trading volumes of any of the company's securities prior to the announcement of material information is embarrassing to company management and damaging to the reputation of the securities market since the investing public may assume that certain persons benefited from access to material information which was not generally disclosed.

Rumor Often a Cause

Unusual market activity is often caused by the presence of rumors. The Exchange recognizes that it is impractical to expect management to be aware of, and comment on, all rumours, but when market activity indicates that trading is being unduly influenced by rumors the Exchange will request that a clarifying statement be made by the company. Prompt clarification or denial of rumors through a news release is the most effective manner of rectifying such a situation. A trading halt may be instituted [by the Exchange] pending a "no corporate developments" statement from the company. If a rumor is correct in whole or in part, immediate disclosure of the relevant material information must be made by the company and a trading halt will be instituted pending release and dissemination of the information.

Contents of announcements of material information should be factual and balanced, neither over-emphasizing favourable news nor under-emphasizing unfavourable news. Unfavourable news must be disclosed just as promptly and completely as favourable news. It is appreciated that news releases may not be able to contain all the details that would be included in a prospectus or similar document. However, news releases should contain sufficient detail to enable media personnel and investors to appreciate the true substance and importance of the information so that investors may make informed investments decisions.

In restricted circumstances disclosure of material information concerning the business and affairs of a listed company may be delayed and kept confidential temporarily where immediate release of the information would be unduly detrimental to the interests of the company.

It is the policy of the Exchange that the withholding of material information on the basis that disclosure would be unduly detrimental to the company's interests must be infrequent. This can only be justified where the potential harm to the company or to the investors caused by immediate disclosure may reasonably be considered to outweigh the undesirable consequences of delaying disclosure, keeping in mind at all times the considerations that have given rise to the Exchange's immediate disclosure policy. While recognizing that there must be a trade-off between the legitimate interests of a company in maintaining secrecy and the right of the investing public to disclosure of corporate information, the Exchange discourages delaying disclosure for a lengthy period of time since it is unlikely that confidentiality can be maintained beyond the short term.

At any time when material information is being withheld from the public, the company is under a duty to take precautions to keep such information completely confidential. Such information should not be disclosed to any officers or employees of the company, or to the company's advisers, except in the necessary course of business. The directors, officers and employees of a listed company should be reminded on a regular basis that confidential information obtained in the course of their duties must not be disclosed.

Insider Rules Urged

Every listed company should have a firm rule prohibiting those who have access to confidential information from making use of such information in trading in the company's securities before it has been fully disclosed to the public and a reasonable period of time for dissemination of such information has passed.

In any situation where material information is being kept confidential because disclosure would be unduly detrimental to the best interests of the company, management is under a duty to take every possible precaution to ensure that no trading whatsoever takes place by any insiders or persons in a "special relationship" with the company, such as lawyers, engineers and accountants, in which use is made of such information before it is generally disclosed to the public. Similarly, undisclosed material information cannot be passed on or "tipped" to others who may benefit by trading on the information.

SOURCE: JOHN W. CARSON, "EQUAL ACCESS TO INFORMATION CORNERSTONE OF TSE POLICY," CORPORATE DISCLOSURE: A SPECIAL REPORT (TORONTO: CANADA NEWSWIRE LTD., 1989). REPRINTED BY PERMISSION.

HOW'S YOUR UNDERSTANDING

Here are two questions you should be able to answer, based on what you have just read:

1. If a particular capital market is described as being "efficient," what does that imply about the role and usefulness of financial accounting information in that market?
2. Why is timely disclosure of financial accounting and other information important to capital markets?

8.5 CONTRACTS AND FINANCIAL ACCOUNTING INFORMATION

The previous sections may have left you with the impression that reporting to capital markets is about all that financial accounting is good for, or that managers worry about. It is not. There are many other roles financial accounting plays that are important to managers and other parties. Financial accounting information is used in resource-allocation decisions made by governments, in assessing income taxes, in negotiations with and by labour unions, and perhaps also in enhancing or attacking the political power of certain groups (such as the corporate sector) in society.

To illustrate the different perspective on accounting you can get from examining another role, this section sets out some of the ideas behind **agency (contract) theory**, an important area of economic and accounting thought that focuses on contractual relationships among people. The area goes by several other names, with differences that aren't important to this discussion, including "principal–agent theory," and "positive accounting theory." Some of the work is quite theoretical and mathematical, and some uses data to predict how people, such as managers or investors, behave in an economic environment that includes accounting information. The research is based in economics and so focuses on economic forces rather than social or psychological ones.[2]

Agency theory is concerned with contractual relationships among people in which one or more people (the *agents*, who might be managers, auditors, lawyers, or physicians) are entrusted with acting on behalf of one or more other people (the *principals*, who might be owners, creditors, defendants, or patients). Contracts may be formally written ones (such as legally binding "indentures" providing protection to bond holders), less formal employment contracts or supplier agreements, or informal arrangements such as a handshake between partners.

Agency theory examines a fundamental characteristic of contracts among self-interested participants: they are unlikely to have the same interests. Conflict of interests is not viewed as being bad, but rather as being the natural state of affairs. For example, if the agent is to provide effort on behalf of the principal, it would be natural for the agent to want to work less hard than the principal wishes. For the agent, effort is costly and, therefore, is to be minimized, whereas for the principal, the agent's effort should improve results and is, therefore, to be maximized. The theory develops ideas about how the agents can be induced to act "properly" on behalf of the principals, for example, to do things that are in the principals' best interests and not shirk their responsibilities or lie about what they've done when the principals cannot observe their actions. (The theory has some quaint phrases: the agent's not doing what the principal wants is called "adverse selection" and the risk that the agent will lie about it is called "moral hazard.")

Agency theory tends to focus on the **stewardship** role of accounting information (in monitoring the stewardship of the agent on behalf of the principal) rather than on the future-oriented, decision-making role of such information that capital market theory emphasizes. It doesn't deny that both roles exist—it just emphasizes the former. The theory views information that is produced by financial accounting, management accounting, or auditing as resulting from the wish by the various parties to provide incentives and controls over each other's behaviour. This wish exists because agents are assumed to want to act in their own interests and, in the absence of appropriate incentives and controls, their interests are assumed not necessarily to coincide with those of their principals.

The theory has very practical implications, proposing that if conditions change between various parties, accounting and auditing will change to meet the new conditions. Accounting information is viewed as an economic good that changes to meet changes in demand, not as something that is in any sense "right" or "wrong." Principals and agents will demand whatever information they require to manage the contractual relationship between them, and information, therefore, can be judged only in terms of that specific relationship. Is it what they need, or isn't it?

Information is "good" to the extent that it helps the contracting parties agree on what each party should do and on how to allocate the positive or negative results that occur. In a typical example, suppose the shareholders of Lakewood Inc. wanted management to work hard to maximize the price of Lakewood's shares, which are traded on a stock exchange. The higher the price, the better the return to the owners from owning the shares and the higher their wealth. The owners might, through their representatives on Lakewood's board of directors, propose a management contract that specifies that the top managers get no salary, but instead get 20% of the change in the company's share price over each year. The top managers might well reply that this is too risky for them because all sorts of things might affect share price, including things they have no control over such as wars, recessions, or other unexpected problems. The share price could go up, but it might as likely go down. The managers may then propose that they should be paid a flat salary of $200,000 each, regardless of changes in share price, believing that the owners should take the risks. This isn't what the owners want, because they are concerned that the managers will not be sufficiently conscientious if they are guaranteed a salary regardless of performance. Therefore, the two parties negotiate. Finally, a contract is agreed upon, according to which the managers will get $150,000 each plus performance bonuses of 5% of the annual net income and 3% of the increase in share price, with no penalty for negative income or negative change in share price, but with no bonuses then either. (The owners, interested in maximizing the share price, and the managers, feeling that they have more control over net income than share price, would in this case have agreed to include both factors in the bonus calculation. Management compensation contracts are often very complex and a subcommittee of the board of directors may be created specifically to design and monitor such contracts. Securities commissions increasingly require public companies to disclose the nature of such contracts and the compensation that results from them, especially for the chief executive officer and other senior managers.)

The result is that the managers, as agents for the owners (the principals), have agreed to work for the owners, and the owners have agreed to employ the managers. Both parties entered into the contract for their own reasons, and both are satisfied with it (or they would not have agreed). Now the financial accounting information can be used by the owners to monitor the managers' performance and to calculate their bonuses based on net income. Both parties, because of their contract, are interested in the accounting information; neither would be satisfied without accounting. They may specify in their contract that GAAP be used to calculate net income, for the sake of convenience or because they prefer it that way. They also may specify other ways of calculating net income that they think are to their mutual advantage.

You can see that if many companies have these sorts of bonus arrangements or other such incentive contracts in which financial accounting information plays a role, there can be strong pressures on the development of GAAP or official accounting standards in directions that improve the effectiveness of such contracts. These pressures are likely to be in similar directions to those of, say, capital markets, because the owners are trading their shares on such markets. They will not be exactly the same, though, because the managers have to agree to the contracts too and may not want, for example, to bear as much risk as the capital market might like them to.

You can also see the role for auditors that we saw earlier: if the managers are responsible for the accounting information and are being paid on the basis of it, the owners (who are perhaps some distance from the company's offices and in any case would not want to have to show up to ask questions about accounting) may not be inclined to trust the managers' figures and would prefer having an outside auditor evaluate them.

There are many kinds of formal and informal contracts that may use financial accounting information. The parties to such contracts will necessarily have an interest in the financial statements, in GAAP, in auditing, and in the other aspects of financial accounting. They will, therefore, act as part of the system of information demand and use that shapes accounting. Some of the contracts that are likely to be of interest from a financial accounting point of view include management compensation contracts, as illustrated above, labour contracts, contracts with suppliers and/or customers, and financial contracts such as those drawn up for issuance of bonds, other debt, or equity. One reason for written contracts is the conflict of interests mentioned earlier. For example, bondholders receive a claim on the company, or its assets, that has a higher legal priority than the shareholders' residual claim. A contract, such as a "bond indenture," is written specifying the exact rights of the bondholders. The indenture might say that if the company's working capital falls below a certain level, the bondholders have the right to demand early payment or some other penalty. This doesn't remove the conflict of interests, but clarifying the situation makes everyone's assessments of the company's performance and prospects more informed.

There are many implications of the agency (contract) theory view. In summary, here are some of the main implications to financial accounting:

a. Financial statements have a role in monitoring actions and understanding past actions to improve control, as well as in the prediction of future results;

b. The ancient stewardship role of financial accounting is alive and well in the modern world of professional managers and remote owners trading their shares on stock markets;

c. Financial accounting information is useful in assessing the likely consequences and risks of potential contractual arrangements and in setting up the specific terms of any contracts, for example, in allocating rewards or penalties;

d. The usefulness of financial statements in particular contracts may or may not coincide with other uses (for example, the contract that would motivate managers most may have undesirable income tax consequences, so a contract that motivates less may be decided upon to reduce tax);

e. The motives of managers (and others) in choosing accounting methods are likely to be complex, because they will include consideration of all sorts of formal and informal contracts the managers are concerned about, in addition to trying to provide information for others to use;

f. Managers' and owners' support for such general financial accounting concepts as fairness, conservatism, adherence to GAAP, and verifiability will depend on whether the results, or costs, of following those concepts improve various contractual relationships.

HOW'S YOUR UNDERSTANDING

Here are two questions you should be able to answer, based on what you have just read:

1. What is the "agency" or "contractual" view of the value of financial accounting information?
2. Green Inc. has a set of management bonus contracts for its senior executives, specifying that their pay will be based partly on how well the company performs. Brown Inc., however, just pays its managers a flat salary. What differences would you expect in the attitudes of the two groups of managers to their company's financial statements?

8.6 "WHAT IF" (EFFECTS) ANALYSIS

Suppose you are a financial analyst trying to determine what a recently released set of financial statements tells you about the company's performance. You can do various standard analyses (as will be described in Chapter 9), but before you do that you find that the company's accounting isn't quite comparable to that of another company you want to compare it to, or that the company has used an accounting method you don't agree with. You therefore want to alter the numbers to show "what if" the company used the other company's accounting method, or a method you do agree with.

Or perhaps you are the president of a company, and are assessing some alternative accounting methods to determine which would be the most appropriate for the company. You know that there are restrictions on the company's debt–equity ratio imposed by a major lender and that there are expectations of the year's net income resulting from a forecast you made during a speech earlier in the year. You also know that various financial analysts examine your company's performance quite closely and that, if that performance declines, your bonus and even your job could be in jeopardy. You therefore want to know what the effects on the company's financial statements would be if the company adopted each alternative accounting method.

Such questions are very common in business. Answering them requires analysis of the accounting information: we'll call this **"what if" (effects) analysis**. The ability to analyze accounting information to tell managers, bankers, and others what difference various accounting choices, or business events in general, would make to the financial statements is very important to accountants. If you are going to be an accountant, you have to develop this skill. If you are not going to be an accountant, you should have some idea of what the accountants are doing in such analyses, so that you can evaluate the results they give you. You may even want to do some basic analysis yourself. Computer spreadsheets are particularly good for this sort of analysis, but you have to know what to tell the spreadsheet to do.

EXAMPLES OF "WHAT IF" EFFECTS ANALYSIS

A good way to think about what would result if one method was used instead of another, or one event happened instead of another, is to figure out the accounting numbers both ways and compare them. There are shortcuts to this, and if you see one, go ahead and use it! But for now, let's take the longer, and hopefully clearer, way.

a. Cash vs. accrual

Back in Section 7.5, we had an example comparing cash and accrual figures for Goblin Consulting Ltd. Suppose Goblin's president said, "I know we use accrual accounting, but what difference would it make to this year's income if we used the cash basis instead?"

This year's accrual income is $11,800 (income statement), and this year's cash from operations is $13,400 (SCFP). Therefore, the answer to the president's question is that income would be $1,600 higher this year on a cash basis.

b. Revenue recognition: during or after production

In Section 7.7, we had the example of Greenway Construction, which uses percentage of completion to recognize its construction revenues and expenses. Suppose the company's banker, more used to revenue recognition at completion of production (completion of the contract, which would be like using the point of sale method), wanted to know what difference there would be to income if the completion of production method were used instead.

The percentage of completion project income (totalling $600,000 over three years) was:

- $120,000 for Year 1;
- $270,000 for Year 2; and
- $210,000 for Year 3.

If revenue and expenses were recognized only at completion of the project, the project income would be:

- $0 in Year 1;
- $0 in Year 2; and
- $600,000 in Year 3.

So the answer to the banker's question would be that income would be:

- $120,000 *lower* in Year 1;
- $270,000 *lower* in Year 2; and
- $390,000 *higher* in Year 3.

There has been no change in the three-year total, but the yearly figures are rearranged if the completion of production method is used.

c. Franchise revenue recognition

In Section 7.8, the accrual and cash basis ways of recognizing income from WonderBurgers Ltd.'s franchising operations were compared. It should be easy for you to see now that if you used the cash basis instead of the accrual basis, you'd have the following effects on income over the three years of the example:

- Year 1 income would be $4,200 *higher*;
- Year 2 income would be $3,100 *lower*; and
- Year 3 income would be $1,100 *lower*.

EXAMPLES OF INCOME TAX EFFECTS IN THIS ANALYSIS

d. Income tax effects on examples (b) and (c)

Suppose Greenway Construction pays income tax at a rate of 35% and WonderBurgers pays at a rate of 30%. What effect would that have on our figures above? The answer is that the income tax reduces all the effects by the tax rate, because that proportion goes to the government. As you'll see below, a useful rule is to just multiply the before-tax effect by (1 – tax rate), in this case (1 – .35) = .65 for Greenway and (1 – .30) = .70 for WonderBurgers.

Here is a table of the effects, before and after income tax (for presentation purposes, Greenway's figures are in thousands of dollars):

	GREENWAY			WONDERBURGERS		
Year	Gross Effect 100%	Tax Effect 35%	After-tax Effect 65%	Gross Effect 100%	Tax Effect 30%	After-tax Effect 70%
1	$(120)	$(42)	$(78)	$4,200	$1,260	$2,940
2	(270)	(94.5)	(175.5)	(3,100)	(930)	(2,170)
3	390	136.5	253.5	(1,100)	(330)	(770)
Total	0	0	0	0	0	0

Income tax reduces both positive and negative differences. The assumption here is that an increased income is taxed, and a decreased income produces tax savings (by reducing tax payable on other income or creating tax credits that can be used to get refunds on past years' taxes or reduce future taxes).

Without knowing the details of the income tax law (which are beyond the scope of this book), we cannot say for sure how much of the income tax effect is current and how much is deferred:

- We know the effect on total income tax expense, as indicated above, but not how to allocate that effect between the current and deferred portions of the expense.
- We know the other side of the overall effect, the increase or decrease in total income tax liability, but not how to allocate that effect between the income tax payable liability and the deferred income tax liability.

e. "Net of tax" analysis

Revenues and expenses can be considered to increase or decrease income taxes on their own, and, therefore, the effects on net income of changes in revenues and expenses can be estimated directly, net of tax, once the income tax rate is known (or approximated). Here's how it works. Suppose Alcatraz Fencing Inc. has one revenue, one expense, and an income tax rate of 35%. Its income statement might look like this:

Revenue	$1,000
Expense	700
Income before income tax	$ 300
Income tax expense (35%)	105
Net income	$ 195

Note that the net income is 65% of the income before tax. We can state this in a formula, as suggested in part (D) above:

Net income = (1 – tax rate) × Income before income tax

You can look at net income as the residual after the income tax has been deducted. But this works just as well for the revenues and expenses. Suppose we recast the income statement as if the revenues and expenses were taxed directly, so that they are shown net of tax and the income tax effect is, therefore, included in them rather than being a separate expense:

	Original	Net of Tax
Revenue (net = $1,000 x (1 – .35))	$1,000	$650
Expense (net = $700 x (1 – .35))	700	455
Income before income tax	$ 300	
Income tax expense (35%)	105	
Net income	$ 195	$195

The net-of-tax way of looking at things can be very useful analytically. Suppose the president of Alcatraz has a plan to increase revenue by $200 without any increase in the $700 expense. What would that do to net income? The new net income would be higher by $200 × (1 – .35) = $130, and so would be $325 ($195 + $130). There is no need to recalculate the whole income statement.

If you are doubtful, you can always do the analysis the longer way, by recalculating the income statement:

New revenue	$1,200
Expense still	700
New income before tax	$ 500
New tax expense (35%)	175
New net income	$ 325

Net-of-tax analysis got us to this answer more quickly by focusing just on what *changes*.

f. Interest expense net of tax

Another net-of-tax example, which will be important for some of the ratio analyses in Chapter 9, concerns interest expense. Suppose $60 of Alcatraz's expense were interest and we wanted to know what the company's net income would be prior to considering the interest (as if it had no debt). The answer is that the net income would go up, but not by $60, because deducting the interest expense saves income tax. The net income would rise by $60 × (1 – .35) = $39. Interest really costs the company only $39, because it brings a tax saving, as does any tax deductible expense.

Again, if you wish, you can calculate the net income effect the long way. Using the original revenue, if the company had no interest expense:

Revenue still	$1,000	
New expense	640	($700 – $60 Interest)
New income before tax	$ 360	
New tax expense (35%)	126	
New net income	$ 234	($39 more than the original $195)

HOW'S YOUR UNDERSTANDING

Here are two questions you should be able to answer, based on what you've just read:

1. The president of a company is thinking about changing the company's method of accounting for insurance expense, and wants to know what the effect of the policy will be on net income. Explain why all you need to know to estimate the effect is the amount of the expense under the present and proposed methods and the company's income tax rate.
2. A Canadian railway company had revenues of $10.4997 billion in a recent year. Its income tax rate was 37%. If its revenues increased by 2%, with no effect on expenses other than income tax, what would be the effect on net income for that year? (Revenue effect = 2% × $10,499.7 = $210.0 million more revenue. Net income effect = $210 (1 – .37) = $132.3 million higher.)

8.7 FRAMEWORK FOR DOING MULTI-YEAR "WHAT IF" (EFFECTS) ANALYSIS

The analysis approach shown in Section 8.6 can be extended to as many years as you need. Some of this was illustrated in the Greenway and WonderBurgers examples, but now let's develop a framework for a complete multi-year analysis.

AN EXAMPLE

Earth Fabrics Inc. manufactures several lines of environmentally friendly dress fabrics, hiking clothes, and other cloth goods. It has been in business three years. There have been more returns of fabrics by retail stores in the current year than in the first two, and, because of this, the president is considering a suggestion by the external auditor to recognize revenue from shipments to retailers a little more conservatively. The company's income tax rate is 34%, and revenue and accounts receivable data for the company's first three years are:

	Year 3	Year 2	Year 1
Revenue for the year	$1,432,312	$943,678	$575,904
Year-end accounts receivable	194,587	148,429	98,346

The auditors suggest that a more appropriate revenue recognition policy would reduce revenues by reducing year-end accounts receivable by 10% at the end of Year 1, 15% at the end of Year 2, and 25% at the end of Year 3. (Recognizing revenue includes a debit to Accounts receivable and a credit to revenue, so reducing receivables implies reducing revenue, and vice versa.) What effect would this have on:

1. accounts receivable at the end of each year?
2. revenue in each year?
3. net income for the year?
4. income tax liability at the end of each year?
5. shareholders' equity at the end of each year?

1. Effects on accounts receivable:

Year 1	Receivables down 10% = $9,835	New balance =	$88,511
Year 2	Receivables down 15% = $22,264	New balance =	$126,165
Year 3	Receivables down 25% = $48,647	New balance =	$145,940

It's important to realize what these receivables changes do. By reducing the receivables at the end of any year, all revenue recognized up to that point is reduced — you might say that the recognition of some of it is being postponed to the next year. So, for example, the Year 1 revenue is reduced $9,835, but because that revenue is postponed to Year 2, that year's revenue is *increased* by $9,835. By the end of Year 3, all the prior revenues are reduced by $48,647. Let's see how that divides up into the three years.

2. Effects on revenue:

Year 1	Revenue down	$ 9,835
Year 2	Revenue down $22,264 and up $9,835, net down	12,429
Year 3	Revenue down $48,647 and up $22,264, net down	26,383
Total decrease in revenue over the three years		$48,647

3. Effects on net income:

Year 1	Net income down $9,835 (1 – .34)	$ 6,491	
Year 2	Net income down $12,429 (1 – .34)		8,203
Year 3	Net income down $26,383 (1 – .34)		17,413
Total decrease in net income over the three years			$32,107

We can check this. If accounts receivable are reduced by an accumulated amount of \$48,647, then the accumulated net income must have gone down by this times (1 – .34). \$48,647 (1 – .34) = \$32,107. The rest is the income tax effect.

4. Effects on income tax liability:
   Income tax is saved on the lower incomes. The amount of the accumulated saving is just the tax rate (.34) times the accumulated change in accounts receivable at the same time:

Year 1 Year-end liability down \$9,835 (.34)	\$ 3,344	
Year 2 Year-end liability down \$22,264 (.34)		\$ 7,570
(Check: this should equal the tax saved on the reductions in revenue in the first two years, or (\$9,835 + \$12,429) (.34) = \$3,344 + \$4,226 = \$7,570)		
Year 3 Year-end liability down \$48,647 (.34)		\$16,540
(Check: (\$9,835 + \$12,429 + \$26,383) (.34) = \$3,344 + \$4,226 + \$8,970 = \$16,540)		

5. Effects on shareholders' equity:
   Shareholders' equity is reduced by the reductions in net income, which reduce retained earnings. Therefore, the effects on shareholders' equity are the accumulations of those listed for income in Part 3:

Year 1 Ending equity down	\$ 6,491
Year 2 Ending equity down (\$6,491 + \$8,203)	\$14,694
Year 3 Ending equity down (\$6,491 + \$8,203 + \$17,413)	\$32,107

AN ANALYTICAL FRAMEWORK

It may help you to keep multiple-year analyses straight if you use the analytical framework below. The framework relies on two important things:

- Because accounting is a double-entry system, all the effects at any point in time must balance out, so that the balance sheet stays in balance. This might help if, for example, you can't remember which way one effect goes; you know that it has to work so that everything stays in balance.
- Because each balance sheet is the accumulation of everything that has gone before, each balance sheet's effects are the sum of whatever the effects were on the previous balance sheet plus the effects on the income statement between the two balance sheets.

Figure 8.1 provides the framework, in blank. We'll fill it in shortly.

FIGURE 8.1

"WHAT IF" EFFECTS ANALYTICAL FRAMEWORK

Balance Sheet End Last Year	+	Income Statement This Year	=	Balance Sheet End This Year
Assets		**Revenue**		**Assets**
Liabilities		**Expenses**		**Liabilities**
Other than tax		Other than tax		Other than tax
Income Tax		Income Tax		Income Tax
Equity		________		**Equity**
Retained Earnings		**Net Inc.** ________		Retained earnings

Notes

1. Without knowledge of the tax law, it may be impossible to separate the tax effects into current and deferred portions.

2. For there to be a cash effect, some cash or cash equivalent account must be affected. For accounting policy changes, error corrections, and most other effects analyses, this will not happen.

Now let's fill the framework in for each of the three years of the Earth Fabrics example. Remember that the company has only existed for three years, so the "end of last year" figures for Year 1 are all zero.

Balance Sheet End Last Year		+	Income Statement This Year		=	Balance Sheet End This Year	
YEAR 1							
Assets			*Revenue*			*Assets*	
Rec. down	$ 0		Down	$ 9,835		Rec. down	$ 9,835
Liabilities			*Expenses*			*Liabilities*	
Other than tax			*Other than tax*			*Other than tax*	
No effect			No effect			No effect	
Income tax			*Income tax*			*Income tax*	
Down	$ 0		Down	$ 3,344		Down	$ 3,344
Equity						*Equity*	
Retained earn.			*Net income*			*Retained earn.*	
Down	$ 0		Down	$ 6,491		Down	$ 6,491
YEAR 2							
Assets			*Revenue*			*Assets*	
Rec. down	$ 9,835		Down	$12,429		Rec. down	$22,264
Liabilities			*Expenses*			*Liabilities*	
Other than tax			*Other than tax*			*Other than tax*	
No effect			No effect			No effect	
Income tax			*Income tax*			*Income tax*	
Down	$ 3,344		Down	$ 4,226		Down	$ 7,570
Equity						*Equity*	
Retained earn.			*Net income*			*Retained earn.*	
Down	$ 6,491		Down	$ 8,203		Down	$14,694
YEAR 3							
Assets			*Revenue*			*Assets*	
Rec. down	$22,264		Down	$26,383		Rec. down	$48,647
Liabilities			*Expenses*			*Liabilities*	
Other than tax			*Other than tax*			*Other than tax*	
No effect			No effect			No effect	
Income tax			*Income tax*			*Income tax*	
Down	$ 7,570		Down	$ 8,970		Down	$16,540
Equity						*Equity*	
Retained earn.			*Net income*			*Retained earn.*	
Down	$14,694		Down	$17,413		Down	$32,107

You should note the following two points about the analytical framework:

- Each year's effects add vertically and horizontally. That is, vertically, the beginning and ending balance sheet effects and income statement effects work out exactly, and horizontally, the ending balance sheet effects are the sum of the beginning ones and the income statement ones.
- You can do the analysis at any point, working forward or backward from there. Probably, the most important analysis would be Year 3, because it accumulates everything from the beginning to now.

The analytical framework will help you think about effects analysis, but you have to consider the specific circumstances of each situation rather than hope for a general solution you can memorize. You have to exercise the knowledge and judgment you've acquired in your studies and experience! We'll do more effects analysis examples below and in Chapters 9 and 10, to help you develop your analytical ability.

JOURNAL ENTRY

You may be interested to know how the revenue recognition change would be entered in the accounts. It is quite straightforward, and uses the figures for the Year 3 analysis, because the company is just finishing Year 3 (let's assume the accounts for Year 3 have not yet been closed). Here is the entry, in the order of the accounts in the analytical framework:

Account	DR	CR
CR Accounts receivable		48,647
DR Income tax liability (we don't know if this is current or deferred)	16,540	
DR Retained earnings (prior years' effects, like a prior period adjustment)	14,694	
DR Revenue (Year 3)	26,383	
CR Income tax expense (Year 3)		8,970

CASH EFFECTS

You'll note that the analysis above and the journal entry to implement the change said nothing about cash. An important point to remember is that *analysis of accounting method changes almost never involves cash.* If we are changing revenue, receivables, inventories, depreciation, etc., we will change net income, working capital, income tax liability, and/or owners' equity (retained earnings), but *unless* cash is being spent or received as part of the change, there is no cash effect. There will eventually be a cash effect through increased income tax or a tax refund, but at the time the accounting change is implemented, there is no tax effect.

It's pretty easy to see that if no cash (or cash equivalent) account is affected in the change, there is no cash effect. Remembering that may be enough for you. But you can also show, via examining effects on the SCFP's Operations section, that even if there appears to be a cash effect because net income is affected, that effect is cancelled out by effects on other account changes used to determine cash from operations. Let's use the Earth Fabrics example to show you how this works.

	Year 1	Year 2	Year 3
Accounts receivable:			
Total reduction at the end of the year	$9,835	$22,264	$48,647
Total reduction at the beginning of the year	0	9,835	22,264
Asset reduction over the year	$9,835	$12,429	$26,383
Income tax liability:			
Total reduction at the end of the year	$3,344	$ 7,570	$16,540
Total reduction at the beginning of the year	0	3,344	7,570
Liability reduction over the year	$3,344	$ 4,226	$ 8,970
Retained earnings:			
Total reduction at the end of the year	$6,491	$14,694	$32,107
Total reduction at the beginning of the year	0	6,491	14,694
Income reduction over the year	$6,491	$ 8,203	$17,413
SCFP's Operations section changes:			
Income reduction appears to hurt cash	–$6,491	–$ 8,203	–$17,413
Receivables reduction appears to help cash	9,835	12,429	26,383
Liability reduction appears to hurt cash	–3,344	–4,226	–8,970
Net effect on cash from operations	$ 0	$ 0	$ 0

A FURTHER EXAMPLE

Rexdon Interiors Ltd. sells decorating supplies and does contract home and office decorating work. The company accounts for revenue at the point of delivery for ordinary sales and on the completed contract basis for contract work. Resulting accounts for 1995 and 1994 are:

	1995	1994
Revenue for 1995	$1,234,530	
Accounts receivable at the end of the year	114,593	$93,438
Bad debts expense for 1995	11,240	
Allowance for doubtful accounts at the end of the year	13,925	6,560

The president, Rex, is thinking of changing the revenue recognition method for contract work to the percentage of completion method. If this were done, accounts receivable would rise to $190,540 at the end of 1994 and $132,768 at the end of 1995. The controller advises that if this were done, revenue/expense matching would also require raising the allowance for doubtful accounts to $14,260 at the end of 1994 and to $16,450 at the end of 1995. No other expense recognition changes would be anticipated. Rexdon's income tax rate is 32%.

Using the analytical framework described in Chapter 8, here is a summary of the effects of the policy change. Explanation for the figures follow.

Balance Sheet End Last Year		+	Income Statement This Year		=	Balance Sheet End This Year	
Assets			*Revenue*			*Assets*	
Rec. up	$97,102		Down	$78,927		Rec. up	$18,175
ADA up	($7,700)					ADA up	($2,525)
Liabilities			*Expenses*			*Liabilities*	
Other than tax			*Other than tax*			*Other than tax*	
No effect			BDs down	$ 5,175			No effect
Income tax			*Income tax*			*Income tax*	
Up	$28,609		Down	$23,601		Up	$ 5,008
Equity						*Equity*	
Retained earn.			*Net income*			*Retained earn.*	
Up	$60,793		Down	$50,151		Up	$10,642

You can see that the effects are much larger at the end of 1994 than at the end of 1995, resulting in effects on the 1995 income statement that might be opposite to what you expected. If a company does try to manipulate its net income through accounting policy changes, it can easily have such unexpected results. Financial statement manipulation is not for the faint of heart: unexpected effects are one reason such manipulation is not a very good idea. Rex should only change revenue recognition policies if he believes the new policy is really better, more appropriate, and fairer, and if he is therefore willing to stick with the new policy even when it produces awkward results, as it does in 1995.

Here are details behind the above framework summary:

a. Retained earnings at the end of 1994 would rise by the increase in receivables minus the increase in income tax expense:
   ([$190,540 – $93,438] – [$14,260 – $6,560]) × (1 – .32)
   = $89,402 × (1 – .32)
   = $60,793 increase.

b. The 1994 income tax liability would increase by
   $89,402 × .32 = $28,609.

c. Revenue for 1995 would *decrease* because more revenue that is now in 1995 would be pushed back to 1994 than would revenue now in 1996 be pushed back to 1995. The increase in 1994 accounts receivable ($190,540 – $93,438 = $97,102) would be transferred out of 1995 revenue and the increase in 1995 accounts receivable ($132,768 – $114,593 = $18,175) would be transferred into 1995 revenue, for a net decrease in 1995 revenue of $78,927 ($97,102 – $18,175).

d. Bad debts expense for 1995 would also decrease because of the corresponding revision in the timing of recognition of the expense. The increase in 1994 allowance ($14,260 – $6,560 = $7,700) would be transferred out of 1995 expense and the increase in 1995 allowance ($16,450 – $13,925 = $2,525) would be transferred into 1995 expense, for a net decrease in 1995 expense of $5,175.

e. Net income for 1995 would decrease due to the combined effect of the revenue decrease and the bad debts expense decrease, minus the tax effect: ($78,927 – $5,175) × (1 – .32) = $73,752 × (1 – .32) = $50,151 decrease.

f. The 1995 income tax expense would decrease by $73,752 × .32 = $23,601.

g. Income tax liability at the end of 1995 would increase $5,008 ($28,609 increase from 1994, minus $23,601 decrease from 1995).

h. There would be no immediate effect on cash or on 1995 cash flow, but eventually the $5,008 increased income tax liability would have to be paid.

Following the above framework summary, the journal entry to record the policy change as at the end of 1995 would be:

DR Accounts receivable	18,175	
CR Allowance for doubtful accounts		2,525
CR Income tax liability (payable or deferred)		5,008
CR Retained earnings (prior period policy change effect)		60,793
DR Revenue for 1995	78,927	
CR Bad debts expense for 1995		5,175
CR Income tax expense for 1995		23,601

HOW'S YOUR UNDERSTANDING

Here are two questions you should be able to answer, based on what you have just read:

1. Hinton Inc. has found an error in its revenue account: an invoice for $1,400 was recorded as revenue in 1994 when it should have been recorded in 1995. The company's income tax rate is 35% and there was no corresponding error in cost of goods sold. What is the effect of the error on: 1994 net income; 1994 cash from operations; 1995 net income; retained earnings at the end of 1994; retained earnings at the end of 1995? ($1,400 [1 – .35] = $910 too high; no cash effect; $910 too low; $910 too high; no effect as the sum of 1994 and 1995's incomes is unaffected)
2. Granby Industrial Inc. decided to change its accounting for warranties, to accrue warranty expense sooner than had been done. The effect on warranty liability as at the end of 1995 was to increase it by $121,000. By the end of 1996, the liability would go up $134,000. The company's income tax rate is 30%. What would be the effect of the change on: 1996 net income; 1996 cash from operations; retained earnings at the end of 1996; income tax liability at the end of 1996? (($134,000 – $121,000) (1 – .30) = $9,100 lower; no cash effect; $134,000 (1 – .30) = $93,800 lower; $134,000 (.30) = $40,200 lower)

8.8 FUTURE CASH FLOWS: PRESENT VALUE ANALYSIS

Earlier in this book, we saw that cash flow is important to a company. In Chapter 9, we will see that assessing cash flow is a significant part of the analysis of a company's financial performance and position. We will also see that sorting out the impact of interest rates on the company's returns is important to understanding how it has performed. This chapter has reviewed ideas about capital markets, which are concerned with the company's expected ability to generate returns in the future, especially cash returns that can be used to pay dividends or reinvest in the company. Many financial contracts, such as for management compensation and supply or service arrangements, focus on future financial performance. Generally, management should be looking forward to the future and trying to combine its asset acquisition, borrowing, and income-generation strategies to produce a good future return for the owners.

An important way of thinking about future performance, especially future cash flows, is **present value** (PV) or **discounted cash flow** (DCF) analysis. Future cash flows are not the same as present ones, because you have to wait for them. Because you have to wait, you lose interest or other returns you could have earned if you had had the cash sooner.

Detailed PV or DCF techniques are examined in management accounting and finance courses, and you may well have seen them already in economics or business mathematics courses. In this section, basic ideas will be outlined to prepare you for the financial analysis to follow in Chapter 9 and to help you think about how traders in capital markets may use expectations of future cash flows and future interest rates when deciding on prices of securities. (Note that such traders don't necessarily do explicit PV or DCF calculations, but research shows that capital market prices behave as if they are doing something like that.)

INTEREST AND THE TIME VALUE OF MONEY

In Western society, it is permissible—even expected—that the owner of capital should charge a person who wants to use that capital a fee for that use. That fee is called interest and is computed by applying a specified percentage rate to the amount lent, which can be referred to as either the investment or the principal. For example, an 8% interest rate on a \$200 loan would produce annual interest of \$16 (\$200 × .08). The existence of interest, which builds up as time passes, gives money a *time value*.

Some simple formulas you probably already know (P = principal or investment, i = interest rate):

Annual interest = $P \times i$
Amount due at the end of one year = $P(1 + i)$
Amount due after *n* years, with annual compounding, if no payments at all are made = $P(1 + i)^n$

Suppose a loan provides for repayment of the principal plus interest after several years, with no payments in the meantime. Two examples of this are Canada Savings Bonds (when you buy them you are lending the government your money) and whole life insurance (some of the premiums you pay are invested on your behalf and you are entitled to the accumulated value if you don't die). If the interest is compounded, which is normally the case, that means interest builds up on the unpaid interest as well as on the unpaid principal. In order to know how this works, you need to know how frequently interest compounds. Do you get interest on the interest:

- as soon as any interest arises ("continuous compounding")? or
- after a day's interest has been added ("daily compounding")? or
- after a month's interest has been added ("monthly compounding")? or
- only after a year's interest has been added ("annual compounding")?

Here's an example of annual compounding. We have the same $200, 8% loan as above, which is to be repaid in five years with *annual* compounding. We can then calculate the amount which the loan has built up to at the end of each year (its "future value", FV below) as follows:

Year	FV at Beginning of Year	Annual Interest at 8%	FV at End of Year
1	$200.00	$16.00	$216.00
2	216.00	17.28	233.28
3	233.28	18.66	251.94
4	251.94	20.16	272.10
5	272.10	21.77	293.87

You can see that the FV increases every year. Using the third formula above, we can calculate the FV at the end of any year:

- End of year 3: $FV = P(1 + i)^n$
  $= \$200\ (1 + .08)^3$
  $= \$251.94$
- End of year 5: $FV = \$200\ (1 + .08)^5$
  $= \$293.87$ (just a rounding difference with above)

INTEREST AND PRESENT VALUE

The concept of interest can be "turned on its head" by considering what you *lose* by waiting some period of time for your money, or, putting it another way, what a future payment is worth in present terms if you assume your money should earn interest between now and when you get it back.

Suppose someone promises to give you $100 a year from now. If you were given the money now instead, you'd be earning 9% interest on it. Therefore, if you'd had some amount of P now and earned 9% on it, you'd be in the same position as you will be after waiting the year. Using the second formula above, $100 = P(1 + .09), where P is the amount you could have earned interest on.

Solving for P we get P = $100/(1.09) = $91.74. If you had $91.74, you could have invested it at 9% and ended up with $100 at the end of the year ($91.74 + [.09 × $91.74] = $100).

We say that $91.74 is the **present value** of $100 received after waiting one year, "discounted at 9%." This present value concept is another way of thinking of the time value of money: it reminds us that as long as we wait for cash that could have earned interest, we lose that interest we could have earned. This idea is referred to as an "opportunity cost," which you may recall from introductory economics. As long as the interest rate is greater than zero, present value is less than the actual future amount of cash that will be received.

Analogous to the above interest formulas are the following present value formulas (where C = future cash flow, and i = interest rate):

Present value waiting one year	=	$\frac{C}{1 + i}$
Present value waiting *n* years with no payments in the meantime, interest compounded annually	=	$\frac{C}{(1 + i)^n}$
Combining these two, present value of a constant cash payment over *n* years, interest compounded annually	=	$\frac{C}{i}\left(1 - \frac{1}{(1 + i)^n}\right)$

(A comment on the derivation of the third formula is at the end of this chapter.[3])

Therefore the present value of $1,000 received three years from now, discounted at an **opportunity cost** interest rate of 12%, would be $711.78 (this is $1,000 divided by $(1.12)^3$). The phrase "opportunity cost" is often used, because by waiting three years for the $1,000, you lose the *opportunity* to invest your money at 12% in the meantime.

Future values of a principal invested at a fixed rate, with interest compounded each period

Present values of a periodic cash flow, at a fixed opportunity cost interest rate

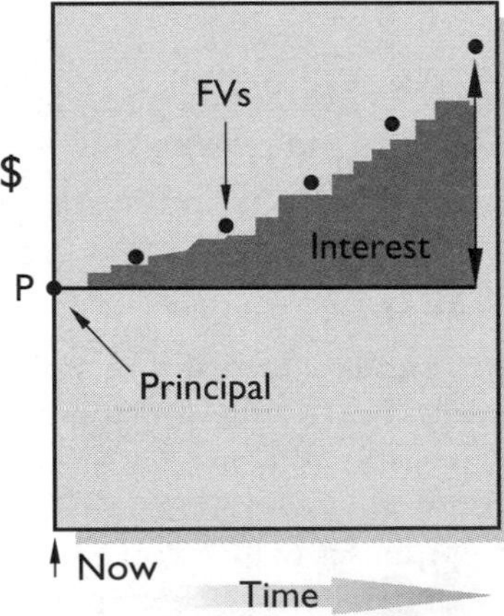

Future value > principal because interest builds up over time.

Present value < cash flows because interest is lost by waiting.

FIGURE 8.2

Here's an example of present value calculations. A company is considering an investment that will cost $10,000 and will return $2,400 at the end of each year for five years. This looks good: 24% of the investment cost received each year, a total of $12,000 back on the $10,000 invested. To make the investment, the company will have to borrow at an interest rate of 7%. Should it go ahead?

Before we do the calculations, note three things about problems like this:

1. What we are trying to determine is if the money coming in is equivalent to a **cost of capital** of 7%. If the company has to raise its money at 7%, it will want the investments it makes to return at least that. A greater rate of return would be desirable, otherwise there would be little point in investing, but 7% is the minimum acceptable return.
2. The idea of present value analysis is to take the future returns and subtract the 7% that the company has to pay on its borrowing, to determine if, after considering the borrowing cost, the returns equal the $10,000 that has to be invested. *Is the present value of the future cash flows equal to the present cost outlay that has to be made in order to get those flows?*
3. The 24% quoted above is irrelevant to the analysis. It compares the annual return to the investment cost, all right, but it does not consider the interest cost of waiting several years for some of that return. The whole idea of present value analysis is to build that interest cost, the time value of money, into the analysis.

Here's the present value analysis:

- Using the second present value formula above:

PV of first year's return is $\$2{,}400/(1.07)^1$	$2,242.99
PV of second year's return is $\$2{,}400/(1.07)^2$	2,096.25
PV of third year's return is $\$2{,}400/(1.07)^3$	1,959.11
PV of fourth year's return is $\$2{,}400/(1.07)^4$	1,830.95
PV of fifth year's return is $\$2{,}400/(1.07)^5$	1,711.17
Total PV	$9,840.47

- Since the annual flows are constant, the third present formula above could have been used instead:

  $PV = (\$2{,}400/.07)(1 - [1/1.07]^5) = \$9{,}840.48$

This is the same answer except for a minor rounding difference.

We can draw the needed conclusion from this and also see the effects of waiting for returns:

- The conclusion is that the investment is *not* a good idea, not quite. It will cost $10,000, but after calculating the interest cost of waiting for the money to be returned, the present value of the $12,000 returned is only $9,840. Therefore, the investment is returning less than the 7% rate the company has to pay to finance it. It's close, but still not attractive.
- You can estimate the "internal rate of return" of the project by equating the cost of $10,000 to the third formula above and solving for i:

  $\$10{,}000 = (\$2{,}400 / i)[1 - (1 /(1 + i)^5])$ produces an i of 6.4%

  So the return of the project is less than 7%. (Don't worry about having to solve for the *n*th root of a denominator as above: there are theoretical problems with calculating the IRR, mainly that it assumes the returns are reinvested at the IRR rate, 6.4% above, so we will not use it further. But you can see the idea that if the IRR is not at least equal to the borrowing cost, the project is not attractive.)

- From the annual calculations above, you can see that the present value of the $2,400 is smaller the longer we wait for it. The $2,400 received after one year has a PV of $2,243, but the $2,400 received after four years has a PV of $1,831. *This is a necessary result*: the longer the wait, the lower the PV because the greater is the amount of interest assumed included in the cash flow and, therefore, the lower is the residual PV.

The chart in Figure 8.2 illustrates the difference between the future values of an investment made now and the present values of future cash flows. You can see that interest gets larger each period. In the future values case, it becomes a larger component of the total value; in the present value case, it becomes a larger component of the cash flow.

SOME PRESENT VALUE EXAMPLES

As we have seen with the example above, the concept of present value is very useful in evaluating investment possibilities ahead of time. Here are some more examples.

1. Suppose you are offered the chance to invest $2,000 in a project that will pay you back $4,500 after six years. Is it a good deal? Suppose, alternatively, you could invest your $2,000 at 11%. The present value of the $4,500 is $\$4{,}500/(1 + .11)^6$, or $2,406. Therefore, the present value of what you'll get ($2,406) exceeds your cost ($2,000), and it does seem a good deal.
2. Gazplatz Ltd. issues bonds at 7% having a total face value of $100,000 that will pay interest every year in cash plus pay the principal back in 10 years. What would you pay for such a set of bonds if you could get 9% on your money elsewhere?

   a. Present value of annual interest $= \dfrac{\$7{,}000}{.09}\left(1 - \dfrac{1}{(1 + .09)^{10}}\right) = \$44{,}924$

   b. Present value of principal payment $= \dfrac{\$100{,}000}{(1 + .09)^{10}} = 42{,}241$

   Total present value $87,165

   (Note that the interest rate in the formula is your opportunity rate of 9%. The company's 7% rate just determines how much interest is paid each year—it does not represent your interest expectations.)

   As a rational investor, you'd be willing to pay $87,165 for the bonds. If the bonds sold for $87,165, they'd be "priced to yield" 9%. They'd sell at a discount below $100,000 to make them sufficiently attractive to investors who want a better return than the stated 7% rate. By paying $87,165, you'd actually earn the 9% you want, as we can show by constructing a table of each year's return:

Date	Cash Paid Each Year	Return on Investment Demanded (9%)	Residual (Growth in Debt)	Effective Principal Balance
Purchase date				$87,165
1 year later	$ 7,000	$7,845*	$ (845)	88,010
2 years later	7,000	7,921	(921)	88,931
3 years later	7,000	8,004	(1,004)	89,935
4 years later	7,000	8,094	(1,094)	91,029
5 years later	7,000	8,193	(1,193)	92,222
6 years later	7,000	8,299	(1,299)	93,521
7 years later	7,000	8,417	(1,417)	94,938
8 years later	7,000	8,544	(1,544)	96,482
9 years later	7,000	8,683	(1,683)	98,165
10 years later	107,000	8,835	98,165	0
	$170,000	$82,835	$87,165	

* $7,845 = $87,165 × .09; $7,921 = $88,010 × .09; and so on.

3. Usually, in modern financial arrangements, "blended" payments are made to cover the specified interest plus some payment on the principal. House mortgages and car loans are two common examples. In such cases, to understand what is going on, we have to separate the return *on* investment (the interest) from the return *of* investment (repayment of the principal). Here is an example: a loan of $7,998 carrying an interest rate of 10% is being repaid by a blended annual payment of $2,110, made at the end of each year, which will cover all interest and pay off the principal as well in five years. In such a case, the interest amount gets smaller every year because the principal balance is falling, but the *rate* of return on investment is a constant 10%.

Date	Total Blended Payment	Return on Investment (Interest)	Residual Paid on Principal	Principal Balance
Loan date				$ 7,998
1 year later	$ 2,110	$ 800*	$1,310	6,688
2 years later	2,110	669	1,441	5,247
3 years later	2,110	525	1,585	3,662
4 years later	2,110	366	1,744	1,918
5 years later	2,110	192	1,918	0
	$10,550	$2,552	$7,998	

* $800 = $7,998 × .10; $669 = $6,688 × .10; and so on.

Using this example, the *present value* of $2,110 paid every year for five years, *discounted* at 10%, compounded annually, is $7,998. This is ($2,110/.10) (1 – 1/[1.10]^5): check it and see.

HOW'S YOUR UNDERSTANDING

Here are two questions you should be able to answer, based on what you have just read:

1. What is the present value of $300 you will receive after two years if your opportunity cost of waiting is 11%? ($243.49, which is $300/[1 + .11] [2])
2. Wildwood Inc. issued a set of $1,000 face-value bonds carrying an interest rate of 10% and payable in eight years. The bonds were priced to yield 12%, which is what the capital market demanded for bonds of that risk and life. Did the bonds sell for more, or less, than $1,000 each? (Less)

8.9 MANAGERS AND PERFORMANCE INFORMATION

One of the main reasons top managers of public companies pay close attention to their companies' financial statements, earnings announcements, and other disclosures is that stock markets and other securities markets respond quickly to information and do so in accordance with the value of that information to the market traders. Markets impose a sort of "discipline" on such corporations and their management. Whatever the managers may hope, the market evaluates the information in accordance with its own lights and quickly applies rewards, by bidding companies' stock or bond prices up, or penalties, by bidding them down, regardless of whether management thinks the reward or penalty is justified.

The less a company is in the public eye and/or the less it is involved in various securities markets, the less it is disciplined by such markets. However, even private companies are not immune to such discipline because they often compete or cooperate with, or are suppliers to or customers of, more directly affected companies, and also because even private owners often wish to sell their companies, borrow heavily, or take other action that brings their performance information under scrutiny. (Common ways of calculating the value of a private business make extensive use of financial statements and of the performance and trends they reveal, for example.)

In the 1960s and 1970s, many smaller companies "went public," listing their shares on stock markets to raise capital in the hope of benefitting from the markets' evaluations of their future prospects. This was sometimes a success, sometimes not. Inflation and interest rates became high for awhile and share prices did not increase accordingly, so many investors sold their shares and put their money into bonds and other debt securities, further depressing share prices. In the more cautious 1980s, a substantial number of public companies withdrew from such markets ("went private"), partly because the benefits were not great enough to compensate for the risks market discipline entails (such as the risk of a takeover if performance falters and other people think they can run the company better) or for the costs of continuing to supply the markets' insatiable demand for information.

Managers also pay close attention to their companies' financial statement figures because important contracts are based on those, explicitly or indirectly. Many top managers are compensated based on the income shown in the financial statements, many own shares in their companies, and if the company is public the top managers may be fired if stock market prices decline or fail to rise as the board of directors wishes.

Managers' stewardship performance in running the company for the owners is scrutinized by the external auditors, so managers are also faced with justifying what the financial statements show. The statements are really the representations of senior management, so in the end, they should be what those managers think is an appropriate reflection of their performance, within the constraints of GAAP and the auditors' scrutiny.

8.10 ACCOUNTING RESEARCH: MANAGING CORPORATE FINANCIAL DISCLOSURE

We have seen that management has good reason to be concerned about the financial information released about their companies. Accounting research has clearly established that financial-statement and related information does matter to corporations and their managers, and that managers do make accounting policy choices, argue for or against accounting standards, and affect the nature of accounting information in other ways. Some recent research has focused on how managers may try to do this, and the following excerpt is from a report on a set of 20 interviews conducted with top managers and observers of the financial disclosure scene.

CA MAGAZINE

Financial disclosure isn't just passive and neutral: it can help, it can hurt, it can clarify, it can confuse.

If Numbers Could Speak

When we asked the controller of a petrochemical company the pros and cons of disclosing more information to the public, he had a single answer: "The pros are, the public has more information so it can understand you better; the cons are, it has more information so it can understand you better."

Because of the obvious effect accounting statements and other financial information about their companies can have on their future prospects, self-preservation dictates that managers have a large hand in managing what gets released. And while the practice of "information management" per se has its good points, provided it serves to enhance the accuracy, timeliness and relevance of the information disclosed for public consumption, the phrase also has something of an Orwellian, manipulative ring to it; we all worry if we think we're on the receiving end of information that has been altered or manipulated in any way.

For accountants, this dilemma is a double-edged sword. Accounting information is important to the world, and we labour hard to make it better, more reliable, more important. But the more important it is, the more corporate managers will be interested in managing what it says about their companies and themselves, and the greater the pressure brought to bear on neutrality —the "tell it like it is" character of accounting reports. Managers, after all, are responsible for managing their companies' production, marketing, personnel and financial condition, so why not financial disclosure as well?

We asked 20 Canadian business executives and accounting professionals to tell us about the process of corporate financial disclosure. Our analysis of the 20 interviews shows managers tend to focus on the control of six interrelated aspects of disclosure—from the most basic to the most sophisticated.

Information categories

Most basic is whether to release any information at all about some event or performance, including the level of aggregation of data and supplementary information.

Recalls a treasurer for a wholesale distributor, "In preparing the prospectus, it was the first time our president had to come to grips with releasing information of that significance and detail. The lawyers were suggesting disclosing product-line gross margins, but he said, 'No.' "

How does one fill in the blanks? Explains an analyst with a brokerage firm, "In some companies, for various reasons, the quarterly releases may not disclose cash flow, so I might phone the company to get a little more explanation on these kinds of things."

The values of numbers

When it's clear an item of information is to be disclosed, the concern shifts to the number value or specific content of a narrative disclosure. This level of disclosure management involves considering accounting policy choices and possible economic decisions affecting the value of key variables.

"We find ourselves under tremendous pressure to get deals closed at the ends of quarters—to get deals far enough along that they can be reported, or indeed to delay them. It happens all the time," says a lawyer with a corporate law firm.

Redundant disclosure

Companies will often release information to different audiences or through multiple media. How much redundancy results is up to management. This primarily involves the categories of information disclosed rather than the value of specific numbers. In most cases, a company will not release different number values to different audiences but may release different categories of information to different audiences, or the same values to different audiences.

Explains a PR officer with a public utility, "I produce a draft of the interim report. We take out the paragraphs that are not newsworthy and then we have our news release."

In the case of a construction company, its controller reports the material is entirely redundant: "The financial section of our 10K [a report that must be filed annually with the U.S. Securities and Exchange Commission if a company is carrying on certain business activities in the U.S.] is identical to our annual report, word for word, period for period."

Timing

The timing of releases can be important to a company, but there's a marked difference between the control exerted over good and bad news: good news may be delayed for weeks, bad news rarely for more than a few days.

"We do try to time good news if we possibly can, and release it at, say, the annual general meeting. That gives you something to talk about. It means you've got the media there, a lot of brokers and bankers—the biggest bang for the buck."

As for bad news, says this controller of an energy conglomerate, it's released "after the exchange is shut, right on Friday afternoon."

A matter of interpretation

Companies may simply release a terse announcement through a wire service, or choose to provide an interpretative context. Such efforts to manage how information is interpreted, either before or at the time of disclosure, include having management analyses printed with the annual report, or holding press conferences or other interactive, face-to-face meetings. Efforts may also be made to manage the visibility of disclosure by, for example, burying sensitive disclosures in footnotes or highlighting certain revenues or expenses.

The controller of a public utility opts for interaction: "We have a good relationship with analysts and bond raters. We invite them out, give them presentations. We're an AAA company and we want to keep it that way."

A lawyer, on the other hand, says, "If there is one area in which we are called upon to give advice, it is almost entirely in the area of non-arm's-length transactions. We are asked to do what we can to keep this issue as low profile as possible."

Interpreting after the fact

The release of financial information may trigger attempts by third parties to interpret results. The company is then faced with the decision of whether to try to manage those interpretations, by calling to correct press stories, for example, or suggesting to analysts that their earnings forecasts are inaccurate.

"We had a specific note and it stuck out like a sore thumb, a big contingent liability," a treasurer for an industrial fabrication company recalls. "We had preset guidelines that were used to answer phone calls about the note."

A vice-president of finance for a retail chain, asked whether she corrects the press if they misquote her, answers, "Oh no. You get into more trouble, and then the issue is in the forefront."

SOURCE: M. GIBBINS, A. RICHARDSON, AND J. WATERHOUSE, "IF NUMBERS COULD SPEAK," *CA MAGAZINE*, OCTOBER 1989, 33–39. REPRINTED BY PERMISSION OF THE CANADIAN INSTITUTE OF CHARTERED ACCOUNTANTS, TORONTO, CANADA.[4]

8.11 CONTINUING DEMONSTRATION CASE

INSTALMENT 8

In this instalment, we'll prepare the first year's financial statements for the company. The statements will be analyzed in Instalment 9, so make sure you are clear about how they are assembled below.

Data for Instalment 8

The February 28, 1995, adjusted trial balance of Mato Inc. prepared at the end of Instalment 7 was (credits are bracketed):

Cash	6,418	Deferred revenue liability	(500)
Accounts receivable	15,671	Share capital	(125,000)
Allowance for doubtful accounts	(1,542)	Revenue	(229,387)
Inventory	33,612	Cost of goods sold expense	138,767
Prepaid insurance	525	Bad debts expense	2,436
Automobile	10,000	Salary—Mavis	0
Accumulated amortization—auto	(2,000)	Salary—Tomas	0
Leasehold improvements	63,964	Salary—Other	0
Accumulated amortization—leasehold	(12,792)	Salaries expense	67,480
Equipment and furniture	32,390	Travel expense	9,477
Accumulated amortization—equipment	(2,364)	Phone expense	4,014
Computer	14,900	Rent expense	24,000
Accumulated amortization—computer	(2,980)	Utilities expense	3,585
Software	4,800	Office and general expense	5,688
Accumulated amortization—software	(960)	Interest expense	6,469
Incorporation cost	1,100	Inventory shortage expense	441
Bank loan	(47,500)	Amortization expense—auto.	2,000
Accounts payable	(37,166)	Amortization expense—leasehold	12,792
Deductions payable	(2,284)	Amortization expense—equipment	2,364
Salaries payable	(2,358)	Amortization expense—computer	2,980
Loan payable	0	Amortization expense—software	960
	71,434		(71,434)

Results for Instalment 8

With the help of the public accountant, Tomas prepared the set of financial statements shown in Exhibits 8.1, 8.2, and 8.3 for the company's first year.

Exhibit 8.1

Mato Inc.
Statement of Income and Deficit
for the Year Ended February 28, 1995

Revenue		$229,387
Cost of goods sold		138,767
Gross profit		$ 90,620
Operating expenses:		
Bad debts	$ 2,436	
Salaries	67,480	
Travel	9,477	
Telephone	4,014	
Rent	24,000	
Utilities	3,585	
Office and general	5,688	
Inventory shortage	441	
Interest	6,469	
Amortization	21,096	144,686
Net loss for the year (no tax)		$ (54,066)
Retained earnings, March 1, 1994		0
Deficit as at February 28, 1995		$ (54,066)

Exhibit 8.2

Mato Inc.
Balance Sheets
at February 28, 1995, and March 1, 1994

Assets			**Liabilities and Equity**		
	1995	**1994**		**1995**	**1994**
Current assets:			Current liabilities:		
Cash	$ 6,418	$130,000	Bank loan	$ 47,500	$ 0
Receivables (net)	14,129	0	Payables	$ 41,808	1,100
Inventory	33,612	0	Loan payable	0	15,000
Prepaid Expense	525	0	Deferred revenue	500	0
	$ 54,684	$130,000		$ 89,808	$ 16,100
Noncurrent assets:			Shareholders' equity:		
Equipment cost	$ 57,290	$ 10,000	Share capital	$125,000	$125,000
Accum. amort.	(7,344)	0	Deficit	(54,066)	0
Leasehold (net)	51,172	0		$ 70,934	$125,000
Software (net)	3,840	0			
Incorp. cost	1,100	1,100			
	$106,058	$ 11,100			
TOTAL	$160,742	$141,100	TOTAl	$160,742	$141,100

Exhibit 8.3

Mato Inc.
Statement of Changes in Financial Position
for the Year Ended February 28, 1995

Operations:		
Net loss for the year		$ (54,066)
Add back amortization for the year		21,096
Changes in noncash working capital accounts:		
Increase in accounts receivable	$(14,129)	
Increase in inventory	(33,612)	
Increase in prepaid expenses	(525)	
Increase in accounts payable	40,708	
Decrease in loan payable	(15,000)	
Increase in deferred revenue	500	(22,058)
Cash used in operations		$ (55,028)
Investing activities:		
Equipment, leasehold improvements, and software acquired		(116,054)
Decrease in cash during the year		$(171,082)
Cash on hand, March 1, 1994		130,000
Cash and equivalents, February 28, 1995		$ (41,082)
Cash and equivalents, February 28, 1995		
Cash on hand	$ 6,418	
Demand bank loan	(47,500)	
Cash and cash equivalents	$(41,082)	

The results for the year were still negative: a loss of $54,066 and a decrease in cash of $171,082. However, there was quite an improvement compared with the first six months:

- The loss for the first six months (Instalment 3) had been $49,378, so the additional loss for the second six months was relatively small at only $4,688.
- The cash decrease for the first six months (Instalment 4) was $200,493, so there was an *addition* to cash of $29,411 during the second six months.
- The working capital at the end of August (Instalment 3) was negative at $38,772 ($96,844 – $135,616) and by February 28, 1995, was still negative at $35,124 ($54,684 – $89,808), but a little less negative.

Further analysis of the results will be conducted in Instalment 9.

8.12 HOMEWORK AND DISCUSSION TO DEVELOP UNDERSTANDING

PROBLEM 8.1* Capital market and agency theories and accounting

1. Briefly describe two important implications capital market theory has for the use of accounting information.
2. Briefly describe two important implications agency (contract) theory has for the use of accounting information.

PROBLEM 8.2* Settle an argument about financial accounting's purpose

Two students are arguing. One says that financial accounting exists in order to provide information to outsiders (for example, capital markets) for assessing company performance. The other says that it exists in order to provide a monitoring and control system over managers who are running the company as the agents of the owners. Settle the argument.

PROBLEM 8.3* Accounting concepts and economic agents

1. Explain why each of the following concepts is important in financial reporting to markets and other economic agents who rely on such reporting.
   a. Economic entity assumption.
   b. Historical cost basis of accounting
   c. Fairness.
   d. Generally accepted accounting principles.
   e. Professional ethics of the accountants and/or auditors involved in producing financial statements.
2. How have each of these concepts been incorporated into the financial statements of a large public company you know about? Give specific examples, if so.
3. Now apply these ideas to a small private company, such as your local nonchain pizza joint, automotive repair company, or clothing store. Are these concepts still relevant? Why?

PROBLEM 8.4* Basic multi-year effects analysis, with income tax

Mistaya Ltd. has decided to change its revenue recognition policy to increase revenue $10,000 in the current year and by a total of $8,000 in prior years (accounts receivable are increased correspondingly). Matched expenses increase $4,000 in the current year and $3,000 in prior years (so accounts payable go up as well). The company's income tax rate is 35%.

Determine all effects of the change on the company's income statement and cash flow statement for the current year and balance sheet as at the end of the current year. Show your calculations and demonstrate that all the effects balance.

PROBLEM 8.5* Basic present value analysis

You have an opportunity to invest $200,000. You will be paid a single interest payment of $100,000 (and get your investment back) at the end of five years.

1. If 8% is the return you require, should you invest? Show all calculations.
2. Describe one other factor you should consider before you invest.

PROBLEM 8.6 How do financial statements help users?

Many external parties rely on statements such as the balance sheet, the income statement, and the statement of changes in financial position produced by a company. Identify two different types of major users of financial information and briefly explain how each of the preceding three financial statements will help them. (This is a similar question to some asked in earlier chapters, but now you should be able to give a more sophisticated answer.)

PROBLEM 8.7 Capital markets and contracts for a corporation

Choose any large, well-known corporation you are interested in and answer the following, based on your choice:

1. What kinds of capital markets are likely to be important to the company?
2. Suppose those capital markets are "efficient" and an unexpected and important piece of information about the company is released. What would likely happen? Would it make a difference if the markets expected the information?
3. List some of the explicit, implicit, or even casual contractual relationships between the company and other internal or external parties that are likely to be important to the company's success.

PROBLEM 8.8 Usefulness of financial statements in modern business

How useful is financial statement information in a modern business setting? In your answer you may consider, among other things, the historical development of accounting practice and the implications of capital market theory and agency theory.

PROBLEM 8.9 Disclosure regulation and management strategy

1. The president of a smallish company, Brandex Ltd., is thinking about listing the company's shares on the Toronto Stock Exchange because doing so might facilitate issuing a large block of new shares, bringing the company needed capital. Describe for the president a few ways in which life might be more difficult if Brandex becomes a publicly listed company.
2. The president feels that if the company becomes listed, a strategy for handling financial disclosure will have to be adopted so that disclosure is managed as other company activities are. What would some likely components of a managed financial disclosure strategy be?

PROBLEM 8.10 Auditors and capital markets

1. Why would the shareholders of a large, publicly traded company want to have the company's financial statements audited?
2. The auditors' report is normally written in a standard wording. The idea is that if things are *not* all right, variations from the standard wording will alert users of the financial statements. Is that consistent, or inconsistent, with capital market theory?

PROBLEM 8.11 Authoritative standards, capital markets, and contracts

Many of the accounting methods we study in this book are based on authoritative standards (*CICA Handbook*, FASB *Statements*, and so on) that attempt to specify how companies' financial accounting should be done. Such standards don't cover everything: companies must still make many choices when they are preparing their financial statements.

Why are there authoritative standards for companies to follow? Why don't they cover everything? Should we have more or less of them? Put your answer in the context of this chapter's theories about information use.

PROBLEM 8.12 Reasons for and against financial disclosure management

1. It appears that some top managers attempt to manage their companies' financial disclosure, including their financial accounting, to alter the story such disclosure tells. Why might managers be motivated to do this?
2. Do you think managers should be prohibited from practising such disclosure management?

PROBLEM 8.13 Some effects analysis concepts

1. Why do changes in accounting methods usually have no effect on cash or cash flow?
2. Since the SCFP begins with net income, any method change that changes net income will appear to change cash flow. How can this happen when the SCFP's total cash flow is unaffected by the change?
3. Can you suggest a situation where an accounting method change *would* affect cash flow as reported on the SCFP?
4. Why is it important to take income tax into account when doing "what if" effects analysis?
5. If a company decides to recognize revenue earlier than had been its practice, its accounts receivable will increase. Does this mean that revenue and net income will increase for every year affected by the policy change?

PROBLEM 8.14 Multi-year effects analysis without considering income tax

Fringle Sales Inc. has the following history for its first three years of existence:

	1993	1994	1995
Revenue:			
Credit sales	$900,000	$600,000	$500,000
Cash sales	80,000	75,000	40,000
Cash collected from customers*	910,000	640,000	420,000
Accounts receivable that became:			
Doubtful during the year	40,000	15,000	10,000
Worthless during the year	10,000	30,000	5,000

* Including cash sales

The president, Fringle, is wondering what difference to the company's working capital and income *before* income tax it would make if the company used one of the following accounts receivable valuation methods:

a. Make no allowance for doubtful or bad debts and just keep trying to collect.
b. Write off worthless accounts, but make no allowance for doubtful ones.
c. Allow for doubtful and worthless accounts when they become known.

Provide an analysis for the president.

PROBLEM 8.15 Multi-year effects analysis with income tax

Amalgamated Buggywhips Inc. has a large amount of excess cash invested temporarily because it is winding down and selling off several of its divisions. Data with respect to its cash and temporary investments are:

	December 31, 1995	December 31, 1994
Cash on hand	$ 2,134,600	$ 1,814,910
Temporary investments (cost)	16,493,220	8,649,270
Temporary investments (market)	15,829,300	10,100,500
Investment revenue for the year	1,492,814	948,653
Income tax rate for the year	37%	36%

The company has been valuing its temporary investments at cost, but this year the company's auditor resigned and the new auditor insists the company value the investments at the lower of cost or market.

1. What effect will the new accounting policy have on net income for 1995?
2. What effect would the new accounting policy have on the 1995 cash flow if:
   a. temporary investments are part of cash and cash equivalents?
   b. temporary investments are *not* part of cash and cash equivalents?

PROBLEM 8.16 Effects of changing doubtful accounts allowance, with tax

"Karl, we have a problem in our accounts receivable. We've provided an allowance for doubtful accounts of 2% of the gross receivables, but during this recession more customers are running into trouble. The allowance should be raised to 5%."

"Tanya, we can't do that. It would wipe out our profitability and ruin our cash flow."

Given the data below, prepare an analysis for Karl and Tanya.

Data:		
	Gross accounts receivable at year end	$8,649,000
	Net income for the year at present	223,650
	Income tax rate	30%

PROBLEM 8.17 Effects of recognizing supplies inventory, with tax

Magnic Manufacturing Co. has large amounts of manufacturing supplies that been recorded as an expense when purchased. Now the company is considering recognizing the supplies on hand as an asset. If this were done, a new supplies inventory account would appear in the current assets. Its balance would be $148,650 at the end of last year and $123,860 at the end of this year. The company's income tax rate is 30%.

Calculate the effect on each of the following that would result if the company changed its accounting to recognize the supplies inventory:

1. Retained earnings at the end of last year.
2. Income tax liability at the end of last year.
3. Supplies expense for this year.
4. Net income for this year.
5. Current assets at the end of this year.
6. Income tax liability at the end of this year.
7. Retained earnings at the end of this year.
8. Cash flow for this year.
9. Cash flow for next year.

PROBLEM 8.18 Effects of change from perpetual to periodic inventory

Frogmorton Fashions began the period with inventory costing $30,000. During the period, $125,000 more inventory was purchased. At the end of the period, a physical count showed that inventory costing $38,000 was on hand. The firm's perpetual inventory system showed that inventory costing $114,000 had been sold during the period.

The president says, "It's a bother keeping track of our inventory the way we do—our perpetual system requires continuous attention to inventory costs. What if we just used the periodic method? What difference would it make?"

PROBLEM 8.19 Basic ideas of present value analysis

1. Explain what the "time value of money" or "present value" concept is all about. Why would business people be sensitive to it?

2. Calculate the present value of each of the following:
   a. $1,000 to be received a year from now. If it were on hand now, it would be invested at 10% interest.
   b. $1,000 to be received at the end of each of the next three years. The opportunity cost of interest or cost of capital in this case is 12%.
   c. Answer (b) again but assume a rate of 10%. Why is the present value *higher* when the rate is *lower*?

PROBLEM 8.20 Present value analysis—market interest and bonds

Dingbat Ltd. issues a set of 9% first-mortgage bonds that have a face value of $100,000 and pay interest at the end of each year for four years. The principal is to be repaid at the end of four years, too.

1. If the market rate of interest for such bonds is 9%, what will the company receive for them? Why?
2. If the market rate is more than 9%, will the company receive more or less than the face value? Why? What if the market rate is less than 9%?

PROBLEM 8.21 Present value analysis—wrestle or play hockey?

Elbows Murphy, a feared hockey player, has come to you for financial advice. The Burlington Stars, in a bid to strengthen their team, have made him a contract offer that would pay a signing bonus now of $90,000, plus a salary of $85,000 for each of the next three years. Elbows is considering turning down the offer, because he thinks he can earn $120,000 per year for the next three years as a professional wrestler.

1. If Elbows could invest his hockey earnings (including signing bonus) at 11%, should he wrestle or play hockey?
2. If Elbows could invest at only 7%, what should he do?
3. At what interest rate would it make no difference to Elbows whether he wrestled or played hockey?

PROBLEM 8.22 Present value analysis—proposed investment in shares

Surprising Sleepwear Ltd. is considering making an investment in shares of a company that makes fibreglass underwear. The investment will cost $110,000 and will return $8,000 cash per year for four years. At the end of four years, Surprising expects to be able to sell the shares for $125,000. Surprising pays 11% to raise financing for such ventures. Based just on this data, should Surprising buy the shares?

PROBLEM 8.23 Present value analysis—buy or lease a truck?

Speedy Trucking is trying to decide whether it should buy a new truck for its business or lease the truck from another company. If Speedy decides to buy the truck, it must pay $140,000 cash immediately, and the truck is expected to last for five years. At the end of the five years, the truck will have no remaining value and will be disposed of. If Speedy decides to lease the truck, it must pay $30,000 at the end of each year for five years, at which point the truck must be returned to the leasing company.

1. If the current market interest rate (which Speedy has to pay to borrow) is 10%, should Speedy lease or buy the truck?

2. Suppose Speedy discovers that if the truck were bought, it could be sold at the end of the five years for $35,000. Would your answer to Question 1 change?
3. Identify one or two important assumptions made in your analyses and explain why those assumptions are important.

PROBLEM 8.24 Effects of an inventory error, with tax

(Challenging)

On December 20, 1995 merchandise amounting to $1,000 was received by the Profit Company Ltd., half of which was counted in its December 31 listing of all inventory items on hand. The invoice was not received until January 4, 1996, at which time the acquisition was recorded as of that date. The acquisition should have been recorded in 1995. Assume that the periodic inventory method is used and that the company's income tax rate is 40%. Indicate the effect (overstatement, understatement, none) and the amount of the effect, if any, on each of the following:

1. Inventory as at December 31, 1995.
2. Inventory as at December 31, 1996.
3. Cost of goods sold expense, 1995.
4. Cost of goods sold expense, 1996.
5. Net income for 1995.
6. Net income for 1996.
7. Accounts payable as at December 31, 1995.
8. Accounts payable as at December 31, 1996.
9. Retained earnings as at December 31, 1995.
10. Retained earnings as at December 31, 1996.

PROBLEM 8.25 Efficient markets and information for users

(Challenging)

1. The efficient market hypothesis is usually discussed in the context of major stock exchanges, such as New York or Toronto. How does the market for getting or giving bank loans in a small branch of a bank in a shopping centre differ from those stock markets?
2. Financial accounting information could be presented in either simple or complex ways. The methods chosen should be simple enough to allow which of the following users to understand and be informed by the information? Why?
   a. Business school students?
   b. A national bank's branch manager in Kingston, Ontario?
   c. The vice-president for corporate lending for the same bank's Ontario region?
   d. A small-time private investor who enjoys "playing the stock market"?
   e. Securities analysts at a major brokerage firm?
3. Cast yourself in the role of a branch bank manager in northern Alberta. A local businessman has come to you to borrow money to build a restaurant adjacent to his service station on Highway 16. He has given you his financial statements for the fiscal year just ended and has asked for a $100,000 loan. Would you attempt to gather any further information before you make a loan decision? In what ways would you be more and less qualified to make this decision than the prairie region vice-president for corporate lending whose office is in a large prairie city?

PROBLEM 8.26 Auditors and forecast information

(Challenging)

Recently, there has been pressure to expand the role of auditors because investors and other groups are demanding more forward-looking information. If these demands are met, auditors may be expected to review the plans and forecasts of a company that will be reporting to the public, and to determine the fairness of such forward-looking financial statements.

Discuss the implications of this expanded role for auditors, using such concepts as fairness, independence, information value, comparability, agency theory, capital market theory, relevance, reliability, objectivity, and any other concepts that you feel are important.

PROBLEM 8.27 Capital markets, auditors, and contracts

(Challenging)

1. On October 31, 1994, analysts predicted that the earnings per share of Laurel Oakes Corp. would equal $4.80 for the year ended December 31, 1994. Actual results were announced on February 27, 1995. Earnings per share for 1994 came to $3.95. Consider the three dates noted above (October 31, 1994, December 31, 1994 and February 27, 1995). At which of these dates would you expect to see share prices react to earnings information? Why? Can you predict the direction in which share prices would react on any of these dates? If yes, explain why; if no, explain why not.
2. Explain the importance of the audit function in the context of a large company where the ownership (composed of a large number of private investors) and the management are separated. To whom are the auditors primarily responsible? By whom are they hired? What would the market investors expect of the auditors? Do your answers indicate anything inconsistent in the auditor's role as an independent party?
3. Agency theory describes the problems inherent in a situation where one party (the principal) hires a second party (the agent) to do work on the former's behalf. Choose one contractual relationship existing between parties connected with a corporation, and describe this relationship in an agency theory context.

PROBLEM 8.28 Can financial statements meet various needs?

(Challenging)

The chairperson of the board of directors of a large public company said in frustration, "The company's written and unwritten contracts with its shareholders are so different from those with its managers, that it's impossible to design financial statements that will meet the needs of both shareholders and managers." What do you think?

PROBLEM 8.29 Present value analysis—investment choices

(Challenging)

You are a rational investor facing a choice of two investment opportunities on December 31, 1995. Your required rate of return is 9%, the current market yield.

The first investment is in corporate bonds issued by Big Conglomerate, Inc. (an old and established firm), which have a face value of $100 and pay 8% annual interest on December 31 of each of the next four years, and repay the $100 principal on December 31 of the fourth year.

1. What is the value of the $100 Big Conglomerate bond to you?

The second alternative is an investment in shares of a small gold mining company recently formed by your uncle. He is quite confident that the company will be able to pay cash dividends according to the following schedule:

Dec. 31/96	Dec. 31/97	Dec. 31/98	Dec. 31/99
$32 per share	$32 per share	$32 per share	$32 per share

2. Based on this schedule, at what price per share would it not matter to you whether you invested some of your money in Big Conglomerate bonds or bought shares in your uncle's mining company?
3. What other factors might you want to consider before you make a decision?

PROBLEM 8.30 Present value analysis—business valuation

(Challenging)

Maranatha Medical Services Ltd. (MMSL) completed its first year of operation on April 30, 1995. Its statement of changes in financial position for the year is shown below. MMSL has no noncash working capital accounts, since all fees are paid in cash by clients, all expenses are paid in cash immediately, and no inventories are held. The owners of MMSL, Doctors A and B, who each own 50% of MMSL, have approached you today, May 1, 1995, to provide an estimate of their share values five years hence (April 30, 2000), when they plan to close their practice and move to other careers. They indicate that net income and cash flow from operations should remain at the 1995 level over the next five years, that no dividends will be paid out, and that no further investment in fixed assets will be made. The fixed assets will have no value at April 30, 2000.

Maranatha Medical Services Ltd.
Statement of Changes in Financial Position
for the Year Ended April 30, 1995

Operations		
Net income for the year		$100,000
Add back amortization, which does not involve cash outflows		25,000
Cash provided from operating activities		$125,000
Investment activities		
Additions to fixed assets		(150,000)
Financing activities		
Issue of common shares (3,000 @ $10)		30,000
Increase in cash during the year, and cash at end of year		$ 5,000
Cash consists of:		
Short-term investments	$2,000	
Cash in bank	3,000	
	$5,000	

Assume a discount rate of 10% in determining solutions to the problems below.

1. Calculate the estimated value of the shares of MMSL at May 1, 1995 (ignore income taxes), by estimating the present value of its expected future cash flows. State any assumptions you feel are necessary.
2. Suppose the fixed assets could be sold for $10,000 at April 30, 2000, and recalculate Question 1.
3. Suppose dividends of $50,000 each will be paid out on April 30 in each of the next four fiscal year, and recalculate Question 1 again.
4. What is the present value of future cash flows up to April 30, 2000, for Dr. A, assuming that the above dividends are paid to him and his shares are sold as at that date?

PROBLEM 8.31 Multiple-issue effects analysis, with tax

(Challenging)

Cranberry Costumes Ltd. has been operating for several years now. So far the income for the current year is $75,000, before income tax at 30%. (The preceding year's income before tax was $62,000 and the tax rate then was also 30%.) Owner Jan Berry is considering a few changes and has asked your advice. The possible changes are:

- Change the revenue recognition policy to recognize revenue earlier in the process. This would increase accounts receivable by $26,000 immediately and $28,000 at the end of the previous year.
- Make a monthly accrual of the bonuses paid to employees at the end of each fiscal year. This would increase accounts payable by $11,000 immediately and $7,000 at the end of the preceding year.
- Postpone for five years repayment of a $19,000 loan (by Jan to the company), which has up to now been classified as a current liability.
- Capitalize as a trademark asset $14,000 of advertising supplies and wages expense recorded in the preceding year.

1. Calculate the net income after income tax for the *current year* that will result if all of the changes are adopted, and discuss the economic reasons for considering each change.
2. Calculate the effect on the amount of cash in the bank account of Cranberry Costumes Ltd. that these changes will have.
3. Explain any difference between results calculated for Question 1 and Question 2 above.

PROBLEM 8.32 Multi-year effects analysis, with tax

(Challenging)

Kitchener Steel Fabricating operates an iron and steel recycling and fabricating business. Sales are to a variety of domestic and foreign industrial companies. Only a small number of products are kept in inventory because much of the work is done to special order, so the company keeps perpetual inventory records for both products in inventory and costs of special orders. When products are sold or orders are filled, the costs are transferred from the inventory asset accounts to cost of goods sold expense. The company pays income tax at a rate of 32% and has a fairly large deferred income tax liability due to large past differences between book amortization and tax capital cost allowances.

The company is considering changing its revenue recognition policy to recognize revenue a little later in the production process. If the change is made, the company's recognition of cost of goods sold expense will change in a parallel way. The change would decrease accounts receivable by $1,200,000 at the end of the present year and $340,000 at the end of the prior year (moving $1,200,000 of revenue from this year to next year and $340,000 of revenue from last year to this year). Parallel to that, inventory would increase $850,000 at the end of the present year and $190,000 at the end of the previous year (moving $850,000 of COGS expense from this year to next year and $190,000 of COGS expense from last year to this year).

1. What would be the after-tax effect of the accounting policy change on net income for this year?
2. What would be the after-tax effect of the change on retained earnings at the end of this year?
3. Show that the answer to Question 2 minus the answer to Question 1 equals the effect on retained earnings at the end of last year.
4. What would be the effect of the change on the following balance sheet accounts at the end of this year:
   a. Cash?
   b. Accounts receivable?
   c. Inventory?
   d. Income tax liability (current and/or deferred)?
5. Show that the answers to Question 2 and Question 4 add up to a balanced effect on the balance sheet at the end of this year.

PROBLEM 8.33 Multi-year effects analysis, with tax

(Challenging)

Kennedy Controls Inc. is considering a change in its accounting for maintenance costs. The chief financial officer proposes that the company capitalize 20% of its maintenance expenses, on the grounds that some of that expenditure has created additional plant assets. The company, the income tax rate for which is 40%, has existed for four years and depreciates its plant assets at 10% of year-end cost.

Here are some relevant account balances for the last four years, before considering the above proposal:

	Year 1	Year 2	Year 3	Year 4
Expenditures on plant assets	$1,243,610	$114,950	$34,770	$111,240
Balance in the plant assets account	1,243,610	1,358,560	1,393,330	1,504,570
Amortization expense	124,361	135,856	139,333	150,457
Accumulated amortization	124,361	260,217	399,550	550,007
Maintenance expense	43,860	64,940	73,355	95,440

Determine the effects of the proposed change on the Year 4 income statement, cash flow statement, and balance sheet at the end of Year 4.

CASE 8A Discussing a real executive compensation plan

Telus Corporation operates largely in the telephone field in Alberta. The company's shares are listed on the Toronto, Montreal, and Alberta stock exchanges. Below is an excerpt from the company's March 4, 1994, "Notice of Annual and Special Meeting," containing the report of the board of directors' executive compensation committee. With capital market and agency (contract) theory as a background, discuss the compensation used by the company. What features of the plan relate to the performance of the company's shares on the stock market? What features relate to management's stewardship of the company on behalf of the shareholders? What role does accounting information play in the compensation?

REPORT ON EXECUTIVE COMPENSATION

The Committee utilizes the services of outside consultants and independent compensation data in determining appropriate compensation levels for its executive officers. In October 1992 the Committee adopted an executive compensation philosophy statement to assist in its evaluation and the application of executive compensation programs.

The primary objective of the executive compensation program is to promote the attainment of the Corporation's business goals and to enhance its competitive position through a clear linkage of executive compensation to results.

In support of this objective, the philosophy further states:

- Plans will be competitive, cost effective, and provide an appropriate standard of living and security;
- Pay for performance will be an underlying theme for all components of the program;
- Variable compensation plans will be emphasized; every executive will have a substantial component of pay at risk relative to attainment of specific performance targets;
- Total direct compensation will be measured against median levels within a competitive group, however the program will offer executives the opportunity to earn above average pay for outstanding performance;
- Long term incentives will be linked to the Corporation's Common Share performance and the factors which contribute to sustainable increases in shareholder value; and
- Executives will be expected and encouraged to maintain certain levels of share ownership in the Corporation.

Individual executive officer compensation is composed of cash, which includes base salary plus a variable component, and long term incentives in the form of stock options. Total compensation for a position is based upon a periodic evaluation of the responsibilities of that position and an annual review of market data for comparable positions in other companies. The companies included in the sample from which the market data is obtained include those in the same or similar businesses and those of comparable size. The total compensation package for each individual is compared to median compensation levels as indicated by market data obtained from the review with the intention that general market comparability be maintained.

Cash compensation

Base salaries are reflective of the particular job responsibilities of an executive officer. Market related base salaries are used as reference points for establishing base salary ranges for particular job functions. Individual base salaries are dependent upon experience levels, actual job responsibilities and market comparability.

The Committee has placed a significant emphasis on the variable "at risk" component of compensation with the result that base salaries tend to be somewhat less than the median of market comparisons. Each year in conjunction with the strategic and operating plan of the Corporation, the Committee establishes performance targets in the areas of financial results, customer satisfaction and team performance, from which the amount of variable compensation payable to executive officers is derived. Upon satisfactory achievement in all areas of measurement, an individual's variable compensation will be payable at the designated percentage for that position.

Financial performance is the main factor in determining the annual variable compensation payable to executive officers. If financial performance does not achieve a minimum level, no variable compensation is payable. At exceptional levels of financial performance the awards payable may increase up to a maximum amount as determined by the Committee. Further, the Committee, upon recommendation from the President and Chief Executive Officer, may vary an individual's variable compensation amount upwards or downwards to reflect the individual performance of a particular executive officer.

Long Term Incentive

The Corporation's long term incentive arrangement is designed to promote sustainable increases in shareholder value by linking the interests of the Corporation's executive officers to those of the shareholders. Additionally, provisions are in place to increase the level of share ownership by executive officers by facilitating the acquisition and retention of Common Shares of the Corporation.

To accomplish these goals, the Executive Stock Option Plan was approved by the shareholders of the Corporation at an Annual and Special Meeting held on May 2, 1991. The Corporation granted options to purchase Common Shares to its executive officers in December 1990, December 1991 and February 1993. The amounts of options granted under the plan take into account the type of businesses in which the Corporation is engaged, market comparability and the present value attributable to such options. The options were granted at the fair market value as at the date of the grant. They have a seven-year term and vest over three years.

The Corporation also granted options with a term of sixty (60) days to certain executive officers in February 1993. The Corporation loaned funds to those executive officers who exercised these options in order to purchase the Common Shares. The loans are interest free and repayable at anytime within five years from the date of this particular grant. The Common Shares are held as security for the loan and all dividends paid theron are utilized to reduce the balance of the outstanding loan.

The Committee views the combination of the above grants as providing encouragement for long term management continuity and providing the appropriate balance between reward for share appreciation and risk to the participants. The Committee further views these long term incentives as consistent with market practice and as an effective means to align the interests of management and shareholders.

CASE 8B Effects analysis on a real company's data

Following are the December 31, 1993, financial statements (without notes) of Telus Corporation, which operates largely in the telephone field in Alberta. Do as complete an analysis as you can of the effects of the following proposed accounting method change, identifying the particular items in the financial statements that you think would be affected. Telus is listed on the Toronto, Montreal, and Alberta stock exchanges: do you think the company's share price on those exchanges would react to the method change if it were announced? Why or why not?

Proposed accounting method change: Faced with increased competition in the long-distance telephone market, Telus has been re-evaluating its approach to that business. A suggestion for changing the pricing structure for such business has been made, and if that were put into practice, it would mean that the company would recognize revenue, but also some associated expenses, a little more conservatively. Relevant data are:

- Accounts receivable would go down by 3% at the end of 1992 and 2% at the end of 1993;
- Inventories for resale would go up by 2% at the end of both years;
- Depreciation and amortization expense would go down by 2% in 1993 and 1% in 1992 (no change for prior years);
- As the income statement shows, the company's income tax rate is very low because of tax deductions carried forward from prior years: only 2.9% in 1993 and 2.3% in 1992. (Just assume an average 2.6% rate in your analysis.)

TELUS CORPORATION

CONSOLIDATED STATEMENT OF INCOME

(thousands of dollars except per share amounts)	Year Ended December 31 1993	1992
Operating Revenues		
Long-distance service	$ 691,847	$ 681,903
Local service	469,948	410,016
Other	100,692	95,447
	1,262,487	1,187,366
Operating Expenses		
Operations	647,983	657,729
Depreciation and amortization	283,268	250,993
Property and business taxes	41,686	42,921
	972,937	951,643
Income from Operations	289,550	235,723
Interest expense, net (Note 2)	95,276	63,472
Other, net	8,383	(9,628)
	103,659	53,844
Income before Income Taxes	185,891	181,879
Income taxes (Note 3)	5,347	4,111
Net Income	$ 180,544	$ 177,768
Earnings per Common Share	$ 1.30	$ 1.28

CONSOLIDATED STATEMENT OF RETAINED EARNINGS

(thousands of dollars)	Year Ended December 31 1993	1992
Retained Earnings, Beginning of Year	$ 152,395	$ 102,150
Net income	180,544	177,768
Dividends on common shares	(128,102)	(127,523)
Retained Earnings, End of Year	$ 204,837	$ 152,395

TELUS CORPORATION

CONSOLIDATED STATEMENT OF CHANGES IN FINANCIAL POSITION

(thousands of dollars)	Year Ended December 31 1993	1992
Operating Activities		
Net income	$180,544	$177,768
Items not affecting cash		
Depreciation and amortization	283,268	250,993
Allowance for funds used during construction	(6,543)	(8,756)
Drawdown of rate stabilization reserve	(1,934)	(6,000)
Amortization of workforce reduction costs	14,081	—
Loss reversal under letter of credit	—	(8,000)
Other	(9,910)	(3,048)
Sinking fund earnngs	(7,489)	(39,031)
Net change in non-cash working capital	(111,978)	50,614
Cash Provided by Operating Activities	340,039	414,540
Dividends	(128,090)	(127,344)
Financing Activities		
Issue of long-term debt	6,271	11,142
Issue of notes payable	36,300	—
Repayment of long-term debt	(17,298)	(170,920)
Sinking fund withdrawals, net	(2,000)	246,676
Financing commitment on investment in Telecential Communications	43,411	—
Issue of common shares	677	27
Cash Provided by Financing Activities	67,361	86,925
Investing Activities		
Capital expenditures	(352,647)	(368,131)
Items not affecting cash	25,013	28,438
Acquisition of interest in Telecential Communications	(44,840)	—
Decrease (increase) in investments	4,162	(23,764)
Other	(4,984)	14,381
Cash Used by Investing Activities	(373,296)	(349,076)
Increase (Decrease) in Cash	(93,986)	25,045
Cash, Beginning of Year	114,247	89,202
Cash, End of Year	$ 20,261	$114,247

For the purpose of this statement, cash is defined as "Cash and short-term deposits."

TELUS CORPORATION
CONSOLIDATED BALANCE SHEET

	December 31	
(thousands of dollars)	**1993**	**1992**
Assets		
Current		
Cash and short-term deposits	$ 20,261	$ 114,247
Accounts receivable	234,937	212,588
Inventories for resale	11,838	12,690
Prepaid expenses	21,995	21,629
	289,031	361,154
Property, Plant and Equipment,		
Net *(Note 4)*	2,798,326	2,728,588
Other Assets		
Deferred charges *(Note 5)*	94,036	64,181
Investments *(Note 6)*	19,374	28,536
Net investment in leases and other	19,487	12,705
Goodwill *(Note 7)*	23,946	—
	156,843	105,422
	$3,244,200	$3,195,164
Liabilities		
Current		
Accounts payable and accrued liabilities	$ 270,518	$ 325,072
Dividends payable	32,027	32,015
Service billed in advance	49,971	44,807
Debt due within one year *(Note 8)*	78,546	983
	431,062	402,877
Deferred Revenue	148,621	166,862
Long-term		
Long-term debt *(Note 9)*	1,066,670	1,069,787
Less Sinking fund assets *(Note 10)*	69,413	59,924
	997,257	1,009,863
Shareholders' Equity		
Share Capital *(Note 11)*	1,463,844	1,463,167
Cumulative Foreign Currency		
Translation Adjustment	(1,421)	—
Retained Earnings	204,837	152,395
	1,667,260	1,615,562
	$3,244,200	$3,195,164

NOTES

1. For good summaries of capital market theory and many of the research findings on it, see Richard Brealey, Stewart Myers, Gordon Sick, and Robert Whaley, *Principles of Corporate Finance*, 1st Canadian ed. (Toronto: McGraw–Hill Ryerson, 1986), especially Chapters 7, 8, and 13; George Foster, *Financial Statement Analysis*, 2nd ed., (Englewood Cliffs, N.J.: Prentice–Hall, 1986), especially Chapters 9 and 11; Ross L. Watts and Jerold L. Zimmerman, *Positive Accounting Theory* (Englewood Cliffs, N.J.: Prentice–Hall, 1986), especially Chapters 2 and 3; William H. Beaver, *Financial Reporting: An Accounting Revolution*, 2nd ed. (Englewood Cliffs, N.J.: Prentice–Hall, 1989); or Thomas R. Dyckman and Dale Morse, *Efficient Capital Markets and Accounting: A Critical Analysis*, 2nd ed. (Englewood Cliffs, N.J.: Prentice–Hall, 1986).

2. For more ideas on agency (contract) theory, see Chapters 8 and 9 of the Watts and Zimmerman book mentioned in Note 1 above. See also John E. Butterworth, Michael Gibbins, and Raymond D. King, "The Structure of Accounting Theory: Some Basic Conceptual and Methodological Issues," in *Research to Support Standard Setting in Financial Accounting: A Canadian Perspective*, ed. S.J. Basu and A. Milburn (Toronto: The Clarkson Gordon Foundation, 1982), 9–17, especially. This article was reprinted in *Modern Accounting Research: History, Survey, and Guide*, ed. R. Mattessich (Vancouver: Canadian Certified General Accountants' Research Foundation, 1984), 209–50.

3. The formula for the present value of a constant cash payment comes from the sum of the following geometric series:

$$\frac{C}{(1+i)^1} + \frac{C}{(1+i)^2} + \frac{C}{(1+i)^3} + \cdots + \frac{C}{(1+i)^n}$$

See an algebra textbook for proof of how this series sums to the formula given.

4. For a more detailed and technical presentation of aspects of the research, see M. Gibbins, A. Richardson, and J. Waterhouse, "The Management of Corporate Financial Disclosure: Opportunism, Ritualism, Policies, and Processes," *Journal of Accounting Research* (Spring 1990): 121–43.

Analysis: Ratios, Cash Flow, and Change Effects

9.1 Chapter Overview

This chapter provides tools for analysis and evaluation of financial position and performance. The main focus is on **ratio analysis**, but analysis of cash flow, which we first encountered in Chapter 4, is revisited and there are more examples of "what if" effects analysis.

In this chapter you'll learn:

Use concepts: how to think about evaluating a company's financial performance, relative to the company's circumstances and to other companies and other years;

Preparation concepts: why it is useful to prepare financial statements that are consistent and comparable so that they may be used in intelligent analysis;

Preparation techniques: little new material here, because this chapter focuses on the use of financial accounting information;

Use techniques: how to do ratio analysis and cash flow analysis, including grouping ratios to provide more complete analysis and spotting trends over time, illustrated using the financial statements of a real corporation, and more practice on "what if" effects analysis.

9.2 Investment and Relative Return

A fundamental economic assumption is that wealth, or capital, has value because it can be used for consumption, to get "all the ... things your little heart pines for," as Fats Waller sang. If our wealth is used up on current consumption, there'll be no consumption next period, so generally we are willing to forego some current consumption by investing some of our wealth in order to obtain consumption in the future. We hope that the investment will earn a return that we can consume in the future.

Because the future consists of many periods, it would be nice if the return were enough to cover each period's desired consumption so that the investment capital wouldn't have to be dipped into (such dipping would reduce the investment and, therefore, the likely level of subsequent returns).

All this has led to the business concept that an investment is made to earn a return. The return is usually thought of in relation to the amount of the investment required to earn it. For example, you might be pleased with a $1,000 annual return if you had invested $2,000, but horrified if you had invested $2,000,000. One way to relate the two components is via **return on**

investment, in which the return is the numerator and the initial investment is the denominator:

$$\text{Relative return (return on investment)} = \frac{\text{Return}}{\text{Investment}}$$

Later, we will examine relative returns, like return on investment (ROI), in more depth. For now, note that we have to have some way of measuring both return and investment if we are to be able to calculate (and evaluate) relative return.

Much of **financial statement analysis** is based on ratios like ROI. Some points you should remember about ratios:

- The purpose of a ratio is to produce a scale-free, relative measure of a company that can be used to compare with other companies, or other years for the company. Such a measure is scale free because both numerator and denominator are measured in the same units (dollars) and are both dependent on the size of the company. A large company will have a larger investment than a small one and should be expected to have a larger return as well, but a ratio like ROI cancels out some of the effects of size and so allows the large and small companies to be compared.
- The ratio will be unreliable as a comparison, or even misleading or useless, unless its numerator is appropriate. This means that the numerator must be properly calculated, as well as suitable for the comparison being made. The word "return" in ROI could be represented by several possible quantities, including net income, cash generated by operations, or interest. The appropriate quantity for the numerator depends on the context of the analysis, as we will see. Also, the role of GAAP and other rules in making figures such as net income meaningful is very important to the conclusions that may be drawn from ratio analysis.
- These same points apply equally to the denominator of the ratio. Additionally, sometimes a doubtful or ambiguous accounting method can create a problem in both the numerator and denominator, bringing the whole ratio into question. An example here is that if a company chooses a revenue recognition method that makes net income doubtfully valid, that will also make the retained earnings figure doubtful, throwing into question one of the most widely used ROI-type ratios, called **return on equity**, which is calculated as net income divided by equity (including retained earnings).

9.3 INTRODUCTION TO FINANCIAL STATEMENT ANALYSIS

The purpose of financial statement analysis is to use the financial statements to evaluate an enterprise's financial performance and financial position. Therefore, the value of the analysis depends on the value of the financial statements.

FINANCIAL EVALUATION IS NOT JUST CALCULATION

When you have completed this chapter, you will be able to take a set of financial statements of pretty well any company and make an evaluation of its performance and prospects. But remember that such an evaluation is not just a calculation, it is a judgment based on the calculations that make sense for that company and based on substantial knowledge of the company. The more you know about a company, its business, its management, and its accounting, the more useful and credible will be your analysis.

You may have noticed that the preceding paragraph used the word "company." Analytical techniques for governments and not-for-profit organizations are more specialized than those illustrated for this book's examples, though many of the ratios and other techniques are useful there too. Some companies, such as banks and insurance companies, also have sufficiently specialized financial statements and business operations that they require particular analytical techniques in addition to, or instead of, those illustrated in this book. Other methods of analysis can always be developed, in order to make the analysis fit the decision-making (use) objective of the user. Therefore, this whole chapter is illustrative: many other techniques exist, and new ones are being invented all the time.

Financial accounting information is not used in a vacuum but is part of a vast array of information available to investors, creditors, managers, and others. Its use is affected by its own quality, such as whether a company's financial statements have been carefully prepared and are comparable to other companies' statements. Use is also affected by the availability of other sources of information that may contain all or part of what is in the financial statements. Remember the idea from the discussion of capital market research in Section 8.3: it is difficult to "beat the market" using financial statement information, because the statements reflect business events people already know something about and because there are many other people, all with their own sources of information, also trying to analyze what is going on and taking action on the basis of their analyses. You should always view financial accounting information as part of a network of information, not as standing alone. To explain and illustrate various techniques, however, this chapter deals with them separately.

PREPARATION FOR INTELLIGENT ANALYSIS

Unless you know why you're doing the analysis, that is, what decision or evaluation is dependent on it, you can't get very far with it. Also, unless you have substantial knowledge of the enterprise, you can't interpret the figures your analysis produces (for example, what is good performance for a new company in a troubled industry may be unsatisfactory for an established company in a prosperous industry).

Much of financial analysis involves ratios, which are boiled-down summaries of the financial statements. Therefore, they have little meaning on their own: they are merely indicators, which can be interpreted and used meaningfully only with a good understanding of the company and the accounting policies used in preparing the financial statements. The scale-free nature of a ratio means that it allows comparisons over certain periods of time, among companies of different sizes, and with other indicators such as interest rates or share prices. But it also can be tempting to think that when you have calculated a ratio, you have something meaningful in itself. While there is some fundamental meaning in each ratio, as we will see, what the comparisons mean to the analyst's decision must be added by the analyst, using knowledge and information beyond the ratios.

Therefore, in order to do an intelligent and useful financial statement analysis, you should do the following:

a. Learn about the enterprise, its circumstances, and its plans. This is essential in any real analysis: don't be misled by the more limited information given for the examples in this book. The annual report's Management Discussion and Analysis section and the footnotes to the financial statements will help you learn about the enterprise.
b. Get a clear understanding of the decision or evaluation to which the analysis will contribute, who the decision maker is, and what assistance he or she requires.
c. Calculate the ratios, trends, and other figures that apply to your specific problem. Don't calculate indiscriminately.
d. Find whatever comparative information you can to provide a frame of reference for your analysis. Industry data, reports by other analysts, results for similar companies or the same company in other years, and other such information is often plentiful.
e. Focus on the analytical results that are most significant to the decision maker's circumstances and integrate and organize the analysis so that it will be of most help to the decision maker.

There are many sources of information about companies to help you become knowledgeable about them and able to place your analysis in context. As you might expect, there is more information about large companies than small ones and more about public companies (those whose shares and other securities are listed on stock exchanges) than about private ones (those that are closely held by a few owners). Companies will often send you their annual reports and other information about them, and many libraries have extensive sources of company, industry, and other economic information, much of it on computer-readable databases. Some popular sources are included in the endnotes.[1]

The preparer of financial statements has a choice from among a number of accounting policies on which to base the financial information. (You've seen this already in Chapter 7 and in some "what if" effects analysis examples in Chapter 8, and you'll see more about it in Chapter 10.) You, as the analyst of these statements, may wish to recast them using other policies that you prefer before computing any of the ratios. For example, some analysts deduct intangible assets, such as goodwill, from assets and owners' equity before computing ratios. They reason that because these assets are not physical in nature, some people may doubt their value; deleting them, therefore, may improve comparability with companies that don't have such assets.

The validity of financial analysis based on accounting ratios has been challenged. Among the criticisms are that future plans and expected results, not historical numbers, should be used in computing ratios, especially liquidity ratios; current market values, not historical numbers, should be used for assets, debts, and shareholders' equity in computing performance ratios; and cash flow, not accounting income, should be used in computing performance ratios. Another objection is that because, at least for public companies, stock markets and other capital markets adjust prices of companies' securities as information comes out, ratios based on publicly available information cannot tell you anything the markets have not already incorporated into security prices. While these criticisms are controversial, they are reminders to use ratios with care and intelligence. Useful additional ideas on the issues raised in this section can be found in many accounting and finance texts. Be careful when reading such material: ratio analysis may be made to appear more cut-and-dried than it is, and some finance authors do not appear to know much about the nature of the accounting information used in the analysis.[2]

9.4 THE NORTH WEST COMPANY, INC.: AN EXAMPLE COMPANY

To help you see how the analyses in this chapter work, they will be illustrated using the financial statements of The North West Company, Inc., a company that is part of northern Canada's social and economic fabric. This company is used in this book because it provides the necessary scope for illustrating a wide variety of analyses. The main reason it is included, though, is to give you a sense of *accomplishment* as you work through this chapter. You will find that, with the accounting knowledge you already have and the techniques outlined in this chapter, you can understand a lot about such a company as North West. While there will be some head scratching as you go, you will be pleased at how knowledgeable you become.

Let's start with an image. In the snows of the long northern winter stands a building with the word "Northern" on it, in big letters. Parked near the building are a pick-up truck and more than a dozen snowmobiles. Inside the building is a store that looks just like any other supermarket you've seen, except usually more compact and selling CDs, carpenter's pencils, electronic gadgets, toys, wheelbarrows, clothing, skates, and all sorts of things besides food. The staff and customers represent a mixture of ages, races, and occupations, with three-piece suits not to be seen. In a network across northern Canada, from Newfoundland to the Yukon, and on into Alaska, more than 150 of these Northern stores serve the vast hinterland. The stores have been there since the first one was built by the Hudson's Bay Company in 1668. In the late 1980s, the company was formed from the Northern Stores division of the Bay and has prospered on its own ever since. In June 1993, the company was designated Innovative Retailer of the Year in the large company category by the Retail Council of Canada.

The company closes its books at the end of the last Saturday in January, not at the end of the month. The fiscal period is therefore measured in weeks. Also, because the period ending near the end of January was mostly in the prior calendar year, the company uses that year to refer to the period's results. Therefore:

- The most recent NorthWest balance sheet in this book is dated January 29, 1994, and is compared to figures for January 30, 1993;
- The most recent statement of earnings and retained earnings and statement of changes in financial position are for the 52 weeks, ended January 29, 1994, and are compared to figures for the 53 weeks ended January 30, 1993; and

- The company refers to the 52 weeks ended January 29, 1994, as *1993* and the 53 weeks ended January 30, 1993, as *1992*.

To ease your referencing the company's information, we will follow the company's dating practice. Therefore, the most recent fiscal period (to January 29, 1994) will be referred to as 1993 and the prior period (to January 30, 1993) will be called 1992. This might be a bit confusing at first, but you'll soon get used to it.

The financial statements and other items from North West's 1994 annual report are at the back of the book. *Before you go further*, read the introductory comments, the Profile, and the History, and then find the financial statements and familiarize yourself with them. Find:

- The 1993 net income number (called "earnings for the year," $17,162 thousand: that is, $17.162 million);
- The January 29, 1994, retained earnings ($46,701 thousand);
- The increase in cash for 1993 ($1,120 thousand);
- The January 29, 1994, total assets ($331,055 thousand); and the January 29, 1994, total liabilities and shareholders' equity (also $331,055 thousand).

It's a good-sized company, but we'll see that we can make sense of its financial position and performance just as we can for a little company, perhaps even more sense because the annual report includes several pages of explanatory notes and a discussion and analysis by management. You might find it useful just to browse through those and see the kinds of things North West wanted to tell us about.

As you familiarize yourself with the general content and format of the financial statements, here are a few things to keep in mind:

a. The financial statements are consolidated because North West is really a group of companies.

b. North West provides figures for the prior year, 1992. In addition, at the end of the notes to the statements, there's a five-year summary. We'll make extensive use of the prior-year figures to help us understand the 1993 ones.

c. In the auditors' report, the auditors state their opinion that the financial statements present the financial story fairly.

d. Two directors signed the financial statements to indicate that the statements were approved by the board of directors.

HOW'S YOUR UNDERSTANDING

Here are two questions you should be able to answer, based on what you have just read:

1. Explain to your friend, who has missed some classes lately, some things that should be done before beginning to analyze a company's financial statements.
2. What kind of business does North West operate: what does it sell, where, and to whom?

9.5 FINANCIAL STATEMENT RATIO ANALYSIS

If you're familiar enough with North West's financial statements to have a good idea of where to look for information, let's turn now to this chapter's first kind of analysis, ratio analysis of the financial statements.

Twenty kinds of ratios that could be used to analyze a company's financial performance and position are outlined in the following pages. (More than this set have been proposed and used. You may wish to invent more yourself if you have particular analytical uses in mind.) Each ratio is illustrated by showing how it is calculated from the North West statements at the back of the book. Some interpretive and comparative comments are made as illustrations, but the main purpose of this section is to show you how to figure out the ratios.

Most figures below are given in thousands of dollars, as they are in North West's statements. Ratios are calculated to three decimal places. They could be done to more decimals, but that would be false accuracy, because the ratios depend on all sorts of judgments and estimates made in assembling the financial statements and, therefore, should not be thought of as precise quantities, but rather as indicators.

PERFORMANCE RATIOS

1. *Return on equity* (sometimes called return on shareholders' investment or return on net worth): calculated as Net income / Owners' equity. ROE indicates how much return the company is generating on the historically accumulated owners' investment (contributed share capital and other capital items plus retained earnings). Owners' equity can be taken straight from the balance sheet or can be computed from the balance sheet equation as Total assets – Total liabilities. The denominator can be year-end equity or average equity over the year; for a growing company, you'd expect a slightly larger ROE figure for the latter.

   For North West, ROE (based on year-end equity) for the last two years has been:

   - $17,162 / $147,652 = .116 for 1993; and
   - $14,954 / $135,346 = .110 for 1992.

   The income return relative to equity is up just a little from 1992. Given the judgments and estimates behind the financial statements, this is probably not a significant increase.

   In the 1993 Financial Highlights (front of the annual report and early in Chapter 5) and the Six-Year Summary (near end of the annual report), North West reports its return on average equity as .123 in 1993 and .146 in 1992. These are calculated by averaging equity over the year, depending on when new shares are issued and dividends are declared, and can't be calculated exactly from the information we have. But we can get close. For example, for 1994, if we do a simple average of the beginning and ending equity, we get: $17,162 / ([$135,346 + $147,652] / 2) = .121. Such differences between versions of ratios are common. They are usually not large and, as long as you calculate your ratio in the same way from year to year, you should be able to spot major changes and trends regardless of how you calculated the ratio. The Six-Year Financial Summary shows the return on average equity to be quite variable: .123 in 1993, .146 in 1992, .149 in 1991, .056 in 1990, .195 in 1989, and .283 in 1988.

2. *Return on assets* (often called return on investment or ROI): usually calculated as (Net income + Interest expense) / Total assets. As with equity in ROE, the total assets figure can be the year-end figure or the average over the year. ROA indicates the company's ability to generate a return on its assets before considering the cost of financing those assets (interest). It helps in judging whether borrowing is worthwhile: presumably if it costs x% to borrow money, the company should expect to earn at least x% on the assets acquired with the money. (This relationship between ROA and borrowing cost is explored further in Section 9.6.)

   We will use a slightly refined version of ROA: we'll calculate the interest expense after income tax, because if interest is just added back to income, the impact of the tax saving it brings is lost. But we will also calculate the ROA without the tax adjustment, because that is the way North West and most other companies do it.

   For our refined ROA, we first have to calculate the after-tax interest cost. You will recall from Chapter 8 that After-tax interest cost = Interest expense × (1 – Tax rate). According to note 8 to the financial statements, the effective income tax rate for 1993 was 42% ($12,435 income tax expense divided by $29,597 income before income taxes). For 1992, it was 39.3% ($9,507 / $24,214). Total interest expense is shown on the income statement as $8,457 for 1993 and $9,157 for 1992. With these figures, the refined ROA on year-end assets was:

   - ($17,162 + $8,457 × [– .420]) / $331,055 = .067 in 1993; and
   - ($14,954 + $9,157 × [– .393]) / $298,412 = .069 in 1992.

   Like ROE, ROA was not significantly different in 1993 from 1992.

   These two "relative return" ratios may be compared. In 1993, ROE was .116 while ROA was .067. The return to owners was .049 higher than the company earned on its assets prior to the interest cost of financing the assets, almost twice as much. In 1992, ROE was .110 while ROA was .069, so the difference was a little smaller. This difference, which was to the benefit of the shareholders (ROE greater than ROA), is called **leverage** and is the subject of Section 9.6. Some other ratios that reflect leverage effects are shown later in this section.

   North West calculates an ROA ratio called "return on net assets from continuing operations" and the Financial Highlights page from Chapter 5 defines this as "pre-tax earnings plus interest as a percentage of net assets employed." For 1993, pre-tax earnings plus interest would be $38,054. It's not clear what "net assets employed" are, but it is common to calculate this as total assets minus current liabilities. Using that calculation, net assets employed were $331,055 – $83,285 = $247,770 at the end of 1993 and $298,412 – $87,142 = $211,270 at the end of 1992. A simple average would be $229,520, and dividing $38,054 by that figure gives 16.6%.

North West's figure is 14.9%, so we again haven't been able to reproduce the company's figure, but have come reasonably close. You can see the value of being able to calculate ratios that you understand yourself, because the versions produced by companies may not be fully clear, since each company fits the ratios to its own circumstances.

3. *Sales return* (or profit margin): usually calculated as Net income/Revenue. Sales return indicates the percentage of sales revenue that ends up as income, so it is the average "bottom line" profit on each dollar of sales. For example, a .10 sales return would mean that 10 cents in net income, after income tax and all other expenses, are generated from each dollar of sales, on average. It is a useful measure of performance and gives some indication of pricing strategy or competition intensity. You might expect a discount retailer in a competitive market to have a low sales return, and an upscale jeweller to have a high return, for example.

   In Section 9.6, we will use an alternative version of the sales return ratio, calculated analogously to that of the refined ROA, that is, by adding interest expense after tax back to net income in order to determine the operating return before the cost of financing that return. Here the usual simpler version will be illustrated.

   For North West, sales return for 1993 was .031 ($17,162 / $548,679) and for 1992 was 0.032 ($14,954 / $472,710). The company made about 3 cents in net income for every dollar of sales. Having already seen that ROE and ROA were each about the same in 1993 compared to 1992, we should not be surprised that return on sales also stayed about the same.

4. *Common size financial statements*: by calculating all balance sheet figures as percentages of total assets and all income statement figures as percentages of total revenue, the size of the company can be approximately factored out. This procedure assists in comparing companies of different sizes and in spotting trends over time for a single company.

   For North West, the common size income statement for 1993 and 1992 would be (rounding to one decimal):

	1993	1992
Sales and other revenue	100.0	100.0
Cost of sales, selling and administrative expenses	91.2	91.3
Depreciation and amortization	1.8	1.6
Operating profit from continuing operations	7.0	7.1
Interest expense	1.6	1.9
Earnings from continuing operations, before income tax	5.4	5.2
Income tax expense	2.3	2.0
Loss from reinstated operations	.0	.0
Net income for the year	3.1	3.2

You can see that the bottom figures are the sales return ratios calculated earlier. The common size income statement shows the same year-to-year stability indicated by ROE and ROA. Only interest expense and income tax expense show any real changes and those are small.

A similar analysis may be done of the balance sheet, dividing all assets, liabilities, and equity items by total assets. You might try that yourself as an exercise and see what is revealed by it.

5. *Gross margin* (or gross profit ratio): calculated as (Revenue – Cost of goods sold) / Revenue. This provides a further indication of the company's product pricing and product mix. For example, a gross margin of 33% indicates that the company's average markup on cost is 50% (revenue equals 150% of cost, so cost is 67% of revenue and gross margin is 33%). This is a rough indicator only, especially for companies with a variety of products or unstable markets.

   This ratio cannot be calculated for North West, because the income statement does not disclose cost of goods sold expense separately from selling and administrative expenses. The common size income statement above showed that the sum of all these was 91.2% of revenue in 1993 and 91.3% in 1992, so it is likely that the gross margin ratio also was stable over the two years.

6. *Average interest rate*: calculated as Interest expense / Liabilities. There are various versions of this ratio, depending on whether interest expense is calculated before or after income tax and on whether all liabilities are included or just the interest-bearing ones, such as bonds and mortgages. If it is calculated on an after-tax basis and applied to all liabilities, it is likely to be quite low: interest is tax-deductible, so income tax savings amount to a third to a half of it and many liabilities, such as deferred income tax, minority interest liability, dividends payable, and most accounts payable, carry no interest. Interest rate calculations are discussed further in Section 9.6, where the rate is calculated on an after-tax basis.

   On a before-tax basis, we have interest expense of $8,457 in 1993 and $9,157 in 1992. Total liabilities were $183,403 at the end of 1993 and $163,066 at the end of 1992. Therefore, the average pre-tax interest rate on all liabilities was .046 in 1993 and .056 in 1992. This is the first ratio to show much of a change. With the information about long-term interest given in the income statement and some thought about which of the liabilities bears interest, and reference to the 1991 balance sheet (not included in this text), we can break the interest rate down approximately as shown on the next page.

   Note 5 to the financial statements indicates that the estimates are a little off the mark. But, given the approximations provided by the averages of beginning and ending debt and the assumption that accounts payable and taxes bear no interest, it can be seen that the overall interest rate decline seemed to happen equally in long-term and short-term debt. It can also be seen that the interest rates on the two kinds of interest-bearing debt are significantly higher than the overall interest rate calculated earlier because the overall rate includes liabilities that do not bear interest.

	1993	1992	1991
Total interest, per income statement	$ 8,457	$ 9,157	
Interest disclosed on long-term debt	5,660	4,685	
Deduced interest on short-term debt	$ 2,797	$ 4,472	
Long-term debt at end of period (including the current portion)	$98,336	$73,870	$50,000
Bank advances and notes at end of period	26,640	33,445	48,694
Noninterest-bearing debts (accounts payable and income taxes payable)	46,645	46,209	41,078
Nondebt liability (deferred income tax)	11,782	9,542	8,310
Total liabilities	$183,403	$163,066	$148,082
Long-term interest as a percentage of *average* of current and last period's long-term debt	6.6%	7.6%	
Short-term interest as a percentage of *average* of current and prior period bank loans and notes	9.3%	10.9%	

7. *Cash flow to total assets*: calculated as Cash generated by operations / Total assets." Cash generated by operations is found in the SCFP and total assets may be the year-end balance sheet figure or an average of the beginning and ending figures. This ratio relates the company's ability to generate cash resources to its size, which approximately factors out size. It provides an alternative return measure to ROA, focusing on cash return rather than on accrual income return as used in ROA.

   For North West, using year-end assets, the ratio was .047 in 1993 ($15,529 / $331,055) and .061 in 1992 ($18,123 / $298,412). The apparent decline is caused by not having the cash inflow from discontinued operations received in 1992: if only cash from continuing operations is used to calculate the ratio, it was .046 in 1992 ($13,773 / $298,412). As with most other ratios, there was little change from 1992 to 1993. (There will be more about this in Section 9.7)

8. *Earnings per share*: conceptually, this ratio is calculated as (Net income – Dividends on preferred shares) / Average number of common shares outstanding. EPS relates earnings attributable to common shares to the number of common shares issued, thereby providing a sort of down-to-earth performance measure. It is also another way of factoring out the company's size. If you have only a 100 shares of a large company, it is not easy to understand what the company's multi-million-dollar income means to you. But if you are told that the EPS are $2.10, you know that your 100 shares earned $210 for the year and can then relate the company's returns to your own circumstances.

   Calculating EPS is a little complicated, so GAAP require that publicly traded companies provide it in their financial statements. That way shareholders may compare the company's return to their circumstances, helping them to evaluate the worth of the shares and to compare various companies' returns to the prices of their shares on the stock market. (See price–earnings ratio below.) Because it is part of the financial statements, it is for most companies the only audited ratio.

For small, closely held companies, however, it is not as meaningful because the owners usually cannot trade their shares readily and are likely to be interested in the value of the overall company more than in that of individual shares. GAAP, consequently, do not require EPS for smaller companies.

More than one version of EPS can appear in the same set of statements. If a company has extraordinary items, discontinued operations, or other anomalies, EPS is calculated both before and after such items, so that the effect of such items may readily be seen. Also, if the company has potential commitments to issue further shares, such as in stock-option plans to motivate senior management or preferred shares convertible to common shares at the option of the holder of the preferred shares, the potential effect of the exercise of such commitments is calculated by showing both ordinary EPS and "fully diluted" EPS. ("Dilution" refers to the potential lowering of return to present shareholders resulting from other people's exercising rights arising from commitments already made by the company.)

For North West, the income statement shows that basic EPS stayed unchanged at $1.06 for both 1992 and 1993. Potential dilution of present shareholders' interests would have no effect in 1994 and only a one cent effect in 1992. The Six-Year Financial Summary at the end of the financial statements shows that EPS have varied from year to year, similar to the pattern for ROE.

9. *Book value per share*: calculated as (Shareholders' equity – Preferred shares) / Number of common shares outstanding. Similar to EPS, this ratio relates the portion of the shareholders' equity attributable to the residual common shareholders to the number of shares outstanding, and so brings the company balance sheet down to the level of the individual shareholder. It is not really a performance ratio, but shareholders' equity does include retained earnings, so it incorporates accumulated performance. Because the balance sheet's figures do not reflect the current market value of most assets or of the company as a whole, many people feel that book value per share is a largely meaningless ratio, but you will see it mentioned in many financial publications.

   For North West, the balance sheet indicates that 16,164 thousand common shares were issued at the end of 1993 and 16,097 thousand at the end of 1992. Book value per share, therefore, equalled $9.13 at the end of 1993 ($147,652 / 16,164) and $8.41 at the end of 1992 ($135,346 / 16,097). These amounts are reported in the Six-Year Financial Summary at the end of the financial statement notes.

   The book value per share and market price per share may be compared to indicate how similar the accounting figures are to the market's evaluation of the company. The two are determined by different processes (book value is measured by GAAP based largely on the historical cost basis, while market price is determined by the market's expectations of future performance as well as current value), so they would be the same only by coincidence. However, a comparison of the two for various companies may indicate companies that appear to be overvalued or undervalued by the market, according to accounting's measure of financial position. North West's shares have been trading at about $15 or higher since 1992, so the market traders see more than the $8 or $9 book value behind the shares. The higher market price will be a function of such factors as traders thinking some assets (such as land) may be more valuable than shown on the balance sheet and their belief that the company will earn greater returns in the future that are worth buying into now. The next ratio focuses on the earnings part of this added value.

10. *Price–earnings ratio*: calculated as Current market price per share / EPS. The PE ratio relates the accounting earnings and market price of the shares, but, since the relationship between such earnings and changes in stock market prices is not straightforward (as noted in Chapter 8 and in other earlier material), the interpretation of PE is controversial. Nevertheless, it is a widely used ratio, appearing in many publications and analyses of companies. Many newspapers include PE in their daily summaries of each company's stock market trades and prices.

    The idea is that, because market price should reflect the market's expectation of future performance, PE compares the present performance with those expectations. A company with a high PE is expected to show greater future performance than its present level, while one with a low PE is not expected to do much better in the future. High-PE companies are those that are popular and have good share prices, while low-PE companies are not so popular, having low share prices relative to their present earnings. PE is highly subject to general increases and decreases in market prices, so it is difficult to interpret over time and is more useful when comparing similar companies listed in the same stock market at the same time.

    For North West, the ordinary shares had an average price on the Toronto Stock Exchange of about $18 in the year ended January 31, 1994, and about $15 in the year ended January 31, 1993 (corresponding to our 1993 and 1992 periods). The average PE ratio was, therefore, about 17 for 1993 ($18 / $1.06) and 14 for 1992 ($15 / $1.06). Because PE changes as share prices change, with each announcement of an EPS number, it can be monitored regularly to track changes in the market's expectations, particularly changes relative to other companies' PEs.

11. *Dividend payout ratio*: calculated as Annual dividends declared per share / EPS. This is a measure of the portion of earnings paid to shareholders. For example, if the dividend payout ratio is .40, 40% of income was distributed to shareholders and the remaining 60% was kept in the company (retained earnings) to finance assets or reduce debts. A stable ratio would suggest that the company has a policy of paying dividends based on earnings, and a variable ratio would suggest that other factors than earnings are important in the board of directors' decisions to declare dividends.

    For North West, the Financial Highlights at the beginning of Chapter 5 indicate that dividends were $.36 per share in each of the last two years. EPS were $1.06 each year, so the dividend payout ratio was a constant 34%. This can be seen also from the total figures on the earnings and retained earnings statement, which shows that dividends of $5,810 were declared in 1993 and $5,182 in 1992. These are 33.9% of net income in 1993 ($5,810 / $17,162) and 34.7% in 1992 ($5,182 / $14,954). The same stability we've seen before is here.

ACTIVITY (TURNOVER) RATIOS

12. *Total asset turnover*: calculated as Revenue / Total assets. This and similar turnover ratios relate the company's dollar sales volume to its size, thereby answering the question: How much volume is associated with a dollar of assets? Turnover and profit-margin ratios are often useful together because they tend to move in opposite directions. Companies with high turnover tend to have low margins, and those with low turnover tend to have high margins. Those extremes represent contrary marketing strategies or competitive pressures: pricing low and trying for high volume vs. pricing high and making more on each unit sold. (There is more about using profit margin and turnover together in Section 9.6.)

    North West's total asset turnover was 1.66 in 1993 ($548,679/$331,055) and 1.58 in 1992 ($472,710/$298,412). Turnover rose in 1993 because revenue grew faster than assets did. The company is getting more business out of each dollar of assets.

13. *Inventory turnover*: calculated as Cost of goods sold expense / Average inventory assets. (If cost of goods sold is not disclosed, it is often replaced by sales revenue in calculating the ratio, which is all right for comparing one year to others for one company, as long as markups and product mixes do not change substantially.) This ratio relates the level of inventories to the volume of activity: a company with low turnover may be risking obsolescence or deterioration in its inventory and/or may be incurring excessive storage and insurance costs. In recent years, many companies have attempted to pare inventories to the bone, keeping just enough on hand to meet customer demand or even ordering inventory as it is demanded by customers (as in the "just in time" method of minimizing inventories without running out of stock and irritating customers).

    For North West, cost of goods sold is not disclosed, but there is so much stability in the other ratios that it is likely useful to compare sales revenue with average inventories. Average inventories for 1993 were $113,658 ([$119,948 + $107,367] / 2) and for 1992 were $97,893 ([$107,367 + $88,419 from the 1991 balance sheet, not included in this book] / 2). (The 1992 average is likely a little distorted by the November 1992 Alaskan acquisition described in financial statement note 10.) These result in turnovers relative to revenue of 4.8 for 1993 ($548,679/$113,658) and 4.8 for 1992 ($472,710 / $97,893). The usual stability! The company appears to have managed its inventories in about the same way in both years.

14. *Collection ratio* (receivables turnover): often called days' sales in receivables: calculated as Accounts receivable/(Revenue/365). This ratio indicates how many days it takes, on average, to collect a day's sales revenue. It becomes large when accounts receivable become larger relative to sales, so its interpretation is the opposite of those of the previous two turnover ratios: a large collection ratio is a negative signal, raising questions about the company's policies of granting credit and the vigour of its collection

attempts. The ratio is subject to significant seasonal changes for many companies, usually rising during heavy selling periods, such as just before Christmas for a retailer, and falling during slow times. (It would be preferable to use only revenue from credit sales in the denominator, since cash sales are collected immediately, but few companies break their revenue figures down to separate cash revenue.)

North West's collection ratio was 35 days at the end of 1993 ($53,034/[$548,679 / 365]) and was also 40 days at the end of 1992 ($51,970/[$472,710 / 365]). It takes the company a little more than a month, on average, to collect from its customers. This is a typical sort of delay: probably you pay your bills about once a month!

FINANCING RATIOS

15. *Debt–equity ratio*: calculated as Total liabilities/Total equity, or sometimes as Total external debt/Total equity to exclude deferred revenue, deferred income tax, and other liabilities that are consequences of accrual accounting's revenue and expense matching more than they are real debt. This ratio measures the proportion of borrowing to owners' investment (including retained earnings) and thus indicates the company's policy of financing its assets. A ratio greater than one indicates the assets are financed mostly with debt, while a ratio less than one indicates the assets are financed mostly with equity. A high ratio, well above one, is a warning about risk: the company is heavily in debt relative to its equity and may be vulnerable to interest rate increases, general tightening of credit, or creditor nervousness. (A high ratio also indicates that the company is leveraged, which means it has borrowed to increase its assets over the amount that could be acquired with owners' funds only and hopes thereby to increase returns and benefit the owners. See the comments on leverage at the end of the discussion of ROA above and in Section 9.6.)

    North West's balance sheet makes this calculation straightforward, by totalling both liabilities and equity. The ratio for 1993 (actually, January 29, 1994) therefore, is 1.24 ($183,403/$147,652) and for 1992 is 1.20 ($163,066/$135,346). These ratios show that the company relies on debt more than on equity and that its relative reliance on debt increased slightly during 1993.

16. *Long-term debt–equity ratio*: calculated as (Long-term loans + Mortgages + Bonds + Similar debts) / Total Equity. This ratio, which has many versions, depending on which specific items the analyst decides to include as debt, is frequently referred to as the debt/equity ratio, under the apparent assumption that longer-term debt is more relevant to evaluating risk and financing strategy than are either the shorter-term debts, such as accounts payable, or the accrual accounting residuals, such as deferred income taxes and minority interest liability included in total liabilities (and therefore included in the version of the debt/equity ratio above).

    For North West, this ratio would involve just the debt described in financial statement note 5. Not including the debt's current portion, the resulting ratio is .60 for 1993 ($88,336/$147,652) and .49 for 1992 ($66,382/$135,346). The company's reliance on long-term debt is not great, but it did increase from 1992 to 1993.

17. *Debt to assets ratio*: if calculated as Total liabilities / Total assets, this ratio is the complement of the debt–equity ratio discussed above and indicates the proportion of assets financed by borrowing. It may also be calculated by just comparing long-term debt or external debt to assets.

    Using total liabilities, the ratio for North West was 0.55 at the end of both 1993 and 1992 ($183,404 / $331,055 and $163,066 / $298,412). The company's use of borrowing to finance assets is unchanged. The long-term debt/equity ratio did increase, so this indicates a somewhat lower reliance on short-term debt in 1993. The balance sheet shows that, while total assets went up about $33 million between 1992 and 1993, current liabilities went down by about $4 million.

LIQUIDITY AND SOLVENCY WARNING RATIOS

18. *Working capital* (current) ratio: calculated as Current assets / Current liabilities. This ratio has already been used several times in this book. It indicates whether the company has enough short-term assets to cover its short-term debts. A ratio above 1 indicates that working capital is positive (current assets exceed current liabilities), and a ratio below 1 indicates that working capital is negative. Generally, the higher the ratio, the greater is the financial stability and the lower is the risk for both creditors and owners. However, the ratio should not be too high because that may indicate the company is not reinvesting in long-term assets to maintain future productivity. Also, a high working capital ratio can actually indicate problems if inventories are getting larger than they should or collections of receivables are slowing down.

    The working capital ratio is a very commonly used indicator. Many analysts use a rough rule that says the working capital ratio should be around 2 (twice as much in current assets as current liabilities), but this is simplistic. Many large companies regularly operate with a working capital ratio closer to 1 than 2. The ratio's interpretation depends on the specific circumstances of each company. Interpretation of it is also complex because it is a static ratio, measuring financial position at a point in time and not considering any future cash flows the company may be able to generate to pay its debts. This ratio is most useful for companies having cash flows that are relatively smooth during the year and hardest to interpret for those that have unusual assets or liabilities or that depend on future cash flows to pay current debts. An example of the latter would be a company that owns a rented building: there may be few current assets and large current liabilities for mortgage payments, but, as long as the building is mostly rented and rental income is steady, the company is not in difficulty even though its working capital ratio is low. However, it is more at risk than a similar company with a higher working capital ratio, because that company could more easily weather a loss of tenants due to recession or the opening of a competing building.

    North West's working capital ratio was 2.19 at the end of 1993 ($182,735/$83,285) and 2.00 at the end of 1992 ($174,486/$87,142). The ratio is now well above 2, which has not been the case before in the company's six years as a separate company. The reason seems to be that the company is using some resources to pay down its bank loans, so the denominator of the ratio is declining while the numerator is growing.

19. *Acid test (quick) ratio*: calculated as (Cash + Temporary investments + Accounts receivable) / Current liabilities. This is a more demanding version of the working capital ratio and indicates whether current liabilities could be paid without having to sell the inventory, in other words, without having to convince more customers to agree to buy what the company has for sale. There is an even harsher version of this ratio, called the "extreme acid test," that uses only cash and cash equivalents in the numerator. A complementary ratio, Inventory / Working capital, is often used to indicate what percentage of working capital is tied up in inventory. These ratios are all used to signal greater degrees of risk than may be revealed by the working capital ratio alone, and so tend to be used when that ratio is deteriorating or is worrisome for some other reason.

    For North West, the acid test ratio was .72 at the end of 1993 ([$7,136 + $53,034]/$83,285) and .75 at the end of 1992 ([$13,385 + $51,970]/$87,142). The company could not have paid its current liabilities out of its more liquid assets at the end of 1992 and was even less able to do so at the end of 1993. The fact that these ratios are so much less than the working capital ratio shows that the company's working capital is greatly influenced by the amount of inventory carried (prepaid expenses are small). This is not unexpected for a retailer, and, as we saw earlier, inventory turnover (related to sales) has not changed over the two years, so the company is gaining increased revenue from its increased inventory. However, the slight decline in the acid test ratio indicates that inventory levels should be watched.

20. *Interest coverage ratio*: usually calculated as (Income before interest expense + Income tax) / Interest expense. This and similar coverage ratios based on cash flow figures from the SCFP indicate the degree to which financial commitments (in this case those to pay interest on debts) are covered by the company's ability to generate income or cash flow. A low coverage ratio (especially below 1) indicates that the company is not operating at a sufficiently profitable level to cover the interest obligation comfortably and may also be a warning of solvency problems (difficulty in meeting obligations over the long haul).

    To calculate North West's interest coverage ratio, we add net income, income tax expense, and interest expense and divide by the latter. The ratio was therefore 4.50 in 1993 ([$17,162 + $12,435 + $8,457]/$8,457) and 3.67 in 1992 ([$14,954 + $9,507 + $9,157]/$9,157). Interest coverage, which was already comfortable, improved further in 1993.

Ratios are a quick method of breaking the information in the financial statements down into a form that allows for comparability with similar companies and with the financial performance of the company over a number of years. Ratios offer another advantage in that different ratios consider different parts of a company's performance. Thus, if you do not want to investigate anything more about a company than its liquidity, you might only calculate liquidity ratios, such as the quick and current ratios.

Users rely on more than ratios and other calculations from the financial statements when analyzing a company's performance. They also rely on the parts of the annual report that precede the financial statements, the auditor's report, notes to the financial statements, reports by various analysts, personal knowledge of management, news media reports, and much more.

Some possible pieces of information that users could find in the first part of an annual report would include management's interpretation of past and prospective performance, new ventures or growth strategies for the company, and indications of the areas of operations that were undergoing stress or change. The people who prepare the nonfinancial-statement (and not audited) parts of the annual report may not be objective about performance and prospects, but users can still get an indication of strengths or troubles in the company from this part of the report. See the Management's Discussion and Analysis section of North West's annual report, preceding the financial statements at the back of this book.

The auditor's report tells users whether or not financial statements fairly represent the company's position. This is not a clean bill of health on the operations of the company; it is simply saying that the current state of the company, good or bad, is fairly represented in the accounting statements. The auditor's report also tells users whether any unusual (non–GAAP or inconsistent) accounting methods have been used in determining the values in the statements.

Notes to financial statements provide further explanations of some key areas in the statements, as we have seen in the calculation of ratios for North West. These can include information about a company's accounting policy for particular accounts, detailed calculations of how some account values were determined, and notifications of any accounting policy changes, significant litigations, and other possibly significant items. All of this information, along with the statements themselves, and any ratios or other analyses, help users get a well-rounded picture of the company.

HOW'S YOUR UNDERSTANDING

Here are two questions you should be able to answer, based on what you've just read:

1. How well did The North West Company perform in 1993 as compared to 1992?
2. How was North West's liquidity at the end of 1993? Is that an improvement over 1992?

9.6 INTEGRATIVE RATIO ANALYSIS: THE SCOTT FORMULA

With knowledge of the company and the purpose of the analysis, the long list of ratios above can be used to reveal many things about a company. We learned much about North West in Section 9.5 above, but it may not be obvious how to pull all the information together into an overall picture of the company's performance. It's clear that the company is performing well, that its performance was very stable across 1992 and 1993, and that, other than for a slight rise in inventories, its liquidity is good. Can we fit the ratios together more systematically? Can we make use of the fact that the ratios are all calculated on the same financial statement figures and thus tend to connect to each other?

In this section, you will see how to do a particularly useful integrative analysis called the **Scott formula**, named after its originator, Professor William R. Scott of the University of Waterloo. This integrative approach is one of many that are, or could be, used. It is described here in detail, both because it tells a great deal about how a company's overall returns have been generated and it is an example of taking advantage of the double-entry financial statements to increase analytical power.

The Scott formula uses the idea of **leverage**, which is an important objective and consequence of borrowing money and then using it to generate returns. Leverage, also called "trading on the equity," "financial leverage," and, in Britain and some other countries, "gearing," works like this:

a. Professor Grunion wants to invest $15,000 in a real estate project;

b. Grunion has $5,000 available in personal funds;

c. So, Grunion borrows $10,000 from the bank at 11% interest;

d. Grunion invests the total $15,000 in the project and receives an annual return of $2,100;

e. The project's return is 14% before tax ($2,100 / $15,000);

f. Out of that, Grunion pays the bank interest (11% of $10,000 = $1,100);

g. Grunion keeps the rest ($2,100 – $1,100 = $1,000);

h. Grunion's before-tax return on the equity invested is 20% ($1,000 / $5,000).

Not bad! The project returns 14%, but Grunion gets 20% on the equity invested. The reason is that Grunion has borrowed at 11% but has used the borrowed funds to earn 14%. The extra 3% return on the borrowed funds is Grunion's to keep in return for taking the risk of investing in the project:

- Overall return = 14% on $15,000 = $2,100
- Paid to the bank = 11% on $10,000 = $1,100
- Kept by Grunion: 14% on $5,000 own funds + 3% on $10,000 borrowed funds
- Grunion's return = the 14% ($700) + the 3% ($300) = $1,000, which is 20% of the $5,000

Grunion has benefitted from leverage: borrowing money to earn money.

Leverage is a good way to increase your return, as long as you can ensure that the project's total rate of return is greater than your borrowing cost. It's a double-edged sword, though, because leverage can hit you hard if returns are low or negative. Suppose Grunion's real estate project returns only 7%. Then look what happens:

- Overall return = 7% on $15,000 = $1,050
- Paid to the bank = 11% on $10,000 = $1,100
- Kept by Grunion: 7% on own funds *minus* 4% on $10,000 borrowed funds
- Grunion's return = the 7% ($350) – the 4% ($400) = – $50, which is –1% of $5,000

Grunion has been hurt by leverage.

So, Grunion in this case loses on every dollar borrowed, because the project returns less than the cost of borrowing. It's not such a great deal any more! Grunion is losing 1% on the equity invested, but if just that equity had been invested, with no borrowing, Grunion would have made 7%, the project's return. Leverage is now hurting, not helping.

When there is any borrowing involved, the return on the equity invested is always the sum of the project's rate of return, applied to the equity invested, plus the leverage return, which is the difference between the project's rate of return and the borrowing cost applied to the proportion borrowed. We would hope both these components are positive, but they may not be, as we saw in the second case above. This way of calculating returns is used in the last point in the two cases and is the basis of the Scott formula. That formula also breaks the overall return down into two parts to reveal how it was generated, producing the following analysis:

Return on equity = Overall operating return before interest cost + Leverage return
= (Sales return before interest) × (Asset turnover) + (Operating return – Interest rate) × (Borrowing proportion)

ROE = SR × AT + (ROA – IN) × D/E

ROE is the same return on equity you saw in the ratio list;
SR is the version of the sales return calculated by adding interest expense after tax back to net income;
AT is the total asset turnover ratio;
ROA is the return on assets you saw previously, the "refined" version computed by adding interest expense after tax back to net income;
IN is the average *after-tax* interest rate, calculated as after-tax interest expense divided by total liabilities;
D/E is the debt–equity ratio.

The Scott formula thus combines several ratios into an integrated analysis of performance and position. Let's see how this formula is calculated from the financial statements and then, how to use it. A brief arithmetic proof of the formula is included in the endnotes, if you're interested.[3]

CALCULATION OF THE SCOTT FORMULA

The formula can be developed using either example figures or symbols. To increase your understanding, let's do it both ways:

		Example Figures	Symbols
Total assets		$100,000	A
Total liabilities		$ 70,000	L
Total equity		$ 30,000	E
Total revenue		$150,000	REV
Net income		$ 6,000	NI
Interest expense		$ 7,000	INT
Income tax rate		40%	TR
After-tax interest expense (Expense × (1 – Tax rate))		$4,200	ATI = INT (1 – TR)
ROE (return on equity)	$6,000/$30,000 = .20		NI / E
SR (sales return before interest)	($6,000 + $4,200)/150,000 = .068		(NI + ATI)/REV
AT (asset turnover)	$150,000/$100,000 = 1.50		REV/A
ROA (return on assets)	($6,000 + $4,200)/$100,000 = .102		(NI + ATI)/A
IN (average interest rate after tax)	$4,200/$70,000 = .06		ATI/L
D/E (debt–equity ratio)	$70,000/$30,000 = 2.333		L/E

Result:

ROE= SR × AT + (ROA – IN) × D/E

.20 = .068 × 1.5 + (.102 – .06) × 2.333

The Scott formula result for this example company shows that the company's 20% return on equity is made up of:

- A 6.8% return on sales;
- An asset turnover of 1.5 times;
- Return on assets of 10.2%;
- Average interest rate of 6%;
- A debt–equity ratio of 2.333 times.

This provides several points of comparison with other companies or other years. Those comparisons could have been made using the individual ratios listed earlier, but now the ratios are tied to one another so that you can see how each affects return on equity.

The terms on the right of the equal sign can be collected together to summarize the two basic components of the return on equity:

- The first is the **operating return**, which indicates the company's ability to make a return on its assets before interest costs (6.8% × 1.5 = 10.2%, the return on assets); and

- The second is the **leverage return** (.102 – .06) × 2.333 = .042 × 2.333 = 9.8%).

So, we have:

Return on equity = Operating return + Leverage return
ROE = ROA + Leverage
20% = 10.2% + 9.8%

The example company's return on equity, therefore, is a little more than half from operations and a little less than half from using borrowed funds to increase the return to owners. *Note that if the two figures on the right don't add up to the figure on the left, there's been an error* (perhaps just a rounding error but maybe something more serious). The Scott formula is based on the double-entry financial statements (as shown in the proof in the endnotes), so if the figures are developed correctly, it has to balance.

SCOTT FORMULA FOR NORTH WEST

To illustrate how to apply the Scott formula to a real company, let's use North West's figures. The formula can be applied to any set of balanced financial statement figures; let's use the figures for 1993 and as at the end of 1994, because they are all incorporated in the 1993 balance sheet (January 29, 1994). To test your knowledge of the financial statements, put a piece of paper over the 1993 figures below and find them yourself in back of the book. (You should recognize most of the ratios as the same ones calculated in Section 9.5.)

	1993 Figures	Symbols
Total assets, end of 1993	$331,055	A
Total liabilities, end of 1993	183,403	L
Total equity, end of 1993	147,652	E
Total revenue for 1993	548,679	REV
Net income for 1993	17,162	NI
Interest expense for 1993	8,457	INT
Income tax rate for 1993 ($12,435/$29,597)	.42	TR
After-tax 1993 interest expense (Expense × (1 – tax rate))	4,905	ATI = INT (1–TR)
ROE (return on equity)	.116	NI/E
SR (sales return before interest)	.040	(NI + ATI)/REV
AT (asset turnover)	1.657	REV/A
ROA (return on assets)	.067	(NI + ATI)/A
IN (average interest rate after tax)	.027	ATI/L
D/E (debt-equity ratio)	1.242	L/E

Result:

ROE = SR × AT + (ROA – IN) × D/E
.116 = .040 × 1.657 + (.067 – .027) ×1.242
.116 = .066 + .050

(Note that there is a slight rounding error. ROA is the first term in the brackets on the right, and it is the product of SR and AT, the first terms right of the equal sign. Therefore, SR × AT should equal .067, but they equal .066 above. If you're doing the calculations, it is a good idea to check that those terms are equal, because a difference may indicate a mistake more serious than just a rounding error!)

Here is the Scott formula applied to North West for 1992. See if you can produce these figures yourself from the financial statements in the Appendix. (If you can't, refer to their derivation as set out in this chapter's notes.[4])

$.110 = .043 \times 1.584 + (.069 - .034) \times 1.205$
$.110 = .068 \quad + .042$
(Slight rounding error: .068 should = .069)

Interpretation of Scott Formula Results

The Scott formula is powerful for a quick analysis of a company's return on equity, because it highlights the individual components of the return as well as the relationships among the components that make up the final return. To demonstrate, let's look at these components.

Operating Component of Return on Equity

We can see how profit margin (SR) and turnover (AT) interact to produce the operating return (return on assets). In one company, a low margin and a high turnover may generate the return. In another, a high margin and a low turnover may generate the return. Profit margin and turnover are likely to offset each other in generating the return on assets, because competitive pressures are likely to force selling prices, and therefore profit margins, down if a high turnover is desired. Conversely, if you want to cater to the high-priced end of the market, you are not likely to have much sales volume. Think of what great results you'd get if you could get *both* high margin and high volume (and so our worry about monopolies), or of how disastrous things are for companies stuck with *both* low margin and low volume.

We already know from the earlier ratio analyses that North West had a good year in 1993. Subject to our small rounding error, the Scott formula shows the operating return (ROA) to be 6.6% in 1993, made up of a 4.0% sales return before tax and an asset turnover of 1.66 times. Results were very similar in 1992, with an ROA of 6.8%, made up of a 4.3% sales return and an asset turnover of 1.58 times. Even though the results were similar, you can see the return–turnover tradeoff: 1993 showed higher turnover but lower sales return than 1992.

Leverage Component of Return on Equity

The Scott formula shows how (or if) companies use financial leverage, defined as the difference between the cost of money borrowed to provide resources (assets) and the return on those assets. If there is a significant positive difference between the operating return and the cost of borrowing, a company may take advantage of this difference and use leverage to enhance its return by large borrowing relative to its owners' equity base. Another company may have a significant leverage potential (difference between return on asset and cost of borrowing), but not borrow as much and so not utilize it to the same extent. A prudently managed company does not borrow too much relative to its equity base. This provides protection against the *negative* effects of leverage (especially a negative difference between return on assets and interest rates), but the trade-off is that the company might also not be taking full advantage of the positive side of leverage when times are good. Management is always having to face the dilemma of being careful in order to avoid serious losses and taking risks to take advantage of opportunities.

North West had positive leverage in both years. The leverage component of ROE was 5.0% in 1993, a little more than the 4.2% in 1992. This happened because of a combination of a greater leverage potential (ROA – IN) in 1993 (.040: .067 – .027, vs. .035: .069 – .034) with a greater degree of borrowing (debt–equity ratio of 1.242 vs. 1.205). Neither difference was great, but both worked in the same direction to help ROE.

RETURN ON EQUITY

The Scott formula shows how financial leverage and operating return combine to produce the overall return on equity. It is a reminder of the business fact that the owners' return is partly a function of day-to-day operations and partly a function of the financial structure of the company. Marketing, production, and finance are *all* important in generating the owners' return.

North West's results for 1993 and 1992 were summarized by the Scott Formula as follows:

	ROE	=	Operating return	+	Leverage return
1993:	.116	=	.066	+	.050
1992:	.110	=	.068	+	.042

Operating return was just a tiny amount less in 1993 than 1992, but, because leverage return was higher, overall return on equity was up over 1992. The company's owners have benefitted from leverage; in fact, the leverage return was 43% of ROE in 1993, vs. 38% in 1992, so they benefitted more than in 1992. As long as the company doesn't extend its borrowing too much and become vulnerable to interest rate increases or operating return declines, the owners should be pleased that the company is using leverage to increase their returns. Without any borrowing (a debt–equity ratio of zero), the company's ROE would just equal the operating return, which is much less in both years.

To interpret North West's results further, more comparative information is needed. Comparisons with other companies in 1993 and 1992 would highlight North West's performance relative to those companies as the economy began to recover from the early 1990s recession. While comparisons with similar companies would be the most informative, the Scott formula allows comparisons with any other company that may be an alternative choice for investors wondering whether to become shareholders or creditors of North West. Calculation of the Scott formula for North West for several years would give an indication of how the company's returns have been managed in good years and poor ones.

CONCLUDING COMMENTS

The Scott formula is an effective tool, but it only analyzes some of the financial data. For example, although it reflects one aspect of risk (borrowing), it does not directly adjust for or incorporate the many risky components of a company's operations that may play a large role in the level of return the company generates. Working capital, liquidity, solvency, and cash flow, all of which relate to risk, are not reflected in the Scott formula. Nor is there any reflection of market rates of return (such as on the company's shares if traded on a stock market, as North West's are) or of such potentially great risks as international currency fluctuations, interest rate policies of governments, and inadequate marketing strategy. While the Scott formula reflects the *historical* results of these sorts of factors and may indicate the company's strengths and limitations as it faces the future, it is not a predictor of the future. The formula is only an example of one of the many tools available for financial analysis and should be used in conjunction with other such tools.

HOW'S YOUR UNDERSTANDING

Here are two questions you should be able to answer, based on what you have just read:

1. You have prepared a Scott-formula analysis for Pembina Manufacturing Ltd. for 1995 and determined that the return on equity was 12%, the return on assets was 7%, and the leverage return was 5%. Explain this result to the company's president.
2. Write a paragraph summarizing North West's financial performance for 1993 compared with 1992.

9.7 INTERPRETATION OF CASH FLOW INFORMATION

Both in the theory of economics and finance and in the practical relationship between businesses and their owners and creditors, cash flow is an important measure of return. Income for the company is all very well, but owners sooner or later want to receive some of it in cash dividends, lenders want cash payments to cover interest and principal due, and so on. Income is revenue minus expenses, but the revenue may be tied up in uncollected receivables and the expenses may either not have been paid yet or have been paid in advance. The cash flow statement (SCFP) is designed to reconcile the net income figure to the amount of cash generated from operations and to provide nonoperating cash flow information.

To refresh your memory of the SCFP and help you think about using it for analysis, a summary of the kinds of effects on cash that the statement can indicate is shown on the next page.

The conceptual basis of the statement and the way it is intended to be used can be seen from the above summary.

- First, the Operations section of the SCFP converts income (profit) from the complex accrual basis used in preparing the income statement to a simpler cash flow basis.
- Second, the conversion from accrual to cash basis reveals something about how the company has managed its current assets and liabilities over the period: for example, have receivables gone up, delaying the inflow of cash from revenue?

	Increase Cash	Decrease Cash
Net income:		
Positive net incomes	X	
Negative net incomes (net losses)		X
Noncash expenses (such as amortization of long-term assets and the deferred portion of income tax expense) are added back to net income and so *appear to*	X	
Noncash revenues (such as share of income of an associated company) are deducted from net income and so *appear to*		X
Changes in noncash working capital accounts:		
Increases in noncash current assets		X
Decreases in such assets	X	
Increases in noncash current liabilities	X	
Decreases in such liabilities		X
Changes in noncurrent assets:		
Increases in cost of (investment in) such assets		X
Proceeds from disposal of such assets	X	
Changes in noncurrent debts and capital:		
Financing obtained from owners and creditors	X	
Repayments, redemptions, dividend payments		X

- Third, the Dividends, Investing, and Financing sections of the SCFP show what the company did with the cash it generated from day-to-day operations, and how much nonoperating cash it raised during the period.
- The SCFP, therefore, gives quite a complete portrayal of how the company raised its cash and spent it, and what its cash position is now. (Remember that "cash" includes anything deemed "equivalent" to cash, such as short-term bank deposits, very liquid investments, and perhaps the deduction of very short-term demand bank loans or bank account overdrafts.)

The SCFP, *in combination with the income statement and balance sheet*, can be used to:[5]

a. Evaluate the relative significance of the cash flow figures by relating them to the size of the company's assets, liabilities, equity, and income;

b. Evaluate the company's relative dependence on internally generated cash (from operations) vs. cash generated from external financing activities;

c. Evaluate solvency (ability to pay debts when due) and liquidity (having adequate reserves of cash and near-cash assets);

d. Evaluate the level of spending on long-term asset acquisitions in relation to the size of the company's assets and the amount of annual amortization, in order to help judge whether the company appears to be keeping its plant and equipment up to date;
e. Evaluate the company's debt vs. equity financing strategy;
f. Evaluate the company's dividend policy by comparing dividends with both income and cash flow, and reviewing the pattern over time;
g. Determine the relationship between income and cash flow to evaluate the "quality" of earnings (income): income should be reasonably consistent with cash flow, after adjusting for normal corrections such as amortization, and should not be so far out of line with cash flow that there's some question about its validity;
h. Identify possible manipulation of the cash flow figures, such as failing to replace inventories or delaying payment of current or noncurrent debts, by comparisons to the way cash flows were generated in past years;
i. Identify either the hazards of success, such as drains on cash flow due to the build-up of inventories or accounts receivable, or the benefits of decline, such as cash increases due to shrinking inventories or receivables.

ILLUSTRATIVE ANALYSIS OF THE NORTH WEST COMPANY

Let's have a look at North West's cash flow information and find out what we can about points such as those listed above. In the process, general comments will be made about the company's financial performance and position with reference to the illustrative ratios and Scott-formula calculations already done for North West.

To interpret North West's SCFP, it is necessary to keep in mind what the company defines as "cash" (cash and cash equivalents). At the bottom of the SCFP, we're told that "cash position" is comprised of cash minus bank advances (short-term bank loans) and short-term notes. Since there are more of the liabilities than there is of cash on hand, the cash position is negative, and has been so since at least the beginning of the 1992 year. But it is slowly climbing toward a positive amount, going from \$(47,650) to \$(19,504) over the two years covered by the SCFP.

As with the other statements, decisions by the company about how to disclose or calculate information can make a big difference in the SCFP. For example, suppose the company had defined cash as just the cash asset. Then the SCFP would have shown a change in cash for 1992 of positive \$8,764 and for 1993 of negative \$6,249 (\$4,621 on hand at the end of 1991, according to earlier financial statements, rising to \$13,385 at the end of 1992 and then falling to \$7,136 at the end of 1993). The repayments of bank advances would have appeared in the Financing, or perhaps Operating, sections of the SCFP as cash outflows.

While this would have shown the cash account changes clearly, it would perhaps have obscured two other things. First, there is a fluid interchange between cash on hand and bank loans. Most companies' banking arrangements provide for lines of credit, by which the company can borrow by just writing cheques that the bank has agreed to honour. To complement this, bank loans can be reduced any time the company has more cash on hand than it needs, so that interest costs can be kept down. Note 4 to the financial statements reports that North West's Canadian lines of credit alone are $80 million, which is far above the total current borrowing of $26.6 million. So, if the SCFP separated cash from this kind of borrowing, it would be arithmetically correct but wrong as a representation of the underlying business affairs. Second, the company's apparent strategy of paying down the bank advances seems to have "plateaued" at a negative cash of about $20 million. Probably that represents the kind of combination of cash on hand and access to bank loans that the company needs for its day-to-day operations. If the cash account had been separated from the bank advances, the stability in that combination during 1993 would not be apparent.

With that introduction, the SCFP may be summarized:

	1993	1992	Difference
Cash generated by operations:			
Continuing operations	$ 15,529	$ 13,773	$ 1,756
Discontinued operations	—	4,350	(4,350)
Cash used in investing activities	(33,705)	(32,754)	(951)
Cash raised by financing activities	25,100	47,050	(21,950)
Cash paid out in dividends	(5,804)	(4,814)	(990)
Change in cash position	$ 1,120	$ 27,605	$(26,485)
Foreign currency translation effect	(564)	(15)	(549)
Increase in cash for the year	$ 556	$ 27,590	$(27,034)
Cash and equivalents, beginning	(20,060)	(47,650)	27,590
Cash and equivalents, end	$(19,504)	$(20,060)	$ 556

Several similarities and differences between 1993 and 1992 are apparent:

- Cash from continuing operations was up in 1993, but not dramatically. This accords with the sort of stability in 1993 that the earlier ratio and Scott-formula analyses showed.
- Discontinued operations raised cash of $4,350 in 1992, but there were none such in 1993. This is an example of the cash perspective of the SCFP. Presumably the activities that were discontinued were poor performers, or they'd have been continued. So getting out of them should help future overall performance by removing their presumably downward impact on net income. But getting out of them also helps right away by bringing in cash that can be used elsewhere, such as to pay down bank loans.
- Spending on investing activities and dividends were both up from 1992, but not much. More evidence of stability!
- Financing activities, however, were very much reduced over 1992. Only about half the financing raised in 1992 was raised in 1993.
- Foreign currency translation adjustments were required to convert the Alaskan revenues, expenses, assets, and liabilities to Canadian dollars

in producing the consolidated financial statements. These had little effect in 1992, soon after the Alaskan acquisition, but were more apparent in 1993 as the Canadian dollar declined somewhat against the U.S. dollar. North West has chosen to separate the translation effect from the other items in the SCFP, but it could have been included in investing, financing, or elsewhere, as many companies do. (You'll remember from Chapter 4 that all balance sheet changes have to go somewhere in the SCFP, but deciding where to put foreign currency translation effects, which are produced just by differences in the way various accounts are converted to Canadian dollars, is as awkward for the SCFP as it is for the balance sheet. North West's balance sheet puts the effects in the equity section as a separate item (as GAAP specify), so it seems consistent to separate them in the SCFP too.)

In Section 9.5, the cash flow to total assets ratio, for continuing operations, was calculated as .047 in 1993 and .046 in 1992, so operating cash flows rose at the same rate as the company grew. A review of the Operating Activities section of the SCFP shows that the reason cash from operations did not grow as much as income did is that increased cash was tied up in noncash working capital in 1993. For both years, working capital increases were nearly as much as net income, so the day-to-day cash inflows and outflows were nearly equal. The increasing noncash working capital is one of the few warning signals in the company's results; as noted earlier, this comes mainly from significant increases in inventories.

The Financing Activities section of the SCFP shows a change in financing between the two years. In 1992, a major cash infusion was provided by a $31 million issue of share capital. Long-term borrowing was $23 million. In 1993, there was no significant issue of shares, but long-term borrowing went up to $36 million. Some of the new borrowing was needed in both years to repay other long-term debt as it became due (see the current portion on the balance sheet) or as it was refinanced to take advantage of declining interest rates.

The Investing Activities section shows roughly equivalent amounts being spent on fixed assets to those raised in financing activities. The company is financing its long-term assets with long-term debt and share capital. This is a common and sensible strategy: financing long-term assets with short-term borrowing can leave a company vulnerable to short-term variations in interest rates and in its own liquidity. The Alaskan acquisition was a big part of the investing in 1992, but in 1993, without such an acquisition, total investing was about the same as 1992, so the company continues to be aggressive about growth through investment. One measure of this is to compare total spending on fixed assets to the depreciation and amortization expenses. We'd expect that a company that is keeping its assets up to date would spend at least as much each year as the loss in economic value that depreciation and amortization estimate. Probably more, because inflation usually means that the cost of replacing an asset is higher than its purchase price was. In North West's case, spending on fixed assets is more than three times depreciation and amortization in both years.

In summary, the SCFP reveals useful information about the company's financial and investment strategy and, overall, presents the same picture of stability that we saw in the earlier analyses. For North West, accrual income and cash income (cash from operations) are very similar, so the company is not accruing profits beyond its ability to collect them. This is part of the picture we'd expect of a retailer: the revenue and expense recognition policies are quite straightforward. The company continues to grow, and its growth is financed mainly through long-term debt and equity. There isn't much cash left over from operations to finance this, because inventory increases (probably associated with the growth in fixed assets: stores and equipment for them) use up about half the cash generated by net income adjusted for depreciation, amortization, and deferred income taxes.

You may have thought of more conclusions than these. Careful use of the SCFP in conjunction with the other financial information can provide many insights and raise useful questions for further investigation.

HOW'S YOUR UNDERSTANDING

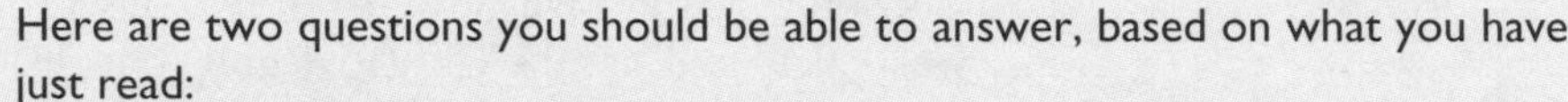

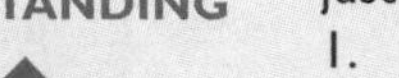

Here are two questions you should be able to answer, based on what you have just read:

1. What were the main components of North West's 1993 cash flow?
2. How does cash flow information contribute to financial statement analysis?

9.8 "WHAT IF" EFFECTS, RATIOS, AND CASH FLOW

This section continues the "what if" effects analysis examples, to include an analysis of effects on ratios and cash flow. As before, this analysis will be done on an after-tax basis. Therefore, remember the following general points:

1. Changes in specific accruals or general accounting policies do not directly affect cash because they do not involve cash. For example, correcting a depreciation expense involves an entry to depreciation expense (for the current year), retained earnings (for past years), and accumulated depreciation. Cash isn't part of the entry. Even when an accrual or accounting policy change is implemented in the accounts, there is no direct cash effect because, by the nature of accrual accounting, such choices are implemented by journal entries involving balance sheet accounts other than cash (such as receivables, payables, inventories, and accumulated depreciation).
2. Such changes *do* generally affect income tax expense and liability, as we have already seen, because tax is assessed on an accrual accounting basis, by and large. The income tax effect on any current or prior year change, X is approximately rX, where r is the tax rate estimated from the financial statements. The after-tax effect is therefore (1 – r)X. Without detailed tax knowledge, it may not be possible to tell whether it is the current or the deferred part of the tax that is affected, but that is unlikely to matter for the purpose of most "what if" analysis.
3. The effect on income tax expense and liability is also an effect on accruals, and so involves no *immediate* cash effect either. However, there will be a cash effect fairly soon, when the extra tax is paid or the tax refund is collected, unless only deferred income tax is affected.

Accounting research has shown that stock market prices tend to reflect the above analysis. If there is no effect on cash at all, now or ever, the stock market is likely to largely ignore the change. If there is a tax effect, the market may react in accordance with it because of its cash implications. For example, if a public company takes a write-down or makes a change in accounting that reduces income, but saves income tax in doing so, the price of its shares might *rise* a bit to recognize the cash saving.

Below we will examine five "what if" effects analysis examples. For each, we will ask eight standard questions, just to help you see the extent of the analysis that is possible. We will ask what is the effect of each on:

		Abbreviation
1.	Net income for the current year	Net income
2.	Retained earnings at the beginning of the current year (Effect on *ending* retained earnings is the sum of 1 and 2.)	Begin R.E.
3.	Income tax liability at the end of the current year (combining current tax payable and deferred income tax liability)	Tax liability
4.	Cash from operations for the current year	Op. cash flow
5.	Working capital ratio at the end of the current year	W/C ratio
6.	Return on equity for the current year	ROE
7.	Return on assets for the current year;	ROA
8.	Debt–equity ratio at the end of the current year	D/E ratio

Here are the five examples (*assume a 40% income tax rate for all*):

A. Handee Hardware Ltd. is considering borrowing a short-term loan of $1,000,000 from the bank.

B. Yukon Crystals Inc. proposes to write an unproductive mine down by $25,000,000.

C. The Rock Manufacturing Company has signed an agreement with its union whereby the company's contribution to the pension plan will be increased immediately by $2,000,000, $480,000 of which will apply to the current year and the rest to prior years. This has been done to correct past unintended undercontributions to the pension plan by the company. Future contributions will be made correctly.

D. An account payable for $8,000 rent expense was forgotten by City Jewellery at the end of the previous year and is recorded in the current year instead.

E. Grand Scenter Perfume is considering changing its method of accounting for bad debts. Under the present method, the allowance for doubtful accounts was $15,000 at the end of last year and is $26,000 at the end of this year. Under the proposed method, the allowance would be recalculated as $23,000 at the end of last year and $38,000 at the end of this year.

If the solution notes that follow are not entirely clear to you, you might try using the change effects analytical framework introduced in Chapter 8 to help you see what is happening.

Solution Notes—Example A

Net income: No effect on current income (until after the borrowing, when interest begins to accumulate).

Begin R.E.: No effect on past incomes.

Tax liability: No effect on income tax (until after the borrowing, when interest incurred becomes a tax-deductible expense).

Op. cash flow: The cash account goes up by $1,000,000. The effect on cash from operations depends on whether the bank loan is considered a cash equivalent liability. If it is, there is no effect on operating cash flow. If it is not, there will be a $1,000,000 cash inflow shown under operations or under financing

W/C ratio: Both the cash asset and the bank loan liability are current liabilities, and both are increased, so there is no effect on working capital. But to think about effects on the working capital ratio, consider the following possible situations:

	Current Assets		Current Liabilities		W.C. Ratio	
	Before	After	Before	After	Before	After
a.	6,000,000	7,000,000	3,000,000	4,000,000	2.00	1.75
b.	6,000,000	7,000,000	5,000,000	6,000,000	1.20	1.17
c.	6,000,000	7,000,000	7,000,000	8,000,000	.86	.88
d.	6,000,000	7,000,000	9,000,000	10,000,000	.67	.70

You can see from these situations that such an event drives the working capital ratio toward 1: down toward 1 if it was higher, up toward it if lower. So, there is no effect on working capital because it is the *difference* between current assets and current liabilities, and the effects on each cancel one another out. But there is an effect on the working capital ratio, because it is current assets *divided* by current liabilities, and the effects on each do not cancel out because there is no subtraction.

ROE: No effect until interest starts to accumulate and any revenues or decreased costs for which the money is used begin. Whether ROE ultimately goes up or down depends on whether the company has borrowed wisely. For example, the money may be used to pay suppliers sooner and get early-payment discounts that are greater than the interest paid to the bank for the money, in which case ROE will go up eventually.

ROA: Like ROE, there is no effect now and future effects depend on how the money is used.

D/E ratio: This will go up because the company has more debt and there has been no immediate effect on equity (no effect on income).

Solution Notes—Example B

Net income: The mine asset cost will be credited, accumulated amortization will be debited, and an expense, loss or “discontinued operations” special loss account will be debited. The full effect would be on current income: a $25,000,000 reduction less whatever portion (if any) of deferred income tax liability applied to the mine. The actual calculation might be complex, but we can say that there would be an immediate reduction in net income between $25,000,000 and $15,000,000 (that is, $25,000,000 × [1 – .40]).

Begin R.E.: No effect on past incomes.

Tax liability: Probably some reduction in income tax liability. The exact effect depends on resolving the tax deduction uncertainty.

Op. cash flow: No effect on cash or cash from operations. The loss included in the net income would be added back on the Operations section of the SCFP.

W/C ratio: No effect on working capital, or on the ratio, unless there was a reduction of current income tax liability or an increase in income tax receivable (refundable). In such a case, working capital and the ratio would increase.

ROE: Income would fall, therefore so would ROE. The write-off would equally reduce income and equity (retained earnings after including the lower income), so the ratio's fall would be reduced a little by the decline in the denominator as well as the numerator.

ROA: Like ROE, this would fall because of the effect on income. The effect on ROA might well be smaller than the effect on ROE, because total assets are probably larger than equity, so the effect on the denominator would likely be proportionately less than for ROE.

D/E ratio: This will go up because the company has less equity. The effect will be reduced by any decrease in income tax liability.

Solution Notes—Example C

This would be recorded by an entry like this (assuming the pension contribution is all tax deductible):

	CR	Cash		$2,000,000
DR		Pension expense (current year)	480,000	
	CR	Income tax expense (40%)		192,000
DR		Retained earnings (past years, $1,520,000 × (1 – .40))	912,000	
DR		Income tax liability (current or deferred: 40%)	800,000	

Net income: Current income would go down $288,000 (that is, $480,000 less income tax).

Begin R.E.: As the entry shows, these would go down $912,000.

Tax liability: The overall liability would go down $800,000.

Op. cash flow: Cash goes down $2,000,000. Cash from operations would go down by the current portion of this ($288,000) plus any portion of the reduction of income tax liability that is current. The rest of the reduction in cash would usually be shown on the SCFP as a special item, affecting cash but not doing so through current operations.

W/C ratio: Working capital would decrease by $2,000,000 less any reduction in current income tax liability. The ratio would fall because the reduction in cash would be greater than any reduction in current income tax liability.

ROE: Income would fall, therefore so would ROE.

ROA: Like ROE, this would fall because of the effect on income. But the effect on ROA might be minimal because income would be reduced $288,000 but assets would go down $2,000,000 (the cash). The first divided by the second is 14.4%, which is probably not too different from the prior ROA, and so the agreement would not affect the ratio much.

D/E ratio: Debt (income tax) is reduced by $800,000 and equity is reduced by a total of $1,200,000. The ratio of these is 66.7%. If that ratio is anywhere near the prior debt–equity ratio, the effect on the ratio will be minor. If the tax effect is a tax receivable (refundable) instead of a reduction in liability, there will be no reduction in debt, so the debt–equity ratio will definitely go up as equity falls.

Solution Notes—Example D

Net income: Current income is too low by $4,800 (that is, $8,000 × (1 – .40).

Begin R.E.: Prior income, and so beginning retained earnings, are too high by $4,800.

Tax liability: No effect on income tax liability now. Tax was assessed in the wrong year, but the error has now, in a sense, corrected itself.

Op. cash flow: No effect on cash or cash from operations. The $4,800 error in income is equalled by errors in the adjustments for changes in income tax liability ($3,200 in the same direction) and accounts payable ($8,000 in the opposite direction).

W/C ratio: No effect on working capital, or on the ratio. The error was last year, and at this point there is no longer an error in any balance sheet account.

ROE: Current year's income would be too low, and so would ROE. (ROE for the previous year would have been too high.)

ROA: Like ROE, this would fall because of the effect on income.

D/E ratio: No effect because there is no error in any balance sheet account at this point.

Solution Notes—Example E

Here's what would happen:

- The allowance previously changed from $15,000 to $26,000, an increase of $11,000, after adjusting for whatever hopeless accounts were written off during the year. It would now change from $23,000 to $38,000, an increase of $15,000.
- There is apparently no change in the method for writing off hopeless accounts, so bad debt expense for the current year would rise by $4,000 (the $15,000 increase in the new policy minus the $11,000 increase under the old policy).
- Past years' incomes would also be affected, because the allowance balance at the beginning of this year would be changed as part of the method change. The beginning allowance (which was the ending allowance for last year) would rise from $15,000 to $23,000, an increase of $8,000.
- The effect on the allowance for doubtful accounts is an increase of $12,000 (revised present balance of $38,000 minus former present balance of $26,000).

- The effect on the income tax liability would include a decrease of \$3,200 (that is, 40% of \$8,000) from prior years and \$1,600 (that is, 40% of \$4,000) from the current year, for a total \$4,800 decrease. This would be a change in the current portion of the income tax liability because the allowance for doubtful accounts is a current liability.

The journal entry to implement the method change would be:

DR		Retained earnings (past years' incomes) (23,000 – 15,000) × (1 – .40)	4,800	
DR		Bad debts expense (current year's income) (38,000 – 23,000) – (26,000 – 15,000)	4,000	
	CR	Income tax expense (current year's income) (4,000 × .40)		1,600
	CR	Allowance for doubtful accounts (38,000 – 26,000)		12,000
DR		Income Tax Liability (current) (12,000 × .40)	4,800	

Net income: Current net income would fall \$2,400 (that is, \$4,000 × [1 – .40]) because bad debts expense would increase.

Begin R.E.: Past incomes would fall \$4,800 (that is, \$8,000 × (1 – .40).

Tax liability: Income tax liability would fall \$4,800 (that is, \$12,000 × .40).

Op. cash flow: No effect on cash or cash from operations. Net income would be reduced \$2,400, but that would equal the \$4,000 smaller change in net accounts receivable minus the \$1,600 smaller change in income tax liability.

W/C ratio: Working capital would go down \$7,200 (that is, the \$12,000 reduction in the allowance for doubtful accounts minus the \$4,800 reduction in income tax liability), so the ratio would fall.

ROE: Income would fall, therefore so would ROE.

ROA: Like ROE, this would fall because of the effect on income. The effect on ROA might be a little smaller than the effect on ROE, because assets will be larger than equity and the allowance account is likely to be a small (negative) part of total assets.

D/E ratio: This will go up because the company has less equity. The effect will be reduced by the decrease in income tax liability.

HOW'S YOUR UNDERSTANDING

Here are two questions you should be able to answer, based on what you have just read:

1. Strapped Ltd., which has $190,000 in current assets and $170,000 in current liabilities, borrows $40,000 from the bank as a long-term loan, repayable in four years. What is the effect of this loan on working capital? On the working capital ratio? On current net income? (Up $40,000; up from 1.12 to 1.35; none immediately, but it should be helped as the money is put to work and hurt as interest is paid.)
2. Slipshod Inc. has discovered that it has not estimated enough warranty expenses because more customers are returning products for repair than had been expected. The company decides to recognize an additional $130,000 in noncurrent warranty liability, and therefore in corresponding expenses: $90,000 in respect to sales recognized in the current year and $40,000 in respect to prior years' sales. The company's income tax rate is 35%. What will this do to the current year's net income? To retained earnings? To cash from operations? To the working capital ratio? (Down by $90,000 × (1 – .35), or $58,500; down by $130,000 × (1 – .35), or $84,500, which is $58,500 for the current year plus $40,000 × (1 – .35) for the prior years; no effect (income decline is offset by a change in the addbacks for noncash warranty provision expense and deferred income tax liability); no effect because no current assets or liabilities are involved.)

9.9 DO FINANCIAL STATEMENTS PROPERLY MEASURE A MANAGER'S PERFORMANCE?

They don't without sensitive and informed interpretation, and even then, seldom fully satisfactorily! For example, if a company follows standard financial accounting methods uncritically, making no attempt to adjust them to fit its own circumstances, the resulting financial statements will provide clear, but very arbitrary, measures of the performance of the company's management. On the other hand, if the company ignores standard methods entirely, designing its own accounting methods for everything, the resulting financial statements will provide a relevant but hard-to-compare measure of management performance. Most companies are in between these extremes, which means their financial statements are partly arbitrary and partly hard to compare! Not a happy situation for managers or the people trying to evaluate them.[6]

It is hard to determine how much a company's performance is really due to management and how much depends on other factors, such as economic trends, product price changes, union pressure, and even pure luck (good or bad). Also, in most companies management is a group, so it is difficult to set one manager's performance apart from the group's. The result is that evaluating a manager's performance (even the president's) with financial statements requires great care and knowledge of the company and its industry—and is probably still substantially arbitrary.

The ratios and other computations used in financial analysis can easily compound the problem. Let's take the example of return on assets. Consider the case of two companies, "A" and "B." A has assets of $100,000 and net income plus after-tax interest of $20,000, for a 20% ROA. Looks great. But the manager is not looking into the future much and so is not keeping the company's assets or maintenance up to date.

B is exactly the same, except that the manager is very aware of the need to stay competitive and look after the assets, and so has spent $10,000 on new assets and $2,000 (after tax) on an improved maintenance program. B's assets are, therefore, $110,000 and its net income plus after-tax interest is $18,000, for a 16% ROA. Consequently, A looks better than B: ROA is reduced both by a smaller numerator and a larger denominator in the case of B.

You can see that, unless the person doing the financial analysis really understands the situation, the prudent and responsible manager of B will look worse than the neglectful manager of A!

9.10 ACCOUNTING RESEARCH: THE ROLE OF FINANCIAL STATEMENT ANALYSIS

Chapter 8 pointed out that immediate release of any significant information is required of larger (public) companies and that markets respond quickly to information. Of what value, then, is analysis of the financial statements, which are usually produced some months after the company's fiscal year end? This is an intriguing issue to researchers who wonder why so much value is placed on the financial statements. Two such researchers note that:

> Even a casual look at the statistics on the number of copies of annual reports distributed by various corporations and the hours spent...preparing and analyzing these reports would lead us to conclude that published statements play an important role in the dissemination of corporate information.[7]

A large number of people make it their business to analyze financial statements, and many forecasts of earnings and other financial statement numbers are made by such analysts. The importance of this activity is demonstrated not only by the resources put into it, but also by the existence of professional associations of financial analysts and by the considerable prominence given to many of the analyses and forecasts by business newspapers and other media. The *Financial Post*'s Annual Report Awards are based partly on how useful the reports and their financial statements are thought to be to people trying to use them in analysis.

Here is some of the evidence about financial statement analysis produced by accounting research:[8]

1. If the financial statements have new or unexpected information (as would those of most private and/or small companies), analysis of them is valuable in order to interpret the results.
2. Ratios computed from financial statements have some value in predicting bankruptcy or other financial problems. Just how this works is controversial (because of deep statistical problems), but research indicates that for some companies, financial problems can be predicted several years in advance using accounting ratios.

3. Financial analysis is an important activity in the monitoring of lending agreements, management bonus plans, and other contractual arrangements. Many such agreements involve analysis because they specify that deterioration of some ratios (such as debt–equity) will trigger penalties or even the termination of the agreement, or because ratios are used in computing bonuses or other payments.
4. Even though annual reports come out rather a long time after the fiscal year end, there is enough reaction by stock markets to them to indicate that analysis of the reports still has something to say to market traders.
5. People cannot cope with masses of disaggregated data: it takes too long and requires too much special expertise. So, summarizing techniques, such as financial analysis, play a major role in users' decision making.
6. Analysts' forecasts of earnings, based partly on financial statement data, do help to predict companies' future earnings performance. The analysts often can anticipate significant changes in earnings because they are following companies closely, so market prices regularly change before the new financial statements are released.
7. Risk and return are generally related. Investments with a higher potential return often are riskier, and those with a low risk usually have a low potential return. Different investors have different risk preferences: some prefer to hold risky shares that may generate high returns (or large losses!), others prefer more secure investments. Financial statement analysis helps to assess risk, and thus helps investors choose the shares that seem appropriate for their risk preferences.
8. Financial statement analysis is useful to corroborate what people already believe about a company's performance, position, or risk. Even if such analysis turns up little that is "new," it acts as a check on the other flows of information about companies, because the validity of that information can be verified later when the financial statements come out. Also, sometimes financial statement analysis does turn up new information, allowing people to fine tune their expectations about future performance.

9.11 CONTINUING DEMONSTRATION CASE

INSTALMENT 9

Data for Instalment 9

In Instalment 8, three financial statements for Mato Inc. were prepared: a Statement of Income and Deficit for the year ended February 28, 1995 (which might have been called the Statement of Loss and Deficit, because the company had a $54,066 loss); Balance Sheets at February 28, 1995, and March 1, 1993; and Statement of Changes in Financial Position for the year ended February 28, 1995.

These statements are the data for this instalment, which will illustrate the calculation of various financial ratios and of the Scott formula. The illustration will not always be straightforward, because the company lost money and is not in a strong financial position. Unfortunately, you may well encounter such less than successful companies. So, seeing how to apply the analyses to them should increase your understanding of the analyses.

Results for Instalment 9

To begin with, here are the ratios set out in Section 9.5, in the order given there. Refer to the statements in Instalment 8 (Section 8.11), and make sure you know where the figures for the ratios below came from. Note that the company has made no provision for an income tax recovery on its first-year loss—such a recovery would depend on having future taxable income to deduct the loss against, and that is not likely enough to warrant creating an income tax recovery asset in the present circumstances.

Other versions of some of the ratios calculated below are quite possible. Dollar signs have been omitted and most ratios are rounded to three decimals.

Performance ratios:

1. Return on year-end equity: (54,066)/70,934 = (.762), negative Return on beginning equity: (54,066)/125,000 = (.433), negative
2. Return on ending assets: ((54,066) + 6,469)/160,742 = (.296), negative
3. Sales return before interest: [(54,066) + 6,469]/229,387 = (.207), negative

   Sales return after interest: (54,066)/229,387 = (.236), negative
4. Common size financial statements: not illustrated here
5. Gross margin: 90,620/229,387 = .395. Cost of goods sold is .605 of sales revenue, so the average markup is .395/.605 = 65% of cost.
6. Average interest rate: 6,469/89,808 = .072
7. Cash flow to total ending assets: (55,028)/160,742 = (.342), negative
8. Earnings per share: number of shares not known, and EPS is not as meaningful for a private company as for a publicly traded one.
9. Book value per share: number of shares not known; however, the owners' original equity of $125,000 is now down to $70,934, which means the book value of the shares is only 56.7% of the amounts the owners contributed.
10. Price–earnings ratio: not determinable because the shares of a private company like this are not traded and their price, therefore, is not known.
11. Dividend payout ratio: no dividends declared since there was a loss.

Activity (turnover) ratios:

12. Total asset turnover: 229,387/160,742 = 1.427 times
13. Inventory turnover: 138,767/33,612 = 4.128 times
14. Collection ratio: 14,129/(229,387/365) = 22.5 days

Financing ratios:

15. Debt–equity ratio: 89,808/70,934 = 1.266

    Beginning debt–equity ratio was: 16,100/125,000 = .129
16. Long-term debt–equity ratio: zero (no long-term debt)
17. Debt to assets ratio: 89,808/160,742 = .559

Liquidity and solvency warning ratios:

18. Working capital ratio: 54,684/89,808 = .609

    Beginning working capital ratio was: 130,000/16,100 = 8.075

19. Acid test ratio: (6,418 + 14,129) / 89,808 = .229
20. Interest coverage ratio: not calculated because with this large a loss there is no coverage!

The ratios tell a grim story:

- The company has lost 43.3% of its beginning equity;
- Its working capital ratio is considerably less than 1 (its working capital is negative);
- Its acid test ratio is less than 25%; and
- Its cash and receivables would carry its operations for less than a month.

But, there are some positive signs:

- The collection ratio is low (only 22.5 days);
- The debt–equity ratio is not high even though equity has been reduced by losses; and,
- With a fairly low debt to assets ratio and no long-term debt, there may be room for some long-term borrowing, should that be necessary to improve the current position.

What does the Scott formula tell us? Using the year-end figures from the above ratios, we have:

$$ROE = SR \times AT + (ROA - IN) \times D/E$$
$$(.762) = (.207) \times 1.427 + (.296) - .072) \times 1.266$$
$$(.762) = (.295) \qquad + (.368) \times 1.266$$
$$(.762) = (.295) \qquad + (.466)$$

The formula works out to within a .001 rounding error. It indicates that the company's woeful ROE is due to the negative effects of leverage compounding poor operating performance: the company was already losing money, and by borrowing, made things worse. Normally, a high asset turnover indicates good performance. But here, as the company was losing on every sale, getting more sales also made things worse. Perhaps Mavis and Tomas tried to do too much in their first year.

This example illustrates that most ratios and such aggregations as the Scott formula can be calculated for losing companies. Financial statement analysis is not limited to profitable, financially solid companies. However, the interpretation of the statements must be made carefully, because negative relationships may exist where they're not expected, as we saw with the effects of asset turnover above.

We should wish Mavis and Tomas well in their second year. If they don't do better, there won't be a third year!

HOMEWORK AND DISCUSSION TO DEVELOP UNDERSTANDING

PROBLEM 9.1* List advantages and disadvantages of ratio analysis

List the advantages and disadvantages you see of using ratio analysis of financial statements (including the Scott formula analysis) as a way of evaluating management's performance. For the disadvantages, try to think of a way around each problem you identify.

PROBLEM 9.2* Ratios to measure different kinds of performance

1. Many financial performance measures are ratios of some return over some investment base. Why is such a concept of performance important in business?
2. With your answer to Question 1 in mind, how might you measure the performance of each of the following investments owned by Professor Ann Mandel:
   a. Her $1,200 in a savings account at Solid Bank.
   b. Her investment of $15,000 in a little consulting business she runs off campus.
   c. Her Slapdash 210 sports car.

PROBLEM 9.3* Comments on leverage and risk

Use nontechnical language to answer the following:

1. What is financial leverage?
2. Why is such leverage risky?
3. How does the Scott formula incorporate leverage?
4. Which is more risky, a company whose Scott formula leverage component is $(.10 - .08) \times 2$, or one whose component is $(.09 - .08) \times 1$? Explain.

PROBLEM 9.4* Answer various questions using ratio analysis

Company A is owned 100% by Mr. A. A summary of Company A's financial statement information is as follows:

Balance Sheet as at September 30, 1995:

Total assets	$80,000
Total liabilities	$35,000
Total shareholder's equity	45,000
Total liabilities and shareholder's equity	$80,000

Income Statement for the year ending September 30, 1995:

Revenue		$30,000
Expenses		
Interest	$ 2,000	
General and operating expenses	19,000	
Income tax (33 1/3%)	3,000	24,000
Net income for the year		$ 6,000

Statement of Retained Earnings for the year ending September 30, 1995:

Balance at beginning of year	$17,000
Net income for year	6,000
Balance at end of year	$23,000

1. Calculate Company A's return on equity for 1995.
2. What contributes more to return on equity: managerial performance (operating return) or leverage return (financial leverage)? Show all calculations.
3. Company A is considering borrowing $50,000 for additional assets that would earn the company the same return on assets it has historically earned, according to the financial statement information above. The cost of borrowing this money is 8%. Should the company borrow the money? (Assume there are no alternative sources of funding.) Show all calculations.
4. Place yourself in the role of the local bank manager. Mr. A has approached you to lend the company the required $50,000 mentioned above. Detailed financial statement information has already been presented to you,
   a. What additional information would you require, if any?
   b. What financial statement ratios, in addition to those calculated in previous parts of this problem, would be useful in aiding your decision? Do not calculate the ratios, just mention or describe them.

PROBLEM 9.5* Change effects analysis, with ratios

Suppose that on December 31, the last day of its fiscal year, a large company sold bonds by which it borrowed $150,000,000 cash, to be paid back in six years. The money was used on the same day to reduce the company's short-term bank loans by $50,000,000 and buy additional equipment for $100,000,000.

Calculate the *changes* to the following that would result from the above:

a. Total current assets.
b. Total assets.
c. Total current liabilities.
d. Working capital ratio.
e. Total shareholders' equity.
f. Net earnings for the year ended on the day of the borrowing.
g. Cash and cash equivalents.
h. Cash used for investments.
i. Cash provided from financing.

Describe how predictions of the effects on the following could be made:

j. Return on equity for the period after the loan.
k. Leverage return.

PROBLEM 9.6 Describe some ratios' value and calculate them for a company

In this chapter we have seen several types of ratios used to analyze financial statements and information.

1. Select two types of ratios and describe what information is conveyed by each.
2. Calculate ratios of these types for any company you are interested in.

PROBLEM 9.7 Calculate and interpret Scott formula for a company

1. Choose any company you are interested in and compute its Scott formula numbers for two recent years.
2. Interpret the Scott formula results. What can you conclude about the company's performance on the basis of those results?
3. List some of the additional data you would require in order to make an intelligent evaluation of the company's performance.

PROBLEM 9.8 Draft a speech on analysis and the use of financial statements

Write the rough notes for a speech you have been asked to give to a local investment club. The members of the club are all experienced stock market investors and want a better understanding of companies' accounting information. The topic of your speech is "Analysis and Use of Financial Accounting Information."

PROBLEM 9.9 Comment on a complaint about financial statement analysis

A senior member of a large public company's management complained,

> Accountants' financial analyses don't seem very useful to me. The analyses don't reveal the business management factors that are important to my company's success. They are biased toward the past rather than the future. And, anyway, the stock market is way ahead of the accountants in judging the company's performance.

Comment on the manager's complaint.

PROBLEM 9.10 Write an overall evaluation of The North West Company

This chapter has presented a variety of ratios and cash flow analyses of The North West Company Inc. Write a few paragraphs summarizing your evaluation of the company's financial performance for 1993 (period ended January 29, 1994) and financial position at the end of that year. Make use of the comments in the chapter, and try to pull it all together into an overall evaluation that would make sense to a person who has not read the chapter.

PROBLEM 9.11 Brief explanations of accounting change effects

Write a brief explanation for each of the following:

a. Why is it true that changing financial accounting accruals does not affect cash flow (ignoring any tax effect)?
b. Why does changing amortization method (that is, changing the amortization numbers in the financial statements) change the debt to equity ratio?
c. A company is considering creating a new account, a liability for warranty repairs, by estimating the costs of warranty repairs not yet done for customers but likely to be necessary. Would such an accounting method change affect the return on assets? Why?

PROBLEM 9.12 Effects analysis of truck fleet purchase and financing

Suppose that on May 1, 1995, Large Corporation decides to purchase a new fleet of delivery trucks at a total cost of $5,800,000. The trucks will be paid for in cash, which Large Corporation will raise by using $2,200,000 cash on hand, issuing shares for $2,000,000, and borrowing $1,600,000 over 20 years from the bank.

1. Using the preceding information, fill in the blanks below, indicating the magnitude and direction of the change in each category the truck purchase will cause.

Large Corporation
***Changes in* Balance Sheet at May 1, 1995**

Cash equivalent assets	$______	Cash equivalent liabilities	$______
Other current assets	______	Other current liabilities	______
Noncurrent assets	______	Noncurrent liabilities	______
		Share capital	______
		Retained earnings	______
Total assets	$______	Total liabilities & owners' equity	$______

2. What effect (if any) will this event have on the Financing Activities section of the statement of changes in financial position for the year?
3. What effect (if any) will this event have on the income statement for the year?
4. Which important financial statement ratios would you expect this event to affect?
5. Record the above event as a journal entry.

PROBLEM 9.13 Calculate and explain return on equity and effect of debt

A neighbour of yours finds out that you are taking business courses and engages you in a conversation to get some cheap investment advice. As it turns out, she was raised during the Depression and is very averse to debt. She believes that solid companies should be debt free and raise all their capital by issuing shares or by retaining earnings. You have handy a set of financial statements for a company she knows about, which you use to discuss the matter with her.

Use the financial information below, extracted from the financial statements, to calculate the company's return on equity. Explain to your neighbour the effect debt has on the company's return on equity, and,specifically, whether this return is helped or hindered by the debt.

Total assets	$251,600
Total liabilities	98,980
Interest-bearing long-term debt	42,580
Share capital	87,150
Income tax rate	43%
Retained earnings	$ 65,470
Total revenues	313,450
Interest expense	5,070
Income before-tax and unusual item	36,100
Net income	28,060

PROBLEM 9.14 Analysis of effects of events on Scott formula

You are the chief accountant for Yummy Cookies Inc. and have just calculated the following Scott-formula analysis for the company:

$$ROE = SR \times AT + (ROA - IN) \times D/E$$
$$.095 = .04 \times 2.00 + (.08 - .07) \times 1.5$$

The president is not happy with a return on equity of 9.5% and has asked you to estimate the effects of each of the following changes and events *separately:*

1. Raising selling prices to increase after-tax sales return by half and asset turnover by 5%.
2. Refinancing the company's debt to reduce the after-tax cost of borrowing to 6%.
3. Reducing operating costs to increase after-tax sales return to 5%.
4. Increasing long-term borrowing and reducing equity to increase the debt–equity ratio to 1.8.

PROBLEM 9.15 Evaluate Telus's financial performance

The 1993 financial statements of Telus Corporation are included with Case 8B in Chapter 8. Using those statements, and making assumptions about any missing information if you need to, calculate the Scott formula and other useful ratios and prepare a short evaluation of the company's performance in 1993, as compared to 1993.

PROBLEM 9.16 Evaluate Microsoft's financial performance

The 1993 financial statements of Microsoft Corporation are included with Case 4A in Chapter 4. Using those statements, and making assumptions about any missing information if you need to, calculate the Scott formula and other useful ratios and prepare a short evaluation of the company's performance in 1993, as compared to 1993.

PROBLEM 9.17 Use Scott formula to explain change in performance

The president of General Products Ltd. is curious about why, in spite of growth in revenue, assets, and net income since last year, the company's return on equity has gone down. Last year's ROE was 9.3%, but this year it was 9.0%.

This year's financial statement information shows:

- As at September 30, 1995: total assets, $5,000,000; total liabilities, $2,000,000; total owners' equity, $3,000,000.
- For the year ended September 30, 1995: revenue, $1,800,000; interest expense, $200,000; other expenses except income tax, $1,150,000; income tax expense (40%), $180,000; net income, $270,000; dividends declared, $50,000.

1. Prepare a Scott–formula analysis for the year ended September 30, 1995.
2. Explain to the president what the results you derived in Question 1 indicate about the company's 1995 performance.
3. The president wants to know what the limitations of the Scott formula for assessing managerial performance are. Remembering that the formula is based on accounting figures, answer the president.

4. Last year's Scott formula for General Products Ltd. (rounded to three decimals) was: .093 = (.164) (.491) + (.080 – .025) (.240). Use this and your answer to Question 1 to explain to the president why return on equity changed from last year to this.

PROBLEM 9.18 Use statement analysis to evaluate president's claims

The president of a medium-sized manufacturing company wants to renew the company's operating loan. In discussions with the bank's lending officer, the president says, "As the accompanying financial statements show, our working capital position has increased during the past year, and we have managed to reduce operating expenses significantly."

The partial financial statements showed the following:

Titan Manufacturing Ltd.
Partial Balance Sheet
as at December 31, 1995 and 1994

	1995	1994
Current Assets		
Cash	$ 50,000	$200,000
Accounts receivable	250,000	100,000
Inventories	500,000	400,000
Total current assets	$800,000	$700,000
Current Liabilities		
Accounts payable	$250,000	$200,000
Operating loan	100,000	100,000
Total current liabilities	$350,000	$300,000

Titan Manufacturing Ltd.
Income Statement
for the Years Ended December 31, 1995 and 1994

	1995	1994
Sales	$1,200,000	$1,500,000
Less cost of goods sold	780,000	900,000
Gross profit	$ 420,000	$ 600,000
Operating expenses	350,000	400,000
Income before taxes	$ 70,000	$ 200,000
Income taxes	14,000	40,000
Net income	$ 56,000	$ 160,000

1. Evaluate the president's comments. Incorporate appropriate ratio analysis into your discussion.
2. What additional financial information (if any) would you request of the president? Why?

PROBLEM 9.19 Cash flow, effects analysis, and ratios

(Challenging)

The following summarized data are from Grantham Inc.'s financial statements. (CEA = cash equivalent assets; OCA = other current assets; NCA = noncurrent assets; CEL = cash equivalent liabilities; OCL = other current liabilities; NCL = non-current liabilities; CAP = share capital; RET = retained earnings; REV = revenue; EXP = general expenses; INT = interest expense; NRE = nonoperating revenues and expenses; TAX = income tax expense; SEI = special and extraordinary items; INC = net income)

Assets			Liabilities & Equity			Income		
	1996	1995		1996	1995		1996	
CEA	$ 2,000	$ 1,000	CEL	$ 2,000	$ 3,000	REV	$125,000	
OCA	9,000	8,000	OCL	4,000	2,000	EXP	(84,000)	(amort. = $5,000)
NCA	37,000	32,000	NCL	17,000	18,000	INT	(2,000)	
			CAP	12,000	10,000	NRE	4,000**	
			RET*	13,000	8,000	TAX	(19,000)	(deferred = $3,000)
						SEI	(13,000)***	
	$48,000	$41,000		$48,000	$41,000	INC	$ 11,000	

* Dividend of $6,000 was declared and paid in 1996.

** $4,000 nonoperating income is a gain on an NCA sale: proceeds $7,000 minus $3,000 book value.

*** $(13,000) special item = $21,000 write-off minus $8,000 deferred tax reduction

1. Show that the following are correct for the 1996 cash flow statement (SCFP):

a. Cash generated from operations	$ 29,000
b. Dividends paid	(6,000)
c. Cash obtained from financing activities	6,000
d. Cash disbursed for investing activities(net)	(27,000)
e. Increase in cash and equivalents	$ 2,000

2. The company is considering an accounting method change that will increase inventory at the end of 1995 by $2,000, and at the end of 1996 by $1,000 (tax rate 44%). If this is implemented retroactively, what will be the effect on:
   a. Retained earnings, end of 1995?
   b. Net income for 1996?
   c. Retained earnings, end of 1996?
   d. Cash generated from operations for 1996?
   e. Return on equity for 1996?
   f. Leverage return for 1996?
3. The company is considering changing its revenue recognition policy to a more liberal one. Accounts receivable would increase by $11,000 at the end of 1995 and by $18,000 at the end of 1996. Answer the same questions as in Part 2.

PROBLEM 9.20 (Challenging)

Use ratios to evaluate relative performance

A friend has asked you to evaluate information about two companies in the same industry. Your friend wants to invest in one or the other, but not both. Both companies are publicly traded, started with $10,000 of cash, have been in operation exactly one year, have paid the interest owing on their long-term debts to date, and have declared dividends of $1 per share.

The beginning balance sheets for the two companies at January 1, 1995, were as follows:

Alpha Company		Omega Company	
Total assets	$10,000	Total assets	$10,000
Long-term debt	$ 1,000	Long-term debt	$ 9,000
Shareholders' equity (900 common shares issued)	9,000	Shareholders' equity (100 common shares issued)	1,000
Total	$10,000	Total	$10,000
Net income for 1995	$ 2,400	Net income for 1995	$ 1,600

Your friend says, "Alpha Company seems the better investment. Its return on investment is 24%, and Omega's is only 16%."

Comment on your friend's observation and on the relative performance of the companies, and give your friend some investment advice.

PROBLEM 9.21 (Challenging)

Ratio analysis of a small company

The balance sheet, income statement, and statement of retained earnings for Whitemud Windsurfing Ltd. are shown at the end of this problem. They were prepared by the company's accountant, I.M. Trying, and although they may not use the best format, the figures are all correct (including the absence of an income tax expense).

1. Whitemud has some interest-bearing debt, so it may be benefiting from financial leverage. Calculate the company's return on equity and then calculate how much, if any, the ROE is helped or hurt by leverage.
2. In comparison with the company's other activities, is the long-term investment a good economic resource? Why or why not?
3. Suppose it is found that the company does owe income tax after all for the year ended February 29, 1996. Without doing any calculations, indicate below what this will do to the following:

	Will Go Up	Will Go Down	Will Not Change
a. Return on equity	______	______	______
b. Return on assets	______	______	______
c. Effective interest rate	______	______	______
d. Asset turnover	______	______	______

4. Calculate the company's working capital ratio as at February 29, 1996, and comment on what this indicates about the company's financial position as at that date. State any assumptions you feel are necessary.

Whitemud Windsurfing Ltd.
Balance Sheet as at February 29, 1996

Assets		**Liabilities and Equity**	
Accounts receivable	$ 25,100	Accounts payable	$ 21,400
Accumulated amortization	(61,600)	Bank loan*	50,500
Building and equipment	187,000	Mortgage payable**	118,900
Cash	1,200	Retained earnings	114,300
Inventory	62,400	Share capital	30,000
Land	71,000		
Long-term investment	50,000		
	$335,100		$335,100

* The bank loan is secured by accounts receivable, inventory, and long–term investment, and is payable on demand.

** The mortgage is secured by land and building and is due in ten years.

Whitemud Windsurfing Ltd.
Income Statement for the Year Ended February 29, 1996

Sales revenue		$323,800
Cost of goods sold expense	$214,100	
Operating expenses	65,200	
Amortization expense	13,400	
Interest expense	22,900	315,600
Operating income		$ 8,200
Revenue from long-term investment		$ 4,000
Income before income tax		12,200
Income tax expense*		0
Net income for the year		$ 12,200

* The company qualifies for tax credits and, therefore, owes no income tax on this year's income.

Whitemud Windsurfing Ltd.
Statement of Retained Earnings
for the Year Ended February 29, 1996

Retained earnings, February 28, 1995	$102,100
Net income for the year ended February 29, 1996	12,200
Retained earnings, February 29, 1996	$114,300

PROBLEM 9.22 Effects of change in revenue recognition

(Challenging)

Tidy Toys Ltd. makes a line of educational toys: grenade launchers, machine guns, nerve gas, and the like. The company makes all of its sales on credit and has been recognizing revenue at the point of completion of production; because the toys sell so well, making them seems to be the "critical event." However, this way of doing things ends upon the retirement of its long-time auditor, Ease E. Going, and the arrival of a new one, Ree L. Stickler, who suggests the company change its revenue recognition policy to recognize revenue at the point of shipment of the toys, which is usual in the educational toy industry. A change in the revenue recognition policy would not affect expenses, but if income were affected, so would be income tax expense (40% rate).

Revenue recognition for each toy would be delayed from completion of production date to shipment date, but the effect each year depends on the specifics of that year's production and sales. The following information has been obtained:

	Estimated for Next Year	This Year	Last Year	All Previous Years
Revenue using present policy	$1,400,000	$1,280,000	$1,040,000	$8,680,000
Revenue using proposed policy	$1,420,000	$1,190,000	$1,120,000	$8,550,000
Proposed minus present	$ 20,000	$ (90,000)	$ 80,000	$ (130,000)

What would be the effect of changing the revenue recognition policy on income for last year? For this year? On retained earnings at the end of this year? On accounts receivable at the end of this year? On return on equity for this year? On the working capital ratio for this year?

PROBLEM 9.23 Performance evaluation using ratios

(Challenging)

International Business Computers (IBC) has enjoyed modest success in penetrating the personal computer market since it began operations a few years ago. A new computer line introduced recently has been received well by the general public. However, the president, who is well-versed in electronics but not in accounting, is worried about the future of the company.

The company's operating loan is at its limit and more cash is needed to continue operations. The bank wants more information before it extends the company's credit limit.

The president has asked you, as vice-president, finance, to do a preliminary evaluation of the company's performance, using appropriate financial statement analysis, and to recommend possible courses of action for the company. The president particularly wants to know how the company can obtain additional cash. Use the following summary financial information to do your evaluation and make your recommendations.

International Business Computers
Balance Sheets as at December 31 (in 000s)

	1995	1994	1993
Current assets:			
Cash	$ 19	$ 24	$ 50
Marketable securities	37	37	37
Accounts receivable—trade	544	420	257
Inventory	833	503	361
Total current assets	$1,433	$ 984	$ 705

continued next page

Fixed assets:			
Land	$ 200	$ 200	$ 100
Buildings	350	350	200
Equipment	950	950	700
	$1,500	$1,500	$1,000
Less: Accumulated amortization, buildings and equipment	(447)	(372)	(288)
Net fixed assets	1,053	1,128	712
Total assets	$2,486	$2,112	$1,417
Current liabilities			
Bank loan	$ 825	$ 570	—
Accounts payable—trade	300	215	$ 144
Other liabilities	82	80	75
Income tax payable	48	52	50
Total current liabilities	$1,255	$ 917	$ 269
Shareholder's equity:			
Common stock	$1,000	$1,000	$1,000
Retained earnings	231	195	148
Total shareholders' equity	$1,231	$1,195	$1,148
Total liabilities and shareholders' equity	$2,486	$2,112	$1,417

International Business Computers
Combined Statements of Income and Retained Earnings
for the Years Ended December 31

	1995	1994	1993
Sales	$3,200	$2,800	$2,340
Cost of goods sold	2,500	2,150	1,800
Gross profit	$ 700	$ 650	$ 540
Expenses	584	533	428
Net income	$ 116	$ 117	$ 112
Opening retained earnings	195	148	96
	$ 311	$ 265	$ 208
Less: Dividends	80	70	60
Closing retained earnings	$ 231	$ 195	$ 148
Other related information included in total expenses:			
Interest expense	$ 89	$ 61	—
Income tax expense	$ 95	$ 102	$ 97

PROBLEM 9.24 Effects analysis, with ratios

(Challenging)

Funtime Toys Inc. invents, manufactures, and sells toys and children's board games. In 1995, financial executives at Funtime decided to change two accounting methods.

- First, they decided to capitalize certain costs related to the development of new educational games, which had previously been expensed as incurred. It was thought that market demand for the games had been strong for several years, and that development costs were sure to provide future benefits.

- The second change was to the amortization method used on one class of equipment, to produce an annual amortization expense that was thought to better match the company's revenue generation process.

The effects of these changes on development and amortization expenses for the fiscal years 1993 and 1995 are shown below. The company's income tax rate is 30% and the method changes would affect deferred, not current, income tax.

Development Expense	**1994**	**1995**
Old method	$ 75,000	$ 85,000
New method	70,000	78,000
Amortization Expense	**1994**	**1995**
Old method	$150,000	$175,000
New method	160,000	170,000

1. Determine the *combined* impact the two method changes have on each of the following items for 1994 and 1995. Decide whether each item increases, decreases, or is not affected. (Check each ratio carefully to determine the impact on both the numerator and the denominator.)
   a. Net income.
   b. Working capital at the end of the year.
   c. Total assets at the end of the year.
   d. Debt–equity ratio at the end of the year.
   e. Return on year-end equity.
   f. Total asset turnover.
2. Look at the changes you have identified. What differences would these changes make to investors, according to the efficient markets hypothesis? Why?

PROBLEM 9.25 Prepare a speech on modern statement analysis

(Challenging)

Prepare a speech for a meeting of local business people, all of whom are active managers and investors, on the following topic: "Methods and value of financial statement analysis in the age of computer spreadsheets and efficient capital markets." There will be a question period after your talk, so include a few notes on any awkward issues you may decide not to deal with directly in your talk.

PROBLEM 9.26 Effects analysis: proposed business venture

(Challenging)

Pretty People Inc. supplies a lot of those good-looking young men and women you see in bathing-suit, beer, and deodorant soap ads. For the last few years, its revenues have been fairly stable at around $3,000,000 per year and its expenses (largely modelling fees and other costs related directly to the revenue) have been about $2,400,000 per year. After income tax totalling about 40%, the company's net income has been about $360,000 per year, a return on sales of 12%.

The company is considering a new venture: providing pretty pets for dog food, cat food, and other "cute creatures" ads. Unlike human models, who only have to look good, the pets will have to bark, purr, jump, and perform on cue. Therefore, such creatures will have to be trained first. Company management estimates that an initial $100,000 will have to be spent for training, but after that the pets should bring in additional revenue of $200,000 per year and incur expenses of about $140,000. It will be two to five years before a trained pet ceases to be cute or just can't stand it any more. Therefore, each year after the first two, the company expects to have to replace and retrain about 25% of its stable of pets. (Assume all the above events begin on January 1, Year 1.)

What will the new venture do to annual net income? Shareholders' equity now? Two years from now? Five years from now? Working capital now? Next year? Two years from now? Performance ratios next year?

PROBLEM 9.27 Effects analysis of business expansion

(Challenging)

The following are the most recent balance sheet and income statement for Smythe Ltd.

Smythe Ltd.
Balance Sheet as at August 31, 1995

Assets		Liabilities and Equity	
Current assets	$ 20,000	Current liabilities	$ 11,000
Fixed assets	120,000	Note payable, 11%, 1998	30,000
Accumulated amortization	(40,000)	Common shares *	40,000
		Retained earnings	19,000
Total assets	$100,000	Total liabilities and equity	$100,000

* 4,000 shares issued and outstanding

Smythe Ltd.
Income Statement for the Year Ended August 31, 1995

Sales		$120,000
Selling and administrative expenses	$91,200	
Amortization expense	5,500	
Interest expense	3,300	
Income taxes	8,000	
Total expenses		108,000
Net income		$ 12,000

Because a major competitor has recently gone out of business, the management of Smythe Ltd. is contemplating a major expansion. With the expansion, annual sales are expected to increase by 35%, and selling and administrative expenses to rise by 30% over the current year. Current liabilities should increase by $22,000 by August 31, 1996.

To accomplish the expansion, the company needs a net $50,000 addition of capital. Two options have been developed to raise the funds; the company can issue 5,000 additional common shares for $50,000 or it can obtain the same amount by issuing 12% bonds (which mature in 2010). The money would be used to buy new equipment and to increase working capital. The company does not pay dividends and pays income tax at a rate of 40%. The shares or bonds would be issued in early September, 1995. The following pro forma income statements and balance sheets have been prepared to show expected results in 1996 under the bond and share issue options.

Smythe Ltd.
Pro Forma Income Statements
for the Year Ending August 31, 1996

	Share Option	Bond Option
Sales	$162,000	$162,000
Selling and administrative expense	$118,560	$118,560
Amortization expense	9,250	9,250
Interest expense	3,300	9,300
Income tax	12,356	9,956
Total expenses	$143,466	$147,066
Net income	$ 18,534	$ 14,934

Smythe Ltd.
Pro Forma Balance Sheets as at August 31, 1996

	Share Option	Bond Option
Current assets	$ 84,784	81,184
Fixed assets	145,000	145,000
Accumulated amortization	(39,250)	(39,250)
Total assets	$190,534	$186,934
Current liabilities	$ 33,000	33,000
Note payable, 11%, 1998	30,000	30,000
Bonds payable, 12%, 2010	—	50,000
Common shares	90,000	40,000
Retained earnings	37,534	33,934
Total liabilities and equity	$190,534	$186,934

1. Calculate the Scott-formula ratios for the Smythe Ltd. financial statements dated August 31, 1995, and for both options as of August 31, 1996. Calculate other ratios, if you think they are important.
2. Analyze the Scott-formula ratios and others you may have used. How does each option affect profitability, return, leverage, and liquidity?
3. Based on the small amount of information provided, which course of action would you favour for Smythe Ltd.?

CASE 9A The financial performance of Moore Corporation

The article that follows, "Moore Shares Poised for Growth," comments on the financial and stock market performance of Moore Corporation, a large manufacturer of business forms and similar products that began in Canada and has become a thoroughly international enterprise. Moore is listed on the Toronto and New York stock exchanges, and because most of its business is now done in the U.S., it reports its financial results in U.S. dollars.

Based on the following article and the material in this chapter and Chapter 8, discuss Moore's financial performance and prospects.

MOORE SHARES POISED FOR GROWTH

Since it was last reviewed in this column a year ago, Moore Corp. Ltd.'s shares have risen 24% to a high of US$21¼, with a recent price at US$20¼. It was then priced at US$17⅛, with a two-year buy recommendation for a target of US$25, and three to five years of US$35 to US$40.

The world's largest manufacturer of business forms and related products, Moore was founded in Canada in 1882. It employs more than 22,000 in 58 countries and has more than 100 manufacturing plants serving business, government and other enterprises.

Paper-based and electronic-based products include business forms and systems, information management services, electronic forms and solutions, and outsourcing services.

In 1990, Moore implemented a poison pill plan to foil any unwanted takeover. It essentially gives the shareholder the right to purchase additional stock at a 50%-discount if an authorized party acquires more than 15% of total shares.

Toppan-Moore Co. Ltd., a 45%-owned joint venture between Moore and Toppan Printing Co. of Japan, supplies a similar range of products throughout Southeast Asia. In 1993, Moore received dividends of US$4.1 million and has a share of US$90 million in undistributed earnings from this venture.

Revenue for 1993 fell 4% to US$2.36 billion from US$2.43 billion a year earlier. The U.S. accounted for 65% of the sales, Canada 8%, Europe 14% and others 13%.

Moore reported a net 1993 loss of US$77.6 million (US78¢ a share) compared with a loss of US$2.3 million (US1¢). Operating income jumped 30% to US$1.3 billion, with the U.S. contributing 87%, Canada 2%, Europe 1%, and others 10%.

Dividends were unchanged at US94¢ a share, but equity per share fell 11.1% to US$13.19 due to the loss.

As a result of new technologies in the information handling businesses (such as laser printers) and changing customer demands, Moore is streamlining and closing plants.

In 1993, the company had a restructuring charge of US$1.66 billion after tax as a result of this rationalization program.

The new president and chief executive Reto Braun, appointed last fall, will oversee the revitalization of the company; and revenues in 1994 are expected to equal last year's levels, with return on equity expected to rise to 8%, and eventually return to 15%.

In the decade from 1983, sales increased 28%, assets rose 76%, while income from operations before restructuring costs fell 23%; per-share statistics show net income at a loss of US78¢ in 1993 compared with a profit of US$1.16; dividends rose 41%; equity is up 58%; cash flow up 9%; working capital down 5%; long-term debt down 30%; and capital expenditures up 137%. The number of shares outstanding increased just 17% while the share price in U.S. terms rose 36% but underperformed the S&P 500 by 56%. In Canada, the price gain was 127% and outperformed the TSE-300 index by 48%.

Today, a US$10,000 investment made in 1974 would be worth US$13,848 and income from dividends would add US$9,562 for a total 20-

year investment performance of US$23,410 or an annual average compound rate of return of 4.34%.

Share Price: From 1945 to 1973 Moore was considered one of the great growth stocks of the era. From a loss of US40¢ in 1945 (adjusted for splits) Moore's shares rose 48 times in value to a record high of US$19 3/8 in 1973, declined 60% to US$8 in 1978 and then rose 4.3 times to a new record high of US$34 1/4 in 1989. Moore's shares then declined 60% to a low of US$14 3/8 in late 1992. A new uptrend began and has seen the shares rise 50% to the late 1993 high of US$21 1/4. Major support lies at US$18, while upward resistance is evident above US$26.

Relative Strength: From 1960 to 1974, Moore performed 300% better than the S&P 500 index but since then it has underperformed the market by 80% to the end of 1992. From mid-1989 until the end of 1992 Moore performed 65% worse than the market but since then has outperformed it by 25%.

Conclusion: Moore shares recently traded at US$20 1/4 and sell at 17.6 times estimated 1994 earnings per share of between US$1.10 and US$1.25 and at 10.1 times estimated 1994 cash flow of US$2 a share to yield 4.64% on the current dividend of US94¢ a share.

Over the past 30 years, Moore has sold at an average of 12.8 times earnings; 9.1 times cash flow; a 4% yield and 182% of book value. Based on those average values and 1994 estimates, Moore would have a current minimum value of US$21.

The balance sheet is strong and highly liquid with virtually no debt. The dividend yield is well above average at 4.64%.

After experiencing eroding margins over the last decade, Moore is finally acting to reverse those trends through rationalization to create a tighter operation that is acquisition oriented. Traditionally the business forms industry leads business out of recession. As business conditions continue to improve, Moore's shares should resume the long-term uptrend interrupted in 1989. At US$20 1/4, the shares are rated as a "buy on any weakness," with a target of between US$35 to US$40 in the next three to five years.

A Six-Year Financial Snapshot

Fiscal years ended Dec. 31	1989	1990	1991	1992	1993	1994
Earnings per share US$...	2.15	1.27	0.91	(0.02)	(0.78)	1.15*
Cash flow per share US$...	2.86	2.41	1.83	1.50	1.75	2.00*
Dividends per share US$...	0.88	0.94	0.94	0.94	0.94	0.94[2]
Working capital per share US$...	8.26	8.06	7.86	7.18	5.62	5.77*
Current assets minus all real liabilities per share US$...	6.22	5.40	5.63	5.23	3.51	4.47*
Long-term debt per share US$...	0.43	0.99	0.77	0.60	0.68	0.82*
Net worth per share US$...	15.27	16.05	16.21	14.83	13.19	14.15*
Mean P/E ratio...	13.5x	20.4x	25.1x	(906.3)x	(23.2)x	18.16x*
Mean price/cash flow ratio...	10.1x	10.8x	13.0x	12.1x	10.4x	10.4x*
Mean yield (%)...	3.04	3.62	3.96	5.19	5.19	4.50*
Average dividend payout (%)...	40.9	74.0	103.3	4700.0	(120.5)	81.7*
Mean share price US$...	28.94	25.94	23.75	18.13	18.13	20.88[1]

*estimate; [1]recent; [2]indicated

SOURCE: A.D.G. REID, "MOORE SHARES POISED FOR GROWTH," *THE FINANCIAL POST*, MARCH 31, 1994, 19. GRAPHS AND ONE PARAGRAPH OF THE ARTICLE DEALING WITH "MOMENTUM" ARE NOT REPRODUCED. REPRODUCED COURTESY OF TONY REID.

CASE 9B Analysis of a company's failure

W.T. Grant Company was a large U.S. retailer that enjoyed considerable success but then went bankrupt in the mid-1970s. The company had grown rapidly in the ten years up to 1973, establishing over 600 new stores in that period. A Canadian subsidiary was Zellers, now owned by the Hudson's Bay Company. It made some strategy changes during this time, for example, moving "upscale" from low-priced soft goods to higher-priced goods in competition with several department store chains. Its strategy was also to lease store space rather than to buy the property.

The company's share price fell dramatically between January 31, 1973, and January 31, 1974. In 1974, the company lost its credit rating, and after rescue attempts by 143 banks, the company was declared bankrupt shortly after the end of its 1975 fiscal year. Within another year, all the company's assets had been liquidated and the company ceased to exist.

Summary financial statements, several ratios, and the Scott formula calculations for W.T. Grant over the period 1970–1975 are shown below.[9] Use those to identify some reasons for the company's share price crash in 1973–74 and its ultimate failure.

W.T. GRANT COMPANY

Some Balance Sheet Items as of January 31 *(in millions $)*

	1970	1971	1972	1973	1974	1975
Cash and marketable securities	33	34	50	31	46	80
Accounts receivable	368	420	477	543	599	431
Inventory	222	260	299	400	451	407
Total current assets	628	720	831	980	1103	925
Total assets	707	808	945	1111	1253	1082
Total current liabilities	367	459	476	633	690	750
Total liabilities	416	506	619	776	929	968
Equity	291	302	326	335	324	114

Some Income, SCFP, and Dividend Numbers *(in millions $)*

	Year Ended January 31					
	1970	1971	1972	1973	1974	1975
Revenue	1220	1265	1384	1655	1861	1772
Cost of goods sold	818	843	931	1125	1283	1303
Income before interest and tax	85	92	76	85	60	(87)
Interest expense	15	19	16	21	51	199
Tax expense	28	33	26	26	1	(119)
Net income	42	40	35	38	8	(177)
Tax rate	.40	.45	.43	.41	.11	.40
Dividends declared	20	21	21	21	21	5
Cash flow from operations	(3)	(15)	(27)	(114)	(93)	(85)
Financing activities	25	33	76	121	138	140
Investment activities	(14)	(17)	(32)	(28)	(29)	(21)

W.T. GRANT COMPANY
Some Summary Numbers (Year Ended January 31)

	1970	1971	1972	1973	1974	1975
Return on equity	0.144	0.132	0.107	0.113	0.025	-1.553
Return on assets	0.072	0.062	0.047	0.045	0.042	-0.057
Sales return	0.042	0.040	0.032	0.030	0.028	-0.035
Total asset turnover	1.73	1.57	1.46	1.49	1.49	1.64
Cash flow to total assets	-0.004	-0.019	-0.029	-0.103	-0.074	-0.079
Average interest rate	0.022	0.038	0.026	0.027	0.055	0.205
Debt/equity ratio	1.43	1.68	1.90	2.32	2.87	8.49
Inventory turnover	3.68	3.24	3.21	2.81	2.84	3.20
Collection ratio	110.1	121.2	125.8	119.8	117.5	88.8
Working capital ratio	1.71	1.57	1.75	1.55	1.60	1.23
Acid test ratio	1.09	0.99	1.11	0.91	0.93	0.67
Gross margin	0.32	0.33	0.33	0.32	0.31	0.26
Interest coverage ratio	5.67	4.84	4.75	4.05	1.33	negative
Earnings per share in $	2.94	2.67	2.50	2.71	0.57	negative
Dividends per share in $	1.40	1.40	1.50	1.50	1.50	zero
January 31 closing share price in $	47.0	47.1	47.8	43.9	10.9	1.1

Scott Formula Components*

	ROE	=	SR	×	AT	+	(ROA	–	IN)	×	(D/E)
1970	0.144	=	0.042	×	1.73	+	(0.072	–	0.022)	×	1.43
1971	0.132	=	0.040	×	1.57	+	(0.062	–	0.021)	×	1.68
1972	0.107	=	0.030	×	1.46	+	(0.047	–	0.015)	×	1.90
1973	0.113	=	0.030	×	1.49	+	(0.045	–	0.016)	×	2.32
1974	0.025	=	0.028	×	1.49	+	(0.042	–	0.049)	×	2.87
1975	-1.553	=	-0.035	×	1.64	+	(-0.057	–	0.119)	×	8.49

*Because of rounding, the numbers don't all satisfy the relationship precisely.

NOTES

1. Some popular sources of information about companies are:
   a. The companies themselves, such as the Management Discussion and Analysis section of the annual report;
   b. Analyses prepared by stock and bond brokers and investment dealers;
   c. Annual rankings of companies according to their size and profitability, such as *The Financial Post Top 500 Companies*, and *The Globe and Mail Report on Business Magazine Top 1000 Companies*;
   d. Detailed descriptions of major companies and summaries of their performance information over several years in written sources, such as the *Financial Post Card Service* (Toronto: The Financial Post Publications), *Blue Book of Canadian Business* (Toronto: Canadian Newspaper Services International), *Blue Book of CBS Stock Reports* (Toronto: Canadian Business Service), and *Value Line Investment Survey* (New York: A. Bernhard);

e. Computer databases, such as *Disclosure Canada* (Bethesda, Md.: Disclosure Incorporated), *Disclosure USA* (Bethesda, Md.: Disclosure Incorporated), and an increasingly large number of other general and specialized databases;
f. Paper and computerized indexes of articles, such as *Info globe* (Toronto: The Globe and Mail), *Canadian Business Index* (Toronto: Micromedia), *Canadian Business and Current Affairs* (Toronto: Micromedia), *Business Periodicals Index* (New York: H.W. Wilson), and *ABI Inform* (Louisville, Ky.: Data Courier).

2. Many intermediate accounting and finance principles textbooks have good sections on financial statement analysis. There are also books with financial statement analysis in the title, going into more details and suggesting more extensive analyses than this book does. A good Canadian source is *Using Ratios and Graphics in Financial Reporting* (Toronto: CICA, 1993).

3. Proof of the Scott Formula (A = Assets, L = Liabilities, E = Equity):
   a. Define ROE = Net income / E
   b. Define ROA = (Net income + After-tax interest expense) / A
   c. Define IN = After-tax interest expense / L
   d. By double-entry accounting, A = L + E
   e. From (a), Net income = ROE × E
   f. From (b), Net income = (ROA × A) – After-tax interest expense
   g. Equate right sides of (e) and (f):
      ROE × E = (ROA × A) – After-tax interest expense
   h. From (d) and (c):
      ROE × E = (ROA × [L + E]) - (IN × L)
      ROE × E = ROA × L + ROA × E – IN × L
      ROE × E = ROA × E + (ROA – IN) × L
   i. Dividing the last through by E produces:
      ROE = ROA + (ROA – IN) × L/E
   j. Break up the first term to the right of the equal sign into two terms by multiplying it by REV / REV:
      ROA = (Net income + After-tax interest expense) / A
      ROA = (Net income + After-tax interest expense) / REV × REV / A
   k. Define the first new term as sales return SR and the second as asset turnover AT
   l. This produces the final version of the formula:
      ROE = SR × AT + (ROA – IN) × L/E

4. Derivation of Scott formula amounts for North West for 1992:

Total assets, end of 1993	$298,412	A
Total liabilities, end of 1993	163,066	L
Total equity, end of 1993	135,346	E
Total revenue for 1993	472,710	REV
Net income for 1993	11,954	NI
Interest expense for 1993	9,157	INT
Income tax rate for 1993 ($9,507 / $24,214)	0.393	TR
After-tax 1993 interest expense (Expense ×[1 – Tax rate])	5,558	ATI = INT (1 – TR)

(continued next page)

ROE (return on equity)	.110	NI / E
SR (sales return before interest)	.043	(NI + ATI) / REV
AT (asset turnover)	1.584	REV / A
ROA (return on assets)	.069	(NI + ATI) / A
IN (average interest rate after tax)	.034	ATI / L
D/E (debt/equity ratio)	1.205	L / E

Result:

ROE = SR × AT + (ROA – IN) × D/E

.110 = .043 × 1.584 + (.069 .034) × 1.205

.110 = .068 + .042

(Slight rounding error: .068 should = .069)

5. The booklet *Reporting Cash Flows: A Guide to the Revised Statement of Changes in Financial Position* (Toronto: Deloitte, Haskins & Sells [now Deloitte & Touche], 1986) was helpful in developing points about interpreting cash flow information.

6. A Canadian research study that examined some aspects of companies' use of "tailored" (special) accounting principles ("TAP") for evaluation under the terms of leading agreements is D.J. Thornton and M. Bryant, *GAAP vs. TAP in Leading Agreements: Canadian Evidence* (Toronto: Canadian Academic Accounting Association, 1986).

7. T.R. Dyckman and D. Morse, *Efficient Capital Markets and Accounting: A Critical Analysis*, 2nd ed. (Englewood Cliffs, N.J.: Prentice–Hall, 1986), 8. Reprinted by permission of Prentice–Hall Inc.

8. For more information on these issues, see P.A. Griffin ed., *Usefulness to Investors and Creditors of Information Provided by Financial Reporting*, 2nd ed. (Stamford, Conn.: Financial Accounting Standards Board, 1987) see several parts of the book, particularly 78–82, 120–28, and 201–208; Dyckman and Morse, *Efficient Capital Markets*, 58–59; Thornton and Bryant, *GAAP vs. TAP*; and W.H. Beaver, *Financial Reporting: An Accounting Revolution*, 2nd ed. (Englewood Cliffs, N.J.: Prentice–Hall, 1989), 165–66.

9. For more information on this case and some interesting charts of various ratios' performance over time, see J.A. Largey, III and C. P. Stickney, "Cash Flows, Ratio Analysis and the W.T. Grant Company Bankruptcy," *Financial Analysts Journal*, July–August, 1980, 51–54.

Accounting Policy Choices: Inventories, Long-term Assets, Liabilities, and Related Expenses

10.1 Chapter Overview

Enterprises have some choices as to how to prepare financial statements to suit their circumstances. Analyzing financial performance and position, and understanding the effects of such **accounting policy choices** require knowledge of accounting methods, the principles of accrual accounting and GAAP that guide and constrain choices, and methods of analysis. Now that you have such knowledge, you are prepared to extend the understanding of accrual accounting's revenue and expense recognition developed in Chapter 7 by examining some important expense recognition accounting policy choices, the GAAP that concern them, and their effects on the financial statements. This will complete the building blocks to the *understanding* of financial statements that the diagram represents and that is the objective of this book.

In this chapter you'll learn:

Use concepts: how the many differences among enterprises, the complexity of both users' demands for information and of the environment, and the reluctance of regulatory authorities to specify a single solution in the face of all this variation and complexity, encourage a diversity of financial accounting methods under the general umbrella of GAAP;

Preparation concepts: how the challenge of producing fair and comparable financial statements when enterprises can make choices about their financial accounting is met by the kinds of acceptable choices that have been developed and by the criteria for choosing among them;

Preparation techniques: how to implement in the financial statements important kinds of accounting policy choices for expenses, particularly the use of inventories and the amortization of long-term assets;

Use techniques: how to extend the techniques of ratio analysis, cash flow analysis, and especially "what if" effects analysis, to explore the consequences of accounting policy choices and to develop an understanding of how to make sense of financial statements that reflect such choices.

10.2 Background to Accounting Policy Choices

This section explains what is meant by "accounting policy choices" and outlines some aspects that are worth thinking about when working through the rest of the chapter.

WHAT IS AN ACCOUNTING POLICY?

Imagine the following scenario: the bookkeeper for MegaMega Stores Inc. has to decide whether or not each sales invoice should be recorded as revenue (credit revenue, debit cash or accounts receivable) and so, each time, phones the president and asks whether that invoice should be recorded. Pretty silly, eh? What the company needs to do is decide, *in advance and in general*, what sort of transaction constitutes a sale that is to be recorded as revenue. Then this decision can be communicated to the bookkeeper, who can apply the criteria to each invoice and so decide what to record without phoning the president. The president can run the company instead of talking to the bookkeeper every few minutes.

An **accounting policy** is a decision made in advance about how, when, and whether to record or recognize something. Typically, companies make policy choices in areas such as:

- When and how to recognize revenue (Chapter 7);
- How to compute amortization, often called depreciation, on plant and equipment assets (this chapter);
- How to value inventories (this chapter);
- How to value receivables, including how to estimate the allowance for doubtful accounts (Chapter 7);
- Which expenditures on fixed assets should be capitalized (added to the asset accounts) and which should be included with expenses such as repairs and maintenance (Chapter 5 and this chapter);
- Which product development expenditures should be expensed and which (if any) should be capitalized (this chapter);
- How to compute amortization on intangible assets (this chapter);
- Which assets and liabilities should be included in cash and cash equivalents for the purpose of preparing the SCFP (Chapter 4);
- How accounts of subsidiary and partly owned companies are to be reflected in the parent company's financial statements (Chapter 5).

When you choose the location of an account in the financial statements (such as putting it in current liabilities rather than noncurrent liabilities), you are making an accounting policy choice!

Accounting policy choices are very important to the interpretation and analysis of the financial statements. Without knowing how the statements were assembled, it is difficult to use them intelligently. For this reason, the first of the notes following the financial statements is usually a summary of the company's significant accounting policies. The other notes provide further details on important policies.

WHY IS THERE A CHOICE?

Accounting, in spite of being numerical, is not mathematically cut-and-dried. Preparers of financial statements are forced to make choices, whether they like it or not, for the following main reasons:

1. There is information value in the location of an account in the statements (for example, current vs. noncurrent or revenue vs. other income). Choice of location ("classification") of accounts is therefore potentially important.

2. Even the basic transactional records of accounting, the bookkeeping records, require decisions about what is a transaction, which accounts should be used, and how and when transactions are to be recorded.
3. The basis of accrual accounting, as we have seen, is to augment the transactional records to produce a more complete (in the economic sense) picture of the enterprise's performance and position. How to do this is a matter of judgment and of criteria such as matching, fairness, and economic substance. Accrual accounting therefore *necessitates* choices about accounting figures, notes, and methods.
4. In Canada, the United States, Britain, Australia, New Zealand, and many other countries, governments and professional accounting standard setters (such as the CICA and the FASB) have been reluctant to specify all solutions and require all enterprises to follow them. Such authorities appear to believe that choices in accounting are appropriate to fit the accounting to each enterprise's circumstances, and perhaps inevitable in our free enterprise economic system. Stock market participants, financial analysts, and others who rely on financial statements are expected to attain sufficient knowledge of accounting and the enterprise to make informed decisions, just as they would when buying the enterprise's products or having other interactions with the enterprise.

   It should be noted that authorities in many countries (such as China, France, Germany, and Japan) specify accounting methods much more strictly than is done in Canada. In such countries, the material covered in this chapter would put more emphasis on how to implement the approved accounting methods and less on how to choose among a variety of acceptable methods.
5. Because the complete financial statements include the figures and the footnotes and other narrative disclosures, there is frequently a decision to be made as to whether to adjust the figures for something or to disclose it in the narrative material instead, or even both. For example, if the company has been sued by a disgruntled customer, should that be recorded as a liability? Should it instead be disclosed only in the notes, or recorded as a liability with an explanatory note? Or are none of these appropriate?

GENERAL CRITERIA FOR ACCOUNTING POLICY CHOICES

When deciding how to account for revenues, inventories, depreciation, and other matters (*including* what to say in footnote disclosures), companies have to consider the following kinds of criteria and how they apply to the specific policy choice situation:

1. Fairness (objectivity, lack of bias, correspondence with economic substance of the situation);
2. Matching (fitting revenue recognition to the economic process, fitting expense recognition to the economic process and to the revenue);
3. Consistency over time;
4. Comparability to other companies (especially in the same industry);
5. Conformance with authoritative standards and less formal aspects of generally accepted accounting principles;

6. Materiality to (significance to decisions of) known or presumed users of the information;
7. Cost of implementing the policy;
8. Conservatism (taking anticipated losses into account before the transaction happens, but not taking anticipated gains into account until the transaction happens).

In addition, various criteria specific to the *particular* accounting policy choice issue must be considered. These were indicated for revenue recognition, consolidation, and other topics in earlier chapters; others will be given in this chapter.

How Much Freedom of Choice Is There?

As the earlier historical material indicated, companies used to have much more freedom to decide what and how to report than they do now. Some laws specify the use of particular reporting methods: for example, information about a corporation's transactions with its shareholders. But, more importantly, there is now a vast array of accounting standards that operate to constrain enterprises' choices about their accounting. Some of these standards (such as which partly owned companies should be consolidated) are specified in authoritative sources, such as the *CICA Handbook*. Others (such as that business enterprises should deduct amortization expense in computing income) are part of a more informal set of traditional, accepted procedures. The authoritative standards and the traditions *together* form generally accepted accounting principles (GAAP).

In some areas the choices have already been largely made by a standard-setting body, legislators, or by accepted practice. In others, there is no such guidance and the enterprise is free to make its own decisions.

- Examples of the first, already set, kind are consolidation method, accounting for income taxes, accounting for pensions, and accounting for leases. (These are still subject to revision when needed. As this book goes to press, income tax accounting is under study by the CICA to determine whether a different approach, used in the United States. and other countries, should be used in Canada.)
- Examples of the second kind, in which choice is allowed, are which of several depreciation methods to use, which of several inventory cost methods to use, and how to determine allowance for doubtful accounts.

Professional Judgment and Professional Standards

Even when there is an authoritative standard or a clear tradition, the necessity of fitting the accounting policy to the particular circumstances of the enterprise necessitates, in turn, the exercise of professional judgment by the preparers and auditors of the information. As the *CICA Handbook*'s Introduction to Accounting Recommendations says:

> No rule of general application can be phrased to suit all circumstances or combination of circumstances that may arise, nor is there any substitute for the exercise of professional judgment in the determination of what constitutes fair presentation or good practice in a particular case.[1]

A research study on professional judgment in financial reporting listed several reasons for professional standards and commented on their relationship to professional judgment.[2] Some of the main points under the two categories of findings are summarized below.

1. Why Have Professional Standards?
   - To carry out the profession's responsibility to society of reducing the risk of error and impropriety;
   - To bring collective wisdom to bear on difficult or complex issues;
   - To remove the inefficiency that would result if everyone had to solve every reporting issue anew on their own;
   - To state the official wisdom of the profession and so provide some protection to accountants and auditors;
   - To develop and communicate a consensus on issues that may lack objectively arrived at "right" answers.
2. Professional Judgment/Professional Standards Relationship
   - Standards reduce the need for (and risk entailed by) unfettered individual judgment;
   - Standards provide a framework within which judgment on unresolved issues may be exercised;
   - Judgment is needed to determine whether a given standard applies to a particular circumstance;
   - Judgment is needed to apply standards, especially where estimates and allocations are involved or materiality (significance of something) is in doubt;
   - Judgment is needed in determining whether the substance of the situation meets the spirit of the standard, or whether affairs have been carefully arranged just to make them fit the standard ("substance vs. form");
   - Judgment is needed to match relatively static standards to ever-changing circumstances.

MANIPULATION

Does accounting policy choice provide a way for company management to alter the picture presented in the financial statements—to present the story they want to tell rather than the truth? The short answer is yes. In fact, the whole idea of accrual accounting is to permit a company to choose how its performance and position are to be depicted. There is a fine line between choosing the accounting policies that suit the company's circumstances and so produce fair reporting, and choosing policies that tell a desired story that may not be fair. *The vast majority of companies and their managers are scrupulous about their accounting* and consider producing fair financial statements to be both ethical and good business practice. But we do learn of companies that have stepped over the line and "doctored" their accounts to make themselves look better or to hide some embarrassing result.

Here are some examples that the user of financial statements may want to think about and evaluate:

- A company may choose accounting methods, for receivables, inventories, amortization, or any other accounts, that tend to make earnings (income) higher than would have been produced by other methods. This could involve optimistic estimates of earned revenue, of the useful life of assets, or of the value of patents or exploration expenditures.
- Another company, concerned about its income tax burden, might make choices that would reduce income and, in this way, put off paying taxes.
- Having promised the bank that working capital would be maintained at a certain level, a company may choose accounting methods that help the working capital look as high as possible, such as classifying longer-term receivables as current assets or likely short-term obligations as noncurrent liabilities.

There may be reasons for manipulating income statement or balance sheet figures in any direction, but good knowledge of the enterprise may be necessary to predict what that direction is likely to be.

A dramatic example of income manipulation and one that may be fairly common is the "Big Bath" (discussed in an earlier chapter). The method works in this way: the management of a company that has a bad year may write off extra costs (for example, writing inventories, receivables, or intangibles way down) on the assumption that the company is already going to be criticized, so the criticism won't be much stronger if the results appear even worse. By transferring such costs to expenses now, instead of in later years, future expenses are reduced and therefore future incomes will look better. The company will appear to have bounced back quickly. Management hopes for praise for this recovery, even though it is not all real because of the manipulation.

Manipulation dangers can be overrated. Few managers are crooked con artists in their accounting: most are honest and anxious that their accounting be fair and truthful. Most consider that good financial reporting is important to the company's reputation and ability to borrow, raise share capital, and generally do business. Most consider good financial reporting to be part of good business and professional ethics. However, the danger of manipulation is always there, so accountants, auditors, and users who rely on income and other measures for their decisions must be vigilant. It is especially dangerous to rely on financial statements that have not been audited, or at least reviewed, by independent public accountants.

A Few Technical Points

1. *Cash flow*. Generally, accounting policy choice does not affect cash flow. We saw the reasons for this in Chapters 8 and 9: policy choices are made by accrual accounting entries, which do not affect cash directly. There may be indirect or eventual effects, especially through income tax. But, at the instant an accounting policy choice is implemented, there is no cash or cash flow effect unless a cash account is involved (as a rare example, a company might reclassify a deposit previously called part of cash and cash equivalents as a long-term investment asset).
2. *General form of policy change journal entry*. You can see the lack of cash effect from the following general form of an entry to implement a change in an accounting policy (cash is not part of the entry):

DR or CR	Some balance sheet account (receivables, payables, inventories, accumulated amortization, etc.)
CR or DR	Some income statement account for the current year's effect of the change (revenue, expenses, amortization, write-off loss, etc.)
DR or CR	Current year's income tax expense (current or deferred portion) for the income tax consequences of the current year's income statement effect
CR or DR	Retained earnings for the after-tax effect on prior years' incomes of the change
CR or DR	Income tax liability (current or deferred portion) for the accumulated amount of current and past years' income tax consequences of the change

3. *Dual effects of changes*. As noted in prior chapters, and as the above entry shows, most accounting policy changes affect both the balance sheet and the income statement. They *must* affect both if they are to affect net income. Here are some examples:

Balance Sheet Accounts	*Main Income Statement Accounts*
Temporary investments	Nonoperating revenue or expense
Accounts receivable	Revenue, bad debts expense
Inventories	Cost of goods sold expense
Prepaid and accrued expenses	Various expense accounts
Property and plant assets	Amortization expense
Intangible and leased assets	Amortization expense
Liabilities	Various expense accounts
Equity	None*

* Transactions with owners, such as share capital issues and redemptions and dividends, are ordinarily not considered part of the measurement of income. However, there are some technicalities in which this may be violated—this book will not cover such technicalities.

4. *Classification and disclosure*. There are accounting policy choices in two areas besides the example of Equity accounts above that do not affect income:

   - *Classification* policies (decisions about where within the balance sheet or where within the income statement to show accounts) do not affect income because they do not involve *both* the balance sheet and income statement, as do recognition policies, but instead affect only one or the other.
   - *Disclosure* policies relate to what is said about the figures in the words used in the statements and in the notes to the statements.

HOW'S YOUR UNDERSTANDING

Here are two questions you should be able to answer, based on what you have just read:

1. Sue Wong, an experienced investor, reacted in frustration on having difficulty comparing the financial statements of two companies she was considering investing in. "There is too much judgment being exercised in financial accounting! Why are companies allowed to choose their accounting policies, not just told how to do it?" What are some pros and cons of allowing enterprises to make accounting policy choices?
2. Indicate the probable direction of the effect of each of the following possible accounting policy changes on the account given:

Policy Change	Effect on?
◆ Accrue greater employee benefits expense	Liabilities
◆ Recognize accounts receivable sooner	Revenue
◆ Capitalize some repairs expenses	Net income
◆ Disclose board's intention to declare dividend	Net income
◆ Separate bank loan into current and long-term	Net income
◆ Recognize doubtful accounts sooner	Net income
◆ Write off spoiled inventories	Operating income

(Increase, increase, increase, no effect, no effect, decrease, decrease)

10.3 EXPENSE RECOGNITION IS EITHER ASSET CONSUMPTION OR LIABILITY INCURRENCE

This chapter will focus on important expense recognition policies, such as those for cost of goods sold and various kinds of amortization. Revenue recognition was covered sufficiently in Chapter 7; now we will examine some ways of matching important expenses to the revenue we think is being produced by incurring those expenses.

Asset consumption. Expense recognition for any asset consumption is produced by a form of the basic entry seen in Chapter 7 to recognize an expense incurred after cash was expended on the asset:

DR Expense
  CR Asset or Asset Contra

This entry recognizes the consumption of some or all of the economic value that was anticipated when the asset was recorded. Several examples of expense recognition and associated asset valuation policies form the bulk of this chapter.

Liability incurrence. If there is no asset being consumed, but instead a liability being incurred, the entry is different, also as shown in Chapter 7, to recognize an expense incurred before cash is expended:

DR Expense
  CR Liability

Liabilities will be reviewed toward the end of this chapter.

10.4 INVENTORY VALUATION AND COST OF GOODS SOLD

Inventory accounting, like accounting for other current assets, uses a modified version of the standard historical cost valuation basis: lower of cost or market. Because inventory is expected to be turned into cash (sold), or otherwise consumed within the next year, it is a current asset, and because it is a current asset, GAAP require that any impairment in the asset's value be recognized in the period the impairment occurred, not later when the asset is sold. Market is used only if it is lower than cost, so the historical cost basis is departed from only in one direction, down, if that is needed. This is an application of accounting conservatism: "anticipate no gains but allow for all losses."

In this section, we'll review briefly how to determine "cost," how to get "market," and how to get "lower" of the two. Inventory accounting affects both the balance sheet (inventory valuation) and the expense recognized for the use of inventory (cost of goods sold expense).

INVENTORY COST FLOW ASSUMPTIONS

Total cost is just the sum of quantity times unit cost for all items of inventory.

- We can get the quantity by counting the items, estimating the quantity, or using records (remember inventory control in Chapter 6).
- We know that unit cost includes the invoiced cost plus inward shipping, preparation, and so on (Section 5.8).
- Finding total cost, therefore, seems easy: just identify each item in inventory, trace it back to the purchase records, figure out its cost, and add all the costs together.

But is it so easy? Imagine the trouble you'd have keeping track of the invoiced cost, shipping, and other cost components for every item in a hardware store's inventory, or the impossibility of keeping track of individual barrels of oil in an oil refinery.

In practice, the actual cost of inventory items is tracked only for high-value items (houses, automobiles, airplanes, expensive jewellery) that can be identified by serial numbers and other methods. As the cost of keeping records decreases due to computerization, more items can be tracked this way. Still, serial numbers or other ways to identify specific inventory items are needed. According to *Financial Reporting in Canada 1993,* only 10 companies in its 1992 survey of 300 companies said they used actual, or "specific items," cost for any inventories.[3]

For most inventories, because it is not worthwhile or even possible to keep track of the cost of individual items in inventory, most companies figure out their balance sheet inventory cost and cost of goods sold expense by *assuming* some flow of costs through the business. We don't want to have to know exactly which ones are on hand, or which have been sold, so we make assumptions.

To illustrate the effects of different assumptions, we will first use a simple example based on the periodic inventory control method, in which no records are kept of changes in inventory levels during the accounting period. If the perpetual control method were used, the calculations would be more complex (we'll see those later). The example involves inventory purchased for resale (such as a retailer would purchase), but the ideas work just as well for inventory manufactured by a company: in that case, cost of *purchases* is replaced by cost of *goods manufactured*. From the graph in Figure 10.1 we can see that there were 330 units available for sale during the period (120 + 210) and, after selling 180, 150 units remained on hand at the end of the period.

FIGURE 10.1

- Inventory at beginning of period: 120 units costing $2 each
- Purchases during period (in the order they happened):
  1. 100 units costing $3 each
  2. 110 units costing $4 each
- Sales during period: (based on an ending inventory of 150 units) 180 units

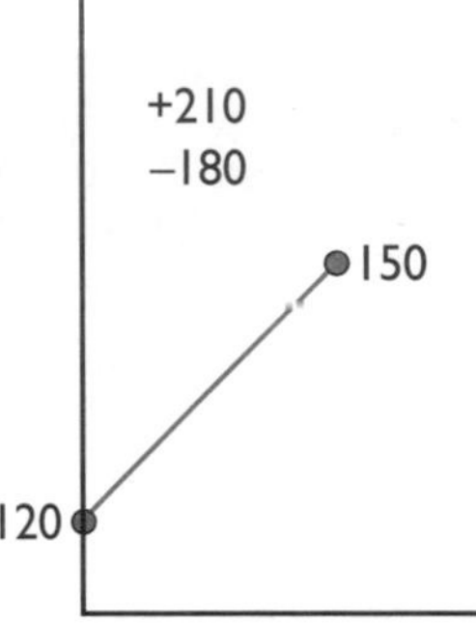

The *cost of goods available for sale* equals the cost of the opening inventory plus the cost of those purchased (or manufactured). So we have 120 × $2 = $240, plus 100 × $3 = $300, plus 110 × $4 = $440, for a total cost of goods available of $980.

Our problem is how to *allocate* the $980 between the income statement for the period (cost of goods sold expense) and the balance sheet at the end of the period (ending inventory asset).

Exhibit 10.1 shows three different assumptions that would underlie decisions about how to do that allocation. *In each case the sum of the ending balance sheet asset valuation and the cost of goods sold expense is $980.* The different cost flow assumptions just allocate this available cost differently between the balance sheet valuation and the income statement expense.

Exhibit 10.1

	Ending Inventory Asset	Cost of Goods Sold Expense
1. **"First in, first out" assumption—** FIFO assumes that the first items acquired are the first ones sold, and, therefore, that any ending inventory on hand consists of the most recently acquired units (recent costs on balance sheet, older costs in COGS expense).	(110 × $4) + (40 × $3) = **$560**	$980 – $50 = **$420** ([120 × $2] + [60 × $3] = $420)
2. **Weighted annual average assumption—**AVGE assumes ending inventory and COGS are composed of a mixture of old and new units.	**Average unit cost = $980/330 = $297** (rounded) 150 × $2.97 = **$445**	$980 – $445 = **$535** (180 × $2.97 = $535)
3. **"Last in, first out" assumption—** LIFO assumes the opposite of FIFO, saying that any inventory on hand consists of the oldest units (older costs on balance sheet, recent costs in COGS expense).	(120 × $2) + (30 × $3) = **$330**	$980 – $330 = **$650** ([110 × $4] + [70 × $30] = 650)

MORE ABOUT INVENTORY COST FLOW ASSUMPTIONS

The above example introduced three cost flow assumptions, FIFO, AVGE, and LIFO. For most purposes, if you can understand the ideas behind the chart above, you know all you need to about the three. But there is an additional wrinkle that you might as well know about, because you may well run into it.

We know from Chapter 6 that internal control over inventory may mean using the periodic or perpetual methods. If we put the three cost flow assumptions against the two control methods, we get the following:

Assumption	Periodic Control	Perpetual Control
FIFO	FIFO	FIFO
AVGE	Weighted annual average	Moving weighted average
LIFO	Periodic LIFO	Perpetual LIFO

FIFO is not affected by the inventory control method, because it just assigns most recent cost to whatever is on hand. But the other two methods are affected by the control method, because they depend on what we know about what happened to inventory levels during the period. This gives us five potential methods: FIFO and two versions each of AVGE and LIFO. (There is a sixth, actual cost, as we have already seen, and, at the end of this section, two more methods will be mentioned briefly. So there are at least eight different ways to account for inventory cost!) In Canada, the weighted annual average and both LIFO methods are rare, but we will include them because the contrast with FIFO and moving average may help you understand the latter ones, and because LIFO is very common in the United States, so you will see it mentioned in many U.S. financial statements.

Let's examine these assumptions and their interaction with internal control methods further. Remember that, because each assumption allocates the available inventory cost between the inventory asset and the cost of goods sold expense differently, the choice of assumption has an effect on both the balance sheet and the income statement. The significance of the effect depends on how much purchase (or manufacturing) costs per unit rise or fall during the period: if there is little change in these costs, the various methods will show very similar results.

FIFO assigns the more *recent* purchase costs to the balance sheet inventory asset account, and, therefore, *older* costs to the cost of goods sold expense account.

- It is used because it is convenient, not affected by internal control method, and produces inventory asset values that are close to current costs, which seems to many people to be appropriate for a current asset.
- It is convenient because all you really need to do is keep your purchase invoices and, when you know how many units are on hand, just go through recent invoices to find the costs.
- For example, suppose there are 620 boxes of chocolates on hand at December 31, and recent purchase invoices showed the following costs: Dec. 29, 260 boxes at \$3.20; Dec 14, 310 boxes at \$3.35; Dec. 1, 210 boxes at \$3; and so on. The FIFO cost is found by starting with the most recent purchase and going back in time until all the ones on hand are accounted for (working on assumption, since we do not really know

when any particular box was purchased). So the FIFO cost here would be (260 × \$3.20) + (310 × \$3.35) + ([620 – 260 – 310 = 50] × \$3), or \$2,020.50. You don't need complicated records, just a pile of invoices. Also, it doesn't matter what the internal control method is, because all you need to know is the quantity on hand, whether determined by count or by perpetual records.

- *Financial Reporting in Canada 1993* indicates that in 1992, 262 of the 300 companies surveyed disclosed the cost flow assumption for inventories, and FIFO was used by 125 of them.[4]
- FIFO is considered appropriate for a current asset by many people because it is the most reasonable method of physically moving inventory, especially inventory that is perishable or subject to changes in style or features, such as groceries, clothing, and other retail products. Picture a shelf in a grocery store: FIFO assumes that new stock is placed behind older stock on the shelf, so that the inventory keeps moving forward on the shelf. That way older items sell first and do not just collect dust and mold at the back of the shelf.

AVGE assigns the available cost equally to the inventory asset and to cost of goods sold expense. In the example in Figure 10.1 above, both inventory asset and cost of goods sold used the same \$2.97 average cost per unit.

- Average cost is used largely for inventories that are a mixture of recent and older purchases and that are not particularly perishable, such as lumber, metals, oil, gas, and other bulk products and raw materials.
- *Financial Reporting in Canada 1993* says that in 1992 the average cost method was the second-most popular, with 92 companies reporting using it.[5] The two versions of the average cost method (the "annual weighted average" method illustrated for the periodic inventory control example above and the "moving weighted average" method, which can be used where the perpetual control method provides the required information) are illustrated below.

LIFO is, on the face of it, a strange valuation method. It assumes that the newer items are sold first and, therefore, that the oldest are the ones left on hand. In the extreme, this would imply that the grocery store's first loaves of bread are still at the back of the shelf, years later.

- LIFO is used for one very practical reason: in the United States, it is an allowable method for income tax purposes. In a period of rising purchase costs (inflation), which is pretty much constantly the case, it produces a higher cost of goods sold expense and a lower inventory asset value than do FIFO or AVGE. Therefore, LIFO also produces lower income and lower income tax, *if* it can be used for tax purposes.
- In Canada, it is not an allowable method for income tax purposes, so a Canadian company using it for the financial statements would have to compute inventory values all over again using one of the other methods when doing its income tax return.
- *Financial Reporting in Canada 1993* indicates that, in 1992, only 10 Canadian companies used LIFO, only two of which used it for all inventories and three of which used it for inventories held by U.S. subsidiaries.[6]

- It can also be argued that LIFO matches revenues with expenses better than do the other two methods. For example, if a company changes its selling prices as its purchase costs change, its revenues reflect recent price changes and it then seems appropriate to deduct the more recent purchase costs as cost of goods sold expense against the revenues. The trouble is that LIFO produces inventory asset values that are based on older purchase costs and this seems awkward for valuing a current asset.
- It would be nice to use current purchase prices for cost of goods sold expense *and* for the balance sheet inventory value. But, that can't be done if we stick to the historical cost accounting basis: the books wouldn't balance because some of the units would have been purchased at older costs and those costs would be in the accounts, too, in the inventory asset or expense accounts. (There are proposals for using current costs, such as replacement costs, to get both balance sheet and income statement figures, but these are not used in practice, at least not yet.)
- LIFO is affected by whether its amounts are determined using the periodic or perpetual control methods, as the example below will show.

AN EXAMPLE: MEEIX INC.

Among the products Meeix Inc. purchases and sells is Gloop. It began last year with 1,000 units of Gloop on hand at a cost of $4 each and during the year its purchase and sales records showed:

Date	Units Purchased	Units Sold	Units on Hand	Purchase Price
Jan. 1			1,000	$4
Feb. 15		350	650	
Mar. 20	600		1,250	$5
Apr. 30		750	500	
Sept. 12	800		1,300	$6
Dec. 11		200	1,100	
	1,400	1,300		

The chart in Figure 10.2 shows how the quantities of Gloop changed during the year. Note that the cost flow assumptions would identify the *ending inventory's* 1,100 units as:

- FIFO: 1,100 = 800 most recently bought + 300 of those bought Mar. 20;
- AVGE:
  Annual weighted: 1,100 = a proportionate mixture of those on hand at the beginning and those bought Mar. 20 and Sept. 12;
  Moving: the first average is the 1,250 on hand at Mar. 20, a proportionate mixture of those on hand at beginning + those bought Mar. 20; second average, the 1,100, is a proportionate mixture of the first average (on hand Apr. 30) and those bought Sept. 12;
- LIFO:
  Periodic: the ups and downs during the year are not known (no records kept), so the 1,100 = 1,000 on hand at beginning + 100 bought Mar. 20;

Perpetual: during the year, the inventory hit a minimum of 500, so that's all of the beginning items that could still be on hand at the end, therefore 1,100 = 500 from beginning + 600 bought Sept. 12.

Inventory Balances and Changes: Meeix's Gloop

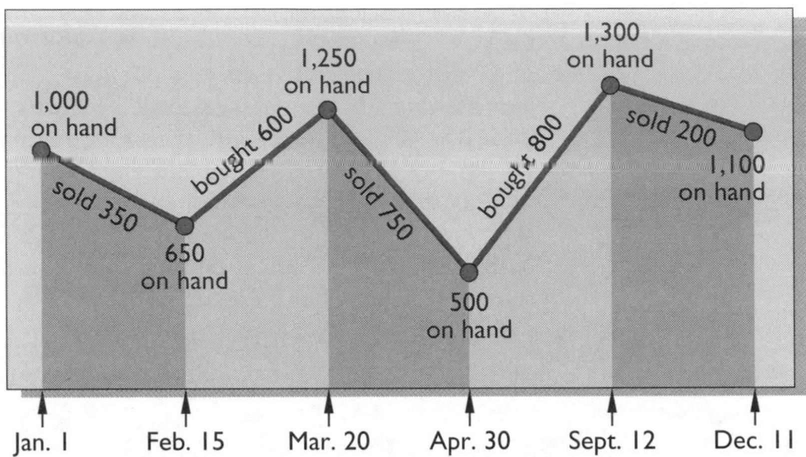

FIGURE 10.2

Now we can go on with the calculations. *Regardless of the cost flow assumption used*, we know that the beginning inventory cost is $4,000 and that purchases costing $7,800 (600 × $5 + 800 × $6) were made. *Available cost*, therefore, is the sum of beginning inventory and purchases, which is $11,800. Consequently, as long as the historical cost basis of accounting is used, any inventory cost allocation method must produce $11,800 as the sum of the ending inventory asset and cost of goods sold expense. You might think of it this way:

Available for sale	=	Gone + Still here
Beginning inventory + Purchases	=	Cost of goods sold expense + Ending inventory

The left side equals $11,800, so the right side must result in the same total. This gives us ways to check our calculations. If we calculate cost of goods sold expense and ending inventory asset cost separately, they must add up to $11,800. As a short cut, we can calculate *either* the expense or the asset value and deduce the other by deducting it from $11,800. This is easier than doing it twice, but the calculations below will include both the expense and the asset so that you can see how it all works.

Based on the patterns shown in Figure 10.2 and the summary of each method's assumption about the ending inventory quantity, here are the calculations for ending inventory cost and cost of goods sold.

a. **FIFO**

Ending inventory cost: (800 × $6) + (remaining 300 × $5)	$ 6,300
Cost of goods sold expense:	
(1,000 × $4) + (remaining 300 × $5)	5,500
	$11,800

b. **AVGE**

Annual weighted average

Average cost = $11,800 / (1,000 + 600 + 800) = $4.917 (rounded)

Ending inventory cost: 1,100 × $4.917	$ 5,408
Cost of goods sold expense: 1,300 × $4.917	6,392
	$11,800

Moving weighted average

The average works the same way as the above weighted average, but it is recalculated after each purchase, weighted in accordance with the inventory on hand at that point.

Weighted average after first purchase
= ([650 × $4]+ [600 × $5]) / (650 + 600) = $4.48

Weighted average after second purchase
= ([500 × $4.48] + [800 × $6]) / (500 + 800) = $5.415

Ending inventory cost (using average at that point):	
1,100 × $5.415	$ 5,957
Cost of goods sold expense:	
(350 × $4) + (750 × $4.48) + (200 × $5.415)	5,843
	$11,800

c. **LIFO**

Periodic basis

Ending inventory cost: (1,000 × $4) + (remaining 100 × $5)	$ 4,500
Cost of goods sold expense: (800 × $6) + (remaining 500 × $5)	7,300
	$11,800

Perpetual basis

The perpetual records allow us to determine whether it is reasonable to assume that all the original 1,000 units are still on hand. In this example it is not, because at one point the inventory was down to 500 units, so that "layer" of cost has been partly used up. The calculation reflects the "cost layer" information available from the records.

Ending inventory cost: (500 × $4) + (remaining 600 bought since × $6)	$ 5,600
Cost of goods sold expense: (350 × $4) + (600 × $5 [layer all gone]) + (further 150 from the original layer × $4) + (200 from the most recent layer × $6)	6,200
	$11,800

EFFECTS ANALYSIS

The following summarizes the Meeix example's results. Whether or not you were able to follow all the calculations, you should be able to understand the effects on the financial statements of choosing among the inventory cost methods, *assuming* that in all cases cost is lower than market value for the ending inventory asset (valued on the balance sheet at lower of cost or market).

Cost Method	Ending Inventory Asset	Cost of Goods Sold Expense	Total Cost Available
FIFO	$6,300	$5,500	$11,800
AVGE - Annual	5,408	6,392	11,800
- Moving	5,957	5,843	11,800
LIFO - Periodic	4,500	7,300	11,800
- Perpetual	5,600	6,200	11,800

This example illustrates a result that is common when using these methods. *In a period of rising purchase prices,* as here:

- FIFO tends to have the highest inventory asset value and lowest cost of goods sold expense (and therefore highest net income);
- LIFO tends to have the lowest inventory asset value and highest COGS (and therefore lowest net income).
- AVGE tends to be between the other two in asset values, COGS, and net income.

If purchase prices are falling, the positions of FIFO and LIFO reverse, with FIFO tending to have the lowest net income and LIFO the highest. AVGE tends again to be between the other two.

The differences among the methods are larger the more purchase cost prices rise (or fall) during the period. The differences tend to be smaller when inventory turnover is high, because price changes occurring during the time inventory is held are smaller and the size of the inventory asset relative to cost of goods sold expense is smaller. If a perpetual LIFO or moving average method is being used, the differences can also be in unexpected directions, depending on coincidental increases or decreases in inventory levels. The LIFO perpetual ending inventory for Meeix is higher than the annual average ending inventory because a large amount of the beginning inventory was sold, so the LIFO perpetual method used this information, but the annual average did not. The relationships among the methods also can stray from the typical pattern if purchase price changes and inventory quantities are moving in opposite directions (for example, if inventory levels are falling but prices are rising, or vice versa).

Let's assume Meeix Inc. is using FIFO for its inventory of Gloop. What would be the effects on Meeix's financial statements if it changed to one of the other four methods *beginning this year* (that is, without changing past years and so without changing the $4 cost of the January 1 inventory)? Meeix's income tax rate is 30%.

If it *changed to moving weighted average:*

- Cost of goods sold expense would go up by $343 ($5,843 – $5,500), so net income would decline by 70% of that, or $240.
- Income tax expense and liability would go down by the other 30%, or $103.
- Working capital would go down by $343 (inventory asset decline) and up by $103 (income tax liability decline) for a net decrease of $240, the same as the net income decline.

◆ There would be no immediate effect on cash or cash flow.

Here are the above effects entered into our analytical framework. (We'll do this just for the above change to moving weighted average, because there are no effects on past years and so the framework doesn't provide great insight. But it might help you see how to analyze a multi-year inventory accounting policy change.)

Balance Sheet End Last Year		+	**Income Statement This Year**		=	**Balance Sheet End This Year**	
Assets			*Revenue*			*Assets*	
Inv. no change	$0		No effect			Inv. down	$343
Liabilities			*Expenses*			*Liabilities*	
Other than tax			*Other than tax*			*Other than tax*	
No effect			COGS up	$343			No effect
Income tax			*Income tax*			*Income tax*	
No effect			Down	$103		Down	$103
Equity						*Equity*	
Retained earn.			Net income			*Retained earn.*	
No effect			Down	$240		Down	$240

You should be able to fill in the analysis for changes to any of the other methods. For your reference, the results for changes to the other three are shown in the chapter endnotes.[7]

INVENTORY MARKET VALUE FOR LOWER OF COST OR MARKET RULE

There are two common perspectives on this:

- For inventory that is not to be sold, but rather to be used up (for example, manufacturing raw materials, factory supplies, and office supplies), the *input* market value or *replacement cost* seems most relevant. Replacement cost is determined by obtaining prices from suppliers and making other estimates of what it would cost to replace the items on hand. The focus is on items whose supply prices are falling because, remember, we're concerned only with cases in which market (replacement cost) is *lower* than the cost originally paid, or assumed to have been paid, for the items.
- For inventory that is to be sold, the *output* market value or *net realizable value* seems most relevant. Net realizable value is determined by taking selling prices and deducting any costs to complete (such as putting it in a box) or sell the items. Again, the focus is on items whose net realizable value is *below* cost, so we're concerned about items whose selling prices are falling or that have been damaged, or have become obsolete, or out of style so that we can't sell them for what we thought we could.

LOWER OF COST OR MARKET

Basically, to calculate the lower of cost or market value, we just take the cost of the items and match those costs against the market values and use the lower as the balance sheet inventory value. In practice, companies usually focus mainly on items whose values are likely to be impaired (as might be identified during the physical count), rather than calculating market value for everything.

Often the kind of inventory suggests both a cost flow assumption and a market value method. For example:

- Raw materials are often shown at the lower of average cost and replacement cost; while
- Goods for sale are usually shown at the lower of FIFO cost and net realizable value.

Thus we tend to see the cost and market methods going together (average with replacement, FIFO with NRV), though there are many exceptions. The retail method of costing inventory (discussed below) is an amalgam of costs and selling prices, so it, too, is an example of costs and market values going together.

Canadian financial accounting standards are not explicit about "lower of cost or cost or market" issues. They are left to the professional judgment of individual accountants and auditors. In the United States there are a number of rules and regulations, including the "floor–ceiling" rule (in which market equals replacement cost as long as that does not exceed a pair of floor and ceiling values calculated from selling price), which provide more specific guidance. The complexities of these rules and guidelines are best left to other books. But what you should know for now is that figuring out lower of cost or market for inventories requires management to make accounting policy decisions about cost, about market, and about combining them.

THE RETAIL INVENTORY AND OTHER METHODS

Financial Reporting in Canada 1993 tells us that in 1992, 12 companies used the retail method, which was mentioned in Section 6.10 as an inventory and cash control method.[8] These 12 are from a sample of large companies; the retail method is probably much more common among smaller companies, so a brief comment about it will be useful. The retail method, which, as you might expect, is most applicable for retailers' inventories, combines purchase costs and selling prices into a single calculation, or estimate.

- What you do is first price the list of inventory items at their selling prices, which is often easy to do because the selling price is marked on the items or is in the computer record connected to the cash registers.
- Then you deduct the markup made by the company on each item (it is usually easier to do this on groups of similar items, or even on all items together if you have a reasonably accurate average markup percentage) and make an estimate of the cost.
- Cost equals selling price minus markup.
- This method allows sales staff to keep track of inventories and cash according to selling prices, while not having to know costs. But maintaining accuracy while using the method requires keeping track of

unusual markups (such as special sales or promotions), markdowns because of slow sales or damaged items, and other complications.

A few other inventory costing methods are used. *Financial Reporting in Canada 1993* says 13 companies reported methods other than the ones described here.[9] One of these, standard costing, which you will learn about if you take a course in management accounting or cost accounting, is applicable to inventories manufactured by the company and uses estimated costs based on standard production costs and volumes.

HOW'S YOUR UNDERSTANDING

Here are two questions you should be able to answer, based on what you have just read:

1. Beyond the general criteria for accounting policy choice, such as fairness, how does a company decide which method to use in determining the cost of inventory?
2. Meeix Inc. also stocks a pet food called Dog's Breakfast, which it controls using the periodic inventory method. Last year, there were 200 crates of Dog's Breakfast on hand at the beginning of the year, and 1,500 crates were purchased and 1,450 crates were sold during the year. The crates on hand at the beginning cost $400 each. There were three purchases: early in the year, 500 crates costing $404 each were purchased; then 600 crates costing $390 each; and near the end of the year, 400 crates costing $384.50 each were purchased. What would be the cost of the inventory at the end of the year and the cost of goods sold expense under (a) FIFO? (b) AVGE? and (c) LIFO? (a) $96,125; $573,675; (b) $98,500; $571,300; (c) $100,200; $569,600)

10.5 AMORTIZATION OF ASSETS AND AMORTIZATION EXPENSE

Fixed assets have value because the company intends to receive economic benefits from using them in the future. However, with the exception of land, all fixed assets must eventually be retired from service. Thus, when purchasing a fixed asset such as a building or equipment, the rational purchaser will at least have an approximate idea of how much benefit the asset will provide. For example, when buying a piece of equipment to slice bread, the baker must have a reasonable idea of how many loaves it will slice, before it wears out. If we can estimate how many loaves it will slice we can then deduct the cost of the machine from revenue (in calculating income) a part at a time, over the number of years it will take to bake that many loaves of bread. This process of allocating the cost over years of benefit is called amortization, and the annual deduction from revenue is amortization expense. All fixed assets except land are amortized if a company is following GAAP.

A short comment on terminology may be helpful here. This section and the book in general use the terms "amortization," "depreciation," and "depletion." Historically, depreciation has been used when physical assets, such as buildings and equipment, are involved; depletion has been used when "wasting assets," such as timber sales or ore bodies, are involved, and amortization has been used when various miscellaneous and intangible assets are involved. The usage is changing: since 1990, the *CICA Handbook* has used amortization as the only term, and this book uses that term most of the time. We may see depreciation and depletion eventually disappear from Canadian financial statements. But then again we may not, because they are deeply entrenched terms, especially depreciation.

Several questions should be answered before examples of amortization methods are presented. These are outlined below.

WHY ALLOCATE THE COST?

Assets are resources of the enterprise, used in order to generate revenue for the owners and, ultimately, a return on their investment. One of the objectives of accrual accounting is to attempt to match expenses with the revenue earned. In the case of long-lived assets, the cost will benefit many periods in which revenue is earned. Therefore, some method is needed to allocate the cost of long-lived assets over their useful lives. If the whole asset cost were deducted from income in the period in which it was acquired, that would make that period's income relatively low, and subsequent periods' incomes relatively high. So, amortization spreads the cost out over all the periods that share in the using up of the asset's economic value.

- The bread slicer costs $5,000 and will have no value after eight years, so amortization of $5,000 over eight years (for example, $625 of amortization expense each year) shows that using up the slicer's value over those eight years costs us something. We have a $5,000 asset now; in eight years we will have no asset.
- This cost allocation system is somewhat arbitrary, since it is based on expectations when the asset is acquired and not on tracking changes in market value, for example, over the time the asset is used. Over that time, the cost and resale value of slicers may keep changing due to inflation, market conditions, or technological change. We may be able to resell the slicer for only $3,000 after one year, so perhaps the economic value used up in that year is $2,000, but if our amortization method specifies $625 per year, that is what we use.

It is *essential* to understand that the accounting concept of amortization involves an *allocation of cost* in order to measure *income: it is not a system to track value changes in the assets or to measure the current value of those assets in the balance sheet.* It recognizes an expense (based on historical cost) that is presumed to *match* the revenue generated by using up the asset's economic value. The balance sheet shows the net of the asset's original cost minus accumulated amortization: it does not mean the asset's current value is that net amount.

In the above example, after one year the balance sheet shows the slicer at $4,375 ($5,000 cost less $625), not at $3,000 or any other measure of current value. The accounting meaning of amortization (and depreciation and depletion) is very specific: *an allocation of historical cost as a deduction from income over the useful life of the asset.*

WHY NOT AMORTIZE LAND?

The basic answer is that land's economic value is not considered to decline through use. Land is not normally susceptible to physical or economic decline.

- As a machine is used in a production process it wears out, like the soles of your shoes as you walk. Other natural processes, such as wind, rain, rust, fatigue, and corrosion, all keep assets from providing benefit indefinitely.
- There are also nonphysical causes of economic amortization. A machine can become obsolete with the advent of newer and faster machines, economic conditions in an area can result in the closure of a plant that has many productive years left but cannot be profitable any more, and the whims of fashion can cause retail merchants to change display racks every two years when they were built to last for 10.

Land is considered immune from all this and so is not depreciated. If evidence of a loss of land value does appear, the land's cost can be reduced to a revised value, but that is a special case and is a "loss" rather than amortization.

WHEN DOES THE COST ALLOCATION (AMORTIZATION EXPENSE) BEGIN?

Amortization is meant to provide an expense to match the economic benefit obtained from the use of the asset. Therefore, when the asset is put to use and the benefit begins to be realized, amortization expense should begin. In Chapter 5 the components of the cost of an asset were listed, and in Chapter 7 journal entries for amortizing assets as part of accrual accounting were explained. The general pattern is to capitalize costs incurred on the asset prior to putting it into service, and then, when the asset is put into service, to amortize those costs.

This pattern is illustrated in the chart in Figure 10.3. The line sloping downward from cost need not be a straight one, as we will see.

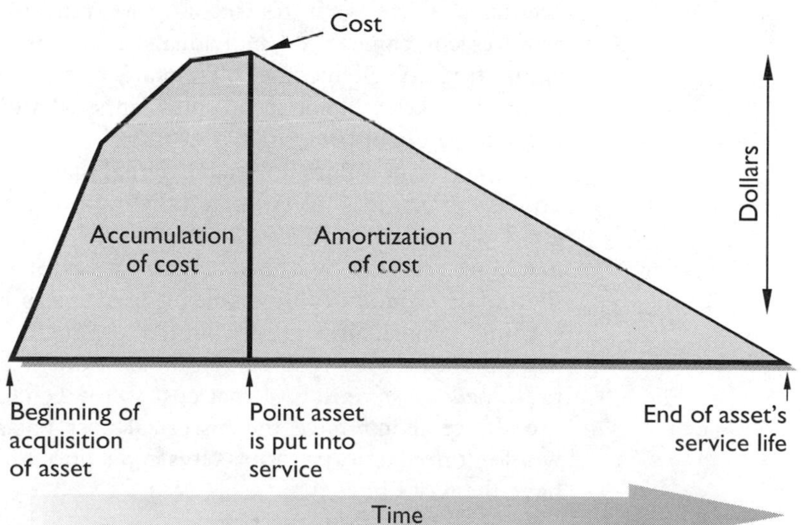

FIGURE 10.3

Once the asset has been put into service, further costs of painting, maintenance, repairs, and so on are now considered expenses—part of the cost of keeping the asset on its *planned path of decline* over its useful life. If a cost incurred subsequent to the asset's going into service significantly changes its economic value in earning revenue or extends its useful life, such a "betterment" may properly be capitalized as part of the asset's cost and then depreciated along with the rest of the asset's cost. In the chart above, a betterment would be shown as an upward jog in the downward sloping amortization line, with the amortization line then resuming from the higher point at the top of the jog.

OTHER QUESTIONS

Does amortization affect cash flow? Is it exact? What effect does it have on income tax?

Amortization is recognized by the following journal entry :

DR Amortization expense
  CR Accumulated amortization contra asset

The entry has no cash component, so amortization has no cash effect. The fact that amortization appears on the cash flow statement (SCFP) often misleads people: because it is added to income, it seems to be a source of cash. But it has no effect on cash one way or the other. It is added back to income at the beginning of the cash flow statement to *remove* its effect from accrual accounting income and so convert that income to cash income.

Amortization, no matter how carefully calculated, is never exact. It involves a prediction of economic use and useful life, and such a prediction can easily be wrong. If assets are grouped together for computing amortization, the errors can be reduced because some assets for which the prediction overshoots may be offset by others for which the prediction undershoots. Any amortization amount is fundamentally arbitrary; for that reason, most companies prefer fairly simple calculations rather than complex guesses!

In Canada, as we saw in Section 7.13, amortization calculated in the accounts is irrelevant for income tax purposes because Revenue Canada requires companies (and individuals) to follow its own rules, not GAAP, in computing taxable income. A company can use whatever GAAP amortization method it likes in its financial statements; whatever that is, it is still irrelevant for income tax purposes.

Amortization does not match actual market value changes in assets, it has no cash effect, it is an estimate only, and it has no income tax effect! What good is it? That's a question often asked, and the answer goes back to the matching criterion and historical cost basis of accrual accounting. We know that some economic value is being used up as a depreciable asset is used in earning revenue. Since we are limited to using cost in measuring that value, we end up with a way of spreading the cost out over the useful life to match the presumed consumption of that cost to the benefits (revenue) gained from the use. If we didn't have the historical cost basis or matching, we probably wouldn't need amortization as it is conventionally calculated. But, since we do have them, we have it!

AMORTIZATION BASES AND METHODS

Several amortization methods are commonly used today. Different methods attempt to approximate different economic use patterns of the assets over their lives. In each case, the purpose is to *match* the amortization expense for each period to the presumed economic benefit obtained during that period, often in a simple way, since amortization is an estimate rather than an exact measure of value changes.

As noted in Section 7.9, which discusses contra accounts, the accumulated amortization account is a balance sheet offset account to the truck asset cost account. Over time, it accumulates the *total* of the amortization expense recorded over the years. As this accumulation rises, book value falls.

There are four basic assumptions about how an asset brings economic benefit, and one general kind of amortization for each:

	Assumption	Kind of Cost Allocation
1.	*Evenly over the asset's life* The asset is assumed to be equally valuable in earning income in each year of its useful life.	*Straight-line* Expense is the same each year of the useful life.
2.	*Falling over the asset's life* The asset's value in its early years is assumed to be greater than that in its later years.	*Accelerated declining balance* Expense is larger in the earlier years than in the later years.
3.	*Rising over the asset's life* Opposite to assumption 2 above.	*Decelerated* Opposite to accelerated.
4.	*Variable over the asset's life* The asset's value in earning income varies according to how much production is achieved each year.	*Units of production, depletion* Expense depends on each year's volume of production.

These four general kinds are compared graphically in Figure 10.4 Each has a different amortization expense per period and a different pattern of book value. (Book value equals cost minus accumulated amortization, so, because cost is constant, the book value pattern comes from the accumulation of the amortization.)

You may be wondering where the names "accelerated" and "decelerated" amortization come from. The reason the methods have been named in this manner is because of their connection with straight-line amortization.

- Accelerated amortization is accelerated (higher expense) in comparison with straight-line amortization in the *early years* of the asset's life.
- Decelerated amortization has a smaller expense than straight-line amortization in the early years of the asset's life.

The reason for the name "units of production" is explained later.

Let's see how to calculate amortization using the four different bases.

1. Straight-Line Amortization

Straight-line amortization, depicted in the top panel of Figure 10.4, is the simplest and most widely used of all the amortization methods. *Financial Reporting in Canada 1993* indicates that 294 of the 300 surveyed companies

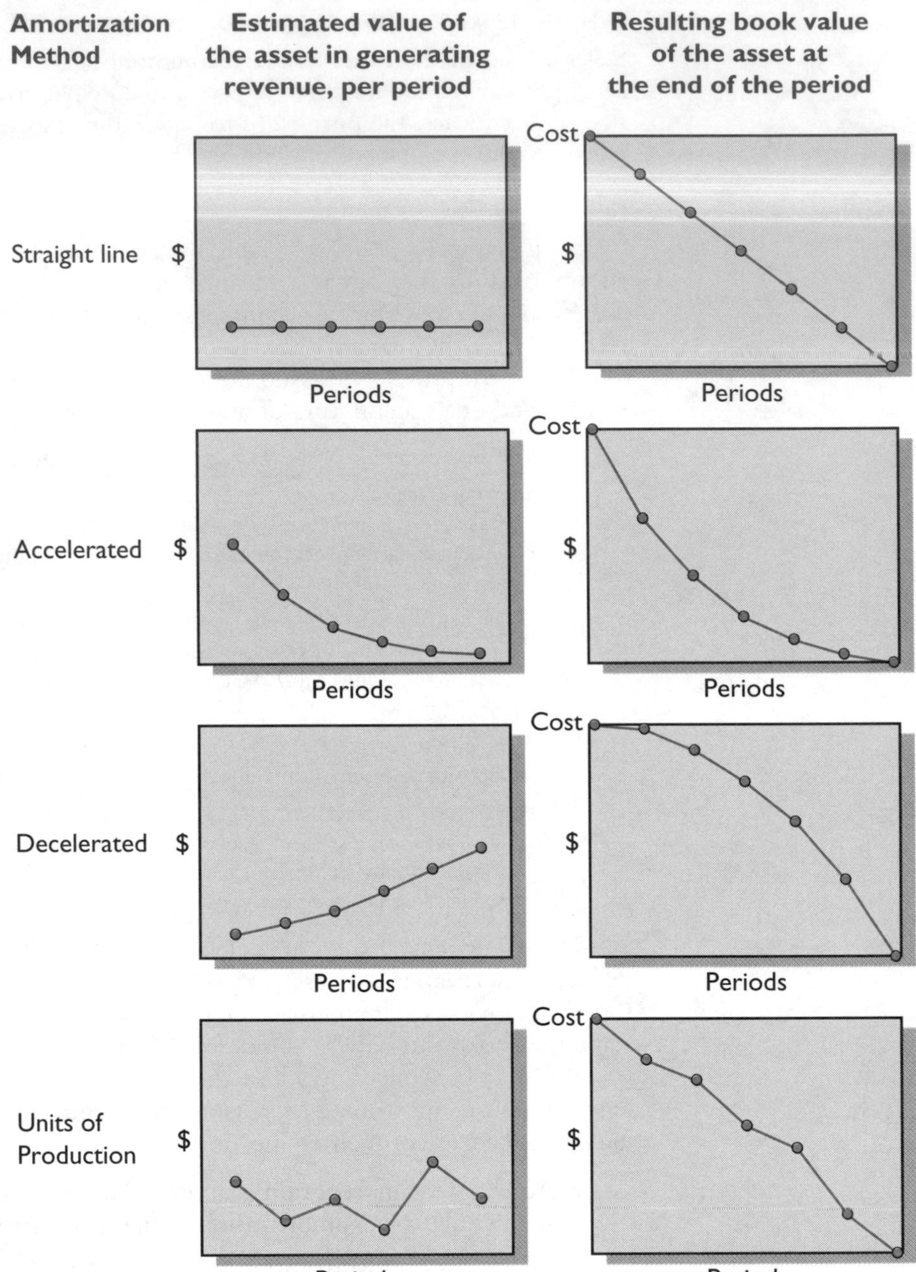
Amortization Method
Estimated value of the asset in generating revenue, per period
Resulting book value of the asset at the end of the period
Straight line
$
Periods
Cost
$
Periods
Accelerated
$
Periods
Cost
$
Periods
Decelerated
$
Periods
Cost
$
Periods
Units of Production
$
Periods
Cost
$
Periods

FIGURE 10.4

in 1992 disclosed their amortization, depletion, or depreciation method. Of those, 143 used only straight-line and 119 more used it for some assets.[10] It is nearly always used for amortization of intangible assets (see Section 10.7). Three pieces of information are necessary in order to compute straight-line amortization.

a. Cost of the asset—the total cost to be amortized over time (the amount capitalized to the date the asset is put into service).
b. Estimated useful life of the asset—the number of periods the asset is expected to benefit the enterprise.
c. Estimated "salvage value"—the amount expected to be recovered via the sale of the asset at the end of its useful life. (This amount is likely to be only an educated guess and is often assumed to be zero for purposes of computing amortization over long periods of time.)

The formula for straight-line amortization is:

$$\text{Amortization for one period} = \frac{\text{Cost minus estimated salvage value}}{\text{Estimated useful life (no. of periods)}}$$

Using the above formula, annual amortization on a delivery truck used by a local business would be calculated this way:

- ◆ Cost of the truck = $5000
- ◆ Estimated useful life = 5 years
- ◆ Estimated salvage value after 5 years = $1000

$$\text{Amortization for one year} = \frac{\$5{,}000 - \$1{,}000}{5} = \$800$$

At the end of the first year, the net book value of the truck will be:

Cost – Total amortization to date = $5,000 – $800 = $4,200

Amortization expense for each of the five years will be $800, reducing the book value by $800 per year. As shown in the chart above, the constant expense produces a linear increase in accumulated amortization and so a linear decline in book value.

A common practice for many firms is to assume the salvage value of the asset to be zero, which then enables amortization to be expressed in terms of percentages instead of years. For example, a company might use straight-line amortization expressed as 20% of historical cost, rather than as a term of five years.

2. Accelerated Amortization

Some assets contribute most of their benefit to the enterprise in the early parts of their lives. For example, a new computer may benefit the company greatly when it is first purchased, but due to quickly changing technology and changing needs as the company grows, this same computer may be relegated to less important tasks within a few years of its purchase, as better computers are acquired. Therefore, even though the computer will continue to benefit the company, most of its economic value has been consumed near the beginning of its life.

In Canada, the most common method of calculating accelerated amortization is the declining balance method. *Financial Reporting in Canada 1993* says that 86 of the 300 companies reported using declining balance amortization in 1992, 16 alone and 70 in combination with other methods (69 of these used it in combination with straight-line).[11] *Capital cost allowance* for income tax purposes (Section 7.13) is also usually calculated using a declining balance procedure.

Information needed for this procedure is:

a. Cost of the asset;
b. Total amortization recorded since the acquisition of the asset (accumulated amortization);
c. Amortization rate—the percentage of the book value (cost minus amortization to date) of the asset that is to be amortized in the period.

The formula for declining balance amortization is:

Amortization for one period = (Cost – Accumulated amortization) × Rate
= Remaining book value of the asset × Rate

Let's use the declining balance method to compute amortization for the five-year life of same truck we had above. With this method, the amortization *rate* is established such that over the asset's life, the cost will be fully depreciated. Doing this exactly requires complex algebra, so approximate rates are usually used. For example, the amortization expense for a "double declining balance" (a particular type of declining balance) uses double the straight-line rate. Double declining balance works reasonably well for assets with an expected life in the ten-year range, but not for shorter lives. Canadian capital cost allowance rates used in computing taxable income were originally based on double declining balance estimates.

Since the truck is not in the ten-year useful life range, double declining balance is not really suitable (double the straight-line rate would be 40%), so we will use 25% instead to approximate the economic consumption pattern.

- Cost = $5,000
- Amortization to date = $0 (at beginning)
- Amortization rate = 25%

Year 1

Amortization for the year	= ($5,000 – $0) × 25%
	= $1,250
Total amortization to date	= $1,250
Remaining book value	= $3,750

Year 2

Amortization for the year	= ($5,000 – $1,250) × 25%
	= $937.50
Total amortization to date	= $2,187.50
Remaining book value	= $2,812.50
Amortization expense gets smaller with each year.	

continued next page

Year 3	
Amortization for the year	= (\$5,000 – \$2,187.50) × 25%
	= \$703.13
Total amortization to date	= \$2,890.63
Remaining book value	= \$2,109.37
Year 4	
Amortization for the year	= (\$5,000 – \$2,890.63) × 25%
	= \$527.34
Total amortization to date	= \$3,417.97
Remaining book value	= \$1,582.03
Year 5	
Amortization for the year	= (\$5,000 – \$3,417.97) × 25%
	= \$395.51
Total amortization to date	= \$3,813.48
Remaining book value	= \$1,186.52

Although in this example the remaining book value of the truck at the end of five years is fairly close to the expected salvage value of the truck, declining balance amortization does not normally take salvage value into account. Consequently, the book value at the end of five years would be the same whether or not the company expected to recover any of the cost of the truck.

The second panel of the chart in Figure 10.4 shows the kind of patterns of amortization expense and book value we calculated for the truck. The expense and book value lines are curves instead of straight lines. Will there be any difference in net income using one method instead of the other? Yes. Will there be any difference in the cash position of the company using declining balance rather than straight-line? No. More will be said about this later.

In the United States, a method of calculating accelerated amortization called "sum of the years' digits" is often used. This is a method of calculating accelerated amortization more exactly than by declining balance that was common before the advent of calculators and computers. Now that calculators are as much a part of daily business as a pencil and computers are becoming very commonplace, sum-of-the-years'-digits amortization is less common. It is rare in Canada (*Financial Reporting in Canada 1993* indicates that only one company of the 300 reported using it in 1992), so it is illustrated only in an endnote.[12]

3. Units-of-Production Amortization and Depletion

The economic consumption of many assets is not necessarily a function of time, but rather of use. For example it may make more sense to say that the delivery truck is expected to last so many kilometres rather than so many years. The consumption of natural resources ("wasting assets") is also often accounted for using units of production, because the value to the enterprise of a stand of timber, or an oil well, is tied to the number of trees remaining to be felled or the amount of oil left to be recovered. Therefore, the units-of-production method of amortization is also used to compute depletion of natural resources.

To compute amortization or depletion per unit of usage, the following information is needed:

a. Cost of the asset;
b. Estimated salvage value;
c. Estimated number of units to be produced during life of asset—the estimated number of board feet of lumber in the timber stand, or the estimated number of kilometres that the delivery truck will travel, or other production measures.

The formula for computing units-of-production amortization is:

$$\text{Amortization or depletion for one unit of use or production (for example, a kilometre)} = \frac{\text{Cost} - \text{Estimated salvage value}}{\text{Estimated no. of units of use or production during life}}$$

To determine amortization for the year, the charge per unit is multiplied by the number of actual units produced or used. Using the delivery truck as an example one more time, amortization of the truck over its expected useful life might be:

- Cost = \$5,000
- Estimated salvage value = \$1,000
- Estimated no. of km to be driven = 200,000

$$\text{Amortization per km} = \frac{\$5{,}000 - \$1{,}000}{200{,}000}$$
$$= \$.02 \text{ amortization/km}$$

Year 1
Suppose the truck is driven 20,000 km during the year; the amortization charge for the year will be:

$\$.02 \times 20{,}000 = \$400$

Year 2
If the truck is driven 80,000 km during the second year, the amortization charge for the year will be:

$\$.02 \times 80{,}000 = \$1{,}600$

Year 3
Let's say the truck is driven 65,000 km during the year. Then the amortization charge for the year will be:

$\$.02 \times 65{,}000 = \$1{,}300$

Year 4
Let's suppose the truck is driven 50,000 km during the year; however, after 35,000 km, the truck will be fully depreciated (it has been driven the estimated 200,000 km). Therefore, the amortization charge for the year will be just the remaining \$700, which is less than $\$.02 \times 50{,}000$ km.

The bottom panel in Figure 10.4 illustrates units of production amortization. It is the only method that can result in the annual amortization expense going up and down from period to period. *Financial Reporting in Canada 1993* says that, in 1992, 14 companies reported using only units of production amortization, depletion, or depreciation, and eight more used it in combination with other methods.[13]

Depletion of a wasting asset and units-of-production amortization of a fixed asset are computed in the same manner, but depletion refers to the *physical* consumption of an asset, rather than just the economic consumption. For the timber stand mentioned earlier, salvage value may be the value of the land after all the timber has been cut. Instead of accumulating depletion in a contra account, the asset itself may be reduced by the amount of the depletion for the period. In this case, the journal entry would look like this:

DR Depletion expense	XXXX	
CR Timber stand asset		XXXX
(instead of Accumulated amortization)		

When an accumulated amortization account is not used, the asset account shows the remaining book value at the present time, not the original cost. This is often the case for amortization of intangible assets (Section 10.7).

4. Decelerated Amortization

If the asset's economic value is expected to decline more slowly in early years and more quickly in later years, a form of decelerated amortization (the opposite of accelerated amortization) may be used. Under decelerated amortization, amortization expense per period rises over the duration of the asset's life. The third panel of the chart in Figure 10.4 illustrates this method. Such an approach is rarely used, because for most assets it does not seem to follow reasonable economic assumptions. *Financial Reporting in Canada 1993* indicates that only four companies reported using a form of decelerated amortization, called the "sinking fund" method, and all those used it for "income-producing real estate assets" in combination with straight-line amortization for other assets.[14] The calculations for this method are complex and so will not be illustrated here.

AMORTIZATION EFFECTS ANALYSIS

Amortization effects analysis is eased a little because

a. Amortization does not affect cash;
b. It does not affect current tax payable, as was explained in Section 7.13; and
c. It does not affect any other working capital accounts either.[15]

Therefore, in general all it *does* affect is:

i. Net book value of noncurrent assets;
ii. Net income (via amortization expense and the deferred portion of income tax expense); and
iii. Deferred income tax liability.

On the cash flow statement, amortization is shown as an add-back to net income (as is the deferred portion of the income tax expense), but the add-back is the same as that deducted on the income statement, so if amortization goes up, income and deferred income tax expense go down. But the amortization add-back and the deferred income tax add-back go up, resulting in no effect on cash from operations.

Here is an example. Greco Inc. has purchased a factory at a cost of $23,000,000 (not including land). The company has not had such a factory before, so the president wants to know what difference it would make if the company used straight-line, declining balance, or units-of-production amortization.

- Estimated useful life is 20 years, during which time the company plans to make about 100 million boxes of its standard product.
- Estimated salvage value after the end of the useful life is $5,000,000.
- If declining balance amortization were used, the probable rate chosen would be 10% per year on the declining balance.
- Production plans call for production over the next six years of 4, 9, 9, 8, 9, and 5 million boxes per year, and likely stable production of about 4 million boxes per year for the remaining 14 years.

The resulting amortization bases would be:

Straight-line: $23,000,000 – $5,000,000 = $18,000,000 over 20 years (5% of base per year)
Declining balance: $23,000,000 – Accumulated amortization × 10% per year
Units-of-production: $18,000,000 / 100,000,000 boxes = $0.18 per box produced

If everything turns out as expected, annual amortization expense for the next 20 years will be as follows:

Year	Straight-Line Expense	Declining Balance		Units-of-Production Expense
		Begin Book Value	Expense	
1	$ 900,000	$23,000,000	$ 2,300,000	$ 720,000
2	900,000	20,700,000	2,070,000	1,620,000
3	900,000	18,630,000	1,863,000	1,620,000
4	900,000	16,767,000	1,676,700	1,440,000
5	900,000	15,090,300	1,509,030	1,620,000
6	900,000	13,581,270	1,358,127	900,000
7	900,000	12,223,143	1,222,314	720,000
8	900,000	11,000,829	1,100,083	720,000
9	900,000	9,900,746	990,075	720,000
10	900,000	8,910,671	891,067	720,000
11	900,000	8,019,604	801,960	720,000
12	900,000	7,217,644	721,764	720,000
13	900,000	6,495,880	649,588	720,000
14	900,000	5,846,292	584,629	720,000
15	900,000	5,261,663	526,166	720,000
16	900,000	4,735,497	473,550	720,000
17	900,000	4,261,947	426,195	720,000
18	900,000	3,835,752	383,575	720,000
19	900,000	3,452,177	345,218	720,000
20	900,000	3,106,959	310,696	720,000
Total	$18,000,000		$20,203,737	$18,000,000

At the end of 20 years, if everything works out as expected, the book value of the factory will be, for each method:

Straight-line:	$23,000,000	–	$18,000,000	=	$5,000,000
Declining balance:	$23,000,000	–	$20,203,737	=	$2,796,263
Units-of-production:	$23,000,000	–	$18,000,000	=	$5,000,000

If at the end of 20 years the factory is sold, there will be a gain or loss on sale equalling the sale proceeds minus the book value. The proceeds may not be the expected $5,000,000. If they are not, there will be a gain or loss on sale for even the simplest method (that is, straight-line).

The declining balance method, however, will be a little off target at the end of 20 years, with a book value of less than $3 million. In fact, it will reach a $5 million book value in the 15th year. If the expected $5,000,000 salvage value is actually obtained at the end of 20 years, the declining balance method will result in a gain on sale at the date of sale of the factory equalling $2,203,737 ($5,000,000 proceeds minus $2,796,263 book value), which is really a correction of the overamortization that the declining balance method produced. The method will have been off target by this $2,203,737 amount.

The units-of-production method will almost certainly result in a book value not exactly equal to $5,000,000, even though it is planned to equal that. This is so because the actual production will be very unlikely to equal exactly 100 million boxes over 20 years.

Whichever method is adopted, the company can always adjust its calculations later, if the expectations about length of useful life or salvage value begin to look seriously incorrect. Methods of doing this are part of more advanced accounting courses. But it can be observed that, like the initial choice of method, the decision to adjust the figures has no effect on cash or other working capital.

The president wants to know what effects the amortization choice has. Some things you could tell the president are:

a.
- ◆ The straight-line method shows the same amortization every year;
- ◆ The declining balance method starts out with much higher amortization than that of the straight-line method and ends up with much lower amortization; and
- ◆ The units-of-production method starts out lower, rises, and then falls back in accordance with production plans.

b. Accordingly,
- ◆ The declining balance method will show lower net incomes than straight-line in the earlier years and higher in the later years.
- ◆ The units-of-production method result is greatly different from that produced by the straight-line method in years two to five, but in other years they are not much different.

c. After subtracting the 40% income tax effect on income, the differential effect on net incomes in a sample of years would be, if everything works out as expected, as shown below.

	Declining Balance Compared with Straight-Line		Units-of-Production Compared with Straight-Line	
Year	Amortization Expense Effect	Net income Effect (60%)	Amortization Expense Effect	Net income Effect (60%)
1	$ 1,400,000	$ (840,000)	$(180,000)	$108,000
5	609,030	(365,418)	720,000	(432,000)
10	(8,933)	5,360	(180,000)	108,000
15	(373,834)	224,300	(180,000)	108,000
20	(589,304)	353,582	(180,000)	100,000
20 (gain)	$(2,203,737)	$1,322,242	0	0

d. The company will look less profitable in the early years, if declining balance or units-of-production is chosen, and more profitable in the later years.

e. The choice has no effect on income tax payable each year or on cash flow, cash balance, or working capital. The balance sheet effects are in the book value of the factory, and therefore also in the book value of the total assets of the business, which decline least rapidly with the straight-line method, and in the deferred income tax liability and retained earnings. The liability will have 40% of the difference in book value, and retained earnings will have the other 60%.

f. The effects on return on equity and return on assets are reduced somewhat because both the numerators and the denominators are affected by the amortization choice. For example, declining balance shows lower net income in year five than does straight-line, but, by then, book value and retained earnings are both also lower and, therefore, ROE and ROA are pushed a little closer to the values they would have under the straight-line method.

g. Greco Inc. should choose the amortization method that would best match its amortization expense to the apparent economic value provided by using the factory. But, since amortization does not affect cash flow or current assets and because in this case the straight-line method provides higher net incomes in the early years, it might be that the president will want to use that method. The president is likely concerned about the reaction to the company's performance over the next few years, and it may take a good deal of explanation to demonstrate that the nonstraight-line methods do result in a fairer way of determining income and balance sheet figures. As we saw earlier, most large Canadian companies use straight-line, so that method likely also has comparability with other companies in Greco's industry in its favour.

HOW'S YOUR UNDERSTANDING

Here are two questions you should be able to answer, based on what you have just read:

1. Explain to the president of Cold Lake Manufacturing Inc., which opened for business at the beginning of this year, what amortization expense is supposed to accomplish and the criteria you would recommend the company use in choosing the most appropriate method.
2. Cold Lake management is trying to decide whether to use straight–line or declining balance amortization for its assets. If it used straight-line, the amortization expense for this first year would be $1,120,000; but if it used declining balance with the rate management believes would be appropriate, the expense would be $1,860,000. The company's income tax rate is 35%. Calculate how much higher or lower each of the following would be if that declining balance method were used rather than the straight-line method: amortization expense, current portion of income tax expense, deferred portion of income tax expense, net income, cash from operations, net book value of assets, deferred income tax liability, retained earnings, working capital ratio. ($740,000 higher; no effect; $259,000 lower; $481,000 lower; no effect; $740,000 lower; $259,000 lower; $481,000 lower; no effect)

10.6 GAINS AND LOSSES ON NONCURRENT ASSET DISPOSALS AND WRITE-OFFS

Gains, losses, and write-offs have been mentioned and illustrated in various ways since Chapter 4. This section is intended to pull the ideas together for you and show you how they are partly the consequences of accounting policy choices.

In the above Greco example, there was a possibility of a gain or loss on the sale of the factory in the 20th year. When a noncurrent asset is sold, it could be handled as ordinary revenues are: the proceeds could be added to revenue and the book value of the asset added to the cost of goods sold. But this would mix day-to-day revenues from the activities for which the enterprise exists with the occasional (and presumably less important economically) revenues from reducing long-term fixed assets or other investments.

Therefore, such events are kept separate from ordinary revenues via the following kind of journal entry, which we have seen before:

DR Cash or nontrade receivables (proceeds)	XXXX		
CR Cost of the noncurrent asset			XXXX
DR Accumulated amortization on that asset (all that has accumulated)	XXXX		
DR or CR loss or gain on sale	XXXX	or	XXXX

The gain or loss is just the difference between the proceeds and the book value (cost minus accumulated amortization, if any). Here is an example: Company X has a truck that cost $84,000. The accumulated amortization at the date of sale is $46,000. Therefore, book value is $38,000 at the date of sale. If the company:

a. sells it for $52,000, there is a gain on sale of $14,000 ($52,000 – $38,000);

b. sells it for \$30,000, there is a loss on sale of \$8,000 (\$38,000 – \$30,000).

The following three reminders may be useful:

1. On the SCFP, the proceeds of the sale are shown (usually) as a deduction from the Investing Activities cash disbursements. That is the *only* cash flow, as can be seen from the preceding example. Because the proceeds are the only cash flow, the gain or loss must be removed from income at the top of the SCFP: it is a noncash item. So a gain is deducted from income and a loss is added back.

   Think of gains and losses as amortization corrections:

   - If the company knew in advance what the proceeds would be and when the sale would happen, it could have amortized the asset down exactly to the proceeds amount by that date. So if the proceeds equal book value, there is no gain or loss.
   - If the proceeds are *less* than book value, there is a loss: in effect, more amortization is needed and that's what the loss really is. Therefore, the loss is *added back* to income on the SCFP, just as amortization is.
   - If the proceeds are *more* than book value, there is a gain: in effect, too much amortization was taken and the gain is really just that excess (which caused the lower book value) being recognized. Therefore, the gain is *deducted* from income on the SCFP; it's just negative amortization.

   These ideas are depicted in Figure 10.5.

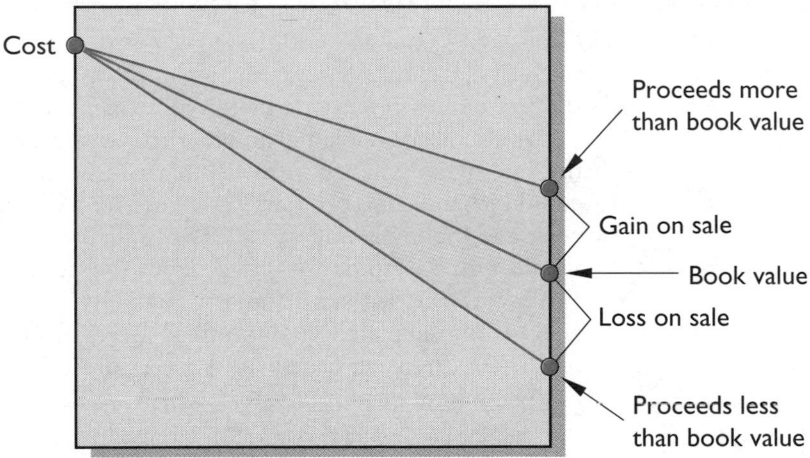

FIGURE 10.5

2. Many assets are depreciated as a group. In such a case, there is usually no gain or loss recognized on the sale of one of the group, because its individual book value is not known. The gain or loss is in effect buried in accumulated amortization by the following journal entry (which is the same as the one above but with no gain or loss):

DR Cash or nontrade receivables (proceeds)	XXXXX	
CR Cost of the noncurrent asset		XXXXX
DR Accumulated amortization (cost minus proceeds)	XXXXX	

This entry wouldn't work very well if proceeds *exceeded* cost, but we'll leave that complication out. Burying any gain or loss in accumulated amortization doesn't work out very well either, if such gains or losses do not average out to zero over time. If they do not, the accumulated amortization will get out of line over time. Dealing with this is a subject for more advanced accounting courses.

3. The above ideas also work for three other situations: sales of nonamortized noncurrent assets (investments or land, for example) and write-offs or write-downs of noncurrent assets, whether already amortized or not:
   - In the first situation, the gain or loss on sale is just the difference between cost and proceeds because there is no accumulated amortization.
   - In the second situation, the asset is being removed from the balance sheet, or being reduced in size, without any cash proceeds. The write-off amount is just cost, or book value if there is accumulated amortization, because there is no "proceeds" line in the journal entry.
   - The write-down amount similarly involves no proceeds.

   All these gains, losses, and write-offs have no effect on cash or working capital, and no effect on cash flow because their effects on income are removed in the adjustments at the top of the SCFP.

10.7 INTANGIBLE ASSETS AND BRIEF COMMENTS ABOUT CAPITAL LEASES

Most of the discussion of noncurrent assets so far has involved intercorporate investments and, especially, "fixed" assets such as land, buildings, and equipment. There are other noncurrent assets on many companies' balance sheets, however:

- First, there is a host of "intangible" assets, which are felt to involve economic value but lack the same "tangible" physical existence that the fixed assets have.
- Second, some land, buildings, and equipment may be leased, not owned, but will appear on the balance sheet anyway.

INTANGIBLE ASSETS

Intangible assets are long term assets that do not have a visible physical existence, as do land, buildings, or equipment. Intangible assets include:

- Patents, copyrights, trademarks, and other such legal property;
- Franchises, distributorships, and other such rights to sell someone else's products in a certain geographical area (McDonald's Restaurants, Speedy Muffler, Arthur Murray Dance Studios, and Canadian Tire are examples in which the local operator has paid for the right to use the name and sell the products);
- Deferred charges such as incorporation costs, leasehold improvements, financing costs, and other items that are really long-term prepaid expenses;
- Product development expenditures (e.g., product-testing costs or computer software development costs) that are capitalized so they can be expensed at the time they earn revenue in the future, thus satisfying the matching principle;

- Purchased goodwill (arising when more is paid for a group of assets, such as a whole business, than the assets seem to be worth individually), similar to the goodwill arising on consolidation as calculated in Section 5.17.

According to *Financial Reporting in Canada 1993*, the 300 surveyed companies reported the following intangible assets in 1992:

149 reported goodwill (mainly on consolidation);
18 reported licences;
11 reported customer lists;
11 reported trademarks;
10 reported patents; and
17 reported franchises, noncompetition agreements or other intangibles.[16]

What Are Intangible Assets Worth?

Because such assets *are* intangible, their existence and value may be doubtful. Generally, the more clearly identifiable and documented the assets are (especially via external evidence such as contracts and legal documents), the less difficulty they pose. However, even for clearly owned assets such as patents and franchises, there may be considerable doubt about their future economic value. For example, what is a Wendy's franchise worth? It depends on ever-changing consumer tastes, on whether a competitor does or doesn't open across the street, and on many other business and economic factors.

For assets lacking clear external documentation, such as product development expenditures, there is often a real question as to whether they belong on the balance sheet at all. Capitalizing expenditures on such items may appear to create better matching and is usually seen to be proper by those making such expenditures, but this depends on whether they will ever return future value. Will the great new product sell? Will it produce revenues greater than costs? This is a difficult judgment to make, and many people have concluded that such assets should not appear, because these people favour conservatism in accounting, are afraid of manipulation, or just feel that recognizing such assets is not fair or appropriate. Expenditures on such things would therefore be expensed immediately and not capitalized. For these sorts of reasons, accounting standards require that general research and development expenditures be expensed as they are made, *not* capitalized as intangible assets.

Purchased Goodwill

Goodwill is a special case, though no less controversial. It arises, in a way, because of the necessity to keep the accounts in balance. Here is an example: Great buys all the business assets of Small for $800,000 cash. The best estimate of the fair market values of those assets are: receivables, $60,000; inventories, $110,000; land, $100,000; building, $260,000; equipment, $130,000; total, $660,000; no liabilities are assumed by Great.
Great would record the purchase as follows:

CR Cash		800,000
DR Accounts receivable	60,000	
DR Inventories	110,000	
DR Land	100,000	
DR Buildings	260,000	
DR Equipment	130,000	

No problem. Except that the entry doesn't balance! So a new account called Goodwill is created and debited with $140,000, which is the $800,000, cost of the whole, minus $640,000, the sum of the fair values of the parts. (You've seen this before, included in the consolidations material in Chapter 5.) This keeps the books in balance but creates an account the value and meaning of which are unclear. If goodwill represents unrecorded assets, what are they? If it represents a good location, good managers, or "synergy" with the operations of Great, what are these things really worth? How much future value do they have? How long will this value last? Does goodwill, at least sometimes, indicate that the purchaser made a bad deal and just paid too much? (By the way, in the reverse situation, if the cost of the whole is *less* than the sum of the parts, no "badwill" is recorded. Instead, the amounts assigned to the parts are reduced so that they add up to the cost of the whole.)

Cost of Intangibles

Goodwill's cost is determined as illustrated above. For other intangibles, cost is determined in the same way as that of any other asset: purchase cost and other expenditures made prior to putting the asset into service (getting economic benefits from it). There may be substantial ambiguity about the cost of internally developed assets, such as product development expenditures, because it may be difficult to determine exactly what was spent to develop the asset, separately from normal expenses incurred, and for this reason many companies decline to recognize (capitalize) such assets. Internally developed goodwill is never capitalized (for example, expenditures on office parties that create happy employees are expensed, not capitalized).

Amortization of Intangibles

Intangible assets are amortized over their useful lives, just like fixed assets. Determining *legal* useful life may be fairly straightforward for assets supported by contracts or other documents (for example, leases have a specified term, as do most franchises, and patents are good for a specific number of years), but whether this is also the *economic* useful life is harder to say. For other assets such as incorporation costs or goodwill, useful life is anyone's guess. Canadian standards specify a *maximum* useful life of 40 years for goodwill, surely an optimistic estimate!

Because of all this ambiguity, intangibles are amortized simply, using the straight-line basis over the estimated useful life, and are usually estimated reasonably conservatively. The asset account itself is usually credited with the amortization, rather than bothering with a contra account for accumulated amortization.

EFFECTS ANALYSIS

Let's look at an example. Checkup Auto Services Inc., which has been in business one year, has a chain of heavily advertised automobile service centres. The company's income tax rate is 30%. The company makes it a practice to capitalize a portion of its advertising costs as a "deferred asset." An accountant suggested to the company's vice-president of finance that the policy of capitalizing advertising should be ended because the future economic benefit from the expenditures is not clearly determinable. The vice-president wants to know what effect such policy changes would have.

Data:

- The amount of advertising capitalized was $75,000 this year.
- The capitalized amount is being amortized at 20% per year.

Present method:

- Amortization expense is $15,000 this year (20% of $75,000);
- Balance sheet asset is $75,000 – $15,000 = $60,000 at end of this year.

Proposed method: Expenses this year would be $75,000.

Effects:
If advertising were *not* capitalized:

- This year's income would be lower by 70% of ($75,000 – $15,000) = $42,000;
- Income tax liability would go down by $18,000 (the other 30%);
- Retained earnings this year would be lower by $42,000;
- Assets would be lower by the removal of $60,000 net capitalized advertising asset;
- Balance sheet proof: $(60,000) = $(18,000) + ($42,000);
- No effect on cash flow, cash balance, or working capital.

CAPITAL LEASES

Some leased assets are included on the balance sheet because the company is deemed to have enough of the rights and obligations of ownership, the assets are significant to the company's economic performance, and leaving them off the balance sheet is thought to misrepresent the company's economic position. This is an example of accrual accounting's moving well beyond just recording transactions: there is no legal exchange of leased assets, but it is thought that there has been an economic exchange of them.

Such **capital leases** are included on the balance sheet (often just mixed in with owned fixed assets) as follows:

- The "cost" is the present value of the future lease payments, using an appropriate interest rate usually deduced from the lease agreement.
- At the same time, the present value of those payments is recorded as a liability.
- So the journal entry to put the leases on the balance sheet is:

DR Capital lease asset	XXXX	
CR Capital lease obligations liability		XXXX

- After that:

  a. The leased asset is amortized, just as the owned assets are, following a policy that is consistent with that used for owned assets but also taking into account the terms of the lease.

b. The liability is reduced as payments are made on the lease. Each payment is divided into deduced principal and interest portions, so that only the principal portion is deducted from the liability and the rest is considered interest expense. This maintains the liability at the present value of the remaining lease payments.
c. The expenses for using the leased asset, therefore, are amortization and interest. Such amounts are usually combined with other amortization and interest expenses because the intent is to represent the economic situation fairly.
d. Various particulars of significant capital leases are usually disclosed in the notes to the financial statements, so that the readers of the statements may judge the effects of such capitalization. Such separate disclosure is usual for: the lease obligations liability, the terms of the lease, and related amortization and interest expenses.

The result of these procedures is that the leased asset is treated essentially as if it were owned. Accrual accounting recognizes the economic value of the asset and disregards the legalities of who owns it.

If the lease does not result in an economic equivalence of ownership (for example, if it is really a rental situation where the owner continues to pay property tax, do the repairs and maintenance, and generally control the asset), the lease is termed an "operating lease." For such leases, there is no asset or lease obligation liability recognized, and the lease payments are just expensed as rent expense. If the operating lease is significant to the company, some of its particulars may be disclosed in the notes to the financial statements.

HOW'S YOUR UNDERSTANDING

Here are two questions you should be able to answer, based on what you have just read:

1. Explain to another classmate why gains on sales of noncurrent assets are deducted from net income in the adjustments at the top of the cash flow statement.
2. Senior management of Telemark Skiing Ltd. wishes to capitalize $2,350,000 in ski hill improvement costs expended this year and amortize the capitalized costs over 10 years, rather than just expensing them all as is now done. The company's income tax rate is 25%, and the company would plan to continue deducting the costs as expenses in computing income tax payable for this year, assuming the tax authorities would permit that. What would be the effect on this year's net income and cash flow from operations if the company capitalized those costs? ([$2,350,000 – $235,000] × 0.75 = $1,586,250 higher income; no effect on cash flow)

10.8 COMMENTS ON LIABILITIES

This book puts more emphasis on the income statement, the SCFP, and the assets side of the balance sheet than it does on the liabilities and equity side. There is more about the liabilities and equity side in finance courses and in more advanced accounting courses.

This and the next section cover a few of the things you should know about accounting policies for liabilities and equity. Only some parts will be very new to you, but you should find the summary useful.

LEGAL DEBTS

Bank loans, trade accounts payable, wages payable, Canada Pension Plan, employees' income tax deducted from their pay and due to governments, sales taxes collected and due to governments, bonded debt, mortgages, asset purchase contracts, and other legal debts are recorded when incurred and are reported at the amounts incurred (minus anything paid so far). Just a few details:

- Historical cost accounting applies here too. The amounts shown are those that arose when the debt was incurred. This is normally the same amount as will actually be paid, but sometimes it is not. For example, if bonds are issued at a discount, the discounted amount is shown initially and is only gradually raised to the cash payable as the due date approaches. In the case of a $1,000 10-year bond issued for $930, for example, the bond liability would start at $930 and rise to $1,000 over the 10 years by recognizing that there is really an extra $70 in interest to be paid over time.
- There is no recognition of nonhistorical interpretations of the debt, even if the economic meaning of the debt would increase because of such recognition. Three things therefore *not* recognized are:
    1. Interest that will have to be paid but has not yet accrued (for example, if a debt is due in two years, only the interest to date is added, not the interest for the next two years);
    2. Inflation (even though being in debt during a period of inflation is a good idea because you pay back with dollars worth less than those you borrowed);
    3. Market value changes in public debt (for example, if interest rates have risen so much that the $1,000 bond is now selling on the bond market for $780, it is still shown at somewhere between the $930 issue price and the $1,000 to be paid).
- Unless there is evidence to the contrary, the company is assumed to be a "going concern" and, therefore, debts are shown at the amounts that would normally be paid, not at some other liquidation value that might be negotiated with creditors if the company got into serious financial trouble.
- For important debts, some of the legal details are disclosed (usually by footnote). The main details here are the interest rate on the debt (especially for long-term debt), any assets or other securities given, repayment terms, and any special conditions such as being convertible to equity.
- Debts are sorted into three classifications: cash-equivalent debts (very short-term or demand loans), current debts (due within the year), and noncurrent debts. Current debts include the portion (if any) of noncurrent debts due within one year. (There's a twist here you should watch

for: in accordance with the above points, it's only the *principal* portion payable in the next year that's called current. Suppose, for example, Jocelyn owes $71,000 on her mortgage and during the next year must make 12 monthly payments of $1,000, including interest. If the interest will amount to $6,400 over the next year, her balance sheet will show a current liability of $5,600 ($12,000 – $6,400) and a noncurrent liability of $65,400 ($71,000 – $5,600). The $6,400 that will be next year's interest is ignored at this point because it has not yet accrued. Her total debt is $71,000 ($5,600 + $65,400), not $77,400.)

SHORT-TERM ACCRUALS

Accrued interest, estimated after-sale service costs, estimated income tax payable, and other such estimated but not yet legally payable short-term liabilities are accounted for by debiting an expense account and crediting a current liability. Although they are not yet actual debts, they are reported in the same way as the legal debts.

LONG-TERM ACCRUALS

These are in principle just longer-term versions of the above. Like the short-term accruals, they are created by debiting an expense account. But, since there will not be a payment for a long time, the credit is to a noncurrent liability. Many of these are quite approximate estimates: they are recorded in order to account for the future consequences of arrangements made to help earn income today, and so their main purpose is income measurement rather than balance sheet valuation.

There is no debt now and it's often anyone's guess as to exactly when a debt will arise and precisely how much it will be. Such accruals often are based on the present value of future estimated cash flows because of the principle, mentioned above, of not recognizing future interest.

Some examples of long-term accruals are:

a. *Warranty liability:* the estimated future cost of providing warranty service for products already sold (revenue already recognized).

b. *Pension liability:* the estimated future cost of providing pensions for work already done by employees, *minus* cash paid to a pension trustee to be invested to fund the eventual pensions. For example, if an employee has worked five years and is already entitled to some part of a pension 30 years from now based on that work, the estimated present value of that pension entitlement is recorded as a liability. Cash paid to the trustee is deducted from the liability. You can see the problems in trying to estimate such a liability when you think of all the things that can change in those 30 years: the employee might die first, be fired, or quit; interest rates (used in the present value calculation) will doubtless vary; the pension plan itself might change, even retroactively; laws governing such plans may change; and so on.

c. *Post-employment benefits other than pensions:* since FASB pronouncements on this in the late 1980s, these are accounted for in the same sort of way as are pension obligations, and with the same sort of difficulties. With Canada's greater state support of medical costs, these obligations are usually not as large for Canadian companies as they are for companies in the United States, where the obligations are often many billions of dollars. (See Case 7B in Chapter 7 for more about health care costs.)

d. *Deferred income taxes:* this liability (which is usually long-term but may be short-term) arises when there are *temporary* differences between the way income is calculated for the financial statements and the way it is calculated for income tax purposes. See details in Section 7.13.

OFF-BALANCE-SHEET FINANCING

Sometimes companies will arrange for sources of financing that do not meet the accounting definition of a liability or an equity and that therefore do not appear on the right-hand side of the balance sheet. There may be a concern among users of financial statements that such sources of financing are sought by management *because* they do not appear on the balance sheet and therefore do not affect the debt–equity ratio, the working capital ratio, or other measures. Perhaps such sources of financing might not be disclosed at all, so that the user would not be aware of the financial commitment they imply. This concern led accounting standards to deem one such source, long-term leasing of important fixed assets, to be equivalent to a liability and require its recognition and disclosure, as described in Section 10.7. This source of financing has therefore been brought onto the balance sheet as a capital lease obligations liability.

New financial arrangements are being invented all the time, and the impact they make on the balance sheet, or might make depending on the company's accounting policies, are likely to be a factor in their acceptability and popularity. Four examples of financing that may or may not be well reported in the balance sheet and/or in the notes to the financial statements include:

- Operating leases (mentioned at the end of Section 10.7);
- The sale of rights to collect accounts receivable so as to speed up the cash inflow in return for taking on potential obligations to the party buying those rights;
- Making long-term purchase commitments to get favourable terms; and
- Using nonconsolidated subsidiaries or effectively controlled companies to borrow money so that the commitments do not show up on the parent company's balance sheet.

10.9 EQUITY

The owner's, or owners', equity for an unincorporated business (sole proprietorship or partnership) is usually shown as just one figure called "capital" and is calculated as:

beginning capital
+ new investment
+ income for the year (or minus loss)
– withdrawals by owner(s)
= ending capital.

Such businesses do not pay income tax on their income; the owners pay it on their shares of the income. Therefore, there is no tax expense or liability.

For an incorporated company (a corporation or limited company), there are several mainly legal requirements that influence the accounting:

- Dividends must ordinarily be paid out of accumulated income only and not out of invested capital. Therefore, owners' (shareholders') equity is divided into invested capital (share capital) and accumulated income (retained earnings: the sum of all net incomes since incorporation minus all dividends declared since then).
- Share capital shows the amounts contributed by shareholders over the years to buy shares *directly* from the company. Share transfers between shareholders are not reflected, nor is the current market value of the shares.
- The company may have more than one class of shares, such as common (voting) shares and preferred (nonvoting) shares, or class A and class B shares, and, if so, the share capital for each class must be disclosed separately, either on the balance sheet or in a note.
- A note must also disclose the number of shares of each class issued by the company, whether any class of shares has special rights or limitations, such as minimum annual dividend, preference on winding up of the company, or convertibility to another class of shares. Any minimum issue price ("par value") or other restriction on the issuing of more shares is also disclosed.
- Retained earnings shows the accumulated income minus dividends declared since incorporation. Restrictions on dividends may be disclosed. Note that when the board of directors declares a dividend, it becomes a liability of the company to the shareholders: debit retained earnings, credit dividends payable current liability.

Three other items should be mentioned here:

1. Owners may lend the company money, for example, by not withdrawing all the salary that has been recorded as an expense, perhaps because the company is short of money. Such a loan is shown under liabilities, not owners' equity, because the owner is acting as a creditor rather than an owner (though the distinction may strike you as rather slight).
2. The company may (in some jurisdictions) buy a few of its own shares. Such an investment is not really an asset because the shares represent an *interest* in the assets and because they cannot vote. Therefore, such shares are called **treasury shares** and are *deducted* from the rest of owners' equity at the cost paid for them.
3. Companies with operations in foreign countries must convert their foreign incomes, assets, and liabilities to the local currency (Canadian dollars, in Canada). Income is converted at average exchange rates over the period, while assets and liabilities are converted at historical rates or current rates, depending on the asset or liability. Because everything is not converted the same way, the result usually does not balance. To keep the financial statements in balance, a "plug" to do so is shown under owners' equity and is called **accumulated foreign currency translation adjustment** or something

similar. It doesn't really belong there, but no one has found a better place for it!

10.10 ACCOUNTING POLICY DISCLOSURE

You have seen that a company may have a variety of accounting policies chosen to fit its circumstances. GAAP require that companies disclose both what their significant policies are and any changes in them since the previous period. The idea is to help the users of the financial statements understand and interpret the figures and notes in the statement, as this chapter has tried to prepare you to do.

A summary of the significant policies usually appears as the first of the notes to the financial statements, or in a special note preceding the financial statements. The user should be able to tell from this note the company's policies for inventory cost and market, amortization, accounting for intercorporate investments, and any other policies the company and its auditors feel are necessary for an understanding of how the financial statements have been prepared. For an example of this accounting policy disclosure, see Note 1, Significant Accounting Policies, to The North West Company's financial statements at the back of the book.

Policy specifics are often not disclosed if the methods used are what you'd expect; for example, if revenue is recognized at the point of sale or delivery, or if normal accruals are made for expenses.

Changes in accounting policies are also disclosed, including a description of the change and a calculation of the effect the change has had on the financial statements. Many changes have to be given retroactive effect. For example, if the revenue recognition method is changed, past years' financial statements have to be recalculated to show them on the new basis. Therefore, if a company has changed its accounting policy in some area, the prior years' figures in this year's annual report may not be the same as the ones you would have seen in last year's annual report.

10.11 MANAGEMENT'S OBJECTIVES IN MAKING ACCOUNTING POLICY CHOICES

Each chapter has included a few words about managers and accounting to bring a managerial perspective to the topics and help to answer the question, "Why should a manager care about financial accounting?"

In the case of accounting policy choice, the answer should not be hard to see. Management is responsible for the financial statements, as it is other aspects of the business, and must see that it chooses the best accounting policies for its company for several reasons:

1. As this book has emphasized, such choices are an inevitable consequence of accrual accounting. They are part of the judgmental fabric that is at the heart of accrual accounting, and, properly made, they add to the value of the financial statements. Improperly made, they detract from the value. In either case, they make a difference!

2. Management is in the best position to make valid accounting policy choices, because management knows the company best. Professional advisors can provide great assistance to management here, but management should have the data that would drive rational accounting policy choices.
3. Management's performance on behalf of the owners is evaluated partly via the financial statements. While this provides a motivation for self-serving managers to abuse accrual accounting in order to make themselves look good, it also provides an opportunity for those more professional managers to create financial measures that show the company's performance in the clearest, most valid light. Such a portrayal should, in the long run, benefit everyone.
4. In the management discussion and analysis (MD&A) section that is in most annual reports, management reviews the year's performance and takes responsibility for it. This naturally leads management to be interested in the policy choices behind the financial statements, for not only do they help determine how management's performance is measured, but also they too are the responsibility of management.
5. Agency (contract) theory, based on the idea that self-interested behaviour is to be expected of everyone, provides a straightforward objective for management's accounting policy choices: to increase managers' share of corporate returns (and therefore decrease the returns of owners, creditors, and employees). Agency theory puts no negative cast on this, simply treating it as a natural function of economically rational behaviour. But many people see this as manipulation and are very critical of managers who appear to put their own interests first. Such behaviour may be prompted by managers' concerns about their performance bonuses, about avoiding complications due to investor or creditor nervousness about apparently poor performance, or about avoiding standing out as being too profitable.[17] Managers' objectives are likely to be complex, including in many cases a simple wish to "tell it like it is" in a fair and unbiased manner.

Readers of this book should now have considerable sensitivity to the position of the manager in the financial accounting situation and be able to interpret or prepare financial statements more intelligently given that sensitivity. If you're a present or future manager, many of the use techniques should be helpful. For example, the ability to do, arrange for, or at least use "what if" effects analysis, forms an important part of the manager's analytical toolkit. Graduates of accounting courses should be in a particularly good position to answer others' "What if?" questions. Financial statements are thus closer to the centre of effective management than you might have imagined. This closeness should motivate managers to pay close attention to their financial statements and should motivate others (users, accountants, and auditors) to understand management's role in preparing any financial statements with which they are involved.

10.12 ACCOUNTING RESEARCH: DOES ACCOUNTING POLICY CHOICE MATTER?

The answer to the question of whether accounting policy choice matters is, as you might already have suspected, a resounding "yes and no." Stock market prices correlate with accounting income as measured by accrual accounting, and that extends to the results of accounting policy choices that affect income. Accrual earnings have a greater association with stock prices than cash flow does, as has been noted earlier. On the other hand, accounting policy choices that have direct cash consequences (such as through higher or lower future tax assessments) are more likely to prompt a stock market response than are choices without direct cash consequences. (The question of how to determine indirect cash consequences has not yet been answered by research. The effects analysis we have done in this book focused on the direct effects of accounting policy choice, and usually there are none. There might be future income tax effects. But also there might be various indirect future cash effects. Two examples: (1) if a manager's bonus is dependent on the company's net income, and a policy choice will affect net income, there will be an effect on the cash paid to the manager; (2) if a policy choice changes the debt–equity ratio, the company's risk might appear enough different to affect interest rates on its debts and so change future interest payments.)

The research here is not complete, but an example of a policy choice having future direct cash consequences is the inventory cost policy choice of FIFO vs. LIFO *in the United States*, where either can be used in calculating income tax. An example of a policy choice without direct cash consequences is the choice of straight-line vs. accelerated amortization in Canada, where the government's rules must be used for the purposes of computing income tax regardless of the company's financial statement accounting policy.

The broader the perspective taken on accounting policy choice, the more ways turn up in which such choice matters. However, the research is still in its early stages, and so far all the ways in which policy choice, and accrual accounting in general, have been investigated *together* explain only a small percentage of the variations in companies' accounting policy choices and in such measures as stock market prices.

The series of "accounting research" sections in this book has outlined many ideas and results about financial accounting, in the hope that they would be interesting and add to your understanding of financial accounting's place in the world. Accounting research is still a young discipline. It includes many topics beyond this book's scope, such as auditing, managerial accounting, accounting theory and aspects of taxation, management information systems, and finance, but there is only a small body of definite findings as yet. Many of the findings that do exist depend on statistical and economic assumptions (such as that the stock market is efficient) that may not be strictly true in many cases. This book has not emphasized the limitations and problems in accounting research, but consumers of such research results should exercise care.

There is much to be done in accounting research. It would be great if some of the readers of this book helped get it done, either by becoming researchers, or by becoming managers or professional accountants who support valid research.

10.13 CONTINUING DEMONSTRATION CASE

INSTALMENT 10

Data for Instalment 10

The financial statements for the company's first year shown in Instalment 8 are incomplete because they lack notes, which are integral to any set of statements. Also, Mavis and Tomas wonder if the financial statements have made their company's performance appear worse than necessary and if some other choice of accounting policies might make things look more optimistic.

Results for Instalment 10

The notes prepared for attachment to the financial statements are below.

Mato Inc.
Notes to the Financial Statements as at February 28, 1995

1. Significant accounting policies:
   a. Inventory is valued at the lower of cost, determined by the first-in, first-out method, and net realizable value.
   b. Noncurrent assets are recorded at cost. Amortization is calculated on a straight-line basis of 20% of cost per annum on automotive equipment, leasehold improvements, and computer equipment and software, and at 10% of cost per annum on other equipment and furniture.
2. The bank loan is secured by receivables, inventories, a general charge on the company's assets, and by the personal guarantees of the shareholders.
3. The company's authorized capital is 1,000,000 shares without par value. At the beginning of the year, 12,500 shares were issued for $10 cash each.
4. No provision for income taxes has been made in the financial statements because the current loss will result in an income tax recovery only if there are future taxable incomes against which that loss may be deducted.
5. Salaries of directors and officers of the company were $54,280 for the year.
6. The company has commitments to purchase goods that will cost $23,430 on delivery, which is expected by April 30, 1995.

Three notes *not* included are:

a. Mavis, Tomas, and their accountant felt that the company's policy of recognizing revenue at the point of delivery is what anyone reading the statements would expect and so requires no mention in the notes.
b. Regarding general expense recognition (bad debts, prepaid expenses, payables), again, there is nothing unusual here. So it was decided not to clutter up the notes by saying anything about it.
c. The company has done sufficiently badly so far that there may be some question as to whether it is a going concern; that is, whether it can be expected to continue. If it cannot and if difficulty realizing assets or even winding up the company may be expected, readers of the statements should

be warned. Mavis and Tomas felt that such a warning was not necessary because they expected the business to be able to continue and because the financial statements already depicted the circumstances quite clearly.

WHAT ABOUT MAKING THINGS LOOK MORE OPTIMISTIC?

Mavis and Tomas's concern regarding changing their accounting policies to make things look rosier is understandable. They have worked hard to make their company succeed, but the first year's results are not positive. If they had paid themselves no salaries for their year's work, the company would have shown a tiny income ($54,280 salaries per note 5 above minus the $54,066 loss would equal $214 income before income tax). But that would have been misleading because it would fail to measure the value added by their efforts—not to mention that they would have starved! Would it make sense to try to find accounting policies that would improve the picture? The answer is no, for the following reasons:

1. Such manipulation would be ethically questionable and perhaps even dangerous, if it obscured the company's real problems and reduced the pressure on Mavis and Tomas to improve Mato's performance. They may feel disappointed, but the thing to do is try harder to manage the company well, not "shoot the messenger" by trying to change the financial accounting "message."
2. Such a change would not likely help in dealing with the parties who are going to be most concerned about the company. The bank already has the company's assets pretty well tied up as security on its loan and is going to be interested in the company's ability to generate cash to repay the loan as well as in its long-term viability. The bank is undoubtedly very concerned about the company and will be on the lookout for desperate actions, so optimistic reporting is unlikely to fool them—or, for that matter, suppliers, other investors, and the company's employee.
3. The SCFP would show the same cash flow figures regardless of accounting policy changes, so users of the financial statements who know how to read the SCFP would see through such changes, and might even become suspicious if the income diverged too much from the cash flow from operations.
4. For this company, there is really not much that could be manipulated even if it were ethical and successful. Receivables are not large, nor is there any obvious reason for the company to recognize revenue sooner than it does without violating GAAP. Inventories are also not large, and, since FIFO is already being used, there is likely to be little room for raising inventory value to increase income. Amortization could be slowed down, but such a move would make little difference to income. Even cutting amortization in half would reduce the year's loss by less than 20%.

This ends the continuing demonstration case. Let's hope that Mavis and Tomas solve their problems and make a success of their fledgling company!

HOMEWORK AND DISCUSSION TO DEVELOP UNDERSTANDING

PROBLEM 10.1* Discuss the conflict between flexible and standard accounting

As you have seen, there is a general conflict between two financial reporting objectives. The first objective is to fit the accounting to each company's circumstances so that the resulting reports are relevant to understanding or evaluating that company. The second is to make accounting consistent from company to company so that intercompany comparisons may be facilitated and the overall credibility of the information maintained.

Write a paragraph giving your views on how important this conflict is and how (if at all) it should be dealt with.

PROBLEM 10.2* Analyze various possible inventory costing policies

Yang Inc. has been in business for three years and pays income tax at 30%. The company manages its inventories well, so that there are no significant inventories for which cost is less than net realizable value. For the past three years, here are the company's inventory asset and COGS expense computed under each of three methods:

	1996	1995	1994
a. FIFO – ending inventory	$112,000	$148,000	$115,000
– COGS expense	636,000	867,000	585,000
b. AVGE – ending inventory	108,000	126,000	106,000
– COGS expense	618,000	880,000	594,000
c. LIFO – ending inventory	104,000	118,000	92,000
– COGS expense	614,000	874,000	608,000
Purchases in each year	600,000	900,000	700,000

1. Determine the inventory cost policy that would produce the highest and lowest income in each year and calculate the effect on net income of choosing the former over the latter.
2. Given the variation of results you observed in Question 1, how should a company choose its inventory cost policy?

PROBLEM 10.3* Amortization calculations, entries, and effects

At the beginning of 1994, Garrison Inc. acquired machinery costing $100,000 and having a useful life of 10 years. The company amortized this machinery during 1994 and 1995 using the straight-line method. During 1996, it decided to change to the declining balance method of amortization for the machinery. Garrison is taxed at an income tax rate of 40%.

1. Calculate the amortization expense Garrison has recognized for 1994 and 1995 and write a journal entry to record either year's amount.

2. Calculate the amortization expense Garrison would have recorded had it been using the declining balance method for 1994 and 1995.
3. Calculate the effects of changing from straight-line to declining balance on the following:
   a. The balance sheet at the end of 1994.
   b. The income statement for 1995.
   c. The balance sheet at the end of 1995.
   d. The SCFP for 1995.

PROBLEM 10.4* Questions about the right-hand side of the balance sheet

Answer the following questions briefly:

1. What is the difference between liabilities and equity?
2. What is the difference, if any, between liabilities and debts?
3. Suggest two examples each of short-term and long-term accruals that require difficult estimates and indicate what the difficulty is in each case.
4. How is a company's purchase of its own shares on the stock market handled in the balance sheet?

PROBLEM 10.5* Effects analysis: expensing vs. capitalizing, plus tax

The controller of Squiffle, Inc. is having some disagreements with senior management about some company accounting policies.

1. Squiffle, in business for only a year, has capitalized $67,000 in development costs. The controller argues that such costs should be expensed instead. Assume this accounting policy affects current income tax liability and that the company's income tax rate is 30%. What would the controller's proposal do to:
   a. The current year's net income?
   b. The current year's cash flow?
   c. Working capital at the end of the current year?
2. Top management is likely to go grudgingly along with the controller regarding Question 1 because of the income tax saving. If that is done, the first year's income statement will show income before income tax of $100,000. The income tax law allows an extra deduction of $25,000, to postpone payment of the tax on that $25,000 for several years—the company has received this as an inducement to locate in a depressed region. Top management wants to take advantage of the income tax inducement by showing income tax expense for the year of only $22,500 (which is 30% of $100,000 – $25,000), because that is all the income tax the company will have to pay. The controller believes that the company should create a deferred income tax liability for the inducement, because the tax will have to be paid after several years. What would the controller's proposal do to:
   a. The current year's net income?
   b. The current year's cash flow?
   c. Working capital at the end of the current year?

PROBLEM 10.6 Whose role should it be to choose accounting policies?

Should management have the responsibility and authority to choose companies' accounting policies, or should that role be someone else's (for example, the government's, the auditor's, an independent board's)? If you think it should be management's role, why? If you think it should be someone else's role, whose? Why?

PROBLEM 10.7 Can the auditor prevent unfair accounting policies?

A commentator on the accounting scene remarked, "Management makes its accounting choices to serve its own interests, and there's no way the poor lonely auditor can hold the fort of fairness when you consider how vague and judgmental accrual accounting's criteria for accounting policy choices are."

What are your views on the commentator's remarks?

PROBLEM 10.8 Question about the significant accounting policies note

1. Outline the kinds of information you would expect to see in a company's significant accounting policies note to the financial statements.
2. How should a company decide what to include in that note?
3. A business commentator suggested that, when a company uses an accounting policy that is unusual, its significant accounting policies note should include a calculation of the effect on income of using that policy as compared to the more usual practice. What do you think of that idea?

PROBLEM 10.9 Comment on various remarks about accounting policies

Comment briefly on the following remarks by a business person:

1. No one cares what our accounting policy choices are because they have no effect on the price of the company's shares.
2. Last year we sold some equipment that had a book value of $70,000 for $54,000. I was really angry at our general manager for losing $16,000 and nearly fired him.
3. I don't allow our company to include any intangible assets on its balance sheet because I prefer a conservative balance sheet that doesn't contain questionable assets.
4. Once we have established proper accounting policies, all those notes at the end of the financial statements are really an irrelevant nuisance.

PROBLEM 10.10 Conceptual questions about inventories and their cost

Discuss each of the following:

1. In accounting for inventories and cost of goods sold, why make cost flow assumptions? Why not just charge the actual cost of items sold to cost of goods sold and keep the actual cost of unsold items in the inventory asset account on the balance sheet?
2. What are the circumstances under which each of the following inventory cost determination policies would be appropriate?
   a. Specific identification (actual cost of items on hand).
   b. LIFO cost flow assumption.

   c. Average cost flow assumption.
   d. FIFO cost flow assumption.
   e. Cost estimate via deduction of markup from selling price (for example, retail method).
3. Are inventories always current assets?
4. What is the connection (if any) between a company's revenue recognition policy and its inventory cost determination policy?
5. Can you suggest some examples of inventory assets that are not supported by physical assets?
6. What is the difference (if any) between an inventory asset and each of the following?
   a. A marketable security asset.
   b. A prepaid expense.
   c. A deferred charge.
   d. A property asset.

PROBLEM 10.11 Conceptual questions about LIFO and its effects

"In the United States, unlike in Canada, the LIFO inventory costing method is acceptable for tax purposes. For this reason, more companies use the LIFO inventory costing method in the United States than in Canada, especially in this time of rising prices [1980]."

1. Explain the above quotation.
2. Suppose you were a shareholder in a company that switched its inventory costing method from FIFO to LIFO and, as a result, its reported net income dropped $2 million. What would be your reaction? Explain.

PROBLEM 10.12 LIFO, FIFO, and AVGE inventory cost calculations

The following purchases of inventory were made by Anvil Corp. in April.

Date	Number of Units Purchased	Per Unit Amount	Total Cost
April 2	100	$5	$ 500
April 15	200	6	1,200
April 23	50	7	350
	350		

Sales of inventory during April were:

Date	Number of Units Sold
April 6	70
April 13	120
April 18	200
	390

Anvil's inventory on April 1 consisted of 150 units valued at $4 each.

1. Calculate cost of goods sold for April, using LIFO, FIFO, and weighted annual average inventory cost flow assumptions, and assume that Anvil uses a periodic inventory control system.
2. Calculate ending inventory values under each of the three methods above as at April 30.
3. Suppose the market price for these units was only $5 per unit at April 30, and the lower of cost or market valuation is applied to each unit individually. Redo Question 2 above.
4. (Optional) Redo Questions 1, 2, and 3, assuming Anvil uses a perpetual inventory control system.

PROBLEM 10.13 Inventory cost and market calculations

Winedark Sea Ltd. sells prints of romantic paintings. The prints are done on expensive paper and are quite costly. Pricing the prints to sell is hard because popularity of a print is difficult to predict. Sometimes prints don't sell well at all and are then disposed of in bulk for use in hotels and motels.

Here are data on two prints:

	Print X		Print Y	
	Units	Cost per Unit	Units	Cost per Unit
Inventory, January 1, 1994	4	$340	11	$500
Purchases during 1994:				
During summer	10	350	25	480
During fall	15	330	30	510
Sales during 1994	23		38	

1. Calculate the following:
   a. Inventory cost, December 31, 1994, for Print X, FIFO basis.
   b. Cost of goods sold, 1994, for Print Y, AVGE basis.
2. Print Y hasn't sold since September. No one seems to like it any more. An out-of-town hotel has offered $100 each for all that Winedark has left, if Winedark will pay the $10 per print shipping cost. What amount would you suggest be used for the inventory of Print Y on the December 31, 1994, balance sheet? Why?

PROBLEM 10.14 Inventory cost and effects calculations

You work for a large local company as inventory manager. The company uses FIFO in accounting for inventory. In June, the company began to stock a new product, Painto. The June inventory record for Painto was:

Date	Purchase Price	Units Purchased	Units Sold	Units on Hand
June 1	$10	1,250		1,250
10	$11	1,000		2,250
12			250	2,000
17	$12	500		2,500
23			2,000	500
27	$13	1,500		2,000

1. Calculate, using FIFO:
   a. The cost of the June 30 inventory of Painto.
   b. The cost of goods sold for Painto for June.
2. Calculate, using LIFO (either perpetual or periodic):
   a. The cost of the June 30 inventory of Painto.
   b. The cost of goods sold for Painto for June.
3. The company's income tax rate is 35%. Based on your calculations in Questions 1 and 2, what would be the effect of changing from FIFO to LIFO on the company's:
   a. Net income for June?
   b. Balance sheet at the end of June?

PROBLEM 10.15 Conceptual questions about amortization

1. Why do companies have such an expense as amortization, depreciation, or depletion? What is the purpose of the accounting principle underlying it?
2. Why does amortization appear as an adjustment on the SCFP?
3. Why record amortization expense by debiting the expense and crediting accumulated amortization? Why not just credit the asset cost so that the balance sheet shows just the remaining unamortized cost? (After all, the latter method is used for prepaid expenses, deferred charges, and many intangible assets such as patents and goodwill.)
4. What are the circumstances under which each of the following amortization policies would be appropriate?
   a. Straight-line (even periodic expenses over asset's life).
   b. Accelerated (declining periodic expenses over asset's life).
   c. Decelerated (increasing periodic expenses over asset's life).
   d. Units of production (variable periodic expenses depending on the use of the asset).

PROBLEM 10.16 Various amortization questions and calculations

1. Your friend Z has just completed the first year of operating a one-truck delivery company. Z explains to you that, because of careful care of the truck, the price the truck would fetch on the used truck market is not much different from the price paid for the truck a year ago. As a result, says Z, no amortization expense on the truck is needed for accounting purposes this year. Next year, Z believes, the truck's value will drop a noticeable amount, but this is not a problem because the cash obtained from deducting tax capital cost allowance will compensate for the decline in market value over the year.

   Explain to Z what the accounting concept of amortization is and how Z's thinking is in error with respect to that concept.
2. Another friend is just starting a yard grooming service and has purchased a group of new lawnmowers for $20,000. The friend expects the mowers to last five years and to have negligible resale value at that point. The friend's business plan projects cutting 5,000 lawns over the five years, with per-year projections of 500, 1,000, 1,200, 1,800, and 500 lawns over the five years.
   a. Calculate the accumulated amortization balance at the end of the *second* year on each of the following amortization bases:

i. Straight-line.
ii. Declining balance (25% rate).
iii. Units-of-production.

b. Based on your calculations, which amortization basis would produce the highest retained earnings at the end of the second year?
c. Your friend has never heard of the units-of-production basis. Explain why companies use it and comment on whether it would make sense for your friend's business.
d. If the 25% declining balance method is used, accumulated amortization will be $15,254 at the end of the fifth year. Suppose that on the first day of the sixth year, all the lawnmowers are sold as junk for $100 cash in total. Ignoring income taxes:
   i. Calculate the loss on sale that would be recorded that day.
   ii. Suppose your friend objects to recording the loss on sale, pointing out that $100 more was received for the lawnmowers than had been expected five years earlier, and claims that, in any case, income for the sixth year should not be reduced by the loss when it happened on the first day on the year. Reply to your friend.

PROBLEM 10.17 Amortization calculations, entries, effects, and choice

SD Corporation acquired machinery at the beginning of 1994, having a cost of $100,000 and an anticipated useful life of 10 years. It amortized this machinery for 1994 and 1995 using the straight-line method. During 1996, it decided to change to the declining balance method of amortization. SD is taxed at an income tax rate of 40%.

1. Prepare the journal entry to record amortization expense for *1995* using the straight-line method.
2. Prepare the journal entry to record amortization expense for *1995* using the declining balance method, at a rate of 20%.
3. Show the effects of changing from straight-line to the 20% declining balance method on: the 1995 income statement, the 1995 SCFP, and the balance sheet at the end of 1995.
4. In what circumstances is the use of declining balance amortization more appropriate than use of the straight-line method?

PROBLEM 10.18 Amortization and gain/loss calculations and effects

Fred's Freighthauling Ltd. has a small fleet of delivery trucks. Each one is amortized on the declining balance method (rate 20%; half that in the year of acquisition and in the year of disposal) with no salvage value. Truck 4 was purchased July 1, 1992, for $46,000 and sold three years later, on June 30, 1995, for $15,000. The company's fiscal year-end is December 31.

1. What was the total amortization on Truck 4 to the date of its disposal?
2. Based on your answer to Question1, write a journal entry to record the disposal of Truck 4.
3. Redo Questions 1 and 2, assuming the company uses straight-line amortization at 15% per year and an estimated salvage value of $6,000.
4. Calculate the difference in effects between the two amortization methods on the company's 1995 income statement and SCFP. Ignore income tax effects.

5. What implications (if any) would the use of different amortization methods by the company have for potential creditors or investors?
6. The use of different amortization methods could affect financial performance comparability between fiscal years of a particular company, and between different companies for the same fiscal year. How are these differences mitigated?

PROBLEM 10.19 Calculate any goodwill on a business purchase

Foofaraw Ltd. paid $200,000 for land, buildings, inventories, and accounts payable of another business that will become a branch. The assets (after deducting the accounts payable of $50,000) had an aggregate fair market value of $187,000.

1. What (if anything) is the resulting asset on Foofaraw's balance sheet?
2. If Foofaraw had paid $185,000, what would be your answer to Question1?

PROBLEM 10.20 Contrast accounting for long-term assets and liabilities

Contrast the methods by which long-term assets and long-term liabilities are reported on the balance sheet of a company.

PROBLEM 10.21 Identify significant information in the notes

Review the notes to The North West Company's financial statements at the end of the book and make a list of as many *significant* pieces of information as you can that are *not* included in the financial statement numbers. Briefly, why do you think each piece is significant?

PROBLEM 10.22 Questions about intangibles and capital leases

Answer the following questions briefly:

1. Why is capitalizing costs such as intangible assets a reasonable idea?
2. Why is it not such a good idea?
3. Explain clearly why and how capitalizing the costs of a development project as a "deferred costs" asset affects the income statement and the balance sheet.
4. Explain why capitalizing such costs does not have any direct effect on the SCFP's cash from operations figure.
5. Suggest some indirect effects on cash flow that such a capitalization policy may have.
6. If an asset is leased, it is not owned. How can accounting standards that require creating a balance sheet account for some such leased assets be justified?
7. If a lease is treated as a capital lease rather than an operating lease, what effects does that have on the balance sheet, income statement, and SCFP?

PROBLEM 10.23 Questions on auditors, judgment, and accounting policies

Write a paragraph on each of the following topics, using the perspective on accounting policy choice and methods provided in this chapter:

1. Why the auditor's report refers to whether the company's financial statements have been prepared in accordance with GAAP.
2. Why professional judgment is needed in preparing financial statements.
3. Whether it is justifiable to use an aggressive (in other words, early in the production-sale-collection cycle process) revenue recognition policy.

4. Why companies should specify what they include as cash and cash equivalents when preparing the SCFP.
5. Why a prior period adjustment is separated from the year's income calculation and shown on the statement of retained earnings.

PROBLEM 10.24 Do accounting policies affect share prices?

(Challenging)

A shareholder in a large public company threatens to sue management, the auditors, and the CICA for "approving conservative accounting policies that have resulted in poor apparent performance and low stock prices that have reduced my investment value."

What do you think of the shareholder's complaint?

PROBLEM 10.25 Questions on accounting values and income

(Challenging)

Pull together your knowledge of how accounting numbers are derived and answer each of the following briefly:

1. Explain why balance sheet valuation and income measurement are linked.
2. Briefly discuss two of the limitations of historical cost balance sheet valuation.
3. During times of rising prices, will the following tend to be overstated or understated? Why?
   a. Assets
   b. Net income
   c. Return on equity

PROBLEM 10.26 Effects of pension accounting on the future

(Challenging)

An accounting professor recently stated, "It's not only our government that's spending our children's inheritance. Accounting standard setters are guilty as well, because they have failed to develop and enforce satisfactory accounting guidelines for the reporting and disclosure of obligations such as pension liabilities in both the public and private sectors. The real cost of pensions is not being recognized in balance sheets."

Explain how the alleged failure of standard setters to address pension accounting issues could take cash out of the hands of future generations.

PROBLEM 10.27 Respond to comments on accounting

(Challenging)

During a lunch with a senior executive of a large public company, you are asked to respond to several comments, including:

1. Accounting standards and principles evolve too slowly to keep up with the rapidly changing needs of businesses such as ours. Why don't we just ignore standards and GAAP, and do our accounting the best way for our needs?
2. I would be glad to see our goodwill assets written off. I can't see the sense in including such a thing with the balance sheet assets anyway. To me, it's not like the other assets.
3. You just referred to judgment in applying accounting principles. That's foolish: judgment is just a word people use when they'd prefer not to follow the rules.
4. I've heard that the auditors may not agree with our planned accounting changes. Who cares? We can always change auditors.

5. You mentioned the stock market's response to changes in our accounting methods. Does the market respond? I thought it pretty well ignores accounting.

PROBLEM 10.28 Contract cash flow and income calculations

(Challenging)

The Swazy Construction Company has secured a contract with the Alberta government for the construction of 15 miles of highway at a contract price of $100,000 a mile. Payments for each mile of highway are to be made according to the following schedule:

- 40% at the time the concrete is poured;
- 50% when all work on that mile is completed;
- 10% when all 15 miles of highway have been completed, inspected, and approved.

At the end of the first period of operation, five miles of highway have been entirely completed and approved, concrete has been poured on a second stretch of five miles, and preliminary grading has been done on the third five-mile stretch.

The job was originally estimated to cost $80,000 a mile. Costs to date have coincided with these original estimates and have totalled the following amounts: on the completed stretch, $80,000 a mile; on the second stretch, $65,000 a mile; and on the third stretch, $10,000 a mile. It is estimated that each unfinished stretch will be completed at the costs originally estimated.

1. How much should the Alberta government have paid Swazy during or at the end of the first period of operation under the terms of the contract? Show computations.
2. How much income would you report for this period? Show your calculations and justify your method.

PROBLEM 10.29 Oil production balance sheet and income

(Challenging)

The Lindleigh Company is in the business of oil production. On January 1, 1989, the company paid $1,000,000 for the lease of an area near MacDonald Lake. The lease area was known to contain a vast amount of oil in the form of tar sands.

During the five years to December 31, 1994, the company spent $5,000,000 on exploratory work in assessing the extent of the deposits, perfecting the extraction technique, and building access roads.

1. Assuming that the company commenced with a capital stock of $3,000,000 and has borrowed $3,000,000 since then, and that the transactions specified are the only ones in which the company has engaged, present a balance sheet for the Lindleigh Company as at December 31, 1994.
2. During 1995, 500,000 barrels of oil were produced. Production costs incurred during the period were $1,000,000. At the end of the period, 100,000 barrels of refined oil remained in storage, and 400,000 barrels had been sold at a price of $4 per barrel.
   a. Assuming that selling expenses were $200,000, prepare an income statement for the Lindleigh Company for 1995. Show your cost of goods sold computation.
   b. How would the Assets portion of the balance sheet appear as at December 31, 1995?

PROBLEM 10.30 (Challenging) Accounting policy change calculations

Humungus Ltd. is a retailer of consumer products. The president of the company had two concerns: the company's worsening cash position ($3,000 cash and no bank loan at the end of 1994, no cash and a $7,000 bank loan at the end of 1995), and what the president believed was an inadequate level of net income.

1. The president was confused because the company had a $9,000 income and yet seemed, as noted above, $10,000 *worse* off in its cash position. Explain briefly how, in general, this difference between income and cash change can happen.
2. The president proposed changes in the company's accounting policies in a few areas in an attempt to show a higher income. He met the company's auditors to discuss these ideas. What do you think the auditors should have said?
3. For each of the proposed changes below, *considered separately and independently*, calculate the effect on 1995 net income *and* total assets as at December 31, 1995. Assume a 30% income tax rate.
   a. The president suggested recognizing revenue at an earlier point. If this were done, net accounts receivable would be increased by $12,000 at December 31, 1994, and by $23,000 at December 31, 1995.
   b. The president suggested changing the inventory cost policy to FIFO (which would still produce costs less than net realizable value). Doing so would increase December 31, 1994, inventories by $4,000 and December 31, 1995, inventories by $1,000.
   c. The president suggested the company not account for deferred income taxes, but rather treat income taxes payable in each year as the income tax expense. The deferred income tax liability was $2,800 at December 31, 1994, and without this change was $2,600 at December 31, 1995.
   d. The president suggested capitalizing more of the company's product development costs and amortizing the additional capitalized amounts over five years, using the straight-line method. If this were done, $4,000 of 1994 expenses would be capitalized at December 31, 1994, and $6,000 of 1995 expenses would be capitalized at December 31, 1995.

PROBLEM 10.31 (Challenging) Identify possible asset valuation methods

Sports Forever Inc. has recently agreed to purchase a local arena at a price of $100,000. The realtor had listed the property at $115,000, but Mark Johnson, SFI's president, managed to talk the present owner, Shattered Dreams Limited, down to the lower price by promising full payment in cash. Mark has seen the city's property tax assessment of the arena, which revealed the following information:

Total assessed value:	$80,000
Land value equal to:	70%
Building value equal to:	30%

Mark is also aware that the arena has firm contracts (regardless of change in ownership of the arena) for the next 20 years with both a popular football team and a highly successful local hockey team. Net total cash flows from the two contracts are expected to be approximately $25,000 per year over the full term of the contracts. This is rather convenient, since the remaining expected life of the arena is projected by a professional estimator to be 20 years.

Upon consultation with a contractor, Mark learned that the cost to replace the arena in its original condition is currently $150,000. The president of Shattered

Dreams Limited felt that the price offered by Mark was more than appropriate, since the net book value of the building on his company's books is only $30,000. Sports Forever Inc. can borrow or invest at an interest rate of 10%.

1. Identify all possible valuations of the arena for which sufficient information has been supplied. Where calculations are required, show your work.
2. List the potential users of each valuation and describe how they would use the information.

PROBLEM 10.32 Asset prices, policies, effects and entries

(Challenging)

Advanced Markets Ltd., a retailer, began business on November 1, 1993. The company's balance sheets then and at October 31, 1994, were (in thousands of dollars):

	Oct. 31/94	Nov. 1/93		Oct. 31/94	Nov. 1/93
Cash	$ 26	$100	Accts. payable	$194	$180
Accts. rec'ble.	314	300	Share capital	500	500
Allow. doubt. accts.	(30)	(20)	Ret. earnings	76	—
Inventory (FIFO)	374	240			
Fixtures	40	—			
Accum. amort.	(8)	—			
Goodwill (net)	54	60			
	$770	$680		$770	$680

The company had receivables, payables, and inventories from the beginning because it was formed to take over the business of another company whose owner had decided to retire to a warmer climate. The company's premises and equipment were all rented, so the company had no fixed assets when it began. The company need not pay any income tax this year.

1. From the information given, calculate the purchase price of the business Advanced Markets purchased November 1, 1993.
2. Net income for the company's first year was $76 (thousand). Calculate cash generated by operations for that year (in thousands).
3. If the company changed to average cost for its inventory, the October 31, 1994, inventory asset would be $316 (thousand). If it did so, what would the following be?
   a. Retained earnings, October 31, 1994.
   b. Cash generated by operations (based on your answer to Question 2)
4. The company buys its inventories in large lots. For the last year, its purchases and sales were:

November 1, 1993, beginning	8,000 units @ $30 = $240 (thousand)
Sales before next purchase	6,000 units
February 15, 1994, purchase	7,000 units @ $36 = $252 (thousand)
Sales before next purchase	4,000 units
July 31, 1994, purchase	7,500 units @ $40 = $300 (thousand)
Sales before October 31, 1994	3,500 units

The company uses the periodic inventory control system.

a. What would its October 31, 1994, inventory cost be on the LIFO (last-in, first-out) basis?

b. What would the 1994 cost of goods sold be on the LIFO basis?

5. On December 31, 1994, in the company's *second year* of operation, several unneeded counters and tables were sold for $15 thousand cash. At that date, those assets (which had cost $18 thousand) had a book value of $12 thousand.

   a. Write a journal entry to record the sale.

   b. Explain why this sale affects the calculation of cash from operations in the company's SCFP for its *second year* of operation.

PROBLEM 10.33 Accounting calculations, effects, entries

(Challenging)

Harriett has been making quilts, aprons, pillows, scarves, and other such items for years. Recently, she took the plunge and opened a shop to sell her products and those of other local craftspeople. Her husband, who is more interested in sports than accounting, keeps her books and prepared the draft financial statements that follow.

Draft Financial Statements for Harriett's Handmades Ltd.
Balance Sheet as at December 31,1994

Assets		Liabilities and Owners' Equity	
Current:		Current:	
Inventory	$ 43,000	Owing to bank	$ 18,000
Owing from customers	2,140	Owing to suppliers	21,000
Cash	4,600	Income tax owing	3,200
	$ 49,740		$ 42,200
Noncurrent:		Store mortgage	110,000
Store	$187,000	Owners' equity:	
Amortization so far	3,740	Shares issued	68,000
	$183,260	Income so far	12,800
	$233,000		$233,000

Income Statement
for the Year Ended December 31,1994

Sales		$152,000
Cost of goods sold:		
Purchases	$118,000	
Less inventory left over	43,000	75,000
Margin		$ 77,000
Expenses:		
Store operations	$ 22,000	
Wages	24,000	
Interest	15,000	61,000
Income before tax		$ 16,000
Estimated income tax owing		$ 3,200
Income for the year		$ 12,800

1. The company's "store" assets cost the following: fixtures and shelving, $19,000; cash register and other equipment, $14,000; building, $114,000; land, $40,000; total, $187,000. Harriett's husband computed amortization at 2% of the total and included the resulting $3,740 in store operations expenses.
   a. Evaluate Harriett's husband's amortization accounting policy.
   b. Propose a more suitable amortization accounting policy, indicating any assumptions you need in order to do that.
   c. Calculate amortization for 1994, based on your proposed policy, and write a journal entry to adjust the accounts to reflect your calculation.
2. Most of the company's inventory and the cost of goods sold are recorded at actual cost because each item is tagged with the name of the person who made it plus an identification number. Harriett uses this information to keep track of which craftspeople make popular items and which do not. However, the store also sells a line of fancy wrapping paper. Purchases and sales of that paper were as follows:

Initial purchase	200 packages @ $1.20	$ 240
Sales to April 24	160 packages	
Purchase April 25	300 packages @ $1.30	390
Sales to August 15	310 packages	
Purchase August 16	500 packages @ $1.40	700
Sales December 31	450 packages	
		$1,330

   Harriett's husband, working from an old accounting text, came up with the following figures for the wrapping paper:

Unit cost:	$1,330 / 1,000 = $1.33
Cost of goods sold:	920 × $1.33 = $1,224
Ending inventory:	80 × $1.33 = $106

   a. What inventory costing method was Harriett's husband using?
   b. Is that an acceptable method for the wrapping paper? Why?
   c. Using the perpetual LIFO method, calculate ending inventory and cost of goods sold for the wrapping paper.
3. Harriett is thinking of buying a kitchenette unit for her store, so that she may sell coffee, cappuccino, cookies, and other such things to browsing customers. She thinks the unit would be a great success, bringing in net cash of $1,000 per year (sales from the unit, less expenses, plus increased sales of handcrafts, less expenses). The unit would cost $4,000 and Harriett would plan to sell it in four years for about $1,500 and buy a bigger one if the idea is a success. The company would pay about 12% interest on a bank loan to cover the cost of the unit.

   Should the company buy the kitchenette unit? Support your answer with relevant calculations.
4. Harriett is thinking of capitalizing $2,000 of the year's wage expenses (spent early in 1994 to build shelving) and include that in the cost of fixtures and shelving.
   a. What does it mean to "capitalize" such expenses?
   b. What would be the effect on 1994 income (*ignoring* income tax) if Harriett decided to capitalize the wages?

5. When Harriett reviewed the draft financial statements, she discovered the following:
   - Net realizable value of the inventory totalled $41,600;
   - One customer account, $150, was uncollectible and three, totalling $280, were doubtful;
   - Cash on hand was overstated by $1,000 because her husband had recorded a $1,000 bank loan twice;
   - A $210 bill for operating expenses not incurred until January 1995 was included in accounts payable;
   - The current portion of the store mortgage was $4,200.

   Taking these items *and* assuming implementation of your amortization policy (Question I above) and Harriett's wage capitalization plan (Question 4), calculate the revised *income before income tax* for 1994.
6. Harriett's husband estimated income taxes payable by just multiplying the income before tax by 20%. In fact, because of accelerated capital cost allowance (tax amortization), taxable income for 1994 was only $1,800. The appropriate income tax rate on the company's income is 25%, not 20%.
   a. Write a journal entry to adjust the estimated income tax recorded by the husband to reflect the above information.
   b. Taking into account (a) above *and* Questions 1, 4, and 5, calculate the following as at December 31, 1994:
      i. Retained earnings.
      ii. Total assets.

PROBLEM 10.34 Accounting policies, effects, and entries

(Challenging)

Refer to the Grandin Ltd. trial balances for 1996 and 1995 in Problem 4.19 and the financial statements you originally prepared. Assume that upon further inquiry, you have discovered the following information:

- At the very end of 1996, some equipment that had cost $4,500 11 years earlier was sold for $1,800. The bookkeeper had debited the sale proceeds to cash and credited service revenue.
- The company's amortization policy for its equipment is straight-line, with an estimated useful life of 15 years and no salvage value. No amortization is recorded in the year of sale. Amortization on the remaining assets has been recorded in the accounts.
- No other equipment was bought or sold during 1996.
- The company uses the average inventory costing policy. There were 2,000 units on hand at the end of 1995 (costing $18.50 each), and during 1996 there were the following purchases, in this order: 800 at $19, 1,200 at $16.20, 2,000 at $17.50, 1,500 at $19.20, and 500 at $20.50. Sales for 1996 were recorded at 5,666 units. On the average cost basis, 1996 cost of goods sold for 5,666 units was $103,190 and inventory at the end of 1996 was $42,500. (Weighted average cost was $18.21; the two figures above are rounded.)
- The company has decided to change its inventory costing policy to FIFO (which will be less than net realizable value, as is cost on the average basis). The change will be implemented for 1996, but the inventory cost per unit at the end of 1995 ($18.50) will not be changed. The bookkeeper has no idea how to implement the accounting policy change.

- The company has failed to correctly accrue bonuses owing to the company president for the last three years. The bonuses, related to the 1994, 1995, and 1996 year ends, were paid and recorded as expenses on the 1996 income statement in service wage expense. The bonuses were as follows:

  1994 $2,000
  1995 $3,000
  1996 $4,000

- Grandin's applicable tax rate is 25%. All income tax adjustments will be paid or refunded currently.

1. Prepare adjusting journal entries to correct the company's records.
2. Calculate the effect of the above entries on:
   a. Net income for 1996.
   b. 1996 beginning retained earnings.
   c. 1996 ending retained earnings.
3. Prepare a corrected balance sheet, statement of income, and statement of retained earnings for 1996.
4. Comment on the company's performance for 1996 and its position at year end.

PROBLEM 10.35 Consolidated accounting policies

(Challenging)

Below are the summarized accounts of Ambitious Inc. for this year and last, prior to closing revenues, expenses, and dividends to retained earnings.

	Debits			Credits	
	This	**Last**		**This**	**Last**
Income tax refundable	$5,000	$3,000	Bank loan	$42,000	$41,000
Bad debts	6,000	8,000	Payables	65,000	59,000
Cash	4,000	10,000	Long-term debt	70,000	76,000
Receivables (net)	60,000	35,000	Def. inc. tax	8,000	6,000
Inventories	88,000	68,000	Accum. amort.	41,000	36,000
Investment	48,000	—	Share capital	75,000	50,000
Land	5,000	15,000	*Begin* ret. earn.	58,000	38,000
Plant assets	189,000	187,000	Sales	316,000	261,000
Cost of sales	179,000	148,000	Other income	16,000	11,000
Other expenses	97,000	84,000	Ext. gain (net)	15,000	—
Income tax expense	15,000	11,000			
Dividends	10,000	9,000			
	$706,000	$578,000		$706,000	$578,000

Other data include:

- Amortization expense was $13,000 last year and $15,000 this year.
- During this year, a piece of equipment costing $18,000 was sold for $8,000. Because amortization is computed on a group basis, no gain or loss was recorded on the sale.
- The investment is an 80% voting interest in Tardy Ltd., acquired earlier this year for $40,000 cash. At date of acquisition, Tardy's net assets had a book

value of $26,000 and an estimated fair market value of $31,000 (due to valuable land). Since acquisition, Tardy has reported net income of $10,000 but has paid no dividends. Ambitious pays no income tax on any income from this kind of investment.

- During the year, a parcel of land was unexpectedly expropriated by the government for $30,000. The company had to pay a capital gains tax of $5,000 on the proceeds.
- The company is contemplating a change in accounting for bad debts. Under the revised policy, last year's net receivables would be reduced by $8,000 and this year's by $14,000. Revised income tax returns would be filed, claiming a refund of $3,000 for last year and $2,000 for this year, for a total of $5,000.

1. Write a journal entry to implement the accounting policy change.
2. Calculate net income for this year after the change in Question 1 is recorded.
3. Calculate the following figures for the consolidated statements of Ambitious and Tardy as at the end of this year (any consolidated goodwill is amortized at $1,000 per year):
   a. Consolidated goodwill asset (net).
   b. Consolidated noncontrolling interest liability.
   c. Consolidated net income.
   d. Consolidated retained earnings.
4. Prepare nonconsolidated balance sheets for Ambitious as at the end of last year and this year.
5. Prepare a nonconsolidated statement of changes in financial position for Ambitious for this year.

CASE 10A Discuss two examples of managing earnings

Business Week magazine reported two cases of companies' attempts to manage earnings, one apparently trying to make earnings better, the other apparently trying to make them worse. Discuss the issues, ethics, and methods involved.

A SUPERSLEUTH RAISES A RED FLAG OVER PYXIS

Howard M. Schilit likes to play detective. And his kind of game is deadly serious: ferreting out corporate trouble. An accounting professor at American University, Schilit has called attention to several cases of shenanigans that resulted in either a bankruptcy filing or a plunge in the stock price. As a result, a number of money managers and analysts have hired Schilit to undertake sleuthing of companies they have invested in—or are contemplating putting money into.

The scorecard for Schilit, president of the Center for Financial Research & Analysis in Rockville, Md., is impressive: He alerted investors in January, 1992, to "misleading" financial statements used by College Bound Inc. Before long, the Securities & Exchange Commission suspended trading in the stock, then at 24. The company later ceased operations and filed for bankruptcy protection. In September, 1993, Schilit questioned the way Kendall Square Research recorded revenues. The stock, then at 24, dropped to 16 after Price Waterhouse told the company it ought to revise its reported revenues. By December, Price "recalled" the prior year's entire revenues. The stock fell to 4 and is now at 5.

Front-loading. What company has caught Schilit's eye now? "Watch out," he says, for Pyxis, a San Diego maker and leaser of automated point-of-use systems that hospitals use to control and distribute medications and supplies. Its stock had more than quadrupled—from 8 in 1992 to 35 in December, 1993. Schilit says the sharp rises in revenues and earnings in the past three years are "misleading" and "unsustainable." Revenues jumped from \$13.4 million in 1991 to \$46.3 in million in 1992—and to \$100.1 million last year. After a loss in 1991, Pyxis posted earnings of 38¢ in 1992 and 69¢ last year.

Here's the hitch, says Schilit: Just before going public in 1992, Pyxis started booking revenues from equipment leases as if they were outright sales, rather than spreading them over the life of the lease. By front-loading revenues, says Schilit, the company "distorts" its true financial condition. He explains that although this sales-type reporting revenues is acceptable under normal accounting rules, it still "exaggerates the actual growth in sales and earnings. Pyxis is in the business of leasing," he says. CEO Taylor says Pyxis must report leasing revenues as sales because of the conditions of the lease contracts.

Another factor that has turned off Schilit on Pyxis: Insiders have been selling stock since November, including Chairman and CEO Ronald Taylor and President and CEO Gerald Forth. The stock, which has continued to slip since December, has fallen to 27.

SOURCE: G.G. MARCIAL, "A SUPERSLEUTH RAISES A RED FLAG OVER PYXIS," *BUSINESS WEEK*, APRIL 4, 1994, 104.

DID PFIZER DOCTOR ITS NUMBERS?

To avoid political heat, it may have tried to "manage down" earnings

William C. Steere Jr. is in a strange bind. As chief executive of Pfizer Inc., one of the nation's healthiest drug companies, he should want to flaunt his company's double-digit earnings prospects. And yet, as chairman of the drug industry's main Washington lobbying group, the Pharmaceutical Manufacturer Assn. (PMA), Steere has to convince skeptical legislators that drugmaker profits already are under pressure. President Clinton's healthcare reform, he argues, could endanger the industry's future.

What to do? Some industry insiders claim that Steere is spending heavily and delaying sales to deliberately dampen Pfizer's profit growth rates. "The company did the politically prudent thing at the beginning of the debate over health-care reform," says Paine Webber Inc. drug analyst Ronald M. Nordmann. "They managed down the numbers."

Cut Jobs. Steere scoffs at the idea as "just not true." Pfizer, he insists, is feeling every bit of the cost-containment pain that the entire industry is feeling. After all, it has cut 1,000 jobs since 1992 and is planning to trim 3,000 more in the next three to five years, moves that cost it more than \$750 million in charges to earnings last year.

But a closer look reveals that Pfizer not only is healthier than most of its peers but is faring better than its latest numbers suggest. Take its 19% slide in 1993 net income, to \$657.5 million. Back out restructuring charges and divestitures, and Pfizer shows a net income from ongoing operations of \$1.18 billion, a 15% rise—twice the increase of some major rivals.

There also is evident that Pfizer inched fourth-quarter sales while boosting expenses. Wholesalers say the company withheld all its medicines from them after mid-December, saying it wanted to prevent buyers from stocking up early in anticipation of a planned 2% rise in prices on Jan. 15.

The result: Wholesale customers couldn't get enough of such medicines as Procardia XL, the billion-dollar blockbuster used to treat angina and hypertension. It wound up logging an 11% decline in sales in the quarter. "We went to them and said, 'Hey, we're running short,' and we offered to let them look at our inventory and check us out," says a drug wholesaling executive. "But they were insistent that [we] just wanted to build up to take advantage of the price increase." A Pfizer spokesman says Pfizer simply has gotten better at "policing" against hoarding before price hikes.

More R&D. Whatever the reason, the effect was to tug down Pfizer's results. For the fourth quarter alone, sales growth for continuing operations fell to a paltry 2%, vs. 24% in the year-ago quarter. For the full year, growth from continuing operations amounted to just 9%, to $7.47 billion. Pfizer also boosted R&D spending more than rivals. These moves helped the company in two ways: Curbing the 1993 growth rate kept Pfier at a level less likely to incur "greedy drugmaker" charges from lawmakers. And pushing more sales into early January will help prop up its results for 1994, when pressure from managed-care buyers hammering away for discounts is likely to build with each quarter.

If Pfizer did manage its earnings, though, it made a critical misstep: failing to warn Wall Street. Analysts had expected a 24% rise in earnings from continuing operations for 1993, and investors reacted badly to the reported 15% gain on Jan. 19. Pfizer's share price dropped $5, to just under $63. Since then, it has recovered only to 64 or so.

Managed or not, Pfizer's prospects are far from gloomy. Salomon Bros. analyst Mariola B. Haggar figures that the company's clutch of older drugs and its new-product stream guarantee earnings growth of 12.6% in 1994—not bad in a year of diminished expectations. How that plays in Washington may be ticklish, but it's a problem Bill Steere's drug-industry rivals can only envy.

SOURCE: J. WEBER, "DID PFIZER DOCTOR ITS NUMBERS?" *BUSINESS WEEK*, FEBRUARY 14, 1994, 34.

CASE 10B Discuss the state of GAAP

Discuss the issues raised in the following *Financial Post* article, "Why accounting standards aren't standard."

WHY ACCOUNTING STANDARDS AREN'T STANDARD

Critics say Canada's Generally Accepted Accounting Principles are not only flexible but easily manipulated

The attitude of some public companies towards financial reporting may have taken a turn for the worse in Canada, with more companies stretching accounting rules beyond their indented limit to give investors a better impression of their strength.

The situation is so bad it's "starting to affect capital markets," according to an Ontario Securities Commission official who did not wish to be identified. Investors may be putting their money into the wrong companies because of what is reported, the official says.

Canadian corporate law does provide safeguards against misleading information—the company's financial reports are reviewed by an auditor, who must render an opinion as to their "fairness." But this system may not be working well, many authorities say.

"Auditing firms tend to be too accommodating of management's wishes in the way financial information is presented," says Dominic Dlouhy, president of Dlouhy Investments Ltd., Montreal. Auditors are approved by shareholders, Dlouhy adds, but they are selected by management.

Competition is another problem. An auditor may be under pressure to go along with management's presentation, or lose the auditing contract to a competing firm. That could be a hard blow in today's hotly competitive auditing-services market.

"I think the pressure on auditors started in the recession of the early 1980s," says Patricia O'Malley, partner of KPMG Peat Marwick Thorne.

"Companies found that if they pushed, they could get accounting that was a little bit more like what they wanted," she says. "And that notion tends to come back in hard times."

It's also much harder for an auditor to detect something wrong than it used to be, says John Pelton, president of Federal Industries Ltd. Accounting files are often electronic now, which makes them easier to manipulate, he says, and auditors check a big company's accounts by statistical sampling—rather than by actually adding up inventory, for example.

A Post analysis indicates three major problems with management's financial reporting:

- Wilful prettying-up of financial results by some companies, acting within the law.
- Accounting that is too sophisticated for investors to understand, and too flexible to prevent abuse.
- Reporting standards that are out of date.

"I came to the conclusion five years ago," O'Malley says, "that a conventional balance sheet is rapidly becoming not all that meaningful.

"For example, by the time a bank gets its balance sheet together, and out, the bank may have significantly changed in the way its assets, liabilities, and interest gaps have moved."

In the future, shareholders may get an "annual report" every quarter, O'Malley says, and may be able to search a database for more information filed continually by the company.

The principal concern today, though , is whether there has been a sea change in attitudes towards the disciplines embodied in Generally Accepted Accounting Principles (GAAP), which were first established in Canada in the late 1930s.

All public companies are required to use GAAP in their financial reporting. But Canadian GAAP is more flexible than, say, U.S. GAAP.

The Canadian Institute of Chartered Accountants (CICA), which writes GAAP, maintains its flexibility to enable executives to communicate nuances of financial reality within the company.

But some corporate accountants are using GAAP's suppleness to cast their companies in a rosy light.

Dorothy Sandford, the OSC's associate chief accountant, says she has noticed a major change in the last year or so. When challenged by the OSC over their too-liberal use of GAAP, Sanford says, many accountants now reply: "Where does it say I can't do that?'

GAAP's flexibility has always been there, Sandford say, "but in the past it was looked at in the right way—to give latitude to the reasonable exercise of appropriate professional judgment."

Not so much now.

"GAAP is wide enough to drive three 747s though, side by side," says Jay Gordon, a leading financial analyst. "I'm in favor of GAAP being flexible, that's reality. You can't have GAAP as a straight-jacket," he says.

"But it's too flexible," Gordon maintains. "There is no shortage of instances in which companies have flagrantly abused the flexibility that GAAP confers upon them."

Alex Milburn, chairman of the CICA Accounting Standards Board, agrees that "some accounting standards don't end up being interpreted the way the standard-setters had in mind.

"Sometimes there's literal or legalistic interpretation of what's in the CICA Handbook that people like the Ontario Securities Commission may not think is within the intent."

"I think the standards are improving," he says, "but management still has considerable latitude..." As for liberal accounting, Milburn says: "In my view the situation is no worse than in the past."

The accounting profession likes to describe GAAP as "a multi-attribute model that is always evolving." Others say GAAP is a hodge-podge of accounting doctrines imposed, one on top of the other, within the same set of rules, over the years.

GAAP has never been given a thorough overhaul in living memory. Evolution occurs because new financial issues and instruments pop up from time to time, and different professional groups want GAAP to do different things for them:

- Company accountants want GAAP flexible to give them room to manoeuvre when they write an annual report.
- Auditors want tight rules, so they can control the accountants, and not be accused of acquiescing in puffy reports.
- Financial analysts want comprehensive information that is relevant to today's values first reliability comes second.
- Lenders prefer information that is reliable first, even if it tends to be historic, to provide an indisputable foundation of "financial fact" on which to settle contract disputes.

The views of corporate accountants tend to prevail because they are the most vocal. That's one reason Canadian GAAP remains flexible experts say.

"When CICA puts a statement out for public comment they hear from the [annual report] preparers, the auditors, and the regulators, O'Malley says. "If they're lucky they'll get a couple of responses from the [report] user community..."

The reason for the mish-mash within GAAP goes far back in history.

Accounting standards were founded on the historic cost approach to valuing assets back in the 1930s, to block the games accountants played in the 1920s, when they wrote the values of a company's assets up or down, at will.

The attraction of historic cost is that it has only one value—what the company originally paid for the asset.

The historic cost approach has now partly (but not wholly) given way to more modern accounting notions. The result, some would argue, is a system that has no coherent vision of a company's value at all.

Here are some of GAAP's underlying concerns, and how they may be stretched by determined accountants:

Current Assets (which the company intends to buy and sell within a year) are accounting for at either their cost, or at today's market value, whichever is lower.

The attraction of this approach is that it's "conservative," meaning it never overstates value. But it is also inconsistent, and sometimes misleading.

Some companies own a lot of securities, which they trade within a year for a quick profit.

In a bull market, when current values rise well above original prices, the value of the firm's holdings of current assets can be understated by GAAP.

When the market collapses, a company can delay recognizing its losses by reclassifying its "current assets" as long-term assets. The only difference between current assets and long-term assets is the company's intentions towards them.

Long-term Assets are those the company intends to hold as a long-term investment rather than as a security traded in the short-term.

Long-term assets must be accounted for at their historic cost, rather than at the lower of their cost or market value.

Historic cost acts as a measure of the company's stewardship. The shareholder can see what the company originally invested in the asset, and can compare that (imperfectly) with the company's earnings.

But cost is not relevant to investors, who want to know what the company and its share are worth today. Real estate companies, in particular, can gain or lose a lot of value, along with their land and buildings, and that is not recognized by historic cost accounting.

Historic cost can also be an attractive haven for managers with low-value stocks on their hands at a time when historic cost is higher than market.

For example, marketable securities were reclassified as long-term investments in a couple of the Hees-Edper group of companies, says Alain Tuchmaier, financial services analyst.

"Basically this switch defers the decision to take a writedown, and recognize a loss," he says. The reason is that long-term assets are only written down when impairment of value is permanent. Current assets are written down when their market price falls below their historic cost.

On the other hand, some companies write their assets down farther, and faster—the "Big Bath" approach.

A Big Bath is often attractive during a bad year. The company brings all the writedowns it can see coming in the future, back into the present, and takes a single big hit.

New management may also favor a Big Bath. It gets future writedowns out of the way, and future earnings, when they occur, look better, reflecting well on the new team.

Accrual Accounting: GAAP tries to match big, infrequent expenses against the company's regular, annual revenues to smooth out earnings, which then gives the company a look (some would say a phoney look) of stability.

The cost of a factory, for example, is not charged as an expense in the year of construction, even though it may be paid in full.

The factory is carried as a long-term asset, and a small portion of its cost is charged to the revenue the factory generates every year for, say, 30 years until the cost is written down. By that time the plant needs replacing.

This process is called depreciation. Companies can cosmetically boost their earnings and their assets by depreciating the value of the factory more slowly than its working life warrants.

GAAP's hodge-podge of past and present values is further confused by assets and liabilities that may or may not exist. These entries can also become the soil in which rosy reports are grown.

Goodwill (an asset) represents money the company has paid out for, say, a subsidiary, over and above the fair value of the subsidiary's identifiable net assets.

At best, goodwill represents today"s value of future earnings that management believes it can generate from the subsidiary over and above what would be a normal return. (A "murky concept," as one expert put it.)

At worst, goodwill is the price the company foolishly paid in excess of the subsidiary's real value, which will never be recovered.

In violation of GAAP's spirit, this wasted money may be carried as an asset (suggesting it has value), which inflates the company's net worth on the balance sheet.

Management's defence may be that it expects the subsidiary to generate high earnings. It's difficult to prove such expectations unreasonable in the short term.

Deferred Tax Liabilities are so baffling some experts say they are real liabilities, other experts say they are not.

Deferred tax liabilities arise when Revenue Canada gives a company a tax break by allowing faster than normal depreciation of an asset. (Deprecation is an expense related to the wearing out of the asset. This depreciation expense can be deducted from a company's profit for tax purposes.)

Faster depreciation means more allowable expense and therefore less taxable profit and lower taxes.

A special balance sheet entry becomes necessary because the company still carries the asset on its balance sheet at its normal depreciated value, which is higher than its value after the "tax" depreciation. The extra "tax" depreciation remains hidden from view.

"Deferred tax" is entered on the "liability" side to offset the asset's value on the opposite side of the balance sheet by the amount of hidden depreciation that has occurred in the asset for tax purposes.

This special liability is necessary because the asset will run out of depreciation for tax purposes before it is fully depreciated for book purposes.

At that time, the company will have to pay more taxes to Revenue Canada than would appear necessary from the book value of the asset.

And those taxes will gradually reduce the deferred tax liability until "tax" depreciation is the same as normal depreciation.

Clearly, a deferred tax liability is not a permanent liability to Revenue Canada it is a possible increase in the rate of tax payments for which the company will be liable in the future.

The flexibility of GAAP gives rise to vigorous debate about specific accounting decisions. Here are a few examples. In every case, the accounting falls within GAAP.

Slow Writedowns

Financial services holding company Trilon Ltd. has not written down its $231 million of preferred shares of Gentra Inc. (formerly Royal Trustco Ltd.). Other major investors have written down the stock because of the widely held view that Gentra's assets, when cashed out, will not cover the preferreds.

Gentra owns a portfolio of loans that was not taken up by Royal Bank of Canada, when the bank bought the assets of Royal Trustco last year.

Trilon president George Myhal says Trilon is holding the preferreds as a "long-term investment."

"In our view there has been no permanent impairment," Myhal says.

But some financial services analysts disagree. Alain Tuchmaier says: "My analysis has led me to believe there is permanent impairment."

Myhal also says other shareholders are holding the preferred shares as marketable securities (which GAAP requires to be carried at the lower of cost or market value) and that's why other investors have written these shares down.

Tuchmaier says that three major banks and two major trust companies are holding the shares as long-term investments and have written them down because they believe their value to be permanently impaired.

"Trilon has always said it is a financial institution, not a holding company," Tuchmaier says. "If an asset appears to be impaired, a normal financial institution takes a provision [which recognizes the loss of value]."

Fast Writedowns

CAE Inc. reported a $40-million loss for the nine months ended Dec. 31, 1993, compared with earnings of $23.6 million in the same period of the previous year.

The loss arose because CAE wrote down its U.S. defence business by almost $400 million, and took a $43.6-million hit on retained earnings for changes in its accounting policies.

A large part of the writedown was elimination of goodwill, which was being amortized at normal periods of up to 40 years.

CAE chief financial officer Paul Renaud says:"Do you want to shorten the goodwill amortization period to 10 years ... and burden every year [with big writedowns] or do you take the one-time hit? I don't think you would prolong it."

CAE will find it easier to maintain its reported earnings in future, because the writedown eliminates $11 million a year annual goodwill amortization (a charge against earnings). That's very useful, one analyst says, because CAE is entering a period of tough competition in the defence industry.

CAE's action also raises questions about its goodwill. CAE once regarded its goodwill as potential profit from its U.S. defence business but now regards the amount written down as worthless. "World events have changed," Renaud says.

Asset Reclassification

Brewer John Labatt Ltd. recently reclassified some current assets as long term, which means they continue to be valued at cost rather than at market.

These assets are shares of two private Hees-Edper group companies, which invest mainly in securities of other Edper group companies. The group's stocks performed poorly in the early 1990s.

Labatt was part of the Hees-Edper group itself until last year when it was sold by parent Brascan Ltd., also part of Hees-Edper.

Labatt says it reclassified the assets because "the selling shareholder [Brascan] will assist with the orderly monetization [of the shares] ... at the company's book value over the next three to five years." This means Brascan has said it will help Labatt get the price of the shares back in full, part of the deal made when Labatt was sold.

A more conservative approach for Labatt, analysts say, would be to write the shares down to market value, and then take a profit if Brascan keeps its promise.

Lorne Stephenson, Labatt's vice-president of corporate affairs, says: "The decisions we took were all reviewed by the board and our auditors."

Slow Depreciation

Steelmaker Ivaco Ltd. of Montreal writes down its rolling-mill equipment over 25 years, although most steel companies depreciate it over 16 and 2/3 years. Analyst Jay Gordon says Ivaco's rolling-mill equipment is "the same as everybody else's."

Slow depreciation reduces the annual charge against earnings, leaving both earnings and assets looking higher. An Ivaco official declined to explain the company's practice.

Gordon adds: "Given the rate at which steel-making equipment has been changing in the last 10–15 years, even 16 and 2/3 years is probably twice as long [a depreciation period] as is realistic."

SOURCE: P. MATHIAS, "WHY ACCOUNTING STANDARDS AREN'T STANDARD," *THE FINANCIAL POST*, APRIL 2, 1994, S16–17.

NOTES

1. Canadian Institute of Chartered Accountants, "Introduction to Accounting Recommendations," in *CICA Handbook* (Toronto: Canadian Institute of Chartered Accountants, version in effect June 30, 1994), 6.
2. See M. Gibbins and A.K. Mason, *Professional Judgment in Financial Reporting* (Toronto: Canadian Institute of Chartered Accountants, 1988), Chapter 5. Reprinted by permission of the Canadian Institute of Chartered Accountants, Toronto, Canada.
3. *Financial Reporting in Canada 1993* (Toronto: Canadian Institute of Chartered Accountants, 1993), 92.
4. Ibid.
5. Ibid.
6. Ibid.
7. *Effects of changing to the annual weighted average method*: cost of goods sold expense would go up $892, so net income would decline by 70% of that, $624. Income tax expense and liability would go down by the other 30%, $268. Working capital would go down by $892 (inventory asset decline) and up by $268 (income tax liability decline) for a net decrease of $624, the same as the net income decline. There is no immediate effect on cash or cash flow.

Effect of changing to the periodic LIFO method: the figures, in the same order as above, are up $1,800, decline $1,260, decline $540, down by $1,800, and up by $540 for net decrease of $1,260. No cash effect.

Effects of changing to the perpetual LIFO method: the figures, in the same order again, are up $700, decline $490, decline $210, down by $700, and up $210 for a net decrease of $490. No cash effect.

8. *Financial Reporting in Canada 1993*, 92.
9. Ibid.
10. Ibid.
11. Ibid.
12. Ibid.

Illustration of sum-of-the-year's digits amortization. The variables needed to compute amortization using this method are:

a. Cost.
b. Estimated salvage value.
c. Estimated life of the asset—calculated in years.
d. The sum of the years—for example, for a three-year life:
   Sum = 1 + 2 + 3 = 6
e. Number of years of life remaining.

The formula for computing sum-of-the-years'-digits amortization is:
Amortization for the year = (C – S) (N / SYD)
Where: Cost (C) and salvage (S) are as usually defined
N = number of useful years remaining
SYD = sum of years' digits

Let's look again at the delivery truck and compute the annual amortization:

- Cost = $5,000
- Salvage value = $1,000
- Years of life = 5
- Sum of the years = 5 + 4 + 3 + 2 + 1 = 15

Amortization for year 1 = ($5,000 – $1,000) × (5 / 15) = $1,333.33
Amortization for year 2 = ($5,000 – $1,000) × (4 / 15) = $1,066.67
Amortization for year 3 = ($5,000 – $1,000) × (3 / 15) = $ 800.00
Amortization for year 4 = ($5,000 – $1,000) × (2 / 15) = $ 533.33
Amortization for year 5 = ($5,000 – $1,000) × (1 / 15) = $ 266.67
$4,000.00

13. *Financial Reporting in Canada 1993*, 154.
14. Ibid.
15. Amortization can affect working capital accounts if amortization expense is part of the cost of goods manufactured and some of those goods are in the inventory asset at the end of the year. This complication will not be included in this book, since it is better dealt with in management accounting and more advanced financial accounting courses.
16. *Financial Reporting in Canada 1993*, 120.
17. For more ideas about managers' motivations, see R.L. Watts and J.L. Zimmerman, *Positive Accounting Theory* (Englewood Cliffs, N.J.: Prentice–Hall, 1986), 208, 216, 235.

APPENDIX I

FINANCIAL STATEMENTS OF THE NORTH WEST COMPANY INC.

The January 29, 1994, financial statements of The North West Company, based in Winnipeg, are included in the following pages. To introduce them, here are a "Profile" and a "History" written by the company's Corporate Communications Office March 30, 1994.

THE NORTH WEST COMPANY: PROFILE

- The North West Company is the dominant retailer in Canada's north, with more than 150 retail outlets located in all provinces except P.E.I., New Brunswick, and Nova Scotia. Alaskan operations include 20 stores, operating as AC Value Centers.
- Northern stores operate in markets with populations from 500 to 5,000. A typical store is 7,500 square feet in size and offers a broad assortment of food, family apparel, housewares, appliances, outdoor products, and special services like cheque cashing, catalogue ordering, and money transfers. Some Northern stores offer Pizza Hut and KFC products in the company's Quickstop convenience outlets.
- The North West Company operates complementary businesses that apply its unique heritage and knowledge of the North. These include the largest Inuit Art Marketing Service in North America; Hudson's Bay Blanket Division; Fur Marketing Division; and Transport Igloolik, which operates a leading shipping service in the eastern Arctic.
- The North West Company has 3,788 employees in Canada and 509 in Alaska and is the largest employer of native people in Canada outside of the federal government. In September 1992, The North West Company took possession of a 360,000 square foot Retail Service Centre in Winnipeg. Opened in April 1993 after extensive technological upgrading, the centre generates more than 175 jobs for Manitobans.
- The North West Company has been consistently profitable, and, despite the current recessionary environment, achieved record earnings of $17.2 million in 1993.
- Total revenues last year were $548.7 million, placing The North West Company within the 15 largest companies headquartered in Manitoba.
- The company's goal is to develop existing operations to their full potential while successfully expanding into similar markets. In September 1992, The North West Company announced the acquisition of Alaska Commercial Company, the largest retail chain in rural Alaska. Through an agreement between The North West Company and KNI Retail A/S (Greenland's largest retail chain), Northern's *Selections* catalogue is being translated and distributed in Greenland, with orders filled and shipped from the Winnipeg Retail Service Centre.

THE NORTH WEST COMPANY: HISTORY

- The North West Company can trace its roots back to the first trading post in North America, established at Waskaganish on the shores of James Bay in 1668 (there is a Northern store operating there today!)
- The original North West Company was a partnership of Montreal-based entrepreneurial traders formed in 1779.
- In 1821, the North West Company and Hudson's Bay Company amalgamated under the Hudson's Bay Company name, creating a fur trading monopoly that covered one-quarter of North America.
- Throughout the 1800s and into this century, the entreprise continued as the Northern Department, and then the Northern Stores

Division, of Hudson's Bay Company.

- In 1987, the Northern Stores Division was acquired by a group of investors including 415 employees.
- In 1990, the company renewed its link to the past and re-established its identity as an independent retailer by changing its corporate name to The North West Company, and the trading name of its retail operations to Northern.
- The North West Company became a public company in the fall of 1990 by listing its shares on the Winnipeg and Toronto stock exchanges.
- "Enterprise '95," a long-range strategic plan completed in 1991, focused The North West Company's business on food, family apparel, and general merchandise retailing in small northern communities.
- As part of this strategic direction, the company has been divesting its stores in larger or less remote markets and developing its core business by adding new products, services, stores, and systems in the North.

The "Financial Highlights" page from the 1993 annual report (containing data to January 29, 1994) is reproduced near the beginning of Chapter 5. (As noted in Section 9.4, the company refers to the 52 weeks ended January 29, 1994, as 1993, and that practice has been followed in this book, too.) Other excerpts from the annual report are reprinted in the following pages in the order they appeared in the report:

- *"Management's Discussion and Analysis";*
- *"Management's Responsibility for Financial Statements";*
- *"Auditors' Report";*
- *The consolidated financial statements and their notes;*
- *"Six-year Financial Summary";*
- *"Shareholder Information."*

MANAGEMENT'S DISCUSSION AND ANALYSIS

◆ ◆ ◆ ◆ ◆

1993 RESULTS

The North West Company improved earnings by 14.8% in 1993 to $17.2 million with a 16.1% increase in revenue to $549 million.

The economy made a modest recovery in southern Canada as a result of increased exports of goods and services and lower interest rates. The decline in cross-border shopping due to a lower Canadian dollar provided stimulus to retail sales in large markets which had been hardest hit during the last two years. The G.D.P. estimate for 1993 was 2.4% following a 0.7% increase in 1992 and after shrinking 1.7% in 1991. The recovery has been weaker in northern Canada because of restructuring in the resource sector and high unemployment in many northern communities.

Revenue for the year ending January 29, 1994 (fiscal 1993) included 52 weeks of sales versus 53 weeks in the previous fiscal year. Certain comparative amounts related to discontinued operations have been restated.

The major corporate highlights of 1993 include:

- Revenues for the year at $549 million increased 16.1% over 1992;
- Earnings from Canadian operations increased $1 million or 7.1%;
- Revenue growth in comparable Northern operations increased 1.0%;
- Earnings before interest and taxes (EBIT) improved 4.4% in Canadian operations with a rate improvement of 0.2%;
- EBIT from Alaskan operations at $4.0 million exceeded our plan for the year;
- Shipping operations produced a 17.1% improvement in EBIT.

Revenue for 1993 included $97.7 million from Alaskan operations compared to $25.1 million contributed last year after these operations were acquired in November 1992. Canadian operations delivered a 0.8% increase in revenue. Northern stores sales were flat with last year, while a 19.9% increase was generated in Diversified Business and revenues from Shipping operations advanced 37.8%.

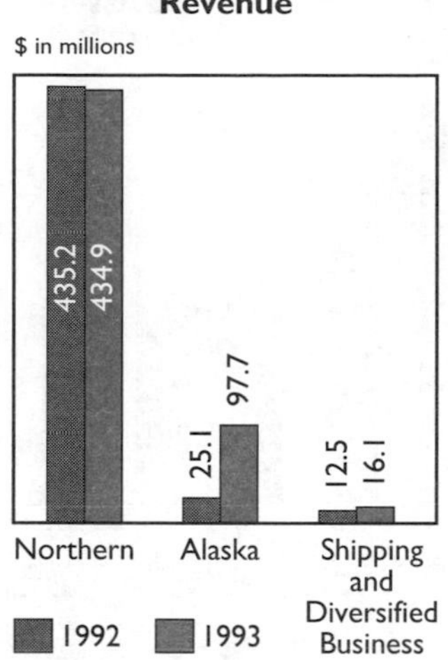

Northern stores operations in Canada accounted for 79.3% of total revenue. Alaskan operations contributed 17.8% of revenue while Shipping and Diversified Business made up 1.6% and 1.3% of the revenue respectively.

EBIT was $38.1 million or 6.9% of revenue compared to $33.4 million or 7.1% of revenue last year. The improvement in earnings was primarily due to the full year contribution from Alaskan operations which generated $4.0 million in EBIT in 1993 on revenue of $97.7 million, compared to $0.8 million on $25.1 million in 1992. Canadian operations increased EBIT to $34.0 million or 7.5% of revenue, versus $32.6 million or 7.3% of revenue last year. The EBIT rate improved by 0.2% in Canadian operations due to improved gross margin rates. This more than offset the increase in the expense rate from higher occupancy costs of expanded and renovated stores. Alaskan operations yielded an EBIT rate of 4.1% which is lower than Canadian operations but in line with our expectations based on a higher percentage of leased assets.

Expenses for the year increased 7.0% after adjusting for the extra week in 1992. Savings in distribution costs were less than planned due to delays experienced in the installation of some labor saving features in the new Winnipeg Retail Service Centre. Debt losses were $1.1 million, or 48.3% higher than last year as a result of financial difficulties encountered by several First Nation bands.

Two unusual items were charged against this year's EBIT. On May 3, 1993, the Obedjiwan, Quebec store was completely lost to fire. A new 7,000 sq. ft. store with an estimated cost of $1.7 million is expected to open in October 1994. The Company incurred a loss of $396,000 in the second quarter of 1993, writing off the cost of the store. The second item was a $807,000 cost related to closing the Montreal buying office and relocating it to Winnipeg in 1993.

Corporate overhead costs increased by 6.2% in 1992. Major initiatives included the continued development of the stores training program, consulting costs related to information systems development and integration problems at the Winnipeg Retail Service Centre, and the buying office relocation from Montreal to Winnipeg.

Canadian operations had 3,788 employees at year-end compared to 3,649 last year. There were 509 employees in Alaska at year end, compared to 467 last year.

Interest expense at $8.5 million was 7.6% lower than 1992 due to the reduced cost of borrowing. The average cost of debt decreased to 7.34% from 8.46% in 1992. Average debt outstanding during the year was $115.1 million, 4.0% higher than 1992. Consolidated debt at the end of January 1994 was $125.0 million, which was 16.5% higher than a year earlier, while net assets employed increased 12.3% to $272.6 million.

The Company's effective income tax rate increased to 42.0% from 39.3% as a result of the increased taxable earning in higher tax jurisdictions. This new rate is expected to continue in 1994. The provision for income taxes of $12.4 million includes $2,229,000 in deferred taxes.

LIQUIDITY AND CAPITAL RESOURCES

On a consolidated basis, the Company had $125 million in debt and $148 million in equity at the end of the year with a debt-to-equity ratio of 46:54 versus 44:56 at January 30, 1993. The Company re-negotiated its Canadian term facilities, increasing the committed amount from $65 million to $80 million and arranged a $10 million facility for Alaska Commercial Company. The Company generated cash flow from operations of $15.5 million in 1993 compared to $18.1 million in 1992.

Capital Structures

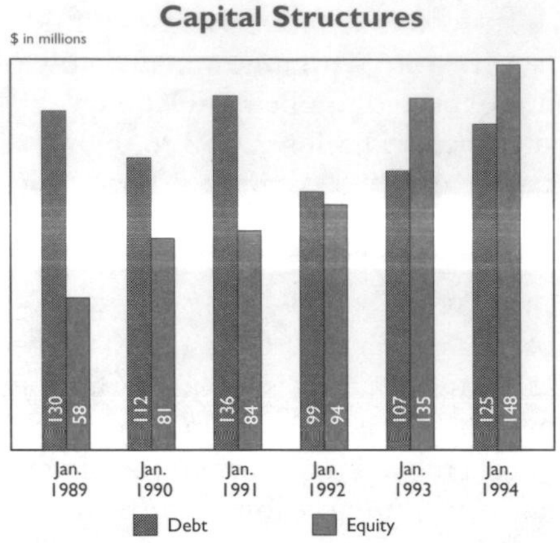

Return on Net Assets and Equity

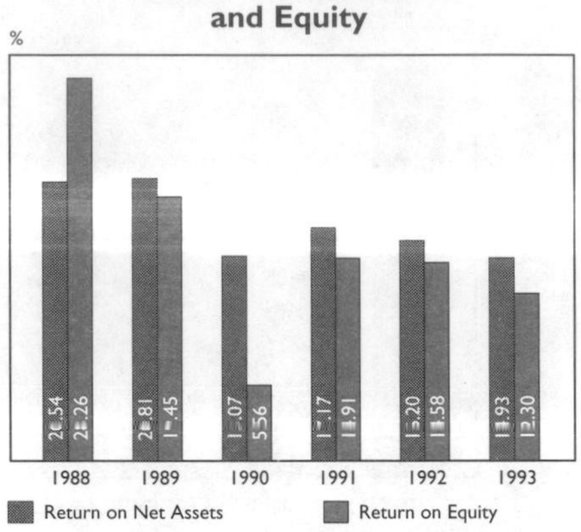

The number of shares outstanding at January 29, 1994, was 16,164,417, while the average shares outstanding for 1993 was 16,129,775 before dilution and 16,233,775 after dilution. There were 348,000 options outstanding which have been issued to officers at exercise prices between $6.75 and $18.75, of which 104,000 have been vested.

Shareholder's Equity

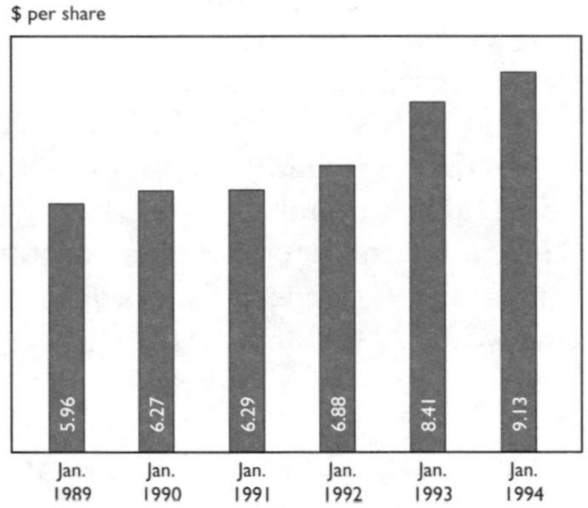

The book value per share at year end was $9.13 increasing $0.72 or 8.6% over last year.

The Company produced a return on net assets (RONA) of 14.93% in 1993 compared to 16.20% in 1992. Return on equity (ROE) was 12.30% versus 14.58% in 1992.

EBIT covered interest expense 4.50 times, up from 3.64 last year.

Canadian Operations

Cash on hand and in transit, at $7.3 million, was $4.6 million less than last year due to lower levels of funds in transit to the stores to accommodate the cashing of government and payroll cheques.

Accounts receivables levels increased 1.5% during the year and are consistent with increases in revenue.

Capital expenditures totaled $26.4 million during the year with $2.5 million spent to complete the new Winnipeg Retail Service Centre and on transportation equipment, $20.2 million on existing store replacements and extensions, $2.1

Capital Expenditures

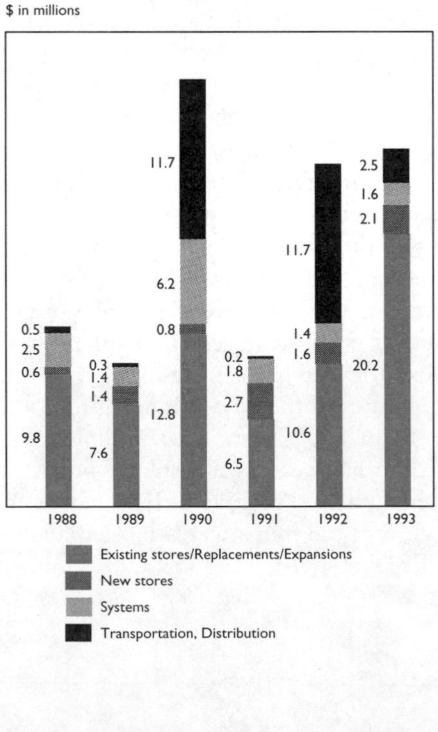

million on new stores and $1.6 million on systems. Capital spending is expected to be $20 million in 1994. Major components are the planned purchase or building of four new stores, renovating or replacing 15 existing stores, and the rollout of *KFC* and *Pizza Hut Quickstop* outlets.

- Existing Stores/Replacements/Expansions
- New Stores
- Systems
- Transportation, Distribution

Northern Stores

All Northern figures for 1992 have been restated to recognize the restatement of nine former Junior Department Stores (JDS) stores to continuing operation effective February 1993.

Revenue from Northern stores at $435 million was flat with last year (1.0% increase on a comparable 52-week basis), while earnings before interest and taxes were up slightly at $32.5 million, compared to $31.3 million in 1992. Food sales increased 5.3% while general merchandise sales slipped by 4.3%, both on a comparable 52-week basis.

Nine former JDS stores were repositioned with Northern effective February 1993. While revenue in this group of stores decreased by 5.6% from 1992 on a comparable 52-week basis, the cash flow contribution was positive and unchanged from last year.

Comparable store revenues increased 6.8% in the first quarter compared to the prior year, 3.0% in the second quarter, 2.2% in the third quarter, and down 3.9% in the fourth quarter. Comparable store revenues were adversely affected in the fourth quarter by the change in the timing of the distribution of federal government child tax credits which were paid on a monthly basis in 1993 instead of the lump sum amount payment in November 1992. This, coupled with difficult economic conditions left little discretionary income available for the purchase of big ticket goods such as snowmobiles, furniture and home entertainment products. In total, Northern hardline sales were down 25% in November 1993 compared to November 1992.

Sales per selling square foot slipped to $876 for food ($878 in 1992) and $257 for general merchandise ($276 in 1992). The decrease in food is attributable to the additional food selling space added late in the year, including a new 14,300 sq. ft. (selling) store in Hay River and two other smaller stores that opened in the fourth quarter. The decline in general merchandise sales per square foot was directly related to poor sales, primarily in the hardlines group. Inventory turnover in the stores, at 4.19 turns, increased over the 3.97 turns in 1992.

Gross margin rates improved in the general merchandise primarily as the impact of the new zone pricing and cost land system took effect. Food margin rates improved significantly as a result of increased rebates and better buying through the expanded use of our warehousing facilities in Winnipeg and Montreal.

One of the Company's key initiatives is to be in stock at all times in basic merchandise. Our customers have few alternatives for basic needs and it is essential to maintain consistent high in-stock levels of basic goods to ensure customer satisfaction and loyalty. Inventory levels were not consistently maintained, especially during the fall season due to numerous changes in the procurement channel. These interruptions in the flow of goods to stores resulted in lower general merchandise stock levels throughout the critical early fall season which contributed to weak sales performance during August and September. Inventory levels at the end of the year were back in line with expectations and 0.4% higher than year end 1992 on a comparable basis.

EBIT margins advanced to 7.5% from 7.2% in 1992 due to improved gross margin rates which offset higher expense rates. Expense rates increased due to increased occupancy costs of store replacements in Nelson House, Sandy Lake and other renovations to existing facilities as well as higher debt losses.

Heavy debt losses were experienced in six communities where First Nation bands ran into financial difficulties. Arrangements have been made subsequent to the year end to repay the majority of the large balances outstanding.

Three stores in new communities were opened during 1993. The Hay River food store was the largest addition in November 1993, a result of the takeover of the lease on this 14,300 sq. ft. (selling) food store. There were no store closures during the year. The Obedjiwan store, lost to fire in May

1993, reduced selling square footage by 1,900 sq. ft. Total selling square footage was increased to 950,000 sq. ft. from 910,000 sq. ft.

Support Activities

Winnipeg Retail Service Centre

Our new 350,000 sq. ft. service centre, which opened in the spring of 1993 is close to full operation using radio frequency and paperless picking devices in a sophisticated systems environment. With its modern materials handling capabilities, this facility will be able to deliver superior service to the stores at a greatly reduced operating cost. While anticipated savings were not realized in 1993 due to transitional problems, this centre will reduce distribution costs by $1.2 million in 1994.

Point-of-Sale Systems

Point-of-sale systems have been installed in all large and medium sized stores accounting for approximately 80% of total revenue. All but two stores are using a PC-based in-store accounts receivable system.

Shipping and Diversified Business

Shipping earnings before interest and taxes increased by 17.1% to $1,114,000 from $951,000 last year on revenues of $8.8 million. Revenue increased 37.8% as a result of increased third party tonnage carried on the Arctic sealift. To take advantage of this demand, a second vessel was chartered for three months over the summer and fall. This also made it possible to successfully bid on federal government contracts for Foxe Basin and Iqaluit zones. While cargo carried into the Arctic increased, operating profits improved at a slower rate due to the higher costs of chartering the second vessel.

Revenues in our Diversified Business group, which includes ten Fur Marketing stores, the Inuit Art Marketing Service and the Blanket Division, reported sales of $7.3 million compared to $6.1 million last year and an operating profit of $407,000 versus $299,000 in 1992. Fur Marketing opened a third *Trading Post* concept gift and quality northern clothing store in November 1993. Outlets are now in Yellowknife, Thompson and Whitehorse. The Fort McMurray, Alberta branch closed in February 1994. Inuit Art and Blanket operations both reported improved earnings in 1993 which were partially offset by a decline in earnings from Fur Marketing stores.

Alaskan Operations

(all dollars in Canadian equivalents)

Alaska Commercial Company (AC Company) completed its first full year of operations under The North West Company ownership. In this year of transition, the management team developed their strategic business plan, laying out a clear direction to improved customer satisfaction and financial performance.

New buying arrangements were negotiated with vendors, allowing AC Company to take a more aggressive stance reducing prices on key items to increase sales while maintaining margins and improving their competitive image with customers in rural Alaska. A *Tomorrow Store* concept was developed with the first store opened in St. Mary's in November 1993. Renovations were completed in stores in McGrath and Fort Yukon during the year. The trading logo was changed to *AC Value Center* to reflect the new competitive positioning.

Competition in AC Company's markets increased in 1993 with the announcement by Carr-Gottstein, an Anchorage-based food retailer and wholesaler, that they will enter our markets with a new 42,500 sq. ft. Eagle store in Dutch Harbor in March 1994. Carr-Gottstein will also be buying stores in Nome and Kotzebue and converting them to Eagle stores. AC Company will accelerate capital expenditure programs in 1994 to protect key markets and aggressively meet the challenge.

At January 29, 1994 AC Company employed net assets of $34.0 million compared to $23.3 million last year, with $13.1 million in bank debt versus $10.6 million. Shareholders' equity increased to $18.3 million from $11.0 million in the previous year.

Comparable stores sales increased 2.1% including a 9.1% increase in the fourth quarter. Overall sales were negatively impacted by a poor fishing season in two key locations, Dutch Harbour and Dillingham.

Earnings before interest and taxes for the 52 weeks ending January 29, 1994 were $4.0 million on revenues of $97.7 million compared to $0.8

million for the 14 weeks ending January 30, 1993 on revenues of $25.1 million. Earnings in Alaska were strongest in the second quarter at $1.7 million reflecting the seasonal nature of rural Alaska's fishing and tourism economy. The traditional Christmas surge produced fourth quarter operating profits of $1.3 million. EBIT margins of 4.1% of sales and other revenue were less than the 7.5% earned in Canada. Gross profit margins earned on sales in Alaska are similar to those achieved in Northern stores, however staff and occupancy costs are higher than Canadian operations.

Capital expenditures in 1993 of $6.9 million included replacement of the old 6,200 sq. ft. store in St. Mary's with 10,000 sq. ft. store opened November 1993; renovations to the stores in McGrath and Fort Yukon, and work in progress on replacement stores in Cordova (20,000 sq. ft. opened April 14, 1994), and Dutch Harbour (33,000 sq. ft. opening June 10, 1994). In February 1994 the Dillingham store and adjacent land were acquired from the landlord to enable AC Company to build a new 20,000 sq. ft. food store and renovate the existing facility for expanded general merchandise selling space.

Capital spending in 1994 is expected to be approximately $19 million.

RISKS

The Company is exposed to the normal business risks of the retail marketplace. Our goods and services are not dependent on any one supplier nor is our success based on any one store or cluster of stores.

Many of our Canadian Aboriginal customers are dependent on the continuation of basic social support programs. We expect to see a continued shift towards Aboriginal self government which the Company believes is in the best interest of the Aboriginal people of Canada.

The recent announcement by some leading American retailers to expand into Canada will increase the competitive intensity in rural and remote markets. Retailers in large markets try to attract customers from secondary markets while retailers in secondary markets will become more aggressive in trying to attract customers from rural and remote markets. Responding with an appropriate marketing strategy to minimize outshopping is a major part of our 1994 marketing plan. These new competitors will put pressure on all retailers to improve efficiencies or be faced with declining market share and earnings.

PROSPECTS FOR 1994

Management expects earnings to improve in 1994 as many of the initiatives undertaken over the last few years will result in increased sales and productivity in new, replacement and expanded stores.

The addition of 31,000 sq. ft. of incremental selling space in Canada in the spring season and 21,000 sq. ft. in Alaska as a result of replacement stores will provide an opportunity to generate strong sales increases in 1994.

The Winnipeg Retail Service Centre is expected to achieve planned benefits. The centralization and upgrading of our buying operations will produce improved margins and a better flow of goods.

MANAGEMENT'S RESPONSIBILITY FOR FINANCIAL STATEMENTS

The management of The North West Company Inc. is responsible for the integrity of the accompanying financial statements and all other information in this annual report. The consolidated financial statements have been prepared by management in accordance with generally accepted accounting principles in Canada and include certain amounts that are based on the best estimates and judgement by management.

In order to meet its responsibility and ensure integrity of financial reporting, management maintains accounting systems and appropriate internal controls and an internal audit function designed to provide reasonable assurance that assets are safeguarded, transactions are authorized and recorded and that the financial records are reliable.

Final responsibility for the financial statements and their presentation to shareholders rests with the Board of Directors. The Audit Committee of the Board, consisting of outside directors, meets periodically with management and with the internal and external auditors to review the audit results, internal controls and accounting policies. The Audit Committee meets separately with management and the Company's external auditors, Price Waterhouse, to review the financial statements and recommend approval by the Board of Directors.

Price Waterhouse, an independent firm of auditors appointed by the shareholders, have completed their audits and submitted their report as follows.

Ian Sutherland
President and Chief Executive Officer

Gary V. Eggertson
Vice-President, Finance and Administration

March 11, 1994

AUDITORS' REPORT

To the Shareholders of The North West Company Inc.

We have audited the consolidated balance sheets of The North West Company Inc. as at January 29, 1994, and January 30, 1993, and the consolidated statements of earnings and retained earnings and changes in financial position for the years then ended. These financial statements are the responsibility of the Company's management. Our responsibility is to express an opinion on these financial statements based on our audits.

We conducted our audits in accordance with generally accepted auditing standards. Those standards require that we plan and perform an audit to obtain reasonable assurance whether the financial statements are free of material misstatement. An audit includes examining, on a test basis, evidence supporting the amounts and disclosures in the financial statements. An audit also includes assessing the accounting principles used and significant estimates made by management, as well as evaluating the overall financial statement presentation.

In our opinion, these consolidated financial statements present fairly, in all material respects, the financial position of the Company as at January 29, 1994, and January 30, 1993, and the results of its operations and the changes in its financial position for the years then ended in accordance with generally accepted accounting principles.

Price Waterhouse
Chartered Accountants
Winnipeg, Canada

March 11, 1994

CONSOLIDATED BALANCE SHEET

(in thousands of Canadian dollars)	*January 29, 1994*	*January 30, 1993*
Assets		
Current assets		
Cash	$7,136	$13,385
Accounts receivable	53,034	51,970
Inventories	119,948	107,367
Prepaid expenses	2,617	1,764
	182,735	174,486
Fixed assets (Note 2)	145,255	122,024
Other assets (Note 3)	3,065	1,902
	$331,055	$298,412
Liabilities		
Current liabilities		
Bank advances and short-term notes (Note 4)	$26,640	$33,445
Accounts payable and accrued	43,181	44,545
Income taxes payable	3,164	1,664
Current portion of long-term debt (Note 5)	10,000	7,488
	83,285	87,142
Long-term debt (Note 5)	88,336	66,382
Deferred income taxes	11,782	9,542
	183,403	163,066
Shareholders' Equity		
Share capital (Note 6)	$100,547	$100,012
Retained earnings	46,701	35,349
Cumulative translation adjustment (Note 7)	404	(15)
	147,652	135,346
	$331,055	$298,412

Approved by the Board — Director — Director

CONSOLIDATED STATEMENT OF EARNINGS AND RETAINED EARNINGS

(in thousands of Canadian dollars)	*52 weeks ended January 29, 1994*	*53 weeks ended January 30, 1993*
Sales and other revenue	$548,679	$472,710
Cost of sales, selling and administrative expenses	(500,526)	(431,466)
Depreciation and amortization	(10,099)	(7,873)
Operating profit from continuing operations	$ 38,054	33,371
Interest, including interest on long-term debt of $5,660 (1993 $4,685)	(8,457)	(9,157)
Earnings from continuing operations before provision for income taxes	29,597	24,214
Provisions for income taxes including deferred of $2,229 (1993 $2,090) (Note 8)	(12,435)	(9,507)
Earnings from continuing operations	17,162	14,707
Loss from reinstated operations charged to provision	—	247
Earnings for the year	17,162	14,954
Retained earnings, beginning of year	35,349	25,577
Dividends	(5,810)	(5,182)
Retained earnings, end of year	$ 46,701	$ 35,349
Earnings per share (Note 9)		
Basic	$ 1.06	$ 1.06
Fully diluted	$ 1.06	$ 1.05

CONSOLIDATED STATEMENT OF CHANGES IN FINANCIAL POSITION

(in thousands of Canadian dollars)	*52 weeks ended January 29, 1994*	*53 weeks ended January 30, 1993*
Cash provided by (used in)		
Operating Activities		
Earnings for the year	$ 17,162	$ 14,954
Non-cash items		
Depreciation and amortization	10,099	7,873
Deferred income taxes	2,229	2,090
(Gain) loss on disposal of fixed assets	(207)	143
Changes in non-cash working capital components	(13,754)	(11,287)
Continuing operations	15,529	13,773
Discontinuing operations	—	4,350
Operating activities	15,529	18,123
Investing Activities		
Alaskan acquisition (Note 10)	—	(8,755)
Purchase of fixed assets	(33,304)	(26,370)
Proceeds from sale of fixed assets	762	2,703
Other assets	(1,163)	(332)
Investing activities	(33,705)	(32,754)
Financing Activities		
Issue of share capital	535	31,447
Proceeds of long-term debt	36,746	23,258
Repayment of long-term debt	(12,181)	(7,655)
Financing activities	25,100	47,050
Dividends	(5,804)	(4,814)
Changes in Cash Position	1,120	27,605
Effect of currency translation adjustment	(564)	(15)
Cash position, beginning of year	(20,060)	(47,650)
Cash Position, End of Year	$(19,504)	$(20,060)
Cash Position is Comprised of		
Cash	$ 7,136	$ 13,385
Bank advances and short-term notes	(26,640)	(33,445)
	$(19,504)	$(20,060)

NOTES TO CONSOLIDATED FINANCIAL STATEMENTS
JANUARY 29, 1994

1. Significant Accounting Policies

General
These consolidated financial statements have been prepared by management in accordance with generally accepted accounting principles in Canada and include the accounts of the Company and its subsidiaries, all of which are wholly owned. All significant intercompany amounts and transactions have been eliminated in consolidation.

Accounts Receivable
In accordance with recognized retail industry practice, accounts receivable classified as current assets include customer installment accounts of which a portion will not become due within one year.

Inventories
Inventories are valued at the lower of cost and net realizable value less normal profit margins. The cost of inventories is determined primarily using the retail method of accounting, with the cost method used in the smaller stores.

Fixed Assets
Fixed assets are stated at cost. Depreciation is provided using the straight-line method at rates which will fully depreciate the assets over their estimated useful lives, as follows:

Buildings	2% – 5%
Leasehold improvements	5% – 20%
Fixtures and equipment	8% – 20%
Transportation equipment	6% – 20%

Other Assets
Other assets include prepayments under lease agreements. These amounts will be amortized over their respective lease terms.

Pensions in Canada
Current service costs under the Company's pension plans are charged to operations as they accrue. The difference between the market value of pension fund assets and the actuarially determined present value of accrued pension obligations, as well as experience gains and losses, are amortized over the expected average remaining service life of the employee group. Actuarial valuations are calculated using the projected benefit method pro-rated on services, based on management's best estimate of future events.

Profit Sharing Plan in Alaska
The company sponsors a deferred compensation plan covering substantially all employees. Under the terms of the plan, the Company is obligated to make a 50% matching contribution up to 3% of eligible compensation. In addition, the Company makes discretionary contributions on behalf of all employees based on eligible compensation. Contributions to this plan are expensed as incurred.

Foreign Currency Translation
The accounts of Alaskan operations have been translated into Canadian dollars as follows: assets and liabilities, at the year-end exchange rate; revenues and expenses, at the average exchange rate for the period. Foreign exchange gains or losses arising from translation are deferred and included in a separate component of shareholders' equity as a cumulative translation adjustment.

2. Fixed Assets

(in thousands of Canadian dollars)

	1994		1993	
	Cost	Accumulated Depreciation and Amortization	Cost	Accumulated Depreciation and Amortization
Land	$ 4,010	$ —	$ 3,675	$ —
Buildings and leasehold improvements	102,722	15,900	84,837	12,153
Fixtures and equipment	62,704	19,569	49,032	14,738
Transportation equipment	15,602	4,314	14,601	3,230
	$185,038	$ 39,783	$152,145	$ 30,121
Net Book Value		$145,255		$122,024

3. Other Assets

(in thousands of Canadian dollars)

	1994	1993
Deferred pension costs	$1,894	$1,467
Prepayments under lease agreements	1,171	435
	$3,065	$1,902

4. Bank Advances and Short-Term Notes

The Company has Canadian operating lines of credit of $80,000,000. As security, the Company has given an assignment of accounts receivable, inventories and a second fixed and floating charge debenture on all fixed and other assets.

The Alaskan operation has an operating line of credit of $4,000,000 US secured by assignments of accounts receivable and inventories. In addition, the Company has guaranteed this operating line of credit.

5. Long-Term Debt

(in thousands of Canadian dollars)

	1994	1993
Canadian term loans	$80,000	$65,000
U.S. term loans	10,000	5,515
Manitoba Development Corporation	5,000	2,813
U.S. obligations under capital lease	2,221	—
Other long-term liabilities	1,115	542
	98,336	73,870
Less: Current portion	(10,000)	(7,488)
	$88,336	$66,382

Canadian chartered bank term loans bearing interest at an average rate of 7.5% (1993 – 8.4%) are repayable $10,000,000 annually and are secured by a first fixed and floating charge debenture against all fixed assets, a first mortgage on the Company's home office, a ship mortgage on the M.V. Aivik and a second charge against accounts receivable and inventories.

U.S. bank term loans, bearing interest at an average rate of 5.2%, are secured by the Company's guarantee and pledge of its Alaska Commercial Company shares. The U.S. bank term loans are repayable $1,000,000 on January 31, 1998; $2,000,000 on January 31, 1999 and on January 31, 2000; and $5,000,000 on January 31, 2001.

The Manitoba Development Corporation loan, provided to assist in the financing of the new Winnipeg Retail Service Centre, bears interest at the rate charged by the Manitoba Government to Crown Corporations and is repayable in four equal annual payments ending December 31, 2003. The loan is secured by a first fixed charge against the leasehold title to the land, a first fixed charge against the building, and a first fixed charge on all present and future processing equipment connected with the project. Interest is forgiven if the Company attains agreed upon annual job creation targets. The Company anticipates that the agreed targets will be met, accordingly, no interest has been accrued.

The U.S. obligation under a capital lease is repayable in blended principal and interest payments of $200,000 US annually. The obligation will be fully repaid on October 31, 2013.

6. Share Capital

Authorized
The Company has an unlimited number of common shares.

(in thousands)	1994 No. of Shares	1994 Share Capital	1993 No. of Shares	1993 Share Capital
Issued				
Class A shares				
Balance, beginning of year	—	—	66	$ 330
Converted to common shares	—	—	(66)	(330)
Balance, end of year	—	—	—	—
Common shares				
Balance, beginning of year	16,097	$100,012	13,607	$ 68,225
Issued				
For cash upon special warrants issue	—	—	2,000	28,613
For cash upon exercise of shareholder options	—	—	323	1,615
Officers share purchase plan	—	—	74	1,061
Officers stock option plan	67	535	17	158
On conversion of class A shares	—	—	66	330
3% stock dividend on exercise of shareholder options	—	—	10	10
Balance, end of year	16,164	$100,547	16,097	$100,012
Total issued shares	16,164	$100,547	16,097	$100,012

Officers stock option plan
From time to time the Board has granted options to certain officers of the Company at the market value of the common shares at that time.

During the year, the Board of Directors approved the following options to officers: 15,000 options at an exercise price of $18.25 with 3,000 options vesting annually commencing August 3, 1994 and expiring August 3, 1999; and 75,000 options at an exercise price of $18.75 with 15,000 options vesting annually commencing November 1, 1994 and expiring November 1, 1999.

Officer stock option transactions were as follows:

	1994	1993
Outstanding, beginning of year	377,500	250,000
Granted	90,000	145,000
Exercised	(67,500)	(17,500)
Cancelled	(52,000)	—
Outstanding, end of year	348,000	377,500

January 29, 1994, 348,000 options issued to nine officers of the Company to acquire common shares were outstanding. Of these, 104,000 options were vested and subject to expiry as follows:

	Number of Shares	
	Outstanding	*Vested*
April 1, 1995, at $9.00 per share	128,000	68,000
April 1, 1995, at $6.75 per share	25,000	15,000
March 19, 1998, at $14.125 per share	105,000	21,000
August 3, 1999, at $18.25 per share	15,000	—
November 1, 1999, at $18.75 per share	75,000	—
	348,000	104,000

7. Cumulative Translation Agreement

The cumulative translation adjustment account represents the net changes due to exchange rate fluctuations in the equivalent Canadian dollar book values of the Company's net investment in self-sustaining Alaskan operations since the date of acquisition. The change in this account in 1994 is attributable to the strengthening of the U.S. dollar relative to the Canadian dollar during the year.

8. Income Taxes

The Company's effective income tax rate is determined as follows:

	1994	1993
Combined income tax rate	41.9%	40.3%
Increase (decrease) in the income tax rate resulting from		
Income not subject to tax	(0.6)	(0.9)
Tax on large corporations	1.2	0.9
Recovery of tax from prior years	(0.2)	(1.0)
Adjustment for U.S. rates	(0.3)	—
Effective income tax rate	42.0%	39.3%

9. Earnings per Share

Earnings per share are based on the weighted average number of common shares outstanding during the year.

Fully diluted earnings per share have been calculated on the assumption that all outstanding vested options were exercised at the beginning of the year. Funds derived from the exercise of options were assumed to have been used to retire debt with an effective annual rate of 5.9%, or 3.4% after tax (1993 – 7.9% or 4.7% after tax).

10. Alaskan Acquisition

Effective November 1, 1992, the Company acquired all of the shares of Alaska Rural Investments (ARI). ARI held majority interests in the Alaska Commercial Company (AC Company) and Frontier Expeditors Inc. (FEI). In concurrent transactions, the Company acquired the minority position in AC Company and FEI from AC Company's employee ownership plan and trust, and FEI's President, respectively.

The acquisition was accounted for using the purchase method. The purchase price has been allocated to the assets and liabilities of the acquired entities based on management's estimate of respective fair values, including appraisals for properties. The operating results of these enterprises from November 1, 1992 are included in these financial statements.

A summary of the assets acquired and the consideration given is as follows:

Assets acquired (in thousands of Canadian dollars)		Consideration given	
Current assets	$16,088	Cash	$8,565
Fixed assets	13,841	Note payable	190
Deferred taxes	853		
Current liabilities	(10,179)		
Bank advances	(3,577)		
Long-term debt	(8,271)		
	$ 8,755		$8,755

11. Segmented Information

The Company operates predominantly within the retail industry in northern Canada and Alaska.

Geographic segmented information in thousands of Canadian dollars is as follows:

		Canada	Alaska	Total
Sales and other revenue	1994	$451,014	$97,665	$548,679
	1993	$447,604	$25,106	$472,710
Operating profit	1994	34,017	4,037	38,054
	1993	32,577	794	33,371
Earnings	1994	15,408	1,754	17,162
	1993	14,621	333	14,954
Identifiable assets	1994	$238,671	$33,957	$272,628
	1993	$219,362	$23,299	$242,661

12. Pensions

The Company maintains defined benefit pension plans for its Canadian employees. The plans provide pensions based on length of service and final average earnings.

The Company's accrued pension benefits and the market value of the plans' net assets were last determined by actuarial valuation as of January 1, 1992. At January 29, 1994, the plans' obligations are estimated to be $26,427,000 (1993 – $24,212,000) and the net assets available to provide these benefits are estimated to be $27,867,000 (1993 – $26,162,000).

13. Operating Lease Commitments

The Company leases the land on which the Winnipeg Retail Service Centre is located from the City of Winnipeg for $1 per year for 15 years subject to attaining agreed-upon job creation targets. The Company anticipates that the agreed targets will be met, accordingly, no additional lease payments have been accrued. The Company is obligated to buy the land for the greater of $1,710,000 or fair market value at August 31, 2007.

The Company has future commitments under operating leases as follows:

Years Ending January	Minimum Lease Payments (000's)
1995	$ 4,887
1996	4,421
1997	3,839
1998	3,509
1999	2,175
Thereafter	35,456
	$54,287

14. Comparative Amounts

In January 1991, the Company announced a plan to sell 26 junior department stores in order to concentrate on core retail operations in the Canadian north. Subsequent to that date, the net assets and operating results of these stores were accounted for as discontinued operations. In February 1993, a decision was made to return 9 remaining stores to continuing operations. The comparative financial statements have been restated to reflect the net assets and operations of those stores with no resulting effect on the previously reported earnings for the year.

SIX-YEAR FINANCIAL SUMMARY

(in thousands of Canadian dollars)	1993	1992	1991	1990	1989	1988
Consolidated Statement of Earnings						
Sales and Other Revenue	$548,679	$472,710	$410,879	$399,698	$392,034	$375,571
Earnings from continuing operations before interest and income tax and unusual items	38,054	33,371	32,054	28,664	34,763	31,548
Unusual item	—	—	772	—	—	2,256
Interest	8,457	9,157	11,297	14,371	13,620	13,279
Income taxes	12,435	9,507	9,130	6,319	8,659	8,301
Earnings from continuing operations	17,162	14,707	12,399	7,974	12,484	12,224
Earnings from discontinued operations	—	—	—	(1,399)	(462)	(529)
Provision from discontinued operations	—	247	524	(2,000)	—	—
Earnings for the year	17,162	14,954	12,923	4,575	12,022	11,695
Cash flow from operating activities	15,529	18,123	36,461	11,021	13,114	9,618
Dividends	5,810	5,182	4,289	4,219	3,732	2,529
Capital expenditures	33,321	26,370	11,275	31,484	10,646	13,387
Consolidated Balance Sheet						
Current assets	$182,735	$174,486	$152,200	$168,730	168,999	167,455
Fixed assets	145,255	122,024	90,014	86,631	62,971	57,983
Other assets	3,065	1,902				
Current liabilities	83,285	87,142	94,772	102,370	96,361	126,343
Long-term debt	88,336	66,382	45,000	61,000	52,000	42,000
Deferred income taxes	11,782	9,542	8,310	7,406	2,122	(820)
Shareholders' equity	147,652	135,346	94,132	83,585	81,487	57,915
Consolidated Per Share ($)						
Net earnings—fully diluted	$ 1.06	$ 1.05	$ 0.93	$ 0.35	$ 0.98	$ 1.02
Cash flow from operations	0.96	1.29	2.73	0.84	1.27	1.19
Dividends paid	0.36	0.36	0.32	0.32	0.30	0.30
Shareholders' equity at end year	9.13	8.41	6.88	6.29	6.27	5.96
Statistics at year end						
Number of stores—continuing operations	156	153	153	149	149	151
Number of stores—discontinued operations	—	—	12	17	17	17
Number of stores—Alaska	20	20	—	—	—	—
Number of employees—Canada	3,788	3,649	3,725	3,801	3,829	3,989
Number of employees—Alaska	509	467	—	—	—	—
Number of common shareholders	1,000	1,000	850	825	800	770
Financial Ratios						
Earnings before interest and taxes (%)	6.9	7.1	7.8	7.2	8.9	8.4
Return on net assets (%)	14.9	16.2	17.2	15.1	20.8	19.8
Return on average equity (%)	12.3	14.6	14.9	5.6	19.5	28.3
Inventory turnover	3.1	3.1	3.0	2.7	2.7	2.6

SHAREHOLDER INFORMATION

Annual Stock Prices and Volumes (TSE)

Fiscal Year Ending	Volume	High	Low	Close
January 1992	2,409,462	16 1/2	5 1/4	16 1/8
January 1993	7,428,817	16 1/8	13 1/4	15 1/8
January 1994	7,351, 617	20 1/4	14 3/4	17 1/4

Transfer Agent and Registrar
The R-M Trust Company
Winnipeg, Montreal, Toronto, Regina, Calgary, Vancouver

Stock Symbol: NWC

Stock Exchange Listings:
The Toronto Stock Exchange
The Winnipeg Stock Exchange

1994 Financial Calendar—Reporting Dates

First Quarter	June 17, 1994
Second Quarter	September 9, 1994
Third Quarter	December 14, 1994
Fourth Quarter	March 24, 1995

Quarterly Dividend Payments
January 31 (record date December 30)
April 30 (record date March 31)
July 31 (record date June 30)
October 31 (record date September 30)

Number of shares outstanding at fiscal year end:
16,164,417

Average number of shares outstanding in 1993:
16,129, 775

CUSIP number: 66329F 10 1

Annual Meeting
The North West Company's Annual Meeting of Shareholders will be held Friday, June 17, 1994 at 11:30 a.m. in the Muriel Richardson Auditorium, Winnipeg Art Gallery, 300 Memorial Boulevard, Winnipeg, Manitoba.

Relative Stock Price Performance
(%)

This chart compares the relative performance of the common shares of The North West Company since 1987, with the TSE 300 composite index and the merchandising sub-index of the TSE 300. Values between June 1987 and listing on the TSE in September 1990 are based on the book value of shares of The North West Company. The index incorporates dividend reinvestment.

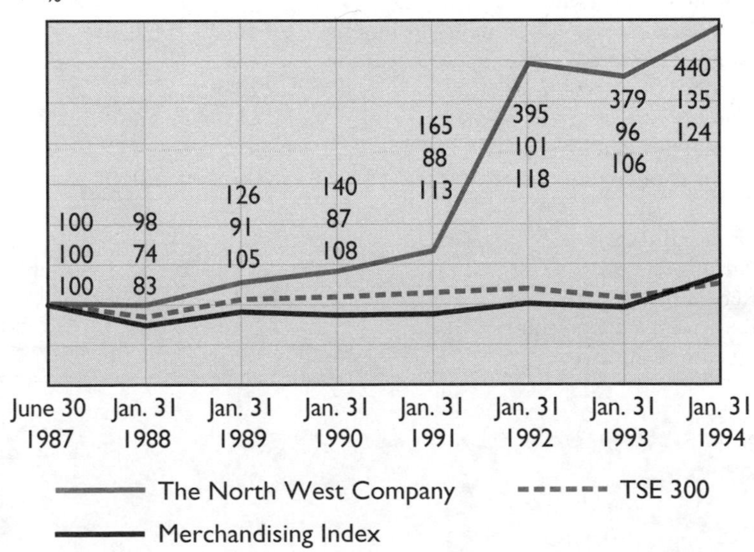

APPENDIX 2

CREATING A COMPUTER SPREADSHEET TO REPRESENT A COMPANY'S ACCOUNTS

SS.1 INTRODUCTION

You should be ready to begin building your spreadsheet any time after about Chapter 3, Section 3.4. This supplement is designed to show you how to create a spreadsheet, but if you choose not to do that but just to read and think about the material, you will still gain accounting knowledge.

This supplement outlines, with examples, how to enter a company's financial statements into a computer spreadsheet and then do three kinds of analysis on those statements:

1. "What if" analysis of the effects on the statements of various events or changes in accounting methods;
2. Cash flow analysis to construct a statement of changes in financial position; and
3. Financial ratio analysis.

Simple summary financial statements are used to build the example spreadsheet so that you can create a tool that is flexible enough to handle most companies you will encounter.

If you are experienced at using spreadsheets, you may see more effective ways of accomplishing the steps below. Please go ahead and use your own ideas: this supplement is just a guide. The objective is to help you build a spreadsheet that works, but the details are up to you.

You should have a real set of financial statements, perhaps those of The North West Company or others in this book, available to work with before you begin to work through this supplement. You can then use this material to assist you, step by step, to build a spreadsheet that fits a real company but that is also a prototype for you to use any time you'd like to analyze another company.

This supplement proceeds as follows:

- Section SS.2 shows you how to enter a single year's balance sheet, income statement, and retained earnings accounts into your spreadsheet and create an initial "workspace";
- Section SS.3 shows you how to format your own version of the company's statements so that your spreadsheet can print out the results of any "what if" analysis you do;
- Section SS.4 illustrates some simple "what if" effects analyses, for which spreadsheets are particularly useful;
- Section SS.5 shows you how to enter the preceding year's accounts into the spreadsheet so that you can do comparisons between years (adding the second year to your own formatted financial statements is left to you as an exercise);

- Section SS.6 shows you how to compute a statement of changes in financial position from the two years' comparisons of balance sheet changes, following the approach used in Chapter 4, especially Sections 4.3 and 4.6;
- Section SS.7 illustrates how to incorporate more cash flow information into your SCFP so that you can fine tune it, following the approach used in Chapter 4, Section 4.4;
- Section SS.8 shows you how to add financial ratio analyses to your spreadsheet that will respond to any "what if" analyses you do; and
- Section SS.9 does one final illustrative "what if" analysis, so that you can see how the balance sheet, retained earnings statement, income statement, SCFP, and ratios all change automatically as part of the analysis. Your spreadsheet is now ready to use for pretty well any company.

Before we begin working on a spreadsheet, some initial comments and cautions:

1. This material is written to apply to any spreadsheet software you might decide to use. There may be places where the example printouts look quite different from those your spreadsheet produces, but it is hoped that this will not be more than a minor nuisance.
2. The example spreadsheet uses simple cell-reference formulas and simple print formatting only, so that you can follow what is going on and so that the peculiarities of any one spreadsheet program do not complicate the illustrations. You are free to use more fancy touches in your own spreadsheet if you wish. You certainly can produce fancier looking financial statements than those used as illustrations in the following pages!
3. **SAVE! SAVE! SAVE! It can't be emphasized too strongly that you should save your work very frequently, so you don't lose hard work when the power goes out, or whatever.**
4. **ALSO, you should save each version of the spreadsheet, especially the part we will call the "workspace," after each version is completed, and then copy it and use the COPY for further work so that you always have the original available. For example, when you have finished Section SS.3, save the spreadsheet; then when you do Section SS.4, start with a COPY of Section SS.3's spreadsheet: use a DIFFERENT FILE NAME for it so you can save that too without copying it on top of your original.**

Chapters 2 and 3 showed examples of entering transactions and accruals into accounts to produce trial balances from which financial statements (balance sheet, income statement, and statement of retained earnings) can be prepared. *Here the objective is different*: to show you how to take a set of such statements, for example the set in a public company's annual report, and create a spreadsheet that will enable you to analyze those statements and understand the consequences of potential changes ("what if" or "effects" analysis). The idea is to show you progressively, over the several parts of this supplement, how to build a spreadsheet that will help you analyze most companies. The example spreadsheet printouts are from *Microsoft Excel®*, but the presentation is intended to be general enough that you can use whatever spreadsheet you wish.

Exhibit SS1 shows a set of financial statements (*not including* the cash flow statement of changes in financial position, which we will see how to generate using the spreadsheet) for a hypothetical company for two years. The statements are presented in summary form and with very simple numbers, so that you will see how to adapt any company's statements to your needs:

- For example, one of the assets below is "Asset A." This is listed under current assets, so it might be cash, or accounts receivable, or inventory, or something else.
- Another is "Asset D," listed under noncurrent assets. It might be land, or equipment, or some other long-term asset.
- "Asset F" is a negative asset, so it would be something like accumulated amortization.
- Expense R might be amortization expense.
- Expense S is near the bottom of the income statement, so it is probably income tax.

At the beginning, it doesn't matter what the accounts are—later, you will see how to incorporate categories of assets and other accounts into your analyses. For now just think of entering whatever the company's assets and other accounts are, using whatever titles the company uses or that you think are appropriate for your purposes.

If you are doubtful about some of your company's accounts, compare that company to the example in Exhibit SS1 and make sure that you know where you would classify all the accounts in the sort of format illustrated below. If your company has some strange accounts, just fit them in somewhere. You can move them around later if necessary. As long as all the accounts are entered into your workspace, you can use formulas and other devices to arrange them in any way you like.

Exhibit SS1

Hypothetical Corp.
Comparative Balance Sheets
for This Year and Last Year

Assets	**This Year**	**Last Year**	**Liabilities and Equity**	**This Year**	**Last Year**
Current assets:			Current liabilities:		
Asset A	$ 173	$ 129	Liability G	$ 70	$ 85
Asset B	292	240	Liability H	264	229
Asset C	302	316	Liability I	156	143
Noncurrent assets:			Noncurrent liabilities:		
Asset D	280	200	Liability J	280	310
Asset E	817	692	Liability K	146	117
Asset F	(283)	(211)	Owners' equity:		
			Capital L	420	300
			Ret. earn. M	245	182
TOTALS	$1,581	$1,366	TOTALS	$1,581	$1,366

Hypothetical Corp.
Comparative Statements of Retained Earnings
for This Year and Last Year

	This Year	Last Year
Retained earnings, beginning of year	$182	$133
Add net income for the year	123	89
Deduct dividends declared (Account N)	(60)	(40)
Retained earnings, end of year	$215	$182

Hypothetical Corp.
Comparative Income Statements
for This Year and Last Year

	This Year	Last Year
Revenue O	$1,106	$953
Expense P	(647)	(581)
Expense Q	(188)	(169)
Expense R (apparently amortization)	(84)	(73)
Expense S (apparently income tax)	(64)	(41)
Net income for the year	$ 123	$ 89

SS.2 GETTING STARTED: CREATING A WORKSPACE

To get started, we will now create a workspace area in the spreadsheet that contains just *this year's* financial statement figures. (You can enter both years' if you wish to do them both at once. See Section SS.5.) The workspace will use reference formulas so that the net income is automatically transferred to retained earnings. Therefore, any changes to revenue or expense accounts will automatically also change retained earnings, and the three financial statements to be produced by the spreadsheet (Section SS.3) will *articulate*, or fit together. This property is a central part of accounting, and making it work in the spreadsheet is a central part of making the spreadsheet useful. (Spreadsheets are designed to accomplish this sort of thing through reference formulas or similar devices, which is one of the main reasons for using them in accounting analysis.)

The workspace can be used as the "input area" of your spreadsheet. The numerical parts of *all other* areas of the spreadsheet will consist *entirely* of formulas referring (ultimately) back to the cells of the workspace. Therefore, if you change a number in the workspace, the rest of the spreadsheet will adjust automatically: you should make sure your spreadsheet works automatically like that, so that you get the full benefit of the spreadsheet's capability.

EXHIBIT SS2

	A	B	C	D
1	Hypothetical Corp. Balance Sheet Accounts			
2				
3			This Year	
4	Asset A	entered	173	
5	Asset B	entered	292	
6	Asset C	entered	302	
7	Asset D	entered	280	
8	Assct E	entered	817	
9	Asset F	entered	-283	
10	Tot Assets	formula	1581	
11	Liab G	entered	-70	
12	Liab H	entered	-264	
13	Liab I	entered	-156	
14	Liab J	entered	-280	
15	Liab K	entered	-146	
16	Capital L	entered	-420	
17	Ret earn M	formula	-245	
18	Tot L & E	formula	-1581	
19				
20	Begin RE	entered	-182	
21	Net inc	formula	-123	
22	Div dec N	entered	60	
23	End RE	formula	-245	
24				
25	Rev O	entered	-1106	
26	Exp P	entered	647	
27	Exp Q	entered	188	
28	Exp R	ontorod	84	
29	Exp S	entered	64	
30	Net inc	formula	-123	
31				

Note the following:

- *Arbitrarily*, debits are recorded in the spreadsheet as positive amounts and credits as negative ones. Thus the net income of -123 is an income, not a loss. This approach is used to help show which is which on the example printouts: you may wish instead to show all your numbers as positive and just remember which ones are debits and which are credits when you're creating your formulas.
- As the words in column B indicate, the amounts in the following lines of column C of the spreadsheet were entered from the financial statements: lines 4, 5, 6, 7, 8, 9, 11, 12, 13, 14, 15, 16, 20, 22, 25, 26, 27, 28, 29.
- Column B also indicates the amounts in column C of the spreadsheet that were *not* entered from the financial statements, but, instead, were produced by *formulas* entered in those lines. This use of formulas is very important, so each of them is listed below:

  Line 10 Is the sum of the amounts are in lines 4 to 9;
  Line 17 Equals whatever is in line 23;
  Line 18 Is the sum of the amounts in lines 11 to 17;

Line 21 Equals whatever is in line 30;
Line 23 Is the sum of the amounts in lines 20 to 22;
Line 30 Is the sum of the amounts in lines 25 to 29.

You could include these calculations in the spreadsheet's financial statements sections instead (see Section SS.3), but putting some of them in the workspace is a good idea. It gives you practice in developing formulas that work and provides useful check figures.

- The important formulas for articulating the financial statements are those in line 30 (which calculates income), line 21 (which transfers income to the retained earnings calculation), line 23 (which calculates ending retained earnings), and line 17 (which transfers the ending retained earnings to the balance sheet). Your spreadsheet must have such a capability if it is to work properly to handle changes and "what if" analysis automatically.
- The other calculations (lines 10 and 18) are useful to ensure that the balance sheet is in balance. These will tell you at a glance if something goes wrong.
- We could also have included other calculations. For example, there could have been a line for total current assets (the sum of lines 4 to 6), and lines for other balance sheet subtotals. There could have been a line for income before income tax (the sum of lines 25 to 28). Any such totals or subtotals could have been used to improve the presentation of the spreadsheet's analysis. We could also have included more headings, full descriptions of the various financial statement accounts, or other things to make the spreadsheet more easily readable. When you do your spreadsheet, try experimenting with such refinements until you come up with an arrangement that you like. There's no "right" way to do this: as in other areas of accounting, make the analysis fit your needs.

SS.3 PREPARING FINANCIAL STATEMENTS FROM THE WORKSPACE

It may seem odd to use the workspace to prepare financial statements, when it was developed *from* a set of statements. But knowing how to set up reports is useful, and when you do "what if" analyses, you may want to print out the revised financial statements that the analyses show.

Exhibit SS3 on page 584 shows a set of financial statements generated from the workspace. The workspace will be used to enter data to produce the financial statements and ratios. The statements are printed out without suppressing printing of all the row and column indicators: they would look better without those, but leaving them in helps in referencing the explanations that follow the statements. The statements could have been located anywhere among the spreadsheet's rows and columns; arbitrarily, they are located in rows below those used in the workspace.

Note the following:

- You may find the formatting of these three statements to be a little rough and ready. No attempt was made to be fancy. All that was done was to print subtotals and totals in bold and to have dollar signs printed in front of the accounting figures. Your own financial statements should be formatted as you like them!
- *The spreadsheet area comprising the three financial statements is* entirely *formulas*, tied back to the workspace above the statements in the spreadsheet. Therefore, *if any number in the workspace is changed, the financial statements will change*, as we will see in the next section. Examples of the formulas behind the financial statements are:
  - The "Asset A" figure in cell B49 on the balance sheet comes from cell C4 of the workspace;
  - The "Liability G" figure in cell D49 on the balance sheet comes from cell C11 of the workspace, with the sign reversed to remove the negative;
  - The "General Expenses" figure in cell D75 on the income statement equals the sum of cells C26 and C27 of the workspace, with the sign reversed to make the sum negative.
- Just for illustration, two ratios have been appended to the set of statements. These ratios use formulas based on the financial statements' cells, so the ratios will change if the statements' figures change. The current (working capital) ratio is cell B52 divided by cell D52. The debt–equity ratio is the sum of cells D52 and D56 divided by cell D60. It is not usual to print ratios right on the financial statements, but with your spreadsheet, you can do whatever suits you.

EXHIBIT SS3

	A	B	C	D
44		Hypothetical Corp.		
45		Balance Sheet at the End of This Year		
46				
47	Assets		Liabilities and Equity	
48	Current assets		Current liabilities	
49	Asset A	$173	Liability G	$70
50	Asset B	$292	Liability H	$264
51	Asset C	$302	Liability I	$156
52		**$767**		**$490**
53	Non-current assets		Non-current liabilities	
54	Asset D	$280	Liability J	$280
55	Asset E	$817	Liability K	$146
56	Less Asset F	($283)		**$426**
57		**$814**	Equity	
58			Capital L	$420
59			Ret'ed earn.	$245
60				**$665**
61	TOTAL	**$1,581**	TOTAL	**$1,581**
62				
63		Hypothetical Corp.		
64		Retained Earnings Statement for This Year		
65				
66	Retained earnings at the beginning of the year			$182
67	Add net income for the year			$123
68	Deduct dividends declared during the year			($60)
69	Retained earnings at the end of the year			**$245**
70				
71		Hypothetical Corp.		
72		Income Statement for This Year		
73				
74	Revenue			$1,106
75	General expenses			($835)
76	Apparent amortization expense			($84)
77	Income before income tax			**$187**
78	Apparent income tax expense			($64)
79	Net income for the year			**$123**
80				
81				
82		**Current ratio**		**1.57**
83		**Debt-equity ratio**		**1.38**

SS.4 SOME SIMPLE ILLUSTRATIVE "WHAT IF" ANALYSES

To illustrate the power of spreadsheets to examine the effects of changes to the accounts, here are just two incidents that we might want to examine:

1. Management of Hypothetical Corp. is considering issuing more share capital and using some of the proceeds to acquire more factory assets and to pay off some debt. The plan is to issue $300 more capital, to use $180 of that for more of Asset E, and to pay off $120 of Liability J.
2. Under pressure from the external auditors, management is also considering changing the way revenue is accounted for. The change would decrease Asset B by $95 and decrease revenue by the same amount. As a

result of this change, income tax expense would also decrease, by $37, as would income tax liability (part of Liability I).

Management is interested in knowing what effect these two changes together would have on the company's financial statements and on the current and debt–equity ratios. All we do is change the figures in *a renamed copy* of our spreadsheet's workspace as follows:

1. Increase Capital L (cell C16) by credit (–) 300;
   Increase Asset E (cell C8) by debit (+) 180;
   Decrease Liability J (cell C14) by debit (+) 120.
2. Decrease Asset B (cell C5) by credit (–) 95;
   Decrease Revenue O (cell C25) by debit (+) 95;
   Decrease Expense S (cell C29) by credit (–) 37;
   Decrease Liability I (cell C13) by debit (+) 37.

Exhibit SS4 shows that workspace with the above changes made. For your assistance, the change calculations for the seven cells in which the above changes were entered are shown to their right. You can see that quite a few other cells changed automatically: these are the ones controlled by formulas referring to the cells in which entries are made.

EXHIBIT SS4

	A	B	C	D
1	Hypothetical Corp. Balance Sheet Accounts			
2				
3			This Year	
4	Asset A	entered	173	
5	Asset B	entered	197	(292-95)
6	Asset C	entered	302	
7	Asset D	entered	280	
8	Asset E	entered	997	(817+180)
9	Asset F	entered	-283	
10	Tot Assets	formula	1666	
11	Liab G	entered	-70	
12	Liab H	entered	-264	
13	Liab I	entered	-119	(-156+37)
14	Liab J	entered	-160	(-280+120)
15	Liab K	entered	-146	
16	Capital L	entered	-720	(-420-300)
17	Ret earn M	formula	-187	
18	Tot L & E	formula	-1666	
19				
20	Begin RE	entered	-182	
21	Net inc	formula	-65	
22	Div dec N	entered	60	
23	End RE	formula	-187	
24				
25	Rev O	entered	-1011	(-1106+95)
26	Exp P	entered	647	
27	Exp Q	entered	188	
28	Exp R	entered	84	
29	Exp S	entered	27	(64-37)
30	Net inc	formula	-65	

Exhibit SS5 shows the revised financial statements, generated automatically via formula references to the workspace. Nothing was entered in these cells, because they all are controlled by formulas and change as the referenced cells change.

EXHIBIT SS5

	A	B	C	D
44		**Hypothetical Corp.**		
45		**Balance Sheet at the End of This Year**		
46				
47	**Assets**		**Liabilities and Equity**	
48	Current assets		Current liabilities	
49	Asset A	$173	Liability G	$70
50	Asset B	$197	Liability H	$264
51	Asset C	$302	Liability I	$119
52		**$672**		**$453**
53	Non-current assets		Non-current liabilities	
54	Asset D	$280	Liability J	$160
55	Asset E	$997	Liability K	$146
56	Less Asset F	($283)		**$306**
57		**$994**	Equity	
58			Capital L	$720
59			Ret'ed earn.	$187
60				**$907**
61	TOTAL	**$1,666**	TOTAL	**$1,666**
62				
63		**Hypothetical Corp.**		
64		**Retained Earnings Statement for This Year**		
65				
66	Retained earnings at the beginning of the year			$182
67	Add net income for the year			$65
68	Deduct dividends declared during the year			($60)
69	Retained earnings at the end of the year			**$187**
70				
71		**Hypothetical Corp.**		
72		**Income Statement for This Year**		
73				
74	Revenue			$1,011
75	General expenses			($835)
76	Apparent amortization expense			($84)
77	Income before income tax			**$92**
78	Apparent income tax expense			($27)
79	Net income for the year			**$65**
80				
81				
82		**Current ratio**		**1.48**
83		**Debt-equity ratio**		**0.84**

We can give management the information required. If the two changes are made, total assets will go up from $1,581 to $1,666, as will total liabilities and equity. Income will go down from $123 to $65, and, consequently, retained earnings will decline from $245 to $187. The current ratio will decline a little, from 1.57 to 1.48, but the debt–equity ratio will decline a lot, from 1.38 to 0.84. The company's short-term financial position will be a little weaker, but its overall financial structure will be stronger, because owners will have more money invested in the company than creditors, which is a reversal of the present situation.

SS.5 ENTERING A SECOND YEAR'S INFORMATION INTO THE WORKSPACE

The financial statements of Hypothetical Corp. were comparative, with figures provided for this year and last year. The workspace in Exhibit SS6 (based on a **copy** of the original spreadsheet) has added last year's amounts in column D. To illustrate one kind of analysis of the figures, column E has been used to calculate the percentage change in each account from last year to this year.

Incorporating last year's figures is a straightforward task. The only complication is in cells C20 and D20, containing the beginning retained earnings. Cell C20 had been entered from the financial statements, but now that we are entering the previous year's beginning amount in cell D20, we should change cell C20 to a formula that just takes last year's ending amount from cell D23. This articulates the two years' statements, so now if we made a "what if" change to *last year's* figures, the results would flow automatically forward to *this year*. (Of course, to keep the accounts in balance, you would have also made a complementary change to one or more balance sheet accounts.) You should always try to set your spreadsheet up so that as many as possible of these sort of automatic connections are made. They're useful in analysis and they help check that you have entered everything correctly, because, for example, if an error is made in entering last year's figures, the error might change this year's figures too, increasing the chance you'd notice the error.

From the above two-year account balances in the workspace, you can change the format of your spreadsheet's financial statements to incorporate last year as well. Just add necessary columns and extend this year's formulas back to last year. *Doing that is left to you as an exercise.*

EXHIBIT SS6

	A	B	C	D	E
1	Hypothetical Corp. Balance Sheet Accounts				
2					
3			This Year	Last Year	% Change
4	Asset A	entered	173	129	34.1
5	Asset B	entered	292	240	21.7
6	Asset C	entered	302	316	-4.4
7	Asset D	entered	280	200	40.0
8	Asset E	entered	817	692	18.1
9	Asset F	entered	-283	-211	34.1
10	Tot Assets	formula	1581	1366	15.7
11	Liab G	entered	-70	-85	-17.6
12	Liab H	entered	-264	-229	15.3
13	Liab I	entered	-156	-143	9.1
14	Liab J	entered	-280	-310	-9.7
15	Liab K	entered	-146	-117	24.8
16	Capital L	entered	-420	-300	40.0
17	Ret earn M	formula	-245	-182	34.6
18	Tot L & E	formula	-1581	-1366	15.7
19					
20	Begin RE	form/ent'd	-182	-133	36.8
21	Net inc	formula	-123	-89	38.2
22	Div dec N	entered	60	40	50.0
23	End RE	formula	-245	-182	34.6
24					
25	Rev O	entered	-1106	-953	16.1
26	Exp P	entered	647	581	11.4
27	Exp Q	entered	188	169	11.2
28	Exp R	entered	84	73	15.1
29	Exp S	entered	64	41	56.1
30	Net inc	formula	-123	-89	38.2

SS.6 COMPUTING THE STATEMENT OF CHANGES IN FINANCIAL POSITION

Now we're ready to see how to use the spreadsheet to compute an SCFP that will automatically reflect any "what if" changes in this year's or last year's accounts. As described in Chapter 4, Sections 4.3 and 4.6, the SCFP's cash flow analysis is based on changes in balance sheet accounts from last year to this year. Therefore, the first step is to convert column E in a **copy** of the spreadsheet's workspace to show *just the changes in the balance sheet.* We ignore the changes in the income and retained earnings statements, because:

- *This* year's income and retained earnings statements are part of the change between last year's balance sheet and this year's, so they are already included when the change in balance sheet retained earnings is calculated; and
- *Last* year's income and retained earnings statements are part of the change between the balance sheet two years ago and last year, so they are irrelevant to computing this year's SCFP.

The resulting revised workspace, *showing balance sheet changes only,* is in Exhibit SS7.

EXHIBIT SS7

	A	B	C	D	E
1	Hypothetical Corp. Balance Sheet Accounts				
2					
3			This Year	Last Year	Change
4	Asset A	entered	173	129	44
5	Asset B	entered	292	240	52
6	Asset C	entered	302	316	-14
7	Asset D	entered	280	200	80
8	Asset E	entered	817	692	125
9	Asset F	entered	-283	-211	-72
10	Tot Assets	formula	1581	1366	215
11	Liab G	entered	-70	-85	15
12	Liab H	entered	-264	-229	-35
13	Liab I	entered	-156	-143	-13
14	Liab J	entered	-280	-310	30
15	Liab K	entered	-146	-117	-29
16	Capital L	entered	-420	-300	-120
17	Ret earn M	formula	-245	-182	-63
18	Tot L & E	formula	-1581	-1366	-215
19					
20	Begin RE	form/ent'd	-182	-133	
21	Net inc	formula	-123	-89	
22	Div dec N	entered	60	40	
23	End RE	formula	-245	-182	
24					
25	Rev O	entered	-1106	-953	
26	Exp P	entered	647	581	
27	Exp Q	entered	188	169	
28	Exp R	entered	84	73	
29	Exp S	entered	64	41	
30	Net inc	formula	-123	-89	

Now we can go on to the SCFP itself, using the "change" calculations set out in Chapter 4, Section 4.3, and illustrated especially in Section 4.6. All we do is set up the format for the SCFP in another part of the spreadsheet (we'll put it directly below the income statement) and enter *formulas* into each cell of the SCFP format to transfer information from the workspace's calculations of balance sheet changes. Just a few complications:

- *Very important*: You should remember that increases in assets reduce cash and so are *negative* on the SCFP. But in our spreadsheet's calculation of balance sheet changes, these are shown as positive because debits are recorded as positive amounts. Similarly, increases in liabilities and equity increase cash and so are *positive* on the SCFP. But in our spreadsheet's calculation of balance sheet changes, these are shown as negative because credits are recorded as negative amounts. *Therefore, given the way the accounts were set up in the workspace, the SCFP's formulas have to reverse the sign of all balance sheet changes* so that they make sense on the SCFP. This is a result of the arbitrary designation of debits as positive and credits as negative: it doesn't have any deeper meaning! It may not apply to the way you set your workspace up.

- This reversal is not needed in the little reconciliation of changes in cash and cash equivalents at the bottom of the SCFP, because now we are using the accounts directly, so a debit change in cash equivalent assets is positive for CCE and a credit change in cash equivalent assets is negative for CCE.
- "Dividends paid" on the SCFP is calculated as dividends declared from the retained earnings statement, adjusted for any changes in unpaid dividends (dividends payable account). We have no information about dividends payable, so let's assume it is zero for now.
- We have to know more about the accounts in order to do a sensible SCFP. Therefore, let's specify the following (you'll have to make similar classifications for the real financial statements you're using):
  - Asset A is cash equivalent assets;
  - Liability G is cash equivalent liabilities;
  - Assets B and C are other current assets;
  - Assets D and E are noncurrent assets;
  - Asset F is accumulated amortization;
  - Liabilities H and I are other current liabilities;
  - Liability J is noncurrent debts;
  - Liability K is noncurrent accruals, such as deferred income tax; and
  - Capital L is owners' contributed capital.

The resulting SCFP, with the formulas used to produce each amount shown on the right, is shown in Exhibit SS8.

EXHIBIT SS8

	A	B	C	D	E
87		Hypothetical Corp.			
88	Statement of Changes in Financial Position for This Year				
89					
90	Cash from operations				
91	Net income		From inc stmt	$123	(-cell C30)
92	Inc adjust's: liab changes		ΔNCLaccrual	$29	(-cell E15)
93	Inc adjust's: asset changes		ΔNCAaccrual	$72	(-cell E9)
94	Other curr liab changes		ΔOCL exc div	$48	(-cells E12+E13)
95	Other curr asset changes		ΔOCA	($38)	(-cells E5+E6)
96				**$234**	
97	Dividends paid				
98	Dividends declared		From RE stmt	($60)	(-cell C22)
99	Changes in div payable		ΔOCL div pay	$0	(no information)
100				**($60)**	
101	Investing activities				
102	Changes in non-curr assets		ΔNCAcost	**($205)**	(-cells E7+E8)
103					
104	Financing activities				
105	Changes in non-curr liab		ΔNCLdebt	($30)	(-cell E14)
106	Changes in capital		ΔCAP	$120	(-cell E16)
107				**$90**	
108					
109	Change in cash and cash equivalents			**$59**	
110					
111	Reconciliation of CCE changes:				
112	ΔCEA	$44			(cell E4)
113	ΔCEL	$15			(cell E11)
114	ΔCCE	**$59**			

SS.7 INCORPORATING MORE CASH FLOW INFORMATION INTO THE SCFP

When you are using your spreadsheet to generate a company's SCFP for use in your analysis, you will encounter the frustration that your SCFP seldom will have exactly the same figures as the company's own SCFP. (We don't know what Hypothetical Corp.'s SCFP might have been like because we are only interested here in developing a spreadsheet that will generate an SCFP automatically.) The reason that your SCFP and the company's SCFP likely differ is that the company's SCFP was prepared using more detailed information than you can ordinarily get from just reading the financial statements. So this isn't something to worry much about as long as you have the basic approach straight in your mind.

But perhaps you are able to find out more details. How can you adapt your SCFP to take those details into account? Following the ideas in Chapter 4, Section 4.4, you just alter the account balances in the workspace and the SCFP's descriptions and formulas accordingly. Here are three illustrations:

1. Let's say we discover that dividends payable is included in Liability I on Hypothetical Corp.'s balance sheet. Dividends payable were $12 at the end of last year and $16 at the end of this year.

   To incorporate this, we can just create a new balance sheet account after Liability I on the workspace, put the above amounts into it, reduce the amounts in Liability I accordingly, and then put a formula in the SCFP's cell D99 to refer to the change in the new liability.
2. We discover that the change in Liability J, down $30, was actually a net of a decrease of $50 and an increase of $20.

   To incorporate this, we can create two "change" cells in the workspace for Liability J, one up $20 and one down $50, and put two lines in the SCFP's "financing" section for the increases and decreases in the liability, referring the two lines to the two change cells.
3. We have thought that Expense R was amortization expense. It was $84 this year, but the change in accumulated amortization (Asset F), which we have used so far to represent amortization expense on the SCFP, is only $72. The reason is that a piece of equipment (Asset E) was sold at a loss during the year: the equipment cost $30 and it had accumulated amortization of $12, so its book value was $18, but it was sold for $15. The loss on sale was therefore $3. This amount was included with Expense Q as a miscellaneous expense. The change in accumulated amortization was therefore $84 amortization expense (which increased accumulated amortization) minus $12 of old accumulated amortization removed when the equipment was sold.

   These alterations in our changes calculations and in our SCFP format will do the job:

   a. Put a new line in the workspace's balance sheet assets section called "disposal" and transfer $12 of the change in accumulated amortization (Asset F) to it. (This change was a reduction of accumulated amortization, so it was a debit. Therefore, the "disposal" account will have a debit balance of $12 now and the change in accumulated amortization will now equal the amortization expense (Expense R: $84).

We will use the disposal account several times. It is shown in line 9 of the revised workspace below, but that workspace printout does not show the intermediate balances in the account, just the final balance. Therefore this discussion will indicate the intermediate balances.

b. Transfer a negative $30 from Asset E to the new disposal account in the workspace. This will leave the Asset E change (cell 8E on the workspace) at $155, which is the cost of the new assets acquired, whereas the previous $125 was the net change in the asset account. This will also leave the disposal account at negative $18, the book value of the asset sold.

c. Divide the disposal account in the workspace into two cells by creating a new line called "proceeds" and transfer negative $15 to it (negative because it is a credit, being the other half of the entry that debited cash when the proceeds were received). In the workspace below, this new line was inserted as line 10. Put a new line in the SCFP "investing" section (line 104 in the revised SCFP below) to report the proceeds on sales of assets. Reference that new line to the "proceeds" cell of the workspace (cell 10E), with sign reversed as always.

d. This leaves $3 in the disposal account, which is the loss on sale. (See cell 9E in the workspace below.) Put a new line in the SCFP "operations" section to adjust income for the loss on sale. (See line 94 on the revised SCFP.) Reference that new line to the workspace's "disposal" cell E9 (with sign reversed, as always).

The resulting changes to the balance sheet workspace and the SCFP are shown in Exhibits SS9 and SS10. Note that the SCFP's internal details have changed to reflect the new information, but its bottom line change in CCE is the same as before, because none of the three pieces of information caused us to change the CCE accounts. You can see from this example that the change in a particular balance sheet account may be reflected in more than one area of the SCFP, but the sum of those detailed components on the SCFP will still equal the account change.

EXHIBIT SS9

	A	B	C	D	E
1		Hypothetical Corp. Balance Sheet Accounts			
2					
3			This Year	Last Year	Change
4	Asset A	entered	173	129	44
5	Asset B	entered	292	240	52
6	Asset C	entered	302	316	-14
7	Asset D	entered	280	200	80
8	Asset E	entered	817	692	155
9	Disposal	new item!			-3
10	Proceeds	new item!			-15
11	Asset F	entered	-283	-211	-84
12	Tot Assets	formula	1581	1366	215
13	Liab G	entered	-70	-85	15
14	Liab H	entered	-264	-229	-35
15	Liab I	entered	-140	-131	-9
16	Div pay'ble	new item!	-16	-12	-4
17	Liab J (decr.)	entered	-280	-310	50
18	Liab J (incr.)	new item!			-20
19	Liab K	entered	-146	-117	-29
20	Capital L	entered	-420	-300	-120
21	Ret earn M	formula	-245	-182	-63
22	Tot L & E	formula	-1581	-1366	-215
23					
24	Begin RE	form/ent'd	-182	-133	
25	Net inc	formula	-123	-89	
26	Div dec N	entered	60	40	
27	End RE	formula	-245	-182	
28					
29	Rev O	entered	-1106	-953	
30	Exp P	entered	647	581	
31	Exp Q	entered	188	169	
32	Exp R	entered	84	73	
33	Exp S	entered	64	41	
34	Net inc	formula	-123	-89	

EXHIBIT SS10

	A	B	C	D	E	F
87			Hypothetical Corp.			
88	Improved Statement of Changes in Financial Position for This Year					
89						
90	Cash from operations					
91	Net income		From inc stmt	$123	(-cell C34 now)	
92	Inc adjust's: liab changes		ΔNCLaccrual	$29	(-cell E19 now)	
93	Inc adjust's: amortization		ΔNCAaccrual	$84	(-cell E11 now)	
94	Inc adjust's: loss on sale			$3	(-cell E9, new)	
95	Other curr liab changes		ΔOCL exc div	$44	(-cells E14+E15 now)	
96	Other curr asset changes		ΔOCA	($38)	(-cells E5+E6)	
97				**$245**		
98	Dividends paid					
99	Dividends declared		From RE stmt	($60)	(-cell C26 now)	
100	Changes in div payable		ΔOCL div pay	$4	(-cell E15, new)	
101				**($56)**		
102	Investing activities					
103	Additions to non-curr assets		ΔNCAcost	($235)	(-cells E7+E8)	
104	Proceeds from disposals			$15	(-cell E10, new)	
105				**($220)**		
106	Financing activities					
107	Decreases in non-curr liab		ΔNCLdebt	($50)	(-cell E17 now)	
108	Increases in non-curr liab			$20	(-cell E18, new)	
109	Changes in capital		ΔCAP	$120	(-cell E20)	
110				**$90**		
111						
112	Change in cash and cash equivalents			**$59**		
113						
114	Reconciliation of CCE changes:					
115	ΔCEA	$44			(cell E4)	
116	ΔCEL	$15			(cell E13)	
117	ΔCCE	**$59**				

At this point, you should check the reference formulas in your three original financial statements (balance sheet, retained earnings statement, income statement). The spreadsheet should follow all your rearrangements, but sometimes it does not. For example, the workspace now has two accounts (lines 15 and 16) that need to be collected together to make Liability I on the balance sheet.

SS.8 INCORPORATING FINANCIAL RATIOS

The earlier set of spreadsheet-generated financial statements contained two ratios. Just to complete the example, several more have been added to those, on a **new copy** of the spreadsheet:

- Return on equity (net income divided by equity);
- Return on sales (net income divided by revenue);
- Dividend payout (dividends declared divided by net income); and
- Cash flow to total assets (cash from operations divided by total assets).

These ratios have all been grouped at the bottom of the income statement, together with the two we had before (current ratio and debt–equity ratio).

The same three financial statements as before, now with six ratios printed out at the bottom of the income statement, are shown in Exhibit SS11.

You can easily calculate more ratios, including the Scott formula ratios, and put them wherever you like on your spreadsheet. You can also produce a common size balance sheet, with each account shown as a percentage of total assets, or a common size income statement, with each account shown as a percentage of revenue. Such statements are useful to compare companies of different sizes, or to identify changes in the financial structure or performance of one company over time. Doing any of these additional analyses is left to you as an exercise.

EXHIBIT SS11

	A	B	C	D	E	F
44		**Hypothetical Corp.**				
45		**Balance Sheet at the End of This Year**				
46						
47	**Assets**		**Liabilities and Equity**			
48	Current assets		Current liabilities			
49	Asset A	$173	Liability G	$70		
50	Asset B	$292	Liability H	$264		
51	Asset C	$302	Liability I	$156		
52		**$767**		**$490**		
53	Non-current assets		Non-current liabilities			
54	Asset D	$280	Liability J	$280		
55	Asset E	$817	Liability K	$146		
56	Less Asset F	($283)		**$426**		
57		**$814**	Equity			
58			Capital L	$420		
59			Ret'ed earn.	$245		
60				**$665**		
61	TOTAL	**$1,581**	TOTAL	**$1,581**		
62						
63		**Hypothetical Corp.**				
64		**Retained Earnings Statement for This Year**				
65						
66	Retained earnings at the beginning of the year			$182		
67	Add net income for the year			$123		
68	Deduct dividends declared during the year			($60)		
69	Retained earnings at the end of the year			**$245**		
70						
71		**Hypothetical Corp.**				
72		**Income Statement for This Year**				
73						
74	Revenue			$1,106		
75	General expenses			($835)		
76	Apparent amortization expense			($84)		
77	Income before income tax			**$187**		
78	Apparent income tax expense			($64)		
79	Net income for the year			**$123**		
80						
81						
82	**Current ratio**		**1.57**	**Return on equity**		**0.18**
83	**Debt-equity ratio**		**1.38**	**Return on sales**		**0.11**
84	**Dividend payout**		**0.49**	**Cash flow to total assets**		**0.15**

SS.9 A FINAL "WHAT IF" ANALYSIS EXAMPLE

Now let's do a final "what if" or "effects" analysis using the spreadsheet, so you can see how the three original statements, the ratios, and the SCFP all reflect the analysis. You'll see from this how powerful an analytical tool the spreadsheet is, once you have built it to accommodate the relationships among the accounts.

Here's the example. Hypothetical Corp. management has decided to bring the company's financial statements into line with some accounting standards relating to accounts receivable (Asset B) and health care and pension accruals (Liability K). These standards had not been followed exactly in the past because the company's circumstances did not quite fit, but now some business changes had removed that problem. The changes are retroactive to past years, but we will change only this year's set of statements because those are all that are built into the spreadsheet so far.

Here are the accounts affected by the accounting change:

a. Last year's accounts:

- Beginning retained earnings (incomes for years before even last year) is reduced by $21;
- Net income for last year is reduced by $11:
  - Revenue O goes down $8 because of the accounts receivable change;
  - Expense Q goes up $6 because of the pension and health care accrual change;
  - Expense S goes down $3 because income tax is saved due to the reduced income.
- Year-end balance sheet account changes:
  - Asset B is reduced $17;
  - Liability I (which includes income tax payable) is reduced $9;
  - Liability K is increased $24.

b. This year's accounts:

- Income statement:
  - Revenue O is reduced $12 due to the accounts receivable change;
  - Expense Q (which includes pensions and health care costs) is increased $14;
  - Expense S (income tax expense) is reduced $7.
- Balance sheet (note that this year's effects are cumulative, that is, they incorporate all the changes happening at the end of last year plus the changes in income occurring this year):
  - Asset B is reduced $29 ($17 from last year plus $12 from this year's income statement—Revenue O);
  - Liability I is reduced $16 ($9 from last year plus $7 from this year's income statement—Expense S);
  - Liability K is increased $38 ($24 from last year plus $14 from this year's income statement—Expense Q).

To make all of this work, and keep the balance sheet in balance, here are the changes we need to make to the accounts in the workspace (all the other areas of the spreadsheet will change automatically):

	This Year	Last Year
Assets		
Asset B reduced (credited)	– $29	– $17
Liabilities and Equity		
Liability I reduced (debited)	$16	$ 9
Liability K increased (credited)	– 38	– 24
Retained earnings:		
Beginning of last year reduced (debited)		21
Revenue O reduced (debited)	12	8
Expense Q increased (debited)	14	6
Expense S reduced (credited)	– 7	– 3
Subtotal of retained earnings effects		32
Spreadsheet will handle this carryover from prior years automatically	32	
	$29	$17

Now that we are sure the effects of the changes are understood and will keep the balance sheet in balance, we can just enter them into a **new copy** of the spreadsheet's workspace and see how all the financial statements (including the SCFP) and the ratios change to reflect them. The results are shown in Exhibits SS12, SS13, and SS14, beginning with the revised-again workspace, revised from before in accordance with the above schedule (accounts with changes are identified in column F for your reference).

Please review the results carefully, in comparison with the statements printed out earlier, and satisfy yourself that you understand what has happened. You might note:

- On the workspace, changes have been made in both years' figures, so the balance sheet changes between years (column E) are also affected. We can expect these changes to carry through to the SCFP, which, you'll remember, is based on balance sheet changes.
- The revised balance sheet at the end of this year is different, as it should be. Asset B is down $29 from $292 to $263; Liability I is down $16 from $156 to $140; Liability K is up $38 from $146 to $184; and Retained earnings are down $51 from $245 to $194.
- The revised retained earnings statement also reflects the effects. Beginning retained earnings are down $32 from $182 to $150, net income is down $19 from $123 to $104, and ending retained earnings are down as already noted.
- The revised income statement shows the details of this year's effects, with revenue down $12 from $1,106 to $1,094, general expenses up $14 from $835 to $849, income tax expense down $7 from $64 to $57, and net income down as already noted.
- The six ratios have all changed, most not much.

EXHIBIT SS12

	A	B	C	D	E	F
1	Hypothetical Corp. Balance Sheet Accounts					
2						Effects
3			This Year	Last Year	Change	(up or down)
4	Asset A	entered	173	129	44	
5	Asset B	entered	263	223	40	dn -29,-17
6	Asset C	entered	302	316	-14	
7	Asset D	entered	280	200	80	
8	Asset E	entered	817	692	155	
9	Disposal	**new item!**			-3	
10	Proceeds	**new item!**			-15	
11	Asset F	entered	-283	-211	-84	
12	Tot Assets	formula	1552	1349	203	
13	Liab G	entered	-70	-85	15	
14	Liab H	entered	-264	-229	-35	
15	Liab I	entered	-124	-122	-2	dn 16, 9
16	Div pay'ble	**new item!**	-16	-12	-4	
17	Liab J (decr.)	entered	-280	-310	50	
18	Liab J (incr.)	**new item!**			-20	
19	Liab K	entered	-184	-141	-43	up -38,-24
20	Capital L	entered	-420	-300	-120	
21	Ret earn M	formula	-194	-150	-44	
22	Tot L & E	formula	-1552	-1349	-203	
23						
24	Begin RE	form/ent'd	-150	-112		last yr dn 21
25	Net inc	formula	-104	-78		
26	Div dec N	entered	60	40		
27	End RE	formula	-194	-150		
28						
29	Rev O	entered	-1094	-945		dn 12,8
30	Exp P	entered	647	581		
31	Exp Q	entered	202	175		up 14,6
32	Exp R	entered	84	73		
33	Exp S	entered	57	38		dn -7,-3
34	Net inc	formula	-104	-78		

EXHIBIT SS13

	A	B	C	D	E	F
44		Hypothetical Corp.				
45		Balance Sheet at the End of This Year				
46						
47	Assets		Liabilities and Equity			
48	Current assets		Current liabilities			
49	Asset A	$173	Liability G	$70		
50	Asset B	$263	Liability H	$264		
51	Asset C	$302	Liability I	$140		
52		**$738**		**$474**		
53	Non-current assets		Non-current liabilities			
54	Asset D	$280	Liability J	$280		
55	Asset E	$817	Liability K	$184		
56	Less Asset F	($283)		**$464**		
57		**$814**	Equity			
58			Capital L	$420		
59			Ret'ed earn.	$194		
60				**$614**		
61	TOTAL	**$1,552**	TOTAL	**$1,552**		
62						
63		Hypothetical Corp.				
64		Retained Earnings Statement for This Year				
65						
66	Retained earnings at the beginning of the year			$150		
67	Add net income for the year			$104		
68	Deduct dividends declared during the year			($60)		
69	Retained earnings at the end of the year			**$194**		
70						
71		Hypothetical Corp.				
72		Income Statement for This Year				
73						
74	Revenue			$1,094		
75	General expenses			($849)		
76	Apparent amortization expense			($84)		
77	Income before income tax			**$161**		
78	Apparent income tax expense			($57)		
79	Net income for the year			**$104**		
80						
81						
82	**Current ratio**		**1.56**	**Return on equity**		**0.17**
83	**Debt-equity ratio**		**1.53**	**Return on sales**		**0.10**
84	**Dividend payout**		**0.58**	**Cash flow to total assets**		**0.16**

EXHIBIT SS14

	A	B	C	D	E	F
87		Hypothetical Corp.				
88	Improved Statement of Changes in Financial Position for This Year					
89						
90	Cash from operations					
91	Net income		From inc stmt	$104	(-cell C34 now)	
92	Inc adjust's: liab changes		ΔNCLaccrual	$43	(-cell E19 now)	
93	Inc adjust's: amortization		ΔNCAaccrual	$84	(-cell E11 now)	
94	Inc adjust's: loss on sale			$3	(-cell E9, new)	
95	Other curr liab changes		ΔOCL exc div	$37	(-cells E14+E15 now)	
96	Other curr asset changes		ΔOCA	($26)	(-cells E5+E6)	
97				**$245**		
98	Dividends paid					
99	Dividends declared		From RE stmt	($60)	(-cell C26 now)	
100	Changes in div payable		ΔOCL div pay	$4	(-cell E15, new)	
101				**($56)**		
102	Investing activities					
103	Additions to non-curr assets		ΔNCAcost	($235)	(-cells E7+E8)	
104	Proceeds from disposals			$15	(-cell E10, new)	
105				**($220)**		
106	Financing activities					
107	Decreases in non-curr liab		ΔNCLdebt	($50)	(-cell E17 now)	
108	Increases in non-curr liab			$20	(-cell E18, new)	
109	Changes in capital		ΔCAP	$120	(-cell E20)	
110				**$90**		
111						
112	Change in cash and cash equivalents			**$59**		
113						
114	Reconciliation of CCE changes:					
115	ΔCEA	$44			(cell E4)	
116	ΔCEL	$15			(cell E13)	
117	ΔCCE	**$59**				

- The SCFP has changed, but also in an important way has not changed. The accounting changes we implemented did not affect cash, so we should not expect the SCFP's totals to change, and they did not. Even cash from operations has not changed, because the cash inflow from day-to-day activities was not affected. The only changes are in the details of the calculation of cash from operations, and all those changes cancel each other out:

Net income is down from $123 to $104	– $19
Income adjustments from liability changes is up from $29 to $43 (that's Liability K)	14
Other current liability changes are down from $44 to $37 (that's Liability I)	– 7
Other current asset changes are down from ($38) to ($26) (that's Asset B)	12
Net effect on cash from operations	$ 0

Well, there you have it! Your spreadsheet should now be a live, adaptable tool you can take away and use in other courses, or even in real life! And in the process of constructing the spreadsheet, you've learned a lot about how accounting works, because you have had to tell the spreadsheet how all the figures fit together—and that's accounting!

APPENDIX 3

SOLUTION OUTLINES TO ASTERISKED HOMEWORK AND DISCUSSION PROBLEMS

The first few homework and discussion problems in each chapter are marked with asterisks. For your use in self-study, outlines of solutions to these problems have been prepared. The outlines are informal and often chatty, and you should take them as suggestions of valid approaches, not as the *only* valid approaches. Students and instructors have various views of the world, and such views colour the way answers to accounting problems, as with other important problems, are developed. Coming up with a coherent personal view of accounting is the responsibility of each student, and the solutions provided here should be fitted to that view, and not override it. The solution outlines are intended to help you, so they are written to be clear, not vague or evasive. But they can never be complete, nor can they anticipate the intelligence and creativity that you will bring to the problems.

Sometimes, the solution to a problem will require some assumptions or data not explicitly given in the problem. That is the way real world problems tend to be formed: not necessarily completely laid out or unambiguously phrased. Become comfortable with stating your assumptions and knowing where they make a difference, because in dealing with the real problems you will face in your career, such assumptions can be replaced by evidence to produce high-quality solutions, but only if you know what the assumptions are and when they matter.

Always try each problem on your own, or with friends, and make rough notes of your solution, before you look at the outline below. If you look at the solution outline before you think about the problem, you will rob the solution of its main value to you, which is feedback on your own learning. Problems always look easier if you look at the solutions prematurely, so if you do that, you can fool yourself about what your ability is.

Solution Outline for Problem 1.1

1. An accountant is a person who prepares an enterprise's financial statements, whereas the auditor verifies the propriety of the statements, once they have been prepared. These roles can be a bit mixed together, because often auditors give advice about the preparation of the statements. Management is responsible for the financial statements, so accountants in effect work for management when doing the statements.

2. Accrual income is a measure of the enterprise's performance in gaining increased resources through sales or services. Accrual procedures are designed to make income a complete measure of this performance, whether or not all cash has yet been received or paid. Cash income is a less complete measure, incorporating only the cash receipts and payments made in connection with operations.

3. Users of financial statements are not all the same in their information needs. They are all different people, with differing objectives, preferences and capabilities, so they are likely to need different information to meet these differences in decision making. Probably most users share an interest in fair, timely information, but the details of that information depend on the decision(s) each user is making.

SOLUTION OUTLINE FOR PROBLEM 1.2

Without knowing much specifically about managers and owners, some thought about them might lead to the following conclusions:

1. The owners will want to measure managers' performance to suit their (the owners') purposes, which will include motivating good managers to agree to work for the owners and do what the owners wish.
2. Managers are people, not machines: they will have their own wishes about such a measurement system and we might predict that managers, especially good managers, will not like a measurement system that is biased in favour of the owners.
3. Only some compromises in the measurement system would likely be acceptable to both owners and managers. Whether the compromises tend to favour the owners or the managers, or are completely neutral, will depend on whether it is easy for the owners to replace the managers, or for the managers to find other jobs, and on personal and ethical considerations. But the compromises might be along the following lines:
   a. The performance measurement should be done carefully and competently: significant errors should be avoided.
   b. The measures should be fair: significant biases in favour of one side or the other should be avoided, or at least clearly identified, so that both the owners and the managers will feel that their interests are being protected.
   c. To enhance fairness and reduce error, the owners and the managers might agree that someone independent of both should prepare the measures, or at least that the calculations should be checked by someone not biased toward either side.
   d. The system should not be too costly. A high-cost system would reduce the business's income and, therefore, result in a smaller "pie" for the owners and managers to share as dividends, bonuses, and so on.
   e. The measures should be verifiable, based on evidence rather than impression or opinion, so that both managers and owners could, if they wanted to, see for themselves that the results are proper.
   f. The system should be stable and the measures themselves "final" at some point, so that neither owners nor managers can go back and try to change the rules or the results afterwards.
   g. It would be helpful if the system were similar to those used by other businesses, so that the owners and the managers could compare the managers' performance to that of the managers of other businesses.
4. More principles could be listed: you may have thought of several. As your accounting knowledge develops, you'll see that the above principles (com-

petence, fairness, verifiability, consistency, comparability, and so on) and others are everyday factors in the way financial accounting works. In its reliance on such principles, accounting isn't too different from other systems of measurement, such as statistics, medical recordkeeping, student course grades, and criminal court records.

5. Which principles would be easy to agree on and which would be more controversial? There is no general answer to this—a lot depends on the particular business and on its particular owners and managers. But we might expect that stability and accuracy would be easier to agree on than fairness and comparability, because the latter depend more on the different viewpoints, and possibly competing interests, of the owners and managers. Similarly, the cost-effectiveness principle depends on who bears the cost—if the owners pay all the costs, the managers would not care much what the costs are, and vice versa.

SOLUTION OUTLINE FOR PROBLEM 1.3

a. Cash in the bank as at the end of 1995:
$12,430 + $1,000 + $68,990 – $1,480 – $36,910 – $28,000 = $16,030.

b. Accrual accounting income for 1995:
$68,990 + $850 – $36,910 – $2,650 – $3,740 = $26,540.

SOLUTION OUTLINE FOR PROBLEM 1.4

Assuming that the outstanding deposit and cheques do eventually reach Wayne's bank account, his "real" bank balance is:

Balance according to the bank	$365
Add outstanding deposit	73
	$438
Deduct outstanding cheques ($145 + $37 + $86 + $92)	360
Balance according to Wayne's records	$ 78

So, if Wayne's records are accurate and there is no hold-up with the bank's crediting the deposit to his account, he can repay the friend's $70.

This little problem is an example of accounting's intuitive basis. Assuming that Wayne is keeping track of his deposits and cheques and so has a record of what his bank balance "should" be, what we've done above is called a bank reconciliation: this is done by most companies at least monthly to try to catch unforeseen problems with their banking records. While such reconciliations can involve thousands of cheques and deposits, they all have the same simple intuitive basis: to get the balance we think is correct, we take the bank's figure and add to or subtract from it items we think the bank has not included in its records. If this adding and subtracting produces the balance we think is right, it makes us confident that it *is* right.

SOLUTION OUTLINE FOR PROBLEM 2.1

Bluebird Bakery (A Partnership)
Balance Sheet as at July 31, 1995

Assets		**Liabilities and Equity**	
Current assets		*Current liabilities*	
Cash on hand	$ 895	Demand bank loan	$ 14,500
Cash in bank	4,992	Accounts payable	11,240
Accounts receivable	3,823	Wages payable	2,246
Inventory of baked goods	245		$ 27,986
Inventory of supplies	13,220	*Partners' equity*	
	$ 23,175	Partner's capital—J. Bird	$ 52,921
Noncurrent assets		Partner's capital—B. Blue	27,425
Equipment (cost)	$129,153		$ 80,346
Accumulated amortization	(43,996)		
	$ 85,157		
TOTAL	$108,332	TOTAL	$108,332

Working capital = $23,175 – $27,986 = –$4,811
Working capital ratio = $23,175 / $27,986 = .83

SOLUTION OUTLINE FOR PROBLEM 2.2

Summary of transactions' effects (dollar signs omitted):

	DR (CR)	Transactions (DR are +, CR are –)	DR (CR)
Cash	24,388	–10,000 + 11,240 + 22,000 – 22,000 – 12,000	13,628
Accts. rec'ble	89,267	–11,240	78,027
Inventories	111,436	+ 5,320	116,756
Prepaid expenses	7,321	no transactions	7,321
Land	78,200	+ 52,000	130,200
Factory	584,211	+ 31,900	616,111
Accum. amort.	(198,368)	no transactions	(198,368)
Bank loan	(53,000)	+ 22,000	(31,000)
Accts. payable	(78,442)	– 5,320 – 13,900	(97,662)
Taxes payable	(12,665)	no transactions	(12,665)
Current mortgage	(18,322)	no transactions	(18,322)
Mortgage payable	(213,734)	– 40,000 – 18,000	(271,734)
Pension liability	(67,674)	no transactions	(67,674)
Share'r loan	(100,000)	+ 10,000	(90,000)
Share capital	(55,000)	– 22,000	(77,000)
Retained earn.	(97,618)	no transactions	(97,618)
	0		0

South Shore Manufacturing Ltd.
Balance Sheet as at August 1, 1995

Assets		**Liabilities and Equity**	
Current assets		*Current liabilities*	
Cash	$ 13,628	Bank loan	$ 31,000
Accounts receivable	78,027	Accounts payable	97,662
Inventories	116,756	Taxes payable	12,665
Prepaid expenses	7,321	Current part of mortgage	18,322
	$215,732		$159,649
Noncurrent assets		*Noncurrent liabilities*	
Land (cost)	$130,200	Mortgage, less current	$271,734
Factory (cost)	616,111	Pension liability	67,674
	$746,311	Loan from shareholder	90,000
Accumulated			$429,408
amortization	(198,368)		
	$547,943	*Shareholders' equity*	
		Share capital	$ 77,000
		Retained earnings	97,618
			$174,618
TOTAL	$763,675	TOTAL	$763,675

SOLUTION OUTLINE FOR PROBLEM 2.3

This problem illustrates the entity principle. In Questions 1, 2, and 3 you are asked to develop a balance sheet for three entities: Janet, Sam, and both Janet and Sam together.

1.

Janet
Statement of Financial Position (Balance Sheet)
as of June 9, 1995

Assets		**Liabilities and Equity**	
Cash	$ 500	Liabilities	$ 0
Stereo	2,000	Janet's equity	2,800
Damage deposit	300		
	$2,800		$2,800

2.

Sam
Statement of Financial Position (Balance Sheet)
as of June 9, 1995

Assets		Liabilities and Equity	
Cash	$1,000	Liabilities	
Prepaid rent	400	Loan	$2,100
Furniture	500	Sam's equity (deficit)	(200)
	$1,900		$1,900

3.

Janet and Sam
Statement of Financial Position (Balance Sheet)
as of June 14, 1995

Assets		Liabilities and Equity	
Cash	$2,500	Liabilities	
Damage deposit	300	American Express	$ 600
Stereo	2,000	Equity	
Furniture	500	Janet and Sam	6,200
Gifts	1,500		
	$6,800		$6,800

We can reconcile their individual equities to their joint equity as follows:

Individually:		
Janet's equity	$2,800	
Sam's equity	(200)	$2,600
Changes due to marriage:		
Wedding presents	$5,600	
Hall rent	(400)	
Band	(1,000)	
Honeymoon	(600)	3,600
Joint equity after honeymoon		$6,200

SOLUTION OUTLINE FOR PROBLEM 2.4

1. Here are the definitions, in enough detail so you can see if you've chosen the appropriate items from the Paychex balance sheet.

   a. A current asset is an item carrying future benefit that will be realized in cash or consumed within a year. This includes "cash equivalent" assets, which are assets that are cash or can be converted at any moment, and other current assets, which can be converted within the year, but not immediately. Examples: cash and cash equivalents, short-term investments, receivables, prepaid expenses, and inventories (Paychex doesn't have inventories).

b. A noncurrent asset is an asset that will be converted to cash or consumed in more than one year. Examples: land, buildings, equipment, long-term investments, and other assets such as development costs.

c. A current liability is any obligation that must be paid in cash within one year, or an estimated payment incorporated as part of accrual accounting. Examples: accounts payable, dividends payable, accrued (estimated) income taxes, portion of long-term debt due within a year, and deferred revenue (revenue or deposits collected from customers before it has been earned, and so still an obligation to the customers).

d. A noncurrent liability is an obligation or accrual that is due to be paid more than one year in the future (minus any part included in current liabilities). Examples: mortgages, long-term bank loans, bonds, pension liabilities, and deferred income taxes. Paychex has also received incentives from landlords to lease space several years into the future: these are being added to income over the terms of the leases and so are like the deferred revenue liability, only long-term.

e. Equity represents the residual ownership interest in a company. It is one of the ways assets such as cash and long-term investments are financed (liabilities are the other way). It is composed of direct investments by owners (such as share capital) and the indirect investment represented by retained earnings, which is accumulated income the owners have chosen to leave in the company rather than withdrawing them as dividends. Paychex has share capital and retained earnings. The share capital has a small legal ("par") value but more than that was received for the shares, which Paychex calls "additional capital."

2. Assets, liabilities, and equity have general definitions such as those above, but each company's particular circumstances may produce variations in how some items are classified. For a manufacturing company, the land its factory is on is a noncurrent asset, but for a real estate company that buys and sells land, land may be a current asset (inventory for sale). For you and Paychex, a bank loan is a liability, but, for a bank, which is a lender rather than a borrower, a bank loan is an asset (an amount receivable from the borrower). Some kinds of debt are so much like shares that they may be classified as equity, while some shares are so much like debt that they may be classified as liabilities. Every company's balance sheet must fit its circumstances so that it will be a valid measure of the company's financial position.

3. Working capital equals current assets minus current liabilities. The working capital ratio equals current assets divided by current liabilities. If you compute these for both years, you can determine if there has been an improvement or a deterioration. (Paychex's 1993 working capital and ratio are calculated in Section 2.5.)

SOLUTION OUTLINE FOR PROBLEM 2.5

1. List your assets and any amounts due to others at one point in time. Anything left over is "owner's equity" or net worth. (Those with negative equity, which is not unusual for students, need a sense of humour!) Just list the assets; don't attempt to match liabilities and assets one for one. For instance, there must once have been $2,000 in cash for a $2,000 loan, but all the cash may have been spent by now. So there may be a liability, but

no remaining asset. Are tuition payments assets? Is an anticipated student loan remission an asset? Are loans from parents liabilities? Try to decide on which items to include so that you get a meaningful measure of your financial position. Such a balance sheet could be used for loan or credit applications. It could also be used to help decide whether to make a major purchase (such as a car).

Pay attention to the title and date of the balance sheet. Identify the *entity*—your name, or that of a married couple, if you can't really separate your assets from those of your spouse.

As an example, imagine a student we know with the following items:

a. $10 — bank account

b. $50 — clothing (purchase price)

c. $1,400 — mountain bike with fancy parts and trim (purchase price)

d. $1,500 — student loan

e. $300 — books (purchase price)

Here is the balance sheet, which will be explained:

Balance Sheet for Student X
as at a Specified Date

Assets		**Liabilities and Equity**	
Current assets		Current liability	
Bank account	$ 10	Student loan	
Clothing	0	(current portion)	$ 500
Books	130		
		Noncurrent liability	
Noncurrent asset		Student loan (rest)	1,000
Bike (with parts)	1,400		
		Equity (deduced)	40
Total assets	$1,540	Total liabilities & equity	$1,540

1. Some explanations:

   a. The bank account is definitely a current asset; more specifically, a cash equivalent asset, because Student X can take out the cash at any time.

   b. Clothing was left out of the balance sheet because we felt there was no remaining value in it—bell-bottom pants and fluorescent shirts aren't "in" any more.

   c. A new mountain bike with such fancy parts would cost about $2,000, but accounting uses the historical cost on the balance sheet ($1,400).

   d. A portion of the student loan must be paid within the year ($500). We therefore took this portion out of the long-term area and placed it in the current liabilities.

e. Student X plans to sell the books at the beginning of the next term and expects to get $130 for them. So, that is the value we used for them on the balance sheet. (Current assets are usually shown at the *lower* of cost or current market value, as this book explains.)

f. Equity here is a calculated (deduced) number, since whatever portion of the assets are not financed by liabilities (A – L) is accounted for in the residual equity figure.

2. Some decision-making information:

   a. There is some threat of immediate cash problems, since cash is only $10 and the balance sheet doesn't show any obvious sources of more cash other than the books.

   b. The current portion of the student loan will have to be paid in a year, and Student X only has enough in current assets to cover $140 of the $500 to be paid, resulting in a $360 shortfall. The need to go out and earn money, or borrow from parents, is clear.

   c. Equity is small but positive—not unusual since Student X has been in school for life! However, the alarm lights would be flashing if this equity position existed after the student had worked for a few years. Therefore, interpreting the financial information depends on other environmental circumstances.

3. Some ideas here are already included above. You can see that the personal balance sheet can be quite revealing. Most students are *not* soundly financed in balance sheet terms because these terms relate to their impoverished past/present—while they are, nevertheless, hoping for a more remunerative future!

SOLUTION OUTLINE FOR PROBLEM 3.1

If you had trouble with any of the terms, the Glossary will help you.

SOLUTION OUTLINE FOR PROBLEM 3.2

1. Land is on the balance sheet because it is an asset, that is, a resource owned or controlled and having economic value. Land carries the potential to produce revenues for the company in the future, as do other assets.
2. Assets = $5,222 + $2,410 = $7,632.
3. Share capital is one of the sources of funds used to acquire the assets on the left side of the balance sheet. Therefore, it is not an asset that can be used to purchase more land, but a co-creator of the assets that now exist. Assets can only be used to buy other assets. Therefore, you must use $3,000 cash or another asset to buy a new asset. The company did not have enough cash, since some had already been used to buy inventory and land, so more cash had to be borrowed.
4. Retained earnings is the accumulation of net income minus dividends for each year of the company's history. It is the accumulated residual undistributed earnings of the company and is on the balance sheet because it is a source of present assets (because assets created in the process of earning income were not all distributed to owners).

5. Net income = \$10,116 – \$9,881 = \$235
6. Ending retained earnings were \$1,222. Subtracting income that had been added (\$235) and adding back dividends that had been deducted (\$120) gives beginning retained earnings of \$1,107. Proof, going the other way: \$1,107 + \$235 – \$120 = \$1,222.
7. Ending retained earnings would be \$1,107 + \$10,116 – \$11,600 = –\$377. There would have been a net loss for the year of \$1,484, and that would have turned the retained earnings at the beginning into a *deficit* at the end of \$377.
8. If the debit for the deficit were shown among the assets, that would indicate that the company had something of value for the future, a resource that could be used to generate income in the future. This is not at all the case: instead, the company has incurred more expenses than revenue and has, therefore, diminished some of the equity (share capital) put into it by the owners. Its resources were decreased by this, not increased as would be indicated by showing it as an asset. That's why a deficit is deducted from other equity (such as share capital) and shown as a negative item on the right–hand side of the balance sheet.

SOLUTION OUTLINE FOR PROBLEM 3.3

Arctic Limo Services Ltd.
Balance Sheet as at September 30, 1995

	1995	1994
Assets		
Current assets		
Cash	\$ 2,000	\$ 4,000
Accounts receivable	0	1,000
	\$ 2,000	\$ 5,000
Noncurrent assets		
Equipment (limos)	\$90,000	\$60,000
Less accumulated depreciation	(30,000)	(20,000)
	\$60,000	\$40,000
Total assets	\$62,000	\$45,000
Liabilities and Equity		
Current liabilities		
Loan	\$ 0	\$10,000
Wages payable	2,000	0
	\$ 2,000	\$10,000
Noncurrent liabilities		
Long-term limo financing	\$50,000	\$30,000
Shareholders' equity		
Share capital	\$ 1,000	\$ 1,000
Retained earnings	9,000	4,000
	\$10,000	\$ 5,000
Total liabilities and equity	\$62,000	\$45,000

Arctic Limo Services Ltd.
Income Statement
for the Year ended September 30, 1995

Revenue		$300,000
Less expenses:		
Wages	$100,000	
Other expenses	70,000	
Amortization	10,000	$180,000
Income before income tax		$120,000
Income tax expense		35,000
Net income		$ 85,000

Arctic Limo Services Ltd.
Statement of Retained Earnings
for the Year Ended September 30, 1995

Beginning balance (September 30, 1994)	$ 4,000
Net income for the year	85,000
Dividends declared	(80,000)
Ending balance (September 30, 1995)	$ 9,000

Assumptions:

- Receivable amount due from Lucky Eddie appears to have been current because he paid it within a year.
- Loan also appears to have been current.
- Wages are payable over a short term; a reasonable assumption is that employees would not allow their wages to remain unpaid for long.
- Noncurrent liabilities have no current portion payable within the next year.

SOLUTION OUTLINE FOR PROBLEM 3.4

Your explanations will have been in your own words, perhaps something like the following.

1. Net income is an increase in cash and other resources produced during a period of time by an enterprise's operating activities, that is, by selling goods and services to customers and incurring the costs of serving the customers.
2. Net income is part of owners' equity because the increase in resources earned as mentioned above belongs to the owners, who may withdraw it as dividends. Until they do withdraw it, it is part of their ownership interest.
3. Net income could be reported on the balance sheet by just showing that owners' equity has increased since the prior period. The income statement

was developed to provide an explanation of the details of the change in owners' equity and to separate that from any dividends withdrawn by the owners during the period.

4. Yes, shareholders have to be kept happy. But keeping them happy involves making an income (so that their ownership interest increases) and/or paying them a dividend, which is a payment to them of some of that increase. Including the dividends in the income calculation would confuse the enterprise's relationships with customers and owners, and would make it less clear whether the enterprise was successful in increasing resources (making income).

SOLUTION OUTLINE FOR PROBLEM 3.5

1. **Fergama Productions Inc.**
Balance Sheet as at the End of Last Year

Assets			**Liabilities and Equity**		
Current assets			**Current liabilities**		
Cash	$23,415		Accounts payable	$37,778	
Accounts receivable	89,455		Taxes payable	12,250	$ 50,028
Supplies inventory	10,240	$ 123,110	Long-term loan		15,000
Noncurrent assets			Shareholders' equity		
Office equip. cost	$24,486		Share capital	$20,000	
Accum. amort.	(11,134)	13,352	Retained earn.	51,434	71,434
TOTAL		$136,462	TOTAL		$136,462

2. Entries to record the activities:

a.	DR Accounts receivable	216,459	CR Revenue	216,459
b.	DR Production expenses	156,320	CR Cash	11,287
			CR Accounts payable	145,033
c.	DR Amortization expense	2,680	CR Accum. amortization	2,680
d.	DR Supplies inventory	8,657	CR Accounts payable	8,657
	DR Cost of supplies used expense	12,984	CR Supplies inventory	12,984
e.	DR Income tax expense	12,319	CR Income tax payable	12,319
f.	DR Retained earnings	25,000	CR Dividend payable	25,000
g.	DR Cash	235,260	CR Accounts receivable	235,260
h.	DR Accounts payable	172,276	CR Cash	172,276
i.	DR Income tax payable	18,400	CR Cash	18,400
j.	DR Long-term loan	5,000	CR Cash	5,000
k.	CR Dividend payable	25,000	CR Cash	25,000

3. Ending trial balance:

	DR	CR
Cash	26,712	
Accounts receivable	70,654	
Supplies inventory	5,913	
Office equipment	24,486	
Accumulated amortization		13,814
Accounts payable		19,192
Income tax payable		6,169
Dividend payable		0
Long-term loan		10,000
Share capital		20,000
Retained earnings—beginning		51,434
Dividend	25,000	
Revenue		216,459
Production expenses	156,320	
Amortization expense	2,680	
Cost of supplies used expense	12,984	
Income tax expense	12,319	
	337,068	**337,068**

4.

Fergama Productions Inc.
Income Statement for This Year

Revenue		$216,459
Expenses		
Production	$156,320	
Amortization	2,680	
Supplies used	12,984	171,984
Income before income tax		$ 44,475
Income tax expense		12,319
Net income for the year		$ 32,156

Fergama Productions Inc.
Statement of Retained Earnings for This Year

Retained earnings, end of last year	$51,434
Add net income for this year	32,156
Deduct dividend declared	(25,000)
Retained earnings, end of this year	$58,590

Fergama Productions Inc.
Balance Sheet as at the End of This Year

Assets			**Liabilities and Equity**		
Current assets			Current liabilities		
Cash	$26,712		Accounts payable	$19,192	
Accounts receivable	70,654		Taxes payable	6,169	$ 25,361
Supplies inventory	5,913	$103,279	Long-term loan		10,000
Noncurrent assets			Shareholders' equity		
Office equip. cost	$24,486		Share capital	$20,000	
Accum. amort.	(13,814)	10,672	Retained earn.	58,590	78,590
TOTAL		$113,951	TOTAL		$113,951

5. Is the company better off than last year? Well, first, substantial net income was earned this year. By the definition of net income, the company has increased its net resources (assets minus liabilities). While most of this income was paid as a dividend to the owners, not all of it was, so the retained earnings are higher than last year. Regarding current position, the working capital was $73,082 last year and is higher, $77,918 this year. The working capital ratio was 2.46 last year and is 4.07 this year. So it appears that the company is better off this year than last. (More ways of answering this question are developed in later chapters.)

SOLUTION OUTLINE FOR PROBLEM 4.1

1. Managing cash flow is important because in our economy cash is the medium of exchange by which business is done. An enterprise must have sufficient cash inflow to cover its need for cash outflow to pay bills, buy new assets, pay dividends, etc. In the short run, or at difficult times of the year, managing cash flow may be more important than managing overall performance as measured by the accrual basis income statement.
2. Yes. A company can show a good net income, but if it does not collect its accounts receivable, or if it buys too much inventory, so cash is either not coming in from customers or is "tied up" in inventory, the cash from operations can be smaller than the net income.
3. Because net income includes substantial noncash expenses (amortization, especially) that depress income but do not affect cash from operations, for most companies net income will be lower than cash income (cash from operations).
4. Cash and cash equivalents are cash on hand and in banks plus assets that are really holding places for temporarily unneeded cash (such as term deposits, investment certificates, and other temporary investments) minus very short-term borrowings, repayment of which could be demanded in cash at any time (such as demand bank loans or loans under lines of credit that are expected to be repaid in a few days when cash comes in).

SOLUTION OUTLINE FOR PROBLEM 4.2

See the SCFP in Section 4.5. That SCFP has sufficient extra detail that you should be able to track down any errors you might make in producing your own version.

SOLUTION OUTLINE FOR PROBLEM 4.3

1. The SCFP's cash flow information covers at least the following:
   a. It tells you what the cash income (cash from operations) is.
   b. It tells you why the cash income differs from the accrual net income.
   c. It reports whether the company's noncash working capital is rising or falling (supplementing the working capital and working capital ratio: if working capital is growing, that may not be good if it is because receivables are not being collected or inventories are increasing, and if such is going on, the SCFP will point out the negative effect of this on cash).
   d. It reports several cash activities that the income statement does not include and that can be determined from the balance sheet only if you know how to do it, such as expenditures on additional noncurrent assets, proceeds from the sale of such assets, and the raising and repayment of noncurrent liabilities and share capital.
   e. It reports how much cash was used to pay dividends.
2. Net change in cash and cash equivalents = \$127,976 – \$40,000 – \$238,040 + \$147,000 = – \$3,064. CCE have gone down \$3,064 during the year.
3. Effects if the event had occurred during the year:
   a. Investing would show an expenditure of \$38,950 and Financing would show a cash inflow of \$28,950 from long-term borrowing. The net change in CCE would be \$10,000 lower.
   b. There would have been a gain on sale of \$880. This gain would have increased the net income but would be deducted in the Operations section of the SCFP to remove the noncash gain from income in calculating cash from operations. The proceeds of \$4,100 would be included as proceeds in the Investing section, reducing the cash expenditure on additional noncurrent assets. The net change in CCE would be \$4,100 higher (the cash received).
   c. The change in accounts receivable would have been \$6,000 higher in the direction of reducing cash in the Operations section of the SCFP, because this revenue is reflected in income but hasn't yet been collected. Cash from operations and the net change in CCE would be \$6,000 lower.
   d. The SCFP reports only dividends actually paid. Therefore this \$15,000 would be ignored on the SCFP. (It might be included as a deduction from dividends declared in calculating the amount of dividends paid, but this calculation is not usually shown.)
   e. The demand loan would go into the cash equivalent assets part of CCE and also into the cash equivalent liabilities part of CCE, so its net effect on CCE would be zero. The amount would not appear anywhere in the body of the SCFP, but it would be included in the reconciliation of CCE at the bottom of the SCFP (both cash equivalent assets and cash equivalent liabilities would be \$25,000 larger).

SOLUTION OUTLINE FOR PROBLEM 4.4

For convenience, this outline refers to the North West Company SCFP (See Appendix 1). If you used another company's SCFP, your comments should be roughly parallel.

1. There aren't many variations. The cash from operations is separated into that from continuing vs. discontinued operations (at least in 1993, when there was some of the latter), but that is done whenever discontinued operations have a significant part of the cash flow. The company puts dividends near the bottom of the SCFP, not right after operations, but then so does Tyson Foods in Section 4.7. One small item is that North West has shown the effect of foreign currency translation (in the equity section of the balance sheet) as a separate item in the SCFP, rather than burying it inside larger items.
2. In the period ended January 29, 1994, cash from operations was \$15,529, while net income was \$17,162. The former is smaller because the increase in noncash working capital (receivables, inventories, etc.), which hurts cash, is smaller than the depreciation, amortization, and deferred income tax corrections, which are added back to net income.
3. CCE is defined as cash minus bank advances and short-term notes, and is negative in both years.
4. The balance sheet indicates that accounts receivable have gone up, as have inventories and prepaid expenses, while accounts payable have gone down. All of these changes reduce cash from operations. Amortization and similar expenses were added back to net income. They had no effect on cash, so the SCFP add-backs corrected net income up toward cash income.
5. Answered with Question 4.
6. Main things going on: \$15 million was generated from operations and \$25 million from financing (mostly new noncurrent debt). This money was spent on additional noncurrent assets (\$34 million net) and on dividends (\$6 million), so CCE ended up almost the same in the most recent period as the previous one.

SOLUTION OUTLINE FOR PROBLEM 4.5

1. To see how this works, assume the inadvertently misclassified dividend payable is \$1,000. When included in the noncash working capital changes, it would have a positive effect on cash from operations of \$1,000, because it would be part of the increases in current liabilities that increase cash from operations. So cash from operations would be \$1,000 too high. Dividends paid, lower down on the SCFP, would be \$1,000 too high because it would appear that all the dividends had been paid. The dividends figure should therefore be \$1,000 lower. There would be no net effect on CCE because the apparently higher cash *inflow* from operations would be equal to the apparently higher cash *outflow* for dividends.
2. a Let x be the acquisitions during the year. Then x – \$236,100 amortization expense – \$840,000 cost removed when building was sold + \$650,000 accumulated amortization removed when building was sold = \$459,200 net change. Solving, x = \$885,300. Going the other way, \$885,300 – \$840,000 – \$236,100 + \$650,000 = \$459,200.

b. The book value of the building was \$840,000 – \$650,000 = \$190,000. The \$200,000 proceeds – \$190,000 book value = \$10,000 gain on sale.

c. Add back amortization of \$236,100; subtract gain on sale of \$10,000.

d. Investing would show \$885,300 acquisitions minus \$200,000 proceeds, for a net expenditure of \$685,300.

SOLUTION OUTLINE FOR PROBLEM 5.1

The set of financial statements is a set and should be interpreted as such because all the statements are prepared, directly or (for the SCFP) indirectly, from the set of balanced accounts. Therefore, they are all portions of the whole set of accounts and the meaning of each is inextricably linked to the others. Some examples:

- Income on the income statement is produced by increasing net resources, so the revenues and expenses are linked to balance sheet accounts such as accounts receivable (uncollected revenue), accounts payable (unpaid expenses), and accumulated amortization (the sum of amortization expenses over time).
- Income is carried from the income statement to the retained earnings statement.
- Dividends on the retained earnings statement are reflected in the balance sheet as either a decrease in cash or an increase in the dividends payable liability.
- Net income from the income statement is used as the beginning figure on the SCFP, which itself is an analysis of changes in balance sheet accounts.

SOLUTION OUTLINE FOR PROBLEM 5.2

Here are some ideas in response to the sentences. You may well think of several other concepts/principles and probably will make additional points about some of them.

1. Three concepts/principles related to this are fairness, reliability, and verifiability. Some effects on financial statements of these are: accountants are careful that all cash transactions and day-to-day events such as credit sales and purchases are reflected in the financial statements; considerable care is taken to minimize errors and omissions in the accounting system that underlies the financial statements; and auditors ensure that important financial statement data can be traced back to underlying events and evidence.
2. Three concepts/principles related to this are conservatism, fairness, and matching. Conservatism results (or should) in financial statements that contain prudent, not overly optimistic estimates of future cash inflows and outflows regarding present assets and liabilities. Fairness has the effect of keeping conservatism in bounds so that the financial statements are not pessimistic (which would be unfair to present owners and managers). Matching says that estimates affecting revenues should be done on comparable bases to those affecting expenses, so that the net income makes sense, so it puts some bounds on conservatism too.

3. Three concepts/principles related to this are conformance with GAAP, consistency, and comparability. Conformance with GAAP ensures that the company's information is prepared in ways the user might expect, to permit meaningful analyses of its performance. The objective of consistency over time results in highlighting inconsistencies so that the user can consider their effects on the information. The goal of comparability refers directly to the idea of "relative performance" because if the previous two principles are met, the company can be evaluated by comparison to others like it, or to others the user might consider investing in or lending to.
4. Two concepts/principles related to this are disclosure and decision relevance. Disclosure has the effect of helping users understand how the accounting numbers were computed and thus helping to make estimates of future effects. Decision relevance is a reminder that the financial statements should be useful both in past-oriented decisions (such as evaluating management's performance or calculating bonuses) and in future-oriented decisions (such as whether to invest in or lend to the company).
5. Three concepts/principles related to this are fairness, reliability, and verifiability. The goal of all three is partly to minimize the effects of human error, biases, and wishes on the information by promoting objective, careful methods of preparing it and making it possible (in principle) for anyone else who prepares it to come up with, and agree with, the same information.

SOLUTION OUTLINE FOR PROBLEM 5.3

1. Independence is considered necessary for it not to matter to the auditors what the financial statements say. Independence helps to ensure that the auditors will bring a detached, professional view to their task. If the auditors were not independent, they might "want" the results to turn out a certain way so that they were better off (for example, if the audit fee was a percentage of net income, then the auditors might go along with methods that make income higher because they would benefit).
2. Independence is difficult to maintain for several reasons. First, the auditors would not have the audit job the next year if the company were to fail, so they are likely to prefer that the company continue to exist, and might be tempted to agree to accounting methods that hide problems. Second, the auditors have to work closely with management, and may depend on management for other business (e.g., tax or accounting advice) that is nice to have. Third, though the auditors are officially appointed by the shareholders, a recommendation by management that the auditors be reappointed (or not) is likely to be accepted by the shareholders, who are not usually very close to the company or to the auditors. Fourth, the auditors are human and get to know and like the people they work with, such as the company management and employees, and usually would like such people to succeed—it's hard to be detached all the time.

SOLUTION OUTLINE FOR PROBLEM 5.1

In order to answer this, let's assume that, at least for some inventories, market is lower than cost. Otherwise, the accountant probably would not have been too concerned. The effects would be:

Balance sheet: the inventory, current assets, and working capital would all be reduced by the difference between cost and market for those inventories whose market is less than cost.

Income statement: that difference would be deducted as an expense on the income statement and therefore would result in a lower net income. (Income tax expense would be smaller on the lower income, which would reduce the negative effect on income somewhat—more about this in later chapters.)

SCFP: the net income figure would be smaller, but that change would be cancelled by a smaller change in the inventories from one year to the next (and in income tax payable, if there is a change in the income tax expense). These effects would all cancel each other out, so that there would be no net effect on cash from operations or on any other SCFP figure.

SOLUTION OUTLINE FOR PROBLEM 5.5

Income from Brassy on cost basis	(.40 × 250,000)	$100,000
Income from Brassy on equity basis	(.40 × 600,000)	240,000
Extra income if equity basis were used		$140,000
Present income of China Sports		800,000
Revised income		$940,000

SOLUTION OUTLINE FOR PROBLEM 5.6

1. Goodwill on consolidation:

a. Net fair value of Piddling's equity ($16,100,000 – $8,300,000)	$ 7,800,000
b. Portion acquired (80% of $7,800,000)	$ 6,240,000
c. Purchase price for that portion	10,800,000
d. Goodwill (c) minus (b)	$ 4,560,000

2. Minority is credited with no goodwill and so is assigned 20% of the book value of Piddling's equity. 20% of $6,400,000 = $1,280,000
3. Consolidated balance sheet figures are on the next page.

		Consolidated
General assets		
Big	$105,000,000	
Piddling	14,600,000	
Portion of fair value changes		
(.80 × [$16,100,000 – $14,600,000])	1,200,000	$120,800,000
Investment in Piddling		
Does not appear on consolidated balance		
sheet because it is an intercompany item		0
Goodwill		
From Question 1		4,560,000
Total consolidated assets		$125,360,000
General liabilities		
Big	$ 83,700,000	
Piddling	8,200,000	
Portion of fair value changes		
(.80 × [$8,300,000 – $8,200,000])	80,000	$ 91,980,000
Minority interest		
From Question 2 above		1,280,000
Equity		
Parent's equity only appears on the consolidated		
balance sheet; subsidiary's equity does not		
appear because it is an intercompany item		32,100,000
Total consolidated liabilities and equity		$125,360,000

SOLUTION OUTLINE FOR PROBLEM 6.1

Users of financial information may want summarized information for several reasons. First of all, they do not have the opportunity or the time to dig up the source documents for a company and to check the ledger and other books themselves. Second, summarization and classification have information value themselves. Third, users like aggregated numbers, which summarize the organization and can be used to trigger actions such as buying or selling shares. Fourth, if the summaries reflect the judgments of experts (for instance, professional accountants), they may be very credible to users.

However, it is very important that users understand the assumptions behind financial data. For example, a company that uses its equipment heavily during the first few years may amortize this equipment rapidly as a consequence. The company's net income and performance ratios will be different from those of a company amortizing its equipment less rapidly. Therefore, the figures being summarized may be different from company to company, as each tries to measure its performance and position appropriately. The summaries themselves follow various procedures that this book describes, so the summarization process should also be well understood if the resulting financial statements are to be understood.

SOLUTION OUTLINE FOR PROBLEM 6.2

a. No transaction so no entry.

b. DR Advertising expense 200
  CR Accounts Payable 200

(This entry may not be recorded until December 31, because there is no economic exchange until the advertisement is run.)

c. DR Bond asset 2,000
  CR Cash 2,000

The interest will be recorded periodically during the three years. In addition to cash interest, entries debiting bond asset and crediting interest revenue will eventually raise the asset value to the $2,500 to be received in three years. (Such entries are beyond the scope of this book.)

d. No transaction yet so no entry.

e. DR Cash 300
  CR Deferred revenue liability 300
(or Customer deposits liability)

f. DR Insurance expense 50 (1/12 × 600)
DR Prepaid insurance 550
  CR Cash 600

Assumption: that the insurance is consumed equally over the twelve months.

SOLUTION OUTLINE FOR PROBLEM 6.3

Journal entry (start with the easy accounts first):

	DR	CR
CR Cash		1,000,000
CR Long-term debt *		3,200,000
DR Inventory	280,000	
DR Land	1,500,000	
DR Building	1,800,000	
DR Equipment	470,000	
DR Rights	40,000	
CR Loan		130,000
DR Loss (Expense)**	240,000	
or		
DR Goodwill (NCA)**		

* Represents the difference between the purchase price and the down payment.

** To balance the journal entry, you must decide whether the additional price paid for the net assets is an expense, or a long-term asset to be amortized over time. Many people prefer to expense it all at once, since Big Ideas has only purchased a few assets of the company and not the entire organization (goodwill cannot come from the individual assets, except the dealer rights), but others would call the difference goodwill asset.

SOLUTION OUTLINE FOR PROBLEM 6.4

1. Cost of goods sold = Beginning inventory $ 246,720
   + Purchases 1,690,000
   − Ending inventory (324,800)
   $1,611,920

Cost of goods sold =	Beginning inventory	$ 246,720
	+ Purchases	1,690,000
	− Ending inventory	(324,800)
		$1,611,920

2. If the correct COGS is $1,548,325, this means that some of what appeared to have been sold was not. It was lost, or stolen, or it strayed! The amount lost is $63,595, which could be left in the COGS expense or could be shown separately, so that the COGS expense would be the accurate, smaller amount. Total expense would not be different; the perpetual method just allows it to be split into $1,548,325 COGS and $63,595 loss, which were lumped together under the periodic method. The need for the $63,595 adjustment indicates that the company has what seems a serious problem somewhere: there are errors in the records, inventories are being lost somehow, or there are more sinister things going on, like employee theft.
3. Companies may not use the perpetual method because of its greater cost to operate. It may be felt that the improved recordkeeping is not worth its cost. Here, the losses are large enough that a reasonable perpetual control system would probably be affordable.

SOLUTION OUTLINE FOR PROBLEM 6.5

1. Journal Entries

a. DR Cash	5,100	
CR Long-term debt		5,000
CR Share capital		100

Although there were no repayment terms on the loan and it is interest free, it is recorded as debt, not equity, since Graham Cline Inc. presumably must pay it back.

b. DR Prepaid expense	120	
CR Cash		120

Storage was prepaid for the year.

DR Storage expense	120	
CR Prepaid expense		120

By the end of the year, the storage had been used. No entry for the $130 until 1996.

c. DR Buns inventory	500	
DR Wieners inventory	1,500	
CR Cash		2,000

Purchase of inventory.

d. DR Hot dog stands expense	600	
CR Cash		100
CR Accounts payable		500

Since the stands were expected only to last this summer, their cost is expensed.

DR Hot dog stands expense	60	
CR Cash		60

The cost of fixing up the stands.

DR Accounts payable	500	
DR Interest expense	29	
CR Cash		529

Payment on December 31, 1995, of the payable and the interest (interest = $500 × .10 × 7/12 = $29).

e. DR Cash	7,000	
CR Revenue		7,000

We assume that sales were for cash only, since people don't usually use credit for hot dog purchases!

f. DR Wages expense	2,400	
CR Cash		2,400

Student employee's wages.

g. DR Cost of goods sold expense	1,960	
DR Left-over products expense	40	
CR Buns inventory		500
CR Wieners inventory		1,500

Ten dozen buns and wieners remain in inventory. Therefore, 490 dozen were sold during the summer. We assumed that the remaining inventory will not last until next summer. Therefore, the inventory on hand is set to 0.

h. DR Income tax expense	358	
CR Cash		358

Income before tax = 7,000 – 120 – 29 – 600 – 60 – 2,400 – 1,960 – 40 = 1,791

Tax = .20 × 1,791 = $358

i. DR Long-term debt	5,000	
CR Cash		5,000

Repayment to Graham's father.

j. DR Dividends declared (Ret. earn.)	500	
CR Cash		500

Dividend: $5 per share × 100 shares

2.

Graham Cline Inc.
Balance Sheet as at December 31, 1995

Assets		Liabilities and Equity	
Cash	$1,033	Common shares	$ 100
		Retained earnings	933
Total Assets	$1,033		$1,033

Graham Cline Inc.
Statement of Income and Retained Earnings
for the year ended December 31, 1995

Sales revenue		$7,000
Cost of goods sold		1,960
Gross margin		$5,040
Operating expenses		
Left-over products	$ 40	
Storage	120	
Wages	2,400	
Interest	29	
Hot dog stands	660	
Total operating expenses		$3,249
Income before income tax		$1,791
Income tax expense		358
Net income for the year		$1,433
Beginning retained earnings		0
Less dividend declared		(500)
Ending retained earnings		$ 933

3. Graham did make some money. His company earned $1,791 ($1,433 after tax) over the summer and repaid his father, but his employee earned more than that for doing less work (one of the two stands, no management). All that Graham actually received was the $500 dividend. Therefore, Graham should consider whether the venture could be made more viable next year. He may have enjoyed being his own boss, but so far the hot dog stand business seems to have been a marginal one.

SOLUTION OUTLINE FOR PROBLEM 7.1

1. Revenue is economic value created through a transaction with a customer, whether or not the customer pays the cash at the time. A cash receipt is the payment by the customer.
2. Revenue but not receipt: credit sales. Receipt but not revenue: a deferred revenue, i.e., down payments or cash advances, for work yet to be performed. Both revenue and receipt: cash sales.

3. Expense: cost of assets used or commitments incurred to pay assets (usually cash) in producing revenue. Matched with revenue, not necessarily with outflow of cash. Recognition of expense may precede, accompany, or follow payment of cash (cash disbursement). Expenses are found on the income statement, cash changes are found on the SCFP.
4. Expense but not disbursement: depreciation, accrued interest, COGS (contrast with cash purchases of inventories). Disbursement but not expense: purchase asset, reduce a payable, pay dividends. Both expense and disbursement: small bills, utilities, donations.

SOLUTION OUTLINE FOR PROBLEM 7.2

	Adjust?	*Journal Entry*		
a.	Y	DR Accounts receivable	3,200	
		CR Revenue		3,200
b.	Y	DR Cost of goods sold expense	1,900	
		CR Inventory		1,900
c.	Y	DR Customer deposits liability	3,900	
		CR Revenue		3,900
d.	Y	DR Store building (asset)	62,320	
		CR Maintenance expense		62,320
e.	Y	DR Warranty expense	4,300	
		CR Warranty liability		4,300
	N	No adjustment seems required for the pain and suffering claim.		
f.	Y	DR Audit expense	2,350	
		CR Accounts payable		2,350
g.	Y	DR Automobile (asset)	17,220	
		CR Accounts payable		17,220
h.	Y	DR Distribution rights amortization expense	500	
		CR Distribution rights (asset)		500

SOLUTION OUTLINE FOR PROBLEM 7.3

Calculation:			
	Revenue (174,320 – 11,380 + 9,440)		$172,380
	Bad debts expense (1,130 – 890 + 520)	$ 760	
	COGS, wages, etc. (165,690 – 12,770 + 15,510 + 21,340 – 24,650)	145,120	
	Interest (12,000 × 8% × 1/12)	80	
	Income tax (2,340 + 3,400 + 1,230)	6,970	152,930
	Accrual net income		$ 19,450

SOLUTION OUTLINE FOR PROBLEM 7.4

1. Revenue recognition points:
   a. As cash is received;
   b. After the outlets have opened, recognize all revenue;
   c. At the signing of the contract, recognize all revenue;
   d. Recognize the full revenue after the down payment is received;
   e. On some other basis.

2. Rank:

a. As cash is received;	*Most Conservative*
b. After the outlets have opened;	*to*
c. After the down payment is received;	
d. After the signing of the contract.	*Least Conservative*

3. Methods of recognizing expenses:
   a. All general and franchise-related costs immediately;
   b. All general expenses, but only 18/28 of the franchise-related costs;
   c. All general expenses, but only 26/28 of the franchise-related costs;
   d. In proportion to the cash received;
   e. Some other formula.

4. Matching:
   a. "Cash received" revenue with "proportion of cash received" expenses (for example, ($5,000 / $20,000) × ($230,000 / 28): after down payment is received);
   b. "After the outlets have opened" with general expenses plus (18 / 28) × $230,000;
   c. "After the down payment is received" with general expenses plus (26 / 28) × $230,000;
   d. "After the signing of the contract" with expensing all general and franchise-related costs immediately.

5. a. After the outlets have opened:

Revenue:		$360,000	($20,000 × 18)
Expenses:			
General	$ 55,000		
Franchise	147,857		(18/28 × $230,000)
Total Expenses		202,857	
Net Income		$157,143	

b. As cash is received:

Revenue:		$130,000	(26 × $5,000)
Expenses:			
General	$55,000		
Franchise	53,393		([$5,000 / $20,000]) ×
Bad Debts	24,643		[$230,000 / 28] × 26)
Total Expenses		133,036	
Net Income (Loss)		$ (3,036)	

Explanation: assuming that the existing $230,000 in franchise-related expenses are evenly distributed to each franchise, the total cost for each franchise to this date is $230,000 / 28 franchises = $8,214.29. Since we are using the cash received basis for income measurement, revenue is 26 × $5,000 = $130,000; franchise expense is ($8,214.29 × ($5,000 / $20,000) × 26).

The reason that only 26 franchises are included is that two have not paid any money ($0 / $20,000 × $8,214.29 = $0 expenses). Bad debt expenses total (4 × $8,214.29 × $15,000 / $20,000) = $24,643, because four franchisees appear to be incapable of ever paying the remaining $15,000 outstanding.

6. The second revenue recognition policy in Question 5 seems to be the best, because The Pie Place and its franchises are new and not really established yet. However, the complexity of its assumptions may be confusing.
7. A typical footnote may read:

   The company recognizes revenue on a cash basis and expenses are deferred and recognized according to the percentage that cash received is of the total franchise price remaining to be received. All general expenses are expensed in the period they are incurred. Remaining deferred expenses for any insolvent or closed franchises are written off.

SOLUTION OUTLINE FOR PROBLEM 7.5

a. Current portion of tax expense:

Income before tax	$ 648,960
Minus non-taxable revenue	(29,650)
Add back amortization	1,149,612
Deduct capital cost allowance	(1,493,114)
Taxable income	$ 275,808

Current tax = $275,808 × .32 = $88,259

b. Deferred portion of tax expense:

Method 1: ($1,493,114 – $1,149,612) × .32 = $109,921
Method 2: Total tax expense = ($648,960 – $29,650) × .32
= $198,179
Deferred portion = $198,179 – $88,259 current portion = $109,920

(The two methods are equivalent: there is just a rounding difference.)

c. Net income = $648,960 – $198,179 total tax expense = $450,781

d. Deferred income tax liability = $329,612 + $109,920 (or $109,921) = $439,532

e. Retained earnings = $3,949,286 + $450,781 = $4,400,067

SOLUTION OUTLINE FOR PROBLEM 8.1

Some of the many points that might be made:

1. a. If the market responds quickly and efficiently to information, it indicates the efficient allocation of capital resources. Money flows toward viable companies and away from less viable ones. So, accounting information assists in this allocation process.

   b. There are systematic and unsystematic risks in a stock market. Accounting information can help in assessing a stock's unsystematic risk.

2. a. Information is used in a "stewardship" role in order to maintain contractual arrangements. Accounting therefore assists in the effective administration of contracts in the economy.

   b. Changes in the contractual arrangements will cause changes in the accounting information that is required. Accounting's use responds to the nature of the control/administration role assigned it.

SOLUTION OUTLINE FOR PROBLEM 8.2

This question can be answered in many ways. You may be cynical and state that accounting is not appropriate for either purpose. Or you may say that external reporting is the most important, or that internal control is. Whatever your position, make sure you can support it with cogent arguments.

One position is to say that financial accounting exists for both purposes, as outlined below.

1. *Information for outsiders*:
   - It allows comparison by investors because each firm is reporting using the same guidelines (GAAP).
   - An independent auditor reviews the information to ensure that it fairly presents the financial position of the company.
   - The information is for everyone, because supposedly it is to be largely understood by the general users who take due diligence to analyze the statements.
2. *Internal*:
   - It assists in such areas as inventory control, which is important for company control.
   - Incentive plans can be based on the accounting information, which provides control.
   - Since the information is prepared for the owners (shareholders), it may eliminate some management bias and promote clearer evaluation of management performance.

SOLUTION OUTLINE FOR PROBLEM 8.3

Some very sketchy comments, intended to generate ideas, are:

1. a. The economic entity that capital markets are presumably interested in is not necessarily the legal entity. For example, a set of consolidated statements is based on the presumed economic entity.

   b. The historical cost basis increases reliability of information but may reduce relevance to current decisions by market participants.

   c. Fairness aims to increase confidence in objectivity or impartiality of information. But is this term too vague? Is fairness open to too wide an interpretation by preparers of information and thus too vague to be really useful to markets and other agents?

   d. Although choice is permitted in the presentation of accounting information, there are guidelines that set boundaries. Therefore, markets can have some confidence about the acceptable range of information being presented.

   e. There is potential for management and/or preparers to have undue influence over accountants and auditors. Users rely on the audit report since the auditors are independent. Professional ethics help ensure this independence and the care and expertise required to do a technically competent job of preparing the accounting information.

2. a. The financial statements are consolidated. The preparers have used a method of consolidation to create financial statements that represent the commonly controlled entity.
   b. Historical cost is the basic measure for most account balances in the large public company's financial statements, including the property, equipment, new debt issued, and so on. Since every company uses the original price under historical cost, the statements satisfy one of the main elements of information: objectivity.
   c. The main piece of evidence relating to fairness is in the audit report. This report gives the external auditor's opinion that the statements are fair.
   d. The auditor's report also says that the statements have been prepared following GAAP.
   e. Professional ethics is implied in the presumably expert, unbiased, independent status of the external auditor. That auditor is expected to act professionally, and not to follow anyone else's dictates in judging the fairness of the financial statements.
3. These concepts are still relevant to a small, private company. While the larger company's information is of interest to market traders and the private company's is not, they otherwise have many similar users: banks, taxation authorities, managers, and perhaps potential owners. Though the use context may differ somewhat, these underlying concepts are still valuable.

SOLUTION OUTLINE FOR PROBLEM 8.4

Balance Sheet End Last Year		+	Income Statement This Year		=	Balance Sheet End This Year	
Assets			*Revenue*			*Assets*	
Rec. up	$8,000		Up	$10,000		Rec. up	$18,000
Liabilities			*Expenses*			*Liabilities*	
Other than tax			*Other than tax*			*Other than tax*	
Pay. up	$3,000		Exp. up	$ 4,000		Pay. up	$ 7,000
Income tax			*Income tax*			*Income tax*	
Up	$1,750		Up	$ 2,100		Up	$ 3,850
Equity						*Equity*	
Retained earn.			*Net income*			*Retained earn.*	
Up	$3,250		Up	$ 3,900		Up	$ 7,150

Note that this question could alternatively have been phrased something like this: "Receivables will increase $18,000 at the end of the current year and $8,000 at the end of the previous year; payables will increase $7,000 at the end of the current year and $3,000 at the end of the previous year." In that case, the current year's net income figures would be deduced from the balance sheet effects, whereas above, the current year's balance sheet effects were deduced from the income figures and the previous balance sheet. In this alternative wording, sometimes people think that the current balance sheet effects will be added to the prior ones (for example, the receivables increase would be *calculated as $26,000). This would be incorrect, because the current balance sheet effects* already *include all prior effects: each balance sheet is the aggregation of everything recorded prior to that.*

There is no effect on cash, but the SCFP's internal numbers will change:

Net income will go up	(positive apparent effect)	$ 3,900
Change in accts. rec'ble will go up	(negative apparent effect)	(10,000)
Change in accts. pay'ble will go up	(positive apparent effect)	4,000
Change in tax pay'ble will go up	(positive apparent effect)	2,100
Net effect on cash from operations		$ 0

SOLUTION OUTLINE FOR PROBLEM 8.5

1. Present value = ($100,000 + $200,000) / $(1 + 0.08)^5$
   = $204,175

   Therefore, the P.V. exceeds the investment cost of $200,000, which means the investment returns more than the 8% required. So you should invest. An investment of $204,175 would return 8%, but you only have to pay $200,000.

2. Other factors:
   - Risk (will the investee pay back what has been promised, on time?);
   - Stability (8% may seem enough today but if interest rates rise, locking up the $200,000 for five years may seem to have been a mistake);
   - Alternative sources of returns (this is barely above 8%; perhaps there are better places to invest the $200,000).

SOLUTION OUTLINE FOR PROBLEM 9.1

Some advantages and disadvantages of ratio analysis are below. You probably will think of others!

Advantages:

- Ratios summarize the financial statements and so provide information in a more concise way, more accessible to decision makers than wading through all the detailed numbers.
- Ratios are scale-free measures so they can be used to compare enterprises of different sizes, or the same enterprise over periods of time in which its size changes.
- Ratios can be aggregated into industry and other groupings, facilitating comparisons of the enterprise to others.
- Because they have both numerators and denominators, ratios can be usefully sensitive to changes in the underlying figures.
- As summarized information, ratios may be easier for less sophisticated people (or nonaccountants in general) to understand than are the detailed financial statements.
- Because they are ratios, the ratios can be related to the "relative return" goal that is presumed to lie behind investors' and creditors' decision-making.

Disadvantages and ways around them:

- Because they are summarizations, ratios are only as good as the underlying data and so will not be meaningful if the data are not (way around: establish that the financial statements are audited, with a "presents fairly" unqualified opinion by the auditors).
- If managers or others know that people will rely on certain ratios, they may strive to produce satisfactory ratios, such as by reducing maintenance expenses or not acquiring new assets, rather than focusing on the fundamental underlying business issues (way around: use ratios with care and find out what managerial actions lie behind them).
- Ratios are just numbers and have no meaning in themselves apart from the phenomena they summarize, for example there is nothing magic about a working capital ratio of 2 (way around: become very knowledgeable about the enterprise and its competitors so that meaningful comparisons may be made).
- There are many different ratios and alternative ways of calculating most of them, so that comparing ratios as calculated by others can be frustrating and not very informative (way around: know how to calculate the ratios that are important to you and use those calculations instead of others' versions if there are problems with those versions).

SOLUTION OUTLINE FOR PROBLEM 9.2

1. Such a concept of performance relates the return to the investment required to earn it, so enabling the relative return to be calculated. This is important because returns do require investment, people usually don't make investments without expecting a return, and the sizes of each have to be related to each other in order to evaluate the quality of the result. A $1,000 return would be great if the investment required was $2,000 (a ratio of 50%) but not so great if the investment were $200,000 (only 0.5%).
2. a. The interest earned could be compared to the $1,200 required to earn it.

   b. The consulting earnings could be compared to the $15,000 invested to earn them.

   c. This is harder because the returns are probably nonfinancial, such as the fun of driving a sports car, and so are not readily comparable to the car's cost—however, this sort of ratio is implicit in many buying decisions, in which we ask ourselves if the benefits we will obtain are worth the cost and we may well choose a cheaper car if the feeling of wind in our hair isn't all that important relative to what we have to pay for a convertible.

SOLUTION OUTLINE FOR PROBLEM 9.3

1. Financial leverage is the use of borrowed money to earn money. The leverage is positive if the money earned is greater than the cost of borrowing (e.g., if $10,000 borrowed at 8% is used to earn a 12% return), and it is negative if the money costs more to borrow than the borrower can earn using it.
2. Such leverage is risky for two main reasons. First, the return earned might not be what is hoped, and, if it is less than the cost of borrowing, then the borrowing ends up making the borrower worse off than without borrow-

ing at all. Second, the money obtained must be repaid, and the lender may take strong action, such as going to court or taking over management or taking assets, if the loan gets into difficulty. So borrowing may result in the loss of more than the money borrowed.

3. The Scott formula incorporates leverage by separating its effect on return on equity from the effect of the operating return (the day-to-day relative return without borrowing: return on assets). Leverage is computed by first of all calculating the difference between the return on assets and the cost of borrowing (in the example above, 12% minus 8%) and then multiplying that by the degree of borrowing relative to equity. If leverage is positive, the more borrowed, the better the effect on return on equity; if it is negative, the more borrowed, the worse the effect on return on equity.
4. The first company's leverage return is 4%; the second's is 1%. The two aspects of risk noted above are present in this comparison. The second company is more in danger of having leverage go negative, but the first company has borrowed relatively more. So the second company is at greater risk of leverage hurting, but the hurt will not be great because not as much is borrowed, whereas the first company has more to repay and so could get into more difficulty if problems do arise.

SOLUTION OUTLINE FOR PROBLEM 9.4

1. Return on equity = $6,000 / $45,000 = .133
2. Calculations (using Scott formula terms):

   ROE = .133 as above
   ROA = ($6,000 + $2,000) / $80,000 = .10
   Interest rate = $2,000 / $35,000 = .057 (IN)
   D/E = $35,000 / $45,000 = .778
   (ROA – IN) = .10 – .057 = .043
   Leverage = (.043) (.778) = .033

   So, managerial performance (ROA) shows a 10% return and leverage shows a 3.3% return, only a third of the ROA.
3. The assets financed would earn 10%, according to the above calculations. The cost of the money borrowed is 8%. Therefore, leverage is positive (2%) and the company should go ahead. This will, however, increase the company's risk because the interest has to be paid and return on assets could decline below that rate.
4. Some possible additional information and ratios (more can be imagined, so this is an outline only):

   - Terms and security of present debts;
   - Quality of management (especially Mr. A);
   - Industry and competition prospects;
   - Personal guarantees Mr. A might offer;
   - Interest coverage ratio;
   - Receivables collection and inventory turnover;
   - Sales return;
   - Income tax information.

SOLUTION OUTLINE FOR PROBLEM 9.5

a. Total current assets are unaffected (the cash came in and went out in one day).

b. Total assets increase by $100,000,000 (the additional equipment).

c. Total current liabilities decrease by $50,000,000 (reduced accounts payable).

d. The working capital ratio would be improved because the denominator, current liabilities, would decrease without there being any effect on the numerator, current assets.

e. No change in shareholders' equity (see (f), however).

f. No direct effect on earnings, but there will be increased interest and amortization expenses in the future. So, unless the additional equipment generates more revenue than that, earnings and shareholders' equity will be reduced in the future.

g. No effect on cash and cash equivalents (no net effect on cash, as noted in (a), and accounts payable are not likely part of cash and cash equivalents). (Cash generated by operations, as shown on the statement of changes in financial position, would decrease by $50,000,000 due to the reduction in accounts payable.)

h. Cash used for investments would increase by $100,000,000 (the additional equipment).

i. Cash provided from financing would increase by $150,000,000 (the borrowing, which would be shown as a noncurrent liability).

j. Effect on return on equity could be estimated by estimating the increased income to be earned from the new equipment and any interest charges on accounts payable that will be saved, and deducting from that the interest costs of the borrowing. All this should be done on an after-tax basis, because return on equity uses net income as its numerator.

k. The leverage return estimate would be done in a similar way. The effect on return on assets that is expected would be compared to the interest rate on the borrowing to determine if the leverage will be positive (presumably it is expected to be positive, otherwise the company would not have borrowed the money).

SOLUTION OUTLINE FOR PROBLEM 10.1

Some points you might consider in drafting your paragraph:

- The clash between the two objectives is real and yet unavoidable in all measurement systems intended for general use (for example, university grading systems).
- Somehow both objectives must be met (at least to some significant degree) or the financial statements will not be useful to anyone outside the company.
- One solution proposed (and used) is to rely on the expert judgment of accounting professionals to find solutions applicable to each company that are still sufficiently comparable to other companies.

- The conflict is important: it occupies much of the time and effort of accountants, auditors, and managers, and court cases have been fought over it. (It was determined in one important U.S. case that it was possible to follow GAAP and still provide financial statements that are unfair in representing the particular company.)
- The large structure of authoritative accounting standards and other development of GAAP began after the 1929 stock market crash and subsequent depression. Has all this helped to prevent repetitions of those problems?
- Perhaps a measurement system that does *not* adjust for individual circumstances (your height measure is not affected by your management objectives) provides, in the end, a more credible, useful measure. Perhaps the accounting objective of fitting the measure to the company is improper. Some countries have quite inflexible rules for financial statements—why not Canada?

SOLUTION OUTLINE FOR PROBLEM 10.2

1.

	1996	1995	1994
Highest income	LIFO	FIFO	FIFO
Lowest income	FIFO	AVGE	LIFO
Difference	$22,000	$13,000	$23,000
Effect on net income (70%)	$15,400	$ 9,100	$16,100

2. The company should choose an inventory cost policy that is fair and appropriate for its circumstances and stick with it. The fact that various methods might produce higher or lower incomes in various years is not a proper criterion for choice of a method. It smacks of manipulation.

SOLUTION OUTLINE FOR PROBLEM 10.3

1. A salvage value has to be assumed to answer this. Assuming it is zero, the amortization would be 10% of cost per year, $10,000 in 1994 and 1995.
   The entry would debit amortization expense and credit accumulated amortization with the $10,000.
2. Here the declining balance rate must be known. Let's assume it is "double declining balance" so that the rate is double the straight-line rate of 10%.
   Amortization for 1994 would be 20% of $100,000 = $20,000.
   Amortization for 1995 would be 20% of ($100,000 – $20,000) = $16,000.

3. Effects analysis:

Balance Sheet End Last Year		+	Income Statement This Year		=	Balance Sheet End This Year	
Assets			*Revenue*			*Assets*	
Acc. amort up	$(10,000)		no effect			Acc. amort up	$(16,000)
Liabilities			*Expenses*			*Liabilities*	
Other than tax			*Other than tax*			*Other than tax*	
no effect			Amort. exp. up	$6,000		no effect	
Income tax			*Income tax*			*Income tax*	
Down	$(4,000)		Down	$(2,400)		Down	$(6,400)
Equity						*Equity*	
Retained earn.			*Net income*			*Retained earn.*	
Down	$(6,000)		Down	$(3,600)		Down	$(9,600)

There is no effect on cash, but the SCFP's internal numbers will change:

Net income will go down (negative apparent effect)	$(3,600)
Amortization expense add-back will go up (positive apparent effect)	6,000
Deferred income tax add-back will go down (negative apparent effect)	(2,400)
Net effect on cash from operations	$ 0

SOLUTION OUTLINE FOR PROBLEM 10.4

1. Liabilities are obligations and estimates of obligations to people outside the enterprise, whereas equity is the residual ownership interest in the enterprise after considering such obligations to have the first claim on the resources (assets). Equity is what would be left after all the bills were paid, assuming that the assets were disposed of at book value and the liabilities were paid off, also at book value. Owners can be creditors too, for example for dividends or management fees, but such obligations will have been deducted from equity (as dividends or expenses) and so, to the extent owners are also creditors, they have less equity.
2. Liabilities include more than just debts. Debts are legally enforceable obligations, based on existing agreements regarding purchases, bank borrowings, and other borrowings. Liabilities also include estimates of future cash expenditures stemming from present activities, especially from present expense incurrence. Such estimates are not yet legal debts, but they are included as part of the expense recognition process in accrual accounting. They include deferred income tax, warranty liability, and short-term accruals for things like interest building up or power being used.
3. Examples of accruals that require difficult estimates:

   Short-term: (1) estimated income tax payable—the actual income tax payable is often not known until months or years have passed and may depend on the resolution of ambiguities in the tax law and even an audit by the tax authorities; (2) deferred revenue on the collection of container deposits by drink manufacturers—it is difficult to know how many containers will be returned for refund because many are lost or broken.

Long-term: (1) estimated pension liability—the actual payment, many years in the future, depends on employees' income levels, their health, future interest rates, and whether they stay employed long enough to qualify for various benefits; (2) estimated warranty liability—this depends on the quality of products sold, changes in laws giving consumers various rights, customers' satisfaction, media coverage, and many other uncertainties.

4. When a company purchases its own shares on the stock market, an account for the shares is created by an entry like: DR Investment, CR Cash. This investment is not an asset, though, because it is an interest in the other assets through its share of the company's ownership. Calling it an asset is like double counting, therefore. GAAP require that such an investment, called Treasury Shares, be instead deducted from the shareholders' equity so that the equity shows the net interest of real owners, after deducting the company's interest in itself represented by the treasury shares.

SOLUTION OUTLINE FOR PROBLEM 10.5

1. a. Net income would go down $46,900 (that is, $67,000 × [1 – .30]).

   b. No immediate cash flow effect, but a cash saving within a year due to lower income tax.

   c. Current tax liability is the only working capital account affected at present. It goes down $20,100 (that is, $67,000 × .30), so working capital is improved by that amount.

2. a. Net income would go down $7,500 (that is, $25,000 × .30)due to the extra income tax expense recognized.

   b. No effect on current cash flow. Net income's decline of $7,500 is offset by an increased deferred income tax add-back of $7,500.

   c. No effect on working capital. No working capital accounts are affected because the deferred tax in this case is noncurrent.

GLOSSARY OF TERMS

The following glossary provides definitions for many terms in financial accounting and refers readers back to those chapter sections in which the terms are discussed. If a good definition or discussion appears in a chapter section, the reference to that section may be provided without repeating the definition. Terms are cross-referenced to other terms where helpful. For additional help in finding things, consult the index at the end of the book.

Some supplementary help in developing this glossary came from: the *CICA Handbook* (Toronto: Canadian Institute of Chartered Accountants, version in effect June 30, 1994); S. Davidson, C.L. Mitchell, C.P. Stickney, and R.L. Weil, *Financial Accounting: An Introduction to Concepts, Methods and Uses* (Toronto: Holt, Rinehart & Winston of Canada, 1986); *Funk & Wagnalls Canadian College Dictionary* (Markham, Ont.: Fitzhenry & Whiteside, 1986); and Ross M. Skinner, *Accounting Standards in Evolution* (Toronto: Holt, Rinehart & Winston of Canada, 1987).

A

Accelerated amortization (depreciation) – an amortization method, such as declining balance, that records more amortization in the earlier years of an asset's life, and less in later years, than does the straight-line method. See **Straight-line amortization, Declining balance amortization,** and Section 10.5.

Account – a summary record of an asset, liability, owners' equity, revenue, or expense, in which the effects of transactions, accruals, and adjustments are indicated in dollars (where dollars are the currency of the country). See **General journal, General ledger, Transaction,** and Sections 3.5 and 6.5.

Accountant – a person who performs accounting functions. Professional accountants are those who are granted designations by self-regulating bodies on the basis of special training and successful examination. For example: CA, or Chartered Accountant (Canada, the United Kingdom); CGA, or Certified General Accountant (Canada); CMA, or Certified Management Accountant (Canada, the United States); and CPA, or Certified Public Accountant (the United States). See Section 1.5.

Accounting – "to account" is to provide a record, such as of funds paid or received for something. Being "accountable" is to be responsible for, as in to *account* for one's actions. These two ideas together describe the practice of accounting as the recordkeeping and reporting of an enterprise's performance and position in monetary terms. Management is responsible for the decisions made in an enterprise. Accounting provides the reports that summarize the economic results of these decisions for inside use and transmit them to outside, interested parties (such as investors, creditors, and regulatory agencies). See **Financial accounting** and **Management accounting.**

Accounting policies – the chosen accounting methods used by a company to recognize economic events on an accrual basis, and to report the financial position and results of operations. For examples, see the notes immediately following the financial statements of any company. See Section 10.2

Accounting policy choice – a decision among acceptable accounting policies is often needed because more than one acceptable policy exists in many areas. See Section 10.2.

Accounting principles – see **Generally accepted accounting principles.**

Accounting standards – The recommending of particular accounting methods or policies by an authoritative body. In Canada this is done by the Accounting Standards Committee of the Canadian Institute of Chartered Accountants; in the United States, by the Financial Accounting Standards Board. See **Accounting policies** and **Generally accepted accounting principles.**

Accounts Payable – liabilities representing amounts owed to short-term trade creditors. (An account payable for the debtor is an account receivable for the creditor.) See Section 10.8.

Accounts Receivable – amounts owing by debtors (customers), usually arising from sales of goods or services. See Section 7.9.

Accrual – entering amounts in the accounts to reflect events or estimates that are economically meaningful but that do not (at present) involve the exchange of cash. An example would be recognizing revenue from credit sales prior to receipt of cash from customers. See Section 7.3 and **Accrual accounting, Revenue recognition,** and **Matching;** see also **Deferral.**

Accrual accounting – the method of making an economically meaningful and comprehensive measurement of performance and position by recognizing economic events regardless of when cash transactions happen; as opposed to the simpler cash basis of accounting. Under this method, revenues and expenses (and related assets and liabilities) are reflected in the accounts in the period to which they relate.See Sections 1.4, 7.2, 7.3, and 10.2.

Accrual income – the result of subtracting expenses from revenue(s), when both kinds of accounts are calculated by accrual accounting. See **Accrual accounting, Net income,** and Sections 1.4, 3.3, 7.2, and 7.3.

Accrued expense – an expense recognized in the accounts prior to paying for it. See Sections 7.2, 7.3, and 10.8.

Accumulated amortization (depreciation) – a balance sheet account that accumulates total amortization (depreciation) expense over a number of years. The account balance is a credit and so is opposite to the debit-balance asset cost account. The difference between cost and accumulated amortization is the "book value" of the asset. See **Book value, Contra accounts, Fixed assets, Amortization, Depreciation,** and Sections 1.4, 7.11, and 10.5.

Accumulated foreign currency translation adjustment – an account arising as a consequence of the method used to convert foreign operations' accounting figures into Canadian dollars for the purpose of combining them with the figures for Canadian operations. Because income statement accounts are generally converted at average foreign exchange rates and balance sheet accounts are generally converted at year-end or historical rates, converted accounts do not quite balance. The difference is put into equity as a separate item because it does not seem to fit anywhere else and it is part of the (converted) residual equity of the owners.

Adjusting (journal) entry – a journal entry to implement accrual accounting by recognizing in the accounts economic events not yet adequately accounted for by the routine transactional accounting system. (For example, if there is no transaction to reveal the gradual wear and tear of a fixed asset, an adjusting entry must be made to recognize this depreciation.) See Section 7.4.

Adjustment(s) – See **Adjusting (journal) entry.**

Agency (contract) theory – is concerned with relationships between people in which one or more of them (the *agents,* such as managers, auditors, lawyers, and physicians) is or are entrusted with acting on behalf of one or more others (*the principals,* such as owners, creditors, defendants, and patients). Agency theory tends to focus on the stewardship role of accounting information (in monitoring and controlling the stewardship of the agent on behalf of the principal). Principals and agents will demand whatever information their specific relationship requires. See Section 8.5.

Aging of accounts receivable – the process of classifying accounts receivable by the time that has passed since the account came into existence. This classification is used as an aid to estimating the required allowance for doubtful accounts for the estimated amount of uncollectible accounts receivable. See Section 7.11.

Allocated, allocating – spread (spreading) the impact of an event out over time, as in amortization of an asset's cost over its useful life or recognition of revenue for a long-term contract over several periods. See **Amortization** and Sections 7.2, 7.3, and 7.7. (Allocation is also used, especially in management accounting, to refer to spreading the impact of an event across activities, such as in allocating the cost of repairs to different departments.)

Allowance for doubtful accounts – the estimated amount of accounts receivable that will not be collected (which are "doubtful"). The allowance, which is a contra account to accounts receivable, is used in order to recognize the bad debts expense related to such doubtful accounts but without removing those accounts from the books because the firm will still try to collect the amounts owing. See Section 7.11.

American Institute of Certified Public Accountants (AICPA) – the national self-regulating body in the United States that sets and monitors the auditing and professional standards by which CPAs practice.

Amortization – allocation of the cost of a noncurrent asset to expense over several accounting periods to recognize the "consumption" of the asset's economic value as it helps to earn revenue over those periods. Amortization expense for a period thus is deducted from revenue in that period, recognizing it as a cost of earning the revenue. The term amortization, and especially the common term depreciation, are used for the allocation of the cost of tangible assets over time; amortization is also used for the allocation of the cost of intangible assets such as patents, franchise rights, and goodwill. See **Depreciation, Intangible assets,** and Section 10.5.

Annual Report – the document provided annually to the shareholders by the officers of a company. It includes the financial statements, the notes to the financial statements, the auditor's report, supplementary financial information such as multi-year summaries, and reports from the company's board of directors and management. See Section 5.2.

Articulation – of the income statement, retained earnings statement, and balance sheet; refers to the fact that because these three statements are prepared from one set of balanced accounts, changes in any one of the three normally affect the others. In particular, recognition of revenue and expense relies on the fact that a revenue causes a change in the balance sheet, as does an expense. See **Recognition, Revenue recognition,** and Sections 3.3 and 10.3.

Asset(s) – an asset is a resource needed to do business in the future, represented by an ownership of or right to expected future economic benefits. Assets have value because they are expected to bring benefits as they are used or sold. See **Cash equivalent assets, Inventory, Accounts receivable, Current assets, Fixed assets, Intangible assets,** and Sections 2.3 and 2.5.

Asset valuation – see **Balance sheet valuation** and Section 5.7.

Attestation – a broader word than "audit," encompassing auditing and similar procedures to confirm or verify reports or events as fair and proper. See **Audit, Auditor's report,** and **Fairness.**

Audit – the examination of accounting records and their supporting documentation with the objective of determining the fairness with which the financial statements present the financial position and performance of the company. See **Auditor, Auditor's report,** and Section 5.4.

Auditor – the person or firm who performs an audit for the purpose of preparing a report on the credibility of the financial statements. See Sections 1.5 and 5.4.

Auditor's report – the document accompanying the financial statements that expresses the auditor's opinion on the fairness of the financial statements. The auditor's report explains what the auditor did and states the auditor's opinion. See Section 5.4.

Average cost (AVGE) – an inventory cost-flow assumption where the cost of an individual unit of inventory is the weighted average cost of the beginning inventory and subsequent purchases. See **Weighted average** and Section 10.4.

B

Bad debts expense – an expense account that results from the reduction in carrying value of those accounts receivable that have been projected to be uncollectible or doubtful. See **Allowance for doubtful accounts** and Section 7.11.

Balance sheet – the "balanced" list of assets, liabilities, and owners' equity constituting the formal statement of a company's financial position at a specified date, summarizing by category the assets, liabilities, and owners' equity. Sometimes referred to as the "Statement of Financial Position." See Sections 2.3, 2.5, and 5.7.

Balance sheet equation – the double-entry arithmetic by which Assets = Liabilities + Owners' Equity. See Section 2.4.

Balance sheet valuation – assigning numerical values to the balance sheet's assets, liabilities and owners' equity accounts. See Section 5.7.

Bankruptcy – the usually involuntary termination of an enterprise due to its inability to pay its debts and continue in operation. Bankruptcy usually involves significant losses to both creditors and owners.

Betterment – an expenditure to improve an asset's value to the business; more than just repairs and maintenance. See Section 5.8.

Big Bath – a way of manipulating reported income to show even poorer results in a poor year in order to enhance later years' results. See Section 3.9.

Board of directors – the senior level of management, representing and directly responsible to the owners (shareholders). Normally elected annually by the shareholders and responsible for hiring and supervising the operating management (president, chief executive officer, etc.).

Bond – a certificate of debt issued by an enterprise in return for cash, in which a promise is made to repay the debt (usually at a particular date or on a specified schedule) plus interest. Many bonds may be sold to other people by those who got them in return for the original cash provided to the enterprise.

Bond markets – capital markets in which debt instruments (bonds and similar items), rather than shares, are traded. See **Capital markets.**

Bookkeeping – the process of recording, classifying, and summarizing transactions in the books of account. See Section 6.4.

Books of original entry – the journals in which transactions are first recorded. See Section 6.6.

Book value – the amount shown in the accounts for any asset, liability, or owners' equity item, after deducting any related contra account (for example, the book value of a truck is the recorded cost minus accumulated amortization [depreciation]). The term is also commonly used to refer to the net amount of total assets less total liabilities (the recorded value of the owners' residual interest, which equals total equity: Assets – Liabilities = Equity). See Sections 2.5, 5.10, and 10.6.

Bottom line – a colloquialism referring to the net income (the "bottom line" on the income statement). See **Net income.**

C

Canada Business Corporations Act (CBCA) – the federal corporations act that provides the authority for the incorporation of federally incorporated companies in Canada and generally sets the requirements for their activities. It requires any such company to prepare annual financial statements.

Canadian Certified General Accountants Association – an association whose members (CGAs) have had training in accounting, taxation, auditing, and other areas of business and have passed qualifying exams. One of the three national professional accounting bodies. See **Accountant.**

Canadian Institute of Chartered Accountants (CICA) – a national self-regulating association of accountants who have met education and examination standards in Canada that sets and monitors the standards by which CAs practice. One of the three national professional accounting bodies. See **Accountant.**

Capital – the owner's contribution to or interest in a business (the equity). Often used specifically to refer to the equity of unincorporated businesses (proprietorships and partnerships). See **Equity** and Section 2.8.

Capital cost allowance – the Canadian Income Tax Act's version of amortization (depreciation). See Section 7.13.

Capitalization, capitalize – the recognition of an expenditure that may benefit a future period as an asset rather than as an expense of the period of its occurrence. Expenditures are capitalized if they are likely to lead to future benefits, and, thus, meet the criterion to be an asset. See Section 5.8.

Capital lease – a lease having the economic character of asset ownership. See Section 10.7.

Capital markets – markets in which financial instruments such as shares and bonds are traded. See Section 8.3.

Capital market theory – deals with the behaviour of aggregate markets (for example, stock markets) and with the role of information in the operation of such markets. See Section 8.3.

Cash – currency and coin on hand, balances in bank accounts, and other highly liquid assets. See Section 6.9.

Cash and cash equivalents – cash equivalent assets minus cash equivalent liabilities. Changes in cash and cash equivalents are explained by the statement of changes in financial position (SCFP). See Section 4.4.

Cash equivalent assets – a term used to describe cash plus liquid assets that can be converted into cash almost immediately on demand. Examples are bonds, stocks, treasury bills, and other financial paper that can be easily and quickly converted to cash. See Section 4.4.

Cash equivalent liabilities – liabilities that are payable on demand and so represent a reduction in the liquidity otherwise apparent from the amount of cash equivalent assets. An example is a bank loan payable on demand, used to acquire short-term investments. See Section 4.4.

Cash flow statement – see **Statement of changes in financial position (SCFP)** and Section 4.2.

Cash from operations – cash generated by day-to-day business activities and highlighted as the first Section in the statement of changes in financial position (SCFP). See Section 4.5.

Cash income – cash receipts minus cash disbursements. Roughly equivalent to the SCFP's cash from operations figure. See Sections 1.4 and 7.5.

Change effects analysis – analysis of the effects on financial statements of economic or accounting policy changes. See Sections 8.6 and 9.8.

Chart of accounts – an organized list of the accounts used in the accounting system. This can be contrasted with the "trial balance," which displays all the accounts and their debit or credit balances.

CICA Handbook – the authoritative source of financial accounting standards in Canada. See Sections 3.2 and 5.3.

Classification policies – accounting policies covering *where* within a financial statement an account or description is to appear.

Classified financial statements – the practice of organizing financial statement accounts under headings that clarify the accounts' meaning to increase the information value of the statements. See Section 4.4.

Closing (entries) – journal entries recorded at year end to transfer the balances in temporary accounts (revenues, expenses, and dividends) to the balance sheet account retained earnings and set those balances to zero in preparation for entering the next year's transactions.

Common Shares – the basic voting ownership interests in a corporation. See **Corporation** and Sections 2.8 and 10.9.

Company – See **Corporation.**

Comparability – information that enables users to identify similarities in and differences between two sets of economic phenomena, such as two different years of a company's financial statements. Comparability between companies and consistency of one company over time are major objectives of financial accounting. See **Fairness, Consistency**, and Section 5.3.

Conservatism – a prudent reaction to uncertainty to ensure that risks inherent in business situations are adequately considered—often phrased as "anticipate possible losses but not possible gains." In situations where the accountant cannot decide on the superiority of one of two accounting treatments on the basis of accounting principles alone, being conservative means choosing the treatment that has the least favourable impact on the income of the current period. See **Historical cost** and **Lower of cost or market** for examples of conservatism, and see also Section 5.3.

Consistency – treatment of like transactions in the same way in consecutive periods so that financial statements will be comparable. The reporting policy implying that procedures, once adopted, should be followed from period to period by a company. See **Accounting policies** and Section 5.3.

Consolidation, consolidated – a method of preparing financial statements for a group of companies linked by ownership as if they were a single company. Consolidated financial statements recognize that the separate legal entities are components of one economic unit. They are distinguishable from the separate parent and subsidiary company statements, and from combined statements of affiliated companies. See **Pooling of interests method** and **Purchase method.** Also see Section 5.10.

Contingency – an economic event (especially a negative one) that is in the process of occurring and so is not yet resolved. Contingencies would include, but are not limited to, pending or threatened litigation, threat of expropriation of assets, guarantees of the indebtedness of others, and possible liabilities arising from discounted bills of exchange or promissory notes. See **Conservatism.**

Contra accounts – accounts established to accumulate certain deductions from an asset, liability, or owners' equity item. See **Book value, Amortization, Depreciation, Allowance for doubtful accounts,** and Section 7.11.

Contract (theory) – see **Agency theory** and Section 8.5. A contract is an oral or written agreement between or among parties, setting out each party's responsibilities and specifying actions agreed to and resulting payments or other settlements.

Corporate group – a group of corporations linked by common or mutual ownership. See **Consolidation** and Sections 2.8 and 5.10.

Corporation – a legal entity with or without share capital, legally separate from those who own it or work as a part of it. It enjoys most of the rights and responsibilities of a person except for those which only an actual person can enjoy. Its main feature is limited liability; in other words, only the assets of the company can be claimed by creditors, not the assets of owners. See **Partnership, Proprietorship,** and Section 2.8.

Cost – the value of an asset when it is acquired by the business. See **Historical cost** and Sections 5.7 and 5.8.

Cost basis – usually used to account for a non-current intercorporate investment when a company owns less than 20% of another company. The investment is carried at cost, and any receipt of dividends or interest is recorded as "other income." See **Equity method, Intercorporate investment,** and Section 5.10.

Cost–benefit – the idea of comparing the benefits of a particular action with its costs, and taking action only if the costs exceed the benefits.

Cost flow assumption – an assumption made about the order in which units of inventory move into and out of an enterprise, used to compute inventory asset value and cost of goods sold expense in cases where the order of flow is not or cannot be identified. Possible assumptions include FIFO, LIFO, and weighted average. See **Cost of goods sold, FIFO, Weighted average,** and **LIFO** for specific examples. See also Section 10.4.

Cost of capital – the cost of raising debt or equity funds (e.g., the cost of borrowed funds is mostly the interest to be paid to the lender). See Section 8.8.

Cost of goods sold (COGS) – an expense account that reflects the cost of goods that generated the revenue (also called cost of sales). The method of calculating COGS depends on the method of inventory costing. See **Gross margin, Cost flow assumption, Inventory costing,** and Sections 3.6, 6.10, and 10.4.

Credit (CR) – the right hand of double-entry accounting. The term credit can be used as a noun to refer to the right-hand side of a journal entry or account, or as a verb referring to the action of making an entry to the right-hand side of an account. Most accounts on the right-hand side of the balance sheets have credit balances (in other words, the credits to them exceed the debits to them). The term credit also refers to the right to buy or borrow on the promise of future payment. A credit journal entry to the liabilities and equity side of the balance sheet causes an increase in the account, while a credit to the assets side of the balance sheet causes a decrease. See **Double-entry accounting, Debit,** and Sections 2.4 and 6.4.

Creditor – one who extends credit (that is, gives someone the right to buy or borrow now in consideration of a promise to pay at a later date). See Section 1.5.

Critical event – a point in the revenue generation and collection process chosen to represent the earning of the revenue, and so the point at which the revenue is recognized in the accounts. This is a simplification: a common critical event is the point at which the customer takes delivery of the goods sold. Not all revenue is accounted for this way: some is allocated over more than one point in the process: long-term construction projects and franchise revenue are examples where the critical event simplification is generally not used. See **Revenue recognition** and Section 7.7.

Current assets – cash and other assets such as temporary investments, inventory, receivables, and current prepayments that are realizable or will be consumed within the normal operating cycle of an enterprise (usually one year). See such current asset categories as **Cash equivalent assets, Inventory,** and **Accounts receivable.** See also Section 2.5.

Current liabilities – debts or estimated claims on the resources of a firm that are expected to be paid within the normal operating cycle of an enterprise (usually one year). See **Cash equivalent liabilities, Accounts payable,** and Section 2.5.

Current market value – the estimated sale value of an asset, settlement value of a debt, or trading value of an equity share. See Section 5.7.

Current ratio – See **Working capital ratio** and Section 9.5.

Cut off – the end of a fiscal period and the procedures used to ensure accuracy in measuring phenomena up to that date. See Section 7.6.

D

Debit (DR) – the left-hand side of double-entry accounting. The term debit can be used as a noun to refer to the left-hand side of a journal entry or account or as a verb referring to the action of making an entry on the left-hand side of an account. Most accounts (except contra accounts) on the left-hand side of the balance sheet have debit balances, which means the debits to them exceed the credits to them. A debit will increase the amounts on the asset side of the balance sheet, but decrease the amounts on the liabilities and equity side. See **Double-entry accounting, Credit,** and Sections 2.4 and 6.4.

Debt – an obligation to make a future payment in return for a benefit already received. See Section 10.8.

Debt–equity ratio – total liabilities divided by total equity. See Sections 9.5 and 9.6.

Decelerated amortization (depreciation) – the opposite of **accelerated amortization (depreciation).** Not acceptable for most enterprises. See **Accelerated amortization (depreciation)** and Section 10.5.

Decision relevance – an accounting objective: information should be available to the user at a time and in a form that is useful to the user's decision–making. See **Relevance** and Section 5.3.

Declining balance – an accelerated amortization (depreciation) method in which the annual amortization (depreciation) expense is calculated as a fixed percentage of the book value of the asset, which declines over time as amortization is deducted. See **Accelerated amortization (depreciation), Amortization,** and Section 10.5.

Deferral – part of accrual accounting but often used as the opposite to an accrual. A deferral involves keeping a *past* cash receipt or payment on the balance sheet, in other words, putting it on the income statement as revenue or expense at a later time. An example is recognizing a deferred revenue liability resulting from a recent cash receipt, such as for a magazine subscription to be delivered later. (In contrast, accruals involve recording a revenue or expense *before* the cash receipt or payment occurs.) See Sections 7.2 and 7.3.

Deferred income tax expense – an expense account intended to recognize the future tax consequences of income reported on the current income statement but not to be reported on the tax return until a future period. See **Deferred income tax liability, Matching,** and Section 7.13.

Deferred income tax liability – a liability (the credit side of deferred income tax expense) that arises when the pretax income shown on the tax return is less than what it would have been had the same accounting principles been used in the tax return as were used in the financial statements. Current reported accounting income is less than the income reported on the tax return, so a liability for income tax is implied for later, when the income *is* reported on the tax return. See Section 7.13.

Deferred revenue – a liability account used for deposits or other cash receipts prior to the completion of the sale (for example, before delivery). See Section 7.3.

Deficit – negative retained earnings. See Section 3.3.

Depletion – an amortization (depreciation) method used for physically wasting assets such as natural resources. See Section 10.5.

Depreciation – the recognition of the expense due to use of the economic value of fixed tangible assets (for example, trucks, building, or plant). Usage appears to be changing to replace the term depreciation with the more general term amortization. See **Amortization, Declining balance, Straight-line, Book value,** and **Accumulated amortization (depreciation)**. See also Sections 1.4 and 10.5.

Disclosure – provision of information about economic events beyond that included in the financial statement figures. Usually given in the notes to the financial statements, but also provided outside the financial statements in press releases, speeches, and other announcements. See **Notes to the financial statements, Management of corporate financial disclosure,** and Section 8.4.

Discontinued operations – portions of the business that the enterprise has decided not to keep going and/or to sell to others. It is good practice to separate the effects of discontinued operations from continuing operations when measuring income and cash flow.

Discounted cash flow – "present value" analysis of future cash flows by removing their presumed interest components. See Section 8.8.

Dividends – distributions of a portion of net income to shareholders in the company. Since this type of payment does not relate to the operating performance of the company, it is placed on the statement of retained earnings and not the income statement. See **Statement of retained earnings.**

Double-entry accounting – the practice of recording two aspects of each transaction or event: the resource effect and the source or story of that effect. Though much expanded since its invention several hundred years ago, it is still the basis of bookkeeping and financial accounting. See Sections 2.2 and 6.4.

E ◆

Earnings – a common synonym for net income. See **Net income** and Section 3.3.

Earnings per share – the ratio of net income to the average number of common (voting) shares outstanding, used to allow the owner of the shares to relate the company's earning power to the size of his or her investment. The calculation of EPS can be quite complex, so most public companies calculate it for the users (as required by GAAP for such companies) and report it on their income statements. See **Ratios** and Section 9.5.

Economic entity – the financial accounting definition of an enterprise, used to determine what is to be included in transactions and in the financial statements. Also used to refer to a group of companies considered to be under the same control and, so, constituting a larger economic group. See **Transaction, Consolidation,** and Sections 2.10 and 5.10.

Effects analysis – see **Change effects analysis** and Sections 8.6 and 9.8.

Efficiency (informational efficiency) – refers to a market's prices quickly and appropriately changing to reflect new information. See Section 8.3.

Efficient capital market – a theoretical description of a capital market whose prices respond quickly and appropriately to information. See Section 8.3.

Efficient market hypothesis – the proposal that capital markets actually are "efficient," responding quickly, smoothly, and appropriately to information. Some seem to be efficient, some do not. See **efficient capital market** and Section 8.3.

Entity – see **Economic entity.**

Entry – see **Journal entry** and Sections 2.2 and 2.7.

Equities – a term sometimes used to refer to the right-hand side of the balance sheet (Equities = Liabilities + Owners' equity).

Equity – the net assets or residual interest of an owner or shareholder (Assets – Liabilities = Equity). See the components of equity under **Shareholders' equity, Retained earnings,** and Sections 2.3, 2.5, and 10.9.

Equity basis – a method of accounting for inter-corporate investments usually used when a company owns between 20% and 50% of another company. The investment is carried at cost, and any profit or loss, multiplied by the percentage ownership of the owned company, is added to or deducted from the investment. Any dividends received are deducted from the investment. See **Cost basis, Consolidation,** and Section 5.10.

Expense – the cost of assets used and/or obligations created in generating revenue. See **Income statement, Revenue, Matching, Expense recognition, Accrual accounting,** and Sections 3.3 and 3.6.

Expense recognition – incorporating measures of expenses incurred into the measurement of income by entering into the accounts the amount of expense determined, according to the firm's accounting policies, to be attributable to the current period. See **Matching, Revenue recognition,** and Sections 7.3 and 7.8.

Expensing – classifying an expenditure or promised expenditure (accrual) as an expense rather than an asset. Opposite of **Capitalization.**

External auditor – an independent outside auditor appointed to review the financial statements. See **Auditor** and Section 5.4.

Extraordinary items – gains and losses that arise out of situations that are not normal to the operations of a firm, not under the control of management, and not expected to recur regularly in the future. See Section 3.4.

F

Fair market value – a value or price determined by an unrelated buyer and a seller who are separate and acting rationally in his or her own self-interest. The value is considered more meaningful if established in an actual transaction than if estimated hypothetically. **Historical cost** is assumed to have been the fair market value of an asset when it was acquired. See two forms of estimated fair market value under **Net realizable value** and **Replacement cost.**

Fairness – because of all the estimations, judgments, and policy choices that go into preparing financial statements, there is no one correct set of figures or disclosures. Instead, there is the idea of fairness, which means playing by the rules and preparing statements honestly, without any intent to deceive or to present any particular view. The opinion paragraph of the auditor's report states that the financial statements "present fairly ... in accordance with generally accepted accounting principles." Attention to fairness in the application of accounting principles requires care and judgment in distinguishing the substance from the form of a transaction and identifying the accepted principles and practices. See **Generally accepted accounting principles, Accounting standards,** and Sections 5.3 and 5.4.

Fair value – an estimate of the fair market values of assets and liabilities of an acquired company used in the purchase method of consolidation accounting. See Section 5.10.

FIFO – an inventory cost flow assumption by which cost of goods sold is determined from the cost of the beginning inventory and the cost of the oldest purchases since—thus the acronym FIFO, which stands for "first in, first out." It follows therefore that under FIFO, ending inventory cost is determined from the cost of the most recent purchases. Since the older inventory is assumed to be sold first, FIFO in a period of inflation usually creates a smaller cost of goods sold and higher income and ending inventory asset value than *LIFO* or **Weighted average.** See **Cost flow assumption** and Section 10.4.

Financial accounting – the reporting in **Financial statements** of the financial position and performance of a firm to users external to the firm on a regular, periodic basis. See **Management accounting** and Section 1.3.

Financial Accounting Standards Board (FASB) – a U.S. body responsible for setting the standards that financial reporting must follow. The Canadian counterpart is the Canadian Institute of Chartered Accountants. See *CICA Handbook*.

Financial leverage – see **Leverage** and Section 9.6.

Financial performance – the enterprise's ability to generate new resources from day-to-day operations over a period of time, via dealing with customers, employees, and suppliers. Measured by the **Net income** figure in the **Income statement** and the **Cash from operations** figure in the **Cash flow statement (SCFP),** as well as by the details of both statements.

Financial position – the enterprise's set of assets, liabilities, and owners' equity at a point in time. Measured by the **Balance sheet,** also called the **Statement of financial position.**

Financial reporting – use of **Financial statements** and **Disclosure** to report to people outside the enterprise on its **Financial performance** and **Financial position.**

Financial statements analysis – use of the financial statements to develop summary measures (ratios) and interpretive comments about an enterprise's financial performance and position. See **Ratios** and Sections 9.3 and 9.5.

Financial statements – the reports for people external to the enterprise (but also of interest to management) referred to in the definition of **Accounting,** which generally comprise a balance sheet, income statement, statement of retained earnings, statement of changes in financial position, and the notes to these statements. See each of these statements in this glossary and Sections 1.3 and 5.2.

Fiscal period – the period (usually a year, a quarter, or a month) over which performance (net income) is measured and at the end of which position (balance sheet) is determined. See Section 7.6.

Fixed assets – tangible noncurrent physical assets that are not expected to be used up in one operating cycle, but are expected to be used in generating revenue for many periods (for example, machines, buildings, land). See **Noncurrent assets** and **Current assets.**

Foreign currency translation – the conversion of foreign monies into domestic monies at a specific date—either a transaction date, if translating a single transaction, or a financial statement date, if translating a foreign operation for consolidation purposes. See **Accumulated foreign currency translation adjustment.**

G ◆

GAAP – see **Generally accepted accounting principles.**

GAAS – see **Generally accepted auditing standards.**

Gain (loss) on sale – a gain on sale occurs when a company receives a larger amount of proceeds for an asset than its book value. An income statement account is then credited with the difference. A loss on sale occurs when the asset's book value is more than the proceeds received from the sale. An income statement account is then debited with the difference. See **Book value** and Section 10.6.

General journal – an accounting record used mainly to record accrual adjustments (journal entries) not provided for in separate specialized journals. See Section 6.6.

General ledger – a collection of individual accounts that summarizes the entire financial accounting system of an enterprise. See Section 6.6.

Generally accepted accounting principles (GAAP) – principles and methods of accounting that have the general support of standard-setting bodies, general practice, texts, and other sources. See **Accounting standards** and Section 5.3.

Generally accepted auditing standards (GAAS) – the professional standards of care and evidence compilation that auditors are expected to follow when preparing their reports on financial statements. See **Auditor's report** and Section 5.4.

Going concern – a fundamental assumption in financial accounting that a firm will be financially viable and remain in business long enough to see all of its current plans carried out. If a firm is *not* a going concern, normal accounting principles do not apply. See **Liquidation value** and Section 5.7.

Goodwill – the difference between the price paid for a group of assets and the sum of their apparent fair (market) values. Arises when a bundle of assets or a whole company is acquired and when the difference is positive. ("Badwill," a negative difference, is not recognized.) "Goodwill on consolidation" often arises when a subsidiary's accounts are consolidated with the parent's. See Sections 5.10 and 10.7.

Governmental accounting – accounting procedures, largely different from GAAP, used to account for governments and their agencies. See Section 5.12.

Gross margin – revenue minus cost of goods sold. Also called gross profit."

H

Historical cost – the dollar value of a transaction on the date it happens, normally maintained in the accounting records from then on because of accounting's reliance on transactions as the basis for recording events. The cost, or historical cost, of an asset is therefore the dollar amount paid for it or promised to be paid as of the date the asset was acquired. See **Cost, Lower of cost or market value,** and **Conservatism.** Also see **Fair market value** and Sections 5.7 and 5.8.

I

Income – the (net) income of a business is the residual after deduction of expenses from revenues. Also referred to as profit or earnings. See **Cash income, Gross margin, Income before income tax, Net income,** and Sections 3.3 and 3.4.

Income before (income) tax – an amount equal to revenue plus other income minus all other ordinary expenses except income tax. Appears quite low down on the income statement. Some nontaxed or special items such as **Extraordinary items** are placed after income tax has been deducted, and are therefore not part of income before income tax.

Income smoothing – the "manipulation" of net income so that the year-to-year variations in reported income are reduced. See Section 3.9.

Income statement – a financial statement that summarizes revenues and expenses of a business for a stated period of time and computes the residual net income (revenues minus expenses). Sometimes referred to as "Statement of Earnings," "Statement of Operations," or "Statement of Income." See components of the income statement such as **Revenue, Expense,** and **(Net) Income;** see also **Financial performance** and Sections 3.3 and 3.4.

Income tax – tax assessed on income, according to laws about the computation of income for income tax purposes. See Sections 7.13, 8.6, and 8.7.

Income tax expense – an estimate of the current and future ("deferred") income tax arising from the income as computed on the income statement and matched to the revenues and expenses shown on the statement. See Section 7.13.

Information system – An organized and systematic way of providing information to decision makers. Accounting is an information system. See also **Management information system.**

Intangible assets – nonphysical noncurrent assets such as copyrights, patents, trademarks, import and export licences, other rights that give a firm an exclusive or preferred position in the marketplace, and goodwill. See **Assets, Amortization, Goodwill,** and Section 10.7.

Intercorporate investments – investments by one company in other companies. See **Consolidation, Equity basis, Cost basis,** and Section 5.10.

Internal control – methods of providing physical security and management control over an enterprise's cash, inventories, and other assets. See Sections 6.7, 6.8, and 6.9.

Inventory(ies) – the goods purchased or manufactured by a company for sale, resale, or further use in operations, including finished goods, goods in process, raw materials, and supplies. See **Current assets, Inventory costing,** and Sections 5.8 and 10.4.

Inventory costing – comprises various methods of determining the cost of inventory for balance sheet valuation purposes and of valuing cost of goods sold. The more common methods are

FIFO, LIFO, and **Weighted average.** See also Sections 5.8 and 10.4.

Investments – usually refers to such assets as shares or bonds held for their financial return (for example, interest or dividends), rather than for their use in the enterprise's operations. See Sections 5.10, 8.3, and 9.2.

Investors – people who own **Investments** and who, because of their interest in the value of those shares or bonds, are interested in information about the enterprises issuing such shares and bonds. See Sections 1.5 and 8.3.

J

Joint venture – a business arrangement between corporations that is like a corporate partnership. See Section 5.10.

Journal entry – a record of a transaction or accrual adjustment that lists the accounts affected and in which the total of the debits equals the total of the credits. See **Account** and Sections 6.4 and 6.6.

Journals – records in which accounting transactions of a similar nature are permanently recorded. See **Books of original entry, General journal,** and Section 6.6.

L

Lease – a contract requiring the user of an asset to pay the owner of the asset a predetermined fee for the use of the asset. See Section 10.7.

Ledger – any book or electronic record that summarizes the transactions from the "books of original entry" in the form of accounts. See **Accounts, General ledger, Journals, Trial balance,** and Section 6.6.

Leverage – financial leverage refers to the increased rate of return on owners' equity when assets earn a return larger than the interest rate paid for debt financing of them. The Scott formula illustrates how part of the return on equity is made up of **Operating return** and **Leverage return.** See **Scott formula** and Sections 9.5 and 9.6.

Leverage return – the portion of **Return on equity** that is due to earning more return on borrowed funds than it costs in interest to borrow them. See **Scott formula, Operating return,** and Section 9.6.

Liability – a debt or obligation, legally existing or estimated via accrual accounting techniques, of the enterprise to another party (creditor) arising from a past transaction (for example, a bank loan, a shareholder loan, an account payable, a mortgage, an accrued expense, or deferred revenue). See **Creditors** and Sections 2.4, 2.5, and 10.8.

LIFO – a cost flow assumption that is the opposite of **FIFO.** "Last in, first out" assumes that the units sold are from the most recent purchases and thus bases cost of goods sold on the most recent purchases and ending inventory on the oldest purchases. Because of this, in a period of inflation the LIFO cost of goods sold figure is usually the highest of the inventory costing methods, and the inventory value on the balance sheet is usually the lowest. See **Cost flow assumption, FIFO, Weighted average, Inventory costing,** and Section 10.4.

Liquidation value – the value of a firm's assets if they are all to be sold off when it is no longer a going concern. See **Historical cost, Fair market value,** and Section 5.7.

Liquidity – the excess of very short-term assets over short-term debts, and so the measure of a company's ability to pay its immediate obligations in cash at the present moment. See **Solvency** and Section 9.5.

Loss on sale – see **Gain (loss) on sale** and Section 10.6.

Lower of cost or market – a method of valuing items of inventory, temporary investments, or other current assets, under which losses inherent in declines of the market prices of items held below their costs are recognized in the period in which such declines become apparent. Gains from market increases above cost are not recognized until the items are sold. Lower of cost or market is a conservative procedure. See some of the different values of assets under **Fair market value, Net realizable value, Replacement cost, Historical cost,** and Sections 5.7 and 10.4.

M

Management – the people who run the day-to-day operations of a firm, in contrast to the investors, who own the firm.

Management accounting – accounting information designed to aid management in its operation and control of the firm, and in its general decision–making. It is different from **Financial accounting,** which is aimed primarily at users external to the firm.

Management information system – the accounting, marketing, production, employee, and other recordkeeping and reporting systems within the enterprise used by management in its internal decision–making. Often abbreviated as MIS and often associated with computer systems. See **Management accounting.**

Management of corporate financial disclosure – steps taken by management to manage the outward flow of information about an enterprise, much as other aspects of the enterprise are managed. See Section 8.10.

Manipulation – the accusation that management, in choosing its accounting and disclosure policies, attempts to make the performance and position measures suit its wishes. See Section 10.2.

Marketable securities – investments having a ready market for resale and held as a way of earning a return from temporarily unneeded cash. See **Temporary investments** and Section 5.10.

Market value – see **Fair market value.**

Matching – the concept of recognizing expenses in the same accounting period in which the related revenues are recognized. See **Accrual accounting, Expense recognition, Revenue recognition,** and Sections 5.3, 7.3, and 7.8.

Materiality, material – the magnitude of an omission or misstatement of accounting information that, in the light of surrounding circumstances, makes it probable that the judgment of a reasonable person relying on the information would have been changed or influenced by the omission or misstatement. Materiality and **Decision relevance** are both defined in terms of what influences or makes a difference to a decision maker. A decision not to disclose certain information may be made because it is believed that investors or other users have no need for that kind of information (it is not relevant) or that the amounts involved are too small to make a difference (it is not material). See **Relevance** and Section 5.3.

Measurement, measuring – the attachment of dollar figures to assets, liabilities, revenues, and expenses in order to produce the figures (values) on the balance sheet and to enable the computation of income (revenues minues expenses) and equity (assets minus liabilities). See **Asset valuation, Balance sheet valuation, Recognition, Income,** and Section 5.7.

Minority interest, noncontrolling interest – an account in the liabilities part of the consolidated balance sheet. The percentage of the subsidiary's equity *not* owned by the parent company is designated as minority (noncontrolling) interest liability. A minority (noncontrolling) interest expense calculated in a similar way is also deducted in computing consolidated net income. See **Consolidation** and Section 5.10.

Moving average cost – See **Average cost** and Section 10.4.

N

Net book value – the cost of an asset minus any accumulated depreciation, amortization, allowance for doubtful accounts, and so on. See **Book value** and Section 2.5.

Net fair value of equity – the fair value of the assets minus the fair value of the liabilities of an acquired firm (used to calculate consolidated goodwill). See **Goodwill** and Section 5.10.

Net income – equals income minus income tax expense, plus or minus extraordinary and special items (each net of any tax). See **Income, Retained earnings, Statement of retained earnings, Revenue recognition, Matching,** and Sections 3.3 and 3.4.

Net loss – negative **Net income.**

Net realizable value – the fair market value that an asset will bring if it is sold through the usual product market minus any completion or disposal costs. See **Fair market value, Replacement cost, Lower of cost of market,** and Section 5.7.

Noncurrent assets – assets expected to bring benefit for more than one fiscal year. See **Fixed assets** and **Current assets.**

Noncurrent liabilities – liabilities expected to be repaid or otherwise removed more than one year in the future. See **Liability** and Sections 2.3, 2.5, and 10.8.

Notes to the financial statements – notes appended to the statements, providing information about the accounting policies chosen and other supplementary information helpful to interpreting the figures. See Sections 5.2 and 10.2.

Not-for-profit accounting – procedures used to account for nonbusiness, nongovernment entities. These procedures increasingly follow **GAAP.** See Section 5.12.

O

Objectivity – the notion that the information in financial statements must be as free from bias as possible, in order that all user groups can have confidence in it. An accountant attempts to record and report data that are based on objective sources to make the data more acceptable to outside parties. Because completed arm's-length transactions are supported by documents that can be verified by any interested observer, these constitute the preferred basis of measurement. See **Fairness, Relevance, Reliability, Timeliness, Verifiability, Materiality,** and Section 5.3.

Off-balance-sheet financing – methods of obtaining financing that avoid having to record the sources as liabilities or equity. See Section 10.8.

Ontario Securities Commission – the securities-trading regulator for Ontario and the leading such regulator in Canada.

Operating return – the return earned by an enterprise before considering the cost of financing and usually also before considering nonrecurring items. See **Leverage return, Scott formula** and Section 9.6.

Opportunity cost – the return that could have been earned if funds were used in another way than the way they are being used or are proposed to be used. It is called a cost because it is the return given up by not adopting that other way. See Section 8.8.

Overhead cost – costs of manufacturing inventories or constructing other assets that are incurred indirectly, such as heat, power, and supervisors' salaries.

Owners – parties who have contributed resources in return for the right to dividends and any residual value (equity) of the enterprise. See Section 1.5.

Owners' equity – See **Equity** and Sections 2.3, 2.4, 2.5, and 10.9.

P

Parent – the dominant company in a corporate group linked by ownership, the name of which is usually used in the consolidated financial statements. See Section 5.10.

Partnership – a contractual agreement among individuals to share resources and operations in a jointly run business. This form of business does not have the privilege of limited liability. See **Corporation, Proprietorship,** and Section 2.8.

Percentage of completion – a method of allocating revenue (and associated expenses) over several fiscal periods during which the revenue is earned. Used for long-term construction contracts, franchise revenue and similar multi-period revenues. See Sections 7.7 and 7.8.

Periodic inventory method – a method of calculating inventory that uses data on beginning inventory, additions to inventory, and an end-of-period count to deduce the cost of goods sold. See **Perpetual inventory method, Retail inventory method,** and Section 6.10.

Periodic reporting – a basic convention of financial accounting that holds that accounting information must be assembled and presented to users at regular intervals (at least yearly and often quarterly or monthly). See Sections 1.5 and 7.6.

Perpetual inventory method – a method of controlling inventory that maintains continuous records on the flow of units of inventory. Thus, there are figures on record for beginning inventory, each unit added to inventory, and each unit removed from inventory for sale. From this an ending inventory figure can be determined and checked against the figure from a physical count. This method provides better control than the periodic inventory method, but it is also more costly to maintain the extra records. See **Periodic inventory method, Retail inventory method,** and Section 6.10.

Plug – the double-entry system requires that debits equal credits. If adding up all the debits and the credits does not produce two equal figures, the statements must be adjusted so that a balance occurs. The amount of adjustment needed is called a plug. This would only be needed if there had been an error somewhere, though sometimes the word plug is used in criticism of accrual, consolidation, or other adjustments.

Pooling of interests method – a type of business combination (compare with **Purchase method**). In pooling of interests, the assets, liabilities, equities, revenues, and expenses of the firms are added together using their book values. See **Consolidation** and Section 5.10.

Posting – transferring journal entries to ledger accounts and thereby making them permanent. The only way to fix a mistake is to use an adjusting or correcting entry and post that. See Sections 2.4 and 6.6.

Preferred shares – ownership shares having special rights in addition to (or instead of) those going with common shares. See Section 2.8.

Prepaid expense – an expenditure recorded as a current asset because the benefit will be obtained in the near future (for example, insurance coverage good for the next year). See Section 7.10.

Preparers – managers and accountants who produce financial statements. See Section 1.5.

Present value analysis – analysis of future cash flows done by removing the presumed interest components of those flows. See Section 8.8.

Price-level-adjusted historical cost – a rarely used asset valuation method in which the historical cost of each asset is revalued for inflation. See **Historical cost, Fair market value,** and Section 5.7.

Principal–agent theory – see **Agency (contract) theory** and Section 8.5.

Prior-period adjustment – a gain or loss specifically identified with and directly related to the activities of particular prior periods, but not attributable to economic events occurring subsequent to those periods (so net income of those later periods is not increased or decreased because doing so could cause a distortion in the later results). The gain or loss is attributable to decisions by persons other than management or owners and could not be reasonably estimated prior to a final decision being made (for example, a lawsuit that takes several years to resolve). See **Statement of retained earnings** and Section 3.4.

Professional ethics – codes of conduct to guide professionals in applying their professional judgment and that are conducive to their professional activities. See Section 5.5

Professional judgment – the judgment of professionals about problems in their domain, for example, that of accountants or auditors about financial accounting matters. See Section 5.14.

Profit – see **Net income.**

Proprietor approach – a way of viewing financial statements from the point of view of the proprietor (owner). See Section 2.10.

Proprietorship – a firm that is neither a corporation nor a partnership but is under the sole control of one individual. Such a firm is not legally separate from that individual. See **Partnership, Corporation,** and Section 2.8.

Prospectus – a formal document that includes detailed financial information, which is required by law when a company invites the public to subscribe to its securities.

Public accounting – offering auditing, accounting, and related services to the public on a professional basis. Some public accounting firms are very large. See Section 1.5.

Public company – a **Corporation** whose shares and related securities are sold widely, to members of the public and other investors, and whose securities are likely to be traded on capital markets.

Purchase method – a type of accounting for business combinations (compare with the **Pooling of interests method**). Under this method, which is the overwhelmingly dominant method of determining consolidated financial statement figures, the assets and liabilities of the acquired company are added to those of the parent at fair values and any difference between the portion of the sum of fair values acquired by the parent and the total price paid is accounted for as goodwill. See Section 5.10.

R

Ratios, ratio analysis – numbers produced by dividing one financial statement figure by another figure, for example, the working capital ratio is the total current assets figure divided by the total current liabilities figure. Standard ratios are used to assess aspects of a firm, particularly profitability, solvency, and liquidity. See Sections 9.2, 9.3, 9.5, and 9.6. Section 9.5 describes 20 common ratios.

Realized – used in this book as a synonym of received, or collected. Revenue is **recognized** when earned, but that is usually before it is collected, or realized. See **Revenue recognition, Recognition,** and Section 7.3.

Reclassification (entry) – a journal entry or repositioning of an account that changes the location of the account within the balance sheet or within the income statement but does not affect income. See **Classification policies.**

Recognition – giving effect in the accounts to revenue believed to be earned, or expenses believed to be incurred, before (or after) the cash is collected or paid. See **Revenue recognition, Expense recognition,** and Sections 7.3, 7.7, and 7.8.

Recordkeeping – the bookkeeping and other methods used to create the underlying records on which accounting information is based. See Sections 6.2, 6.3, 6.4, and 6.6.

Relevance – the capacity of information to make a difference in a decision by helping users to form predictions about the outcomes of past, present, and future events or to confirm or correct prior expectations. See **Decision relevance, Materiality, Reliability, Timeliness,** and **Objectivity.**

Reliability – a characteristic of information that is represented faithfully and is free from bias and verifiable. See **Relevance, Timeliness, Materiality,** and **Objectivity.**

Replacement cost – the price that will have to be paid in order to replace an existing asset with a similar asset. This is likely to be a different amount than that of **Fair market value** or of **Net realizable value.** See also **Lower of cost or market** and Sections 5.7 and 10.4.

Resources – in financial accounting, the recognized assets of the enterprise as shown on the balance sheet. See Section 2.3.

Retail inventory method – providing internal control and deducing inventory amounts for financial statements by using ratios of cost to selling price; for example, deducing cost of goods sold from sales revenue minus the markup on cost. Ending inventory cost can be determined by measuring inventory at retail prices minus markup. See **Perpetual inventory method, Periodic inventory method, Inventory costing,** and Sections 6.10 and 10.4.

Retained earnings – earnings not yet distributed to owners; the sum of net incomes earned over the life of a company, less distributions (dividends declared) to owners. See **Equity** and Sections 2.3 and 3.3.

Retained earnings statement – see **Statement of retained earnings** and Section 3.3.

Return – some amount of gain (income or performance) usually measured in relation to the amount invested to get the return. See **Risk,** Sections 8.3 and 9.2, and such ratios as **Return on equity** and **Return on assets** in Sections 9.5 and 9.6.

Return on assets – net income, before considering interest expense or the tax saving provided by interest expense, divided by total assets. This measures the **Operating return** before the cost of financing. See Sections 9.2, 9.5, and 9.6.

Return on equity – net income divided by owners' equity. The most frequently used **Ratio** for measuring the business's return to owners. See Sections 9.2, 9.5, and 9.6.

Return on investment – a general term for measures of return related to the investment needed to earn the return. See **Return on assets, Return on equity,** and Section 9.2.

Revenue – the amount of benefit received or promised from the sale of goods or services, before any deductions for the cost of providing the goods or services. See **Income statement, Revenue recognition,** and Sections 3.3 and 3.4.

Revenue recognition – the entering into the accounts of the amount of revenue determined, according to the firm's accounting policies, to be attributable to the current period. See **Accrual accounting, Accounts receivable, Revenue,** and Sections 7.3, 7.7, and 7.9.

Risk – the probable variability in possible future outcomes above and below the expected level of outcomes (for example, returns), but especially below. Risk and return go hand in hand, because a high risk should mean a higher potential **Return** and vice versa. See Section 8.3 and **Return.**

S ◆

SCFP – see **Statement of changes in financial position** (Cash flow statement).

Scott formula – a financial analysis technique of combining a group of **Ratios** into a more comprehensive explanation of performance. The formula separates **Return on equity** into **Operating return** and **Leverage return.** See Section 9.6.

Securities – shares, bonds, and other financial instruments issued by corporations and governments and usually traded on **Capital markets.**

Securities and Exchange Commission (SEC) – an agency of the U.S. government that supervises the registration of security issues, prosecutes fraudulent stock manipulations, and regulates securities transactions in the United States.

Segmented information – financial statement information desegregated by geographical or economic area of activity in order to provide greater insight into financial performance and position. Segmented information is usually placed at the end of the notes to the financial statements.

Share capital – the portion of a corporation's equity obtained by issuing shares in return for cash or other considerations. See Sections 2.8 and 10.9.

Shareholders – the holders of a corporation's **Share capital,** and so the owners of the corporation. See Section 1.5.

Shareholders' equity – the sum of shareholders' direct investment (share capital) and indirect investment (retained earnings). See **Share capital, Equity,** and **Retained earnings.** See also Sections 2.3 and 10.9.

Shares (stock) – units of **Share capital,** evidenced by certificates and, for **Public companies,** traded on **Capital markets** with other **Securities.**

Society of Management Accountants of Canada (SMAC) – a society whose members have had training in tax, accounting, internal audit, and other related areas, with a particular focus on internal management accounting, and have passed qualifying exams. One of the three national professional accounting bodies. See **Accountant.**

Solvency – the condition of being able to meet all debts and obligations. See **Statement of changes in financial position, Liquidity,** and Section 9.5.

Source documents – the evidence required to record a **Transaction.** See Section 6.6.

Sources – the right-hand side of the balance sheet (liabilities and equity) are the sources of the enterprise's assets. See Section 2.3.

Spreadsheet – A computer program used to display and analyze numerical information, such as accounting numbers. A spreadsheet is particularly useful for showing the effects of changes within the numbers. See the appendix on creating a computer spreadsheet to represent a company's accounts.

Standard cost – a method of determining manufactured inventory costs that uses expected normal production costs rather than actual costs.

Statement of changes in financial position (SCFP), cash flow statement – a statement that explains the changes in cash equivalent balances during a fiscal period. Also referred to as a "Statement of Sources and Uses of Funds," "Funds Statement," "Statement of Changes in Cash Resources," or "Statement of Cash Flows." See Sections 4.2, 4.3, and 9.7.

Statement of financial position – a synonym for **Balance sheet.**

Statement of retained earnings – a financial statement that summarizes the changes in retained earnings for the year. Change in retained earnings equals **Net income** minus **Dividends** plus or minus any retained earnings adjustments, such as **Prior-period adjustments.** See Sections 3.3 and 3.4.

Stewardship – the concept that some persons (for example, management) are responsible for looking after the assets and interests of other persons (for example, shareholders), and that reports should be prepared that will be suitable to allow the "stewards" to be held accountable for the actions taken on behalf of the other persons. See **Agency theory** and Section 2.2.

Stock dividend – a **Dividend** paid by issuing more shares to present shareholders rather than paying them cash.

Stock exchange – a place where **Shares** and other **Securities** are traded.

Stock market – a **Capital market** in which equity shares are traded. Often used as a generic term for capital markets.

Stockholder – an alternative term for **Shareholder,** particularly used in the United States.

Stocks – used to mean **Shares,** but also sometimes used to mean **Inventories,** as in "stocktaking" for counting inventories.

Straight-line amortization (depreciation) – a method of computing amortization (depreciation) simply by dividing the difference between the asset's cost and its expected salvage value by the number of years the asset is expected to be used. It is the most common amortization method used in Canada. See **Depreciation** and Section 10.5.

Subsidiary – a company a majority of whose voting shares are owned by another company (the **Parent**). See **Consolidation** and Section 5.10.

Sum-of-years'-digits depreciation – an **accelerated** method of computing amortization (depreciation) that produces a declining annual expense. Used in the United States but rare in Canada. See **Accelerated amortization (depreciation)** and endnote 12 to Chapter 10.

Synoptic – a bookkeeping record listing cash transactions of the business.

T ◆

Temporary investments – investments made for a short term, often used as a place to put temporarily excess cash to work. See Section 5.10.

Timeliness – timely information is usable because it relates to present decision needs. Information received late may be too late to be usable, since decisions pass it by. See **Relevance, Reliability, Objectivity, Materiality,** and Section 5.3.

Time value of money – money can earn interest, so money received in the future is worth less in "present value" terms because the lower amount can be invested to grow to the future amount. Money has a time value because interest accrues over time. See **Present value analysis** and Section 8.8.

Transaction – an accounting transaction is the basis of bookkeeping and is defined by four criteria: (1) Exchange: there must be an exchange of money, goods, or other items that have economic value. (2) External: the exchange must be with an outsider; it is not a transaction if it has occurred within the firm. (3) Evidence: there must be an invoice, computer printout, or some other source document to show that a transaction has taken place. (4) Dollars: the transaction must be quantifiable in dollars. See Section 6.3.

Treasury shares (stock) – share capital issued and then reacquired by the firm that issued the shares. The result is a reduction of shareholders' equity because resources have been used to reduce the actual amount of outstanding equity. See Section 10.9.

Trial balance – a list of all the general ledger accounts and their balances. The sum of the accounts with debit balances should equal the sum of those with credit balances. This is contrasted with the **Chart of accounts,** which lists only the account names. See **Account** and Section 6.6.

U ◆

Units-of-production amortization (depreciation) – an amortization (depreciation) method in which the annual amortization expense varies directly with the year's production volume. See Section 10.5.

Users – people who use financial statements to assist them in deciding whether to invest in the enterprise, lend it money, or take other action involving financial information. See Section 1.5.

V ◆◆◆◆◆◆◆◆◆◆◆◆◆◆◆◆◆◆◆◆◆◆◆

Value in use – the value of an asset determined by the future cash flows it brings in, or the future expenses that will be avoided by owning the asset. See **Historical cost, Fair market value,** and Section 5.7.

Verifiability – ability to trace an accounting entry or figure back to the underlying evidence of its occurrence and validity. See **Source documents** and Sections 5.3 and 6.6.

W ◆◆◆◆◆◆◆◆◆◆◆◆◆◆◆◆◆◆◆◆◆◆◆

Weighted average – an inventory cost flow assumption that determines cost of goods sold and ending inventory cost by averaging the cost of all of the inventory available during the period. See **Average, LIFO, FIFO, Inventory costing,** and Section 10.4.

"What if" effects analysis – see **Change effects analysis** and Sections 8.6, 8.7, and 9.8. See also Sections SS.4 and SS.9 of the computer spreadsheet supplement following this glossary.

Working capital – the difference between current assets and current liabilities. See **Current assets, Current liabilities,** and Section 2.5.

Working capital ratio – current assets divided by current liabilities. See Sections 2.5 and 9.5.

Write-off – refers to the elimination of an asset from the balance sheet. If there is a **Contra account** against the asset already, the write-off is made against the contra and expense (and income) is not affected. If there is no contra account, the write-off is made to expense and income is reduced. See Sections 7.11 and 10.6.

BIBLIOGRAPHY

American Accounting Association. *Accounting Education: Problems and Prospects*. Sarasota, Fla.: American Accounting Association, 1974.

Beaver, W.H. *Financial Reporting: An Accounting Revolution*, 2nd ed. Englewood Cliffs, N.J.: Prentice-Hall, 1989.

Canadian Institute of Chartered Accountants. *Corporate Reporting: Its Future Evolution*. Toronto: CICA, 1980.

Canadian Institute of Chartered Accountants. 1979 National CA Uniform Final (Qualifying) Examination. Toronto, Canada.

Canadian Institute of Chartered Accountants. 1984 National CA Uniform (Qualifying) Examination. Toronto, Canada.

Canadian Institute of Chartered Accountants. *Financial Reporting in Canada 1993*. Toronto: Canadian Institute of Chartered Accountants, 1993.

Carson, J.W. "Equal Access to Information Cornerstone of TSE Policy." *Corporate Disclosure: A Special Report*. Toronto: Canada Newswire Ltd., 1989.

Chatfield, M. "English Medieval Bookkeeping: Exchequer and Manor." In *Contemporary Studies in the Evolution of Accounting Thought*, edited by Michael Chatfield. Belmont, Calif.: Dickenson Publishing Company Inc., 1968.

CICA Handbook. "Introduction to accounting recommendations." Toronto: Canadian Institute of Chartered Accountants, version in effect June 30, 1994, 6.

CICA Handbook, Paragraph 5200.05. Toronto: Canadian Institute of Chartered Accountants, version in effect at December 31, 1993.

Coustourous, George J. *Accounting in the Golden Age of Greece: A Response to Socioeconomic Changes*. Champaign, Ill.: Center for International Education and Research in Accounting, University of Illinois, 1979.

Drummond, Christina S.R., and A.K. Mason. *Guide to Accounting Pronouncements & Sources*, 3rd ed. Toronto: Canadian Institute of Chartered Accountants, 1992.

Dyckman, T.R., and D. Morse. *Efficient Capital Markets and Accounting: A Critical Analysis*, 2nd ed. Englewood Cliffs, N.J.: Prentice-Hall, 1986.

Editorial. "It's time to narrow the GAAP gap." *Financial Post*, January 29–31, 1994, S1.

Gates, B. "Reports Deliver Message with Style and Pizzazz." *Financial Post*, November 27, 1990, 17.

Gibbins, M., and A.K. Mason. *Professional Judgment in Financial Reporting*. Toronto: Canadian Institute of Chartered Accountants, 1988.

Gibbins, M., A.J. Richardson, and J.H. Waterhouse. "If Numbers Could Speak." *CA Magazine*, October 1989, 33–39.

Griffin, P.A., ed. *Usefulness to Investors and Creditors of Information Provided by Financial Reporting*, 2nd ed. Stamford, Conn.: Financial Accounting Standards Board, 1987.

Hasson, C.J. "The South Sea Bubble and M. Shell." In *Contemporary Studies in the Evolution of Accounting Thought*, edited by M. Chatfield, pp. 86–94. Belmont, Calif.: Dickenson Publishing Company Inc., 1968.

Ten Have, O. *The History of Accounting*. Palo Alto, Calif.: Bay Books, 1976.

Heinzl, J. "Scott's serves up lean profit." *Globe and Mail*, September 9, 1993, B1.

"Honest Balance Sheets, Broken Promises." *Business Week*, November 22, 1992, 106–107.

"It's time to narrow the GAAP gap," *Financial Post*, January 29–31, 1994, S1.

Kang, G.M. "It's Corporate America's Spring Hornblowing Festival." *Business Week*, April 12, 1993, 31.

Keister, O.R. "The Mechanics of Mesopotamian Record-Keeping." In *Contemporary Studies in the Evolution of Accounting Thought*, edited by M. Chatfield, pp. 12–20. Belmont, Calif.: Dickenson Publishing Company Inc., 1968.

Kilpatrick, I. "Companies in Convalescence," *CA Magazine* (April 1993): 18–19.

Lemke, K.W. "Asset Valuation and Income Theory." *The Accounting Review* (January 1966): 32–41.

Mactaggart, Sandy A., Chancellor, University of Alberta. Letter to the author, January 24, 1991.

Marcial, G.G. "A Supersleuth Raises a Red Flag Over Pyxis." *Business Week*, April 4, 1994, 104.

Mahood, C. "Companies rush to come clean," *Globe and Mail*, April 26, 1993, B1.

Mathias, P. "Why accounting standards aren't standard." *Financial Post*, April 2, 1994, S16–17.

Miller, M.W., and L. Berton. "How IBM played the numbers game." *Globe and Mail*, April 10, 1993, B1, B4 (from *The Wall Street Journal*).

Murphy, George, ed. *A History of Canadian Accounting Thought and Practice*. New York: Garland Publishing Inc., 1993.

Murphy, George. "Corporate Reporting Practices in Canada: 1900–1970." In *The Academy of Accounting Historians, Working Paper Series*, vol 1. The Academy of Accounting Historians, 1979.

Newman, Peter C. *Company of Adventurers*, xii. Markham, Ont.: Viking/Penguin Books, 1985.

Noakes, S. "Reports Gain New Prominence." *Financial Post*, December 2, 1993, 16.

Ponemon, L.A., and D.R.L. Gabhart. *Ethical Reasoning in Accounting and Auditing*. Vancouver: CGA–Canada Research Foundation, 1993.

Power, C. "Let's Get Fiscal." *Forbes*, April 30, 1984, 102–103.

Reid, A.D.G. "Moore shares poised for growth." *Financial Post*, March 31, 1994, 19.

Reuter. "McDonald's Serves Up Annual Report Video." *Financial Post*, April 13, 1993, 7.

Ronen J., and S. Sadan. *Smoothing Income Numbers: Objectives, Means, and Implications*. Reading, Mass.: Addison-Wesley, 1981.

Royal Bank of Canada. "Starting Out Right." *Your Business Matters* series, 1990, 37.

"Setting New Standards." *CGA Magazine*, February 1991, 36–43.

Skinner, Ross M. *Accounting Standards in Evolution*. Toronto: Holt, Rinehart and Winston, 1987.

Stone, J. "Big Brewhaha of 1800 B.C." *Discover*, January 1991, 14.

The Spicer & Oppenheim Guide to Financial Statements Around the World. New York: John Wiley & Sons, 1989.

Trites, G.D. "Read It in the Annual Report." *CA Magazine* (December 1990): 45–48.

United Dominion Industries. "Notes to Consolidated Financial Statements," in 1992 annual report.

Watts, R.L., and J.L. Zimmerman. *Positive Accounting Theory*. Englewood Cliffs, N.J.: Prentice-Hall, 1986.

Weber, J. "Did Pfizer Doctor Its Numbers?" *Business Week*, February 14, 1994, 34.

INDEX

A

B

J

L

R

S

T

U

V

W

To the owner of this book

We hope that you have enjoyed *Financial Accounting: An Integrated Approach, Second Edition,* and we would like to know as much about your experiences with this text as you would care to offer. Only through your comments and those of others can we learn how to make this a better text for future readers.

School ________________ Your instructor's name ______________________

Course ___________ Was the text required? _______ Recommended? _____

1. What did you like the most about *Financial Accounting*?

____

____

____

2. How useful was this text for your course?

____

____

____

3. Do you have any recommendations for ways to improve the next edition of this text?

____

____

____

4. In the space below or in a separate letter, please write any other comments you have about the book. (For example, please feel free to comment on reading level, writing style, terminology, design features, and learning aids.)

____

____

____

____

Optional

Your name ______________________________ Date __________________

May Nelson Canada quote you, either in promotion for *Financial Accounting* or in future publishing ventures?

Yes _______ No _______

Thanks!

FOLD HERE

Canada Post Corporation / Société canadienne des postes

Postage paid if mailed in Canada	Port payé si posté au Canada
Business Reply	**Réponse d'affaires**

0107077099 01

Nelson

TAPE SHUT

0107077099-M1K5G4-BR01

TAPE SHUT

Nelson Canada
College Editorial Department
1120 Birchmount Rd.
Scarborough, ON M1K 9Z9

PLEASE TAPE SHUT. DO NOT STAPLE.